ANTHROPOLOGY 90/91

Editor

Elvio Angeloni
Pasadena City College

Elvio Angeloni received his B.A. from UCLA in 1963, his
M.A. in anthropology from UCLA in 1965, and his M.A. in
communication arts from Loyola Marymount University in
1976. He has produced several films, including "Little
Warrior," winner of the Cinemedia VI Best Bicentennial
Theme, and "Broken Bottles," shown on PBS. He most
recently served as an academic advisor on the instructional
television series, "Faces of Culture."

Annual Editions
A Library of Information from the Public Press

Cover illustration by Mike Eagle

The Dushkin Publishing Group, Inc.
Sluice Dock, Guilford, Connecticut 06437

The Annual Editions Series

Annual Editions is a series of over fifty volumes designed to provide the reader with convenient, low-cost access to a wide range of current, carefully selected articles from some of the most important magazines, newspapers, and journals published today. Annual Editions are updated on an annual basis through a continuous monitoring of over 200 periodical sources. All Annual Editions have a number of features designed to make them particularly useful, including topic guides, annotated tables of contents, unit overviews, and indexes. For the teacher using Annual Editions in the classroom, an Instructor's Resource Guide with test questions is available for each volume.

VOLUMES AVAILABLE

Africa
Aging
American Government
American History, Pre-Civil War
American History, Post-Civil War
Anthropology
Biology
Business and Management
Business Ethics
Canadian Politics
China
Comparative Politics
Computers in Education
Computers in Business
Computers in Society
Criminal Justice
Drugs, Society, and Behavior
Early Childhood Education
Economics
Educating Exceptional Children
Education
Educational Psychology
Environment
Geography
Global Issues
Health
Human Development

Human Resources
Human Sexuality
Latin America
Macroeconomics
Marketing
Marriage and Family
Middle East and the Islamic World
Money and Banking
Nutrition
Personal Growth and Behavior
Psychology
Public Administration
Social Problems
Sociology
Soviet Union and Eastern Europe
State and Local Government
Third World
Urban Society
Violence and Terrorism
Western Civilization,
  Pre-Reformation
Western Civilization,
  Post-Reformation
Western Europe
World History, Pre-Modern
World History, Modern
World Politics

Library of Congress Cataloging in Publication Data
Main entry under title: Annual editions: Anthropology. 1990–91.
    1. Anthropology—Addresses, essays, lectures. I. Angeloni, Elvio, *comp*. II. Title:
Anthropology.
301.2   74–84595   ISBN 0-87967-833-X
GN 325.A53

Thirteenth Edition

Manufactured by The Banta Company, Harrisonburg, Virginia 22801

To The Reader

In publishing ANNUAL EDITIONS we recognize the enormous role played by the magazines, newspapers, and journals of the *public press* in providing current, first-rate educational information in a broad spectrum of interest areas. Within the articles, the best scientists, practitioners, researchers, and commentators draw issues into new perspective as accepted theories and viewpoints are called into account by new events, recent discoveries change old facts, and fresh debate breaks out over important controversies.

Many of the articles resulting from this enormous editorial effort are appropriate for students, researchers, and professionals seeking accurate, current material to help bridge the gap between principles and theories and the real world. These articles, however, become more useful for study when those of lasting value are carefully *collected, organized, indexed,* and *reproduced* in a *low-cost format*, which provides easy and permanent access when the material is needed. That is the role played by *Annual Editions*. Under the direction of each volume's *Editor*, who is an expert in the subject area, and with the guidance of an *Advisory Board*, we seek each year to provide in each *ANNUAL EDITION* a current, well-balanced, carefully selected collection of the best of the public press for your study and enjoyment. We think you'll find this volume useful, and we hope you'll take a moment to let us know what you think.

The thirteenth edition of *Annual Editions: Anthropology* contains a variety of articles on contemporary issues in social and cultural anthropology. In contrast to the broad range of topics and minimum depth typical of standard textbooks, this anthology provides an opportunity to read firsthand accounts by anthropologists of their own research. By allowing scholars to speak for themselves about the issues on which they are expert, we are better able to understand the kinds of questions anthropologists ask, the ways in which they ask them, and how they go about searching for answers. Where there is disagreement among anthropologists, this format allows readers to draw their own conclusions.

Given the very broad scope of anthropology—in time, space, and subject matter—the present collection of highly readable articles has been selected according to certain criteria. The articles have been chosen from both professional and nonprofessional publications for the purpose of supplementing the standard cultural anthropology textbook that is used in introductory courses. Some of the articles are considered classics in the field, while others have been selected for their timely relevance.

Included in this volume are a number of features designed to make it useful for students, researchers, and professionals in the field of anthropology. While the articles are arranged along the lines of broadly unifying themes, the *topic guide* can be used to establish specific reading assignments tailored to the needs of a particular course of study. Other useful features include the *table of contents abstracts*, which summarize each article and present key concepts in italics, and a comprehensive *index*. In addition, each unit is preceded by an overview which provides a background for informed reading of the articles, emphasizes critical issues, and presents *challenge questions*.

Annual Editions: Anthropology 90/91 will continue to be updated annually. Those involved in producing the volume wish to make the next one as useful and effective as possible. Your criticism and advice is welcomed. Please fill out the article rating form on the last page of the book and let us know your opinions. Any anthology can be improved. This continues to be—annually.

Elvio Angeloni

Elvio Angeloni
Editor

Contents

Unit 1

Anthropological Perspectives

Five selections examine the role of anthropologists in studying different cultures. The innate problems in developing productive relationships between anthropologists and exotic cultures are considered by reviewing a number of fieldwork experiences.

Unit 2

Culture and Communication

Four selections discuss communication as an element of culture. Ingrained social and cultural values have a tremendous effect on an individual's perception or interpretation of both verbal and nonverbal communication.

The concepts in bold italics are developed in the article. For further expansion please refer to the Topic Guide and the Index.

Unit 3

The Organization of Society and Culture

Six selections discuss the influence of the environment and the culture on the organization of the social structure of groups.

The concepts in bold italics are developed in the article. For further expansion please refer to the Topic Guide and the Index.

Unit 4

Other Families, Other Ways

Five selections examine some of the influences on the family structure of different cultures. The strength of the family unit is affected by both economic and social pressures.

Unit 5

Sex Roles and Statuses

Seven selections discuss some of the sex roles prescribed by the social, economic, and political forces of a culture.

The concepts in bold italics are developed in the article. For further expansion please refer to the Topic Guide and the Index.

Unit 6

Religion, Belief, and Ritual

Six selections examine the role of ritual, religion, and belief in a culture. The need to develop a religion is universal among societies.

The concepts in bold italics are developed in the article. For further expansion please refer to the Topic Guide and the Index.

Unit 7

Sociocultural Change: The Impact of the West

Seven articles examine the influence that the developed world has had on primitive cultures. Exposure to the industrialized West often has disastrous effects on the delicate balance of a primitive society.

The concepts in bold italics are developed in the article. For further expansion please refer to the Topic Guide and the Index.

Topic Guide

This topic guide suggests how the selections in this book relate to topics of traditional concern to anthropology students and professionals. It can be very useful in locating articles which relate to each other for reading and research. The guide is arranged alphabetically according to topic. Articles may, of course, treat topics that do not appear in the topic guide. In turn, entries in the topic guide do not necessarily constitute a comprehensive listing of all the contents of each selection.

TOPIC AREA	TREATED AS AN ISSUE IN:	TOPIC AREA	TREATED AS AN ISSUE IN:
Acculturation	26. Between Two Worlds 35. Growing Up as a Fore 37. The Aborigines' Search for Justice 38. Bicultural Conflict 39. Inuit Youth in a Changing World 40. Back on the Land	Cultural Relativity and Ethnocentrism (cont'd)	5. Confessions of a Former Cultural Relativist 8. Social Time 9. How Not to Lose the Trade Wars 31. A Writer in a World of Spirits 33. Body Ritual Among the Nacirema 38. Bicultural Conflict
Aggression and Violence	4. Myth of the Man-Eaters 22. What Keeps Women "in Their Place"? 36. Dark Dreams About the White Man 37. The Aborigines' Search for Justice 38. Bicultural Conflict	Culture Shock	1. Fieldwork Among the Yanomamö 32. You've Gotta Have "Wa" 38. Bicultural Conflict 39. Inuit Youth in a Changing World
Cannibalism	4. Myth of the Man-Eaters	Ecology and Society	10. The Blood in Their Veins 12. Murders in Eden 14. Mystique of the Masai 16. When Brothers Share a Wife 24. Women, Food, and Hospitality 34. Why Can't People Feed Themselves? 39. Inuit Youth in a Changing World 40. Back on the Land
Children and Child Care	11. Memories of a !Kung Girlhood 17. Young Traders of Northern Nigeria 18. Child Care in China 21. Woman the Gatherer 28. The Mbuti Pygmies 38. Bicultural Conflict 39. Inuit Youth in a Changing World		
Cooperation, Sharing, and Altruism	3. Eating Christmas in the Kalahari 10. The Blood in Their Veins 18. Child Care in China 21. Woman the Gatherer 22. Men and Women 39. Inuit Youth in a Changing World	Economic and Political Systems	2. Doctor, Lawyer, Indian Chief 9. How Not to Lose the Trade Wars 14. Mystique of the Masai 16. When Brothers Share a Wife 17. Young Traders of Northern Nigeria 19. Free Enterprise and the Ghetto Family 21. Woman the Gatherer 23. What Keeps Women "in Their Place"? 24. Women, Food, and Hospitality 27. Blaming the Victim 34. Why Can't People Feed Themselves? 37. The Aborigines' Search for Justice
Cross-Cultural Experience	1. Fieldwork Among the Yanomamö 2. Doctor, Lawyer, Indian Chief 3. Eating Christmas in the Kalahari 5. Confessions of a Former Cultural Relativist 7. Shakespeare in the Bush 8. Social Time 9. How Not to Lose the Trade Wars 24. Women, Food, and Hospitality 26. Between Two Worlds 31. A Writer in a World of Spirits 32. You've Gotta Have "Wa" 36. Dark Dreams About the White Man 38. Bicultural Conflict 39. Inuit Youth in a Changing World	Ethnographic Fieldwork	1. Fieldwork Among the Yanomamö 2. Doctor, Lawyer, Indian Chief 3. Eating Christmas in the Kalahari 4. Myth of the Man-Eaters 22. Men and Women
		Health and Welfare	33. Body Ritual Among the Nacirema 34. Why Can't People Feed Themselves? 37. The Aborigines' Search for Justice 39. Inuit Youth in a Changing World
Cultural Diversity	8. Social Time 38. Bicultural Conflict 39. Inuit Youth in a Changing World	Hunter-Collectors	10. The Blood in Their Veins 11. Memories of a !Kung Girlhood 12. Murders in Eden 21. Woman the Gatherer 22. Men and Women 28. The Mbuti Pygmies 39. Inuit Youth in a Changing World 40. Back on the Land
Cultural Identity	14. Mystique of the Masai 20. The Gypsies 26. Between Two Worlds 37. The Aborigines' Search for Justice 38. Bicultural Conflict 39. Inuit Youth in a Changing World		
		Language	6. Language, Appearance, and Reality 7. Shakespeare in the Bush 8. Social Time 9. How Not to Lose the Trade Wars 38. Bicultural Conflict
Cultural Relativity and Ethnocentrism	1. Fieldwork Among the Yanomamö 3. Eating Christmas in the Kalahari 4. Myth of the Man-Eaters		

Anthropological Perspectives

For at least a century the goals of anthropology have been to describe societies and cultures throughout the world and to compare the differences and similarities between them. Anthropologists study in a variety of settings and situations, ranging from small hamlets and villages to neighborhoods and corporate offices of major urban centers throughout the world. They study hunters and gatherers, peasants, farmers, labor leaders, politicians, and bureaucrats. They examine religious life in Latin America as well as revolutionary movements.

Wherever practicable, anthropologists take on the role of the "participant observer," for it is through active involvement in the lifeways of the people that they hope to gain an insider's perspective without sacrificing the objectivity of the trained scientist. Sometimes the conditions for achieving such a goal may seem to form an almost insurmountable barrier, but anthropologists' persistence, adaptability, and imagination may be employed to overcome the odds against them.

The diversity of focus in anthropology means that it is earmarked less by its particular subject matter than by its perspective. Although the discipline relates to both the biological and social sciences, anthropologists also know that the boundaries drawn between such disciplines are highly artificial. For example, although it may be possible to examine only the social organization of a family unit or the organization of political power in a nation-state, in reality, it is impossible to separate the biological from the social from the economic from the political. The explanatory perspective of anthropology, as the articles in this section exemplify, is to seek out interrelationships among all these factors.

The first three articles in this section illustrate the varying degrees of difficulty an anthropologist may encounter in taking on the role of the participant observer. Napoleon Chagnon's "Doing Fieldwork Among the Yąnomamö" shows, for instance, the hardships imposed by certain physical conditions, the unwillingness of the people to provide needed information, and the vast differences in values and attitudes that must be bridged by the anthropologist just in order to get along. While Richard Kurin ("Doctor, Lawyer, Indian Chief") and Richard Lee ("Eating Christmas in the Kalahari") apparently had fewer problems with the physical conditions and the personalities of the people they were studying, they were not completely accepted by the communities until they found ways to participate as equals in the socioeconomic exchange systems.

Since the way in which fieldwork is conducted may have a great deal to do with conclusions reached, and since anthropologists are their own toughest critics, controversy over objectivity has frequently arisen. Witness, for example, William Arens's calling into question historical and anthropological reports of cannibalism. Even the concept of "cultural relativity," calling for tolerance of other people's customs, carries with it a disturbing streak of subjectivity, claims Henry H. Bagish in "Confessions of a Former Cultural Relativist."

Much is at stake in these discussions, since the purpose of anthropology is not only to describe and explain, but to develop a special vision of the world in which cultural alternatives (past, present, and future) can be measured against one another and used as a guide for human action.

Looking Ahead: Challenge Questions

What is culture shock?

How can anthropologists who become personally involved with a community through participant observation maintain their objectivity as scientists?

In what ways do the results of fieldwork depend on the kinds of questions asked?

How does cross-cultural experience help us to understand ourselves?

In what sense is sharing intrinsic to egalitarianism?

How is it that a phenomenon such as cannibalism can be elevated from myth to fact without concrete evidence?

How can we avoid the pitfalls of cultural relativity and ethnocentrism in dealing with what we think of as harmful practices in other cultures?

Doing Fieldwork among the Yanomamö

Napoleon A. Chagnon

VIGNETTE

The Yanomamö[1] are thinly scattered over a vast and verdant Tropical Forest, living in small villages that are separated by many miles of unoccupied land. They have no writing, but they have a rich and complex language. Their clothing is more decorative than protective: well-dressed men sport nothing more than a few cotton strings around their wrists, ankles, and waists. They tie the foreskin of their penises to the waistring. Women dress about the same. Much of their daily life revolves around gardening, hunting, collecting wild foods, collecting firewood, fetching water, visiting with each other, gossiping, and making the few material possessions they own: baskets, hammocks, bows, arrows, and colorful pigments with which they paint their bodies. Life is relatively easy in the sense that they can 'earn a living' with about three hours' work per day. Most of what they eat they cultivate in their gardens, and most of that is plantains—a kind of cooking banana that is usually eaten green, either roasted on the coals or boiled in pots. Their meat comes from a large variety of game animals, hunted daily by the men. It is usually roasted on coals or smoked, and is always well done. Their villages are round and open—and very public. One can hear, see, and smell almost everything that goes on anywhere in the village. Privacy is rare, but sexual discreetness is possible in the garden or at night while others sleep. The villages can be as small as 40 or 50 people or as large as 300 people, but in all cases there are many more children and babies than there are adults. This is true of most primitive populations and of our own demographic past. Life expectancy is short.

The Yanomamö fall into the category of Tropical Forest Indians called 'foot people'. They avoid large rivers and live in interfluvial plains of the major rivers. They have neighbors to the north, Carib-speaking Ye'kwana, who are true 'river people': they make elegant, large dugout canoes and travel extensively along the major waterways. For the Yanomamö, a large stream is an obstacle and can only be crossed in the dry season. Thus, they have traditionally avoided larger rivers and, because of this, contact with outsiders who usually come by river.

They enjoy taking trips when the jungle abounds with seasonally ripe wild fruits and vegetables. Then, the large village—the *shabono*—is abandoned for a few weeks and everyone camps out a day or so away from the village and garden. On these trips, they make temporary huts from poles, vines, and leaves, each family making a separate hut.

Two major seasons dominate their annual cycle: the wet season, which inundates the low-lying jungle making travel difficult, and the dry season—the time of visiting other villages to feast, trade, and politic with allies. The dry season is also the time when raiders can travel and strike silently at their unsuspecting enemies. The Yanomamö are still conducting intervillage warfare, a phenomenon that affects all aspects of their social organization, settlement pattern, and daily routines. It is not simply 'ritualistic' war: at least one-fourth of all adult males die violently.

Social life is organized around those same principles utilized by all tribesmen: kinship relationships, descent from ancestors, marriage exchanges between kinship/descent groups, and the transient charisma of distinguished headmen who attempt to keep order in the village and whose responsibility it is to determine the village's relationships with those in other villages. Their positions are largely the result of kinship and marriage patterns—they come from the largest kinship groups within the village. They can, by their personal wit, wisdom, and charisma, become autocrats but most of them are largely "greaters" among equals. They, too, must clear gardens, plant crops, collect wild foods, and hunt. They are simultaneously peacemakers and valiant warriors. Peacemaking often requires the threat or actual use of force, and most headmen have an acquired reputation for being *waiteri*: fierce.

The social dynamics within villages are involved with giving and receiving marriageable girls. Marriages are arranged by older kin, usually men, who are brothers, uncles, and the father. It is a political process, for girls are promised in marriage while they are young, and the men who do this attempt to create alliances with other men via marriage exchanges. There is a shortage of women due in part to a sex-ratio imbalance in the younger age categories, but also complicated by the fact that some men have multiple wives. Most fighting within the village stems from sexual affairs or failure to deliver a promised woman—or out-and-out seizure of a married woman by some other man. This can lead to internal fighting and conflict of such an intensity that villages split up and fission, each group then becoming a new village and, often, enemies to each other.

But their conflicts are not blind, uncontrolled violence. They have a series of graded forms of violence that ranges from chest-pounding and club-fighting duels to out-and-out shooting to kill. This gives them a good deal of flexibility in settling disputes without immediate resort to killing. In addition, they have developed patterns of alliance and friendship that serve to limit violence—trading and feasting with others in order to become friends. These alliances can, and often do, result in intervillage exchanges of marriage-able women, which leads to additional amity between villages. No good thing lasts forever, and most alliances crumble. Old friends become hostile and, occasionally, treacherous. Each village must therefore be keenly aware that its neighbors are fickle and must behave accordingly. The thin line between friendship and animosity must be traversed by the village leaders, whose political acumen and strategies are both admirable and complex.

Each village, then, is a replica of all others in a broad sense. But each village is part of a larger political, demographic, and ecological process and it is difficult to attempt to understand the village without knowing something of the larger forces that affect it.

COLLECTING THE DATA IN THE FIELD

I spent 41 months with the Yąnomamö, during which time I acquired some proficiency in their language and, up to a point, submerged myself in their culture and way of life.[2] The thing that impressed me most was the importance of aggression in their culture. I had the opportunity to witness a good many incidents that expressed individual vindictiveness on the one hand and collective bellicosity on the other hand. These ranged in seriousness from the ordinary incidents of wife beating and chest pounding to dueling and organized raids by parties that set out with the intention of ambushing and killing men from enemy villages. One of the villages discussed in the chapters that follow was raided approximately twenty-five times during my first 15 months of fieldwork—six times by the group among whom I was living.

The fact that the Yąnomamö live in a chronic state of warfare is reflected in their mythology, ceremonies, settlement pattern, political behavior, and marriage practices. Accordingly, I have organized this case study in such a way that students can appreciate the effects of warfare on Yąnomamö culture in general and on their social organization and political relationships in particular.

I collected the data under somewhat trying circumstances, some of which I will describe to give the student a rough idea of what is generally meant when anthropologists speak of "culture shock" and "fieldwork." It should be borne in mind, however, that each field situation is in many respects unique, so that the problems I encountered do not necessarily exhaust the range of possible problems other anthropologists have confronted in other areas. There are a few problems, however, that seem to be nearly universal among anthropological fieldworkers, particularly those having to do with eating, bathing, sleeping, lack of privacy, loneliness, or discovering that primitive man is not always as noble as you originally thought—or you yourself not as culturally or emotionally 'flexible' as you assumed.

This is not to state that primitive man everywhere is unpleasant. By way of contrast, I have also done limited fieldwork among the Yąnomamö's northern neighbors, the Carib-speaking Ye'kwana

Indians. This group was very pleasant and charming, all of them anxious to help me and honor bound to show any visitor the numerous courtesies of their system of etiquette. In short, they approached the image of primitive man that I had conjured up, and it was sheer pleasure to work with them. Other anthropologists have also noted sharp contrasts in the people they study from one field situation to another. One of the most startling examples of this is in the work of Colin Turnbull, who first studied the Ituri Pygmies (1965, 1983) and found them delightful, but then studied the Ik (1972) of the desolate outcroppings of the Kenya/Uganda/Sudan border region, a people he had difficulty coping with intellectually, emotionally, and physically. While it is possible that the anthropologist's reactions to a particular people are personal and idiosyncratic, it nevertheless remains that there *are* enormous differences between whole peoples, differences that affect the anthropologist in often dramatic ways.

Hence, what I say about some of my experiences is probably equally true of the experiences of many other fieldworkers. I think I could have profited by reading about the pitfalls and field problems of my teachers; at least I might have been able to avoid some of the more stupid errors I made. In this regard there is a growing body of excellent descriptive work on field research. Students who plan to make a career in anthropology should consult these works, which cover a wide range of field situations in the ethnographic present.[3]

The First Day: The Longest One My first day in the field illustrated to me what my teachers meant when they spoke of "culture shock." I had traveled in a small, aluminum rowboat propelled by a large outboard motor for two and a half days. This took me from the territorial capital, a small town on the Orinoco River, deep into Yąnomamö country. On the morning of the third day we reached a small mission settlement, the field "headquarters" of a group of Americans who were working in two Yąnomamö villages. The missionaries had come out of these villages to hold their annual conference on the progress of their mission work and were conducting their meetings when I arrived. We picked up a passenger at the mission station, James P. Barker, the first non-Yąnomamö to make a sustained, permanent contact with the tribe (in 1950). He had just returned from a year's furlough in the United States, where I had earlier visited him before leaving for Venezuela. He agreed to accompany me to the village I had selected for my base of operations to introduce me to the Indians. This village was also his own home base, but he had no been there for over a year and did not plan to join me for another three months. Mr. Barker had been living with this particular group about five years.

We arrived at the village, Bisaasi-teri, about 2:00 P.M. and docked the boat along the muddy bank at the terminus of the path used by the Indians to fetch their drinking water. It was hot and muggy, and my clothing was soaked with perspiration. It clung uncomfortably to my body, as it did thereafter for the remainder of the work. The small biting gnats were out in astronomical numbers, for it was the beginning of the dry season. My face and hands were swollen from the venom of their numerous stings. In just a few moments I was to meet my first Yąnomamö, my first primitive man. What would he be like? I had visions of entering the village and seeing 125 social facts running about calling each other kinship terms and sharing food, each waiting and anxious to have me collect his genealogy. I would wear them out in turn. Would they like me? This was important to me; I wanted them to be so fond of me that they would adopt me into their kinship system and way of life. I had heard that successful anthropologists always get adopted by their people. I had learned during my seven years of anthropological training at the University of Michigan that kinship was equivalent to society in primitive tribes and that it was a moral way of life, "moral" being something "good" and "desirable." I was determined to work my way into their moral system of kinship and become a member of their society—to be 'accepted' by them.

How Did They Accept You? My heart began to pound as we approached the village and heard the buzz of activity within the circular compound. Mr. Barker commented that he was anxious to see if any changes had taken place while he was away and wondered how many of them had died during his absence. I felt into my back pocket to make sure that my notebook was still there and felt personally more secure when I touched it.

The entrance to the village was covered over with brush and dry palm leaves. We pushed them aside to expose the low opening to the village. The excitement of meeting my first Yąnomamö was almost unbearable as I duck-waddled through the low passage into the village clearing.

I looked up and gasped when I saw a dozen burly, naked, sweaty, hideous men staring at us down the shafts of their drawn arrows! Immense wads of green tobacco were stuck between their lower teeth and lips making them look even more hideous, and strands of dark-green slime dripped or hung from their nostrils—strands so long that they clung to their pectoral muscles or drizzled down their chins. We arrived at the village while the men were blowing a hallucinogenic drug up their noses. One of the side effects of the drug is a runny nose. The mucus is always saturated with the green powder and they usually let it run freely from their nostrils. My next discovery was that there were a dozen or so vicious, underfed dogs snapping at my legs, circling me as if I were to be their next meal. I just stood there holding my notebook, helpless and pathetic. Then the stench of the decaying vegetation and filth hit me and I almost got sick. I was horrified. What kind of welcome was this for the person who came here to live with you and learn your way of life, to become friends with you? They put their weapons down when they recognized Barker and returned to their chanting, keeping a nervous eye on the village entrances.

We had arrived just after a serious fight. Seven women had been abducted the day before by a neighboring group, and the local men and their guests had just that morning recovered

five of them in a brutal club fight that nearly ended in a shooting war. The abductors, angry because they had lost five of their seven new captives, vowed to raid the Bisaasi-teri. When we arrived and entered the village unexpectedly, the Indians feared that we were the raiders. On several occasions during the next two hours the men in the village jumped to their feet, armed themselves, and waited nervously for the noise outside the village to be identified. My enthusiasm for collecting ethnographic facts diminished in proportion to the number of times such an alarm was raised. In fact, I was relieved when Barker suggested that we sleep across the river for the evening. It would be safer over there.

As we walked down the path to the boat, I pondered the wisdom of having decided to spend a year and a half with this tribe before I had even seen what they were like. I am not ashamed to admit that had there been a diplomatic way out, I would have ended my fieldwork then and there. I did not look forward to the next day—and months—when I would be left alone with the Indians; I did not speak a word of their language, and they were decidedly different from what I had imagined them to be. The whole situation was depressing, and I wondered why I ever decided to switch from physics and engineering in the first place. I had not eaten all day, I was soaking wet from perspiration, the gnats were biting me, and I was covered with red pigment, the result of a dozen or so complete examinations I had been given by as many pushy Yąnomamö men. These examinations capped an otherwise grim day. The men would blow their noses into their hands, flick as much of the mucus off that would separate in a snap of the wrist, wipe the residue into their hair, and then carefully examine my face, arms, legs, hair, and the contents of my pockets. I asked Barker how to say, "Your hands are dirty"; my comments were met by the Indians in the following way: They would 'clean' their hands by spitting a quantity of slimy tobacco juice into them, rub them together, grin, and then proceed with the examination.

Mr. Barker and I crossed the river

and slung our hammocks. When he pulled his hammock out of a rubber bag, a heavy, disagreeable odor of mildewed cotton came with it. "Even the missionaries are filthy," I thought to myself. Within two weeks, everything I owned smelled the same way, and I lived with that odor for the remainder of the fieldwork. My own habits of personal cleanliness declined to such levels that I didn't even mind being examined by the Yąnomamö, as I was not much cleaner than they were after I had adjusted to the circumstances. It is difficult to blow your nose gracefully when you are stark naked and the invention of handkerchiefs is millenia away.

Life in the Jungle: Oatmeal, Peanut Butter, and Bugs It isn't easy to plop down in the Amazon Basin for a year and get immediately into the anthropological swing of things. You have been told about horrible diseases, snakes, jaguars, quicksand, and getting lost. Some of the dangers are real, but your imagination makes them more real and threatening than many of them really are. What my teachers never bothered to tell me about, however, was the mundane, nonexciting and trivial stuff—like eating, defecating, sleeping, or keeping clean. These turned out to be the bane of my existence during the first several months of field research. I set up my household in Barker's abandoned mud hut, a few yards from the village of Bisaasi-teri, and immediately set to work building my own mud/thatch hut with the help of the Yąnomamö. Meanwhile, I had to eat and try to do my 'field research'. I soon discovered that it was an enormously time-consuming task to maintain my own body in the manner to which it had grown accustomed in the relatively antiseptic environment of the northern United States. Either I would be relatively well fed and relatively comfortable in a fresh change of clothes and do very little fieldwork, or I could do considerably more fieldwork and be less well fed and less comfortable.

It is appalling how complicated it can be to make oatmeal in the jungle. First, I had to make two trips to the river to haul the water. Next, I had to prime my kerosene stove with alcohol to get it burning, a tricky procedure when you are trying to mix powdered milk and fill a coffee pot at the same time: the alcohol prime always burned out before I could turn the kerosene on, and I would have to start all over. Or, I would turn the kerosene on, optimistically hoping that the element was still hot enough to vaporize the fuel, and start a small fire in my palm-thatched hut as the liquid kerosene squirted all over the table and walls and then ignited. Many amused Yąnomamö onlookers quickly learned the English phrase "Oh, Shit!" . . . and, once they discovered that the phrase offended and irritated the missionaries, they used it as often as they could in their presence. I usually had to start over with the alcohol. Then I had to boil the oatmeal and pick the bugs out of it. All my supplies, of course, were carefully stored in rat-proof, moisture-proof, and insect-proof containers, not one of which ever served its purposed adequately. Just taking things out of the multiplicity of containers and repacking them afterward was a minor project in itself. By the time I had hauled the water to cook with, unpacked my food, prepared the oatmeal, milk, and coffee, heated water for dishes, washed and dried the dishes, repacked the food in the containers, stored the containers in locked trunks, and cleaned up my mess, the ceremony of preparing breakfast had brought me almost up to lunch time!

Eating three meals a day was simply out of the question. I solved the problem by eating a single meal that could be prepared in a single container, or, at most, in two containers, washed my dishes only when there were no clean ones left, using cold river water, and wore each change of clothing at least a week—to cut down on my laundry problem—a courageous undertaking in the tropics. I reeked like a jockstrap that had been left to mildew in the bottom of some dark gym locker. I also became less concerned about sharing my provisions with the rats, insects, Yąnomamö, and the elements, thereby eliminating the need for my complicated storage process. I was able to last most of the day on *café con leche*, heavily sugared espresso coffee diluted about five to one with hot milk. I would prepare this in the evening and store it in a large thermos. Frequently, my single meal was no more complicated than a can of sardines and a package of soggy crackers. But at least two or three times a week I would do something 'special' and sophisticated, like make a batch of oatmeal or boil rice and add a can of tuna fish or tomato paste to it. I even saved time by devising a water system that obviated the trips to the river. I had a few sheets of tin roofing brought in and made a rain water trap; I caught the water on the tin surface, funneled it into an empty gasoline drum, and then ran a plastic hose from the drum to my hut. When the drum was exhausted in the dry season, I would get a few Yąnomamö boys to fill it with buckets of water from the river, 'paying' them with crackers, of which they grew all too fond all too soon.

I ate much less when I traveled with the Yąnomamö to visit other villages. Most of the time my travel diet consisted of roasted or boiled green plantains (cooking bananas) that I obtained from the Yąnomamö, but I always carried a few cans of sardines with me in case I got lost or stayed away longer than I had planned. I found peanut butter and crackers a very nourishing 'trail' meal, and a simple one to prepare. It was nutritious and portable, and only one tool was required to make the meal: a hunting knife that could be cleaned by wiping the blade on a convenient leaf. More importantly, it was one of the few foods the Yąnomamö would let me eat in relative peace. It looked suspiciously like animal feces to them, an impression I encouraged.

I referred to the peanut butter as the feces of babies or 'cattle'. They found this disgusting and repugnant. They did not know what 'cattle' were, but were increasingly aware that I ate several canned products of such an animal. Tin cans were thought of as containers made of 'machete skins', but how the cows got inside was always a mystery to them. I went out of my way to describe my foods in such a way as to make them sound unpalatable to them, for it gave me some peace of mind while I ate: they wouldn't beg for a share of something that was too horrible to contemplate. Fieldworkers develop strange defense mechanisms and strategies, and this was one of my own forms of adaptation to the fieldwork. On another occasion I was eating a can of frankfurters and growing very weary of the demands from one of the onlookers for a share in my meal. When he finally asked what I was eating, I replied: "Beef." He then asked: "Shaki![4] What part of the animal are you eating?" To which I replied, "Guess." He muttered a contemptuous epithet, but stopped asking for a share. He got back at me later, as we shall see.

Meals were a problem in a way that had nothing to do with the inconvenience of preparing them. Food sharing is important to the Yanomamö in context of displaying friendship. "I am hungry!" is almost a form of greeting with them. I could not possibly have brought enough food with me to feed the entire village, yet they seemed to overlook this logistic fact as they begged for my food. What became fixed in their minds was the fact that I did not share my food with whomsoever was present—usually a small crowd—at each and every meal. Nor could I easily enter their system of reciprocity with respect to food: every time one of them 'gave' me something 'freely', he would dog me for months to 'pay him back', not necessarily with food but with knives, fishhooks, axes, and so on. Thus, if I accepted a plantain from someone in a different village while I was on a visit, he would most likely visit me in the future and demand a machete as payment for the time that he 'fed' me. I usually reacted to these kinds of demands by giving a banana, the customary reciprocity in their culture—food for food— but this would be a disappointment for the individual who had nursed visions of that single plantain growing into a machete over time. Many years after beginning my fieldwork I was approached by one of the prominent men who demanded a machete for a piece of meat he claimed he had given me five or six years earlier.

Despite the fact that most of them knew I would not share my food with them at their request, some of them always showed up at my hut during meal-

time. I gradually resigned myself to this and learned to ignore their persistent demands while I ate. Some of them would get angry because I failed to give in, but most of them accepted it as just a peculiarity of the subhuman foreigner who had come to live among them. If or when I did accede to a request for a share of my food, my hut quickly filled with Yanomamö, each demanding their share of the food that I had just given to one of them. Their begging for food was not provoked by hunger, but by a desire to try something new and to attempt to establish a coercive relationship in which I would accede to a demand. If one received something, all others would immediately have to test the system to see if they, too, could coerce me.

A few of them went out of their way to make my meals downright unpleasant—to spite me for not sharing, especially if it was a food that they had tried before and liked, or a food that was part of their own cuisine. For example, I was eating a cracker with peanut butter and honey one day. The Yanomamö will do almost anything for honey, one of the most prized delicacies in their own diet. One of my cynical onlookers—the fellow who had earlier watched me eating frankfurters—immediately recognized the honey and knew that I would not share the tiny precious bottle. It would be futile to even ask. Instead, he glared at me and queried icily, "Shaki! What kind of animal semen are you pouring onto your food and eating?" His question had the desired effect and my meal ended.

Finally, there was the problem of being lonely and separated from your own kind, especially your family. I tried to overcome this by seeking personal friendships among the Yanomamö. This usually complicated the matter because all my 'friends' simply used my confidence to gain privileged access to my hut and my cache of steel tools and trade goods—and looted me when I wasn't looking. I would be bitterly disappointed that my erstwhile friend thought no more of me than to finesse our personal relationship exclusively with the intention of getting at my locked up possessions, and my depression would hit new

lows every time I discovered this. The loss of the possessions bothered me much less than the shock that I was, as far as most of them were concerned, nothing more than a source of desirable items. No holds were barred in relieving me of these, since I was considered something subhuman, a non-Yanomamö.

The hardest thing to learn to live with was the incessant, passioned, and often aggressive demands they would make. It would become so unbearable at times that I would have to lock myself in my hut periodically just to escape from it. Privacy is one of our culture's most satisfying achievements, one you never think about until you suddenly have none. It is like not appreciating how good your left thumb feels until someone hits it with a hammer. But I did not want privacy for its own sake; rather, I simply had to get away from the begging. Day and night for the entire time I lived with the Yanomamö I was plagued by such demands as: "Give me a knife, I am poor!"; "If you don't take me with you on your next trip to Widokaiya-teri, I'll chop a hole in your canoe!"; "Take us hunting up the Mavaca River with your shotgun or we won't help you!"; "Give me some matches so I can trade with the Reyaboböwei-teri, and be quick about it or I'll hit you!"; "Share your food with me, or I'll burn your hut!"; "Give me a flashlight so I can hunt at night!" "Give me all your medicine, I itch all over!"; "Give me an ax or I'll break into your hut when you are away and steal all of them!" And so I was bombarded by such demands day after day, month after month, until I could not bear to see a Yanomamö at times.

It was not as difficult to become calloused to the incessant begging as it was to ignore the sense of urgency, the impassioned tone of voice and whining, or the intimidation and aggression with which many of the demands were made. It was likewise difficult to adjust to the fact that the Yanomamö refused to accept "No" for an answer until or unless it seethed with passion and intimidation—which it did after a few months. So persistent and characteristic is the begging that the early 'semi-official' maps made by the Venezuelan

Malaria Control Service (Malarialogia) designated the site of their first permanent field station, next to the village of Bisaasi-teri, as *Yababuhii*; "Gimme." I had to become like the Yąnomamö to be able to get along with them on their terms: somewhat sly, aggressive, intimidating, and pushy.

It became indelibly clear to me shortly after I arrived there that had I failed to adjust in this fashion I would have lost six months of supplies to them in a single day or would have spent most of my time ferrying them around in my canoe or taking them on long hunting trips. As it was, I did spend a considerable amount of time doing these things and did succumb often to their outrageous demands for axes and machetes, at least at first, for things changed as I became more fluent in their language and learned how to defend myself socially as well verbally: I was learning the Yąnomamö equivalent of a left jab to the jawbone. More importantly, had I failed to demonstrate that I could not be pushed around beyond a certain point, I would have been the subject of far more ridicule, theft, and practical jokes than was the actual case. In short, I had to acquire a certain proficiency in their style of interpersonal politics and to learn how to imply subtly that certain potentially undesirable, but unspecified, consequences might follow if they did such and such to me. They do this to each other incessantly in order to establish precisely the point at which they cannot goad or intimidate an individual any further without precipitating some kind of retaliation. As soon as I realized this and gradually acquired the self-confidence to adopt this strategy, it became clear that much of the intimidation was calculated to determine my flash point or my 'last ditch' position—and I got along much better with them. Indeed, I even regained some lost ground. It was sort of like a political, interpersonal game that everyone had to play, but one in which each individual sooner or later had to give evidence that his bluffs and implied threats could be backed up with a sanction. I suspect that the frequency of wife beating is a component in this syndrome, since men can display their *waiteri* (ferocity) and

'show' others that they are capable of great violence. Beating a wife with a club is one way of displaying ferocity, one that does not expose the man to much danger—unless the wife has concerned, aggressive brothers in the village who will come to her aid. Apparently the important thing in wife beating is that the man has displayed his presumed potential for violence and the intended message is that other men ought to treat him with circumspection, caution, and even deference.

After six months, the level of Yąnomamö demand was tolerable in the village I used for my base of operations. We had adjusted somewhat to each other and knew what to expect with regard to demands for food, trade goods and favors. Had I elected to remain in just one Yąnomamö village for the entire duration of my first 15 months of fieldwork the experience would have been far more enjoyable than it actually was. However, as I began to understand the social and political dynamics of this village, it became patently obvious that I would have to travel to many other villages to determine the demographic bases and political histories that lay behind what I could understand in the village of Bisaasi-teri. I began making regular trips to some dozen neighboring Yąnomamö villages as my language fluency improved. I collected local genealogies there, or rechecked and cross-checked those I had collected elsewhere. Hence, the intensity of begging was relatively constant and relatively high for the duration of my fieldwork, for I had to establish my personal flashpoint position in each village I visited and revisited.

For the most part, my own 'fierceness' took the form of shouting back at the Yąnomamö as loudly and as passionately as they shouted at me, especially at first, when I did not know much of the language. As I became more fluent and learned more about their political tactics, I became more sophisticated in the art of bluffing and brinksmanship. For example, I paid one young man a machete (then worth about $2.50) to cut a palm tree and help me make boards from the wood. I used these to fashion a flooring in the bottom of my dugout

canoe to keep my possessions out of the water that always seeped into the canoe and sloshed around. That after noon I was working with one of my informants in the village. The long-awaited mission supply boat arrived and most of the Yąnomamö ran out of the village to see the supplies and try to beg items from the crew. I continued to work in the village for another hour or so and went down to the river to visit with the men on the supply boat. When I reached the river I noticed, with anger and frustration, that the Yąnomamö had chopped up all my new floor boards to use them as crude paddles to get their own canoes across the river to the supply boat.[5] I knew that if I ignored this abuse I would have invited the Yąnomamö to take even greater liberties with my possessions in the future. I got into my canoe, crossed the river, and docked amidst their flimsy, leaky craft. I shouted loudly to them, attracting their attention: they were somewhat sheepfaced, but all had mischievous grins on their impish faces. A few of them came down to the canoe, where I proceeded with a spirited lecture that revealed my anger at their audacity and license: I explained that I had just that morning paid one of them a machete for bringing me the palmwood, how hard I had worked to shape each board and place it in the canoe, how carefully and painstakingly I had tied each one in with vines, how much I perspired, how many gnat bites I had suffered, and so on. Then, with exaggerated drama and finality, I withdrew my hunting knife as their grins disappeared and cut each one of their canoes loose and set it into the strong current of the Orinoco River where it was immediately swept up and carried downstream. I left without looking back and huffed over to the other side of the river to resume my work.

They managed to borrow another canoe and, after some effort, recovered their dugouts. Later, the headman of the village told me, with an approving chuckle, that I had done the correct thing. Everyone in the village, except, of course, the culprits, supported and defended my actions—and my status increased as a consequence.

Whenever I defended myself in such

ways I got along much better with the Yanomamö and gradually acquired the respect of many of them. A good deal of their demeanor toward me was directed with the forethought of establishing the point at which I would draw the line and react defensively. Many of them, years later, reminisced about the early days of my fieldwork when I was timid and *mobode* ("stupid") and a little afraid of them, those golden days when it was easy to bully me into giving my goods away for almost nothing.

Theft was the most persistent situation that required some sort of defensive action. I simply could not keep everything I owned locked in trunks, and the Yanomamö came into my hut and left at will. I eventually developed a very effective strategy for recovering almost all the stolen items: I would simply ask a child who took the item and then I would confiscate that person's hammock when he was not around, giving a spirited lecture to all who could hear on the antisociality of thievery as I stalked off in a faked rage with the thief's hammock slung over my shoulder. Nobody ever attempted to stop me from doing this, and almost all of them told me that my technique for recovering my possessions was ingenious. By nightfall the thief would appear at my hut with the stolen item or send it over with someone else to make an exchange to recover his hammock. He would be heckled by his covillagers for having got caught and for being embarrassed into returning my item for his hammock. The explanation was usually, "I just borrowed your ax! I wouldn't think of stealing it!"

Collecting Yanomamö Genealogies and Reproductive Histories My purpose for living among the Yanomamö was to systematically collect certain kinds of information on genealogy, reproduction, marriage practices, kinship, settlement pattern, migrations, and politics. Much of the fundamental data was genealogical—who was the parent of whom, tracing these connections as far back in time as Yanomamö knowledge and memory permitted. Since 'primitive' society is largely organized by kinship relationships, figuring out the social organization of the Yanomamö es-

sentially meant collecting extensive data on genealogies, marriage, and reproduction. This turned out to be a staggering and very frustrating problem. I could not have deliberately picked a more difficult tribe to work with in this regard. They have very stringent name taboos and eschew mentioning the names of prominent living people as well as all deceased friends and relatives. They attempt to name people in such a way that when the person dies and they can no longer use his or her name, the loss of the word in their language is not inconvenient. Hence, they name people for specific and minute parts of things, such as "toenail of sloth," "whisker of howler monkey," and so on, thereby being able to retain the words "toenail" or "whisker" but somewhat handicapped in referring to these anatomical parts of sloths and monkeys respectively. The taboo is maintained even for the living, for one mark of prestige is the courtesy others show you by not using your name publicly. This is particularly true for men, who are much more competitive for status than women in this culture, and it is fascinating to watch boys grow into young men, demanding to be called either by a kinship term in public, or by a teknonymous reference such as 'brother of Himotoma'. The more effective they are at getting others to avoid using their names, the more public acknowledgement there is that they are of high esteem. Helena Valero, a Brazilian woman who was captured as a child by a Yanomamö raiding party, was married for many years to a Yanomamö headman before she discovered what his name was (Biocca, 1970). The sanctions behind the taboo are more complex than just this, for they involve a combination of fear, respect, admiration, political deference, and honor.

I tried to use kinship terms alone to collect genealogies at first, but Yanomamö kinship terms, like the kinship terms in all systems, are ambiguous at some point because the include so many possible relatives (as the term "uncle" does in our own kinship system). Again, their system of kin classification merges many relatives that we 'separate' by using different terms: they

call both their actual father and their father's brother by a single term, whereas we call one "father" and the other "uncle." I was forced, therefore, to resort to personal names to collect unambiguous genealogies or 'pedigrees'. They quickly grasped what I was up to and that I was determined to learn everyone's 'true name', which amounted to an invasion of their system of prestige and etiquette, if not a flagrant violation of it. They reacted to this in a brilliant but devastating manner: They invented false names for everybody in the village and systematically learned them, freely revealing to me the 'true' identities of everyone. I smugly thought I had cracked the system and enthusiastically constructed elaborate genealogies over a period of some five months. They enjoyed watching me learn their names and kinship relationships. I naively assumed that I would get the 'truth' to each question and the best information by working in public. This set the stage for converting my serious project into an amusing hoax of the grandest proportions. Each 'informant' would try to outdo his peers by inventing a name even more preposterous or ridiculous than what I had been given by someone earlier, the explanations for discrepancies being "Well, he has two names and this is the other one." They even fabricated devilishly improbable genealogical relationships, such as someone being married to his grandmother, or worse yet, to his mother-in-law, a grotesque and horrifying prospect to the Yanomamö. I would collect the desired names and relationships by having my informant whisper the name of the person softly into my ear, noting that he or she was the parent of such and such or the child of such and such, and so on. Everyone who was observing my work would then insist that I repeat the name aloud, roaring in hysterical laughter as I clumsily pronounced the name, sometimes laughing until tears streamed down their faces. The 'named' person would usually react with annoyance and hiss some untranslatable epithet at me, which served to reassure me that I had the 'true' name. I conscientiously checked and rechecked the names and relationships with multiple informants, pleased to see the inconsistencies disappear as my genealogy sheets filled with those desirable little triangles and circles, thousands of them.

My anthropological bubble was burst when I visited a village about 12 hours' walk to the southwest of Bisaasi-teri. I was chatting with the local headman of this village and happened to casually drop the name of the wife of the Bisaasi-teri headman. A stunned silence followed, and then a villagewide roar of uncontrollable laughter, choking, gasping, and howling followed. It seems that the Bisaasi-teri headman was married to a woman named "hairy cunt." It also seems that the Bisaasi-teri headman was called "long dong" and his brother "eagle shit." The Bisaasi-teri headman had a son called "asshole" and a daughter called "fart breath." And so on. Blood welled up to my temples as I realized that I had nothing but nonsense to show for my five months' of dedicated genealogical effort, and I had to throw away almost all the information I had collected on this the most basic set of data I had come there to get. I understood at that point why the Bisaasi-teri laughed so hard when they made me repeat the names of their covillagers, and why the 'named' person would react with anger and annoyance as I pronounced his 'name' aloud.

I was forced to change research strategy—to make an understatement of a serious situation. The first thing I did was to begin working in private with my informants to eliminate the horseplay and distraction that attended public sessions. Once I did this, my informants, who did not know what others were telling me, began to agree with each other and I managed to begin learning the 'real' names, starting first with children and gradually moving to adult women and then, cautiously, adult men, a sequence that reflected the relative degree of intransigence at revealing names of people. As I built up a core of accurate genealogies and relationships—a core that all independent informants had verified repetitiously—I could 'test' any new informant by soliciting his or her opinion and knowledge about these 'core' people whose names and relationships I was confident were accurate. I

was, in this fashion, able to immediately weed out the mischievous informants who persisted in trying to deceive me. Still, I had great difficulty getting the names of dead kinsmen, the only accurate way to extend genealogies back in time. Even my best informants continued to falsify names of the deceased, especially closely related deceased. The falsifications at this point were not serious and turned out to be readily corrected as my interviewing methods improved. Most of the deceptions were of the sort where the informant would give me the name of a living man as the father of some child whose actual father was dead, a response that enabled the informant to avoid using the name of a deceased kinsman or friend.

The quality of a genealogy depends in part on the number of generations it embraces, and the name taboo prevented me from making any substantial progress in learning about the deceased ancestors of the present population. Without this information, I could not, for example, document marriage patterns and interfamilial alliances through time. I had to rely on older informants for this information, but these were the most reluctant informants of all for this data. As I became more proficient in the language and more skilled at detecting fabrications, my informants became better at deception. One of them was particularly cunning and persuasive, following a sort of Mark Twain policy that the most effective lie is a sincere lie. He specialized in making a ceremony out of false names for dead ancestors. He would look around nervously to make sure nobody was listening outside my hut, enjoin me never to mention the name again, become very anxious and spooky, and grab me by the head to whisper a secret name into my ear. I was always elated after a session with him, because I managed to add several generations of ancestors for particular members of the village. Others steadfastly refused to give me such information. To show my gratitude, I paid him quadruple the rate that I had been paying the others. When word got around that I had increased the pay for genealogical and demographic information volunteers be-

gan pouring into my hut to 'work' for me, assuring me of their changed ways and keen desire to divest themselves of the 'truth'.

Enter Rerebawä; Inmarried Tough Guy I discovered that the old man was lying quite by accident. A club fight broke out in the village one day, the result of a dispute over the possession of a woman. She had been promised to a young man in the village, a man named Rerebawä, who was particularly aggressive. He had married into Bisaasi-teri and was doing his 'bride service'—a period of several years during which he had to provide game for his wife's father and mother, provide them with wild foods he might collect, help them in certain gardening and other tasks. Rerebawä had already been given one of the daughters in marriage and was promised her younger sister as his second wife. He was enraged when the younger sister, then about 16 years old, began having an affair with another young man in the village, Bäkotawä, making no attempt to conceal it. Rerebawä challenged Bäkotawä to a club fight. He swaggered boisterously out to the duel with his 10-foot-club, a roof-pole he had cut from the house on the spur of the moment, as is the usual procedure. He hurled insult after insult at both Bäkotawä and his father, trying to goad them into a fight. His insults were bitter and nasty. They tolerated them for a few moments but grew enraged. They came out of their hammocks and ripped out roof-poles, now returning the insults verbally, and rushed to the village clearing. Rerebawä continued to insult them, goading them into striking him on the head with their equally long clubs. Had either of them struck his head—which he held out conspicuously for them to swing at—he would then have the right to take his turn on their heads with his club. His opponents were intimidated by his fury, and simply backed down, refusing to strike him, and the fight ended. He had outbluffed them. All three returned pompously to their respective hammocks, exchanging nasty insults as they departed. But Rerebawä had won the showdown and thereafter swaggered around the village, insulting the two men behind their backs at every opportunity. He was genuinely angry with them, to the point of calling the older man by the name of his long-deceased father. I quickly seized on this incident as an opportunity to collect an accurate genealogy and pumped Rerebawä about this adversary's ancestors. Rerebawä had been particularly 'pushy' with me up to this point, but we soon became warm friends and staunch allies: we were both 'outsiders' in Bisaasi-teri and, although he was a Yanomamö, he nevertheless had to put up with some considerable amount of pointed teasing and scorn from the locals, as all inmarried "sons-in-law" must. He gave me the information I requested of his adversary's deceased ancestors, almost with devilish glee. I asked about dead ancestors of other people in the village and got prompt, unequivocal answers: he was angry with everyone in the village. When I compared his answers to those of the old man, it was obvious that one of them was lying. I then challenged his answers. He explained, in a sort of "you damned fool, don't you know better?" tone of voice that everyone in the village knew the old man was lying to me and gloating over it when I was out of earshot. The names the old man had given to me were names of dead ancestors of the members of a village so far away that he thought I would never have occasion to check them out authoritatively. As it turned out, Rerebawä knew most of the people in that distant village and recognized the names given by the old man.

I then went over the complete genealogical records with Rerebawä, genealogies I had presumed to be close to their final form. I had to revise them all because of the numerous lies and falsifications they contained, much of it provided by the sly old man. Once again, after months of work, I had to recheck everything with Rerebawä's aid. Only the living members of the nuclear families turned out to be accurate; the deceased ancestors were mostly fabrications.

Discouraging as it was to have to recheck everything all over again, it was a major turning point in my fieldwork. Thereafter, I began taking advantage of local arguments and animosities in selecting my informants, and used more extensively informants who had married into the village in the recent past. I also began traveling more regularly to other villages at this time to check on genealogies, seeking out villages whose members were on strained terms with the people about whom I wanted information. I would then return to my base in the village of Bisaasi-teri and check with local informants the accuracy of the new information. If the informants displayed annoyance when I mentioned the new names that I had acquired from informants in distant villages, I was almost certain that the information was accurate. I had to be careful, though, and scrupulously select my local informants in such a way that I would not be inquiring about *their* closely related kin. Thus, for each of my local informants, I had to make lists of names of certain deceased people that I dared not mention in their presence. But despite this precaution, I would occasionally hit a new name that would put my informant into a rage, or into a surly mood, such as that of a dead brother or sister whose existence had not been indicated to me by other informants. This usually terminated my day's work with that informant, for he or she would be too touchy or upset to continue any further, and I would be reluctant to take a chance on accidentally discovering another dead close kinsman soon after discovering the first.

These were always unpleasant experiences, and occasionally dangerous as well, depending on the temperament of my informant. On one occasion I was planning to visit a village that had been raided recently by one of their enemies. A woman, whose name I had on my census list for that village, had been killed by the raiders. Killing women is considered to be bad form in Yanomamö warfare, but this woman was deliberately killed for revenge. The raiders were unable to bushwhack someone who stepped out of the village at dawn to urinate, so they shot a volley of arrows over the roof into the village and beat a hasty retreat. Unfortunately, one of the arrows struck and killed a woman, an accident. For that reason, her village's raiders *deliberately* sought out and killed a woman in retaliation—whose name was on my list. My reason for going to the village was to update my census data on a name-by-name basis and estimate the ages of all the residents. I knew I had the name of the dead woman in my list, but nobody would dare to utter her name so I could remove it. I knew that I would be in very serious trouble if I got to the village and said her name aloud, and I desperately wanted to remove it from my list. I called on one of my regular and usually cooperative informants and asked him to tell me the woman's name. He refused adamantly, explaining that she was a close relative—and was angry that I even raised the topic with him. I then asked him if he would let me whisper the names of *all* the women of that village in his ear, and he would simply have to nod when I hit the right name. We had been 'friends' for some time, and I thought I was able to predict his reaction, and thought that our friendship was good enough to use this procedure. He agreed to the procedure, and I began whispering the names of the women, one by one. We were alone in my hut so that nobody would know what we were doing and nobody could hear us. I read the names softly, continuing to the next when his response was a negative. When I ultimately hit the dead woman's name, he flew out of his chair, enraged and trembling violently, his arm raised to strike me: "You son-of-a-bitch!" he screamed. "If you say her name in my presence again, I'll kill you in an instant!" I sat there, bewildered, shocked, and confused. And frightened, as much because of his reaction, but also because I could imagine what might happen to me should I unknowingly visit a village to check genealogy accuracy without knowing that someone had just died there or had been shot by raiders since my last visit. I reflected on the several articles I had read as a graduate student that explained the "genealogical method," but could not recall anything about its being a potentially hazardous technique. My furious informant left my hut, never again to be invited back to be an informant. I had other similar experiences in different villages, but I was always fortunate in that the dead person had been dead for some time, or was not very closely related to the individual into whose ear I whispered the forbidden name. I was cautioned to desist from saying any more names lest I get people 'angry'.

Kąobawä: The Bisaasi-teri Headman Volunteers to Help Me I had been working on the genealogies for nearly a year when another individual came to my aid. It was Kąobawä, the headman of Upper Bisaasi-teri. The village of Bisaasi-teri was split into two components, each with its own garden and own circular house. Both were in sight of each other. However, the intensity and frequency of internal bickering and argumentation was so high that they decided to split into two separate groups, but would remain close to each other for protection in case they were raided. One group was downstream from the other; I refer to that group as the "Lower" Bisaasi-teri and call Kąobawä's group "Upper" (upstream) Bisaasi-teri, a convenience they themselves adopted after separating from each other. I spent most of my time with the members of Kąobawä's group, some 200 people when I first arrived there. I did not have much contact with Kąobawä during the early months of my work—he was a somewhat retiring, quiet man, and among the Yąnomamö, the outsider has little time to notice the rare quiet ones when most everyone else is in the front row, pushing and demanding attention. He showed up at my hut one day after all the others had left. He had come to volunteer to help me with the genealogies. He was "poor," he explained, and needed a machete. He would work only on the condition that I did not ask him about his own parents and other very close kinsmen who had died. He also added that he would not lie to me as the others had done in the past.

This was perhaps the single most important event in my first year and a half of field research, for out of this incidental meeting evolved a very warm friendship, and what followed from it was a wealth of accurate information on the political history of Kąobawä's village and related villages, highly detailed genealogical information, and hundreds of valuable insights into the Yąnomamö way of like, Kąobawä's familiarity with his group's history and his candidness were remarkable. His knowledge of details was almost encyclopedic, his memory almost photographic. More than that, he was enthusiastic about making sure I learned the truth, and he encouraged me, indeed, demanded that I learn all details I might otherwise have ignored. If there were subtle details he could not recite on the spot, he would advise me to wait until he could check things out with someone else in the village. He would often do this clandestinely, giving me a report the next day, telling me who revealed the new information and whether or not he thought they were in a position to know it. Between Kąobawä and Rerebawä, I made enormous gains in information and understanding toward the end of my first field trip and became lifelong friends with both. And both men knew that I had to get his genealogy from the other one. It was one of those understandings we all had and none of us could mention.

Once again I went over the genealogies with Kąobawä to recheck them, a considerable task by this time: they included about two thousand names, representing several generations of individuals from four different villages. Rerebawä's information was very accurate, and Kąobawä's contribution enabled me to trace the genealogies further back in time. Thus, after nearly a year of intensive effort on genealogies, Yąnomamö demographic patterns and social organization began to make a good deal of sense to me. Only at this point did the patterns through time begin to emerge in the data, and I could begin to understand how kinship groups took form, exchanged women in marriage over several generations, and only then did the fissioning of larger villages into small ones emerge as a chronic and important feature of Yąnomamö social, political, demographic, economic, and ecological adaptation. At this point I was able to begin formulating more sophisticated questions, for there was now a pattern to work from and one to flesh out. Without the help of Rerebawä

and Kacaobawä it would have taken much longer to make sense of the plethora of details I had collected from not only them, but dozens of other informants as well. . . .

Kąobawä was about 40 years old when I first came to his village in 1964. I say "about 40" because the Yąnomamö numeration system has only three numbers: one, two, and more-than-two. It is hard to give accurate ages or dates for events when the informants have no means in their language to reveal such detail. Kąobawä is the headman of his village, meaning that he has somewhat more responsibility in political dealings with other Yąnomamö groups, and very little control over those who live in his group except when the village is being raided by enemies. . . . Most of the time men like Kąobawä are like the North American Indian 'chief' whose authority was characterized in the following fashion: "One word from the chief, and each man does as he pleases." There are different 'styles' of political leadership among the Yąnomamö. Some leaders are mild, quiet, inconspicuous most of the time, but intensely competent. They act parsimoniously, but when they do, people listen and conform. Other men are more tyrannical, despotic, pushy, flamboyant, and unpleasant to all around them. They shout orders frequently, are prone to beat their wives, or pick on weaker men. Some are very violent. I have met headmen who run the entire spectrum between these polar types, for I have visited some 60 Yąnomamö villages. Kąobawä stands at the mild, quietly competent end of the spectrum. He has had six wives thus far—and temporary affairs with as many more, at least one of which resulted in a child that is publicly acknowledged as his child. When I first met him he had just two wives: Bahimi and Koamashima. Bahimi had two living children when I first met her; many others had died. She was the older and enduring wife, as much a friend to him as a mate. Their relationship was as close to what we think of as 'love' in our culture as I have seen among the Yąnomamö. His second wife was a girl of about 20 years, Koamashima. She had a new baby boy when I first met her, her first child. There was speculation that Kąobawä was planning to give Koamashima to one of his younger brothers who had no wife; he occasionally allows his younger brother to have sex with Koamashima, but only if he asks in advance. Kąobawä gave another wife to one of his other brothers because she was *beshi* ("horny"). In fact, this earlier wife had been married to two other men, both of whom discarded her because of her infidelity. Kąobawä had one daughter by her. However, the girl is being raised by Kąobawä's brother, but acknowledged to be Kąobawä's child.

Bahimi, his oldest wife, is about five years younger than he. She is his cross-cousin—his mother's brother's daughter. Ideally, all Yąnomamö men should marry a cross-cousin, as we shall discuss in a later chapter. Bahimi was pregnant when I began my fieldwork, but she destroyed the infant when it was born—a boy in this case—explaining tearfully that she had no choice. The new baby would have competed for milk with Ariwari, her youngest child, who was still nursing. Rather than expose Ariwari to the dangers and uncertainty of an early weaning, she chose to terminate the newborn instead. By Yąnomamö standards, this has been a very warm, enduring marriage. Kąobawä claims he only beats Bahimi 'once in a while, and only lightly' and she, for her part, never has affairs with other men.

Kąobawä is a quiet, intense, wise, and unobtrusive man. It came as something of a surprise to me when I learned that he was the headman of his village, for he stayed at the sidelines while others would surround me and press their demands on me. He leads more by example than by coercion. He can afford to be this way at his age, for he established his reputation for being forthright and as fierce as the situation required when he was younger, and the other men respect him. He also has five mature brothers or half-brothers in his village, men he can count on for support. He also has several other mature 'brothers' (parallel cousins, whom he must refer to as 'brothers' in his kinship system) in the village who frequently come to

his aid, but not as often as his 'real' brothers do. Kąobawä has also given a number of his sisters to other men in the village and has promised his young (8-year-old) daughter in marriage to a young man who, for that reason, is obliged to help him. In short, his 'natural' or 'kinship' following is large, and with this support, he does not have to display his aggressiveness to remind his peers of his position.

Rerebawä is a very different kind of person. He is much younger—perhaps in his early twenties. He has just one wife, but they have already had three children. He is from a village called Karohi-teri, located about five hours' walk up the Orinoco, slightly inland off to the east of the river itself. Kąobawä's village enjoys amicable relationships with Rerebawä's, and it is for this reason that marriage alliances of the kind represented by Rerebawä's marriage into Kąobawä's village occur between the two groups. Rerebawä told me that he came to Bisaasi-teri because there were no eligible women for him to marry in his own village, a fact that I later was able to document when I did a census of his village and a preliminary analysis of its social organization.[6]

Rerebawä is perhaps more typical than Kąobawä in the sense that he is chronically concerned about his personal reputation for aggressiveness and goes out of his way to be noticed, even if he has to act tough. He gave me a hard time during my early months of fieldwork, intimidating, teasing, and insulting me frequently. He is, however, much braver than the other men his age and is quite prepared to back up his threats with immediate action—as in the club fight incident just described above. Moreover, he is fascinated with political relationships and knows the details of intervillage relationships over a large area of the tribe. In this respect he shows all the attributes of being a headman, although he has too many competent brothers in his own village to expect to easily move into the leadership position there.

He does not intend to stay in Kąobawä's group and refuses to make his own garden—a commitment that would reveal something of an intended long-

term residence. He feels that he has adequately discharged his obligations to his wife's parents by providing them with fresh game for several years. They should let him take his wife and return to his own village with her, but they refuse and try to entice him to remain permanently in Bisaasi-teri to continue to provide them with game when they are old. It is for this reason that they promised to give him their second daughter, their only other child, in marriage. Unfortunately, the girl was opposed to the marriage and ultimately married another man.

Although Rerebawä has displayed his ferocity in many ways, one incident in particular illustrates what his character can be like. Before he left his own village to take his new wife in Bisaasi-teri, he had an affair with the wife of an older brother. When it was discovered, his brother attacked him with a club. Rerebawä responded furiously: he grabbed an ax and drove his brother out of the village after soundly beating him with the blunt side of the single-bit ax. His brother was so intimidated by the thrashing and promise of more to come that he did not return to the village for several days. I visited this village with Kąobawä shortly after this event had taken place; Rerebawä was with me as my guide. He made it a point to introduce me to this man. He approached his hammock, grabbed him by the wrist, and dragged him out on the ground: "This is the brother whose wife I screwed when he wasn't around!" A deadly insult, one that would usually provoke a bloody club fight among more valiant Yąnomamö. The man did nothing. He slunk sheepishly back into his hammock, shamed, but relieved to have Rerebawä release his grip.

Even though Rerebawä is fierce and capable of considerable nastiness, he has a charming, witty side as well. He has a biting sense of humor and can entertain the group for hours with jokes and clever manipulations of his language. And, he is one of few Yąnomamö that I feel I can trust. I recall indelibly my return to Bisaasi-teri after being away a year—the occasion of my second field trip to the Yąnomamö. When I reached Bisaasi-teri, Rerebawä was in his own village visiting his kinsmen. Word reached him that I had returned, and he paddled downstream immediately to see me. He greeted me with an immense bear hug and exclaimed, with tears welling up in his eyes, "Shąki! Why did you stay away so long? Did you not know that my will was so cold while you were gone that I could not at times eat for want of seeing you again?" I, too, felt the same way about him—then, and now.

Of all the Yąnomamö I know, he is the most genuine and the most devoted to his culture's ways and values. I admire him for that, although I cannot say that I subscribe to or endorse some of these values. By contrast, Kąobawä is older and wiser, a polished diplomat. He sees his own culture in a slightly different light and seems to even question aspects of it. Thus, while many of his peers enthusiastically accept the 'explanations' of things given in myths, he occasionally reflects on them—even laughing at some of the more preposter-

ous of them. Probably more of the Yąnomamö are like Rerebawä than like Kąobawä, or at least try to be. . . .

FOOTNOTES

1. The word Yąnomamö is nasalized through its entire length, indicated by the diacritical mark ˋ. When this mark appears on any Yąnomamö word, the whole word is nasalized. The vowel 'ö' represents a sound that does not occur in the English language. It is similar to the umlaut 'o' in the German language or the 'oe' equivalent in German, as in the poet Goethe's name. Unfortunately, many presses and typesetters simply eliminate diacritical marks, and this leads to multiple spellings of the word Yąnomamö and multiple mispronunciations. Some anthropologists have chosen to introduce a slightly different spelling of the word Yąnomamö since my work began appearing in print, such as Yąnomami, leading to additional misspellings as diacritics are eliminated by some presses, and to the *incorrect* pronunciation "Yanomameee." Words with a vowel indicated as 'ä' are pronounced as the 'uh' sound in the word 'duck'. Thus, the name Kąobawä would be pronounced "cow-ba-wuh," but entirely nasalized.

2. I spent a total of 41 months among the Yąnomamö between 1964 and 1983. The first edition of this case study was based on the first 15 months I spent among them in Venezuela. By the time the

first edition had gotten to press, I had made another field trip of four months' duration and the first edition indicated that the work was based, as it technically was, on 19 months of field research. I have, at the time of this writing, made 10 field trips to the Yąnomamö and plan to return regularly to continue my long-term study.

3. See Spindler (1970) for a detailed discussion of field research by anthropologists who have worked in other cultures.

4. They could not pronounce "Chagnon." It sounded to them like their name for a pesky bee, *shąki*, and that is what they called me: pesky, noisome bee.

5. The Yąnomamö in this region acquired canoes very recently. The missionaries would purchase them from the Ye'kwana Indians to the north for money, and then trade them to the Yąnomamö in exchange for labor, produce, or 'informant' work in translating. It should be emphasized that those Yąnomamö who lived on navigable portions of the Upper Orinoco River moved there from the deep forest in order to have contact with the missionaires and acquire the trade goods the missionaries (and their supply system) brought.

6. In 1980 word reached me from a friend who was doing medical work among the Yąnomamö that Kąobawä's village attacked a village that was a splinter group of Rerebawä's and killed a large number of men. This was confirmed for me in 1982 by an ecologist who was working near that area. What this will do to the relationships between Kąobawä's village and Rerebawä's village in the future is problematic, but their groups are probably on very strained terms now.

Doctor, Lawyer, Indian Chief

*As Punjabi villagers say, "You never really know who a man is
until you know who his grandfather and his ancestors were"*

Richard Kurin

*Richard Kurin is the Deputy Director
of Folklife Programs at the Smithsonian Institution.*

I was full of confidence when—
equipped with a scholarly proposal,
blessings from my advisers, and
generous research grants—I set out
to study village social structure in the
Punjab province of Pakistan. But
after looking for an appropriate
fieldwork site for several weeks without success, I began to think that my
research project would never get off
the ground. Daily I would seek out
villages aboard my puttering motor
scooter, traversing the dusty dirt
roads, footpaths, and irrigation
ditches that crisscross the Punjab.
But I couldn't seem to find a village
amenable to study. The major problem was that the villagers I did approach were baffled by my presence.
They could not understand why anyone would travel ten thousand miles
from home to a foreign country in
order to live in a poor village, interview illiterate peasants, and then
write a book about it. Life, they were
sure, was to be lived, not written
about. Besides, they thought, what of
any importance could they possibly

tell me? Committed as I was to ethnographic research, I readily understood their viewpoint. I was a *babu
log*—literally, a noble; figuratively, a
clerk; and simply, a person of the city.
I rode a motor scooter, wore tight-
fitting clothing, and spoke Urdu, a
language associated with the urban
literary elite. Obviously, I did not
belong, and the villagers simply did
not see me fitting into their society.

The Punjab, a region about the size
of Colorado, straddles the northern
border of India and Pakistan. Parti-
tioned between the two countries in
1947, the Punjab now consists of a
western province, inhabited by Muslims, and an eastern one, populated in
the main by Sikhs and Hindus. As its
name implies—*punj* meaning "five"
and *ab* meaning "rivers"—the region
is endowed with plentiful resources to
support widespread agriculture and a
large rural population. The Punjab
has traditionally supplied grains,
produce, and dairy products to the
peoples of neighboring and considerably more arid states, earning it a
reputation as the breadbasket of
southern Asia.

Given this predilection for agriculture, Punjabis like to emphasize that
they are earthy people, having values
they see as consonant with rural life.
These values include an appreciation
of, and trust in, nature; simplicity and

directness of expression; an awareness of the basic drives and desires
that motivate men (namely, *zan, zar,
zamin*—"women, wealth, land"); a
concern with honor and shame as
abiding principles of social organization; and for Muslims, a deep faith in
Allah and the teachings of his prophet
Mohammad.

Besides being known for its fertile
soils, life-giving rivers, and superla-
tive agriculturists, the Punjab is also
perceived as a zone of transitional
culture, a region that has experienced
repeated invasions of peoples from
western and central Asia into the
Indian subcontinent. Over the last
four thousand years, numerous
groups, among them Scythians, Par-
thians, Huns, Greeks, Moguls, Per-
sians, Afghans, and Turks, have
entered the subcontinent through the
Punjab in search of bountiful land,
riches, or power. Although Punjabis—notably Rajputs, Sikhs, and
Jats—have a reputation for courage
and fortitude on the battlefield, their
primary, self-professed strength has
been their ability to incorporate new,
exogenous elements into their society
with a minimum of conflict. Punjabis
are proud that theirs is a multiethnic
society in which diverse groups have
been largely unified by a common
language and by common customs
and traditions.

Given this background, I had not expected much difficulty in locating a village in which to settle and conduct my research. As an anthropologist, I viewed myself as an "earthy" social scientist who, being concerned with basics, would have a good deal in common with rural Punjabis. True, I might be looked on as an invader of a sort; but I was benevolent, and sensing this, villagers were sure to incorporate me into their society with even greater ease than was the case for the would-be conquering armies that had preceded me. Indeed, they would welcome me with open arms.

I was wrong. The villagers whom I approached attributed my desire to live with them either to neurotic delusions or nefarious ulterior motives. Perhaps, so the arguments went, I was really after women, land, or wealth.

On the day I had decided would be my last in search of a village, I was driving along a road when I saw a farmer running through a rice field and waving me down. I stopped and he climbed on the scooter. Figuring I had nothing to lose, I began to explain why I wanted to live in a village. To my surprise and delight, he was very receptive, and after sharing a pomegranate milkshake at a roadside shop, he invited me to his home. His name was Allah Ditta, which means "God given," and I took this as a sign that I had indeed found my village.

"My" village turned out to be a settlement of about fifteen hundred people, mostly of the Nunari *qaum*, or "tribe." The Nunaris engage primarily in agriculture (wheat, rice, sugar cane, and cotton), and most families own small plots of land. Members of the Bhatti tribe constitute the largest minority in the village. Although traditionally a warrior tribe, the Bhattis serve in the main as the village artisans and craftsmen.

On my first day in the village I tried explaining in great detail the purposes of my study to the village elders and clan leaders. Despite my efforts, most of the elders were perplexed about why I wanted to live in their village. As a guest, I was entitled to the hospitality traditionally bestowed by Muslim peoples of Asia, and during the first evening I was assigned a place to stay. But I was an enigma, for guests leave, and I wanted to remain. I was also perceived as being strange, for I was both a non-Muslim and a non-Punjabi, a type of person not heretofore encountered by most of the villagers. Although I tried to temper my behavior, there was little I could say or do to dissuade my hosts from the view that I embodied the antithesis of Punjabi values. While I was able to converse in their language, Jatki, a dialect of western Punjabi, I was only able to do so with the ability of a four-year-old. This achievement fell far short of speaking the *t'et'*, or "genuine form," of the villagers. Their idiom is rich with the terminology of agricultural operations and rural life. It is unpretentious, uninflected, and direct, and villagers hold high opinions of those who are good with words, who can speak to a point and be convincing. Needless to say, my infantile babble realized none of these characteristics and evoked no such respect.

Similarly, even though I wore indigenous dress, I was inept at tying my *lungi*, or pant cloth. The fact that my *lungi* occasionally fell off and revealed what was underneath gave my neighbors reason to believe that I indeed had no shame and could not control the passions of my *nafs*, or "libidinous nature."

This image of a doltish, shameless infidel barely capable of caring for himself lasted for the first week of my residence in the village. My inability to distinguish among the five varieties of rice and four varieties of lentil grown in the village illustrated that I knew or cared little about nature and agricultural enterprise. This display of ignorance only served to confirm the general consensus that the mysterious morsels I ate from tin cans labeled "Chef Boy-ar-Dee" were not really food at all. Additionally, I did not oil and henna my hair, shave my armpits, or perform ablutions, thereby convincing some commentators that I was a member of a species of subhuman beings, possessing little in the form of either common or moral sense. That the villagers did not quite grant me the status of a person was reflected by their not according me a proper name. In the Punjab, a person's name is equated with honor and respect and is symbolized by his turban. A man who does not have a name, or whose name is not recognized by his neighbors, is unworthy of respect. For such a man, his turban is said to be either nonexistent or to lie in the dust at the feet of others. To be given a name is to have one's head crowned by a turban, an acknowledgment that one leads a responsible and respectable life. Although I repeatedly introduced myself as "Rashid Karim," a fairly decent Pakistani rendering of Richard Kurin, just about all the villagers insisted on calling me *Angrez* ("Englishman"), thus denying me full personhood and implicitly refusing to grant me the right to wear a turban.

As I began to pick up the vernacular, to question villagers about their clan and kinship structure and trace out relationships between different families, my image began to change. My drawings of kinship diagrams and preliminary census mappings were looked upon not only with wonder but also suspicion. My neighbors now began to think there might be a method to my madness. And so there was. Now I had become a spy. Of course it took a week for people to figure out whom I was supposedly spying for. Located as they were at a cross-roads of Asia, at a nexus of conflicting geopolitical interests, they had many possibilities to consider. There was a good deal of disagreement on the issue, with the vast majority maintaining that I was either an American, Russian, or Indian spy. A small, but nonetheless vocal, minority held steadfastly to the belief that I was a Chinese spy. I thought it all rather humorous until one day a group confronted me in the main square in front of the nine-by-nine-foot mud hut that I had rented. The leader spoke up and accused me of spying. The remainder of the group grumbled *jahsus! jahsus!* ("spy! spy!"), and I realized that this ad hoc committee of inquiry had the potential of becoming a mob.

To be sure, the villagers had good reason to be suspicious. For one, the times were tense in Pakistan—a national political crisis gripped the country and the populace had been anxious for months over the uncertainty of elections and effective governmental functions. Second, keenly aware of their history, some of the villagers did not have to go too far to imagine that I was at the vanguard of some invading group that had designs upon their land. Such intrigues, with far greater sophistication, had been played out before by nations seeking to expand their power into the Punjab. That I possessed a gold seal letter (which no one save myself could read) from the University of Chicago to the effect that I was pursuing legitimate studies was not enough to convince the crowd that I was indeed an innocent scholar.

I repeatedly denied the charge, but to no avail. The shouts of *jahsus! jahsus!* prevailed. Confronted with this I had no choice.

"Okay," I said. "I admit it. I am a spy!"

The crowd quieted for my long-awaited confession.

"I am a spy and am here to study this village, so that when my country attacks you we will be prepared. You see, we will not bomb Lahore or Karachi or Islamabad. Why should we waste our bombs on millions of people, on factories, dams, airports, and harbors? No, it is far more advantageous to bomb this strategic small village replete with its mud huts, livestock, Persian wheels, and one light bulb. And when we bomb this village, it is imperative that we know how Allah Ditta is related to Abdullah, and who owns the land near the well, and what your marriage customs are."

Silence hung over the crowd, and then one by one the assemblage began to disperse. My sarcasm had worked. The spy charges were defused. But I was no hero in light of my performance, and so I was once again relegated to the status of a nonperson without an identity in the village.

I remained in limbo for the next week, and although I continued my attempts to collect information about village life, I had my doubts as to whether I would ever be accepted by the villagers. And then, through no effort of my own, there was a breakthrough, this time due to another Allah Ditta, a relative of the village headman and one of my leading accusers during my spying days.

I was sitting on my woven string bed on my porch when Allah Ditta approached, leading his son by the neck. "Oh, *Angrez!*" he yelled, "this worthless son of mine is doing poorly in school. He is supposed to be learning English, but he is failing. He has a good mind, but he's lazy. And his teacher is no help, being more intent upon drinking tea and singing film songs than upon teaching English. Oh son of an Englishman, do you know English?"

"Yes, I know English," I replied, "after all, I am an *Angrez.*"

"Teach him," Allah Ditta blurted out, without any sense of making a tactful request.

And so, I spent the next hour with the boy, reviewing his lessons and correcting his pronunciation and grammar. As I did so, villagers stopped to watch and listen, and by the end of the hour, nearly one hundred people had gathered around, engrossed by this tutoring session. They were stupefied. I was an effective teacher, and I actually seemed to know English. The boy responded well, and the crowd reached a new consensus. I had a brain. And in recognition of this achievement I was given a name—"Ustad Rashid," or Richard the Teacher.

Achieving the status of a teacher was only the beginning of my success. The next morning I awoke to find the village sugar vendor at my door. He had a headache and wanted to know if I could cure him.

"Why do you think I can help you?" I asked.

Bhai Khan answered, "Because you are a *ustad,* you have a great deal of knowledge."

The logic was certainly compelling. If I could teach English, I should be able to cure a headache. I gave him two aspirins.

An hour later, my fame had spread. Bhai Khan had been cured, and he did not hesitate to let others know that it was the *ustad* who had been responsible. By the next day, and in fact for the remainder of my stay, I was to see an average of twenty-five to thirty patients a day. I was asked to cure everything from coughs and colds to typhoid, elephantiasis, and impotency. Upon establishing a flourishing and free medical practice, I received another title, *hakim,* or "physician." I was not yet an anthropologist, but I was on my way.

A few days later I took on yet another role. One of my research interests involved tracing out patterns of land ownership and inheritance. While working on the problem of figuring out who owned what, I was approached by the village watchman. He claimed he had been swindled in a land deal and requested my help. As the accused was not another villager, I agreed to present the watchman's case to the local authorities.

Somehow, my efforts managed to achieve results. The plaintiff's grievance was redressed, and I was given yet another title in the village—*wakil,* or "lawyer." And in the weeks that followed, I was steadily called upon to read, translate, and advise upon various court orders that affected the lives of the villagers.

My roles as teacher, doctor, and lawyer not only provided me with an identity but also facilitated my integration into the economic structure of the community. As my imputed skills offered my neighbors services not readily available in the village, I was drawn into exchange relationships known as *seipi. Seipi* refers to the barter system of goods and services among village farmers, craftsmen, artisans, and other specialists. Every morning Roshan the milkman would deliver fresh milk to my hut. Every other day Hajam Ali the barber would stop by and give me a shave. My next-door neighbor, Nura the cobbler, would repair my sandals when required. Ghulam the horse-cart driver would transport me to town when my motor scooter was in disrepair. The parents of my students would send me sweets and sometimes delicious meals. In return, none of my neighbors asked for direct payment for the specific actions performed. Rather, as they told me, they would call upon me when they had need of my services. And they did. Nura needed cough syrup for his children, the milkman's brother needed a job contact in the city, students wanted to continue their lessons, and so on. Through *seipi* relations, various neighbors gave goods and services to me, and I to them.

Even so, I knew that by Punjabi standards I could never be truly accepted into village life because I was not a member of either the Nunari or Bhatti tribe. As the villagers would say, "You never really know who a man is until you know who his grandfather and his ancestors were." And to know a person's grandfather or ancestors properly, you had to be a member of the same or a closely allied tribe.

The Nunari tribe is composed of a number of groups. The nucleus consists of four clans—Naul, Vadel, Sadan, and More—each named for one of four brothers thought to have originally founded the tribe. Clan members are said to be related to blood ties, also called *pag da sak,* or "ties of the turban." In sharing the turban, members of each clan share the same name. Other clans, unrelated by ties of blood to these four, have become attached to this nucleus through a history of marital relations or of continuous political and economic interdependence. Marital relations, called *gag da sak,* or "ties of the skirt," are conceived of as relations in which alienable turbans (skirts) in the form of women are exchanged with other, non-turban-sharing groups. Similarly, ties of political and economic domination and subordination are thought of as relations in which the turban of the client is given to that of the patron. A major part of my research work was concerned with reconstructing how the four brothers formed the Nunari tribe, how additional clans became associated with

it, and how clan and tribal identity were defined by nomenclature, codes of honor, and the symbols of sharing and exchanging turbans.

To approach these issues I set out to reconstruct the genealogical relationships within the tribe and between the various clans. I elicited genealogies from many of the villagers and questioned older informants about the history of the Nunari tribe. Most knew only bits and pieces of this history, and after several months of interviews and research, I was directed to the tribal genealogists. These people, usually not Nunaris themselves, perform the service of memorizing and then orally relating the history of the tribe and the relationships among its members. The genealogist in the village was an aged and arthritic man named Hedayat, who in his later years was engaged in teaching the Nunari genealogy to his son, who would then carry out the traditional and hereditary duties of his position.

The villagers claimed that Hedayat knew every generation of the Nunari from the present to the founding brothers and even beyond. So I invited Hedayat to my hut and explained my purpose.

"Do you know Allah Ditta son of Rohm?" I asked.

"Yes, of course," he replied.

"Who was Rohm's father?" I continued.

"Shahadat Mohammad," he answered.

"And his father?"

"Hamid."

"And his?"

"Chigatah," he snapped without hesitation.

I was now quite excited, for no one else in the village had been able to recall an ancestor of this generation. My estimate was that Chigatah had been born sometime between 1850 and 1870. But Hedayat went on.

"Chigatah's father was Kamal. And Kamal's father was Nanak. And Nanak's father was Sikhu. And before him was Dargai, and before him Maiy. And before him was Siddiq. And Siddiq's father was Nur. And Nur's Asmat. And Asmat was of Channa.

And Channa of Nau. And Nau of Bhatta. And Bhatta was the son of Koduk."

Hedayat had now recounted sixteen generations of lineal ascendants related through the turban. Koduk was probably born in the sixteenth century. But still Hedayat continued.

"Sigun was the father of Koduk. And Man the father of Sigun. And before Man was his father Maneswar. And Maneswar's father was the founder of the clan, Naul."

This then was a line of the Naul clan of the Nunari tribe, ascending twenty-one generations from the present descendants (Allah Ditta's sons) to the founder, one of four brothers who lived perhaps in the fifteenth century. I asked Hedayat to recite genealogies of the other Nunari clans, and he did, with some blanks here and there, ending with Vadel, More, and Saddan, the other three brothers who formed the tribal nucleus. I then asked the obvious question, "Hedayat, who was the father of these four brothers? Who is the founding ancestor of the Nunari tribe?"

"The father of these brothers was not a Muslim. He was an Indian rajput [chief]. The tribe actually begins with the conversion of the four brothers," Hedayat explained.

"Well then," I replied, "who was this Indian chief?"

He was a famous and noble chief who fought against the Moguls. His name was Raja Kurin, who lived in a massive fort in Kurinnagar, about twenty-seven miles from Delhi."

"What!" I asked, both startled and unsure of what I had heard.

"Raja Kurin is the father of the brothers who make up—"

"But his name! It's the same as mine," I stammered. "Hedayat, my name is Richard Kurin. What a coincidence! Here I am living with your tribe thousands of miles from my home and it turns out that I have the same name as the founder of the tribe! Do you think I might be related to Raja Kurin and the Nunaris?"

Hedayat looked at me, but only for an instant. Redoing his turban, he tilted his head skyward, smiled, and asked, "What is the name of your father?"

I had come a long way. I now had a name that could be recognized and respected, and as I answered Hedayat, I knew that I had finally and irrevocably fit into "my" village. Whether by fortuitous circumstances or by careful manipulation, my neighbors had found a way to take an invading city person intent on studying their life and transform him into one of their own, a full person entitled to wear a turban for participating in, and being identified with, that life. As has gone on for centuries in the region, once again the new and exogenous had been recast into something Punjabi.

Epilogue: There is no positive evidence linking the Nunaris to a historical Raja Kurin, although there are several famous personages identified by that name (also transcribed as Karan and Kurran). Estimated from the genealogy recited by Hedayat, the founding of the tribe by the four brothers appears to have occurred sometime between 440 and 640 years ago, depending on the interval assumed for each generation. On that basis, the most likely candidate for Nunari progenitor (actual or imputed) is Raja Karan, ruler of Anhilvara (Gujerat), who was defeated by the Khilji Ala-ud-Din in 1297 and again in 1307. Although this is slightly earlier than suggested by the genealogical data, such genealogies are often telescoped or otherwise unreliable.

Nevertheless, several aspects of Hedayat's account make this association doubtful. Hedayat clearly identifies Raja Kurin's conquerors as Moguls, whereas the Gujerati Raja Karan was defeated by the Khiljis. Second, Hedayat places the Nunari ancestor's kingdom only twenty-seven miles from Delhi. The Gujerati Raja Karan ruled several kingdoms, none closer than several hundred miles to Delhi.

Other circumstances, however, offer support for this identification of the Nunari ancestor. According to Hedayat, Raja Kurin's father was named Kam Deo. Although the historical figure was the son of Serung Deo, the use of "Deo," a popular title for the rajas of the Vaghela and Solonki dynasties, does seem to place the Nunari founder in the context of medieval Gujerat. Furthermore, Hedayat clearly identifies the saint (*pir*) said to have initiated the conversion of the Nunaris to Islam. This saint, Mukhdum-i-Jehaniyan, was a contemporary of the historical Raja Karan.

Also of interest, but as yet unexplained, is that several other groups living in Nunari settlement areas specifically claim to be descended from Raja Karan of Gujerat, who is said to have migrated northward into the Punjab after his defeat. Controverting this theory, the available evidence indicates that Raja Karan fled, not toward the Punjab, but rather southward to the Deccan, and that his patriline ended with him. It is his daughter Deval Devi who is remembered: she is the celebrated heroine of "Ashiqa," a famous Urdu poem written by Amir Khusrau in 1316. She was married to Khizr Khan, the son of Karan's conqueror; nothing is known of her progeny.

Eating Christmas in the Kalahari

Richard Borshay Lee

Richard Borshay Lee is a full professor of anthropology at the University of Toronto. He has done extensive field-work in southern Africa, is coeditor of Man the Hunter *(1968) and* Kalahari Hunter-Gatherers *(1976), and author of* The !Kung San: Men, Women, and Work in a Foraging Society.

how it got there

The !Kung Bushmen's knowledge of Christmas is thirdhand. The London Missionary Society brought the holiday to the southern Tswana tribes in the early nineteenth century. Later, native catechists spread the idea far and wide among the Bantu-speaking pastoralists, even in the remotest corners of the Kalahari Desert. The Bushmen's idea of the Christmas story, stripped to its essentials, is "praise the birth of white man's god-chief"; what keeps their interest in the holiday high is the Tswana-Herero custom of slaughtering an ox for his Bushmen neighbors as an annual goodwill gesture. Since the 1930's, part of the Bushmen's annual round of activities has included a December congregation at the cattle posts for trading, marriage brokering, and several days of trance-dance feasting at which the local Tswana headman is host.

As a social anthropologist working with !Kung Bushmen, I found that the Christmas ox custom suited my purposes. I had come to the Kalahari to study the hunting and gathering subsistence economy of the !Kung, and to accomplish this it was essential not to provide them with food, share my own food, or interfere in any way with their food-gathering activities. While liberal handouts of tobacco and medical supplies were appreciated, they were scarcely adequate to erase the glaring disparity in wealth between the anthropologist, who maintained a two-month inventory of canned goods, and the Bushmen, who rarely had a day's supply of food on hand. My approach, while paying off in terms of data, left me open to frequent accusations of stinginess and hard-heartedness. By their lights, I was a miser.

The Christmas ox was to be my way of saying thank you for the cooperation of the past year; and since it was to be our last Christmas in the field, I determined to slaughter the largest, meatiest ox that money could buy, insuring that the feast and trance-dance would be a success.

Through December I kept my eyes open at the wells as the cattle were brought down for watering. Several animals were offered, but none had quite the grossness that I had in mind. Then, ten days before the holiday, a Herero friend led an ox of astonishing size and mass up to our camp. It was solid black, stood five feet high at the shoulder, had a five-foot span of horns, and must have weighed 1,200 pounds on the hoof. Food consumption calculations are my specialty, and I quickly figured that bones and viscera aside, there was enough meat—at least four pounds—for every man, woman, and child of the 150 Bushmen in the vicinity of /ai/ai who were expected at the feast.

Having found the right animal at last, I paid the Herero £20 ($56) and asked him to keep the beast with his herd until Christmas day. The next morning word spread among the people that the big solid black one was the ox chosen by /ontah (my Bushman name; it means, roughly, "whitey") for the Christmas feast. That afternoon I received the first delegation. Ben!a, an outspoken sixty-year-old mother of five, came to the point slowly.

"Where were you planning to eat Christmas?"

"Right here at /ai/ai," I replied.

"Alone or with others?"

"I expect to invite all the people to eat Christmas with me."

"Eat what?"

"I have purchased Yehave's black ox, and I am going to slaughter and cook it."

"That's what we were told at the well but refused to believe it until we heard it from yourself."

"Well, it's the black one," I replied expansively, although wondering what she was driving at.

"Oh, no!" Ben!a groaned, turning to her group. "They were right." Turning back to me she asked, "Do you expect us to eat that bag of bones?"

"Bag of bones! It's the biggest ox at /ai/ai."

"Big, yes, but old. And thin. Everybody knows there's no meat on that old ox. What did you expect us to eat off it, the horns?"

Everybody chuckled at Ben!a's one-liner as they walked away, but all I could manage was a weak grin.

That evening it was the turn of the young men. They came to sit at our evening fire. /gaugo, about my age, spoke to me man-to-man.

"/ontah, you have always been square with us," he lied. "What has happened to change your heart? That sack of guts and bones of Yehave's will hardly feed one camp, let alone all the Bushmen around /ai/ai." And he proceeded to enumerate the seven camps in the /ai/ai vicinity, family by family. "Perhaps you have forgotten that we are not few, but many. Or are you too blind to tell the difference between a proper cow and an old wreck? That ox is thin to the point of death."

"Look, you guys," I retorted, "that is a beautiful animal, and I'm sure you will eat it with pleasure at Christmas."

"Of course we will eat it; it's food. But it won't fill us up to the point where we will have enough strength to dance. We will eat and go home to bed with stomachs rumbling."

That night as we turned in, I asked my wife, Nancy: "What did you think of the black ox?"

"It looked enormous to me. Why?"

"Well, about eight different people have told me I got gypped; that the ox is nothing but bones."

"What's the angle?" Nancy asked. "Did they have a better one to sell?"

"No, they just said that it was going to be a grim Christmas because there won't be enough meat to go around. Maybe I'll get an independent judge to look at the beast in the morning."

Bright and early, Halingisi, a Tswana cattle owner, appeared at our camp. But before I could ask him to give me his opinion on Yehave's black ox, he gave me the eye signal that indicated a confidential chat. We left the camp and sat down.

"/ontah, I'm surprised at you: you've lived here for three years and still haven't learned anything about cattle."

"But what else can a person do but choose the biggest, strongest animal one can find?" I retorted.

"Look, just because an animal is big doesn't mean that it has plenty of meat on it. The black one was a beauty when it was younger, but now it is thin to the point of death."

"Well I've already bought it. What can I do at this stage?"

"Bought it already? I thought you were just considering it. Well, you'll have to kill it and serve it, I suppose. But don't expect much of a dance to follow."

My spirits dropped rapidly. I could believe that Ben!a and /gaugo just might be putting me on about the black ox, but Halingisi seemed to be an impartial critic. I went around that day feeling as though I had bought a lemon of a used car.

In the afternoon it was Tomazo's turn. Tomazo is a fine hunter, a top trance performer . . . and one of my most reliable informants. He approached the subject of the Christmas cow as part of my continuing Bushman education.

"My friend, the way it is with us Bushmen," he began, "is that we love meat. And even more than that, we love fat. When we hunt we always search for the fat ones, the ones dripping with layers of white fat: fat that turns into a clear, thick oil in the cooking pot, fat that slides down your gullet, fills your stomach and gives you a roaring diarrhea," he rhapsodized.

"So, feeling as we do," he continued, "it gives us pain to be served such a scrawny thing as Yehave's black ox. It is big, yes, and no doubt its giant bones are good for soup, but fat is what we really crave and so we will eat Christmas this year with a heavy heart."

The prospect of a gloomy Christmas now had me worried, so I asked Tomazo what I could do about it.

"Look for a fat one, a young one . . . smaller, but fat. Fat enough to make us //gom ('evacuate the bowels'), then we will be happy."

My suspicions were aroused when Tomazo said that he happened to know of a young, fat, barren cow that the owner was willing to part with. Was Tomazo working on commission, I wondered? But I dispelled this unworthy thought when we approached the Herero owner of the cow in question and found that he had decided not to sell.

The scrawny wreck of a Christmas ox now became the talk of the /ai/ai water hole and was the first news told to the outlying groups as they began to come in from the bush for the feast. What finally convinced me that real trouble might be brewing was the visit from u!au, an old conservative with a reputation for fierceness. His nickname meant spear and referred to an incident thirty years ago in which he had speared a man to death. He had an intense manner; fixing me with his eyes, he said in clipped tones:

"I have only just heard about the black ox today, or else I would have come here earlier. /ontah, do you honestly think you can serve meat like that to people and avoid a fight?" He paused, letting the implications sink in. "I don't mean fight you, /ontah; you are a white man. I mean a fight between Bushmen. There are many fierce ones here, and with such a small quantity of meat to distribute, how can you give everybody a fair share? Someone is sure to accuse another of taking too much or hogging all the choice pieces. Then you will see what happens when some go hungry while others eat."

The possibility of at least a serious argument struck me as all too real. I had witnessed the tension that surrounds the distribution of meat from a kudu or gemsbok kill, and had documented many arguments that sprang up from a real or imagined slight in meat distribution. The owners of a kill may spend up to two hours arranging and rearranging the piles of meat under the gaze of a circle of recipients before handing them out. And I also knew that the Christmas feast at /ai/ai would be bringing together groups that had feuded in the past.

Convinced now of the gravity of the situation, I went in earnest to search for a second cow; but all my inquiries failed to turn one up.

The Christmas feast was evidently going to be a disaster, and the incessant complaints about the meagerness of the ox had already taken the fun out of it for me. Moreover, I was getting bored with the wisecracks, and after losing my temper a few times, I resolved to serve the beast anyway. If the meat fell short, the hell with it. In the Bushmen idiom, I announced to all who would listen:

"I am a poor man and blind. If I have chosen one that is too old and too thin, we will eat it anyway and see if there is enough meat there to quiet the rumbling of our stomachs."

On hearing this speech, Ben!a offered me a rare word of comfort. "It's thin," she said philosophically, "but the bones will make a good soup."

At dawn Christmas morning, instinct told me to turn over the butchering and cooking to a friend and take off with Nancy to spend Christmas alone in the bush. But curiosity kept me from retreating. I wanted to see what such a scrawny ox looked like on butchering, and if there *was* going to be a fight, I wanted to catch every word of it. Anthropologists are incurable that way.

The great beast was driven up to our dancing ground, and a shot in the forehead dropped it in its tracks. Then, freshly cut branches were heaped around the fallen carcass to receive the meat. Ten men volunteered to help with the cutting. I asked /gaugo to make the breast bone cut. This cut, which begins the butchering process for most large game, offers easy access for removal of the viscera. But it also allows the hunter to spot-check the amount of fat on the animal. A fat game animal carries a white layer up to an inch thick on the chest, while in a thin one, the knife will quickly cut to bone. All eyes fixed on his hand as /gaugo, dwarfed by the great carcass, knelt to the breast. The first cut opened a pool of solid white in the black skin. The second and third cut widened and deepened the creamy white. Still no bone. It was pure fat; it must have been two inches thick.

"Hey /gau," I burst out, "that ox is loaded with fat. What's this about the ox being too thin to bother eating? Are you out of your mind?"

"Fat?" /gau shot back, "You call that fat? This wreck is thin, sick,

dead!" And he broke out laughing. So did everyone else. They rolled on the ground, paralyzed with laughter. Everybody laughed except me; I was thinking.

I ran back to the tent and burst in just as Nancy was getting up. "Hey, the black ox. It's fat as hell! They were kidding about it being too thin to eat. It was a joke or something. A put-on. Everyone is really delighted with it!"

"Some joke," my wife replied. "It was so funny that you were ready to pack up and leave /ai/ai."

If it had indeed been a joke, it had been an extraordinarily convincing one, and tinged, I thought, with more than a touch of malice as many jokes are. Nevertheless, that it was a joke lifted my spirits considerably, and I returned to the butchering site where the shape of the ox was rapidly disappearing under the axes and knives of the butchers. The atmosphere had become festive. Grinning broadly, their arms covered with blood well past the elbow, men packed chunks of meat into the big cast-iron cooking pots, fifty pounds to the load, and muttered and chuckled all the while about the thinness and worthlessness of the animal and /ontah's poor judgment.

We danced and ate that ox two days and two nights; we cooked and distributed fourteen potfuls of meat and no one went home hungry and no fights broke out.

But the "joke" stayed in my mind. I had a growing feeling that something important had happened in my relationship with the Bushmen and that the clue lay in the meaning of the joke. Several days later, when most of the people had dispersed back to the bush camps, I raised the question with Hakekgose, a Tswana man who had grown up among the !Kung, married a !Kung girl, and who probably knew their culture better than any other non-Bushman.

"With us whites," I began, "Christmas is supposed to be the day of friendship and brotherly love. What I can't figure out is why the Bushmen went to such lengths to criticize and belittle the ox I had bought for the feast. The animal was

perfectly good and their jokes and wisecracks practically ruined the holiday for me."

"So it really did bother you," said Hakekgose. "Well, that's the way they always talk. When I take my rifle and go hunting with them, if I miss, they laugh at me for the rest of the day. But even if I hit and bring one down, it's no better. To them, the kill is always too small or too old or too thin; and as we sit down on the kill site to cook and eat the liver, they keep grumbling, even with their mouths full of meat. They say things like, 'Oh this is awful! What a worthless animal! Whatever made me think that this Tswana rascal could hunt!'"

"Is this the way outsiders are treated?" I asked.

"No, it is their custom; they talk that way to each other too. Go and ask them."

/gaugo had been one of the most enthusiastic in making me feel bad about the merit of the Christmas ox. I sought him out first.

"Why did you tell me the black ox was worthless, when you could see that it was loaded with fat and meat?"

"It is our way," he said smiling. "We always like to fool people about that. Say there is a Bushman who has been hunting. He must not come home and announce like a braggard, 'I have killed a big one in the bush!' He must first sit down in silence until I or someone else comes up to his fire and asks, 'What did you see today?' He replies quietly, 'Ah, I'm no good for hunting. I saw nothing at all [pause] just a little tiny one.' Then I smile to myself," /gaugo continued, "because I know he has killed something big.

"In the morning we make up a party of four or five people to cut up and carry the meat back to the camp. When we arrive at the kill we examine it and cry out, 'You mean to say you have dragged us all the way out here in order to make us cart home your pile of bones? Oh, if I had known it was this thin I wouldn't have come.' Another one pipes up, 'People, to think I gave up a nice day in the shade for this. At home we may be hungry but at least we have nice cool water to drink.' If the horns are big, someone says, 'Did you think that somehow you were going to boil down the horns for soup?'

"To all this you must respond in kind. 'I agree,' you say, 'this one is not worth the effort; let's just cook the liver for strength and leave the rest for the hyenas. It is not too late to hunt today and even a duiker or a steenbok would be better than this mess.'

"Then you set to work nevertheless; butcher the animal, carry the meat back to the camp and everyone eats," /gaugo concluded.

Things were beginning to make sense. Next, I went to Tomazo. He corroborated /gaugo's story of the obligatory insults over a kill and added a few details of his own.

"But," I asked, "why insult a man after he has gone to all that trouble to track and kill an animal and when he is going to share the meat with you so that your children will have something to eat?"

"Arrogance," was his cryptic answer.

"Arrogance?"

"Yes, when a young man kills much meat he comes to think of himself as a chief or a big man, and he thinks of the rest of us as his servants or inferiors. We can't accept this. We refuse one who boasts, for someday his pride will make him kill somebody. So we always speak of his meat as worthless. This way we cool his heart and make him gentle."

"But why didn't you tell me this before?" I asked Tomazo with some heat.

"Because you never asked me," said Tomazo, echoing the refrain that has come to haunt every field ethnographer.

The pieces now fell into place. I had known for a long time that in situations of social conflict with Bushmen I held all the cards. I was the only source of tobacco in a thousand square miles, and I was not incapable of cutting an individual off for noncooperation. Though my boycott never lasted longer than a few days, it was an indication of my strength. People resented my presence at the water hole, yet simultaneously dreaded my leaving. In short I was a perfect target for the charge of arrogance and for the Bushmen tactic of enforcing humility.

I had been taught an object lesson by the Bushmen; it had come from an unexpected corner and had hurt me in a vulnerable area. For the big black ox was to be the one totally generous, unstinting act of my year at /ai/ai, and I was quite unprepared for the reaction I received.

As I read it, their message was this: There are no totally generous acts. All "acts" have an element of calculation. One black ox slaughtered at Christmas does not wipe out a year of careful manipulation of gifts given to serve your own ends. After all, to kill an animal and share the meat with people is really no more than Bushmen do for each other every day and with far less fanfare.

In the end, I had to admire how the Bushmen had played out the farce—collectively straight-faced to the end. Curiously, the episode reminded me of the *Good Soldier Schweik* and his marvelous encounters with authority. Like Schweik, the Bushmen had retained a thorough-going skepticism of good intentions. Was it this independence of spirit, I wondered, that had kept them culturally viable in the face of generations of contact with more powerful societies, both black and white? The thought that the Bushmen were alive and well in the Kalahari was strangely comforting. Perhaps, armed with that independence and with their superb knowledge of their environment, they might yet survive the future.

Myth of the Man-Eaters

An Interview with Dr. William Arens

Elisabeth Rosenthal

Elisabeth Rosenthal, Science Digest assistant editor, has written for the Christian Science Monitor *and for* United Press International.

In 1979, William Arens gave the normally staid and slightly stuffy world of anthropology a slap in the face: There was no good evidence, he said, that cannibalism had been practiced routinely by any tribe, in any nation, in any form—ever. Cannibalism—that unspeakable act of man eating man—seemed to be taboo among "primitives," just as it is among "civilized folks." It was a conclusion that contradicted two centuries of anthropological wisdom.

An anthropologist at the State University of New York, Stony Brook, Arens started his study of man-eating when a student asked him to lecture on something interesting, "cannibalism or witchcraft." The more Arens researched the subject, the more convinced he became that the custom never existed.

Then the anthropologist became a sociologist. He turned the microscope around, and examined the motives and methods of his colleagues. How was it that anthropologists in pursuit of truth had managed to perpetuate a lie?

He put all his research together in a book that challenges a herd of sacred cows: *The Man-Eating Myth: Anthropology and Anthropophagy* (Oxford University Press, 1979, hardcover and paperback). Its publication initially elicited audible gasps from anthropologists; it was called "dangerous" and Arens "ignorant." But popular critics were impressed with Arens's "bold exploration"; the book, wrote the *New Yorker,* "is a model of disciplined and fair argument."

Despite the power of Arens's work, I traveled to Stony Brook half expecting a fraud; I left a believer.

Science Digest: Dr. Arens, many people—explorers, missionaries, even anthropologists—claim to have traveled among cannibals. In light of such evidence, one reviewer said you had to be "malicious" to suggest that cannibalism had never existed. How do you respond to that charge?

Arens: Everyone's just fascinated by the subject of cannibalism. In *Moby Dick,* one of the sailors says to the other as they're about to sail for the South Pacific: "Every Christian wishes he were a heathen on a cannibal island." The idea of a society which lacks the basic rules that we have provides a sense of relief and release. If it doesn't exist, it will be made up. I think it has been in many instances.

When I first started researching the subject, I believed that cannibalism existed. You sort of imbibe cannibalism as the mother's milk of anthropology. But I quickly became dubious about the descriptions of cannibalism I was reading. They were clearly colorful stories: "Then the body was rolled down the pyramid and an orgy of cannibalism took place." It just wasn't anthropological. So I looked at the sources, and found out they were not original sources; then I went back further and found that the people they were citing were not original sources either. When I got to the end, I couldn't tell who, if anyone, had seen cannibalism.

SD: So you're saying there have been no reliable reports of cannibalism?

Arens: There have been few, very few eyewitness accounts of cannibalism. That is, people saying they saw someone killed, then cooked and eaten. And let me remind you that anthropologists have never seen it. My own feeling, my personal feeling, is that people aren't cannibals and weren't cannibals—not in the customary sense. I can't prove that, but that's what I believe.

SD: What about the explorers Stanley and Livingstone? People always think of the old cartoon of Livingstone in the stewpot. What of that?

1. ANTHROPOLOGICAL PERSPECTIVES

Arens: Stanley and Livingstone never saw it; they never saw cannibalism. But they portrayed almost all Africans as cannibals. Not Stanley so much. But Livingstone . . . Livingstone, who shot Africans by the score, saw cannibals everywhere. He would say, "today we passed among a group of cannibals" and "tomorrow we're entering more cannibal country." Look, I know Africa better than anyplace else. There's no good evidence for cannibalism existing in Africa. None. People like Stanley and Livingstone walked around Africa in perfect safety. No one ate them. And Africa has played such an important role in the myth of cannibalism.

As I mentioned in the book, one of the interesting things about confrontations between "cannibals" and non-cannibals is that, inevitably, the "cannibals" disappear. Look at the infamous "cannibal" tribes today: The Caribs [of the Caribbean] don't exist; the Aztecs don't exist; the culture of the New Guinea highlands is disappearing.

SD: Dr. Arens, what about the anthropologist Ronald Berndt? He's written vivid descriptions of cannibal practices in New Guinea. Surely he's seen it . . .

Arens: It's pure sensationalism. In his book *Excess and Restraint,* he says that the practice of cannibalism was suppressed sometime before his arrival on the scene. But, yes, he does provide some rather explicit descriptions of cannibalism. Apparently what he is doing is reporting something that he heard. As far as I know, he's never seen cannibalism—that is, the act itself.

SD: How do you know?

Arens: The scenes he describes are so fantastic. For example, he describes a scene in which a married couple is butchering a dead body. The wife is butchering the top half of the body, and the husband is copulating with the bottom half. This is described in detail. As the wife begins to move down the body, in the process of butchering, she cuts off her husband's penis. He says, "Look what you've

done!" She pops it in her mouth and eats it. I don't care if Berndt claims to have seen this. I think it's beyond normal human capability. His material is bizarre. To a very great extent it's insulting to the people themselves and insulting to the intelligence of anyone who reads that book.

SD: Do you think Berndt fabricated all this?

Arens: I don't think Berndt made it clear that the material he was presenting was from folktales, from informants' conversations about folktales. He gives the impression that he's seen it—that bothers me—when what he's doing is reporting tales like those in our own culture about monsters and people eating each other: "Hansel and Gretel" or "Jack and the Beanstalk."

SD: Dr. Arens, what about informants? Foré tribesmen in New Guinea have told anthropologists, "Yes, we do—or did—practice cannibalism." Why don't you believe them?

Arens: What if informants say, "Yes, there are cannibals here who eat human flesh?" Ah, you think, it's easy. That you can just write this down and assume it to be the case. But it's not always as simple as that. In one particular report, an informant tells an anthropologist that there are cannibals, and also that the cannibals are women who are able to turn themselves into birds. It's also a strange account because the cannibal eats part of a person and then the person wakes up and walks away. So here's an informant saying that there are cannibals, but also that people are birds. It's like a vampire story: Yes, he turns into a bat and sucks blood. It's a metaphorical account, it's folklore. It's not the type we're used to dealing with as if it were a description of reality.

SD: Dr. Arens, you can tell me that these women aren't sorcerers; you know objectively that people can't fly—so you're safe there. But it is possible that people would eat other humans.

Arens: It's true. We don't believe people can fly; we do believe that

people can eat each other.

If it's a custom, it should be observed. That's an anthropologist's job. If only one anthropologist would see it, I would be satisfied. I really would be. Just one anthropologist. New Guinea highlanders are to some extent still eating human flesh today. So why the hell doesn't somebody see it?

SD: Why the insistence on observation? Anthropologists frequently rely on people telling about their lives. When you study incest, you don't sit by the bedside waiting to see who jumps in . . .

Arens: Then you don't report it as fact. I know in the southern Sudan, where I do fieldwork, the people I worked with believed that their neighbors were cannibals. They said, "Oh, be careful, they eat people." I never reported that to be the case. They call those people every nasty name in the book in addition to calling them cannibals. They always portray them in a negative way. It's always people of another clan, or in-laws, or members of the other sex, or people on the other side of the river who are cannibals. It seems to be a projection of difference as evil.

SD: I hate to harp on circumstantial evidence, but if you're out in the field and see charred human bone with human teeth marks all over, what do you think if you don't think cannibalism? That sort of evidence has been uncovered.

Arens: There are a variety of explanations. Skulls could be crushed by falling rocks; bone could be chewed by animals or charred by cremation. I should make something else clear: We know that at certain times in certain places people have eaten other human beings. There's evidence for all cultures. There's evidence for our culture. But that does not make cannibalism a *custom* anywhere. Anthropologists miss that distinction.

SD: In our culture, you're referring to the Donner Pass incident, I presume. In the nineteenth century a party of settlers got caught in a blizzard in the high Sierras and resorted to cannibalism in order to survive.

Arens: Right. And if one were to find in a particular spot a broken charred bone with human teeth marks all over it, you could assume it was cannibalism in the sense of people having eaten human flesh. You cannot presume it was custom until you find all bones like that. And in "cannibal territory" you find bones and bodies buried properly. You can't say that people two thousand years ago were cannibals on the basis of a single find any more than you can say that all Californians are cannibals because in the nineteenth century a bunch of people went there and ate each other.

You know, one anthropologist who works with the Foré tribe in New Guinea says that she knows of people, very recently, who were arrested and later tried and convicted of cannibalism. There's the evidence. So what am I going on about? Well, if you're arrested and tried and convicted for it, then it's not a custom. And cannibalism has always been portrayed as a sanctioned practice. I mean this is entirely different.

SD: So when other anthropologists dismissed your book, saying that the evidence for cannibalism is "overwhelming," what are they referring to?

Arens: There's an interesting pattern. Most anthropologists admit that the evidence for cannibalism has been overplayed. They respond that the evidence in most of the work is not very good—but [they often add] "for my own region of expertise, the evidence is better." They'll say, "He's right, there's no good evidence for, say, Africa, but Arens is wrong about the Aztecs." So one says, "He's wrong about the Aztecs"; another, "He's wrong about New Guinea"; another, "He's wrong for Africa"; another "He's wrong on South America." You add all these up and you know what happens? The world is full of cannibals. That's peculiar.

SD: In particular, critics say you should have looked more at the South Seas.

Arens: It was my responsibility to deal with the strongest cases of can-nibalism, and I think I dealt with the best. Look, South Americanists will know more about the South American Indian and culture than I do. And my colleagues who work in New Guinea will know far more about society and culture in the New Guinea highlands. Those who work on Aztecs will know more about Aztecs than I do. But nobody knows more about cannibalism than me. I've looked at all of it, and I see a pattern emerging that they can't see: the inability to document in any sort of satisfactory way the notion that almost everybody in the world but us was once a cannibal.

There are literally thousands of reported cases of cannibalism. And I couldn't deal with all of them. And that includes, for example, reports on the Irish and the French and the Germans and the Christians and the Jews.

SD: But the medieval claim that Jews were cannibals that you discuss in your book has not withstood scrutiny.

Arens: Right. We dismiss that. Why? Don't forget that these reports are based on confessions, eyewitness accounts and "pictures"—that is, drawings of Jews actually doing this. Why do we dismiss that? We dismiss it because it seems unlikely to us that people who are part of the Judeo-Christian tradition would do such a thing. Why do we think that other people would do it? At some point in time it was decided that if a black or a brown or a red person was accused of cannibalism, there must be something there. But in the event that a white person was accused of cannibalism, it was absurd.

SD: To what extent do you think racism is involved—past or present?

Arens: I think racism has always played a part—a nicer term might be cultural eccentricity or prejudice. But it has always played a part. And it goes both ways. When I was in Africa, they thought I was a cannibal. In the field, they thought all white people went around and sucked blood. The Africans thought all Europeans did it. In fact, their argument for cannibalism is much better than ours; Europeans actually once went around Africa collecting people and shipping them off. And they never came back. One rather amusing story: In Zambia, I was told by an anthropologist about a copper-mining company that employed African workers. The company store stocked tinned beef that had a picture of someone like Aunt Jemima on it. And, according to him, a lot of Africans had now solved the riddle of where all those Africans had gone. The Europeans had not only killed those people, but were now trying to sell them back in cans. Now that's ridiculous and it's absurd and it's nonsense and it makes us laugh. But, on the other hand, when we start talking about Africans being cannibals, instead of laughing at the quality of the evidence, anthropologists shake their heads wisely and talk about how progress is needed, how these people have to be helped, administered or converted to Christianity. It's a joke when it's about us; it's serious business when it's about them.

SD: Dr. Arens, few anthropologists see a cannibal around every corner. Are you perhaps attacking straw men? Do you think you're a bit too extreme in stating your case?

Arens: I don't think I've gone too far. No, I think I was naive—terribly naive—in not realizing how anthropologists would respond. People have taken the book very personally. At meetings, I've encountered something very close to violence. I have been interrupted by screaming anthropologists, extremely aggressive questioning, insults. And then I ask myself, "Gee, why should they do that?" Then I realize that they've all told cocktail party stories and lectured to undergraduates about cannibalism. It's such an affront to these anthropologists to find out that someone is saying: "You've perpetuated a myth about other cultures." The stated purpose of anthropology is to eradicate myths. Maybe I should have put my case more gently, but I'm convinced now that I should have been much more adamant and open in disputing some of the evidence, particularly the idea that a disease called *kuru* is transmitted by cannibalism.

SD: The pathologist Carlton Gajdusek won a Nobel Prize in medicine for his work in New Guinea on *kuru.* In his Nobel lecture, he said he believes "that contamination during the cannibalistic ritual is the sole source of transmission of *kuru* from man to man."

Arens: Gajdusek never saw cannibalism. What Gajdusek really means is that the tribesmen get contaminated during what he thinks is a cannibalistic ritual, while they were handling the body in the process of cannibalism, not by the eating itself. In the introduction to the 1981 edition of his *Letters From the Field,* he writes: "It seems unlikely that eating the bodies caused the spread of the disease."

You see, you don't get *kuru* by eating human flesh. You get it by contact. *Gajdusek never made that clear.* They've been feeding chimps infected brain tissue of people who died from *kuru* for nine years, and the chimps haven't gotten it. They have been able to transmit the disease by direct inoculation though. Which means to the layman that if you were to get infected brain tissue on your hands, the best thing to do would be to eat it and then suck your fingers until everything had gone down. But never to touch your nose or eyes or any open sore.

SD: Gajdusek lived with the Foré for ten months. Why would he believe they were cannibals if he hadn't seen it?

Arens: Because everybody believes they're cannibals. I don't think this is intellectual duplicity or dishonesty or malice. It's just somehow trying to support what's "known." In Gajdusek's Nobel Prize article there are two photographs, one on top of the other. In the top picture there is a dead person, and in the lower scene, something is being eaten with at least the implicit message that the body in the first photograph was being eaten in the second. By Gajdusek's own admission, the two pictures are not related. He was only trying, in his own

words, "to portray or depict a scene." So we all revert to artistry at some point. If Gajdusek has seen cannibalism, if he has photographs, this material has still never been presented.

SD: Dr. Arens, people like Berndt and Gajdusek have lived in these places and say cannibalism exists. You're telling me that, *based on the literature,* no such thing ever existed. Why should I believe you?

Arens: Yes. Right. There's a line from a Groucho Marx film, in which Lady Teasdale goes into a room and catches Groucho under the bed. She says to him, "What are you doing in my room?" And he answers: "Lady, who are you going to believe—me or your eyes?" I realize there's a problem here since Berndt's been there and says he's seen it. I haven't been there, and I say it doesn't exist. All I can do is repeat what I've been saying: They did not see it.

SD: Why do all these normally rational scientists all of a sudden become unscholarly when a discussion turns to this particular topic?

Arens: That's a very broad question and a very deep question. Anthropologists have revived cannibalism generation after generation. So you have to ask anthropologists why they need cannibals. I would argue that anthropologists have an implicit, possibly unconscious, vested interest in maintaining the notion of cannibalism among exotic peoples. Cannibalism points to the fact that there are people so radically different from us that their social systems are worth studying.

SD: But there are many cross-cultural differences that could legitimize anthropology.

Arens: I agree with you. But if you look at the cultural differences that were posited at the beginning of the century, most of these differences have fallen by the wayside. A good example is incest. Around the turn of the century, there was a notion that many people didn't have incest taboos—that they were mating father and daughter, mother and son, brother and sister. But anthropologists did

some fieldwork and were able to show that these people, like us, had incest taboos. So the issues have fallen one by one. Indeed, if cultures become more universally unified there is fear that we anthropologists are going to have to start scratching around for differences. We might turn out to be sociologists or historians. The notion that there's always a cannibal somewhere is, I think, very important to anthropology.

SD: You know you're stepping on a lot of toes. A reviewer in the British journal *Man* called your book "dangerous."

Arens: It wasn't clear what he meant. The fellow's name is Peter Rivière; he's a very good anthropologist at Oxford. Why would any scholar say the work of another scholar was dangerous? Is he afraid that some young anthropologist will believe me, go off to South America and get eaten? Or will the book bring anthropology into disrepute? Is that dangerous?

I couldn't write a book about cannibalism if I was prone to paranoia, but there have been times when I've felt like there was something like an organized front against this book.

The reason I think the idea of cannibalism is dangerous is that people who have been labeled cannibals have been exterminated. With cannibalism, you can legitimize the extermination, enslavement or eradication of a culture—colonialism and cultural genocide. If these people did practice something as horrible as cannibalism, then, to a great extent, they were another species, not human beings.

SD: Do you think that someday anthropologists will decide that cannibalism never existed?

Arens: I think what will happen is the idea that other people were cannibals will slowly recede rather than be confronted. This might take twenty, thirty, forty, fifty years, but who cares? Not necessarily because of this book, but because of changing social, political and economic conditions. There has been a subtle shift toward greater appreciation of African cultures, especially when, all of a sudden, these states, which were once presumed to contain cannibals, became politically and economically significant to us. For example, once Nigeria became a supplier of oil, no anthropologist was going to go over there and look for cannibals.

And now that New Guinea is independent, I think anthropologists who go to New Guinea and start talking about the quest for cannibals are going to find themselves in a very difficult position. The government might take exception to the fact that Westerners consider them cannibals.

SD: Since the publication of your book, has anyone written to you who claims to have seen cannibalism?

Arens: My assumption is that anthropologists are so fascinated by cannibalism that they will make every effort, including possibly jumping into the pot themselves, to see it. The book's been out close to four years, and no anthropologist has responded with an observation.

You know, I have nightmares that some anthropologist will knock at my door and say, "I've seen it. I've lived among these people for years and they are cannibals." But I just don't think it will happen.

Confessions of a Former Cultural Relativist

Henry H. Bagish

Henry H. Bagish is a professor of sociology and anthropology at Santa Barbara City College. In addition to teaching, Mr. Bagish served as adviser for student activities and student government. An ardent advocate of a strong faculty voice in the formulation of college policies, he participated in the creation of the Instructors Association and, later, the Academic Senate. He served as the first president of the Instructors Association and the second president of the Academic Senate. He has also served as chairman of the Social Science Division, the Sociology/ Anthropology Department, and has been a member of most college and Academic Senate committees. He has been involved in the creation of many college policies, such as the institution's sabbatical leave policy.

On the state and regional levels, Mr. Bagish served on a liaison committee linking community colleges and the University of California. He has participated as a member of many accreditation teams for colleges in California and Hawaii. On the national level, he delivered a paper on decision-making in community college education to a national conference of the American Association for Higher Education, and was later appointed by that organization to its Task Force on Faculty Representation and Academic Negotiations, which conducted a nationwide study—publishing the results under the title, "Faculty Participation in Academic Governance." He also served on an advisory committee for the College Entrance Examination Board in establishing the College-Level Examination Program, designed to provide a national system of college credit by examination.

It's true. I confess it. I *was* a cultural relativist once. What's more, I still believe in some of it, even though I've rejected most of it—but let me give it to you from the start. I suppose I first ought to explain what cultural relativity is, for those of you who may not know, and how I became one. Then, I'll explain how I gradually became disillusioned, and end up with where I stand now.

ETHNOCENTRISM

Did you know that the Eskimos don't call themselves Eskimos? That's an Indian name for them, meaning "eaters of raw flesh," a custom that the Indians found disgusting. The Eskimo name for themselves is "Innuit," which translates as "The People." In fact, that sort of thing is quite common; many tribal names translate as "human beings." And if each tribe thinks of itself as "human beings," you know what that must mean to other tribes—they, obviously, must be something less than human. For an example, here's a story concerning the origin of the human races, told by the Cherokee Indians of the Great Smoky Mountains: "The Creator fashioned man by first making and firing an oven and then, from dough he had prepared, shaping three figures in human form. He placed the figures in the oven and waited for them to get done. But his impatience to see the result of this, his crowning experiment in the work of creation, was so great that he removed the first figure too soon. It was sadly underdone—pale, an unlovely color, and from it descended the white people. His second figure had fared well. The timing was accu-

rate, the form, richly browned, that was to be the ancestor of the Indians, pleased him in every way. He so admired it, indeed, that he neglected to take out of the oven the third form, until he smelled it burning. He threw open the door, only to find this last one charred and black. It was regrettable, but there was nothing to be done; and this was the first Negro." You see? Each group feels that, somehow, it is the best, God's chosen people—and others?—well, that's too bad, but obviously they're inferior.

Actually, this kind of attitude is found universally. Early in this century, the American sociologist William Graham Sumner coined a word for it. He called it "ethnocentrism"—the universal tendency for every human group to believe that its own ways, its own customs and beliefs, are the right ways, the best ways—and everybody else's ways are distinctly inferior.

Throughout human history this ethnocentric attitude has been the typical reaction of most travelers who have ever come in contact with people of foreign lands. And it was also the reaction of the early anthropologists of the 19th century, who believed that other cultures represented more primitive, more backward ways, while our Western culture, in Europe and the United States, represented the most advanced, highest pinnacle of evolutionary cultural development.

CULTURAL RELATIVITY

It was against this background that Franz Boas, an American anthropologist of German birth, developed the concept of cultural relativity. He rejected the ethnocentric judgments of the 19th century evolutionists, and

Originally presented as the Second Annual Faculty Lecture, in 1981. Santa Barbara City College. Reprinted with the permission of Henry H. Bagish.

insisted that each culture should be intensively studied as a separate entity. He also insisted that each culture needs to be understood in terms of its own unique background and circumstances. Rather than judging another culture, or even any practice of another culture, by our own ethnocentric standards, Boas said that the practices and customs of another culture should be understood only in terms of its *own* context and its *own* standards. This, then, was the doctrine of cultural relativity: that all customs are relative to a particular cultural context; that is, they stem from that context, are meaningful only in that context, and should be understood only in terms of that context.

Franz Boas has sometimes been called the father of American anthropology, and he certainly set the predominant tone of the field for the first half of this century. The cultural relativity that he espoused became the dominant philosophical stance of both anthropology and sociology. My own training in those fields included that philosophical position, becoming an outlook that I adopted wholeheartedly, and advocated in my teaching—even defending its merits in a College Forum debate many years ago with Bob Casier, Tim Fetler, and Laura Boutilier.

Probably one of the more vigorous exponents of the doctrine of cultural relativity was Melville Herskovits, a student of Franz Boas. He formulated what has become one of the basic statements of cultural relativity: "Evaluations are relative to the cultural background out of which they arise." Herskovits rejected the notion that our culture, or any culture, has exclusive possession of a set of absolute standards by which all other cultures can be judged. He rejected any such claim as just another example of ethnocentrism.

All such evaluations, Herskovits insisted, are relative—not just evaluations that involve judgments of what is good and bad, but also evaluations as to what is right and wrong, beautiful and ugly, normal and abnormal. Even our perception of the world around us is conditioned and influenced by culture, so that truth and reality themselves become relative, each culture with its own unique view of reality, again with no way to prove that any one view is superior to any other.

Herskovits went on to draw one more important conclusion from these premises. Since there are no absolute values, since all values are relative, since there is no way to demonstrate that any one set of values, or practices, or customs, or morals, or truths is any more valid than any other, it behooves us then to have tolerance and respect for other cultures. Herskovits put it this way: "Cultural relativism is a philosophy which, in recognizing the values set up by every society to guide its own life, lays stress on the dignity inherent in every body of custom, and on the need for tolerance of conventions though they may differ from one's own."

RELATIVITY IN AMERICAN SOCIETY

This philosophy of respect for and tolerance of differences has struck a deeply responsive chord in the intellectual life of our society. In fact, the development of such a philosophy is easily understandable in the context of our democratic, liberal, pluralistic society. Certainly, if we are not to be constantly at each others' throats over our differences as Catholics and Protestants, Gentiles and Jews, Republicans and Democrats, blacks and whites, etc., we *need* to have a national philosophy of toleration, of "live and let live," of "to each his own," "one man's meat is another man's poison."

So, in many ways, this philosophy of cultural relativity has permeated our thinking and our social lives. This has become a relativistic era. The very term has become a cliche, thanks in no small part to Albert Einstein and his theory of relativity in physics, which few of us understand but virtually everyone has heard of. You can frequently hear people say, "Everything's relative," "it's all relative."

This principle of relativity is extended in everyday life to the individual level as well. Whenever a moral or ethical question comes up in my anthropology classes, or even more so in my sociology class on marriage, whether it's a question about sex or abortion or almost any other question, a very common response by students is "it's all up to the individual," or "it's that person's choice to make." I find students generally very reluctant to *judge* anyone's behavior, to evaluate it in any way. Most of them resist saying that anyone's else's ideas or behavior are *wrong*, or *bad*. One student said recently in class that he doesn't even use the words "good" or "bad"—it's all relative.

To summarize what we've said about the concept of cultural relativity so far, it says that there are no absolute standards for judging customs, that a society's customs and ideas should be viewed and understood in the context of that society's culture. It further says that all cultures and cultural practices are equally valid, of equal worth and equal dignity, and so we should have tolerance and respect for cultural practices and ideas, even if they happen to differ from ours, or even if they're considered "bad" by our society's standards.

WHAT'S WRONG WITH CULTURAL RELATIVITY?

Well, what could possibly be wrong with that? How could any right-thinking person find anything wrong with tolerance and respect for other people's ideas, with granting them the dignity and validity that surely all the world's peoples are entitled to? To question tolerance and respect is like questioning God, motherhood, and apple pie—but I'd like to give it a try, and in so doing, show you how I became disillusioned with cultural relativity.

Let's do it this way: let's peek and eavesdrop, in imagination, on my Cultural Anthropology class at various times during the semester, as the class and I proceed on our journey of exploration of human cultures.

1. ANTHROPOLOGICAL PERSPECTIVES

First, the students read in their textbook about cultural relativity; there they learn that all customs of a society should be viewed in terms of that society, rather than in terms of their own. They are told that the relativistic attitude fosters empathy and understanding, and respect for other cultures, and that one should avoid making value judgments about other cultures. They also learn about ethnocentrism, and the problems and misunderstandings that arise from the ethnocentric attitude—an attitude that in fact many students bring with them when they first sign up for the course.

Thus equipped, we're ready for the first visit of our journey, to the Tlingit Indians of the 19th century who lived in southeastern Alaska. We listen to a recorded drama that tells of a Tlingit Indian—a warrier, who's also a husband and father—who willingly lets himself be killed in order to avenge a murder committed, not by him, but by another, more high-ranking member of his clan. It seems a very strange custom from our perspective, but we learn that it's perfectly understandable within the total context of the Tlingit Indian culture.

Next, we see a film about life—and death—among the Dani, a Stone-Age people in a remote valley in New Guinea. By this time, the students aren't even fazed by the unusual clothing of the Dani: for the men, feathers in the hair, and a long, slim gourd over the penis; for the women, net bags draped over their heads and down their backs, leaving their breasts exposed.

But the Dani have other interesting customs and beliefs too. They believe in ghosts, and that the ghosts of people slain in war or ambush must be avenged—because unavenged ghosts bring sickness, unhappiness and disaster. Therefore, at the time the film was made, in 1961, the Dani were still fighting a seemingly endless series of retaliatory wars fought with spears, bows and arrows—wars that we can watch in the film with fascination. One side would manage to kill a member of the enemy, and then could celebrate the killing. But then

the enemy had to avenge *that* killing—and so, back and forth it went. Nor was it only warriors in battle who might be killed to avenge the ghosts. Anyone—a woman, a child caught unawares in an ambush, was equally fair game. In the film, we see the funeral of a young boy killed in just such an ambush.

How do the students react to this apparently "senseless" killing? They understand that it's *not* "senseless," that in fact it "makes sense" within the context of Dani beliefs and Dani culture. When I ask them whether such warfare and killing should be stopped by, say, some outside authority, their answer is almost unanimously a vehement "no!" Most of them have by now developed a thoroughly relativistic attitude.

There is one other Dani custom, however, that gives us pause. There is one more ritual that must be performed in order to placate the ghosts of the slain. Early in the morning, two or three young girls who are closely related to the dead person are brought to the funeral site, and there, with a sharp blow from a stone adze just like this one, each girl has two fingers chopped off. Virtually all Dani women have lost two to six fingers in this way. Just as you wince at the thought, so do the students. This custom they find harder to accept. Is it just ethnocentric narrow-mindedness and squeamishness, or is it something more?

Then, a bit later in the course, we read an account by Viktor Frankl of his experiences in the Nazi extermination camp at Auschwitz. Viktor Frankl managed to survive the horrors of the camps, along with a handful of other gaunt, emaciated near-skeletons of human beings—but some eleven million others died in the Nazi attempt at mass extermination of Jews and other so-called "inferior races." Well, I ask the students, what about this "quaint" cultural practice of the Nazis? Would anyone have been justified in trying to intervene in this practice—as, indeed, the Allies finally did? Shouldn't we simply try to understand this practice within the context of that culture, and not at-

tempt to judge it by our own ethnocentric standards? Isn't this practice of equal dignity, equally valid, equally worthy of tolerance and respect?

Since virtually no one by this point is ready to grant respect and tolerance for *that* cultural practice, we have ourselves a conflict. How are we going to reconcile our acceptance of Dani killing with our rejection of Nazi killing?

—But wait: here is something else to read, a story by Nadine Gordimer that tells about life in South Africa under the policy of "apartheid," a story that shows a black man robbed of rights, of identity, even in death—a story that reveals some of the consequences of a policy of racism. Again I ask the students their reaction to *this* cultural practice—and again they have trouble granting it respect and tolerance.

By this point one of the basic tenents of cultural relativity is in trouble. Being non-judgmental, having respect and tolerance, accepting and not intervening, seem to be all right up to a point—but beyond that ill-defined point, we are having difficulty with the concept.

Now we see another film, one that shows us another aspect of the problem. This film is about the Nuer of southwestern Ethiopia, a black, handsome, cattle-herding people. But we see some Nuer children dying of smallpox, their faces and bodies covered with the eruptions and lesions of the disease. The Nuer hold a special ceremony, asking the gods to relieve them of this scourge. They dance, they fire precious bullets into the air, they sacrifice goats to the goddess of the river. This is the Nuer way of dealing with smallpox. I ask: what's *our* way? Vaccination, comes the answer. Which way is *better*?, I ask. Whoops—we good relativists don't like questions like that. We've been taught not to judge, not to evaluate one way as better or worse than another. All ways, after all, are equally valid, and to claim that our way is better than others is to slip into the old trap of ethnocentrism. Besides, now you're challenging the validity of somebody's *religious* beliefs, and that

32

violates an even more deeply-rooted taboo.

But I press them. Which way is more *effective*? Which way, prayers and sacrifices on the one hand, or vaccination on the other, does a more effective job of accomplishing the goal of eliminating smallpox? Now the answer comes, even if a bit reulctantly, and almost with embarrassment: yes, it is true that our way *is* more effective. In fact, this has just recently been demonstrated, in one of the most dramatic triumphs of modern Western medicine. Just one year ago this coming Friday, on May 8, 1980, the World Health Organization declared the total and complete eradication of the disease of smallpox all over the world. The smallpox virus had always been a major killer of mankind. In 1967 there had been an estimated 10 million cases of smallpox, 2 million of those fatal. Smallpox, being a highly contagious disease, respecting no national or societal boundaries, could be attacked only on a world-wide scale. That's what happened. Through a 13-year program of massive vaccination, almost two and a half billion people were vaccinated, eradicating the disease in one area of the globe after another, until the last remaining cases were tracked down in Somalia and southern Ethiopia—the very area we had seen in our film. Those cases were cured, the last remaining people vaccinated—and after a two-year waiting period to be sure there would be no new cases, smallpox, that age-old killer of mankind, was declared eliminated from the face of the earth. Apparently, then, it *can* be demonstrated that some ways *are* better than others. We'll come back to the underlying principle involved in a little bit.

Let's join the class again. Here we're learning that the Arunta, an Australian aboriginal people, believed that women conceived babies by going too near trees or rocks where various totemic spirits lived. A frog spirit or lizard spirit would enter her body, and in time a baby would be born. The Trobriand Islanders, living on small islands off the east coast of New Guinea, had a similar belief, that

pregnancy was caused by spirits that lurk in the water. If a woman waded in too deep, a spirit would enter her vagina, and thus she'd have a baby. The Tobrianders had plenty of experience with sexual intercourse, since premarital sex was freely indulged in, as well as sexual promiscuity after marriage on certain occasions as well—but the Tobrianders didn't make any connection between sexual intercourse and pregnancy. If a Trobriand woman didn't want to get pregnant, the rule was simple: "Don't go near the water."

Once again I ask a series of questions: are the Arunta and Trobriand beliefs that babies are caused by frog or water spirits entering the body of a woman *true* or *false*? That question is really a no-no, I find; I'm violating that same deep-seated taboo against questioning anyone's religious beliefs. It's *true*, I hear in chorus, it's *true*—at least, it's true for *them*. What do they, the students, believe causes babies here in the U.S.A.? I hear something about sperm from a man meeting an ovum in a woman, stemming from an activity called sexual intercourse. Yes, I've heard of that theory—supposedly a natural, biological process that constitutes reproduction in our species. Gee, I wonder aloud, I wonder whether the Arunta and the Trobiranders are also members of our human species, and subject to the same biological process of reproduction—or do they perhaps do it differently, with frog or water spirits? Well, the students agree they're fellow human beings, and so likely to reproduce via the same biological process that we do.

I pose the question a bit differently: are the sperm/ovum theory and the frog/water-spirit theory of equal validity—or do they differ in validity, and if so, how and why? Well, it turns out that the Trobrianders themselves have already answered the question for us, it seems. About a year and a half ago my wife and I went to the Trobriand Islands, to try to find out whether beliefs and customs have changed there, or remained the same. We learned that the Trobrianders are as sexually active as ever, both pre-

maritally and extramaritally—that hasn't changed, despite the best efforts of missionaries. A Trobriander told us: "What's ours is *ours!*" But they've apparently found that the Western sperm/ovum theory does have a certain advantage over the water-spirit theory—namely, it *works* better when you want to slow down the rate of arrival of new little Trobrianders. We learned that there were two family-planning people on the island who visit the villages and provide contraceptives—and the Trobrianders find that method of controlling births a lot more effective than simply staying out of the water. So now these girls on their way home from school can safely "go near the water."

EVALUATION OF CULTURAL RELATIVITY

Well, these questions and problems that I confront my class with are pretty much the same kinds of questions that ultimately led me to become disillusioned with cultural relativity. At this point, let me now give you my present overall evaluation of the principle of cultural relativity. Let me show you what I think is right and good about it, and then what I think is wrong and bad about it—because like so much in life, it has, I think, both good and bad, and I wouldn't want us to throw out the baby with the bath water.

What's good and right about cultural relativity? Well, as a working rule for the anthropologist, I think it's very useful, even necessary, in order to gain as much objective understanding as possible about the culture he's studying. Chad Oliver has put it very well in his latest book: "An anthropologist in the field cannot go about exclaiming, 'How monstrous! How awful! Why, you people are *terrible!*' Moreover, the anthropologist cannot think this way either. There is no hope of understanding how a culture works if it is approached with contempt or loathing. At the very least, a suspension of judgment is required." I'd like to put it this way: *if* you want an objective, accurate understanding of another culture, *then* you'd do well to suspend value judgments about what you see and hear, and try to get an "inside" view of what the culture is all about, in its own terms. As a scientific tool, cultural relativity is demonstrably useful for achieving that goal.

OK, now, what's wrong, bad, invalid, insufficient about cultural relativity? Basically, there are two conclusions that relativists have drawn that I think are in error: the first is that all cultural practices are equally *valid*, and the second is that all cultural practices are equally *worthy of tolerance and respect*. Let's consider each in turn.

ARE ALL CULTURAL PRACTICES EQUALLY VALID?

I believe that the relativist conclusion that all cultures and all cultural practices are equally valid is based upon certain hidden, unstated assumptions that I believe just aren't correct. The first of these is the assumption that each culture, and each cultural practice, by performing positive functions for the people, "meets the needs" of that society, and thus in that sense is "valid."

Now it's true that every practice probably has *some* positive functions, some advantages for its practitioners. For instance, even the Nazi killing of six million Jews performed some beneficial functions for the Nazis—all the psychological and material benefits of scapegoating. But does that make the practice "valid?" The truth is that most practices, in addition to positive functions, have negative functions as well, disadvantages—the price that must be paid for the benefits. "There's no such thing as a free lunch," says the old slogan, and I believe it.

Also, I doubt that any culture meets all the needs of all its members. In short, I believe that all cultures are, to some greater or lesser extent, *imperfect*, and thus could be improved. But then, if all cultures are to some extent imperfect, must we conclude that all are *equally* imperfect?

This, then, brings us to the second

hidden assumption of the relativist, namely, that there is no scientifically valid way to compare cultures, to rate or rank them, to say that one is better or worse than another. Now, in one way I agree—in the sense that I don't know of any valid way to compare *entire* cultures. But I do believe that many specific cultural practices and beliefs *can* be compared, *can* be demonstrated to be clearly better or worse, on a non-ethnocentric basis.

In fact, human societies have been doing this all through history. Despite the universal tendency to to ethnocentrism, when societies have come in contact with other societies that had better tools, or weapons, or practices, ones that *worked* better than their own, most of the time, sooner or later, they have given up the old and adopted the new.

Examples? We've already seen two in our eavesdropping on my class. Which is better when it comes to eradicating smallpox: the Nuer way of shooting bullets and sacrificing goats, or our way of vaccination? Clearly, vaccination; it did work, the other did not. Which is better when it comes to controlling births: the Arunta/Trobriand way of avoiding rocks, trees, and water, or our way of contraceptives—and that's not just our own biased ethnocentric view, but the conclusion reached by the Trobrianders themselves, because they also, just as we did, learned that contraceptives enabled them to *predict* and *control* that aspect of their lives better than they could by dodging spirits in the water.

THE PRAGMATIC PRINCIPLE

What's the basic principle underlying this kind of comparison? It's very simple: it's the *pragmatic* principle. That which *works* is "better" than that which *doesn't* work. Or more accurately, when people are given a choice, that which *works better*, to *achieve certain valued ends*, is what most people end up choosing, most of the time.

But what do I mean by "work better"? Any belief or practice that enables human beings to *predict* and

control events in their lives, with a higher degree of success than previous beliefs or practices did, can be said to "work better." Better *prediction* and better *control* of events—those are the two essential ingredients that enable human beings to adapt better to the world around them.

I'd like to put that somewhat differently, in the form of a general formula that can then have even broader applicability—although I'll caution you right now that it won't work for everything, by any means—but we'll come back to that. Here's the formula (*Fig. 1*):

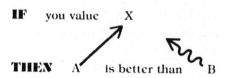

Figure 1.

Further examples are many, but let me show you just two more. Here are two axes (*Figs. 2 and 3*). More accurately, the first is an adze, since the blade is transverse to the handle, rather than parallel to it—but that's not the point. It's from the Dani, in New Guinea, and in addition to being used for chopping off little girls' fingers, it was more often used for chopping wood. Here, on the other hand, is an American steel axe, ground to a sharp edge. Which is better? In terms of the pragmatic formula, it's obvious: *If* you value being able to chop down trees and chop up wood with a minimum of human effort, *then* the steel axe is better than the stone adze. Nor is this just an ethnocentric notion of ours. The greater efficiency and utility of steel axes has never gone unnoticed by those peoples who had been previously using stone axes. In every case, once they've learned about steel axes, they've eagerly sought the more efficient steel tools —as, indeed, did two Dani men with whom I became friends. They each asked me, separately, to send them steel tools—an axe, and a machete— which they had learned about from missionaries. And in fact, when we returned home, I did send them—but not the baby cow they also requested.

Figure 2.

One more example (*Figs. 4 and 5*): here's a Dani arrow, given to me by one of my Dani friends. Look at it closely. See anything "missing"? Yes —it has no feathers on the end. Here's an American arrow for comparison; it's fletched with feathers, because long ago someone discovered that putting feathers on the end

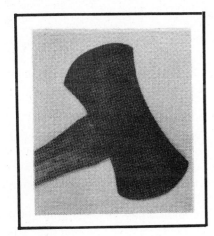

Figure 3.

of an arrow will make it fly straighter and more steadily.

In other words, *if* you want to kill your adversary (be it human or animal) before he or it kills you, *then* putting feathers on the arrow is better than having no feathers. It just so happens that the Dani, who live in an

incredibly remote valley deep in the interior of western New Guinea, have never discovered or learned from others about the principle of feathers on arrows—and so their warfare was somewhat less efficiently lethal than it might have been, as these arrows wobbled and fluttered and slowed in their flight.

However, the pragmatic principle can't be applied in *all* areas of culture. All the areas we've considered so far have been ones in which we've been concerned with choosing instrumental means toward specified ends: "If you want *this* end, then A will achieve it better than B." But some kinds of

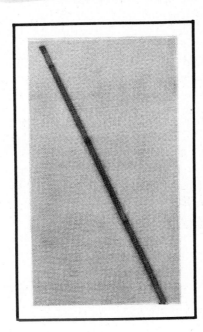

Figure 4.

cultural activities are basically not instrumental, not means toward further ends, but rather they're performed as ends in themselves. When that's the case, the pragmatic test can't be applied. For example, take art. If a culture thinks of art as something that exists only for its own sake, but not as a means of achieving anything else, then I see no way of objectively demonstrating that one art form is better or worse than another. There it's strictly a matter of taste, of meeting whatever the local criteria might be for good art. In other words, there it's relative.

One further warning: so far I've given you examples in which, strangely enough, *our* ways seem to be the ones that are better than those of other people. One might almost suspect a hidden strain of ethnocentrism lurking in all this objective-sounding verbiage. However, we aren't always the winners. In some cases it might be a toss-up, and in others our way might be worse than others. Some examples:

We in the U.S. drive on the right, while the British drive on the left (the "wrong" side, as Americans sometimes ethnocentrically put it). Which is better? For the life of me, I can't think of any way in which either can be said to be better than the other. They're just *different* customs that seem to work equally well. Another: for a number of forms of mental illness and emotional disturbance, it's not at all clear that Western psychotherapy has achieved any better record of success than the practices of

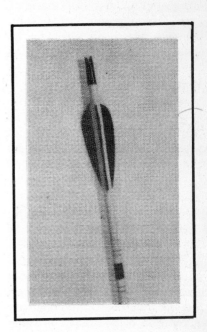

Figure 5.

medicine men and so-called "witch-doctors" in other parts of the world. In fact, they may even have a *better* record of cures than we do. Finally, when it comes to dealing with the aged, I suspect that an awful lot of societies all around the world have devised much better ways of coping with the problems of aging than we have here in America.

So much for the relativists' conclusion that all cultural practices are equally valid. I've tried to show you why I don't agree with that conclusion, and how I believe we can demonstrate, in an objective, non-ethnocentric way, how some cultural practices are actually "better" than others.

ARE ALL PRACTICES EQUALLY WORTHY OF TOLERANCE AND RESPECT?

Now let's turn our attention to the relativists' other major conclusion, that all cultural practices are equally worthy of tolerance and respect.

First of all, it should be noted that the doctrine of cultural relativity purports to be one of scientific objectivity and neutrality, designed to keep our investigations value-free. Various writers, however, have pointed out that cultural relativity, behind its facade of objectivity and neutrality, is actually a *moral* theory, one that is *not* objective and does *not* exclude value judgments. Raymond Firth, for instance, points out that "the affirmation that we should have respect and tolerance for the values of other cultures is itself a value which is not derivable from the proposition that all values are relative." Paul Schmidt points out that an "ought" statement cannot logically be derived from an "is" statement; that is, just because there *is* a wide variety of values and customs in the world does not logically require that we therefore *ought* to tolerate any of them. In fact, says Frank Hartung, cultural relativity is actually a moral theory that gives a central place to one value: *tolerance.*

Nor is it true that cultural relativity is a position of neutrality on value questions. In its tolerance and acceptance of whatever *is*, relativity is essentially lending its approval and support to the *status quo*, whatever that might be, as against any attempts to change or intervene in the *status quo*. Relativity ends up, then, as a basically conservative doctrine. As such, it's often opposed by would-be agents of change, of widely varying ideological persuasions—from religious missionaries, on the one hand, to radical reformers and revolutionaries on the other.

Be that as it may, cultural relativity still does stand for tolerance and respect. What could be wrong with that? *Aren't* all cultural practices equally worthy of tolerance and respect?

Well, in our classroom journey we encountered three cultural practices that I suspect many of us may have had trouble granting tolerance and respect: the Dani practice of chopping off little girls' fingers, the Nazi extermination of eleven million human beings, the South African practice of apartheid. Chal Oliver put our dilemma well: "It is one thing to try to understand a culture in its own terms and recognize its values. It is quite another thing to stand idly by and watch Nazis stacking human beings in gas ovens, saying only, 'well, that's the way they do things in that culture.'" In other words, to tolerate anything and everything that's done in the world around us leads to a paralyzing inability to do anything at all to defend our own conceptions of the good and the right.

But if we do agree that not all cultural practices are equally worthy of respect and tolerance, we're then faced with a very real problem: where and how do we draw the line? If we're to avoid the opposite extreme of complete ethnocentric *in*tolerance, wiping out every custom that's not an identical clone of our own, how do we decide? And isn't tolerance, after all, a good and worthwhile value for a person who believes in liberal democracy, and the idea that people should be free to live as they choose?

TOLERANCE IN ONE'S HIERARCHY OF VALUES

I look at it this way. Yes, I do value tolerance, and tolerance happens to be high up on my personal list of values. But we human beings have many values, not just one, and these values, when we stop to think about them, are arranged in our heads or hearts in a kind of hierarchy, a rank order, with some of our values being much more important to us than others. Sure, I value and enjoy strawberry ice cream, and I suppose it's there somewhere in my personal hierarchy of values. But compassion for my fellow human beings is a value that is much, much higher up on my list, being much more important to me than any flavor of ice cream.

Figure 6.

Now, the advantage of thinking of values as existing in a hierarchy is that when we realize that if we should ever experience a *conflict* of values—something that happens frequently in life—the value that is lower in our hierarchy will have to yield to the one that is higher.

And this is precisely what's happening with our dilemma concerning tolerance. I imagine that many of us here, probably most of us, do value tolerance. After all, it's part of our liberal democratic heritage. But what happens when we encounter cultural practices such as the ones I've shown you today, the finger-chopping, the ovens for humans? Something very important, I think; let me explain.

To do so, I'm going to give you one more example, one that I warn you you'll probably not enjoy, but it will help to make my point. This is a photograph of a seven-year-old African girl who has just had a ritual clitoridectomy (*Fig. 6*); that is, her clitoris and labia minora have just been cut out, without benefit of any anesthesia. She is one of some 30 million females in the world, most of them in Africa and Arab countries, who have undergone this removal of the focal point of female sexual pleasure. Many explanations are given for this ritual practice, but most of them seem to boil down to an attempt to reduce female sexual pleasure and thus ensure sexual fidelity. Now, how do you react to *this* custom? Do you find it "quaint," "interesting,"—or something else?

First of all, please notice that all these things—the finger-chopping, the ovens, the clitoridectomies—aren't being done to *us*, after all; so it could fairly be asked, why is it even any of our business?

Well, I believe that sometimes some of our most dearly held values, ones that are toward the very top of our hierarchy of values, are *deeply* outraged by events out there in the world, even though they don't threaten us personally or directly. What happens when our values are outraged in this way is that our circle of concern broadens. It widens beyond the limits of our own personal bodily self, or even our own family, our own community, even our own society. What we do then is to extend the boundaries, the limits of our sense of identity, of community, of who is included in the circle of "us." We now identify with those people "out there" as well. We empathize with them, we feel with them. Did you wince when I showed you the clitoridectomized girl? I know I did. Did you want to clutch yourself *there*? What hurts those people hurts us. "Compassion" is what it's called; we "suffer with" those others—and when that happens, respect and tolerance, both good but *lesser* values, have to go by the boards. Those practices we cannot accept, cannot tolerate. Somehow, in some way, we are moved to want to change them.

CONCLUSION: GOING BEYOND CULTURAL RELATIVITY

I feel that the doctrine of cultural relativity has served, and even continues to serve, a valuable function, that of gaining objective understanding. But in its refusal to compare, to evaluate, to judge, in its insistence on indiscriminate tolerance of every possible practice, it has tended to paralyze us in our ability to cope with the world we live in. This isn't a world composed only of small, isolated tribes with benign, quaint practices. The real world we inhabit is a rapidly shrinking one, with its peoples in increasingly close contact with each other. Some of those people have cultural practices that either threaten us directly, or else represent an assault on our most deeply-held values. What are we to do? How can we go *beyond* cultural relativity to cope with this world that presses in upon us?

First, I urge that we recognize that it's not only possible, but indeed desirable to compare, evaluate, and judge many cultural practices, not on the basis of a naive ethnocentrism, or on the presumed possession of absolute standards, but rather from an objective, cross-cultural perspective. Such judging can be done in terms of the pragmatic "if. . .then. . ." formula that I presented earlier. Another example to remind you: "*If* you value your children's life, and don't want them to die of smallpox, *then* vaccination is better than goat sacrifice."

Please notice the way this approach employs values. It doesn't *impose* any one set of values on anyone; rather, it *asks*, what *do* you value? *If* you value X, then. . .and so on. Once the value has been established, then there's a basis for evaluations and judgments.

To be sure, not everyone in the world has the same values, as we all know. But on the other hand, in many areas of life we may find more consensus on basic values than we thought, and therefore we may develop greater agreement on means toward those

ends as well—as was the case with the example I just gave you. It turned out that an awful lot of the world's people *did* value their children's lives, and *did* want them not to die of smallpox—and so they went along with vaccination instead of their former practices. Might we achieve other consensuses in the future as well, on other values that are also dear to our hearts?

Interestingly enough, human history *has* shown some value convergences, some achievement of consensus. Headhunting is practically a thing of the past—and even though a dyed-in-the-wool relativist might regret the passing of this "noble" custom that undoubtedly performed important functions for those who hunted heads, I suspect that the potential *victims*—the "donors" for this quaint practice—were happy to see the passing of the custom. Slavery, too, is virtually eliminated from the earth—so it *is* possible to achieve *some* consensus on important values.

Second, I urge that as we compare, evaluate, and judge, that we make our values explicit. We need to be aware of what our values are, of course; examine them, think them through, become aware of what order they stand in our own personal hierarchy of values. But then I urge that we not be bashful; let's speak up for our values, each of us; let's express them, even attempt to persuade others to share them with us. I don't fear this process; rather, I welcome it. If it should turn out that our values are actually narrow and parochial and are only self-serving, I'm sure that others will rapidly let us know by their reaction. If, on the other hand, our values should touch a responsive chord in others, if they should agree, "Yes, that *would* be good, that *would* make for a better world," why, then perhaps we'd all be a little bit closer to achieving consensus on the kind of world we *could* all live in, in peace and harmony.

Culture and Communication

Anthropologists are interested in all aspects of human behavior and how they interrelate with each other. Language is a form of such behavior (albeit primarily verbal behavior), and therefore worthy of study. It is patterned and passed down from one generation to the next through learning, not instinct, and it is integral to human social interaction.

It has long been recognized that human communication through language is by its nature different from the kind of communication found among other animals. Central to this difference is the fact that humans communicate abstractly, with symbols that have meaning independent of the immediate sensory experiences of either the sender or the receiver of messages. Thus, for instance, humans are able to refer to the future and the past, instead of just the here and now.

Recent experiments have shown that anthropoid apes can be taught a small portion of Ameslan, the sign language used to overcome hearing and speech disabilities. It must be remembered, however, that their very rudimentary ability has to be tapped by painstaking human effort, and that the degree of difference between apes and humans serves only to emphasize the peculiarly human need for and development of language.

Just as the abstract quality of symbols lifts our thoughts beyond immediate sense perception, it also inhibits our ability to think about and convey the full meaning of our personal experience. No categorical term can do justice to its referents—the variety of forms to which the term refers. The degree to which this is an obstacle to clarity of thought and communication relates to the degree of abstraction in the symbols involved. The word "chair," for instance, would not present much difficulty since it has rather objective referents. Consider the trouble we have, however, in thinking and communicating with words whose referents are not quite so tied to immediate sense perception—words such as "freedom," "democracy," and "justice." At best, the likely result is symbolic confusion: an inability to think or communicate in objectively definable symbols. At its worst, language may be used to purposefully obfuscate, as is shown in the article "Language, Appearance, and Reality."

A related issue has to do with the fact that languages differ as to what is relatively easy to express within the restrictions of their particular vocabularies. Thus, although a given language may not have enough words to allow one to cope with a new situation or a new field of activity, the typical solution is to invent or borrow words. In this way, it may be said that any language can be used to teach anything. This point is illustrated by Laura Bohannan's attempt to convey the "true" meaning of Shakespeare's *Hamlet* to the West African Tiv. Much of her task is devoted to finding the most appropriate words in the Tiv language to convey her Western thoughts. At least part of her failure is due to the fact that some of the words are just not there, and her inventions are, to the Tiv at least, unacceptable.

Even our sense of time should not be taken for granted, but must be seen in the context of the "pace of life," as discussed in "Social Time: The Heartbeat of Culture." And finally, intercultural misunderstandings may even contribute to the imbalance of trade between nations, as shown in "How Not to Lose the Trade Wars by Cultural Gaffes."

Taken collectively, therefore, the articles in this section show how symbolic confusion may occur between individuals or groups on a verbal and nonverbal level. They also demonstrate the tremendous potential of recent research to enhance effective communication among all of us.

Looking Ahead: Challenge Questions

Does language restrict our thought processes?

In what ways is communication difficult in a cross-cultural situation?

What kinds of messages are transmitted through nonverbal communication? How may ethnic differences create misunderstandings?

How is the "pace of life" of a culture reflected in its vocabulary of time?

How are differences in bargaining style affecting trade relations between Japan and the United States?

How has this section enhanced your ability to communicate more effectively?

Unit 2

Language, Appearance, and Reality: Doublespeak in 1984

William D. Lutz

William D. Lutz, chair of the Department of English at Rutgers University, is also chair of the National Council of Teachers of English (NCTE) Committee on Public Doublespeak and editor of the Quarterly Review of Doublespeak.

There are at least four kinds of doublespeak. The first kind is the euphemism, a word or phrase that is designed to avoid a harsh or distasteful reality. When a euphemism is used out of sensitivity for the feelings of someone or out of concern for a social or cultural taboo, it is not doublespeak. For example, we express grief that someone has *passed away* because we do not want to say to a grieving person, "I'm sorry your father is dead." The euphemism *passed away* functions here not just to protect the feelings of another person but also to communicate our concern over that person's feelings during a period of mourning.

However, when a euphemism is used to mislead or deceive, it becomes doublespeak. For example, the U.S. State Department decided in 1984 that in its annual reports on the status of human rights in countries around the world it would no longer use the word *killing*. Instead, it uses the phrase *unlawful or arbitrary deprivation of life*. Thus the State Department avoids discussing the embarrassing situation of the government-sanctioned killings in countries that are supported by the United States. This use of language constitutes doublespeak because it is designed to mislead, to cover up the

unpleasant. Its real intent is at variance with its apparent intent. It is language designed to alter our perception of reality.

A second kind of doublespeak is jargon, the specialized language of a trade, profession, or similar group. It is the specialized language of doctors, lawyers, engineers, educators, or car mechanics. Jargon can serve an important and useful function. Within a group, jargon allows members of the group to communicate with each other clearly, efficiently, and quickly. Indeed, it is a mark of membership in the group to be able to use and understand the group's jargon. For example, lawyers speak of an *involuntary conversion* of property when discussing the loss or destruction of property through theft, accident, or condemnation. When used by lawyers in a legal situation, such jargon is a legitimate use of language, since all members of the group can be expected to understand the term.

However, when a member of the group uses jargon to communicate with a person outside the group, and uses it knowing that the nonmember does not understand such language, then there is doublespeak. For example, a number of years ago a commercial airliner crashed on takeoff, killing three passengers, injuring twenty-one others, and destroying the airplane, a 727. The insured value of the airplane was greater than its book value, so the airline made a profit of three million dollars on the destroyed airplane. But the airline had two problems: it did not want to talk about one if its airplanes crashing and it had to account for the three million dollars when it issued its annual report to its stockholders. The

airline solved these problems by inserting a footnote in its annual report explaining that this three million dollars was due to "the involuntary conversion of a 727." Note that airline officials could thus claim to have explained the crash of the airplane and the subsequent three million dollars in profit. However, since most stockholders in the company, and indeed most of the general public, are not familiar with legal jargon, the use of such jargon constitutes doublespeak.

A third kind of doublespeak is gobbledygook or bureaucratese. Basically, such doublespeak is simply a matter of piling on words, of overwhelming the audience with words, the bigger the better. For example, when Alan Greenspan was chairman of the President's Council of Economic Advisors, he made this statement when testifying before a Senate committee:

It is a tricky problem to find the particular calibration in timing that would be appropriate to stem the acceleration in risk premiums created by falling incomes without prematurely aborting the decline in the inflation-generated risk premiums.

Did Alan Greenspan's audience really understand what he was saying? Did he believe his statement really explained anything? Perhaps there is some meaning beneath all those words, but it would take some time to search it out. This seems to be language that pretends to communicate but does not.

The fourth kind of doublespeak is inflated language. Inflated language designed to make the ordinary seem extraordinary, the common, uncommon; to make everyday things seem impressive; to give an air of importance to people, situations, or things

From *ETC* (Et Cetera), Winter 1987, pp. 383-391. Excerpt from *The Legacy of Language—A Tribute to Charlton Laird*, edited by Philip C. Boardman. Copyright © University of Nevada Press.

that would not normally be considered important; to make the simple seem complex. With this kind of language, car mechanics become *automotive internists,* elevator operators become members of the *vertical transportation corps,* used cars become not just *preowned* but *experienced cars.* When the Pentagon uses the phrase *pre-emptive counterattack* to mean that American forces attacked first, or when it uses the phrase *engage the enemy on all sides* to describe an ambush of American troops, or when it uses the phrase *tactical redeployment* to describe a retreat by American troops, it is using doublespeak. The electronics company that sells the television set with *nonmulticolor capability* is also using the doublespeak of inflated language.

Doublespeak is not a new use of language peculiar to the politics or economics of the twentieth century. Thucydides in *The Peloponnesian War* wrote that

revolution thus ran its course from city to city. . . . Words had to change their ordinary meanings and to take those which were now given them. Reckless audacity came to be considered the courage of a loyal ally; prudent hesitation, specious cowardice; moderation was held to be a cloak for unmanliness; ability to see all sides of a question, inaptness to act on any. Frantic violence become the attribute of manliness; cautious plotting, a justifiable means of self-defense. The advocate of extreme measures was always trustworthy; his opponent, a man to be suspected.[1]

Caesar in his account of the Gallic Wars described his brutal conquest as "pacifying" Gaul. Doublespeak has a long history.

Military doublespeak seems always to have been with us. In 1947 the name of the War Department was changed to the more pleasing if misleading *Defense Department.* During the Vietnam War the American public learned that it was an *incursion,* not an invasion; a *protective reaction strike* or a *limited duration protective reaction strike* or *air support,* not bombing; and *incontinent ordinance,* not bombs and artillery shells, fell on civilians. This use of language continued with the invasion of Grenada, which was conducted not by the United States Army, Navy, or Air Force, but by the Caribbean Peace Keeping Forces. Indeed, according to the Pentagon, it was not an invasion of Grenada, but a *predawn, vertical insertion.* And it wasn't that the armed forces lacked intelligence data on Grenada before the invasion, it was just that "we were not micromanaging Grenada intelligencewise until about that time frame." In today's army forces, it's not a shovel but a *combat emplacement evacuator,* not a toothpick but a *wood interdental stimulator,* not a pencil but a portable, handheld communications inscriber, not a bullet hole but a *ballistically induced aperture in the subcutaneous environment.*

Members of the military and politicians are not the only ones who use doublespeak. People in all parts of society use it. Take educators, for example. On some college campuses what was once the Department of Physical Education is now the *Department of Human Kinetics* or the *College of Applied Life Studies.* Home Economics is now the *School of Human Resources and Family Studies.* College campuses no longer have libraries but *learning resource centers.* Those are not desks in the classroom, they are *pupil stations.* Teachers—*classroom managers* who apply an *action plan* to a *knowledge base*—are concerned with the *basic fundamentals,* which are *inexorably linked* to the *education user's* (not student's) *time-on-task.* Students don't take tests; now it is *criterion referencing testing* which measures whether a student has achieved the *operational curricular objectives.* A school system in Pennsylvania uses the following grading system on report cards: "no effort, less than minimal effort, minimal effort, more than minimal effort, less than full effort, full effort, better than full effort, effort increasing, effort decreasing." Some college students in New York come from *economically nonaffluent* families, while the coach at a Southern university wasn't fired, "he just won't be asked to continue in that job." An article in a scholarly journal suggests teaching students three approaches to writing to help them become better writers: "concretization of goals, procedural facilitation, and modeling planning." An article on family relationships entitled "Familial Love and Intertemporal Optimality" observes that "an altruistic utility function promotes intertemporal efficiency. However, altruism creates an externality that implies that satisfying the condition for efficiency, does not insure intertemporal optimality." A research report issued by the U.S. Office of Education contains this sentence: "In other words, feediness is the shared information between toputness, where toputness is at a time just prior to the inputness." Educations contributes more than its share to current doublespeak.

The world of business has produced large amounts of doublespeak. If an airplane crash is one of the worst things that can happen to an airline company, a recall of automobiles because of a safety defect is one of the worst things that can happen to an automobile company. So a few years ago, when one of the three largest car companies in America had to recall two of its models to correct mechanical defects, the company sent a letter to all those who had bought those models. In its letter, the company said that the rear axle bearings of the cars "can deteriorate" and that "continued driving with a failed bearing could result in disengagement of the axle shaft and adversely affect vehicle control." This is the language of nonresponsibility. What are "mechanical deficiencies"—poor design, bad workmanship? If they do, what causes the deterioration? Note that "continued driving" is the subject of the sentence and suggests that it is not the company's poor manufacturing which is at fault but the driver who persists in driving. Note, too, "failed bearing," which implies that the bearing failed, not the company. Finally, "adversely affect vehicle control" means nothing more than that the driver could lose control of the car and get killed.

If we apply Hugh Rank's criteria for examining such language, we quickly discover the doublespeak here. What the car company should be saying to its customers is that the car the company sold them has a serious defect which should be corrected immediately—otherwise the customer runs the risk of being killed. But the reader of the letter must find this message beneath the doublespeak the company has used to disguise the harshness of its message. We will probably never know how many of the customers never brought their cars in for the necessary repairs because they did not think the problem serious enough to warrant the inconvenience involved.

When it come time to fire employees, business has produced more than enough doublespeak to deal with the unpleasant situation. Employees are, of course, never fired. They are *selected out, placed out, non-retained, released, dehired, non-renewed.* A corporation will *eliminate the redundancies in the human resources area,* assign *candidates for derecruitment* to a *mobility pool, revitalize the department* by placing executives on *special assignment, enhance the efficiency of operations, streamline the field sales organization,* or *further rationalize marketing efforts.* The reality behind all this doublespeak is that companies are firing employees, but no one wants the stockholders, public, or competition to know that times are tough and people have to go.

Recently the oil industry has been hard hit by declining sales and a surplus of oil. Because of *reduced demand for product,* which results in *spare refining capacity* and problems in *down-stream operations,* oil companies have been forced to *re-evaluate and consolidate their operations* and take *appropriate cost reduction actions,* in order to *enhance the efficiency of operations,* which has meant the *elimination of marginal outlets, accelerating the divestment program,* and the *disposition of low throughput marketing units.* What this doublespeak really means is that oil companies have fired employees, cut back on expenses, and closed gas stations and oil refineries because there's surplus of oil and people are not buying as much gas and oil as in the past.

One corporation faced with declining business sent a memorandum to its employees advising them that the company's "business plans are under revi-

sion and now reflect a more moderate approach toward our operating and capital programs." The result of this "more moderate approach" is a "surplus of professional/technical employees." To "assist in alleviating the surplus, selected professional and technical employees" have been "selected to participate" in a "Voluntary Program." Note that individuals were selected to "resign voluntarily." What this memorandum means, of course, is that expenses must be cut because of declining business, so employees will have to be fired.

It is rare to read that the stock market *fell.* Members of the financial community prefer to say that the stock market *retreated, eased, made a technical adjustment* or a *technical correction,* or perhaps that *prices were off due to profit taking,* or *off in light trading,* or *lost ground.* But the stock market never falls, not if stockbrokers have their say. As a side note, it is interesting to observe that the stock market never rises because of a *technical adjustment* or *correction,* nor does it ever *ease* upwards.

The business sections of newspapers, business magazines, corporate reports, and executive speeches are filled with words and phrases such as *marginal rates of substitution, equilibrium price, getting off margin, distribution coalition, non-performing assets,* and *encompassing organizations.* Much of this is jargon or inflated language designed to make the simple seem complex, but there are other examples of business doublespeak that mislead, that are designed to avoid a harsh reality. What should we make of such expressions as *negative deficit* or *revenue excesses* for profit, *invest in* for buy, *price enhancement* or *price adjustment* for price increase, *shortfall* for a mistake in planning or *period of accelerated negative growth* or *negative economic growth* for recession?

Business doublespeak often attempts to give substance to wind, to make ordinary actions seem complex. Executives *operate* in *timeframes* within the *context* of which a *task force* will serve as the proper *conduit* for all the necessary *input* to *program a scenario* that,

within acceptable *parameters,* and with the proper *throughput,* will *generate* the *maximum output* for a *print out* of *zero defect terminal objectives* that will *enhance the bottom line.*

There are instances, however, where doublespeak becomes more than amusing, more than a cause for a weary shake of the head. When the anesthetist turned the wrong knob during a Caesarean delivery and killed the mother and unborn child, the hospital called it a *therapeutic misadventure.* The Pentagon calls the neutron bomb "an efficient nuclear weapon that eliminates an enemy with a minimum degree of damage to friendly territory." The Pentagon also calls expected civilian casualties in a nuclear war *collateral damage.* And it was the Central Intelligence Agency which during the Vietnam War created the phrase *eliminate with extreme prejudice* to replace the more direct verb *kill.*

Identifying doublespeak can at times be difficult. For example, on July 27, 1981, President Ronald Reagan said in a speech televised to the American public: "I will not stand by and see those of you who are dependent on Social Security deprived of the benefits you've worked so hard to earn. You will continue to receive your checks in the full amount due you." This speech had been billed as President Reagan's position on Social Security, a subject of much debate at the time. After the speech, public opinion polls revealed that the great majority of the public believed that President Reagan had affirmed his support for Social Security and that he would not support cuts in benefits. However, five days after the speech, on July 31, 1981, an article in the *Philadelphia Inquirer* quoted White House spokesman David Gergen as saying that President Reagan's words had been "carefully chosen." What President Reagan did mean, according to Gergen, was that he was reserving the right to decide who was "dependent" on those benefits, who had "earned" them, and who, therefore, was "due" them.[2]

The subsequent remarks of David Gergen reveal the real intent of President Reagan as opposed to his apparent intent. Thus Hugh Rank's criteria for analyzing language to determine whether it is doublespeak, when applied in light of David Gergen's remarks, reveal the doublespeak of President Reagan. Here indeed is the insincerity of which Orwell wrote. Here, too, is the gap between the speaker's real and declared aim.

In 1982 the Republican National Committee sponsored a television advertisement which pictured an elderly, folksy postman delivering Social Security checks "with the 7.4% cost-of-living raise that President Reagan promised." The postman then added that "he promised that raise and he kept his promise, in spite of those sticks-in-the-mud who tried to keep him from doing what we elected him to do." The commercial was, in fact, deliberately misleading. The cost-of-living increases had been provided automatically by law since 1975, and President Reagan tried three times to roll them back or delay them but was overruled by congressional opposition. When these discrepancies were pointed out to an official of the Republican National Committee, he called the commercial "inoffensive" and added, "Since when is a commercial supposed to be accurate? Do women really smile when they clean their ovens?"

Again, applying Hugh Rank's criteria to this advertisement reveals the doublespeak in it once we know the facts of past actions by President Reagan. Moreover, the official for the Republican National Committee assumes that all advertisements, whether for political candidates or commercial products, are lies, or in his doublespeak term, *inaccurate.* Thus, the real intent of the advertisement was to mislead while the apparent purpose was to inform the public of President Reagan's position on possible cuts in Social Security benefits. Again there is insincerity, and again there is a gap between the speaker's real and declared aims.

In 1981 Secretary of State Alexander Haig testified before congressional committees about the murder of three American nuns and a Catholic lay worker in El Salvador. The four

women had been raped and shot at close range, and there was clear evidence that the crime had been committed by soldiers of the Salvadoran government. Before the House Foreign Affairs Committee, Secretary Haig said,

I'd like to suggest to you that some of the investigations would lead one to believe that perhaps the vehicle the nuns were riding in may have tried to run a roadblock, or may accidentally have been perceived to have been doing so, and there'd been an exchange of fire and then perhaps those who inflicted the casualties sought to cover it up. And this could have been at a very low level of both competence and motivation in the context of the issue itself. But the facts on this are not clear enough for anyone to draw a definitive conclusion.

The next day, before the Senate Foreign Relations Committee, Secretary Haig claimed that press reports on his previous testimony were inaccurate. When Senator Claiborne Pell asked whether Secretary Haig was suggesting the possibility that "the nuns may have run through a roadblock." Secretary Haig replied, "You mean that they tried to violate . . .? Not at all, no, not at all. My heavens! The dear nuns who raised me in my parochial schooling would forever isolate me from their affections and respect." When Senator Pell asked Secretary Haig, "Did you mean that the nuns were firing at the people, or what did 'exchange of fire' mean?" Secretary Haig replied, "I haven't met any pistol-packing nuns in my day, Senator. What I meant was that if one fellow starts shooting, then the next thing you know they all panic." Thus did the secretary of state of the United States explain official government policy on the murder of four American citizens in a foreign land.

Secretary Haig's testimony implies that the women were in some way responsible for their own fate. By using such vague wording as "would lead one to believe" and "may accidentally have been perceived to have been," he avoids any direct assertion. The use of "inflicted the casualties" not only avoids using the word *kill* but also implies that at the worst the kill-

ings were accidental or justifiable. The result of this testimony is that the secretary of state has become an apologist for murder. This is indeed language in defense of the indefensible; language designed to make lies sound truthful and murder respectable; language designed to give an appearance of solidity to pure wind.

These last three examples of doublespeak should make it clear that doublespeak is not the product of careless language or sloppy thinking. Indeed, most doublespeak is the product of clear thinking and is language carefully designed and constructed to appear to communicate when in fact it does not. It is language designed not to lead but to mislead. It is language designed to distort reality and corrupt the mind. It is not a tax increase but *revenue enhancement* or *tax base broadening,* so how can you complain about higher taxes? It is not acid rain, but *poorly buffered precipitation,* so don't worry about all those dead trees. That is not the Mafia in Atlantic City, New Jersey, those are *members of a career offender cartel,* so don't worry about the influence of organized crime in the city. The judge was not addicted to the painkilling drug he was taking, it was just that the drug had "established an interrelationship with the body, such that if the drug is removed precipitously, there is a reaction," so don't worry that his decisions might have been influenced by his drug addiction. It's not a Titan II nuclear-armed, intercontinental ballistic missile with a warhead 630 times more powerful than the atomic bomb dropped on Hiroshima, it is just a *very large, potentially disruptive re-entry system,* so don't worry about the threat of nuclear destruction. It is not a neutron bomb but a *radiation enhancement device,* so don't worry about escalating the arms race. It is not an invasion but a *rescue mission,* or a *predawn vertical insertion,* so don't worry about any violations of United States or international law.

Doublespeak has become so common in our everyday lives that we fail to notice it. We do not protest when we are asked to check our packages at the desk "for our convenience" when it is not for our convenience at all but for someone else's convenience. We see advertisements for *genuine imitation leather, virgin vinyl,* or *real counterfeit diamonds* and do not question the language or the supposed quality of the product. We do not speak of slums or ghettos but of the *inner city* or *substandard housing where the disadvantaged* live and thus avoid talking about the poor who have to live in filthy, poorly heated, ramshackle apartments or houses. Patients do not die in the hospital; it is just *negative patient care outcome.*

Doublespeak which calls cab drivers *urban transportation specialists,* elevator operators *members of the vertical transportation corps,* and automobile mechanics *automotive internists* can be considered humorous and relatively harmless. However, doublespeak which calls a fire in a nuclear reactor building *rapid oxidation,* an explosion in a nuclear power plant an *energetic disassembly,* the illegal overthrow of a legitimate administration *destablizing a government,* and lies *inoperative statements* is language which attempts to avoid responsibility, which attempts to make the bad seem good, the negative appear positive, something unpleasant appear attractive, and which seems to communicate but does not. It is language designed to alter our perception of reality and corrupt our minds. Such language does not provide us with the tools needed to develop and preserve civilization. Such language breeds suspicion, cynicism, distrust, and, ultimately, hostility.

Doublespeak is insidious because it can infect and ultimately destroy the function of language, which is communication between people and social groups. If this corrupting process does occur, it can have serious conse-

quences in a country that depends upon an informed electorate to make decisions in selecting candidates for office and deciding issues of public policy. After a while we may really believe that politicians don't lie but only *misspeak,* that illegal acts are merely *inappropriate actions,* that fraud and criminal conspiracy are just *miscertification.* And if we really believe that we understand such language, then the world of *Nineteen Eighty-four* with its control of reality through language is not far away.

The consistent use of doublespeak can have serious and far-reaching consequences beyond the obvious ones. The pervasive use of doublespeak can spread so that doublespeak becomes the coin of the political realm with speakers and listeners convinced that they really understand such language. President Jimmy Carter could call the aborted raid to free the hostages in Tehran in 1980 an "incomplete success" and really believe that he had made a statement that clearly communicated with the American public. So, too, President Ronald Reagan could say in 1985 that "ultimately our security and our hopes for success at the arms reduction talks hinge on the determination that we show here to continue our program to rebuild and refortify our defenses" and really believe that greatly increasing the amount of money spent building new weapons will lead to a reduction in the number of weapons in the world.

The task of English teachers is to teach not just the effective use of language but respect for language as well. Those who use language to conceal or prevent or corrupt thought must be called to account. Only by teaching respect for and love of language can teachers of English instill in students

the sense of outrage they should experience when they encounter doublespeak. But before students can experience that outrage, they must first learn to use language effectively, to understand its beauty and power. Only then will we begin to make headway in the fight against doublespeak, for only by using language well will we come to appreciate the perversion inherent in doublespeak.

In his book *The Miracle of Language,* Charlton Laird notes that

language is . . . the most important tool man ever devised. . . . Language is [man's] basic tool. It is the tool more than any other with which he makes his living, makes his home, makes his life. As man becomes more and more a social being, as the world becomes more and more a social community, communication grows ever more imperative. And language is the basis of communication. Language is also the instrument with which we think, and thinking is the rarest and most needed commodity in the world.[3]

In this opinion Laird echoes Orwell's comment that "if thought corrupts language, language can also corrupt thought."[4] Both men have given us a legacy of respect for language, a respect that should prompt us to cry "Enough!" when we encounter doublespeak. The greatest honor we can do Charlton Laird is to continue to have the greatest respect of language in all its manifestations, for, as Laird taught us, language is a miracle.

NOTES AND REFERENCES

1. Thucydides, *The Peloponnesian Way,* 3.82.
2. David Hess, "Reagan's Language on Benefits Confused, Angered Many," *Philadelphia Inquirer,* July 31, 1981, p. 6-A.
3. Charlton Laird, *The Miracle of Language* (New York: Fawcett, Premier Books, 1953), p. 224.
4. Orwell, *The Collected Essays,* 4:137.

Shakespeare in the Bush

Laura Bohannan

Laura Bohannan is a professor of anthropology at the University of Illinois, at Chicago.

Just before I left Oxford for the Tiv in West Africa, conversation turned to the season at Stratford. "You Americans," said a friend, "often have difficulty with Shakespeare. He was, after all, a very English poet, and one can easily misinterpret the universal by misunderstanding the particular."

I protested that human nature is pretty much the same the whole world over; at least the general plot and motivation of the greater tragedies would always be clear—everywhere—although some details of custom might have to be explained and difficulties of translation might produce other slight changes. To end an argument we could not conclude, my friend gave me a copy of *Hamlet* to study in the African bush: it would, he hoped, lift my mind above its primitive surroundings, and possibly I might, by prolonged meditation, achieve the grace of correct interpretation.

It was my second field trip to that African tribe, and I thought myself ready to live in one of its remote sections—an area difficult to cross even on foot. I eventually settled on the hillock of a very knowledgeable old man, the head of a homestead of some hundred and forty people, all of whom were either his close relatives or their wives and children. Like the other elders of the vicinity, the old man spent most of his time performing 'ceremonies seldom seen these days in the more accessible parts of the tribe. I was delighted. Soon there would be three months of enforced isolation and leisure, between the harvest that takes place just before the rising of the swamps and the clearing of new farms when the water goes down. Then, I thought, they would have even more time to perform ceremonies and explain them to me.

I was quite mistaken. Most of the ceremonies demanded the presence of elders from several homesteads. As the swamps rose, the old men found it too difficult to walk from one homestead to the next, and the ceremonies gradually ceased. As the swamps rose even higher, all activities but one came to an end. The women brewed beer from maize and millet. Men, women, and children sat on their hillocks and drank it.

People began to drink at dawn. By midmorning the whole homestead was singing, dancing, and drumming. When it rained, people had to sit inside their huts: there they drank and sang or they drank and told stories. In any case, by noon or before, I either had to join the party or retire to my own hut and my books. "One does not discuss serious matters when there is beer. Come, drink with us." Since I lacked their capacity for the thick native beer, I spent more and more time with *Hamlet*. Before the end of the second month, grace descended on me. I was quite sure that *Hamlet* had only one possible interpretation, and that one universally obvious.

Early every morning, in the hope of having some serious talk before the beer party, I used to call on the old man at his reception hut—a circle of posts supporting a thatched roof above a low mud wall to keep out wind and rain. One day I crawled through the low doorway and found most of the men of the homestead sitting huddled in their ragged cloths on stools, low plank beds, and reclining chairs, warming themselves against the chill of the rain around a smoky fire. In the center were three pots of beer. The party had started.

The old man greeted me cordially. "Sit down and drink." I accepted a large calabash full of beer, poured some into a small drinking gourd, and tossed it down. Then I poured some more into the same gourd for the man second in seniority to my host before I handed my calabash over to a young man for further distribution. Important people shouldn't ladle beer themselves.

Reprinted from *Natural History*, August/September 1966 by permission of the author.

2. CULTURE AND COMMUNICATION

"It is better like this," the old man said, looking at me approvingly and plucking at the thatch that had caught in my hair. "You should sit and drink with us more often. Your servants tell me that when you are not with us, you sit inside your hut looking at a paper."

The old man was acquainted with four kinds of "papers": tax receipts, bride price receipts, court fee receipts, and letters. The messenger who brought him letters from the chief used them mainly as a badge of office, for he always knew what was in them and told the old man. Personal letters for the few who had relatives in the government or mission stations were kept until someone went to a large market where there was a letter writer and reader. Since my arrival, letters were brought to me to be read. A few men also brought me bride price receipts, privately, with requests to change the figures to a higher sum. I found moral arguments were of no avail, since in-laws are fair game, and the technical hazards of forgery difficult to explain to an illiterate people. I did not wish them to think me silly enough to look at any such papers for days on end, and I hastily explained that my "paper" was one of the "things of long ago" of my country.

"Ah," said the old man. "Tell us."

I protested that I was not a story-teller. Story telling is a skilled art among them; their standards are high, and the audiences critical—and vocal in their criticism. I protested in vain. This morning they wanted to hear a story while they drank. They threatened to tell me no more stories until I told them one of mine. Finally, the old man promised that no one would criticize my style "for we know you are struggling with our language." "But," put in one of the elders, "you must explain what we do not understand, as we do when we tell you our stories." Realizing that here was my chance to prove *Hamlet* universally intelligible, I agreed.

The old man handed me some more beer to help me on with my story-telling. Men filled their long wooden pipes and knocked coals from the fire to place in the pipe bowls; then, puffing contentedly, they sat back to listen. I began in the proper style, "Not yesterday, not yesterday, but long ago, a thing occurred. One night three men were keeping watch outside the homestead of the great chief, when suddenly they saw the former chief approach them."

"Why was he no longer their chief?"

"He was dead," I explained. "That is why they were troubled and afraid when they saw him."

"Impossible," began one of the elders, handing his pipe on to his neighbor, who interrupted, "Of course it wasn't the dead chief. It was an omen sent by a witch. Go on."

Slightly shaken, I continued. "One of these three was a man who knew things"—the closest translation for scholar, but unfortunately it also meant witch. The second elder looked triumphantly at the first. "So he spoke to the dead chief saying, 'Tell us what we must do so you may rest in your grave,' but the dead chief did not answer. He vanished, and they could see him no more. Then the man who knew things—his name was Horatio—said this event was the affair of the dead chief's son, Hamlet."

There was a general shaking of heads round the circle. "Had the dead chief no living brothers? Or was this son the chief?"

"No," I replied. "That is, he had one living brother who became the chief when the elder brother died."

The old men muttered: such omens were matters for chiefs and elders, not for youngsters; no good could come of going behind a chief's back; clearly Horatio was not a man who knew things.

"Yes, he was," I insisted, shooing a chicken away from my beer. "In our country the son is next to the father. The dead chief's younger brother had become the great chief. He had also married his elder brother's widow only about a month after the funeral."

"He did well," the old man beamed and announced to the others, "I told you that if we knew more about Europeans, we would find they really were very like us. In our country also," he added to me, "the younger brother marries the elder brother's widow and becomes the father of his children. Now, if your uncle, who married your widowed mother, is your father's full brother, then he will be a real father to you. Did Hamlet's father and uncle have one mother?"

His question barely penetrated my mind; I was too upset and thrown too far off balance by having one of the most important elements of *Hamlet* knocked straight out of the picture. Rather uncertainly I said that I thought they had the same mother, but I wasn't sure—the story didn't say. The old man told me severely that these genealogical details made all the difference and that when I got home I must ask the elders about it. He shouted out the door to one of his younger wives to bring his goatskin bag.

Determined to save what I could of the mother motif, I took a deep breath and began again. "The son Hamlet was very sad because his mother had married again so quickly. There was no need for her to do so, and it is our custom for a widow not to go to her next husband until she has mourned for two years."

"Two years is too long," objected the wife, who had appeared with the old man's battered goatskin bag. "Who will hoe your farms for you while you have no husband?"

"Hamlet," I retorted without thinking, "was old enough to hoe his mother's farms himself. There was no need for her to remarry." No one looked convinced. I gave up. "His mother and the great chief told Hamlet not to be sad, for the great chief himself would be a father to Hamlet. Furthermore, Hamlet would be the next chief: therefore he must stay to learn the things of a chief. Hamlet agreed to remain, and all the rest went off to drink beer."

While I paused, perplexed at how to render Hamlet's disgusted soliloquy to an audience convinced that Claudius and Gertrude had behaved in the best possible manner, one of the younger men asked me who had married the other wives of the dead chief.

"He had no other wives," I told him.

"But a chief must have many wives! How else can he brew beer and prepare food for all his guests?"

I said firmly that in our country even chiefs had only one wife, that they had servants to do their work, and that they paid them from tax money.

It was better, they returned, for a chief to have many wives and sons who would help him hoe his farms and feed his people; then everyone loved the chief who gave much and took nothing—taxes were a bad thing.

I agreed with the last comment, but for the rest fell back on their favorite way of fobbing off my questions: "That is the way it is done, so that is how we do it."

I decided to skip the soliloquy. Even if Claudius was here thought quite right to marry his brother's widow, there remained the poison motif, and I knew they would disapprove of fratricide. More hopefully I resumed, "That night Hamlet kept watch with the three who had seen his dead father. The dead chief again appeared, and although the others were afraid, Hamlet followed his dead father off to one side. When they were alone, Hamlet's dead father spoke."

"Omens can't talk!" The old man was emphatic.

"Hamlet's dead father wasn't an omen. Seeing him might have been an omen, but he was not." My audience looked as confused as I sounded. "It *was* Hamlet's dead father. It was a thing we call a 'ghost.' " I had to use the English word, for unlike many of the neighboring tribes, these people didn't believe in the survival after death of any individuating part of the personality.

"What is a 'ghost?' An omen?"

"No, a 'ghost' is someone who is dead but who walks around and can talk, and people can hear him and see him but not touch him."

They objected. "One can touch zombis."

"No, no! It was not a dead body the witches had animated to sacrifice and eat. No one else made Hamlet's dead father walk. He did it himself."

"Dead men can't walk," protested my audience as one man.

I was quite willing to compromise. "A 'ghost' is the dead man's shadow."

But again they objected. "Dead men cast no shadows."

"They do in my country," I snapped.

The old man quelled the babble of disbelief that arose immediately and told me with that insincere, but courteous, agreement one extends to the fancies of the young, ignorant, and superstitious, "No doubt in your country the dead can also walk without being zombis." From the depths of his bag he produced a withered fragment of kola nut, bit off one end to show it wasn't poisoned, and handed me the rest as a peace offering.

"Anyhow," I resumed, "Hamlet's dead father said that his own brother, the one who became chief, had poisoned him. He wanted Hamlet to avenge him. Hamlet believed this in his heart, for he did not like his father's brother." I took another swallow of beer. "In the country of the great chief, living in the same homestead, for it was a very large one, was an important elder who was often with the chief to advise and help him. His name was Polonius. Hamlet was courting his daughter, but her father and her brother . . .[I cast hastily about for some tribal analogy] warned her not to let Hamlet visit her when she was alone on her farm, for he would be a great chief and so could not marry her."

"Why not?" asked the wife, who had settled down on the edge of the old man's chair. He frowned at her for asking stupid questions and growled, "They lived in the same homestead."

"That was not the reason," I informed them. "Polonius was a stranger who lived in the homestead because he helped the chief, not because he was a relative."

"Then why couldn't Hamlet marry her?"

"He could have," I explained, "but Polonius didn't think he would. After all, Hamlet was a man of great importance who ought to marry a chief's daughter, for in his country a man could have only one wife. Polonius was afraid that if Hamlet made love to his daughter, then no one else would give a high price for her."

"That might be true," remarked one of the shrewder elders, "but a chief's son would give his mistress's father enough presents and patronage to more than make up the difference. Polonius sounds like a fool to me."

"Many people think he was," I agreed. "Meanwhile Polonius sent his son Laertes off to Paris to learn the things of that country, for it was the homestead of a very great chief indeed. Because he was afraid that Laertes might waste a lot of money on beer and women and gambling, or get into trouble by fighting, he sent one of his servants to Paris secretly, to spy out what Laertes was doing. One day Hamlet came upon Polonius's daughter Ophelia. He behaved so oddly he frightened her. Indeed"—I was fumbling for words to express the dubious quality of Hamlet's madness—"the chief and many others had also noticed that when Hamlet talked one could understand the words but not what they meant. Many people thought that he had become mad." My audience suddenly became much more attentive. "The great chief wanted to know what was wrong with Hamlet, so he sent for two of Hamlet's age mates [school friends would have taken long explanation] to talk to Hamlet and find out what troubled his heart. Hamlet, seeing that they had been bribed by the chief to betray him, told them nothing. Polonius, however, insisted that Hamlet was mad because he had been forbidden to see Ophelia, whom he loved."

"Why," inquired a bewildered voice, "should anyone bewitch Hamlet on that account?"

"Bewitch him?"

"Yes, only witchcraft can make anyone mad, unless, of course, one sees the beings that lurk in the forest."

2. CULTURE AND COMMUNICATION

I stopped being a storyteller, took out my notebook and demanded to be told more about these two causes of madness. Even while they spoke and I jotted notes, I tried to calculate the effect of this new factor on the plot. Hamlet had not been exposed to the beings that lurk in the forests. Only his relatives in the male line could bewitch him. Barring relatives not mentioned by Shakespeare, it had to be Claudius who was attempting to harm him. And, of course, it was.

For the moment I staved off questions by saying that the great chief also refused to believe that Hamlet was mad for the love of Ophelia and nothing else. "He was sure that something much more important was troubling Hamlet's heart."

"Now Hamlet's age mates," I continued, "had brought with them a famous storyteller. Hamlet decided to have this man tell the chief and all his homestead a story about a man who had poisoned his brother because he desired his brother's wife and wished to be chief himself. Hamlet was sure the great chief could not hear the story without making a sign if he was indeed guilty, and then he would discover whether his dead father had told him the truth."

The old man interrupted, with deep cunning, "Why should a father lie to his son?" he asked.

I hedged: "Hamlet wasn't sure that it really was his dead father." It was impossible to say anything, in that language, about devil-inspired visions.

"You mean," he said, "it actually was an omen, and he knew witches sometimes send false ones. Hamlet was a fool not to go to one skilled in reading omens and divining the truth in the first place. A man-who-sees-the-truth could have told him how his father died, if he really had been poisoned, and if there was witchcraft in it; then Hamlet could have called the elders to settle the matter."

The shrewd elder ventured to disagree. "Because his father's brother was a great chief, one-who-sees-the-truth might therefore have been afraid to tell it. I think it was for that reason that a friend of Hamlet's father—a witch and an elder—sent an omen so his friend's son would know. Was the omen true?"

"Yes," I said, abandoning ghosts and the devil; a witch-sent omen it would have to be. "It was true, for when the storyteller was telling his tale before all the homestead, the great chief rose in fear. Afraid that Hamlet knew his secret he planned to have him killed."

The stage set of the next bit presented some difficulties of translation. I began cautiously. "The great chief told Hamlet's mother to find out from her son what he knew. But because a woman's children are always first in her heart, he had the important elder Polonius hide behind a cloth that hung against the wall of Hamlet's mother's sleeping hut. Hamlet started to scold his mother for what she had done."

There was a shocked murmur from everyone. A man should never scold his mother.

"She called out in fear, and Polonius moved behind the cloth. Shouting, 'A rat!' Hamlet took his machete and slashed through the cloth." I paused for dramatic effect. "He had killed Polonius!"

The old men looked at each other in supreme disgust. "That Polonius truly was a fool and a man who knew nothing! What child would not know enough to shout, 'It's me!' " With a pang, I remembered that these people are ardent hunters, always armed with bow, arrow, and machete; at the first rustle in the grass an arrow is aimed and ready, and the hunter shouts "Game!" If no human voice answers immediately, the arrow speeds on its way. Like a good hunter Hamlet had shouted, "A rat!"

I rushed in to save Polonius's reputation. "Polonius did speak. Hamlet heard him. But he thought it was the chief and wished to kill him earlier that evening. . . ." I broke down, unable to describe to these pagans, who had no belief in individual after-life, the difference between dying at one's prayers and dying "unhousel'd, disappointed, unaneled."

This time I had shocked my audience seriously. "For a man to raise his hand against his father's brother and and the one who has become his father—that is a terrible thing. The elders ought to let such a man be bewitched."

I nibbled at my kola nut in some perplexity, then pointed out that after all the man had killed Hamlet's father.

"No," pronounced the old man, speaking less to me than to the young men sitting behind the elders. "If your father's brother has killed your father, you must appeal to your father's age mates; *they* may avenge him. No man may use violence against his senior relatives." Another thought struck him. "But if his father's brother had indeed been wicked enough to bewitch Hamlet and make him mad that would be a good story indeed, for it would be his fault that Hamlet, being mad, no longer had any sense and thus was ready to kill his father's brother."

There was a murmur of applause. *Hamlet* was again a good story to them, but it no longer seemed quite the same story to me. As I thought over the coming complications of plot and motive, I lost courage and decided to skim over dangerous ground quickly.

"The great chief," I went on, "was not sorry that Hamlet had killed Polonius. It gave him a reason to send Hamlet away, with his two treacherous mates, with letters to a chief of a far country, saying that Hamlet should be killed. But Hamlet changed the writing on their papers, so that the chief killed his age mates instead." I encountered a reproachful glare from one of the men whom I had told undetectable forgery was not merely immoral but beyond human skill. I looked the other way.

"Before Hamlet could return, Laertes came back for his father's funeral. The great chief told him Hamlet had killed Polonius. Laertes swore to kill Hamlet because of this, and because his sister Ophelia, hearing her father had been killed by the man she loved, went mad and drowned in the river."

"Have you already forgotten what we told you?" The old man was reproachful. "One cannot take vengeance on a madman; Hamlet killed Polonius in his madness. As for the girl, she not only went mad, she was drowned. Only witches can make people drown. Water itself can't hurt anything. It is merely something one drinks and bathes in."

I began to get cross. "If you don't like the story, I'll stop."

The old man made soothing noises and himself poured me some more beer. "You tell the story well, and we are listening. But it is clear that the elders of your country have never told you what the story really means. No, don't interrupt! We believe you when you say your marriage customs are different, or your clothes and weapons. But people are the same everywhere; therefore, there are always witches and it is we, the elders, who know how witches work. We told you it was the great chief who wished to kill Hamlet, and now your own words have proved us right. Who were Ophelia's male relatives?"

"There were only her father and her brother." *Hamlet* was clearly out of my hands.

There must have been many more; this also you must ask of your elders when you get back to your country. From what you tell us, since Polonius was dead, it must have been Laertes who killed Ophelia, although I do not see the reason for it."

We had emptied one pot of beer, and the old men argued the point with slightly tipsy interest. Finally one of them demanded of me, "What did the servant of Polonius say on his return?"

With difficulty I recollected Reynaldo and his mission. "I don't think he did return before Polonius was killed."

"Listen," said the elder, "and I will tell you how it was and how your story will go, then you may tell me if I am right. Polonius knew his son would get into trouble, and so he did. He had many fines to pay for fighting, and debts from gambling. But he had only two ways of getting money quickly. One was to marry off his sister at once, but it is difficult to find a man who will marry a woman desired by the son of a chief. For if the chief's heir commits adultery with your wife, what can you do? Only a fool calls a case against a man who will someday be his judge. Therefore Laertes had to take the second way: he killed his sister by witchcraft, drowning her so he could secretly sell her body to the witches."

I raised an objection. "They found her body and buried it. Indeed Laertes jumped into the grave to see his sister once more—so, you see, the body was truly there. Hamlet, who had just come back, jumped in after him."

"What did I tell you?" The elder appealed to the others. "Laertes was up to no good with his sister's body. Hamlet prevented him, because the chief's heir, like a chief, does not wish any other man to grow rich and powerful. Laertes would be angry, because he would have killed his sister without benefit to himself. In our country he would try to kill Hamlet for that reason. Is this not what happened?"

"More or less," I admitted. "When the great chief found Hamlet was still alive, he encouraged Laertes to try to kill Hamlet and arranged a fight with machetes between them. In the fight both the young men were wounded to death. Hamlet's mother drank the poisoned beer that the chief meant for Hamlet in case he won the fight. When he saw his mother die of poison, Hamlet, dying, managed to kill his father's brother with his machete."

"You see, I was right!" exclaimed the elder.

"That was a very good story," added the old man, "and you told it with very few mistakes. There was just one more error, at the very end. The poison Hamlet's mother drank was obviously meant for the survivor of the fight, whichever it was. If Laertes had won, the great chief would have poisoned him, for no one would know that he arranged Hamlet's death. Then, too, he need not fear Laertes' witchcraft; it takes a strong heart to kill one's only sister by witchcraft."

"Sometime," concluded the old man, gathering his ragged toga about him, "you must tell us some more stories of your country. We, who are elders, will instruct you in their true meaning, so that when you return to your own land your elders will see that you have not been sitting in the bush, but among those who know things and who have taught you wisdom."

Social Time: The Heartbeat of Culture

*TO UNDERSTAND A SOCIETY,
YOU MUST LEARN ITS SENSE OF TIME.*

Robert Levine
with Ellen Wolff

Robert Levine is a professor of psychology at California State University at Fresno. Ellen Wolff is a freelance writer in Los Angeles.

"If a man does not keep pace with his companions, perhaps it is because he hears a different drummer." This thought by Thoreau strikes a chord in so many people that it has become part of our language. We use the phrase "the beat of a different drummer" to explain any pace of life unlike our own. Such colorful vagueness reveals how informal our rules of time really are. The world over, children simply "pick up" their society's time concepts as they mature. No dictionary clearly defines the meaning of "early" or "late" for them or for strangers who stumble over the maddening incongruities between the time sense they bring with them and the one they face in a new land.

I learned this firsthand, a few years ago, and the resulting culture shock led me halfway around the world to find answers. It seemed clear that time "talks." But what is it telling us?

My journey started shortly after I accepted an appointment as visiting professor of psychology at the federal university in Niteroi, Brazil, a midsized city across the bay from Rio de Janeiro. As I left home for my first day of class, I asked someone the time. It was 9:05 a.m., which allowed me time to relax and look around the campus before my 10 o'clock lecture. After what I judged to be half an hour, I glanced at a clock I was passing. It said 10:20! In panic, I broke for the classroom, followed by gentle calls of "Hola, professor" and "Tudo bem, professor?" from unhurried students, many of whom, I later realized, were my own. I arrived breathless to find an empty room.

Frantically, I asked a passerby the time. "Nine forty-five" was the answer. No, that couldn't be. I asked someone else. "Nine fifty-five." Another said: "Exactly 9:43." The clock in a nearby office read 3:15. I had learned my first lesson about Brazilians: Their timepieces are consistently inaccurate. And nobody minds.

My class was scheduled from 10 until noon. Many students came late, some very late. Several arrived after 10:30. A few showed up closer to 11. Two came after that. All of the latecomers wore the relaxed smiles that I came, later, to enjoy. Each one said hello, and although a few apologized briefly, none seemed terribly concerned about lateness. They assumed that I understood.

The idea of Brazilians arriving late was not a great shock. I had heard about "mãnha," the Portuguese equivalent of "mañana" in Spanish. This term, meaning "tomorrow" or "the morning," stereotypes the Brazilian who puts off the business of today until tomorrow. The real surprise came at noon that first day, when the end of class arrived.

Back home in California, I never need to look at a clock to know when the class hour is ending. The shuffling of books is accompanied by strained expressions that say plaintively, "I'm starving. . . . I've got to go to the bathroom. . . . I'm going to suffocate if you keep us one more second." (The pain usually becomes unbearable at two minutes to the hour in undergraduate classes and five minutes before the close of graduate classes.)

When noon arrived in my first Brazilian class, only a few students left immediately. Others slowly drifted out during the next 15 minutes, and some continued asking me questions long after that. When several remaining students kicked off their shoes at 12:30, I went into my own "starving/bathroom/suffocation" routine.

I could not, in all honesty, attribute

BRAZILIANS SAID THEY WOULD WAIT 33 MINUTES BEFORE CONSIDERING SOMEONE LATE. NORTH AMERICANS DREW THE LINE AT 19 MINUTES.

---

their lingering to my superb teaching style. I had just spent two hours lecturing on statistics in halting Portuguese. Apparently, for many of my students, staying late was simply of no more importance than arriving late in the first place. As I observed this casual approach in infinite variations during the year, I learned that the "mānha" stereotype oversimplified the real Anglo/Brazilian differences in conceptions of time. Research revealed a more complex picture.

With the assistance of colleagues Laurie West and Harry Reis, I compared the time sense of 91 male and female students in Niteroi with that of 107 similar students at California State University in Fresno. The universities are similar in academic quality and size, and the cities are both secondary metropolitan centers with populations of about 350,000.

We asked students about their perceptions of time in several situations, such as what they would consider late or early for a hypothetical lunch appointment with a friend. The average Brazilian student defined lateness for lunch as 33½ minutes after the scheduled time, compared to only 19 min-

utes for the Fresno students. But Brazilians also allowed an average of about 54 minutes before they'd consider someone early, while the Fresno students drew the line at 24.

Are Brazilians simply more flexible in their concepts of time and punctuality? And how does this relate to the stereotype of the apathetic, fatalistic and irresponsible Latin temperament? When we asked students to give typical reasons for lateness, the Brazilians were less likely to attribute it to a lack of caring than the North Americans were. Instead, they pointed to unforeseen circumstances that the person couldn't control. Because they seemed less inclined to feel personally responsible for being late, they also expressed less regret for their own lateness and blamed others less when they were late.

We found similar differences in how students from the two countries characterized people who were late for appointments. Unlike their North American counterparts, the Brazilian students believed that a person who is consistently late is probably more successful than one who is consistently on time. They seemed to accept the idea that someone of status is expected to arrive late. Lack of punctuality is a badge of success.

Even within our own country, of course, ideas of time and punctuality vary considerably from place to place. Different regions and even cities have their own distinct rhythms and rules. Seemingly simple words like "now," snapped out by an impatient New Yorker, and "later," said by a relaxed Californian, suggest a world of difference. Despite our familiarity with these homegrown differences in tempo, problems with time present a major stumbling block to Americans abroad. Peace Corps volunteers told researchers James Spradley of Macalester College and Mark Phillips of the University of Washington that their greatest difficulties with other people, after language problems, were the general pace of life and the punctuality of others. Formal "clock time" may be a standard on which the world agrees, but "social time," the heartbeat of society, is something else again.

How a country paces its social life is a mystery to most outsiders, one that we're just beginning to unravel. Twenty-six years ago, anthropologist Ed-

ward Hall noted in *The Silent Language* that informal patterns of time "are seldom, if ever, made explicit. They exist in the air around us. They are either familiar and comfortable, or unfamiliar and wrong." When we realize we are out of step, we often blame the people around us to make ourselves feel better.

Appreciating cultural differences in time sense becomes increasingly important as modern communications put more and more people in daily contact. If we are to avoid misreading issues that involve time perceptions, we need to understand better our own cultural biases and those of others.

When people of different cultures interact, the potential for misunderstanding exists on many levels. For example, members of Arab and Latin cultures usually stand much closer when they are speaking to people than we usually do in the United States, a fact we frequently misinterpret as aggression or disrespect. Similarly, we assign personality traits to groups with a pace of life that is markedly faster or slower than our own. We build ideas of national character, for example, around the traditional Swiss

---

WESTERNERS LIKE OURSELVES DEFINE PUNCTUALITY USING PRECISE MEASURES OF TIME: 5 MINUTES, 15 MINUTES, AN HOUR.

---

and German ability to "make the trains run on time." Westerners like ourselves define punctuality using precise measures of time: 5 minutes, 15 minutes, an hour. But according to Hall, in many Mediterranean Arab cultures there are only three sets of time: no time at all, now (which is of varying duration) and forever (too long). Because of this, Americans often find difficulty in getting Arabs to distinguish between waiting a long time and a very long time.

According to historian Will Durant,

*E*ACH LANGUAGE *HAS ITS OWN VOCABULARY OF TIME, ONE THAT DOES NOT ALWAYS SURVIVE LITERAL TRANSLATION.*

"No man in a hurry is quite civilized." What do our time judgments say about our attitude toward life? How can a North American, coming from a land of digital precision, relate to a North African who may consider a clock "the devil's mill"?

Each language has a vocabulary of time that does not always survive translation. When we translated our questionnaires into Portuguese for my Brazilian students, we found that English distinctions of time were not readily articulated in their language. Several of our questions concerned how long the respondent would wait for someone to arrive, as compared with when they hoped for arrival or actually expected the person would come. In Portuguese, the verbs "to wait for," "to hope for" and "to expect" are all translated as "esperar." We had to add further words of expla-

nation to make the distinction clear to the Brazilian students.

To avoid these language problems, my Fresno colleague Kathy Bartlett and I decided to clock the pace of life in other countries by using as little language as possible. We looked directly at three basic indicators of time: the accuracy of a country's bank clocks, the speed at which pedestrians walked and the average time it took a postal clerk to sell us a single stamp. In six countries on three continents, we made observations in both the nation's largest urban area and a medium-sized city: Japan (Tokyo and Sendai), Taiwan (Taipei and Tainan), Indonesia (Jakarta and Solo), Italy (Rome and Florence), England (London and Bristol) and the United States (New York City and Rochester).

What we wanted to know was: Can we speak of a unitary concept called "pace of life"? What we've learned suggests that we can. There appears to be a very strong relationship between the accuracy of clock time, walking speed and postal efficiency across the countries we studied.

We checked 15 clocks in each city, selecting them at random in downtown banks and comparing the time they showed with that reported by the local telephone company. In Japan, which leads the way in accuracy, the clocks averaged just over half a minute early or late. Indonesian clocks, the least accurate, were more than three minutes off the mark.

*L*OOKING *CAREFULLY AT DIFFERENT PACES OF LIFE MAY HELP US DISTINGUISH MORE ACCURATELY BETWEEN SPEED AND PROGRESS.*

I will be interested to see how the digital-information age will affect our perceptions of time. In the United States today, we are reminded of the exact hour of the day more than ever, through little symphonies of beeps emanating from people's digital watches. As they become the norm, I fear our sense of precision may take an absurd twist. The other day, when I asked for the time, a student looked at his watch and replied, "Three twelve and eighteen seconds."

" 'Will you walk a little faster?' said a whiting to a snail. 'There's a porpoise close behind us, and he's treading on my tail.' "

So goes the rhyme from *Alice in Wonderland*, which also gave us that famous symbol of haste, the White Rabbit. He came to mind often as we measured the walking speeds in our experimental cities. We clocked how long it took pedestrians to walk 100 feet along a main downtown street during business hours on clear days. To eliminate the effects of socializing, we observed only people walking alone, timing at least 100 in each city. We found, once again, that the Japanese led the way, averaging just 20.7 seconds to cover the distance. The English nosed out the Americans for second place—21.6 to 22.5 seconds—and the Indonesians again trailed the pack, sauntering along at 27.2 seconds. As you might guess, speed was greater in the larger city of each nation than in its smaller one.

Our final measurement, the average time it took postal clerks to sell one stamp, turned out to be less straightforward than we expected. In each city, including those in the United States, we presented clerks with a note in the native language requesting

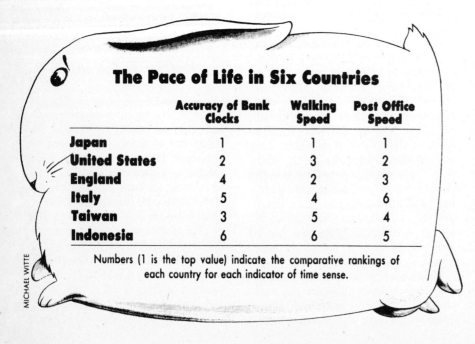

The Pace of Life in Six Countries

	Accuracy of Bank Clocks	Walking Speed	Post Office Speed
Japan	1	1	1
United States	2	3	2
England	4	2	3
Italy	5	4	6
Taiwan	3	5	4
Indonesia	6	6	5

Numbers (1 is the top value) indicate the comparative rankings of each country for each indicator of time sense.

MICHAEL WITTE

a common-priced stamp—a 20-center in the United States, for example. They were also handed paper money, the equivalent of a $5 bill. In Indonesia, this procedure led to more than we bargained for.

At the large central post office in Jakarta, I asked for the line to buy stamps and was directed to a group of private vendors sitting outside. Each of them hustled for my business: "Hey, good stamps, mister!" "Best stamps here!" In the smaller city of Solo, I found a volleyball game in progress when I arrived at the main post office on Friday afternoon. Business hours, I was told, were over. When I finally did get there during business hours, the clerk was more interested in discussing relatives in America. Would I like to meet his uncle in Cincinnati? Which did I like bet-

ter: California or the United States? Five people behind me in line waited patiently. Instead of complaining, they began paying attention to our conversation.

When it came to efficiency of service, however, the Indonesians were not the slowest, although they did place far behind the Japanese postal clerks, who averaged 25 seconds. That distinction went to the Italians, whose infamous postal service took 47 seconds on the average.

"A man who wastes one hour of time has not discovered the meaning of life. . . ."

That was Charles Darwin's belief, and many share it, perhaps at the cost of their health. My colleagues and I have recently begun studying the relationship between pace of life and well-being. Other researchers have demonstrated that a chronic sense of

urgency is a basic component of the Type A, coronary-prone personality. We expect that future research will demonstrate that pace of life is related to rate of heart disease, hypertension, ulcers, suicide, alcoholism, divorce and other indicators of general psychological and physical well-being.

As you envision tomorrow's international society, do you wonder who will set the pace? Americans eye Japan carefully, because the Japanese are obviously "ahead of us" in measurable ways. In both countries, speed is frequently confused with progress. Perhaps looking carefully at the different paces of life around the world will help us distinguish more accurately between the two qualities. Clues are everywhere but sometimes hard to distinguish. You have to listen carefully to hear the beat of even your own drummer.

How Not to Lose the Trade Wars by Cultural Gaffes

*A California professor works to make the bargaining table
a 'level playing field' for all*

John Pfeiffer

Mr. Pfeiffer is writing a book whose thesis is that business executives are leaders in social science research.

Seven executives are trying to do business in a Tokyo conference room: four Americans (a vice president in charge of sales and his associates) and three Japanese middle managers. The Japanese are deferring to their visitors, nodding and listening with pointed respect, especially to the vice president. The Americans respond with the same formality even though they tend to avoid hierarchical behavior, preferring to put everyone on an equal footing. Things are off to a bad start—and about to get worse.

Three more Japanese enter the room, all senior executives in their late 50s, all obviously outranking their compatriots, and all treated with due respect. This puts the Americans in a bind. Having worked hard to be the middle managers' equals, they must readjust to a new situation. In the midst of their efforts, in comes another Japanese, the president of the corporation. The Americans are now caught in an escalating confusion of statuses, of who defers to whom and, sure enough, the rattled vice president makes a major tactical blunder, suggesting an inappropriate meeting at an inappropriate time and place, as negotiations grind to an embarrassing halt.

One of the Americans, a 31-year-old graduate student, never forgot this 1979 debacle. John Graham, professor of marketing at the University of

Southern California's School of Business Administration, has made a career of studying bargaining styles throughout the world. He is interested in business dealings, of course, but beyond that he sees successful bargaining—negotiations in which both parties come away feeling good—as a basic model for social and political progress on the world scene. He has gathered a mass of data from direct observation, interviews, questionnaires and, above all and uniquely, from videotapes of executives role-playing with real-life fervor. His library contains 150 cassettes recording behavior not only in the United States and Japan, but also in ten other cultures.

Graham's main focus, however, has been on our dealings with the Japanese, and no wonder. They are murdering us at the bargaining table. In 1980 the difference between what they sold us and what we managed to sell them amounted to about $12 billion, a figure that today has soared to $58 billion. Many factors help account for this staggering trade gap, notably Japan's aggressive marketing of reasonably priced, high-quality products, coupled with the difficulties foreign firms face trading with Japan: import-restricting regulations, complex distribution systems and unfamiliar business practices.

But Graham, who has studied anthropology as well as business, stresses the influence of clashes between the natives of radically different "tribes" and believes that cultural factors outweigh economic factors: "U.S. com-

panies are sending some of our best executives on suicide missions. They're totally unprepared to bargain with the Japanese. It's kamikaze-style marketing." Two proverbs highlight the difference between Americans and Japanese. Ours: The squeaking wheel gets the grease. Theirs: The pheasant would not be shot but for its cry.

When it comes to understanding the other culture, they are light-years ahead of us. They have been studying us for a long time, since 1853 when America's Commodore Matthew Perry in a memorable display of gunboat diplomacy kicked open Japan's closed door. The Japanese promptly sent a delegation of Samurai warriors to America, not to fight but to fathom the ways of the "red-faced" foreigners.

Present-day descendants of these early observers are still at it. Almost all of the 10,000 to 15,000 Japanese executives living in the United States speak English, while only a few hundred of our innocents abroad have bothered to become conversational in Japanese (although the number is increasing). Furthermore, Japanese firms make a special point of studying our ways of doing business. During the past five years they have sent several thousand young executives over here to earn MBA degrees at American universities. American firms have done nothing comparable.

Graham's research is part of the effort to catch up culturally, to understand the Japanese at least as well as they understand us. His business-game program includes Japanese and American students as well as established executives representing many of the Fortune 500 corporations and Japanese companies such as Toyota, Toshiba (electronics) Daiei (the Japanese equivalent of Safeway), Suntory (alcoholic beverages) and Dentsu (the world's largest ad agency). Japanese players bargain with Americans, selling toys (trucks, dolls, airplanes) or buying citrus fruits (oranges, lemons, grapefruit) under the watchful eyes of three remote-controlled video cameras—one to provide wide-angled views of posture and body movements, and the other two for close-ups of each participant's face.

The games document a deep undercurrent of awkwardness and discomfort. Americans are fast workers—with one another, that is—and complete deals in an average of 25 minutes. Cross-cultural sessions last longer. When buying, the Japanese come up with innumerable questions about the product; when selling, they go into considerable detail to explain their own offerings. A typical American response: "Fine, OK—now let's get down to the numbers." Still, the Japanese pace prevails. Americans must adapt, anticipating sessions that last for 40 or more minutes.

Real life presents similar problems. Americans are quite comfortable with what Graham calls "nontask sounding"—light personal conversation before getting down to the immediate business at hand—provided it doesn't last too long. For them, ten minutes seems appropriate, about the limit for what they consider killing time. For the Japanese, however, such nontask sounding is the heart of the matter, an essential element in the bargaining process, at least as crucial as the final deal itself. Concerned with long-term, personal relationships, they are ready to chat for an hour, for an entire morning or for more. The bigger the deal and the more important the dealers, the longer the preliminaries.

Graham participated in one top-level encounter that involved the purchase of gas turbines. It started with a night on the town—a deluxe Tokyo restaurant and nightclub, then more restaurants and nightclubs, the theater, a visit to a geisha house—followed by an extensive tour of the plant and an afternoon of golf. Graham shot in the upper 90s and still beat his Japanese partner, obviously a far superior player but too polite to show it. "It's practically impossible to lose to your Japanese host," he says. And that is typical. A statistic to mull over: the Japanese spend about 1.2 percent of their gross national product (about \$13 billion) on business entertainment, more than they spend on national defense.

Split-screen studies highlight major cultural differences. Several videotapes reveal a fascinating dance of the eyes, an "out-of-sync bobbing of heads." An American looks across the bargaining table at his Japanese counterpart, who promptly lowers his gaze, only to look up when the American looks down to take notes. As soon as the American raises his eyes again, the Japanese reassumes the head-down position, and so on.

There are cultural reasons for this up-and-down interaction. Japanese children are expected to bow their heads while being scolded, to show that they are humbled and ashamed, while American children must keep their heads up to show they're paying attention ("Look at me when I'm talking to you!"). This sort of body language is difficult to change and easy to misinterpret. Japanese executives cannot help regarding the "forthright" American eye-to-eye posture as impolite and insensitive, while Americans consider looking down as a sign of shiftiness.

Video records also have something to tell us about the subtleties of Oriental "inscrutability." Interviewed after business (and social) encounters, Americans often complain that you can't tell where you stand with the Japanese because they hide their feelings behind poker faces. Observations fail to confirm this impression. Take frowning, for example. It turns out that the Japanese in the study actually frown more often than Americans do, by precise playback count 5.3 times versus 3.8 times for every ten minutes of bargaining. The count for smiling is 11.7 versus 10.8.

What's happening is that Americans tend to be blind to what they consider inappropriate facial expressions. At a particularly sticky point in negotiations, say when bids are far apart and prospects for settlement seem slim, an American executive naturally expects to see a serious expression on his opposite number's face. Instead he sees a broad, cheerful smile, a disconcerting mark of two traditions that are worlds apart. The Japanese smile is a very special thing. By way of explanation Graham cites the following comment of a perceptive 19th-century observer: "The most agreeable face is the smiling face, and to present always the most agreeable face possible . . . is a rule of life." With our most successful overseas rivals, it's inscrutable, yes—but poker-faced, no.

In the same spirit of maintaining harmony, the Japanese tradition is to avoid a direct "no" at practically any cost. They may ask a counterquestion, promise an answer at some later date, change the subject and even occasionally leave the room. Another common response is no response at all, a dead silence. "This drives Americans up the wall," Graham comments. He recalls how one American reacted during a taped bargaining session held at Toyota's U.S. headquarters in California. The executive had just made a proposal involving the opening of new production facilities in Brazil and waited for a reply . . . and waited . . . and waited.

In ordinary conversation the usual response time is a few tenths of a second, and a five- to ten-second delay can be puzzling. This time 15, 20, 25 seconds passed as three Japanese executives sat tight, eyes lowered and hands folded on the table. Finally the American blurted: "I don't think this is getting us anywhere!" He was right. The meeting ended in a stalemate. He should have bided his time and, in due course, quietly asked another question.

According to Graham, ignorance of native bargaining rituals accounts more than any other single factor for our unimpressive sales efforts with the

Japanese and, of all rituals, the buyer-seller relationship is most crucial. The buyer is king in all countries, but more so and with a vengeance in Japan. Special courtesy words mark the difference in status. For a buyer, the seller's firm is referred to as *otaku* (your company), while the seller traditionally responds with *onsha* (your great company). So Americans, who rarely mind being deferred to, do fine as buyers. But being deferential is hardly their style and they tend to play the seller's expected role reluctantly.

You can see the results on videotape. One episode starts with a few minutes of amicable small talk, only to turn sour when the Japanese buyer opens the bidding with a flagrantly lower offer for a citrus shipment. The American responds bluntly as he would to a fellow countryman: "That's not possible at all! There's no way we can negotiate!" The Japanese has never been spoken to that way. He bows his head, flashes a smile of pain and immediately offers a considerably higher price. They finally arrive at a deal, but that American will have a lot of trouble selling anything in Japan.

For their part, the Japanese are capable of behavior that may well strike an American as rude. While he is trying to get an important point across, they may suddenly start talking to one another, in Japanese of course, or get up and leave the room. Upon occasion, even senior executives may be observed "listening with their eyes shut," a Japanese euphemism for dozing off. The recommended response is to keep cool during such episodes, which, Graham assures us, "are not to be taken personally, but simply reflect a different view of appropriate behavior."

Ours is a typically ethnocentric problem. We believe that our way of doing business—informal, cards on the table, get to the point, take me as I am—is the only right way and that the world would be a much better place if everyone were just like us. This John Wayne style can be our undoing overseas: "We must learn to adjust our behavior," Graham emphasizes, "and gain an appreciation for subtler forms of negotiation."

These are lucrative times for experts on how to bargain with the Japanese and Graham qualifies as an expert. But he prefers doing research to cashing in on the consultant's role. (For one thing, he is working closely with his wife, also a professor of marketing at the University of California, Irvine, on a study of male and female bargaining styles.) *Smart Bargaining: Doing Business with the Japanese,* a book on the subject coauthored with Los Angeles business consultant Yoshihiro Sano, is available in American and Japanese editions, since it includes advice for executives on both sides of the Pacific. Here are four of their major pointers on bargaining with those inscrutable Americans:

• Americans do not understand why nontask sounding is so important to us. They consider it small talk. But we arrive at trust primarily through personal relationships, while they rely on lawyers to write tight contracts and settle disputes. We strongly recommend American-style written contracts with Japanese jurisdiction. The written contract is your only assurance of compliance.

• Americans often present proposals backward. Instead of explaining why they want something and then saying what they want and using persuasive tactics, they do things the other way around. They want first and explain later. And sometimes they don't bother explaining at all. Therefore, you must not hesitate to ask questions, even though you may get short, impatient answers.

• Watch out for *akushitsu na teguchi* (dirty tricks). Americans are generally honest and frank, the latter even to a fault. However, you should be aware that a few Americans may use dirty tricks: bringing you into a stark meeting room filled with uncomfortable chairs; escalating demands; raising prices, say 5 percent a day, to hasten negotiations; price padding, particularly by those who think "they know the Orient"; ambiguous authority, saying they'll have to talk that over with their superiors. How to handle all this: speak up, ask for a more comfortable room and chair, call their bluff.

• Last—but very much not least—America is a most heterogeneous culture. Not everyone acts like John Wayne. The roles of minorities and women are changing fast in the United States. You should anticipate key negotiating roles being filled by women and minority executives. They should not be treated any differently than the Caucasian male executives to whom you are accustomed.

The California investigator is winding down the intense phase of his Japanese research and beginning to concentrate increasingly on the behavior of other nationalities. He is part of an expanding network of colleagues at Dortmund University in West Germany; the University of California, Berkeley; the Institute of Technology and Higher Education in Monterrey, Mexico; Korea University in Seoul; the Université de Grenoble Institut d'Etudes Commerciales in France; McGill University in Montreal; and other institutions.

Preliminary observations of the Canadians, our No. 1 trade partners (the Japanese rank No. 2) indicate that they take their low-key time, selecting words deliberately, rather like the British and in marked contrast to Americans whom they often consider pushy and a bit on the reckless side. An outstanding characteristic of the Mexicans, our No. 4 partners, is that the buyer enjoys high status as he does among the Japanese, although not quite to the same hyper-polite degree. Also, kinship weighs heavily in Mexican business circles, often at least as heavily as economics. You buy from your first cousin and sell to your sister's husband, for example, even at some financial sacrifice. Interestingly, family ties are also crucial in Japan, only there the "family" consists of business colleagues rather than blood relatives.

With an eye on mounting competition among Far Eastern nations, Graham and his associates are undertaking special studies of Japan's neighbors. The South Koreans, already No. 7 on our trading list and definitely on the rise, "show us not to generalize about Orientals." They resemble the Mexicans and Japanese in giving the buyer superior status, often speak out even more frankly and bluntly than Americans and are more emotional than the Japanese, much readier to laugh and get angry. One of the most intriguing things about the Chinese in the People's Republic of China, potentially the world's largest market, is the difference between their bargaining style and that of Chinese businessmen from Taiwan. Graham has videotaped experimental games in Tianjin, China's third largest city. Judging by the tapes I saw, the mainland Chinese appear to be more aggressive than the Japanese, occasionally finding themselves talking at the same time; but otherwise, they are very much like Americans.

The Taiwan Chinese, on the other hand, are notable for an out-of-phase quality unlike anything Graham has observed elsewhere. He refers to it as "no reciprocity" behavior. What happens is that one Taiwanese bargainer may be in a cooperative mode, well on the way to reaching an agreement, only to see that for no particular reason his counterpart across the bargaining table is unenthusiastic, annoyed or even downright angry. The strange thing is that often this anti-social behavior pays off: the initially cooperative negotiator gives in across the board.

Of all bargaining styles on file in Graham's cassette library, the Brazilians' is by far the most dynamic. Our No. 1 trade partners in South America do not know the meaning of silence. They are nonstop talkers and it would be something to view them bargaining with the Japanese on videotape. They make physical contact with one another frequently. Japanese and Americans never touch one another, while the Brazilians make a habit of touching, poking, patting. Also, they are the world's top naysayers, uttering "no" more than 40 times per half hour as compared with 4.7 times for Americans and only 1.9 times for the Japanese.

Graham regards his work in the broad perspective of current efforts toward world peace. An eminently practical idealist, he sees a rapidly growing change in international competition, an emphasis due largely to the Japanese: "They have changed the whole game in world leadership, a complete switch from the military game, which is no good, to the economic game—from guns to butter." Moreover, he is convinced that Gorbachev and the Soviets are beginning to see things in the same light and plans to invest heavily on that hunch.

The Organization of Society and Culture

Human beings do not interact with one another or think about their world in random fashion. Instead, they engage in both structured and recurrent physical and mental activities. In this section, such patterns of behavior and thought—referred to here as the organization of society and culture—may be seen in a number of different contexts, from the hunter-collectors of the Arctic to the cattle-herding Masai of East Africa ("Mystique of the Masai").

Of special importance are the ways in which people make a living—in other words, the production, distribution, and consumption of goods and services. It is only by knowing the basic subsistence systems that we can hope to gain insight into the other levels of social and cultural phenomena, for, as anthropologists have found, they are all inextricably bound together.

Noting the various aspects of a sociocultural system in harmonious balance, however, does not imply an anthropological seal of approval. To understand abortion in the manner that it is practiced among the Yąnomamö is neither to condone nor condemn it. Nevertheless, the adaptive patterns that have been in existence for a long time, such as many of the patterns of hunters and gatherers, probably owe their existence to their contributions to long-term human survival. It is for this reason that some anthropologists seek the origins of such patterns in our biological past.

The articles in this section demonstrate that anthropologists are far more interested in problems than they are in place. "The Blood in Their Veins" conveys the hardships of living in the Arctic in such personal terms that the reader cannot help but understand the actions of Eskimos from their viewpoint. Meanwhile, the first-person narrative of "Memories of a !Kung Girlhood" serves as a needful reminder of our common humanity.

Anthropologists, however, are not content with the data derived from individual experience. On the contrary, personal descriptions must become the basis for sound anthropological theory. Otherwise, they remain meaningless, isolated relics of culture in the manner of museum pieces. Thus, "Murders in Eden" expresses the constant striving in anthropology to develop a general perspective from particular events by showing that early forms of population control were intricately related to breast-feeding in the context of the hunter-gatherer way of life.

Articles in this volume offer evidence that anthropologists are not always in agreement, even when they are studying and analyzing the very same cultures. For example, in some ways Napoleon Chagnon's "Doing Fieldwork Among the Yąnomamö" (Unit 1) is a direct contradiction of Shelly Kellman's description of the very same people in "The Yąnomamis: Portrait of a People in Crisis." In addition, Marvin Harris certainly provides a different perspective than has generally been held about the Kwakiutl Indians in "Potlatch."

While the articles in this section are to some extent descriptive, they also serve to challenge both academic and common sense notions about why people behave and think as they do. These clashes of opinion remind us that assumptions are never really safe. Any time anthropologists are kept on their toes, the field as a whole is the better for it.

Looking Ahead: Challenge Questions

What traditional Eskimo practices do you find contrary to values professed in your society, but important to Eskimo survival under certain circumstances?

In what ways is !Kung childhood similar to childhood in American culture?

What can contemporary hunter-collector societies tell us about the quality of life in the prehistoric past?

How has population control been maintained in hunter-collector societies?

In what ways can the Masai be seen as ecological conservationists?

How does the game of waiting in modern society relate to who has the power?

How does competitive feasting contribute to survival among Northwest Coast Indians?

The Blood in Their Veins

Farley Mowat

Barely visible from Gene Lushman's rickety dock at the mouth of Big River, Anoteelik stroked his kayak to seaward on the heaving brown waters of Hudson Bay. Vanishing, then reappearing on the long, slick swells, the kayak was so distant it might have been nothing more than an idle gull drifting aimlessly on the undulating waters.

I had helped Anoteelik prepare for that journey. Together we had carried the skin-wrapped packages of dress goods, food and tobacco down from Lushman's trading shack. Then the squat, heavy-bodied Eskimo, with his dreadfully scarred face, lashed the cargo to the afterdeck and departed. I watched him until the bright flashing of his double-bladed paddle was only a white flicker against the humped outlines of a group of rocky reefs lying three miles offshore.

This was the third time I had seen Anoteelik make his way out of the estuary to the farthest islet on the sombre rim of the sea but it was the first time I understood the real reason behind his yearly solitary voyage.

Gene Lushman, barrenland trapper and trader, had first drawn my attention to him three years earlier.

"See that old Husky there? Old Ano . . . tough old bugger . . . one of the inland people and queer like all of them. Twenty years now, every spring soon as the ice clears, Ano, he heads off out to the farthest rock, and every year he takes a hundred dollars of my best trade goods along. For why? Well, me son, that crazy old bastard is taking the stuff out there to his dead wife! That's

true, so help me God! He buried her there . . . far out to sea as there was a rock sticking up high enough to hold a grave!

"Father Debrie, he's tried maybe a half dozen times to make the old fellow quit his nonsense. It has a bad influence on the rest of the Huskies—they're supposed to be Christians, you know—but Ano, he just smiles and says: 'Yes, Father,' and every spring he turns in his fox skins to me and I sell him the same bill of goods, and he takes it and dumps it on that rock in the Bay."

It was the waste that bothered and puzzled Gene. Himself the product of a Newfoundland outport, he could not abide the waste . . . a hundred dollars every spring as good as dumped into the sea.

"Crazy old bastard!" he said, shaking his head in bewilderment.

Although he had traded with the Big River people for a good many years, Gene had never really bridged the gap between them and himself. He had learned only enough of their language for trade purposes and while he admired their ability to survive in their harsh land he had little interest in their inner lives, perhaps because he had never been able to stop thinking of them as a "lesser breed." Consequently, he never discovered the reason for Anoteelik's strange behaviour.

During my second year in the country, I became friendly with Itkut, old Anoteelik's son—indeed his only offspring. Itkut was a big, stocky man still in the full vigour of young manhood; a man who laughed a lot and liked making jokes. It was he who gave me my Eskimo name, *Kipmetna,* which translates as "noisy little dog." Itkut and I spent a lot of time together

that summer, including making a long boat trip north to Marble Island after walrus. A few days after our return, old Ano happened into Itkut's tent to find me struggling to learn the language under his son's somewhat less-than-patient guidance. For a while Ano listened to the garbled sounds I was making, then he chuckled. Until that moment the old man, with his hideously disfigured face, had seemed aloof and unapproachable, but now the warmth that lay hidden behind the mass of scar tissue was revealed.

"Itkut gave you a good name," he said smiling. "Indeed, the dog-spirit must live in your tongue. *Ayorama—* it doesn't matter. Let us see if we can drive it out."

With that he took over the task of instructing me, and by the time summer was over we had become friends.

One August night when the ice fog over the Bay was burning coldly in the long light of the late-setting sun, I went to a drum dance at Ano's tent. This was forbidden by the priest at Eskimo Point, who would send the R.C.M.P. constable down to Big River to smash the drums if he heard a dance was being held. The priest was a great believer in an ever-present Devil, and he was convinced the drums were the work of that Devil. In truth, these gatherings were song-feasts at which each man, woman or child took the drum in turn and sang a song. Sometimes it was an ancient song from far out of time, a voice from the shadowy distances of Innuit history; or perhaps it might be a comic song in which the singer made fun of himself. Often it was the story of a spectacular hunting incident; or it

epic song

might be a song of tragic happenings and of the spirits of the land.

That night Itkut sang a song of the Hunting of Omingmuk, the muskox. As the story unwound, Ano's face came alight with pride—and with love.

Toward dawn people began to drift away and Ano suggested we walk to the shore and have a smoke. Flocks of plover, grey and ephemeral in the half light, fled shrilling before us, and out on the dim wastes of the sea spectral loons yapped at one another.

Ano's face was turned to the sea.

"I know you wonder at me, Kipmetna, yet you look at this torn face of mine and your questions are never heard. You watch as I make my spring journey out to the rock in the sea and your questions remain silent. That is the way also with my People. Tonight, perhaps because Itkut sang well and brought many memories to me from a long time ago, I would tell you a story."

Once there was a woman, and it was she who was my belly and my blood. Now she waits for me in that distant place where the deer are as many as the stars.

She was Kala, and she was of the Sea People, and not of my People who lived far from the sea on the great plains where no trees grow. But I loved her beyond all things in the sea or on the land. Some said I loved her too much, since I could never find the strength to share her, even with my song-cousin, Tanugeak. Most men respected my love and the *angeokok*, Mahuk, said that the sea-mother, Takanaluk Arnaluk, was pleased by the love I had for my wife.

My mother was Kunee and my father was Sagalik. I was born by the shore of Tulemaliguak, Lake of the Great Bones, far west of here, in the years when the camps of the inland people were almost emptied of life by the burning breath of the white man's sickness. My father died of it soon after my birth.

I was born in the late summer months, and Kunee, my mother, was dead before autumn. Then I was taken into the childless tent of Ungyala and his wife Aputna. They were not young people. Once they had lived very far to the south but their camps too had been stricken by the sickness and they had fled north. They too had been burned by the flame in the lungs, and their sons and daughters had died.

Soon after they took me into their tent, Ungyala and Aputna made ready to flee again, for there were not enough people left in our camps even to bury the dead. So we three went west . . . far off to the west into a land where the Innuit had never lived for fear of the Indians who sometimes came out of the forests into the plains. The deer were plentiful in that place and we lived very well while I grew toward the age of a man and learned to hunt by myself and to drive the long sled over the hard-packed snow.

All the same, it was a lonely land we had come to. There were not even any Indians—perhaps they too, had been burned by the plague. We saw no *inukok*, little stone men set on the hills to tell us that other men of our race had travelled those long, rolling slopes. It was a good land but empty, and we hungered to hear other voices.

In the winter of the year when I became *angeutnak*, almost a man, the blizzards beat upon us for a very long time. Ungyala and I had made good kills of deer in the autumn so we three did not suffer; yet we longed for the coming of spring, the return of the deer and the birds. We yearned for the voices of life, for the voices we heard were of wind and, sometimes I thought, of those spirits who hide in the ground.

In the month when the wolves begin to make love there came a break in the storms. Then I, in the pride of my youth and filled with a hunger I could not yet name, decided to make a journey to the northwest. I said I hoped to kill muskox and bring fresh meat to the camp. Ungyala agreed to my going, though he was not very willing for he was afraid of the lands to the northwest. I took seven dogs and drove the komatik over the snow-hidden hills for three days, and saw no living thing. That land was dead, and my heart was chilled, and only

because I was stubborn and young did I go on.

On the fourth day I came to the lip of a valley, and as I began to descend my lead dog threw up her head. In a moment the dogs were plunging into soft snow, the traces all tangled, and all of them yelling like fiends. I stopped them and walked cautiously forward until I could look down into the flat run of a gulley that lay sheltered by walls of grey stone. There was movement down there. It was *kakwik*, the wolverine, digging with his slashing front claws into the top of what looked like a drift. I ran back to my team and tried to unleash a few of the dogs so they could chase him, but now they were fighting each other; and before I could free them, kakwik was gone, lumbering up the long slope and over the rocks.

I kicked at the dogs, jumped on the sled, and drove headlong into the gulley; but when I slowed past the place where kakwik had dug, my heart went out of the chase.

He had been digging into the top of a buried snowhouse.

Ungyala believed that no men lived to the west and north of our land, yet here was a house. The door tunnel was snowed in and drifts had almost buried the place. I took my snow probe and slid it into a crack between blocks in the roof. It went in so easily I could tell the inside was empty of snow.

I grew cautious and more than a little afraid. The thought came that this might be the home of an *Ino*, a dwarf with knives where his hands should be. Yet the thought that this might instead be the home of true men gave me courage.

With my snowknife I cut a hole in the dome . . . squeezed through it and dropped to the floor. As my eyes grew used to the gloom, I saw that this had been a shelter for men . . . only now it was a tomb for the dead.

There were many bones lying about and even in that dim light I could see that not all had belonged to deer or muskox. One was a skull with black hair hanging down over gleaming white bone where the flesh of the cheeks had been cut away with a knife.

I was about to leap up to the hole in the roof and drag myself out of that terrible place when I saw a shudder of movement under a pile of muskox robes at the back of the sleeping ledge. I was sure something terrible crouched there in the darkness and I raised my snowknife to strike, and fear was a sliver of ice in my belly.

But it was no devil that crawled painfully out from under that pile of rotting hides.

Once, I remember, I found the corpse of a fawn wedged in a deep crevice among some great rocks. It had been missed by the ravens, foxes and wolves and, because it was autumn, the maggots had not eaten the meat. It had dried into a bundle of bones bound around the skin.

The girl who lay helpless before me on the ledge of the snowhouse looked like that fawn. Only her eyes were alive.

Although I was young, and greatly afraid, I knew what I must do. There was a soapstone pot on the floor. I slid the blade of my knife into the flesh of my left arm and let the hot blood flow into the bowl.

Through the space of one day and night I fed the thing I had found with the blood from my veins. Drop by drop was she fed. In between feedings I held here close in my arms under a thick new robe I had fetched from my sled, and slowly the warmth from my body drove the chill from her bones.

Life came back to her but it was nearly three days before she could sit up at my side without aid. Yet she must have had hidden strength somewhere within her for later that day when I came back into the snowhouse after feeding my dogs, all the human bones on the floor, to the last fragment, had vanished. She had found strength, even though death still had his hands on her throat, to bury those things under the hard snow of the floor.

On the fifth day she was able to travel so I brought her back to Ungyala's camp and my parents-by-right took her in and were glad she had come. Neither one made any comment when I told how I had found her and what else I had found in the snowhouse. But later, when Ungyala and I were on a journey away from the camp picking up meat from an autumn cache, he spoke to me thus:

"Anoteelik, my son, this person has eaten the flesh of the dead . . . so much you know. Yet until you too have faced death in the way that he came to this girl, do not judge of her act. She has suffered enough. The spirits of those she has eaten will forgive her . . . the living must forgive her as well."

The girl quickly recovered her youth—she who had seemed beyond age—and as she grew fat she grew comely and often my heart speeded its beat when she was near. She spoke almost no words except to tell us her name was Kala and that her family, who were Sea People, had come inland from the north coast in the fall to hunt muskox.

It was not until the ravens returned that one day when we men were far from camp, she broke into speech to my mother-by-right. Then she told how the family dogs had died of the madness which is carried by foxes and wolves, and how, marooned in the heart of the dark frozen plains, her parents and brother had followed the Snow Walker. She told how she also had waited for death until hunger brought its own madness . . . and she began to eat the flesh of the dead. When she finished her tale she turned from my mother-by-right and cried, "I am unworthy to live!" She would have gone into the night and sought her own end had my mother not caught her and bound her and held her until we returned.

She was calmer by the next day, but she asked that we build her a snowhouse set apart from the camp, and we followed her wish. She lived alone there for many days. Aputna took food to her and talked to her, but we two men never saw her at all.

It was good that spring came so soon after, for spring is the time for forgetting the past. The deer streamed back into our land. The ptarmigan mated and called from the hills, and the male lemmings sought out the females deep in the moss.

The snowhouses softened under the sun and then Kala came back and lived with us in the big skin tent that we built. She seemed to have put out of mind the dark happenings of the winter, and she willingly helped with the work . . . but it was seldom she laughed.

My desire for the girl had become heavy and big during the days she had kept out of sight. It was more than the thrust of my loins; for I had known pity for her, and pity breeds passion in men.

One evening after the snow was all gone, I came and sat by her side on a ridge overlooking our camp where she had gone to watch the deer streaming by. I spoke awkwardly of my love. Kala turned her face from me, but one hand crept to my arm and touched the place where I had thrust the knife into my vein. That night, as we all lay together inside the big tent, she came into my arms and we became husband and wife.

Such was my finding of Kala—a finding that brought me the happiest days of my life, for she was a woman of women. Her sewing was gifted by spirits, and her cooking made even Ungyala grow fat. She could hunt nearly as well as a man. And she was avid for love, as one who has once nearly drowned is avid for air. We four lived a good life all that summer and it seemed as if Kala had brought many good things to our land. The deer were never so fat, the muskox never so many, the trout in the rivers never so large. Even our two bitch dogs, which had been fruitless for over two years, gave birth to big litters and raised eleven fine pups that became the best sled dogs I ever owned. So we believed the girl was forgiven . . . that the spirits wished her to suffer no more.

On a day of the following winter, Ungyala and I were sent out of the snowhouse and we sat and shivered in the lee of some rocks until we heard the voice of my mother-by-right singing birth songs to the Whispering Ones who flame in the sky.

After the birth of Itkut, our son, a restlessness seemed to come over us all. Kala yearned to return to the sea. Aputna was feeling her years, and longed once again to hear the voices and see the faces of people she had known long ago. As for me, I was anxious to visit some trader and buy the things Ungyala had told me about; especially guns, for I thought that hunting with spears, bows and arrows did not let me show what a fine hunter I had become. Only Ungyala thought that perhaps we should stay where we were. He remembered too well that he and Aputna had twice had to flee for their lives when the people in the camps where they were living were struck down by the new kind of dying that came from beyond the borders of the Innuit lands. Yet in his heart he too wished to see people again, so we decided to go.

We had two good teams and two sleds. We drove north and then east, making a broad detour around the now empty camps where I had been born. We saw no sign of living men until we finally came to Big River. There we met two families who spent their summers near Eskimo Point and their winters inland on the edge of the plains. We stayed with them for the rest of that winter, hearing much about the world Ungyala and Aputna had almost forgotten and that Kala and I had never known. In the spring, before the ice softened, we followed Big River down to the coast.

So we took up a new way of life. Every autumn we journeyed in a big canoe, with our dogs running free on the shore, up Big River to a lake near its head where the southbound deer crossed a narrows. Here Ungyala and I speared fat bucks in the water and shot more of them out on the bare, rocky plains with the rifles we had traded for at the coast. By the time the first snows drove the deer out of the land, we would have more than enough meat for the winter, plenty of fat for our lamps, and the best of hides for our clothing and robes.

In the late days of autumn, after the deer had passed and before we began trapping white foxes, there was little to do. Sometimes then I would sit and think and weigh up the worth of my life. It was good, but I understood that its goodness dwelt mainly in Kala. I loved her for the son she had borne, for the clothes that she made me, for the help that she gave me . . . but it went beyond that. I do not know how to explain it, but Kala held me in her soul. The love she gave me passed far beyond respect for a husband and entered that country of pleasure which we of the People do not often know. Such was our life as the child, Itkut, grew with the years.

Now I must tell how it was when we came to the coast. There we met the first white man we had ever seen. It was he who built the wood house at the mouth of Big River. He seemed a good man in some ways, but he was crazy for women. Before he had lived in the country a year, there were few women who had not spent a night in his house, for it was still our law then that a man might not refuse any gift that lay in his giving if another man asked. Kala never went to the house of the white man, though he asked me for her many times. He put shame upon me, for I was forced to refuse.

In the autumn of our fourth year in the new land, we had gone up the river as usual and made our camp at the lake of the Deer Crossing. Ours was the farthest camp from the sea, for we had come from the inland plains and they held no terrors for us. The coast dwellers did not care to go as far as we went. Our tent was pitched within sight of the ford and from the door we could look to see if the deer had arrived.

The time came when the forerunners of the big herd should have appeared, but the crossing remained empty of life. The darkening lichens on the bank were unmarked by the feet of the deer. The dwarf shrubs began to burn red in the first frosts. Ungyala and I walked many miles over the land, climbing the hills and staring out to the north. We saw none of the usual harbingers of the great herds—no ravens floating black in the pale sky, no wolves drifting white on the dark land.

Although we were worried, nothing was said. Kala and Aputna became very busy fishing for trout, suckers and char in the river. They caught little, for the autumn run was nearly over, yet they fished night and day. The dogs began to grow hungry and their howling became so loud we had to move them some miles from the camp in case they frightened the deer. Thinking back to those days I wonder if it was hunger alone that made them so distressed. Maybe they already knew what we would not believe could be true.

The morning came when snow blew in the air . . . only a thin mist of fine snow but enough to tell us that winter had come and it had not brought the deer.

But a few days afterwards the deer came. Ungyala and I went out with light hearts but only a few deer had come to the river. These few were so poor and lacking in fat that we knew they were not the forerunners of the great herds but stragglers that lagged behind, being either too weak or too sick to keep up. We knew then that the deer spirit had led the herds southward by some different path.

The next day there were no deer at the crossing and none to be seen anywhere upon the sweep of the plains and we had killed barely enough meat to feed ourselves and the dogs for two months.

The real snows came and we began the winter with hearts that were shaken by misgivings. We thought of abandoning our camp and trying to make our way to the coast but we could not do this until enough snow had fallen to make sled travel possible. So we stayed where we were, hoping we would find some of the solitary winter deer that sometimes remain in the land. Ungyala and I roamed with pack dogs over the country for many long miles. A few hares and ptarmigan fell to our guns, but these were no more than food for our hopes.

Before long we ran out of fat, then there was neither light nor heat in the snowhouse. One day Ungyala and I resolved to travel southeast on a journey to some distant islands of little trees where in times past deer used to winter. We took only one

3. ORGANIZATION OF SOCIETY AND CULTURE

small team of dogs, but even these we could not feed and they soon weakened until after a few days they could go no farther. That night we camped in the lee of some cliffs and it was too cold to sleep so we sat and the old man talked of the days of his youth. He was very weak and his voice almost too low to hear. At last he dozed and I covered him with both our robes; but before the dawn he had ceased to breathe, and so I buried my father-by-right in the snow in a grave I cut with my snowknife.

I turned back, but before I reached the snowhouse I heard women's voices singing the song of the dead. Aputna had seen the death of Ungyala in the eye of her mind, and the two women were mourning.

A little time after the death of Ungyala, I wakened one night to the muted whispering of the women. I lay with my face turned to the wall and listened to what Kala was saying to my mother-by-right.

"My mother, the time is not yet come for you to take your old bones to sleep in the snow. Your rest will come after. Now comes a time when I have need of your help."

I knew then that Aputna had decided to take the way of release, and had been held from it by Kala. I did not understand why my wife had restrained her, for it is the right of the old ones that they be the first to die when starvation comes to a camp. But I had small time to wonder, for Kala moved over beside me and spoke softly in my ear, and she told me what I dreaded to hear—that now I must take the few dogs that were left and make my way eastward, down river, until I found a camp that had meat to spare.

I refused, and I called her a fool, for she knew the other camps could be no better off then we were. Kala had always been a woman of sense yet I could not make her see that such a trip would be useless. I knew, and she knew, I could not hope to find help until I reached the coast camps where people depended more on seal meat than on deer, and such a trip, there

and back with weak dogs, could not take less than a month. It would be better, I told her, if we killed and ate all the dogs, let my mother-by-right go to her rest, and wait where we were, eking out our lives by fishing for what little could be caught through holes in the ice. Then, if it came to the worst, we three, Kala and Itkut and I, would at least lie down for the last time together.

She would not heed what I said and I heard for the first time the hard edge of anger in her voice.

"You *will* go!" she whispered fiercely. "If you do not, I shall myself put the noose of release on your son when you are gone out of the snowhouse and so save him from the torments that were mine in a time you remember."

And . . . oh, Kipmetan . . . though I knew she was wrong, I could no longer refuse. No, and I did not, although I should have guessed at that which was hidden deep in her thoughts.

At parting next day only the old woman wept. There were no tears from Kala who knew what she knew, and none from young Itkut who was still too young to know what was afoot.

That was a journey! I walked eight days to the nearest camps of the people, for the dogs were too weak to do more than haul the empty sled along at a crawl. In that first camp I found it was as I had feared. Famine had got there before me. Things were nearly as bad all the way down the river. One by one I killed my dogs to keep me and their remaining brothers and sisters alive, and sometimes I shared a little of that lean, bitter meat with people in the camps that I passed.

I was almost in sight of the sea when I came to the camp of my song-cousin, Tanugeak. He and those with him were in good health for they had been living on the meat and the fat of seals Tanugeak had speared far out on the sea ice. They had none too much, though, for they had been helping feed many people who had already fled east from the inland camps. All the same, Tanugeak

proved his friendship. He gave me four seals and loaned me five of his own strong dogs, together with fish enough to feed them on the long journey home.

My strength was not much, but I began the up-river journey at once and I sang to the dogs as they ran strongly to the west. I had been away from my camp only two weeks, and now I hoped to return there in eight days at the most. So I sang as the sled ran smoothly over the hard river ice.

Two days up river and a few miles north of my track was a lake and by it two camps where I had stopped overnight on my way to the sea. In those camps I had been given soup made of old bones by people who were almost old bones themselves. Now, with much food on my sled, I did not turn off to give them at least a little of my meat and fat. I told myself I could spare neither the time nor the food if I was to save my own family from death . . . but I knew I did wrong. As my sled slipped into the darkening west I felt a foreboding and I almost turned back. If only I had . . . but such thoughts are useless, and they are a weakness in man; for he does what he does, and he must pay what he pays.

I decided to drive all that night, but when darkness came on it brought a blizzard that rose, full blown, right in my face. The thundering wind from the northwest lashed me with piercing arrows of snow until I could not tell where I was, and the dogs would face it no more. At last I made camp, turning the sled on its side and making a hole in a snowbank nearby for myself. I did not unharness the dogs but picketed them in their traces some way from the sled. Then I crawled into my robes, intending only to doze until the wind dropped. But I was more weary than I knew and I was soon so sound asleep that even the roar of the blizzard faded out of my mind.

All unknowing because of the storm, I had made my camp less than a mile upwind from another camp of the people. The surviving dogs of that camp were roaming about, a famished

64

and half-mad pack. As I slept, they winded my load of seal meat.

I heard nothing until the damage was done. Only when the marauders attacked my own dogs did I awake. In my anguish and rage I flung myself on those beasts with only my small knife as a weapon. The dogs turned upon me and, though I killed some, the smell of fresh blood drove the remainder to fury. They tore the deerskin clothes from my body, savaged one arm until I dropped the knife, and slashed my face until the flesh hung down over my chin. They would have killed me if the fight with my own dogs had not drawn them off, leaving me to crawl back to my hole in the snow.

The morning broke clear and calm, as if no wind had ever blown. I could only manage to stand and shuffle about, and I went to the sled, but the meat was all gone. Nothing was left but some shreds of skin and some bones. Two of my own dogs had been killed and the remainder were hurt.

There was nothing to do. I began to look for my rifle in the debris near the sled but before I could find it I heard dogs howl in the distance and when I looked to the west I saw the domes of three snowhouses below the bank of the river. I turned and shuffled toward them.

I remember but little of the days I spent in that camp because my wounds festered and I was often unconscious. Those people were kind and they fed me with food they could ill spare—though in truth it was partly my food, for it was the meat of the dogs who had eaten the seals. Before I could travel again, the sun had begun to grow warm and to rise higher up in the sky. Yet the warmth of the oncoming spring could not thaw the chill in my heart.

I made a light sled for the two dogs I had left and prepared to depart. Those in the camps tried to keep me with them for they said that by now there would be no life in my snowhouse that stood by the lake of the deer crossing, and I would only die there myself if I returned before spring brought the deer herds back to the land.

But I did not fear death anymore so I set out. Weak as we were, the dogs and I made the journey home in ten days. We had luck, for we found a deer cache that must have been lost by some hunter in the spring of the previous year. It was a foul mess of hair, bones, and long-rotted meat, but it gave us the strength to continue.

When we came in sight of the lake my belly grew sick and my legs weakened and I could hardly go on; yet when I neared the camp life pounded back through my veins . . . for the snowhouse still stood and snow had recently been dug away from the door!

I shouted until my lungs crackled in the bright, cold air and when none answered, I began to run. I reached the passage and scrambled inside.

Abruptly Anoteelik ceased speaking. He sat staring out over the lightening waters of the Bay . . . out toward the islands that were still no more than grey wraiths on the shifting horizon. Tears were running down his disfigured cheeks . . . running like rain. Then with his head bowed forward over his knees, very quietly he finished the tale.

I was greeted by Aputna, my mother-by-right, and by Itkut. The old woman had shrunk to a miserable rag of a thing that should have been gone long ago; but Itkut seemed strong and his body was firm to the touch when I took him up in my arms.

I looked over his shoulder, and asked, "Where is Kala?" though I knew what the answer would be.

Aputna's reply was no louder than the whisper of wind on the hills.

"What was done . . . was done as she wished. As for me, I will not go away from this place, yet I only did what she said must be done . . . and Itkut still lives . . . Where is Kala? Hold your son close in your arms, love him well for the blood in his veins. Hold him close, oh, my son, for you hold your wife too in your arms."

When the ice left the river, Itkut and I came back down to the coast. Kala was of the Sea People, so I took her bones out to that island which lies far from the shore. While I live I shall take gifts to her spirit each spring . . . in the spring, when the birds make love on the slopes and the does come back to our land, their bellies heavy with fawn.

Memories of a !Kung Girlhood

A woman of the hunter-gatherers recalls her childhood; the differences in her way of life fade in the face of basic human similarities.

Mother asks father to discipline daughter

Marjorie Shostak

Marjorie Shostak is a writer and photographer who first became interested in the !Kung while working with her husband, an anthropologist. For two years, from 1969 to 1971, she lived and worked among the !Kung San of Botswana as a research assistant to Irven DeVore, an anthropologist at Harvard University. After developing fluency in the !Kung language, Shostak began to tape interviews with !Kung women. In 1975 she returned to Botswana for six months to complete the life histories of several women and to correct ambiguous translations. At the same time she collaborated with four other researchers in a study of hormone level and mood fluctuations in relation to menstrual cycles.

I remember when my mother was pregnant with Kumsa. I was still small (about four years old) and I asked, "Mommy, that baby inside you . . . when that baby is born, will it come out from your bellybutton?" She said, "No, it won't come out from there. When you give birth, a baby comes from here." And she pointed to her genitals.

When she gave birth to Kumsa, I wanted the milk she had in her breasts, and when she nursed him, my eyes watched as the milk spilled out. I cried all night . . . cried and cried.

Once when my mother was with him and they were lying down asleep, I took him away from her and put him down on the other side of the hut. Then I lay down beside her. While she slept I squeezed some milk and started to nurse, and nursed and nursed and nursed. Maybe she thought it was him. When she woke and saw me she cried, "Where . . . tell me . . . what did you do with Kumsa? Where is he?"

I told her he was lying down inside the hut. She grabbed me and pushed me hard away from her. I lay there and cried. She took Kumsa, put him down beside her, and insulted me by cursing my genitals.

"Are you crazy? Nisa-Big Genitals, what's the matter with you? What craziness grabbed you that you took a baby, dropped him somewhere else, and then lay down beside me and nursed? I thought it was Kumsa."

When my father came home, she told him, "Do you see what kind of mind your daughter has? Hit her! She almost killed Kumsa. This little baby, this little thing here, she took from my side and dropped him somewhere else.

I was lying here holding him and fell asleep. She came and took him away, left him by himself, then lay down where he had been and nursed. Now, hit her!"

I said, "You're lying! Me . . . daddy, I didn't nurse. Really I didn't. I don't even want her milk anymore."

He said, "If I ever hear of this again, I'll hit you. Now, don't ever do that again!"

I said, "Yes, he's my little brother, isn't he? My little baby brother and I *love* him. I won't do that again. He can nurse all by himself. Daddy, even if you're not here, I won't try to steal Mommy's breasts. They belong to my brother."

We lived and lived, and as I kept growing, I started to carry Kumsa around on my shoulders. My heart was happy and I started to love him. I carried him everywhere. I would play with him for a while, and whenever he started to cry, I'd take him over to mother to nurse. Then I'd take him back with me and we'd play together again.

That was when Kumsa was still little. But once he was older and started to talk and then to run around, that's when we were mean to each other all

From *Human Nature*, June 1978, pp. 80, 82-88. From KALAHARI HUNTER-GATHERERS: STUDIES OF THE !KUNG SAN AND THEIR NEIGHBORS, by Marjorie Shostak.

(handwritten margin notes: "children play", "Age grade", "GRANDMA lives ALONE Collects for herself")

the time. Sometimes we hit each other. Other times I grabbed him and bit him and said, "Ooooh . . . what is this thing that has such a horrible face and no brains and is so mean? Why is it so mean to me when I'm not doing anything to it?" Then he said, "I'm going to *hit* you!" And I said, "You're just a *baby!* I, *I* am the one who's going to hit *you.* Why are you so miserable to me?" I insulted him and he insulted me and then I insulted him back. We just stayed together and played like that.

Once, when our father came back carrying meat, we both called out, "Ho, ho, Daddy! Ho, ho, Daddy!" But when I heard him say, "Daddy, Daddy," I yelled, "Why are you greeting my father? He's *my* father, isn't he? You can only say, 'Oh, hello Father.' " But he called out, "Ho, ho . . . Daddy!" I said, "Be quiet! Only *I* will greet him. Is he your father? I'm going to hit you!"

We fought and argued until Mother finally stopped us. Then we just sat around while she cooked the meat.

This was also when I used to take food. It happened over all kinds of food—sweet *nin* berries or *klaru* bulbs . . . other times it was mongongo nuts. Sometimes before my mother left to go gathering, she'd leave food inside a leather pouch and hang it high on one of the branches inside the hut.

But as soon as she was gone, I'd take some of whatever food was left in the bag. If it was *klaru,* I'd find the biggest bulbs and take them. I'd hang the bag back on the branch and go sit somewhere to eat them.

One time I sat down in the shade of a tree while my parents gathered food nearby. As soon as they had moved away from me, I climbed the tree where they had left a pouch hanging, full of *klaru,* and took the bulbs.

I had my own little pouch, the one my father had made me, and I took the bulbs and put them in the pouch. Then I climbed down and sat waiting for my parents to return.

They came back. "Nisa, you ate the *klaru!*" What do you have to say for yourself?" I said, "Uhn uh, I didn't eat them."

I started to cry. Mother hit me and yelled, "Don't take things. You can't seem to understand! I tell you but you

don't listen. Don't your ears hear when I talk to you?"

I said, "Uhn uh. Mommy's been making me feel bad for too long now. She keeps saying I steal things and hits me so that my skin hurts. I'm going to stay with Grandma!"

But when I went to my grandmother, she said, "No, I can't take care of you now. If I try you will be hungry. I am old and just go gathering one day at a time. In the morning I just rest. We

would sit together and hunger would kill you. Now go back and sit beside your mother and father."

I said, "No, Daddy will hit me. Mommy will hit me. I want to stay with you."

So I stayed with her. Then one day she said, "I'm going to bring you back to your mother and father." She took me to them, saying, "Today I'm giving Nisa back to you. But isn't there someone here who will take good care of

---

About the !Kung

Nisa is a 50-year-old !Kung woman, one of an estimated 13,000 !Kung San living on the northern fringe of the Kalahari Desert in southern Africa. Much of her life—as daughter, sister, wife, mother, and lover—has been spent in the semi-nomadic pursuit of food and water in the arid savanna.

Like many !Kung, Nisa is a practiced storyteller. The !Kung have no written language with which to record their experiences, and people sit around their fires for hours recounting recent events and those long past. Voices rise and fall, hands move in dramatic gestures, and bird and animal sounds are imitated as stories are told and retold, usually with much exaggeration.

I collected stories of Nisa's life as part of my anthropological effort to record the lives of !Kung women in their own words. Nisa enjoyed working with the machine that "grabs your voice" and the interviews with her produced 25 hours of tape and 425 pages of transcription. The excerpts included here are faithful to her narrative except where awkward or discontinuous passages have been modified or deleted, and where long passages have been shortened.

Although most of Nisa's memories are typical of !Kung life, her early memories, like those of most people, are probably idiosyncratic mixtures of fact and fantasy. Her memories of being hit for taking food are probably not accurate. The !Kung tend to be lenient and indulgent with their children, and researchers have rarely

observed any physical punishment or the withholding of food.

Strong feelings of sibling rivalry, like those that Nisa describes, are common. !Kung women wean their children as soon as they find they are pregnant again because they believe the milk belongs to the fetus. Children are not usually weaned until they are three or four years old, which tends to make them resent their younger siblings. Nisa's complaints about being given too little food probably stem from her jealousy of her little brother.

Despite the lack of privacy, !Kung parents are generally discreet in their sexual activity. As children become aware of it, they engage each other in sexual play. Parents say they do not approve of this play but do little to stop it.

Many !Kung girls first marry in their early teens, but these relationships are not consummated until the girls begin menstruating around the age of 16. Early marriages are relatively unstable. Nisa was betrothed twice before marrying Tashay.

The exclamation point at the beginning of !Kung represents one of the many click sounds in the !Kung language. Clicks are made by the tongue breaking air pockets in different parts of the mouth; but the notation for clicks has been eliminated from the translation in all cases except for the name of the !Kung people. Nisa, for instance, should be written as N≠isa.

Marjorie Shostak

3. ORGANIZATION OF SOCIETY AND CULTURE

her? You don't just hit a child like this one. She likes food and likes to eat. All of you are lazy and you've just left her so she hasn't grown well. You've killed this child with hunger. Look at her now, how small she still is."

Oh, but my heart was happy! Grandmother was scolding Mother! I had so much happiness in my heart that I laughed and laughed. But then, when Grandmother went home and left me there, I cried and cried.

My father started to yell at me. He didn't hit me. His anger usually came out only from his mouth. "You're so senseless! Don't you realize that after you left, everything felt less important? We wanted you to be with us. Yes, even your mother wanted you and missed you. Today, everything will be all right when you stay with us. Your mother will take you where she goes; the two of you will do things together and go gathering together."

Then when my father dug *klaru* bulbs, I ate them, and when he dug *chon* bulbs, I ate them. I ate everything they gave me, and I wasn't yelled at any more.

Mother and I often went to the bush together. The two of us would walk until we arrived at a place where she collected food. She'd set me down in the shade of a tree and dig roots or gather nuts nearby.

Once I left the tree and went to play in the shade of another tree. I saw a tiny steenbok, one that had just been born, hidden in the grass and among the leaves. It was lying there, its little eye just looking out at me.

I thought, "What should I do?" I shouted, *"Mommy!"* I just stood there and it just lay there looking at me.

Suddenly I knew what to do—I ran at it, trying to grab it. But it jumped up and ran away and I started to chase it. It was running and I was running and it was crying as it ran. Finally, I got very close and put my foot in its way, and it fell down. I grabbed its legs and started to carry it back. It was crying, "Ehn . . . ehn . . . ehn. . . ."

Its mother had been close by and when she heard it call, she came running. As soon as I saw her, I started to run again. I wouldn't give it back to its mother!

I called out, "Mommy! Come! Help me with this steenbok! Mommy! The steenbok's mother is coming for me! Run! Come! Take this steenbok from me."

But soon the mother steenbok was no longer following, so I took the baby, held its feet together, and banged it hard against the sand until I killed it. It was no longer crying; it was dead. I felt wonderfully happy. My mother came running and I gave it to her to carry.

The two of us spent the rest of the day walking in the bush. While my mother was gathering, I sat in the shade of a tree, waiting and playing with the dead steenbok. I picked it up. I tried to make it sit up, to open its eyes. I looked at them. After mother had dug enough *sha* roots, we left and returned home.

My father had been out hunting that day and had shot a large steenbok with his arrows. He had skinned it and brought it back hanging on a branch.

"Ho, ho. Daddy killed a steenbok!" I said. "Mommy! Daddy! I'm not going to let anyone have any of *my* steenbok. Now *don't* give it to anyone else. After you cook it, just my little brother and I will eat it, just the two of us."

I remember another time when we were traveling from one place to another and the sun was burning. It was the hot, dry season and there was no water anywhere. The sun was burning! Kumsa had already been born and I was still small.

After we had been walking a long time, my older brother Dau spotted a beehive. We stopped while he and my father chopped open the tree. All of us helped take out the honey. I filled my own little container until it was completely full.

We stayed there, eating the honey, and I found myself getting very thirsty, Then we left and continued to walk, I carrying my honey and my digging stick. Soon the heat began killing us and we were all dying of thirst. I started to cry because I wanted water so badly.

After a while, we stopped and sat down in the shade of a baobab tree. There was still no water anywhere. We just sat in the shade like that.

Finally my father said, "Dau, the rest of the family will stay here under this baobab. But you, take the water

containers and get us some water. There's a well not too far away."

Dau collected the empty ostrich eggshell containers and the large clay pot and left. I lay there, already dead from thirst and thought, "If I stay with Mommy and Daddy, I'll surely die of thirst. Why don't I follow my big brother and go drink water with him?"

With that I jumped up and ran after him, crying out, calling to him, following his tracks. But he didn't hear me. I kept running . . . crying and calling out.

Finally, he heard something and turned to see. There I was. "Oh, no!" he said. "Nisa's followed me. What can I do with her now that she's here?" He just stood there and waited for me to catch up. He picked me up and carried me high up on his shoulder, and along we went. He really liked me!

The two of us went on together. We walked and walked and walked and walked. Finally, we reached the well. I ran to the water and drank, and soon my heart was happy again. We filled the water containers, put them in a twine mesh sack, and my brother carried it on his back. Then he took me and put me on his shoulder again.

We walked the long way back until we arrived at the baobab where our parents were sitting. They drank the water. Then they said, "How well our children have done, bringing us this water!" We are alive once again!"

We just stayed in the shade of the baobab. Later we left and traveled to another water hole where we settled for a while. My heart was happy . . . eating honey and just living.

We lived there, and after some time passed, we saw the first rain clouds. One came near but just hung in the sky. More rain clouds came over and they too just stood there. Then the rain started to spill itself and it came pouring down.

The rainy season had finally come. The sun rose and set, and the rain spilled itself and fell and kept falling. It fell without ceasing. Soon the water pans were full. And my heart! My heart within me was happy and we lived and ate meat and mongongo nuts. There was more meat and it was all delicious.

And there were caterpillars to eat, those little things that crawl along going

68

"mmm . . . mmmmm . . . mmmmm. . . ." People dug roots and collected nuts and berries and brought home more and more food. There was plenty to eat, and people kept bringing meat back on sticks and hanging it in the trees.

My heart was bursting. I ate lots of food and my tail was wagging, always wagging about like a little dog. I'd laugh with my little tail, laugh with a little donkey's laugh, a tiny thing that is. I'd throw my tail one way and the other, shouting, "Today I'm going to eat caterpillars . . . *cat-er-pillars!*" Some people gave me meat broth to drink, and others prepared the skins of caterpillars and roasted them for me to eat, and I ate and ate and ate. Then I went to sleep.

But that night, after everyone was dead asleep, I peed right in my sleeping place. In the morning, when everyone got up, I just lay there. The sun rose and had set itself high in the sky, and I was still lying there. I was afraid of people shaming me. Mother said, "Why is Nisa acting like this and refusing to leave her blankets when the sun is sitting up in the sky? Oh . . . she has probably wet herself!"

When I did get up, my heart felt miserable. I thought, "I've peed on myself and now everyone's going to laugh at me." I asked one of my friends, "How come, after I ate all those caterpillars, when I went to sleep I peed in my bed?" Then I thought, "Tonight, when this day is over, I'm going to lie down separate from the others. If I pee in my bed again, won't mother and father hit me?"

When a child sleeps beside her mother, in front, and her father sleeps behind and makes love to her mother, the child watches. Her parents don't fear her, a small child, because even if the child sees, even if she hears, she is unaware of what it is her parents are doing. She is still young and without sense. Perhaps this is the way the child learns. The child is still senseless, without intelligence, and just watches.

If the child is a little boy, when he plays with other children, he plays sex with them and teaches it to himself, just like a baby rooster teaches itself. The little girls also learn it by themselves.

Little boys are the first ones to know its sweetness. Yes, a young girl, while she is still a child, her thoughts don't know it. A boy has a penis, and maybe, while he is still inside his mother's belly, he already knows about sex.

When you are a child you play at nothing things. You build little huts and play. Then you come back to the village and continue to play. If people bother you, you get up and play somewhere else.

Once we left a pool of rain water where we had been playing and went to the little huts we had made. We stayed there and played at being hunters. We went out tracking animals, and when we saw one, we struck it with our make-believe arrows. We took some leaves and hung them over a stick and pretended it was meat. Then we carried it back to our village. When we got back, we stayed there and ate the meat and then the meat was gone. We went out again, found another animal, and killed it.

Sometimes the boys asked if we wanted to play a game with our genitals and the girls said no. We said we didn't want to play that game, but would like to play other games. The boys told us that playing sex was what playing was all about. That's the way we grew up.

When adults talked to me I listened. Once they told me that when a young woman grows up, she takes a husband. When they first talked to me about it, I said: "What? What kind of thing am I that I should take a husband? Me, when I grow up, I won't marry. I'll just lie by myself. If I married a man, what would I think I would be doing it for?"

My father said: "Nisa, I am old. I am your father and I am old; your mother's old, too. When you get married, you will gather food and give it to your husband to eat. He also will do things for you and give you things you can wear. But if you refuse to take a husband, who will give you food to eat? Who will give you things to have? Who will give you things to wear?"

I said to my father and mother, "No. There's no question in my mind—I refuse a husband. I won't take one. Why should I? As I am now, I am still a child and won't marry."

Then I said to Mother, "Why don't you marry the man you want for me and sit him down beside Father? Then you'll have two husbands."

Mother said: "Stop talking nonsense. I'm not going to marry him; you'll marry him. A husband is what I want to give you. Yet you say I should marry him. Why are playing with me with this talk?"

We just continued to live after that, kept on living and more time passed. One time we went to the village where Old Kantla and his son Tashay were living. My friend Nhuka and I had gone to the water well to get water, and Tashay and his family were there, having just come back from the bush. When Tashay saw me, he decided he wanted to marry me. He called Nhuka over and said, "Nhuka, that young woman, that beautiful young woman . . . what is her name?"

Nhuka told him my name was Nisa, and he said, "That young woman . . . I'm going to tell Mother and Father about her. I'm going to ask them if I can marry her."

The next evening there was a dance at our village, and Tashay and his parents came. We sang and danced into the night. Later his father said, "We have come here, and now that the dancing is finished, I want to speak to you. Give me your child, the child you gave birth to. Give her to me, and I will give her to my son. Yesterday, while we were at the well, he saw your child. When he returned he told me in the name of what he felt that I should come and ask for her today so I could give her to him."

My mother said, "Yes . . . but I didn't give birth to a woman, I bore a child. She doesn't think about marriage, she just doesn't think about the inside of her marriage hut."

Then my father said, "Yes, I also conceived that child, and it is true: She just doesn't think about marriage. When she marries a man, she leaves him and marries another man and leaves him and gets up and marries another man and leaves him. She refuses men completely. There are two men whom she has already refused. So when I look at Nisa today, I say she is not a woman."

Then Tashay's father said, "Yes, I have listened to what you have said.

69

That, of course, is the way of a child; it is a child's custom to do that. She gets married many times until one day she likes one man. Then they stay together. That is a child's way." *She does not discuss marry*

They talked about the marriage and agreed to it. In the morning Tashay's parents went back to their camp, and we went to sleep. When the morning was late in the sky, his relatives came back. They stayed around and his parents told my aunt and my mother that they should all start building the marriage hut. They began building it together, and everyone was talking and talking. There were a lot of people there. Then all the young men went and brought Tashay to the hut. They stayed around together near the fire. I was at Mother's hut. They told two of my friends to get me. But I said to myself, "Ooooh . . . I'll just run away."

When they came, they couldn't find me. I was already out in the bush, and I just sat there by the base of a tree. Soon I heard Nhuka call out, "Nisa . . . Nisa . . . my friend . . . there are things there that will bite and kill you. Now leave there and come back here."

They came and brought me back. Then they laid me down inside the hut. I cried and cried, and people told me: "A man is not something that kills you; he is someone who marries you, and becomes like your father or your older brother. He kills animals and gives you things to eat. Even tomorrow he would do that. But because you are crying, when he kills an animal, he will eat it himself and won't give you any. Beads, too. He will get some beads, but he won't give them to you. Why are you afraid of your husband and why are you crying?"

I listened and was quiet. Later Tashay lay down by the mouth of the hut, near the fire, and I was inside. He came in only after he thought I was asleep. Then he lay down and slept. I woke while it was still dark and thought,

"How am I going to jump over him? How can I get out and go to Mother's hut?" Then I thought, "This person has married me . . . yes." And, I just lay there. Soon the rain came and beat down and it fell until dawn broke.

In the morning, he got up first and sat by the fire. I was frightened. I was so afraid of him, I just lay there and waited for him to go away before I got up.

We lived together a long time and began to learn to like one another before he slept with me. The first time I didn't refuse. I agreed just a little and he lay with me. But the next morning my insides hurt. I took some leaves and wound them around my waist, but it continued to hurt. Later that day I went with the women to gather mongongo nuts. The whole time I thought "Ooooh . . . what has he done to my insides that they feel this way."

That evening we lay down again. But this time I took a leather strap, held my skin apron tightly against me, tied up my genitals with it, and then tied the strap to the hut's frame. I didn't want him to take me again. The two of us lay there and after a while he started to touch me. When he reached my stomach, he felt the leather strap. He felt around to see what it was. He said, "What is this woman doing? Yesterday she lay with me so nicely when I came to her. Why has she tied up her genitals this way?

He sat me up and said, "Nisa . . . Nisa . . . what happened? Why are you doing this?" I didn't answer him.

"What are you so afraid of that you tied your genitals?"

I said, "I'm not afraid of anything."

He said, "No, now tell me what you are afraid of. In the name of what you did, I am asking you."

I said, "I refuse because yesterday when you touched me my insides hurt."

He said, "Do you see me as someone who kills people? Am I going to eat you? I am not going to kill you. I have

married you and I want to make love to you. Have you seen any man who has married a woman and who just lives with her and doesn't have sex with her?"

I said, "No, I still refuse it! I refuse sex. Yesterday my insides hurt, that's why."

He said, "Mmm. Today you will lie there by yourself. But tomorrow I will take you."

The next day I said to him, "Today I'm going to lie here, and if you take me by force, you will have me. You will have me because today I'm just going to lie here. You are obviously looking for some 'food,' but I don't know if the food I have is food at all, because even if you have some, you won't be full."

I just lay there and he did his work.

We lived and lived, and soon I started to like him. After that I was a grown person and said to myself, "Yes, without doubt, a man sleeps with you. I thought maybe he didn't."

We lived on, and then I loved him and he loved me, and I kept on loving him. When he wanted me I didn't refuse and he just slept with me. I thought, "Why have I been so concerned about my genitals? They are, after all, not so important. So why was I refusing them?"

I thought that and gave myself to him and gave and gave. We lay with one another, and my breasts had grown very large. I had become a woman.

FOR FURTHER INFORMATION:

Lee, Richard, B., and Irven DeVore, eds. *Kalahari Hunter-Gatherers: Studies of the !Kung San and Their Neighbors.* Harvard University Press, 1976.

Lee, Richard B., and Irven DeVore, eds. *Man the Hunter.* Aldine, 1968.

Marshall, Lorna. *The !Kung of Nyae Nyae.* Harvard University Press, 1976.

Shostak, Marjorie. "Life before Horticulture: An African Gathering and Hunting Society." *Horticulture,* Vol. 55, No. 2, 1977.

2 families build of marriage hut together

Man marries you & becomes like your father & brother

TRADITIONAL MARRIAGE LOVE AFTER TIME

BREASTS GROW LARGE PREGNANT → WOMAN

Murders in Eden

Marvin Harris

Marvin Harris has taught at Columbia University since 1953 and from 1963 to 1966 was Chairman of the Department of Anthropology. In addition to fieldwork in Brazil, Mozambique, and Ecuador on the subjects of cross-cultural aspects of race and ethnic relations, the effects of colonialism, and problems of underdevelopment seen in ecological perspective, Harris has pioneered in the use of videotape techniques in the study of family life in this country.

The accepted explanation for the transition from band life to farming villages used to go like this: Hunter-collectors had to spend all their time getting enough to eat. They could not produce a "surplus above subsistence," and so they lived on the edge of extinction in chronic sickness and hunger. Therefore, it was natural for them to want to settle down and live in permanent villages, but the idea of planting seeds never occurred to them. One day an unknown genius decided to drop some seeds in a hole, and soon planting was being done on a regular basis. People no longer had to move about constantly in search of game, and the new leisure gave them time to think. This led to further and more rapid advances in technology and thus more food—a "surplus above subsistence"—which eventually made it possible for some people to turn away from farming and become artisans, priests, and rulers.

The first flaw in this theory is the assumption that life was exceptionally difficult for our stone age ancestors. Archaeological evidence from the upper paleolithic period—about 30,000 B.C. to 10,000 B.C.—makes it perfectly clear that hunters who lived during those times enjoyed relatively high standards of comfort and security. They were no bumbling amateurs. They had achieved total control over the process of fracturing, chipping, and shaping crystalline rocks, which formed the basis of their technology, and they have aptly been called the "master stoneworkers of all times." Their remarkably thin, finely chipped "laurel leaf" knives, eleven inches long but only four-tenths of an inch thick, cannot be duplicated by modern industrial techniques. With delicate stone awls and incising tools called burins, they created intricately barbed bone and antler harpoon points, well-shaped antler throwing boards for spears, and fine bone needles presumably used to fashion animal-skin clothing. The items made of wood, fibers, and skins have perished, but these too must have been distinguished by high craftsmanship.

Contrary to popular ideas, "cave men" knew how to make artificial shelters, and their use of caves and rock overhangs depended on regional possibilities and seasonal needs. In southern Russia archaeologists have found traces of a hunter's animal-skin dwelling set in a shallow pit forty feet long and twelve feet wide. In Czechoslovakia winter dwellings with round floor plans twenty feet in diameter were already in use more than 20,000 years ago. With rich furs for rugs and beds, as well as plenty of dried animal dung or fat-laden bones for the hearth, such dwellings can provide a quality of shelter superior in many respects to contemporary inner-city apartments.

As for living on the edge of starvation, such a picture is hard to reconcile with the enormous quantities of animal bones accumulated at various paleolithic kill sites. Vast herds of mammoth, horses, deer, reindeer, and bison roamed across Europe and Asia. The bones of over a thousand mammoth, excavated from one site in Czechoslovakia, and the remains of 10,000 wild horses that were stampeded at various intervals over a high cliff near Solutré, France, testify to the ability of paleolithic peoples to exploit these herds systematically and efficiently. Moreover, the skeletal remains of the hunters themselves bear witness to the fact that they were unusually well-nourished.

The notion that paleolithic populations worked round the clock in order to feed themselves now also appears ludicrous. As collectors of food plants they were certainly no less effective than chimpanzees. Field studies have shown that in their natural habitat the great apes spend as much time grooming, playing, and napping as they do foraging and eating. And as hunters our upper paleolithic ancestors must have been at least as proficient as lions—animals which alternate bursts of intense activity with long periods of rest and relaxation. Studies of how present-day hunters and collectors allocate their time have shed more light on this issue. Richard Lee of the University of Toronto kept a record of how much time the modern Bushman hunter-collectors spend in the quest for food. Despite their habitat—the edge of the Kalahari, a desert region whose lushness is hardly comparable to that of France during the upper paleolithic period—less than three hours per day per adult is all that is needed for the Bushmen to obtain a diet rich in proteins and other essential nutrients.

The Machiguenga, simple horti-culturalists of the Peruvian Amazon studied by Allen and Orna Johnson, spend a little more than three hours per day per adult in food production and get less animal protein for this effort than do the Bushmen. In the rice-growing regions of eastern Java, modern peasants have been found to spend about forty-four hours per week in productive farm work—something no self-respecting Bushman would ever dream of doing—and Javanese peasants seldom eat animal proteins. American farmers, for whom fifty-and-sixty-hour work weeks are commonplace, eat well by Bushman standards but certainly cannot be said to have as much leisure.

I do not wish to minimize the difficulties inherent in comparisons of this sort. Obviously the work associated with a particular food-production system is not limited to time spent in obtaining the raw product. It also takes time to process the plants and animals into forms suitable for consumption, and it takes still more time to manufacture and maintain such instruments of production as spears, nets, digging sticks, baskets, and plows. According to the Johnsons' estimates, the Machiguenga devote about three additional hours per day to food preparation and the manufacture of essential items such as clothing, tools, and shelter. In his observations of the Bushmen, Lee found that in one day a woman could gather enough food to feed her family for three days and that she spent the rest of her time resting, entertaining visitors, doing embroidery, or visiting other camps. "For each day at home, kitchen routines, such as cooking, nut cracking, collecting firewood, and fetching water, occupy one to three hours of her time."

The evidence I have cited above leads to one conclusion: The development of farming resulted in an increased work load per capita. There is a good reason for this. Agriculture is a system of food production that can absorb much more labor per unit of land than can hunting and collecting. Hunter-collectors are essentially dependent on the natural rate of animal and plant reproduction; they can do very little to raise output per unit of land (although they can easily decrease it). With agriculture, on the other hand, people control the rate of plant reproduction. This means that production can be intensified without immediate adverse consequences,

especially if techniques are available for combating soil exhaustion.

The key to how many hours people like the Bushmen put into hunting and collecting is the abundance and accessibility of the animal and plant resources available to them. As long as population density—and thus exploitation of these resources—is kept relatively low, hunter-collectors can enjoy both leisure and high-quality diets. Only if one assumes that people during the stone age were unwilling or unable to limit the density of their populations does the theory of our ancestors' lives as "short, nasty, and brutish" make sense. But that assumption is unwarranted. Hunter-collectors are strongly motivated to limit population, and they have effective means to do so.

Another weakness in the old theory of the transition from hunting and collecting to agriculture is the assumption that human beings naturally want to "settle down." This can scarcely be true given the tenacity with which people like the Bushmen, the aborigines of Australia, and the Eskimo have clung to their old "walkabout" way of life despite the concerted efforts of governments and missionaries to persuade them to live in villages.

Each advantage of permanent village life has a corresponding disadvantage. Do people crave company? Yes, but they also get on each other's nerves. As Thomas Gregor has shown in a study of the Mehinacu Indians of Brazil, the search for personal privacy is a pervasive theme in the daily life of people who live in small villages. The Mehinacu apparently know too much about each other's business for their own good. They can tell from the print of a heel or a buttock where a couple stopped and had sexual relations off the path. Lost arrows give away the owner's prize fishing spot; an ax resting against a tree tells a story of interrupted work. No one leaves or enters the village without being noticed. One must whisper to secure privacy—with walls of thatch there are no closed doors. The village is filled with irritating gossip about men who are impotent or who ejacu-

late too quickly, and about women's behavior during coitus and the size, color and odor of their genitalia.

Is there physical security in numbers? Yes, but there is also security in mobility, in being able to get out of the way of aggressors. Is there an advantage in having a larger cooperative labor pool? Yes, but larger concentrations of people lower the game supply and deplete natural resources.

As for the haphazard discovery of the planting process, hunter-collectors are not so dumb as this sequence in the old theory would suggest. The anatomical details in the paintings of animals found on the walls of caves in France and Spain bear witness to a people whose powers of observation were honed to great accuracy. And our admiration for their intellects has been forced to new heights by Alexander Marshak's discovery that the faint scratches on the surface of 20,000-year-old bone and antler artifacts were put there to keep track of the phases of the moon and other astronomical events. It is unreasonable to suppose that the people who made the great murals on the walls of Lascaux, and who were intelligent enough to make calendrical records, could have been ignorant of the biological significance of tubers and seeds.

Studies of hunter-collectors of the present and recent past reveal that the practice of agriculture is often forgone not for lack of knowledge but as a matter of convenience. Simply by gathering acorns, for example, the Indians of California probably obtained larger and more nutritious harvests than they could have derived from planting maize. And on the Northwest coast the great annual migrations of salmon and candlefish rendered agricultural work a relative waste of time. Hunter-collectors often display all the skills and techniques necessary for practicing agriculture minus the step of deliberate planting. The Shoshoni and Paiute of Nevada and California returned year after year to the same strands of wild grains and tubers, carefully refrained from stripping them bare, and sometimes even weeded and watered them. Many other hunter-collectors use fire to deliberately promote the growth of preferred species and to retard the growth of trees and weeds.

Finally, some of the most important archaeological discoveries of recent years indicate that in the Old World the earliest villages were built 1,000 to 2,000 years before the development of a farming economy, whereas in the New World plants were domesticated long before village life began. Since the early Americans had the idea for thousands of years before they made full use of it, the explanation for the shift away from hunting and collecting must be sought outside their heads. I'll have more to say about these archaeological discoveries later on.

What I've shown so far is that as long as hunter-collectors kept their population low in relation to their prey, they could enjoy an enviable standard of living. But how did they keep their population down? This subject is rapidly emerging as the most important missing link in the attempt to understand the evolution of cultures.

Even in relatively favorable habitats, with abundant herd animals, stone age peoples probably never let their populations rise above one or two persons per square mile. Alfred Kroeber estimated that in the Canadian plains and prairies the bison-hunting Cree and Assiniboin, mounted on horses and equipped with rifles, kept their densities below two persons per square mile. Less favored groups of historic hunters in North America, such as the Labrador Naskapi and the Nunamuit Eskimo, who depended on caribou, maintained densities *below* .3 persons per square mile. In all of France during the late stone age there were probably no more than 20,000 and possibly as few as 1,600 human beings.

"Natural" means of controlling population growth cannot explain the discrepancy between these low densities and the potential fertility of the human female. Healthy populations interested in maximizing their rate of

growth average eight pregnancies brought to term per woman. Child-bearing rates can easily go higher. Among the Hutterites, a sect of thrifty farmers living in western Canada, the average is 10.7 births per woman. In order to maintain the estimated .001 percent annual rate of growth for the old stone age, each woman must have had on the average less than 2.1 children who survived to reproductive age. According to the conventional theory such a low rate of growth was achieved, despite high fertility, by disease. Yet the view that our stone age ancestors led disease-ridden lives is difficult to sustain.

No doubt there were diseases. But as a mortality factor they must have been considerably less significant during the stone age than they are today. The death of infants and adults from bacterial and viral infections—dysenteries, measels, tuberculosis, whooping cough, colds, scarlet fever—is strongly influenced by diet and general body vigor, so stone age hunter-collectors probably had high recovery rates from these infections. And most of the great lethal epidemic diseases—smallpox, typhoid fever, flu, bubonic plague, cholera—occur only among populations that have high densities. These are the diseases of state-level societies; they flourish amid poverty and crowded, unsanitary urban conditions. Even such scourges as malaria and yellow fever were probably less significant among the hunter-collectors of the old stone age. As hunters they would have preferred dry, open habitats to the wetlands where these diseases flourish. Malaria probably achieved its full impact only after agricultural clearings in humid forests had created better breeding conditions for mosquitoes.

What is actually known about the physical health of paleolithic populations? Skeletal remains provide important clues. Using such indices as average height and the number of teeth missing at time of death, J. Lawrence Angel has developed a profile of changing health standards during the last 30,000 years. Angel found

that at the beginning of this period adult males averaged 177 centimeters (5' 11") and adult females about 165 centimeters (5' 6"). Twenty thousand years later the males grew no taller than the females formerly grew—165 centimeters—whereas the females averaged no more than 153 centimeters (5' 0"). Only in very recent times have populations once again attained statures characteristic of the old stone age peoples. American males, for example, averaged 175 centimeters (5' 9") in 1960. Tooth loss shows a similar trend. In 30,000 B.C. adults died with an average of 2.2 teeth missing; in 6500 B.C., with 3.5 missing; during Roman times, with 6.6 missing. Although genetic factors may also enter into these changes, stature and the condition of teeth and gums are known to be strongly influenced by protein intake, which in turn is predictive of general well-being. Angel concludes that there was "a real depression of health" following the "high point" of the upper paleolithic period.

Angel has also attempted to estimate the average age of death for the upper paleolithic, which he places at 28.7 years for females and 33.3 years for males. Since Angel's paleolithic sample consists of skeletons found all over Europe and Africa, his longevity estimates are not necessarily representative of any actual band of hunters. If the vital statistics of contemporary hunter-collector bands can be taken as representative of paleolithic bands, Angel's calculations err on the low side. Studies of 165 !Kung Bushman women by Nancy Howell show that life expectancy at birth is 32.5 years, which compares favorably with the figures for many modern developing nations in Africa and Asia. To put these data in proper perspective, according to the Metropolitan Life Insurance Company the life expectancy at birth for non-white males in the United States in 1900 was also 32.5 years. Thus, as paleodemographer Don Dumond has suggested, there are hints that "mortality was effectively no higher under conditions of hunting than under those of a more sedentary life, including agriculture." The increase in disease accompanying sedentary living "may mean that the mortality rates of hunters were more often significantly lower" than those of agricultural peoples.

Although a life span of 32.5 years may seem very short, the reproductive potential even of women who live only to Angel's 28.7 years of age is quite high. If a stone age woman had her first pregnancy when she was sixteen years old, and a live baby every two and a half years thereafter, she could easily have had over five live births by the time she was twenty-nine. This means that approximately three-fifths of stone age children could not have lived to reproductive age if the estimated rate of less than .001 percent population growth was to be maintained. Using these figures, anthropological demographer Ferki Hassan concludes that even if there was 50 percent infant mortality due to "natural" causes, another 23 to 35 percent of all potential offspring would have to be "removed" to achieve zero growth population.

If anything, these estimates appear to err in exaggerating the number of deaths from "natural" causes. Given the excellent state of health the people studied by Angel seemed to enjoy before they became skeletons, one suspects that many of the deceased died of "unnatural" causes.

Infanticide during the paleolithic period could very well have been as high as 50 percent—a figure that corresponds to estimates made by Joseph Birdsell of the University of California in Los Angeles on the basis of data collected among the aboriginal populations of Australia. And an important factor in the short life span of paleolithic women may very well have been the attempt to induce abortions in order to lengthen the interval between births.

Contemporary hunter-collectors in general lack effective chemical or mechanical means of preventing pregnancy—romantic folklore about herbal contraceptives notwithstanding. They do, however, possess a large repertory of chemical and me-

chanical means for inducing abortion. Numerous plant and animal poisons that cause generalized physical traumas or that act directly on the uterus are used throughout the world to end unwanted pregnancies. Many mechanical techniques for inducing abortion are also employed, such as tying tight bands around the stomach, vigorous massages, subjection to extremes of cold and heat, blows to the abdomen, and hopping up and down on a plank placed across a woman's belly "until blood spurts out of the vagina." Both the mechanical and chemical approaches effectively terminate pregnancies, but they are also likely to terminate the life of the pregnant woman. I suspect that only a group under severe economic and demographic stress would resort to abortion as its principal method of population regulation.

Hunter-collectors under stress are much more likely to turn to infanticide and geronticide (the killing of old people). Geronticide is effective only for short-run emergency reductions in group size. It cannot lower long-term trends of population growth. In the case of both geronticide and infanticide, outright conscious killing is probably the exception. Among the Eskimo, old people too weak to contribute to their own subsistence may "commit suicide" by remaining behind when the group moves, although children actively contribute to their parents' demise by accepting the cultural expectation that old people ought not to become a burden when food is scarce. In Australia, among the Murngin of Arnhem Land, old people are helped along toward their fate by being treated as if they were already dead when they become sick; the group begins to perform its last rites, and the old person responds by getting sicker. Infanticide runs a complex gamut from outright murder to mere neglect. Infants may be strangled, drowned, bashed against a rock, or exposed to the elements. More commonly, an infant is "killed" by neglect; the mother gives less care than is needed when it gets sick, nurses it less often, refrains from trying to find supplementary foods,

or "accidentally" lets it fall from her arms. Hunter-collector women are strongly motivated to space out the age difference between their children since they must expend a considerable amount of effort merely lugging them about during the day. Richard Lee has calculated that over a four-year period of dependency a Bushman mother will carry her child a total of 4,900 miles on collecting expeditions and campsite moves. No Bushman woman wants to be burdened with two or three infants at a time as she travels that distance.

The best method of population control available to stone age hunter-collectors was to prolong the span of years during which a mother nursed her infant. Recent studies of menstrual cycles carried out by Rose Frisch and Janet McArthur have shed light on the physiological mechanism responsible for lowering the fertility of lactating women. After giving birth, a fertile woman will not resume ovulation until the percentage of her body weight that consists of fat has passed a critical threshold. This threshold (about 20-25 percent) represents the point at which a woman's body has stored enough reserve energy in the form of fat to accommodate the demands of a growing fetus. The average energy cost of a normal pregnancy is 27,000 calories—just about the amount of energy that must be stored before a woman can conceive. A nursing infant drains about 1,000 extra calories from its mother per day, making it difficult for her to accumulate the necessary fatty reserve. As long as the infant is dependent on its mother's milk, there is little likelihood that ovulation will resume. Bushman mothers, by prolonging lactation, appear to be able to delay the possibility of pregnancy for more than four years. The same mechanism appears to be responsible for delaying menarche—the onset of menstruation. The higher the ratio of body fat to body weight, the earlier the age of menarche. In well-nourished modern populations menarche has been pushed forward to about twelve years of age, whereas in populations chronically on the edge of caloric deficits it may take eighteen or more years for a girl to build up the necessary fat reserves.

What I find so intriguing about this discovery is that it links low fertility with diets that are high in proteins and low in carbohydrates. On the one hand, if a woman is to nurse a child successfully for three or four years she must have a high protein intake to sustain her health, body vigor, and the flow of milk. On the other hand, if she consumes too many carbohydrates she will begin to put on weight, which will trigger the resumption of ovulation. A demographic study carried out by J. K. Van Ginneken indicates that nursing women in underdeveloped countries, where the diet consists mostly of starchy grains and root crops, cannot expect to extend the interval between births beyond eighteen months. Yet nursing Bushman women, whose diet is rich in animal and plant proteins and who lack starchy staples, as I have said, manage to keep from getting pregnant four or more years after each

birth. This relationship suggests that during good times hunter-collectors could rely on prolonged lactation as their principal defense against overpopulation. Conversely, a decline in the quality of the food supply would tend to bring about an increase in population. This in turn would mean either that the rate of abortion and infanticide would have to be accelerated or that still more drastic cuts in the protein ration would be needed.

I am not suggesting that the entire defense against overpopulation among our stone age ancestors rested with the lactation method. Among the Bushmen of Botswana the present rate of population growth is .5 percent per annum. This amounts to a doubling every 139 years. Had this rate been sustained for only the last 10,000 years of the old stone age, by 10,000 B.C. the population of the earth would have reached 604,463,-000,000,000,000,000,000.

Suppose the fertile span were from sixteen years of age to forty-two. Without prolonged nursing, a woman might experience as many as twelve

pregnancies. With the lactation method, the number of pregnancies comes down to six. Lowered rates of coitus in older women might further reduce the number to five. Spontaneous abortions and infant mortality caused by disease and accidents might bring the potential reproducers down to four—roughly two more than the number permissible under a system of zero population growth. The "extra" two births could then be controlled through some form of infanticide based on neglect. The optimal method would be to neglect only the girl babies, since the rate of growth in populations that do not practice monogamy is determined almost entirely by the number of females who reach reproductive age.

Our stone age ancestors were thus perfectly capable of maintaining a stationary population, but there was a cost associated with it—the waste of infant lives. This cost lurks in the background of prehistory as an ugly blight in what might otherwise be mistaken for a Garden of Eden.

Largest known culturally intact indigenous group (handwritten annotation)

The Yanomamis:
Portrait of a People in Crisis

Shelly Kellman

It is 1973. The Brazilian government is cutting through the rain forest, the Amazon jungle. The whine of chain saws reverberates through the dense tangle of trees and vines: "the green wall," it has been called. Trees fall 150 feet with a slashing, tearing sound. The animals flee; exotic birds nervously retreat from branch to branch as their nests fall, too, and are crushed. Some species will perish as a result.

And there are people here as well—most of whom have never seen a human being unlike themselves. They emerge into the clearing curious and unafraid, naked and unashamed. They are Yanomami Indians, members of the largest known culturally intact native tribe in the Americas. The highway workers, mostly illiterate peasants recruited from the poorest parts of the country with the promise of good wages for "easy" work, are unprepared for this encounter. They gape and shout in Portuguese: "You people are naked! Are you crazy?"

The tribespeople are not so surprised: ironically, they are friendlier to the light-skinned intruders than they would be to strangers of their own kind. The roadworkers, they think, must be the long-gone "foreigners" who left at the time of Creation. The hero Omam, their legend says, created all people from the foam of the rapids. Sitting on a rock by the river one day, chanting, Omam scooped up handfuls of foam and shaped them into human beings. Those who settled in the surrounding territory became the Yanomami; those who traveled downriver, far away, became the foreigners.

Creation myth (handwritten annotation)

The Yanomami were given the land, the forest, and the animals, and the foreigners other kinds of goods. Someday, the legend said, the foreigners would return, coming up the river in canoes laden with goods for their Yanomami relatives.

And goods these newcomers have in abundance: elaborate cloth coverings for their bodies, knives that gleam unlike any knife ever cut from forest cane, and similarly gleaming cooking pots—much lighter and stronger than the Yanomamis' own clay vessels. Eagerly, the Indians initiate a trade: they offer the workers their harvest of bananas, yams, and manioc. Eventually, they will end up bargaining with their culture and with their very lives.

During the ensuing two years, from 1973 to 1975, hundreds of Yanomamis would die as a result of their friendly curiosity, and the Brazilian government's indifference. The government had known of the Yanomamis' presence in the area, and the locations of their villages, for many years prior to the highway project, and it had seen the devastating effects on many other tribes of sudden, uncontrolled contact with outsiders. Missionaries and anthropologists who had been working in the area since the early 1960s had already submitted five proposals for creating a protected Yanomami reserve or park, as provided by Brazilian law. Yet the government did not prepare the highway workers to meet the indigenous people, nor even screen the workers for health problems. Dysentery, influenza, measles, and the complications of the common cold were fatal to the Yanomami, who had developed no immunities to these ailments. Tuberculosis, malaria, and onchocerciasis ("river blindness," an

African import) also swept through the area.

In one river valley, fifty percent of the people fell victim to the highway plagues, and the survivors inhabited a shattered world. Many tribespeople developed a consuming fascination with the road, becoming nomads who hitchhiked from construction site to construction site, begging or trading their labor for food and goods. The remnants of entire villages left their *malocas* (communal houses) to live in roadside shacks, their fields abandoned, their traditional routines of planting, harvesting, and feasting seemingly forgotten. Gone too were a rich mythology and the once-central healing arts of shamanism. In July 1975 Brazilian anthropologist Alcida Ramos observed despairingly in her field diary that the roadside Indians seemed to be a people in shell shock: "None of them," she wrote, "is willing to admit that he/she knows his language enough to teach us. They play deaf, dumb, uninterested . . . They have no basketry, no hammocks of their own; all of them wear something [western]—from rags to real clothes . . . If they stay around here, and if they survive physically, they'll become the most desperate beggars of the whole country!"

Today, the majority of Yanomamis have escaped the fate Ramos predicted, thanks largely to the efforts of anthropologists like him, and missionaries. These groups, with a little cooperation and sometimes active interference from FUNAI (the Brazilian Indian agency), have carried out large-scale vaccination programs, cared for the sick, attracted native people deeper into the forest (away from the road), and have continuously tried to mediate between the Yanomami and the intrusions of resource "development." It is probably due to the efforts of these intervenors that the tribe remains to this day our hemisphere's largest known culturally intact indigenous group, with 20,000 members inhabiting more than 25 million acres in and around the Parima Mountains on the Brazilian-Venezuelan border.

The tribe's future remains nonetheless uncertain: the Yanomamis are caught in a tug-of-war between the call for human rights and cultural diversity, and the relentless push of industry to dig up, process, reshape, commoditize and monetize every cubic inch of the planet. Moreover, the threat to their land is ultimately a threat to the entire world, and a more immediate one than most people realize. According to Britain's Alan Grainger and other "tree experts," the net loss of just 1-2 percent more of the world's tree cover may render the planet unable to reprocess enough oxygen to support human life. "The fate of the [Brazilian] Indians," writes British journalist Norman Lewis "cannot be separated from the fate of the trees." And the fate of the trees is central to the fate of all humanity.

A WANING WAY OF LIFE

In a very real sense, the Yanomami represent the last chance for survival of Brazilian Indians. Since the Europeans landed in 1500, the native population has been reduced from an estimated 6 million to, at most, 240,000 today. Dozens of tribes have been exterminated. The war against them has taken many forms: officially sanctioned slavery (abolished, in 1755) "pacification" carried out by religious orders (which meant befriending Indians and "helping" them to abandon their culture and get in step with "national" norms); the seizure and destruction of Indian lands; military attacks, bombings, and even the use of napalm.

The Yanomami were spared all of this, until recently, because of their remote location, far away from any major tributary of the Amazon. Even the appearance during the 1950s, of

rubber tree tappers, nut gatherers, and hunters seeking ocelot, jaguar, and tropical birds in Yanomami lands did not cause significant problems. Yet the missionaries who established outposts at Surucucu in 1963 and Catrimani in 1965 (intending not to "pacify" the Indians but to respect and support their culture) had an uneasy sense that these people's time was running out. "There was a certain feeling that we had been called there," says Father Giovanni Saffirio, who lived among the Yanomami from 1968 to 1978, "although nobody quite knew why."

In 1968, the first epidemic—measles—struck the Yanomami on both sides of the Parima Mountains. While the missionaries were able to save all but one stricken Indian on the Brazilian side, the Venezuelan Yanomami had no health assistance: between 8 and 15 percent of their number died. During this period, a young anthropologist named Napoleon Chagnon was living with the Venezuelan groups; with the publication of his book, *The Fierce People,* the tribe's name became, briefly, a household word throughout the U.S. Focusing on the Yanomamis' inter-village raids, battle preparations, and competitive male rituals (e.g., chest pounding and spear dancing), Chagnon gave them a reputation for violence that other observers would dispute. Chagnon's critics don't quarrel with his descriptions of Yanomami customs, but with the impression he created that fighting is a constant, undertaken for enjoyment. Father Saffirio agrees that the Yanomami are well able to defend themselves; however, he considers the warfare which Chagnon observed to be a direct result of the measles epidemic. "Traditionally, the Yanomami believe that when someone dies suddenly and inexplicably, it's because someone from another, unrelated village has cast a spell on the victim," he explains. "The shaman then determines which village was responsible, and the victim's relatives often retaliate with a raid, in which they might kill, at most, three men." Today, says the priest, most of the Indians understand the biological spread of disease.

Father Saffirio recalls only three raids during his ten-year stay. In striking contrast to Chagnon's portrait, he describes his adopted people as warm and affectionate. The Catrimani mission, where Father Saffirio served, had only two or three nonnative people at a time, so the missioners were immersed in the Yanomamis' way of life.

"The most amazing aspect of Yanomami culture is their togetherness," says Saffirio. "They never feel isolated, as we do; one is never alone with a problem. Anything you need, you can find.

"Of course," he chuckles, "everybody knows *everything* you do. If you leave the house to pee, if a husband and wife are going out to the forest to make love—everybody knows it." He recalls a fun-loving animated people: "They always have *so much* to talk about! They will talk for a week about how 'the Bald One' (their nickname for me) fell down, or about something a child or an animal has done."

Each extended Yanomami family of twenty to eighty people lives in a large communal house, and the smaller, "nuclear" families are apportioned outer sections of the house and separate entrances. Built by the men from poles and woven leaves, the Yanomami houses are comfortable and watertight, but must be abandoned and replaced every four or five years when the cockroach population in the walls and ceilings grows to such proportions that not a scrap of food can be stored overnight. Each *maloca* centers on an open area used for fires, ceremonies, and feasts: almost a monthly event, these feasts (featuring spider monkey as the preferred delicacy) may bring 120 people together under one roof for a week.

Men definitely have the upper hand in this culture. Between the ages of fifteen and forty, they spend most of their time hunting; when they're older, they turn to gardening. Women work in the house, garden, and collect fruit in the forest. Marriages are generally monogamous, though a few men, usually shamans or leaders of the group, may have two or three wives. "This increases the leader's power and status, because it increases his potential kinship ties," says Father Saffirio. "Each marriage gives his group ties with another family or village; and he can have more children, which further increases his relationships, and his share in posterity.

"Children get the best of everything, especially food," Saffirio notes, and both children and the elderly get a great deal of physical affection, although adults are not affectionate with one another in public.

Child-bearing is highly regulated to assure that each child will be well taken care of. Women nurse their babies for two and a half to three years, and the nursing, Saffirio observes, "usually" prevents pregnancy. If a nursing mother should become pregnant, the milk is then considered to be unhealthy, and she will try to abort, using herbal and spiritual remedies. Such attempts usually succeed. Traditionally, the few babies born before they are wanted—or born with no man to take responsibility for them—have been put to death. "Their single question is, Who will be responsible for the child?," according to Father Saffirio. "There is no place in the culture for a child without a father."

This is one of the very few aspects of Yanomami culture that the Catramani missionaries have tried to influence: a family that finds itself with a baby it can't care for may leave the infant at the mission, which later may place the baby with an older couple. "We respect their culture and try not to interfere with it," says Father Saffirio, "but in this case we felt that it's important to try to replace the many people killed in the epidemics."

The soft-spoken, Italian-born priest found the Yanomami culture in no way lacking in comparison to "modern, westernized" ways. He found no cruelty or random violence among the forest people; rather, he was deeply touched by their warmth, their animation and enjoyment of life, and their acceptance of people strange and different from them.

"It was very hard to leave them," admits Saffirio, 42, who is now working towards a Ph.D. in anthropology at the University of Pittsburgh. "If you are trying to help, if you care about them, they know it—and they give it all back. Everyone who really *stays,* and works there awhile, has a hard time leaving the Indians."

THE POLITICAL BATTLE FOR SURVIVAL

Beginning in 1968, the tribe's advocates both outside and inside the Brazilian government began preparing carefully documented reports on the location and condition of the Yanomami, and proposals for their future protection, including the creation of a Yanomami reserve or park. To date there have been twelve such proposals; all but the last two have been tabled or mysteriously "lost" in a labyrinth of governing agencies. The missionaries and anthropologists trying to intervene on the Indians' behalf have dogged the footsteps of officials at every level—local, federal and military—and have encountered contradictory responses and mixed results. A University of Brasilia health team organized by Scottish anthropologist Kenneth I. Taylor, for example, waited nine months for FUNAI funds, then received only a fraction of the promised amount; when FUNAI pulled out, the Yanomami Project went forward on its own, limited resources and achieved at least one clear success. Acting as consultant to a company doing mineral exploration, the team showed that with proper screening, preparation, and supervision, outsiders *could* work in Yanomami territory without harmful effects.

But by this time the trickle of "foreigners" had become a flood. In 1975 government mineral surveyors confirmed that there was gold in that thar' rainforest—as well as diamonds, uranium, and a rich tin ore called cassiterite. The Brazilian government, looking to unbridled resource development as a quick-fix solution to its $60 billion foreign debt, was overjoyed. Surucucu, where most of the minerals—as well as most of the Yanomami (4,500)—are concentrated, looked like a promising prospect for a boom town. The attitudes of local officials were typified in a remark made by the governor of Roraima Territory (where most Yanomami land is located): "An area such as this cannot afford the luxury of having a half dozen Indian tribes obstruct development."

How the People Got the Fire from the IYO

The Yanomami assume a lot of free flow and transmutation between people and animals; people have animal alter-egos; they can become animals, and vice versa. In one myth a Yanomami had become IYO ("*eewoe*"), a big alligatorlike creature who lived on land and had fire. But IYO was selfish with the fire, so everyone else had to eat raw meat. The people noticed that IYO cooked his meat by spitting fire on it, so they tried to make him smile; if he did, they thought, the fire would fall out of his mouth. Finally, the people in bird form (Seis, Kore) did something to make the IYO open his mouth. (There are many versions of what the birds did: let their droppings fall on him, threw dust at him, made him laugh, etc.) The fire fell out of the IYO's mouth, and the people grabbed it up and hid it in the Poronaihi, or cocoa tree (the Yanomami still start fires with the hard wood of a cocoa tree). The IYO was so ashamed of himself that he went to the river and became an alligator (represented by the spirit Caiman). There he has stayed to this day, only showing his eyes, because he is afraid of the Yanomami, and still ashamed.

The unsupervised influx of 500 tin prospectors and placer (surface) miners in 1975 had much the same impacts as the highway incursion in 1973. Though placer mining by non-indigenous people is against the law, the Brazilian authorities waited eighteen months—until fighting broke out between Indians and miners—before evacuating the miners. Currently, according to the ARC, at least 1,500 gold prospectors are illegally present in Yanomami territory.

Pressure on the Yanomami and their environment has recently been escalating from many directions: one government bureau has clear-cut part of their territory so that corporate cattle ranching could move in; another agency is encouraging poor peasants to become landowners by "colonizing" the jungle. The usual complement of Brazilian state-owned companies and multinational interests are busily acquiring permits to go in and dig up the minerals. There are plans on government and business drawing boards for dozens of massive hydroelectric plants on the Amazon and its tributaries, gas and oil wells in the jungle, and even a proposal for liquefying most of the remaining 415 billion cubic feet of the Amazon forest for fuel.

If there's any hope for protecting the Yanomamis, as well as their territory, it lies in a dedicated international human rights movement organized by Brazilian native rights advocates in 1979, with the creation of the Commission for the Creation of a Yanomami Park (CCPY). Aided by the Anthropology Resource Center (ARC), the American Anthropological Association, Cultural Survival, Survival International, and the Indian Law Resource Center (CCPY) brought the Yanomamis' plight to the attention of the world community and to human rights forums in the United Nations, the Organization of American States, and the Fourth Russell Tribunal on the Rights of Indians in the Americas (held in Rotterdam, Holland, in November 1980). The effort has been a resounding success: more than 15,000 letters, petitions, and telegrams have been sent to the Bra-

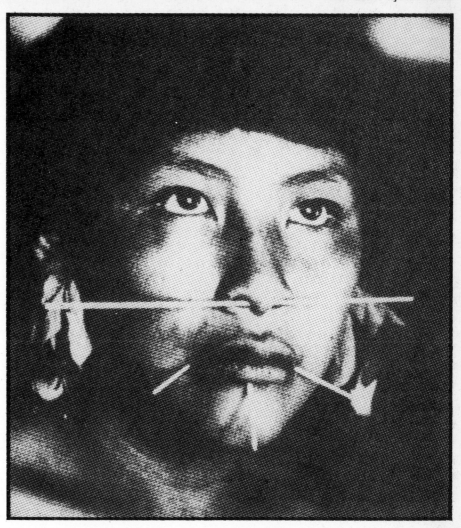

zilian government in support of CCPY's proposal for a Yanomami Park that would include most of the tribe's natural range.

This spring, in mid-March, FUNAI agreed to do just that: it interdicted 17 million acres to be set aside for the Yanomamis, with the federal government having the only right of outside access.

While those who have created and fought for the park are deservedly rejoicing in this victory, they emphasize that the government must go further to make the Yanomami park a reality. "It's an election year in Brazil," ARC's Robin Wright points out. "On several occasions in the past, the government has interdicted Indian areas, but has later revoked them. The most important step has yet to be taken: that of *delimiting* (formally

mapping) Yanomami land. It's important now for people to pressure FUNAI to take this step immediately."

If and when a park plan goes into effect, its proponents have no illusions about its vulnerabilities. Under Brazilian law, the tribe's "exclusive use and control" is only of the land's *surface:* the minerals below still belong to the government and can be taken by the authority of the Ministry of Mines and Energy. The National Institute of Forestry Development, the Special Secretariat for the Environment, and other agencies are also typically given certain kinds of rights on reservation lands. All of this external pressure on the Park will theoretically be strictly supervised and regulated by FUNAI, but FUNAI's effectiveness depends both on the commitment of its personnel and on the amount of power and recognition accorded to it by higher levels of officialdom.

"We are aware that there are no guarantees," says Father Saffirio. "But this really is the best we can hope for. At least it gives us some official protection we can work with. Anything stronger has simply never been an option."

Support organizations are hoping that continued international observation and pressure can be exerted to keep Brazil's administration of the reserve in line with the tribe's rights. However, Saffirio's statement points up a tragedy both moral and ecological, which will remain no matter how well the Yanomami Park is administered: that to leave a relatively tiny segment of the vast Amazon basin just as it's been for hundreds of years, in the hands of people who live there, is not, and has never been, an option. There are laws on the books in Brazil, in many other nations, and in international covenants which talk lavishly about preserving cultural diversity and which guarantee autonomy and self-determination to every indigenous people left on earth. Yet any proposal that would make these principles a reality, anywhere, by allowing a people and their habitat to continue as they were before "civilization" discovered them, has been categorically superseded by the demands of development. It seems to be a given that the reshaping of the physical world into money or items having monetary value is always—everywhere—a priority to which all other considerations must bow. There is overwhelming evidence that this policy is damaging—ethically, ecologically, psychologically, spiritually, and in the long run, even economically. Yet those people who don't understand or don't want to see this evidence are still making the decisions about how land is used on our globe. It is up to the rest of us—somehow—to call the current path of "progress" into question before the damage is irreversible.

Mystique of the Masai

Pastoral as well as warlike, they have persisted in maintaining their unique way of life

Ettagale Blauer

Ettagale Blauer is a New York-based writer who has studied the Masai culture extensively in numerous trips to Africa and who specializes in writing about Africa and jewelry.

The noble bearing, self-assurance, and great beauty of the Masai of East Africa have been remarked upon from the time the first Europeans encountered them on the plains of what are now Kenya and Tanzania. (The word 'Masai' derives from their spoken language, Maa.) Historically, the Masai have lived among the wild animals on the rolling plains of the Rift Valley, one of the most beautiful parts of Africa. Here, the last great herds still roam freely across the plains in their semiannual migrations.

Although the appearance of people usually marks the decline of the game, it is precisely the presence of the Masai that has guaranteed the existence of these vast herds. Elsewhere in Kenya and Tanzania, and certainly throughout the rest of Africa, the herds that once roamed the lands have been decimated. But the Masai are not hunters, whom they call *iltorrobo*—poor men—because they don't have cattle. The Masai do not crave animal trophies, they do not value rhinoceros horns for aphrodisiacs, meat is not part of their usual diet, and they

don't farm the land, believing it to be a sacrilege to break the earth. Traditionally, where Masai live, the game is unmolested.

In contrast to their peaceful and harmonious relationship to the wildlife, however, the Masai are warlike in relationship to the neighboring tribes, conducting cattle raids where they take women as well as cattle for their prizes, and they have been fiercely independent in resisting the attempts of colonial governments to change or subdue them. Although less numerous than the neighboring Kikuyu, the Masai have a strong feeling of being "chosen" people, and have been stubborn in maintaining their tribal identity.

However, that traditional tribal way of life is threatened by the exploding populations of Kenya and Tanzania (41 million people), who covet the vast open spaces of Masai Mara, Masai Amboseli, and the Serengeti Plain. Today, more than half of the Masai live in Kenya, with a style of life that requires extensive territory for cattle herds to roam in search of water and pastureland, and the freedom to hold ceremonies that mark the passage from one stage of life to the next. The Masai's need for land for their huge herds of cattle is not appreciated by people who value the land more for agriculture than for pasturage and for herds of wild animals.

The Masai live in countries that are attractive to tourists and whose leaders have embraced the values and life-style of the Western world. These two facts make it increasingly difficult for the Masai to live according to traditional patterns. The pressure to change in Kenya comes in part from their proximity to urban centers, especially the capital city of Nairobi, whose name is a Masai word meaning cool water.

Still, many Masai live in traditional homes and dress in wraps of bright cloth or leather, decorated with beaded jewelry, their cattle nearby. But the essence of the Masai culture—the creation of age-sets whose roles in life are clearly delineated—is under constant attack. In both Kenya and Tanzania, the governments continually try to "civilize" the Masai, to stop cattle raiding, and especially to put an end to the *morani*—the warriors—who are seen as the most disruptive of the age-sets.

TRADITIONAL LIFE

Masai legends trace the culture back some 300 years, and are recited according to age-groups, allowing fifteen years for each group. But anthropologists believe they arrived in the region some 1,000 years ago, having migrated from southern Ethiopia. As a racial group, they are considered a Nilo-Hamitic mix.

3. ORGANIZATION OF SOCIETY AND CULTURE

Although deep brown in color, their features are not negroid. (Their extensive use of ochre may give their skin the look of American Indians but that is purely cosmetic.)

Traditional Masai people are governed by one guiding principle: that all the cattle on earth are theirs, that they were put there for them by *Ngai,* who is the god of both heaven and earth, existing also in the rains which bring the precious grass to feed the cattle. Any cattle they do not presently own are only temporarily out of their care, and must be recaptured. The Masai do not steal material objects; theft for them is a separate matter from raiding cattle, which is seen as the *return* of cattle to their rightful owners. From this basic belief, an entire culture has grown. The grass that feeds the cattle and the ground on which it grows are sacred; to the Masai, it is sacrilege to break the ground for any reason, whether to grow food or to dig for water, or even to bury the dead.

Cattle provide their sole sustenance: milk and blood to drink, and the meat feast when permitted. Meat eating is restricted to ceremonial occasions, or when it is needed for gaining strength, such as when a woman gives birth or someone is recovering from an illness. When they do eat meat at a ceremony they consume their own oxen, which are sacrificed for a particular reason and in the approved way. Hunting and killing for meat are not Masai activities. It is this total dependence on their cattle, and their disdain for the meat of game animals, that permits them to coexist with the game, and which, in turn, has kept intact the great herds of the Masai Mara and the Serengeti Plain. Their extraordinary diet of milk, blood, and occasionally, meat, keeps them sleek and fit, and Westerners have often noted their physical condition with admiration.

In 1925 Norman Leys wrote, "Physically they are among the handsomest of mankind, with slender bones, narrow hips and shoulders and most beautifully rounded muscles and limbs." That same description holds today. The Masai live on about 1,300 calories a day, as opposed to our consumption of nearly 3,000. They are invariably lean.

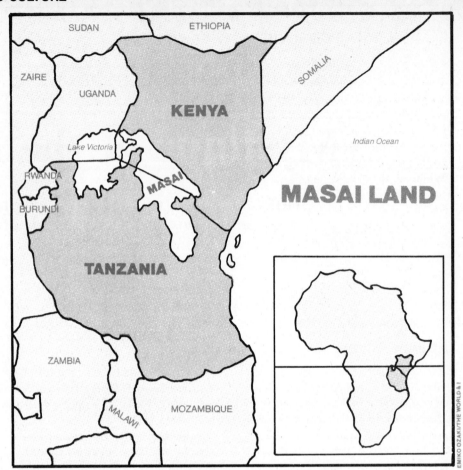

A map of Masai Land. The Masai's traditional territory exists within the two countries of Kenya and Tanzania.

Traditional nomadic life of the Masai, however, was ferocious and warlike in relation to other tribes. The warriors (*morani*) built *manyattas,* a type of shelter, throughout the lands and used each for a few months at a time, then moved to another area when the grazing was used up. As the seasons changed, they would return to those manyattas. They often went out raiding cattle from neighboring tribes whom they terrorized with their great ferocity.

A large part of that aggressiveness is now attributed to drugs; the morani worked themselves into a frenzy as they prepared for a raid, using the leaves and barks of certain trees known to create such moods. A soup was made of fat, water, and the bark of two trees, *il kitosloswa* and *il kiluretti.* From the description, these seem to act as hallucinogens. As early as the 1840s, Europeans understood that the morani's extremely ag-

gressive behavior derived from drug use. Drugs were used for endurance and for strength throughout warriorhood. During a meat feast, which could last a month, they took stimulants throughout, raising them to a virtual frenzy. This, combined with the natural excitement attendant to crowd behavior, made them formidable foes.

Having gained this supernatural energy and courage, they were ready to go cattle raiding among other tribes. To capture the cattle, the men of the other tribe had to be killed. Women were never touched in battle, but were taken to Masailand to become Masai wives. The rate of intermarriage was great during these years. Today, intermarriage is less frequent and the result mostly of chance meetings with other people. It is likely that intermarriage has actually prolonged the life of the Masai as a people; many observers from the early

1900s remarked upon the high rate of syphilis among the Masai, attributable to their habit of taking multiple sexual partners. Their birthrate is notably lower than the explosive population growth of the other peoples of Kenya and Tanzania. Still, they have increased from about 25,000 people at the turn of the century to the estimated 300,000-400,000 they are said to number today.

While the ceaseless cycle of their nomadic life has been sharply curtailed, many still cross the border between the two countries as they have for hundreds of years, leading their cattle to water and grazing lands according to the demands of the wet and dry seasons. They are in tune with the animals that migrate from the Serengeti Plain in Tanzania to Masai Mara in Kenya, and back again.

MALE AGE-SETS

The life of a traditional Masai male follows a well-ordered progression through a series of life stages.

Masai children enjoy their early years as coddled and adored love objects. They are raised communally, with great affection. Children are a great blessing in Africa. Among the Masai, with the lack of emphasis on paternity, and with a woman's prestige tied to her children, natural love for children is enhanced by their desirability in the society. Children are also desired because they bring additional cattle to a family, either as bride-price in the case of girls or by raiding in the case of boys.

During their early years, children play and imitate the actions of the elders, a natural school in which they learn the rituals and daily life practices of their people. Learning how to be a Masai is the lifework of every one in the community. Infant mortality in Africa remains high; catastrophic diseases introduced by Europeans, such as smallpox, nearly wiped them out. That memory is alive in their oral traditions; having children is a protection against the loss of the entire culture, which they know from experience could easily happen. Africans believe that you must live to see your face reflected in that of a child; given the high infant mortality rate, the only way to protect that human chain is by having as many children as possible.

For boys, each stage of life embraces an age-group created at an elaborate ceremony, the highlight of their lives being the elevation to moran. Once initiated, they learn their age-group's specific duties and privileges. Males pass through four stages: childhood, boyhood, warriorhood, and elderhood. Warriors, divided into junior and senior, form one generation, or age-set.

Four major ceremonies mark the passage from one group to another: boys who are going to be circumcised participate in the *Alamal Lenkapaata* ceremony, preparation for circumcision; *Emorata* is followed by initiation into warriorhood—status of moran; the passage from warrior to elderhood is marked by the *Eunoto* ceremony; and total elderhood is confirmed by the *Olngesherr*. All ceremonies have in common ritual head shaving, continual blessings, slaughter of an animal, ceremonial painting of face or body, singing, dancing, and feasting. *Laibons*—spiritual advisers—must be present at all ceremonies, and the entire tribe devotes itself to these preparations.

Circumcision is a rite of passage and more for teenage boys. It determines the role the boy will play throughout his life, as leader or follower. How he conducts himself during circumcision is keenly observed by all; a boy who cries out during the painful operation is branded a coward and shunned for a long time; his mother is disgraced. A boy who is brave, and who had led an exemplary life, becomes the leader of his age-group.

It takes months of work to prepare for these ceremonies so the exact date of such an event is rarely known until the last minute. Westerners, with contacts into the Masai community, often stay ready for weeks, hoping to be on hand when such a ceremony is about to take place. Each such ceremony may well be the last, it is thought.

Before they can be circumcised, boys must prove themselves ready. They tend the cattle—the Masai's only wealth—and guard them from predators whose tracks they learn to recognize. They know their cattle individually, the way we know people. Each animal has a name and is treated as a personality. When they feel they are ready, the boys approach the junior elders and ask them to open a new circumcision period. If this is approved, they begin a series of rituals, among them the Alamal Lenkapaata, the last step before the formal initiation. The boys must have a laibon, a leader with the power to predict the future, to guide them in their decisions. He creates a name for this new generation. The boys decorate themselves with chalky paint, and spend the night out in the open. The elders sing and celebrate and dance through the night to honor the boys.

An Alamal Lenkapaata held in 1983 was probably the most recent to mark the opening of a new age-set. Ceremonies were held in Ewaso Ngiro, in the Rift Valley. As boys joined into groups and danced, they raised a cloud of dust around themselves. All day long, groups would form and dance, then break apart and later start again.

Under a tree, elders from many areas gathered together and their discussion was very intense. John Galaty, professor of anthropology from McGill University in Montreal, who has studied the Masai extensively, flew in specifically to attend this ceremony. He is fluent in Masai and translated the elders' talk. "We are lucky," they said, "to be able to have this ceremony. The government does not want us to have it. We have to be very careful. The young men have to be warned that there should be no cattle raiding." And there wasn't any.

An ox was slaughtered, for meat eating is a vital element of this ceremony. The boys who were taking part cut off hunks of meat which they cooked over an open fire. Though there was a hut set aside for them, the boys spent little time sleeping. The next day, all the elders gathered to receive gifts of sugar and salt from John Keen, a member of Kenya's parliament, and himself a Masai. (Kenya has many Masai in government, including the Minister of Finance, George Saitoti.) The dancing, the meat eating, all the elements of the ceremony continued for several days. If this had been a wealthy group, they might have kept up the celebration for as long as a month.

Once this ceremony is concluded, the boys are allowed to hold councils and to discuss important matters. They choose one from their own group to be their representative. The Alamal Lenkapaata ceremony includes every boy of suitable age, preparing him for circumcision and then warriorhood. The circumcisions will take place over the next few years, beginning with the older boys in this group. The age difference may be considerable in any age-group since these ceremonies are held infrequently; once a circumcision period ends, though, it may not be opened again for many years.

THE MORAN

The Masai who exemplifies his tribe is the moran. This is the time of life that expresses the essence of the Masai—bravery, willingness to defend their people and their cattle against all threats, confidence to go out on cattle raids to increase their own herds, and ability to stand up to threats even from Europ-eans, whose superior weapons subdued the Masai but never subjugated them. The Masai moran is the essence of that almost mythical being, the noble savage, a description invented by Europeans but here actually lived out. With his spear, his elaborately braided and reddened hair, his bountiful beaded jewelry, his beautiful body and proud bearing, the moran is the symbol of everything that is attractive about the Masai. When a young man becomes a moran, his entire culture looks upon him with reverence.

The life a moran enjoys as his birthright is centered on cattle raiding, enhancing his appearance, and sex. The need to perform actual work, such as building fences, rescuing a cow that has gone astray, and standing ready to defend their homeland—Masailand—is only occasionally required. Much of his time is devoted to the glorification of his appearance. His body is a living showcase of Masai art.

From the moment a boy undergoes the circumcision ceremony, he looks ahead to the time when he will be a moran. He grows his hair long so it can be braided into myriad tiny plaits, thickened with ochre and fat. The age-mates spend hours at this, the whole outdoors being their salon. As they work, they chat, always building the bonds between them. Their beaded jewelry is made by their girlfriends. Their bare legs are ever-changing canvases on which they trace patterns, using white chalk and ochre. Though nearly naked, they are a medley of patterns and colors.

After being circumcised, the young men "float" in society for up to two years, traveling in loose groups and living in temporary shelters called *inkangitie*. After that time they can build a manyatta. Before fully becoming a moran, however, they must enter a "holy house" at a special ceremony. Only a young man who has not slept with a circumcised woman can enter the holy house. The fear of violating this taboo is very strong, and young men who do not enter the house are beaten by their parents and carry the disrespect of the tribe all their lives.

The dancing of the morani celebrates everything that they consider beautiful and strong: morani dance competitively by jumping straight into the air, knees straight, over and over again, each leap trying to go higher than the last, as they sing and chant and encourage each

Masai ceremony of the Alamal Lenkapaata which is part of the Morani (warrior) coming of age for young Masai men.

Young Masai Morani (warriors) dancing traditionally with their hair caked with red ochre mud and their legs in an abstract pattern in a traditional Masai Manyatta with long mud huts in the Rift Valley, Kenya.

other. The morani also dance with their young girlfriends. Each couple performs sinuous motions repeatedly, then breaks off and another couple takes their place. A hypnotic rhythm develops as they follow the chanting and hand clapping of their mates.

Although they are now forbidden by the governments of Kenya and Tanzania to kill a lion—a traditional test of manhood—or to go cattle raiding, they retain all the trappings of a warrior, without the possibility of practicing their skill. They occasionally manage a cattle raid, but even without it, they still live with pride and dignity. Masai remain morani for about fifteen years, building up unusually strong relationships among their age-mates with whom they live during that time. Hundreds of boys may become morani at one time.

Traditionally, every fifteen years saw the advent of a new generation of warriors. Now, both colonial governments and independent black-ruled governments have tampered with this social process, and have been successful in reducing the time men spend as warriors. By forcing this change, the governments hope to mold the Masai male into a more tractable citizen, especially by forbidding such disruptive activities as lion killing and cattle raiding. But tinkering with the Masai system can have unforeseen and undesirable consequences. It takes a certain number of years before a moran is ready to take on the duties of that age-group. They need time to build up herds of cattle to be used for bride-price and to learn to perform the decision-making tasks expected. This change also leaves the younger boys without warriors to keep them in check, and to guide them through the years leading up to the circumcision ceremony.

More significantly, since 1978 it has been illegal to build a manyatta, and warriors from that time have been left with no place to live. Their mothers cannot live with them, they cannot tend their cattle or increase their herds, they have no wives or jobs. Since, once they become warriors, they are not allowed to enter another person's house to eat, they are forced to steal other peoples' cattle and live off the land.

Circumcision exists for women as well as for men. From the age of nine until puberty, young girls live with the morani as sexual partners; it is an accepted part of Masai life that girls do not reach puberty as virgins. It is because of this practice that syphilis causes the most serious problems for the Masai. The girls, unfamiliar with their bodies, contract the disease and leave it untreated until sterility results. This sexual activity changes dramatically when a girl reaches puberty. At that time, she is circumcised and forbidden to stay with the warriors. This is to prevent her from becoming pregnant before she is married. As soon as she recovers from the circumcision, or clitoridectomy, an operation that destroys her ability to experience orgasm, she is considered ready for marriage. Circumcision is seen as a means of equalizing men and women. By removing any vestige of the appearance of the organs of the opposite sex, it purifies the gender. Although female circumcision has long been banned by the Kenyan government, few girls manage to escape the operation.

While the entire tribe devotes itself to the rituals that perpetuate the male age-set system, girls travel individually through life in their roles as lovers, wives, and child bearers, in all instances subservient to the boys and men. They have no comparable age-set system and hence do not develop the intensely felt friendships of the men who move through life together in groups, and who, during the period of senior warriorhood live together, away from their families.

It is during this period that the mothers move away from their homes. They build manyattas in which they live with their sons who have achieved the status of senior morani, along with their sons' girlfriends, and away from their own small children. The husbands, other wives, and the other women of the tribe, take care of these children.

The male-female relationship is dictated according to the male age-sets. When a newly circumcised girl marries, she joins the household of her husband's family, and likely will be one among several of his wives. Her role is to milk the cows, to build the house, and to bear children, especially male children. Only through childbirth can she achieve high status; all men, on the other hand, achieve status simply by graduating from one age-set to the next.

A childless Masai woman is virtually without a role in her society. One of the rarest ceremonies among the Masai is a blessing for women who have not given birth and for women who want more children. While the women play a peripheral role in the men's ceremonies, the men are vital to the women's, for it is a man who blesses the women. To prepare for the ritual, the women brew great quantities of beer and offer beer and lambs to the men who are to bless them.

In their preparation for this ceremony, and in conducting matters that pertain to their lives, the women talk things out democratically, as do the men. They gather in the fields and each woman presents her views. Not until all who want to speak have done so does the group move toward a consensus. As with the men, a good speaker is highly valued and her views are listened to attentively. But these sessions are restricted to women's issues; the men have the final say over all matters relating to the tribe. Boys may gather in councils as soon as they have completed the Alamal Lenkapaata; girls don't have similar opportunities. They follow their lovers, the morani, devotedly, yet as soon as they reach the age when they can marry, they are wrenched out of this love relationship and given in marriage to much older men, men who have cattle for bride-price.

Because morani do not marry until they are elevated to elderhood, girls must accept husbands who are easily twice their age. But just as the husband has more than one wife, she will have lovers, who are permitted as long as they are members of her husband's circumcision group, not the age group for whom she was a girlfriend. This is often the cause of tension among the Masai. All the children she bears are considered to be her husband's even though they may not be his biologically. While incest taboos are clearly observed and various other taboos also pertain, multiple partners are expected. Polygamy in Masailand (and anywhere it prevails) dictates that some men will not marry at all. These men are likely to be those without cattle, men who cannot bring bride-price. For the less traditional, the payment of bride-price is sometimes made in cash, rather than in cattle, and to earn money, men go to the cities to seek work. Masai tend to find jobs that permit them to be outside and free; for this reason, many of the night watchmen in the capital city of Nairobi are Masai. They sit around fires at night, chatting, in an urban version of their life in the countryside. . . .

RAIDING, THEFT, AND THE LAW

Though now subject to national laws, the Masai do not turn to official bodies or courts for redress. They settle their own disputes democratically, each man giving his opinion until the matter at hand is settled. Men decide all matters for the tribe (women do not take part in these discussions), and they operate virtually without chiefs. The overriding concern is to be fair in the resolution of problems because kinship ties the Masai together in every aspect of their lives. Once a decision is made, punishment is always levied in the form of a fine. The Masai have no jails, nor do they inflict physical punishment. For a people who value cattle as much as they do, there is no greater sacrifice than to give up some of their animals.

The introduction of schools is another encroachment upon traditional life which was opposed by the Masai. While most African societies resisted sending their children to school, the Masai reacted with particular intensity. They compared school to death or enslavement; if children did go to school, they would be lost to the Masai community. They would forget how to survive on the land, how to identify animals by their tracks, and how to protect the cattle. All of these things are learned by example and by experience.

David Read is a white Kenyan, fluent in Masai who said that, as a boy: "I may not have been able to read or write, but I knew how to live in the bush. I could hunt my dinner if I had to."

The first school in their territory was opened in 1919 at Narok but few children attended. The Masai scorned the other tribes, such as the Kikuyu, who later embraced Western culture and

soon filled the offices of the government's bureaucracies. The distance between the Masai and the other tribes became even greater. The Masai were seen as a painful reminder of the primitivism that Europeans as well as Africans had worked so hard to erase. Today, however, many Masai families will keep one son at home to maintain traditional life, and send another one to school. In this way, they experience the benefits of literacy, opportunities for employment, money, connections to the government, and new knowledge, especially veterinary practices, while keeping their traditions intact. Masai who go to school tend to succeed, many of them graduating from college with science degrees. Some take up the study of animal diseases, and bring this knowledge back to help their communities improve the health of their cattle. The entire Masai herd was once nearly wiped out during the rinderpest epidemic in the late nineteenth century. Today, the cattle are threatened by tsetse flies. But where the Masai were able to rebuild their herds in the past, today, they would face tremendous pressure to give up cattle raising entirely.

LIVING CONDITIONS

While the Masai are admired for their great beauty, their living conditions are breeding grounds for disease. Since they keep their small livestock (sheep and goats) in the huts where they live, they are continually exposed to the animals' excrement. The cattle are just outside, in an open enclosure, and their excrement is added to the mix. Flies abound wherever cattle are kept, but with the animals living right next to the huts, they are ever-present. Like many tribal groups living in relative isolation, the Masai are highly vulnerable to diseases brought in by others. In the 1890s, when the rinderpest hit their cattle, the Masai were attacked by smallpox which, coupled with drought, reduced their numbers almost to the vanishing point.

For the most part, the Masai rely on the remedies of their traditional medicine and are renowned for their extensive knowledge and use of natural plants to treat illnesses and diseases of both people and cattle. Since they live in an

area that had hardly any permanent sources of water, the Masai have learned to live without washing. They are said to have one bath at birth, another at marriage. Flies are pervasive; there is scarcely a picture of a Masai taken in their home environment that does not show flies alit on them.

Their rounded huts, looking like mushrooms growing from the ground, are built by the women. On a frame of wooden twigs, they begin to plaster mud and cow dung. Layers and layers of this are added until the roof reaches the desired thickness. Each day, cracks and holes are repaired, especially after the rains, using the readily available dung. Within the homes, they use animal hides. Everything they need can be made from the materials at hand. There are a few items such as sugar, tea, and cloth that they buy from the *dukas,* or Indian shops, in Narok, Kajiado, and other nearby towns, but money is readily obtained by selling beaded jewelry, or simply one's own image. Long ago, the Masai discovered their photogenic qualities. If they cannot survive as warriors by raiding, they will survive as icons of warriors, permitting tourists to take their pictures for a fee, and that fee is determined by hard bargaining. One does not simply take a picture of a Masai without payment; that is theft.

Their nomadic patterns have been greatly reduced; now they move only the cattle as the seasons change. During the dry season, the Masai stay on the higher parts of the escarpment and use the pastures there which they call *osukupo*. This offers a richer savannah with more trees. When the rains come, they move down to the pastures of the Rift Valley to the plains called *okpurkel*.

Their kraals are built a few miles from the water supply. The cattle drink on one day only, then are grazed the next, so they can conserve the grazing by using a larger area than they would be able to if they watered the cattle every day. But their great love of cattle has inevitably brought them to the point of overstocking. As the cattle trample their way to and from the waterhole, they destroy all vegetation near it, and the soil washes away. Scientists studying Masai land use have concluded that with the change from a totally nomadic way of life, the natural environmental resistance of this system was destroyed; there is no self-regulating mechanism left. Some Masai have permitted wheat farming on their land for the exploding Kenyan population, taking away the marginal lands that traditionally provided further grazing for their cattle.

PRESSURE TO CHANGE

In June 1901, Sir Charles Eliot, colonial governor of Kenya, said, "I regard the Masai as the most important and dangerous of the tribes with whom we have to deal in East Africa and I think it will be long necessary to maintain an adequate military force in the districts which they inhabit."

The traditional Masai way of life has been under attack ever since. The colonial British governments of Kenya and Tanzania (then Tanganyika) outlawed Masai cattle raiding and tried to stifle the initiation ceremony; the black governments that took over upon independence in the 1960s continued the process. The Masai resisted these edicts, ignored them, and did their best to circumvent them throughout the century. In some areas, they gave in entirely—cattle raiding, the principal activity of the morani—rarely occurs, but their ceremonies, the vital processes by which a boy becomes a moran and a moran becomes an elder, remain intact, although they have been banned over and over again. Stopping these ceremonies is more difficult than just proclaiming them to be over, as the Kenyan government did in 1985.

Some laws restrict the very essence of a Masai's readiness to assume the position of moran. Hunting was banned entirely in Kenya and nearly so in Tanzania (except for expensive permits issued to tourists, and restricted to designated hunting blocks), making it illegal for a moran to kill a lion to demonstrate his bravery and hunting skills. Although the Masai ignore the government whenever possible, at times such as this, conflict is unavoidable. Lions are killed occasionally, but stealthily; some modern Masai boys say, "Who needs to kill a lion? It doesn't prove anything."

The Kenyan governments requirement that Masai children go to school has also affected the traditional roles of girls and women, who traditionally married at age twelve or thirteen and left school. Now the government will send fathers and husbands to jail for taking these girls out of school. There was a case in Kenya in 1986 of a girl who wrote to the government protesting the fact that her father had removed her from school to prepare her for marriage. Her mother carries the letter to the appropriate government officials, the father was tried, and the girl was allowed to return to school.

Sometimes there is cooperation between governmental policy and traditional life-style. Ceremonies are scheduled to take place in school holidays, and while government policies continue to erode traditional customs, the educated and traditional groups within the Masai community try to support each other.

TRADITION IN THE FACE OF CHANGE

Although the Masai in both countries are descended from the same people, national policies have pushed the Kenyan Masai further away from their traditions. The Tanzanian Masai, for example, still dress occasionally in animal skins, decorated with beading. The Kenyan Masai dress almost entirely in cloth, reserving skins for ceremonial occasions.

In 1977, Kenya and Tanzania closed their common border, greatly isolating the Tanzanian Masai from Western contact. Though the border has been reopened, the impact on the Masai is clear. The Kenyan Masai became one of the sights of the tourist route while the Tanzanian Masai were kept from such interaction. This has further accelerated change among the Kenyan Masai. Tepilit Ole Saitoti sees a real difference in character between the Masai of Kenya and Tanzania. "Temperamentally," he says, "the Tanzanian Masai tend to be calmer and slower than those in Kenya."

Tribal people throughout Africa are in a constant state of change, some totally urbanized, their traditions nearly forgotten; others are caught in the middle, part of the tribe living traditionally, some moving to the city and adopting Western ways. The Masai have retained their culture, their unique and distinctive way of life, longer than virtually all the other tribes of East Africa, and they have done so while living in the very middle of the tourist traffic. Rather than disappear into the bush, the Masai use their attractiveness and mystique to their own benefit. Masai Mara and Amboseli, two reserves set aside for them, are run by them for their own profit.

Few tribes in Africa still put such a clear cultural stamp on an area; few have so successfully resisted enormous efforts to change them, to modernize and "civilize" them, to make them fit into the larger society. We leave it to Tepilit Ole Saitoti to predict the future of his own people: "Through their long and difficult history, the Masai have fought to maintain their traditional way of life. Today, however, they can no longer resist the pressures of the modern world. The survival of Masai culture has ceased to be a question; in truth, it is rapidly disappearing."

BIBLIOGRAPHY

Bleeker, Sonia, *The Masai, Herders of East Africa*, 1963.

Fedders, Andrew, *Peoples and Cultures of Kenya*, TransAfrica Books, Nairobi, 1979.

Fisher, Angela, *Africa Adorned*, Harry N. Abrams Inc., New York, 1984.

Kinde, S.H., *Last of the Masai*, London, 1901.

Kipkorir, B., *Kenya's People, People of the Rift Valley*, Evans Bros. Ltd., London, 1978

Lamb, David, *The Africans*, Vintage Books, New York, 1984.

Moravia, Alberto, *Which Tribe Do You Belong To?*, Farrar, Straus & Firous, New York, 1974.

Read, David, *Barefoot Over the Serengeti*, Read, Nairobi, 1979.

Ole Saitoti, Tepilit, *Masai*, Barry N. Abrams, Inc., New York 1980.

—,*The Worlds of a Masai Warrior*, Random House, New York, 1986.

Ricciardi, Mirella, *Vanishing Africa*, Holt, Rinehard Winston, 1971.

Sankan, S.S., *The Masai*, Kenya Literature Bureau, Nairobi, 1971.

Thomson, Joseph, *Through Masai Land*, Sampson Low, Marston & Co., London 1885.

Tignor, Robert, *The Colonial Transformation of Kenya, The Kamba, Kikuyu and Masai from 1900 to 1939*, Princeton, NJ 1976.

Potlatch

Marvin Harris

Marvin Harris has taught at Columbia University since 1953 and from 1963 to 1966 was Chairman of the Department of Anthropology.

Some of the most puzzling life-styles on exhibit in the museum of world ethnography bear the imprint of a strange craving known as the "drive for prestige." Some people seem to hunger for approval as others hunger for meat. The puzzling thing is not that people hunger for approval, but that occasionally their craving seems to become so powerful that they begin to compete with each other for prestige as others compete for land or protein or sex. Sometimes this competition grows so fierce that it appears to become an end in itself. It then takes on the appearance of an obsession wholly divorced from, and even directly opposed to, rational calculations of material costs.

Vance Packard struck a responsive chord when he described the United States as a nation of competitive status seekers. Many Americans seem to spend their entire lives trying to climb further up the social pyramid simply in order to impress each other. We seem to be more interested in working in order to get people to admire us for our wealth than in the actual wealth itself, which often enough consists of chromium baubles and burdensome or useless objects. It is amazing how much effort people are willing to spend to obtain what Thorstein Veblen described as the vicarious thrill of being mistaken for members of a class that doesn't have to work. Veblen's mordant phrases "conspicuous consumption" and "conspicuous waste" aptly convey a sense of the peculiarly intense desire for "keeping up with the Joneses" that lies behind the ceaseless cosmetic alterations in the automotive, appliance, and clothing industries.

Early in the present century, anthropologists were surprised to discover that certain primitive tribes engaged in conspicuous consumption and conspicuous waste to a degree unmatched by even the most wasteful of modern consumer economies. Ambitious, status-hungry men were found competing with each other for approval by giving huge feasts. The rival feast givers judged each other by the amount of food they provided, and a feast was a success only if the guests could eat until they were stupefied, stagger off into the bush, stick their fingers down their throats, vomit, and come back for more.

The most bizarre instance of status seeking was discovered among the American Indians who formerly inhabited the coastal regions of Southern Alaska, British Columbia, and Washington. Here the status seekers practiced what seems like a maniacal form of conspicuous consumption and conspicuous waste known as *potlatch*. The object of potlatch was to give away or destroy more wealth than one's rival. If the potlatch giver was a powerful chief, he might attempt to shame his rivals and gain everlasting admiration from his followers by destroying food, clothing, and money. Sometimes he might even seek prestige by burning down his own house.

Potlatch was made famous by Ruth Benedict in her book *Patterns of Culture*, which describes how potlatch operated among the Kwakiutl, the aboriginal inhabitants of Vancouver Island. Benedict thought that potlatch was part of a megalomaniacal lifestyle characteristic of Kwakiutl culture in general. It was the "cup" God had given them to drink from. Ever since, potlatch has been a monument to the belief that cultures are the creations of inscrutable forces and deranged personalities. As a result of reading *Patterns of Culture*, experts in many fields concluded that the drive for prestige makes a shambles of attempts to explain lifestyles in terms of practical and mundane factors.

I want to show here that the Kwakiutl potlatch was not the result of maniacal whims, but of definite economic and ecological conditions. When these conditions are absent, the need to be admired and the drive for prestige express themselves in completely different lifestyle practices. Inconspicuous consumption replaces conspicuous consumption, conspicuous waste is forbidden, and there are no competitive status seekers.

The Kwakiutl used to live in plank-house villages set close to the shore in the midst of cedar and fir rain forests. They fished and hunted along the island-studded sounds and fiords of Vancouver in huge dugout canoes. Always eager to attract traders, they made their villages conspicuous by erecting on the beach the carved tree trunks we erroneously call "totem poles." The carvings on these poles symbolized the ancestral titles to which the chiefs of the village laid claim.

A Kwakiutl chief was never content with the amount of respect he was getting from his own followers and from neighboring chiefs. He was always insecure about his status. True enough, the family titles to which he laid claim belonged to his ancestors. But there were other people who could trace descent from the same ancestors and who were entitled to vie with him for recognition as a chief. Every chief therefore felt the obligation to justify and validate his chiefly pretensions. The prescribed manner for doing this was to hold potlatches. Each potlatch was given by a host chief and his followers to a guest chief and his followers. The object of the potlatch was to show that the host chief was truly entitled to chiefly status and that he was more exalted than the guest chief. To prove this point, the host chief gave the rival chief and his followers quantities of valuable gifts. The guests would belittle what they received and vow to hold a return potlatch at which their own chief would prove that he was greater than the former host by giving back even larger quantities of more valuable gifts.

Preparations for potlatch required the accumulation of fresh and dried fish, fish oil, berries, animal skins, blankets, and other valuables. On the appointed day, the guests paddled up to the host village and went into the chief's house. There they gorged themselves on salmon and wild berries while dancers masked as beaver gods and thunderbirds entertained them.

The host chief and his followers arranged in neat piles the wealth that was to be given away. The visitors stared at their host sullenly as he pranced up and down, boasting about how much he was about to give them. As he counted out the boxes of fish oil, baskets full of berries, and piles of blankets, he commented derisively on the poverty of his rivals. Laden with gifts, the guests finally were free to paddle back to their own village. Stung to the quick, the guest chief and his followers vowed to get even. This could only be achieved by inviting their rivals to a return potlatch and obliging them to accept even greater amounts of valuables than they had given away. Considering all the Kwakiutl villages as a single unit, potlatch stimulated a ceaseless flow of prestige and valuables moving in opposite directions.

An ambitious chief and his followers had potlatch rivals in several different villages at once. Specialists in counting property kept track of what had to be done in each village in order to even the score. If a chief managed to get the better of his rivals in one place, he still had to confront his adversaries in another.

At the potlatch, the host chief would say things like, "I am the only great tree. Bring your counter of property that he may try in vain to count the property that is to be given away." Then the chief's followers demanded silence from the guests with the warning: "Do not make any noise, tribes. Be quiet or we shall cause a landslide of wealth from our chief, the overhanging mountain." At some potlatches blankets and other valuables were not given away but were destroyed. Sometimes successful potlatch chiefs decided to hold "grease feasts" at which boxes of oil obtained from the candlefish were poured on the fire in the center of the house. As the flames roared up, dark grease smoke filled the room. The guests sat impassively or even complained about the chill in the air while the wealth destroyer ranted, "I am the only one on earth—the only one in the whole world who makes this smoke rise from the beginning of the year to the end for the invited tribes." At some grease feasts the flames ignited the planks in the roof and an entire house would become a potlatch offering, causing the greatest shame to the guests and much rejoicing among the hosts.

According to Ruth Benedict, potlatching was caused by the obsessive status hunger of the Kwakiutl chiefs. "Judged by the standards of other cultures the speeches of their chiefs are unabashed megalomania," she wrote. "The object of all Kwakiutl enterprises was to show oneself superior to one's rivals." In her opinion, the whole aboriginal economic system of the Pacific Northwest was "bent to the service of this obsession."

I think that Benedict was mistaken. The economic system of the Kwakiutl was not bent to the service of status rivalry; rather, status rivalry was bent to the service of the economic system.

All of the basic ingredients of the Kwakiutl giveaways, except for their destructive aspects, are present in primitive societies widely dispersed over different parts of the globe. Stripped down to its elementary core, the potlatch is a competitive feast, a nearly universal mechanism for assuring the production and distribution of wealth among peoples who have not yet fully acquired a ruling class.

Melanesia and New Guinea present the best opportunity to study competitive feasting under relatively pristine conditions. Throughout this region, there are so-called big men who owe their superior status to the large number of feasts that each has sponsored during his lifetime. Each feast has to be preceded by an intensive effort on the part of an aspiring big man to accumulate the necessary wealth.

Among the Kaoka-speaking people of the Solomon Islands, for example, the status-hungry individual begins his career by making his wife and children plant larger yam gardens. As described by the Australian anthropologist Ian Hogbin, the Kaoka who wants to become a big man then gets his kinsmen and his age-mates to help him fish. Later he begs sows from his friends and increases the size of his pig herd. As the litters are born he boards additional animals among his neighbors. Soon his relatives and friends feel that the young man is going to be a success. They see his large gardens and his big pig herd and they redouble their own efforts to make the forthcoming feast a memorable one. When he becomes a big man they want the young candidate to remember that they helped him. Finally, they all get together and build an extra-fine house. The men go off on one last fishing expedition. The women harvest yams and collect firewood, banana leaves, and coconuts. As the guests arrive (as in the case of potlatch), the wealth is stacked in neat piles and put on display for everyone to count and admire.

On the day of the feast given by a young man named Atana, Hogbin counted the following items: 250 pounds of dried fish, 3,000 yam and coconut cakes, 11 large bowls of yam pudding, and 8 pigs. All this was the direct result of the extra work effort organized by Atana. But some of the guests themselves, anticipating an important occasion, brought presents to be added to the giveaway. Their contributions raised the total to 300 pounds of fish, 5,000 cakes, 19 bowls of pudding, and 13 pigs. Atana proceeded to divide this wealth into 257 portions, one each for every person who had helped him or who had brought gifts, rewarding some more than others. "Only the remnants were left for Atana himself," notes Hogbin. This is normal for status seekers in Guadalcanal, who always say: "The giver of the feast takes the bones and the stale cakes; the meat and the fat go to the others."

The feast-giving days of the big man, like those of the potlatch chiefs, are never over. On threat of being reduced to commoner status, each big man is obliged to busy himself with plans and preparations for the next feast. Since there are several big men per village and community, these plans and preparations often lead to complex competitive maneuvering for the allegiance of relatives and neighbors. The big men work harder, worry more, and consume less than anybody else. Prestige is their only reward.

The big man can be described as a worker-entrepreneur—the Russians call them "Stakhanovites"—who renders important services to society by raising the level of production. As a result of the big man's craving for status, more people work harder and produce more food and other valuables.

Under conditions where everyone has equal access to the means of subsistence, competitive feasting serves the practical function of preventing the labor force from falling back to levels of productivity that offer no margin of safety in crises such as war and crop failures. Furthermore, since there are no formal political institutions capable of integrating independent villages into a common economic framework, competitive feasting creates an extensive network of economic expectations. This has the effect of pooling the productive effort of larger populations than can be mobilized by any given village. Finally, competitive feasting by big men acts as an automatic equalizer of annual fluctuations in productivity among a series of villages that occupy different microenvironments—seacoast, lagoon, or upland habitats. Automatically, the biggest feasts in any given year will be hosted by villages that have enjoyed

conditions of rainfall, temperature, and humidity most favorable to production.

All of these points apply to the Kwakiutl. The Kwakiutl chiefs were like Melanesian big men except that they operated with a much more productive technological inventory in a richer environment. Like big men, they competed with each other to attract men and women to their villages. The greatest chiefs were the best providers and gave the biggest potlatches. The chief's followers shared vicariously in his prestige and helped him to achieve more exalted honors. The chiefs commissioned the carving of the "totem poles." These were in fact grandiose advertisements proclaiming by their height and bold designs that here was a village with a mighty chief who could cause great works to be done, and who could protect his followers from famine and disease. In claiming hereditary rights to the animal crests carved on the poles, the chiefs were actually saying that they were great providers of food and comfort. Potlatch was a means of telling their rivals to put up or shut up.

Despite the overt competitive thrust of potlatch, it functioned aboriginally to transfer food and other valuables from centers of high productivity to less fortunate villages. I should put this even more strongly: Because of the competitive thrust, such transfers were assured. Since there were unpredictable fluctuations in fish runs, wild fruit and vegetable harvests, intervillage potlatching was advantageous from the standpoint of the regional population as a whole. When the fish spawned in nearby streams and the berries ripened close at hand, last year's guests became this year's hosts. Aboriginally, potlatch meant that each year the haves gave and the have-nots took. To eat, all a have-not had to do was admit that the rival chief was a great man.

Why did the practical basis of potlatch escape the attention of Ruth Benedict? Anthropologists began to study potlatch only long after the aboriginal peoples of the Pacific

Northwest had entered into commercial and wage-labor relations with Russian, English, Canadian, and American merchants and settlers. This contact rapidly gave rise to epidemics of smallpox and other European diseases that killed off a large part of the native population. For example, the population of the Kwakuitl fell from 23,000 in 1836 to 2,000 in 1886. The decline automatically intensifed the competition for manpower. At the same time, wages paid by the Europeans pumped unprecedented amounts of wealth into the potlatch network. From the Hudson's Bay Company, the Kwakiutl received thousands of trade blankets in exchange for animal skins. At the great potlatches these blankets replaced food as the most important item to be given away. The dwindling population soon found itself with more blankets and other valuables than it could consume. Yet the need to attract followers was greater than ever due to the labor shortage. So the potlatch chiefs ordered the destruction of property in the vain hope that such spectacular demonstrations of wealth would bring the people back to the empty villages. But these were the practices of a dying culture struggling to adapt to a new set of political and economic conditions; they bore little resemblance to the potlatch of aboriginal times.

Competitive feasting thought about, narrated, and imagined by the participants is very different from competitive feasting viewed as an adaptation to material constraints and opportunities. In the social dreamwork—the lifestyle consciousness of the participants—competitive feasting is a manifestation of the big man's or potlatch chief's insatiable craving for prestige. But from the point of view followed in this book, the insatiable craving for prestige is a manifestation of competitive feasting. Every society makes use of the need for approval, but not every society links prestige to success in competitive feasting.

Competitive feasting as a source of prestige must be seen in evolutionary perspective to be properly understood. Big men like Atana or the Kwakiutl chiefs carry out a form of economic exchange known as redistribution. That is, they gather together the results of the productive effort of many individuals and then redistribute the aggregated wealth in different quantities to a different set of people. As I have said, the Kaoka redistributor-big man works harder, worries more, and consumes less than anybody else in the village. This is not true of the Kwakiutl chief-redistributor. The great potlatch chiefs performed the entrepreneurial and managerial functions that were necessary for a big potlatch, but aside from an occasional fishing or sea-lion expedition, they left the hardest work to their followers. The greatest potlatch chiefs even had a few war captives working for them as slaves. From the point of view of consumption privileges, the Kwakiutl chiefs had begun to reverse the Kaoka formula and were keeping some of the "meat and fat" for themselves, leaving most of the "bones and stale cakes" for their followers.

Continuing along the evolutionary line leading from Atana, the impoverished worker-entrepreneur big man, to the semihereditary Kwakiutl chiefs, we end up with state-level societies ruled over by hereditary kings who perform no basic industrial or agricultural labor and who keep the most and best of everything for themselves. At the imperial level, exalted divine-right rulers maintain their prestige by building conspicuous palaces, temples, and megamonuments, and validate their right to hereditary privileges against all challengers—not by potlatch, but by force of arms. Reversing direction, we can go from kings to potlatch chiefs to big men, back to egalitarian lifestyles in which all competitive displays and conspicuous consumption by individuals disappear, and anyone foolish enough to boast about how great he is gets accused of witchcraft and is stoned to death.

In the truly egalitarian societies that have survived long enough to be studied by anthropologists, redistribution in the form of competitive feasting does not occur. Instead, the mode of exchange known as reciprocity predominates. Reciprocity is the technical term for an economic exchange that takes place between two individuals in which neither specifies precisely what is expected in return nor when they expect it. Superficially, reciprocal exchanges don't look like exchanges at all. The expectation of one party and obligation of the other remain unstated. One party can continue to take from the other for quite a while with no resistance from the giver and no embarrassment in the taker. Nonetheless, the transaction cannot be considered a pure gift. There is an underlying expectation of return, and if the balance between two individuals gets too far out of line, eventually the giver will start to grumble and gossip. Concern will be shown for the taker's health and sanity, and if the situation does not improve, people begin to suspect that the taker is possessed by malevolent spirits or is practicing witchcraft. In egalitarian societies, individuals who consistently violate the rules of reciprocity are in fact likely to be psychotic and a menace to their community.

We can get some idea of what reciprocal exchanges are like by thinking about the way we exchange goods and services with our close friends or relatives. Brothers, for example, are not supposed to calculate the precise dollar value of everything they do for each other. They should feel free to borrow each other's shirts or phonograph albums and ought not to hesitate to ask for favors. In brotherhood and friendship both parties accept the principle that if one has to give more than he takes, it will not affect the solidary relationship between them. If one friend invites another to dinner, there should be no hesitation in giving or accepting a second or a third invitation even if the first dinner still remains unreciprocated. Yet there is a limit to that sort of thing, because after a while unreciprocated gift-giving begins to feel suspiciously like exploitation. In other words, everybody likes to be thought generous, but nobody wants to be taken for a sucker. This is precisely the quandary we get ourselves into at Christmas when we attempt to revert to the principle of reciprocity in drawing up our shopping lists. The gift can neither be too cheap nor too expensive; and yet our calculations must appear entirely casual, so we remove the price tag.

But to really see reciprocity in action you must live in an egalitarian society that doesn't have money and where nothing can be bought or sold. Everything about reciprocity is opposed to precise counting and reckoning of what one person owes to another. In fact, the whole idea is to deny that anybody really owes anything. One can tell if a lifestyle is based on reciprocity or something else by whether or not people say thank you. In truly egalitarian societies it is rude to be openly grateful for the receipt of material goods or services. Among the Semai of central Malaya, for example, no one ever expresses gratitude for the meat that a hunter gives away in exactly equal portions to his companions. Robert Dentan, who has lived with the Semai, found that to say thank you was very rude because it suggested either that you were calculating the size of the piece of meat you had been given, or that you were surprised by the success and generosity of the hunter.

In contrast to the conspicuous display put on by the Kaoka big man, and the boastful ranting of potlatch chiefs, and our own flaunting of status symbols, the Semai follow a lifestyle in which those who are most successful must be the least conspicuous. In their egalitarian lifestyle, status seeking through rivalrous redistribution or any form of conspicuous consumption or conspicuous waste is literally unthinkable. Egalitarian peoples are repelled and frightened by the faintest suggestion that they are being treated generously or that one person thinks he's better than another.

Professor Richard Lee of the University of Toronto tells an amusing story about the meaning of reciprocal exchange among egalitarian hunters and gatherers. For the better part of a year, Lee had been following the Bushmen around the Kalahari Desert observing what they ate. The Bushmen were very cooperative and Lee wanted to show his gratitude, but he had nothing to give them that would not disturb their normal diet and pattern of activity. As Christmas approached he learned that the Bushmen were likely to camp at the edge of the desert near villages from which they sometimes obtained meat through trade. With the intention of giving them an ox for a Christmas present, he drove about in his jeep from one village to another, trying to find the biggest ox that he could buy. In a remote village, Lee finally located an animal of monstrous proportions, one covered with a thick layer of fat. Like many primitive peoples, the Bushmen crave fatty meat because the animals they obtain by hunting are usually lean and stringy. Returning to camp, Lee took his Bushmen friends aside and told them one by one that he had bought the largest ox he had ever seen and that he was going to let them slaughter it at Christmas time.

The first man to hear the good news became visibly alarmed. He asked Lee where he had bought the ox, what color it was, and what size its horns were, and then he shook his head. "I know that ox," he said. "Why, it is nothing but skin and bones! You must have been drunk to buy such a worthless animal!" Convinced that his friend didn't really know what ox he was talking about, Lee confided in several other Bushmen, but continued to meet with the same astonished reaction: "You bought that worthless animal? Of course we will eat it," each would say, "but it won't fill us up. We will eat and go home to bed with stomachs rumbling." When Christmas came and the ox was finally slaughtered, the beast turned out to be covered with a thick layer of fat, and it was devoured with great gusto. There was more than enough meat and fat for everybody. Lee went over to his friends and insisted upon an explana-

tion. "Yes, of course we knew all along what the ox was really like," one hunter admitted. "But when a young man kills much meat he comes to think of himself as a chief or big man, and he thinks of the rest of us as his servants or inferiors. We cannot accept this," he went on. "We refuse one who boasts, for someday his pride will make him kill somebody. So we always speak of his meat as worthless. This way we cool his heart and make him gentle."

The Eskimos explained their fear of boastful and generous gift-givers with the proverb "Gifts make slaves just as whips make dogs." And that is exactly what happened. In evolutionary perspective, the gift-givers at first gave gifts that came from their own extra work; soon people found themselves working harder to reciprocate and to make it possible for the gift-givers to give them more gifts; eventually the gift-givers became very powerful, and they no longer needed to obey the rules of reciprocity. They could force people to pay taxes and to work for them without actually redistributing what was in their storehouses and palaces. Of course, as assorted modern big men and politicians occasionally recognize, it is still easier to get "slaves" to work for you if you give them an occasional big feast instead of whipping them all the time.

If people like the Eskimo, Bushmen, and Semai understood the dangers of gift-giving, why did others permit the gift-givers to flourish? And why were big men permitted to get so puffed up that they could turn around and enslave the very people whose work made their glory possible? Once again, I suspect that I am on the verge of trying to explain everything at once. But permit me to make a few suggestions.

Reciprocity is a form of economic exchange that is primarily adapted to conditions in which the stimulation of intensive extra productive effort would have an adverse effect upon group survival. These conditions are found among certain hunters and gatherers such as the Eskimo, Semai, and Bushmen, whose survival de-

pends entirely on the vigor of the natural communities of plants and animals in their habitat. If hunters suddenly engage in a concerted effort to capture more animals and uproot more plants, they risk permanently impairing the supply of game in their territory.

Lee found, for example, that his Bushmen worked at subsistence for only ten to fifteen hours a week. This discovery effectively destroys one of the shoddiest myths of industrial society—namely that we have more leisure today than ever before. Primitive hunters and gatherers work less than we do—without benefit of a single labor union—because their ecosystems cannot tolerate weeks and months of intensive extra effort. Among the Bushmen, Stakhanovite personalities who would run about getting friends and relatives to work harder by promising them a big feast would constitute a definite menace to society. If he got his followers to work like the Kaoka for a month, an aspiring Bushman big man would kill or scare off every game animal for miles around and starve his people to death before the end of the year. So reciprocity and not redistribution predominates among the Bushmen, and the highest prestige falls to the quietly dependable hunter who never boasts about his achievements and who avoids any hint that he is giving a gift when he divides up an animal he has killed.

Competitive feasting and other forms of redistribution overwhelmed the primordial reliance upon reciprocity when it became possible to increase the duration and intensity of work without inflicting irreversible damage upon the habitat's carrying capacity. Typically this became possible when domesticated plants and animals were substituted for natural food resources. Within broad limits, the more work you put into planting and raising domesticated species, the more food you can produce. The only hitch is that people don't usually work harder than they have to. Redistribution was the answer to this problem. Redistribution began to appear as people worked harder in order to maintain a reciprocal balance with prestige-hungry, over-zealous producers. As the reciprocal exchanges became unbalanced, they became gifts; and as the gifts piled up, the gift-givers were rewarded with prestige and counter-gifts. Soon redistribution predominated over reciprocity and highest prestige went to the most boastful, calculating gift-givers, who cajoled, shamed, and ultimately forced everybody to work harder than the Bushman ever dreamed was possible.

As the example of the Kwakiutl indicates, conditions appropriate for the development of competitive feasting and redistribution some-times also occurred among nonagri-cultural populations. Among the coastal peoples of the Pacific North-west, annual runs of salmon, other migratory fish, and sea mammals provided the ecological analogue of agricultural harvests. The salmon or candlefish ran in such vast numbers that if people worked harder they could always catch more fish. More-over, as long as they fished with the aboriginal dip net, they could never catch enough fish to influence the spawning runs and deplete next year's supply.

Stepping away for the moment from our examination of reciprocal and redistributive prestige systems, we can surmise that every major type of political and economic system uses prestige in a distinctive manner. For example, with the appearance of capitalism in Western Europe, com-petitive acquisition of wealth once more became the fundamental cri-terion for big-man status. Only in this case, the big men tried to take away each other's wealth, and highest prestige and power went to the indi-vidual who managed to accumulate and hold onto the greatest fortune. During the early years of capitalism, highest prestige went to those who were richest but lived most frugally. After their fortunes had become more secure, the capitalist upper class resorted to grand-scale conspicuous consumption and conspicuous waste in order to impress their rivals. They built great mansions, dressed in exclusive finery, adorned themselves with huge jewels, and spoke con-temptuously of the impoverished masses. Meanwhile, the middle and lower classes continued to award highest prestige to those who worked hardest, spent least, and soberly re-sisted all forms of conspicuous con-sumption and conspicuous waste. But as the growth of industrial capac-ity began to saturate the consumer market, the middle and lower classes had to be weaned away from their frugal habits. Advertising and mass media joined forces to induce the middle and lower classes to stop saving and to buy, consume, waste, destroy, or otherwise get rid of ever-larger quantities of goods and ser-vices. And so among middle-class status seekers, highest prestige now goes to the biggest and most con-spicuous consumer.

But in the meantime, the rich found themselves threatened by new forms of taxation aimed at redistributing their wealth. Conspicuous consump-tion in the grand manner became dangerous, so highest prestige now once again goes to those who have most but show least. With the most prestigious members of the upper class no longer flaunting their wealth, some of the pressure on the middle class to engage in conspicuous con-sumption has also been removed. This suggests to me that the wearing of torn jeans and the rejection of overt consumerism among middle-class youth of late has more to do with aping the trends set by the upper class than with any so-called cultural revolution.

One final point. As I have shown, the replacement of reciprocity by competitive status seeking made it possible for larger human popula-tions to survive and prosper in a given region. One might very well wish to question the sanity of the whole pro-cess by which mankind was tricked and cajoled into working harder in order to feed more people at sub-stantially the same or even lower levels of material well-being than that enjoyed by people like the Eskimo or Bushmen. The only answer that I see to such a challenge is that many primitive societies refused to expand their productive effort and failed to increase their population density precisely because they discovered that the new "labor-saving" tech-nologies actually meant that they would have to work harder as well as suffer a loss in living standards. But the fate of these primitive people was sealed as soon as any one of them—no matter how remotely situated—crossed the threshold to redistribu-tion and the full-scale stratification of classes that lay beyond. Virtually all of the reciprocity-type hunters and gatherers were destroyed or forced into remote areas by bigger and more powerful societies that maximized production and population and that were organized by governing classes. At bottom, this replacement was essentially a matter of the ability of larger, denser, and better-organized societies to defeat simple hunters and gatherers in armed conflict. It was work hard or perish.

Other Families, Other Ways

Since most people in small-scale societies of the past spent their whole lives within a local area, it is understandable that their primary interactions—economic, religious, and otherwise—were with their relatives. Every age group, from children to the very old, played an active and indispensable role in the survival of the collective unit. It also makes sense that, through marriage customs, they strengthened those kinship relationships that clearly defined their mutual rights and obligations. Indeed, the resulting family structure may be surprisingly flexible and adaptive, as witnessed in "When Brothers Share a Wife," by Melvyn C. Goldstein. It is for these reasons that anthropologists have looked upon family and kinship as the key mechanisms through which culture is transmitted from one generation to the next. Since social changes would have been slow to take place throughout the world, and as social horizons have widened accordingly, family relationships and community alliances are increasingly based upon new sets of principles. There is no question that kinship networks have diminished in size and strength as we have increasingly become involved with others as co-workers in a market economy. Our associations depend more and more upon factors such as personal aptitudes, educational backgrounds, and job opportunities. Yet, the family is still there. It is smaller, but it still functions in its age-old nurturing and protective role. Beyond the immediate family, the situation is still in a state of flux. Certain ethnic groups, especially those living in poverty, still have a need for a broader network, and in some ways seem to be reformulating those ties.

Where the changes described in this section will lead us, and which ones will ultimately prevail, we do not know.

One thing is certain: anthropologists will be there to document the trends, for the discipline of anthropology has had to change as well. One important feature of the essays in this section is that they are all representative of the growing interest of anthropologists in the study of complex societies—especially American society, where old theoretical perspectives are increasingly inadequate.

Current trends do not necessarily mean the eclipse of the kinship unit, however, as "Free Enterprise and the Ghetto Family," "Young Traders of Northern Nigeria," and "The Gypsies" illustrate. The message is that the large family network is still the best guarantee of individual survival and well-being in an urban setting. According to the Bruce Dollar article, even in China, where a mere 40 years ago women's feet were bound, jobs for women and day care for children have made home life easier and have actually strengthened the family.

Looking Ahead: Challenge Questions

Why is "fraternal polyandry" socially acceptable in Tibet, but not in our society?

Why are large numbers of children important to people in poverty?

How are attitudes of cooperation, sharing, and altruism instilled in individuals in an industrial society?

How do differences in child care relate to economic circumstances?

Do poor people value work in the same way as the well-off?

Should Gypsies be forced to follow in the mainstream of modern society?

Unit 4

When Brothers Share a Wife

Among Tibetans, the good life relegates many women to spinsterhood

Melvyn C. Goldstein

Melvyn C. Goldstein, now a professor of anthropology at Case Western Reserve University in Cleveland, has been interested in the Tibetan practice of fraternal polyandry (several brothers marrying one wife) since he was a graduate student in the 1960s.

Eager to reach home, Dorje drives his yaks hard over the 17,000-foot mountain pass, stopping only once to rest. He and his two older brothers, Pema and Sonam, are jointly marrying a woman from the next village in a few weeks, and he has to help with the preparations.

Dorje, Pema, and Sonam are Tibetans living in Limi, a 200-square-mile area in the northwest corner of Nepal, across the border from Tibet. The form of marriage they are about to enter—fraternal polyandry in anthropological parlance—is one of the world's rarest forms of marriage but is not uncommon in Tibetan society, where it has been practiced from time immemorial. For many Tibetan social strata, it traditionally represented the ideal form of marriage and family.

The mechanics of fraternal polyandry are simple. Two, three, four, or more brothers jointly take a wife, who leaves her home to come and live with them. Traditionally, marriage was arranged by parents, with children, particularly females, having little or no say. This is changing somewhat nowadays, but it is still unusual for children to marry without their parents' consent. Marriage ceremonies vary by income and region and range from all the brothers sitting together as grooms to only the eldest one formally doing so. The age of the brothers plays an important role in determining this: very young brothers almost never participate in actual marriage ceremonies, although they typically join the marriage when they reach their midteens.

The eldest brother is normally dominant in terms of authority, that is, in managing the household, but all the brothers share the work and participate as sexual partners. Tibetan males and females do not find the sexual aspect of sharing a spouse the least bit unusual, repulsive, or scandalous, and the norm is for the wife to treat all the brothers the same.

Offspring are treated similarly. There is no attempt to link children biologically to particular brothers, and a brother shows no favoritism toward his child even if he knows he is the real father because, for example, his other brothers were away at the time the wife became pregnant. The children, in turn, consider all of the brothers as their fathers and treat them equally, even if they also know who is their real father. In some regions children use the term "father" for the eldest brother and "father's brother" for the others, while in other areas they call all the brothers by one term, modifying this by the use of "elder" and "younger."

Unlike our own society, where monogamy is the only form of marriage permitted, Tibetan society allows a variety of marriage types, including monogamy, fraternal polyandry, and polygyny. Fraternal polyandry and monogamy are the most common forms of marriage, while polygyny typically occurs in cases where the first wife is barren. The widespread practice of fraternal polyandry, therefore, is not the outcome of a law requiring brothers to marry jointly. There is choice, and in fact, divorce traditionally was relatively simple in Tibetan society. If a brother in a polyandrous marriage became dissatisfied and wanted to separate, he simply left the main house and set up his own household. In such cases, all the children stayed in the main household with the remaining brother(s), even if the departing brother was known to be the real father of one or more of the children.

The Tibetans' own explanation for choosing fraternal polyandry is materialistic. For example, when I asked Dorje why he decided to marry with his two brothers rather than take his own wife, he thought for a moment, then said it prevented the division of his family's farm (and animals) and thus facilitated all of them achieving a higher standard of living. And when I later asked Dorje's bride whether it wasn't difficult for her to cope with three brothers as husbands, she laughed and echoed the rationale of avoiding fragmentation of the family and land, adding that she expected to be better off economically, since she would have three husbands working for her and her children.

Exotic as it may seem to Westerners, Tibetan fraternal polyandry is thus in many ways analogous to the way primogeniture functioned in nineteenth-century England. Primogeniture dictated that the eldest son inherited the family estate, while younger sons had to leave home and seek their own employment—for example, in the military or the clergy. Primogeniture maintained family estates intact over generations by permitting only one heir per generation. Fraternal polyandry also accomplishes this but does so by keeping all the brothers together with just one wife so that there is only one *set* of heirs per generation.

While Tibetans believe that in this way fraternal polyandry reduces the risk of family fission, monogamous marriages among brothers need not necessarily precipitate the division of the family estate: brothers could continue to live together, and the family land could continue to be worked jointly. When I asked Tibetans about this, however, they invariably responded that such joint families are unstable because each wife is primarily oriented to her own children and interested in their success and well-being over that of the children of the other wives. For example, if the youngest brother's wife had three sons while the eldest brother's wife had only one daughter, the wife of the youngest brother might begin to demand more resources for her children since, as males, they represent the future of the family. Thus, the children from different wives in the same generation are competing sets of heirs, and this makes such families inherently unstable. Tibetans perceive that conflict will spread from the wives to their husbands and consider this likely to cause family fission. Consequently, it is almost never done.

Although Tibetans see an economic advantage to fraternal polyandry, they do not value the sharing of a wife as an end in itself. On the contrary, they articulate a number of problems inherent in the practice. For example, because authority is customarily exercised by the eldest brother, his younger male siblings have

Family Planning in Tibet

An economic rationale for fraternal polyandry is outlined in the diagram below, which emphasizes only the male offspring in each generation. If every wife is assumed to bear three sons, a family splitting up into monogamous households would rapidly multiply and fragment the family land. In this case, a rule of inheritance, such as primogeniture, could retain the family land intact, but only at the cost of creating many landless male offspring. In contrast, the family practicing fraternal polyandry maintains a steady ratio of persons to land.
Joe LeMonnier

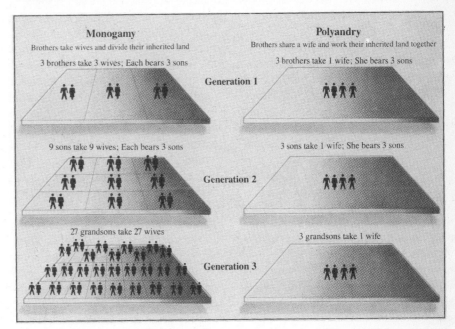

to subordinate themselves with little hope of changing their status within the family. When these younger brothers are aggressive and individualistic, tensions and difficulties often occur despite there being only one set of heirs.

In addition, tension and conflict may arise in polyandrous families because of sexual favoritism. The bride normally sleeps with the eldest brother, and the two have the responsibility to see to it that the other males have opportunities for sexual access. Since the Tibetan subsistence economy requires males to travel a lot, the temporary absence of one or more brothers facilitates this, but there are also other rotation practices. The cultural ideal unambiguously calls for the wife to show equal affection and sexuality to each of the brothers (and vice versa), but deviations from this ideal occur, especially when there is a sizable difference in age between the partners in the marriage.

Dorje's family represents just such a potential situation. He is fifteen years old and his two older brothers are twenty-five and twenty-two years old. The new bride is twenty-three years old, eight years Dorje's senior. Sometimes such a bride finds the youngest husband immature and adolescent and does not treat him with equal affection; alternatively, she may find his youth attractive and lavish special attention on him. Apart from that consideration, when a younger male like Dorje grows up, he may consider his wife "ancient" and prefer the company of a woman his own age or younger. Consequently, although men and women do not find the idea of sharing a bride or a bridegroom repulsive, individual likes and dislikes can cause familial discord.

Two reasons have commonly been offered for the perpetuation of fraternal polyandry in Tibet: that Tibetans practice female infanticide and therefore have to marry polyandrously, owing to a shortage of females; and that Tibet, lying at extremely high altitudes, is so barren and bleak that Tibetans would starve without resort to this mechanism. A Jesuit who lived in Tibet during the eighteenth century articulated this second view: "One reason for this most odious custom is the sterility of the soil, and the small amount of land that can be cultivated owing to the lack of water. The crops may suffice if the brothers all live together, but if they form separate families they would be reduced to beggary."

Both explanations are wrong, however. Not only has there never been institutionalized female infanticide in Tibet, but Tibetan society gives females considerable rights, including inheriting the family estate in the absence of brothers. In such cases, the woman takes a bridegroom who comes to live in her family and adopts her family's name and identity. Moreover, there is no demographic evidence of a shortage of females. In Limi, for example, there were (in 1974) sixty females and fifty-three males in the fifteen- to thirty-five-year age category, and many adult females were unmarried.

The second reason is also incorrect. The climate in Tibet is extremely harsh, and ecological factors do play a major role perpetuating polyandry, but polyandry is not a means of preventing starvation. It is characteristic, not of the poorest segments of the society, but rather of the peasant landowning families.

In the old society, the landless poor could not realistically aspire to prosperity, but they did not fear starvation. There was a persistent labor shortage throughout Tibet, and very poor families with little or no land and few animals could subsist through agricultural labor, tenant farming, craft occupations such as carpentry, or by working as servants. Although the per person family income could increase somewhat if brothers married polyandrously and pooled their wages, in the absence of inheritable land, the advantage of fraternal polyandry was not generally sufficient to prevent them from setting up their own households. A more skilled or energetic younger brother could do as well or better alone, since he would completely control his income and would not have to share it with his siblings. Consequently, while there was and is some polyandry among the poor, it is much less frequent and more prone to result in divorce and family fission.

An alternative reason for the persistence of fraternal polyandry is that it reduces population growth (and thereby reduces the pressure on resources) by relegating some females to lifetime spinsterhood. Fraternal polyandrous marriages in Limi (in 1974) averaged 2.35 men per woman, and not surprisingly, 31 percent of the females of child-bearing age (twenty to forty-nine) were unmarried. These spinsters either continued to live at home, set up their own households, or worked as servants for other families. They could also become Buddhist nuns. Being unmarried is not synonymous with exclusion from the reproductive pool. Discreet extramarital relationships are tolerated, and actually half of the adult unmarried women in Limi had one or more children. They raised these children as single mothers, working for wages or weaving cloth and blankets for sale. As a group, however, the unmarried woman had far fewer offspring than the married women, averaging only 0.7 children per woman, compared with 3.3 for married women, whether polyandrous, monogamous, or polygynous. While polyandry helps regulate population, this function of polyandry is not consciously perceived by Tibetans and is not the reason they consistently choose it.

If neither a shortage of females nor the fear of starvation perpetuates fraternal polyandry, what motivates brothers, particularly younger brothers, to opt for this system of marriage? From the perspective of the younger brother in a landholding family, the main incentive is the attainment or maintenance of the good life. With polyandry, he can expect a more secure and higher standard of living, with access not only to this family's land and animals but also to its inherited collection of clothes, jewelry, rugs, saddles, and horses. In addition, he will experience less work pressure and much greater security because all responsibility does not fall on one "father." For Tibetan brothers, the question is whether to trade off the greater personal freedom inherent in monogamy for the real or potential economic security, affluence, and social prestige associated with life in a larger, labor-rich polyandrous family.

A brother thinking of separating from his polyandrous marriage and taking his own wife would face various disadvantages. Although in the majority of Tibetan regions all brothers theoretically have rights to their family's estate, in reality Tibetans are reluctant to divide their land into small fragments. Generally, a younger brother who insists on leaving the family will receive only a small plot of land, if that. Because of its power and wealth, the rest of the family usually can block any attempt of the younger brother to increase his share of land through litigation. Moreover, a younger brother may not even get a house and cannot expect to receive much above the minimum in terms of movable possessions, such as furniture, pots, and pans. Thus, a brother contemplating going it on his own must plan on achieving economic security and the good life not through inheritance but through his own work.

The obvious solution for younger brothers—creating new fields from virgin land—is generally not a feasible option. Most Tibetan populations live at high altitudes (above 12,000 feet), where arable land is extremely scarce. For example, in Dorje's village, agriculture ranges only from about 12,900 feet, the lowest point in the area, to 13,300 feet. Above that altitude, early frost and snow destroy the staple barley crop. Furthermore, because of the low rainfall caused by the Himalayan rain shadow, many areas in Tibet and northern Nepal that are within the appropriate altitude range for agriculture have no reliable sources of irrigation. In the end, although there is plenty of unused land in such areas, most of it is either too high or too arid.

Even where unused land capable of being farmed exists, clearing the land and building the substantial terraces necessary for irrigation constitute a great undertaking. Each plot has to be completely dug out to a depth of two to two and half feet so that the large rocks and boulders can be removed. At best, a man might be able to bring a few new fields under cultivation in the first years after separating from his brothers, but he could not expect to acquire substantial amounts of arable land this way.

In addition, because of the limited farmland, the Tibetan subsistence economy characteristically includes a strong emphasis on animal husbandry. Tibetan farmers regularly maintain cattle, yaks, goats, and sheep, grazing them in the areas too high for agriculture. These herds produce wool, milk, cheese, butter, meat, and skins. To obtain these resources, however, shepherds must accompany the animals on a daily basis. When first setting up a monogamous household, a younger brother like Dorje would find it difficult to both farm and manage animals.

In traditional Tibetan society, there was an even more critical factor that operated to perpetuate fraternal polyandry—a form of hereditary servitude somewhat analogous to serfdom in Europe. Peasants were tied to large estates held by aristocrats, monasteries, and the Lhasa government. They were allowed the use of some farmland to produce their own subsistence but were required to provide taxes in kind and corvée (free labor) to their lords. The corvée was a substantial hardship, since a peasant household was in many cases required to furnish the lord with one laborer daily for most of the year and more on specific occasions such as the harvest. This enforced labor, along with the lack of new land and ecological pressure to pursue both agriculture and animal husbandry, made polyandrous families particularly beneficial. The polyandrous family allowed an internal division of adult labor, maximizing economic advantage. For example, while the wife worked the family fields, one brother could perform the lord's corvée, another could look after the animals, and a third could engage in trade.

Although social scientists often discount other people's explanations of why they do things, in the case of Tibetan fraternal polyandry, such explanations are very close to the truth. The custom, however, is very sensitive to changes in its political and economic milieu and, not surprisingly, is in decline in most Tibetan areas. Made less important by the elimination of the traditional serf-based economy, it is disparaged by the dominant non-Tibetan leaders of India, China, and Nepal. New opportunities for economic and social mobility in these countries, such as the tourist trade and government employment, are also eroding the rationale for polyandry, and so it may vanish within the next generation.

Young Traders of Northern Nigeria

Enid Schildkrout

Thirty years ago, Erik Erikson wrote that "the fashionable insistence on dramatizing the dependence of children on adults often blinds us to the dependence of the older generation on the younger one." As a psychoanalyst, Erikson was referring mainly to the emotional bonds between parents and children, but his observation is a reminder that in many parts of the world, adults depend on children in quite concrete ways. In northern Nigeria, children with trays balanced on their heads, carrying and selling a variety of goods for their mothers or themselves, are a common sight in villages and towns. Among the Muslim Hausa, aside from being a useful educational experience, this children's trade, as well as children's performance of household chores and errands, complements the activity of adults and is socially and emotionally significant.

Children's services are especially important to married Hausa women, who, in accordance with Islamic practices, live in purdah, or seclusion. In Nigeria, purdah is represented not so much by the wearing of the veil but by the mud-brick walls surrounding every house or compound and by the absence of women in the markets and the streets. Women could not carry out their domestic responsibilities, not to mention their many income-earning enterprises, without the help of children, who are free from the rigid sexual segregation that so restricts adults.

Except for elderly women, only children can move in and out of their own and other people's houses without violating the rules of purdah. Even children under three years of age are sent on short errands, for example, to buy things for their mothers.

Hausa-speaking people are found throughout West Africa and constitute the largest ethnic group in northern Nigeria, where they number over eighteen million. Their adherence to Islam is a legacy of the centuries during which Arabs came from the north to trade goods of North African and European manufacture. The majority of the Hausa are farmers, but markets and large commercial cities have existed in northern Nigeria since long before the period of British colonial rule. The city of Kano, for example, which was a major emporium for the trans-Saharan caravan trade, dates back to the eighth century. Today it has a population of about one million.

Binta is an eleven-year-old girl who lives in Kano, in a mud-brick house that has piped water, but no electricity. The household includes her father and mother, her three brothers, her father's second wife and her three children, and a foster child, who is the daughter of one of Binta's cousins. By Kano standards, it is a middle-income family. Binta's father sells shoes, and her mother cooks and sells bean cakes and *tuwo*, the stiff porridge made of guinea corn (*Shorghum vulgare*), which is the Hausa's staple. Binta described for me one day's round of activities, which

began very early when she arose to start trading.

"After I woke up, I said my prayers and ate breakfast. Then I went outside the house to sell the bean cakes my mother makes every morning. Soon my mother called me in and asked me to take more bean cakes around town to sell; she spoke to me about making an effort to sell as much as I usually do. I sold forty-eight bean cakes at one kobo each [one kobo is worth one and a half cents]. After I returned home, some people came to buy more cakes from me. Then I went out for a second round of trading before setting out for Arabic school. I study the Koran there every morning from eight to nine.

"When school was over, I washed and prepared to sell *tuwo*. First my mother sent me to another neighborhood to gather the customers' empty bowls. I also collected the money from our regular customers. My mother put the *tuwo* in the bowls and told me the amount of money to collect for each. Then I delivered them to the customers.

"On my way home, a man in the street, whom I know, sent me on an errand to buy him fifteen kobo worth of food; he gave me a reward of one kobo. I then sold some more *tuwo* outside our house by standing there and shouting for customers. When the *tuwo* was finished, I was sent to another house to buy some guinea corn, and one of the women there asked me to bring her one of my mother's big pots. The pot was too heavy for me to carry, but finally one of my brothers helped me take it to her.

"When I returned, my mother was busy pounding some grain, and she sent me out to have some locust beans pounded. She then sent me to pick up three bowls of pounded guinea corn, and she gave me money to take to the woman who had pounded it. The woman told me to remind my mother that she still owed money from the day before.

"When I came home I was sent out to trade again, this time with salt, bouillon cubes, and laundry detergent in small packets. Afterward I prepared some pancakes using ingredients I bought myself—ten kobo worth of flour, one kobo worth of salt, five kobo worth of palm oil, and ten kobo worth of firewood. I took this food outside to sell it to children.

"My mother then gave me a calabash of guinea corn to take for grinding; my younger sister also gave me two calabashes of corn to take. The man who ran the grinding machine advised me that I should not carry so large a load, so I made two trips on the way back. He gave me and my younger brothers, who accompanied me, on kobo each.

"I was then told to take a bath, which I did. After that I was sent to visit a sick relative who was in the hospital. On the way I met a friend, and we took the bus together. I also bought some cheese at the market for five kobo. I met another friend on the way home, and she bought some fish near the market for ten kobo and gave me some. I played on the way to the hospital. When I got home, I found the women of the house preparing a meal. One of them was already eating, and I was invited to eat with her.

"After nightfall, I was sent to take some spices for pounding, and I wasted a lot of time there. The other children and I went to a place where some fruits and vegetables are sold along the street. We bought vegetables for soup for fifty kobo, as my mother had asked me to do. By the time I got home it was late, so I went to sleep."

Binta's many responsibilities are typical for a girl her age. Like many women, Binta's mother relies upon her children in carrying out an occupation

at home. Although purdah implies that a woman will be supported by her husband and need not work, most Hausa women do work, keeping their incomes distinct from the household budget. Women usually cook one main meal a day and purchase their other meals from other women. In this way they are able to use their time earning a living instead of performing only unpaid domestic labor.

Among the Hausa, men and women spend relatively little time together, eating separately and, except in certain ritual contexts, rarely doing the same things. Differences in gender are not as important among children, however. In fact, it is precisely because children's activities are not rigidly defined by sex that they are able to move between the world of women, centered in the inner courtyard of the house, and the world of men, whose activities take place mainly outside the home. Children of both sexes care for younger children, go to the market, and help their mothers cook.

Both boys and girls do trading, although it is more common for girls. From the age of about five until marriage, which is very often at about age twelve for girls, many children like Binta spend part of every day selling such things as fruits, vegetables, and nuts; bouillon cubes, bread, and small packages of detergent, sugar, or salt; and bowls of steaming rice or *tuwo*. If a woman embroiders, children buy the thread and later take the finished product to the client or to an agent who sells it.

Women in purdah frequently change their occupations depending on the availability of child helpers. In Kano, women often trade in small commodities that can be sold in small quantities, such as various kinds of cooked food. Sewing, embroidery, mat weaving, and other craft activities (including, until recently, spinning) are less remunerative occupations, and women pursue them when they have fewer children around to help. Unlike the situation common in the United States, where children tend to hamper a woman's ability to earn money, the Hausa woman finds it difficult to earn income without children's help. Often, if a

woman has no children of her own, a relative's child will come to live with her.

Child care is another service children perform that benefits women. It enables mothers to devote themselves to their young infants, whom they carry on their backs until the age of weaning, between one and two. Even though women are always at home, they specifically delegate the care of young children to older ones. The toddler moves from the mother's back into a group of older children, who take the responsibility very seriously. Until they are old enough, children do not pick up infants or very young children, but by the age of nine, both boys and girls bathe young children, play with them, and take them on errands. The older children do a great deal of direct and indirect teaching of younger ones. As soon as they can walk, younger children accompany their older siblings to Arabic school. There the children sit with their age-mates, and the teacher gives them lessons according to their ability.

Much of a child's activity is directed toward helping his or her parents, but other relatives—grandparents, aunts, uncles, and stepmothers—and adults living in the same house as servants or tenants may call on a child for limited tasks without asking permission of the parents. Like other Muslims, Hausa men may have up to four wives, and these women freely call on each other's children to perform household chores. Even strangers in the street sometimes ask a child to do an errand, such as delivering a message, particularly if the chore requires entering a house to which the adult does not have access. The child will be rewarded with a small amount of money or food.

Adults other than parents also reprimand children, who are taught very early to obey the orders of grownups. Without ever directly refusing to obey a command, however, children do devise numerous strategies of non-compliance, such as claiming that another adult has already co-opted their time or simply leaving the scene and ignoring the command. Given children's greater mobility, there is little an adult can do to enforce compliance.

4. OTHER FAMILIES, OTHER WAYS

Besides working on behalf of adults, children also participate in a "children's economy." Children have their own money—from school allowances given to them daily for the purchase of snacks, from gifts, from work they may have done, and even from their own investments. For example, boys make toys for sale, and they rent out valued property, such as slide viewers or bicycles. Just as women distinguish their own enterprises from the labor they do as wives, children regard the work they do for themselves differently from the work they do on behalf of their mothers. When Binta cooks food for sale, using materials she has purchased with her own money, the profits are entirely her own, although she may hand the money over to her mother for safekeeping.

Many girls begin to practice cooking by the age of ten. They do not actually prepare the family meals, for this heavy and tedious work is primarily the wives' responsibility. But they do carry out related chores, such as taking vegetables out for grinding, sifting flour, and washing bowls. Many also cook food for sale on their own. With initial help from their mothers or other adult female relatives, who may given them a cooking pot, charcoal, or a small stove, children purchase small amounts of ingredients and prepare various snacks. Since they sell their products for less than the adult women do, and since the quantities are very small, their customers are mainly children. Child entrepreneurs even extend credit to other children.

Aisha is a ten-year-old girl who was notoriously unsuccessful as a trader. She disliked trading and regularly lost her mother's investment. Disgusted, her mother finally gave her a bit of charcoal, some flour and oil, and a small pot. Aisha set up a little stove outside her house and began making small pancakes, which she sold to very young children. In three months she managed to make enough to buy a new dress, and in a year she bought a pair of shoes. She had clearly chosen her occupation after some unhappy trials at street trading.

Hausa women usually engage in some form of enterprise; most of their profits are invested in their children's marriage expenses. Working at home, a woman weaves a mat for sale.

In the poorest families, as in Aisha's, the profit from children's work goes toward living expenses. This may occur in households that are headed by divorced or widowed women. It is also true for the *almajirai*, or Arabic students, who often live with their teachers. The proceeds of most children's economic activity, however, go to the expenses of marriage. The income contributes to a girl's dowry and to a boy's bridewealth, both of which are considerable investments.

The girl's dowry includes many brightly painted enamel, brass, and glass bowls, collected years before marriage. These utensils are known as *kayan daki*, or "things of the room." After the wedding they are stacked in a large cupboard beside the girl's bed. Very few of them are used, but they are always proudly displayed, except during the mourning period if the husband dies. *Kayan daki* are not simply for conspicuous display, however. They remain the property of the woman unless she sells them or gives them away. In the case of divorce or financial need, they can provide her most important and immediate source of economic security.

Kayan daki traditionally consisted of brass bowls and beautifully carved calabashes. Today the most common form is painted enamel bowls manufactured in Nigeria or abroad. The styles and designs change frequently, and the cost is continually rising.

Among the wealthier urban women and the Western-educated women, other forms of modern household equipment, including electric appliances and china tea sets, are becoming part of the dowry.

The money a young girl earns on her own, as well as the profits she brings home through her trading, are invested by her mother or guardian in *kayan daki* in anticipation of her marriage. Most women put the major part of their income into their daughters' *kayan daki* as well as helping their sons with marriage expenses. When a woman has many children, the burden can be considerable.

For girls, marriage, which ideally coincides with puberty, marks the transition to adult status. If a girl marries as early as age ten, she does not cook for her husband or have sexual relations with him for some time, but she enters purdah and loses the freedom of childhood. Most girls are married by age fifteen, and for many the transition is a difficult one.

Boys usually do not marry until they are over twenty and are able to support a family. They also need to have raised most of the money to cover the cost of getting married. Between the ages of eight and ten, however, they gradually begin to move away from the confines of the house and to regard it as a female domain. They begin taking their food outside and eating it with friends, and they roam much farther than girls in their play activities. By the onset of puberty, boys have begun to observe the rules of purdah by refraining from entering the houses of all but their closest relatives. In general, especially if they have sisters, older boys spend less time than girls doing chores and errands and more time playing and, in recent years, going to school. Traditionally, many boys left home to live and study with an Arabic teacher. Today many also pursue Western education, sometimes in boarding school. Although the transition to adulthood is less abrupt for boys, childhood for both sexes ends by age twelve to fourteen.

As each generation assumes the responsibilities of adulthood and the restrictions of sexual separation, it must rely on the younger members of society who can work around the purdah system. Recently, however, the introduction of Western education has begun to threaten this traditional arrangement, in part just by altering the pattern of children's lives.

The Nigerian government is now engaged in a massive program to provide Western education to all school-age children. This program has been undertaken for sound economic and political reasons. During the colonial period, which ended in the early 1960s, the British had a "hands-off"

policy regarding education in northern Nigeria. They ruled through the Islamic political and judicial hierarchy and supported the many Arabic schools, where the Koran and Islamic law, history, and religion were taught. The British discouraged the introduction of Christian mission schools in the north and spent little on government schools.

The pattern in the rest of Nigeria was very different. In the non-Muslim areas of the country, mission and government schools grew rapidly during the colonial period. The result of this differential policy was the development of vast regional imbalances in the extent and level of Western education in the country. This affected the types of occupational choices open to Nigerians from different regions. Despite a longer tradition of literacy in Arabic in the north, few northerners were eligible for those civil service jobs that required literacy in English, the language of government business.

This was one of the many issues in the tragic civil war that tore Nigeria apart in the 1960s. The current goal of enrolling all northern children in public schools, which offer training in English and secular subjects, has, therefore, a strong and valid political rationale.

Western education has met a mixed reception in northern Nigeria. While

it has been increasingly accepted for boys—as an addition to, not a substitute for, Islamic education—many parents are reluctant to enroll their daughters in primary school. Nevertheless, there are already more children waiting to get into school than there are classrooms and teachers to accommodate them. If the trend continues, it will almost certainly have important, if unintended, consequences for purdah and the system of child enterprise that supports it.

Children who attend Western school continue to attend Arabic school, and thus are removed from the household for much of the day. For many women this causes considerable difficulty in doing daily housework. It means increased isolation and a curtailment of income-producing activity. It creates a new concern about where to obtain the income for children's marriages. As a result of these practical pressures, the institution of purdah will inevitably be challenged. Also, the schoolgirl of today may develop new skills and new expectations of her role as a woman that conflict with the traditional ways. As Western education takes hold, today's young traders may witness a dramatic change in Hausa family life— for themselves as adults and for their children.

Child Care in China

Bruce Dollar

Societies differ as to how they characteristically raise (socialize) their children. The following selection describes some of the cultural values, beliefs, and institutions of modern China that directly affect the development of its children and the roles of other family members. The institutionalized child care programs in China will be of particular interest to those concerned with the growing use of day care centers in the United States.

The old art of China watching is giving way to China witnessing, and one quality of the new China seems inevitably to impress all recent visitors is the extraordinary vibrancy of Chinese children, from the very youngest to the adolescents, who already tower so noticeably over their grandparents. During my own recent trip within China, my companions and I saw for ourselves the exuberant self-confidence that seems to infuse all Chinese kids, whether they are performing for strangers, participating in a classroom exercise, or playing by themselves.

"Ours is a socialist society; everything is done according to plan." This pronouncement, with which our various Chinese hosts so frequently prefaced their answers to our questions, provides a starting point for understanding how this spirit of exuberance has been achieved. Although Chinese society is largely decentralized to encourage local self-sufficiency and diversification, the whole is knit together by an administrative structure that is more or less uniform from city to city and, somewhat less, from commune (or network of villages) to commune. It is a framework that provides an efficient system of communication and has helped produce a remarkable social cohesion based on commonly held goals and values—which themselves are informed by the teachings of Mao Tse-tung.

The consensus is particularly apparent with respect to the care and training of the young. This is hardly surprising when one considers the enormous stock the Chinese place in producing what they call "revolutionary successors," an apt phrase in a country where revolutionary consciousness has been maintained largely through vivid comparisons with the "bitter past," and where the problem of continuing the revolution into succeeding generations is paramount.

Thus, throughout our visit we constantly encountered—with amazing consistency at various points along a 2,500-mile itinerary—several major ideas about child rearing in the numerous conversations we had with people in child-related institutions: families, nurseries, kindergartens, and schools. These themes—especially the subordination of personal to social needs, respect for productive labor, altruism, cooperation, and the integration of physical with intellectual labor—together describe the kind of citizen China hopes to produce. The techniques employed to achieve these values are in practice virtually from infancy.

During the years before primary schools, which begins at the age of seven, a series of public child care facilities is available to parents who wish to use them. In the cities, where patterns are more uniform, a mother's maternity leave (paid) usually terminates 56 days after birth. Since breast-feeding is the rule in China, the mother may then place her child in the nursing room at her place of work. Most work institutions—factories, hospitals, and government offices, for example—provide this facility for their employees. In a typical arrangement the mother has two half hour breaks, plus lunch, to visit and nurse her baby during the work day. After work the baby returns home with the mother.

Nursing rooms provide care for infants up to one and a half years old; then they may be sent to one of the various kinds of nurseries. Some of these are attached to the work place or located in the home neighborhood; they may be open only during the work day, or they may be "live-in" nurseries, where children stay overnight and go home on weekends. Kindergartens, usually located in the residential areas, generally care for children from three and a half to seven years old and may also be either part-time or full-time.

In a country in which over 90 per cent of all women of working age do work, it might be expected that a similar percentage of children would therefore receive some kind of institutional care. But there are options. The most common is to leave the child in the care of grandparents, who frequently live with the family. Another alternative is to make arrangements with a friend or neighbor. Estimates vary from place to place, but in most cities no more than half the children of nursery school age are in attendance. For kindergarten the figures are higher, especially in the cities, where attendance is over 80 per cent.

Since child care is decentralized, different localities often make their own arrangements, which may not conform to the usual patterns. This is particularly true of rural areas, where a lack of resources and the persistence of custom probably account for a lower incidence of public child care facilities. One small village we visited, the Sha Shih Yu Brigade in northeast China, had no permanent facility; only during harvest time, when all hands were needed in the fields, was there organized care for small children. A child care center located in a coalmining area near Tangshan, on the other hand, served 314 children divided into at least five separate age groups, from 56 days to six years old.

How do these institutions work to socialize the children under their care? And what are they like for the kids? In spite of the diversity in organizational structure, the remarkable similarity from place to place, both in the values espoused and the methods used to inculcate them, seems to support a number of generalizations.

One quality that is sure to strike an American observer is the preponderance and the style of group activities. A common example is the "cultural performance," usually presented for visitors. Whether they are songs from a revolutionary opera, dances to celebrate a harvest, or a program of folk melodies played on traditional Chinese instruments, these performances are always presented by groups, and it is impossible to pick out a "star."

Although there were exceptions, many early child care facilities we visited seemed rather poorly supplied with the variety of toys and materials that the conventional wisdom in the United States says should be on hand to enrich and enliven a child's environment. Although this may have been due to a simple inability to pay for more equipment, the teachers we spoke to did not seem to consider it a shortcoming. Perhaps this is because Chinese children are generally expected to rely on each other for stimulation—at any rate, this seems to be the effect. The situation provides an interesting contrast to that in the United States, where

the highly desired "rich environment" often means that kids interact with inanimate materials more than they do with other people.

The small children we saw were not without playthings, however. There was always at least one toy for each child—typically a rubber or plastic doll of a worker, a peasant, or a soldier. Rocking horses were also common, as were military toys and playground equipment that could accommodate many children. But in general the emphasis was on group play. One recent American visitor to a Chinese nursery school reports noticing that the blocks seemed awfully heavy for the small children. "Exactly!" beamed the teachers. "That fosters mutual help."

Chinese teachers actively encourage such group behavior as cooperation, sharing, and altruism. "We praise a child when he shows concern for others' interests," said one kindergarten teacher. "For example, at meal time teachers give out bowls and chop sticks. If a youngster gets a nicer bowl and gives it to someone else, we praise him for it. Or when the children are asked to select a toy and a child gives the best one to a classmate, we praise that, too."

Even in a competitive situation, this teacher said, helping another is more important than winning. "When the children run in a relay race, sometimes one will fall down, especially if he's small. If another child stops to help him get up or to see if he's all right, even though his own team might fall behind, we encourage this." The approach contrasts markedly with methods used in the Soviet Union, another country that stresses the collective in its child-rearing practices. There, competition is discouraged between individuals but promoted between groups. Each child is made aware of his importance within his group—say, a row in his classroom—and then competes fiercely for the rewards of a group victory. The Chinese seem genuinely to eschew even this form of competition in favor of straightforward mutual help and cooperation.

But how do teachers deal with improper behavior and matters of discipline? Here is how the question was answered in a conversation with three staff members of a full-time kindergarten in Peking:

Q: What kinds of behavior do you discourage in the children?
A: We criticize those who take toys or other things from others. Or if children beat each other—we criticize that.
Q: Exactly how do you handle such a situation—say, two kids fighting?
A: First, the teacher must understand the reason for the fight. For instance, one might have taken a toy from the other, and the second child hit him. In that case, the teacher will criticize both. This criticism is carried out alone, unless it took place in the class; in that case it will be done in front of the class so that all the children will understand what was wrong. Criticism is to make children understand what was wrong and why.
Q: What kind of punishment do you use?
A: There is no punishment.
Q: Well, what if a child were really intractable? Would you use some mild sanction, such as depriving him of some free play time on the playground?
A: (At this point all three women broke into smiles at our incredulity. Waving their hands back and forth to underscore their words, they said): No, no, nothing like that. We believe in persuasion.
Q: Do other children ever participate in criticism?
A: Generally, no. Unless a third child saw what happened—then he'll be asked to tell.
Q: Let's say the incident was unobserved by any third party and the two kids involved give conflicting versions of what happened. Then how does the teacher act?
A: If the teacher finds a contradiction when both tell what happened, she will try to educate the children. She will note that everyone can make a mistake, including teachers. The mistake that led to the fight is not important, she will say, but telling the truth is very important. At this point the children will probably tell the truth.

This sounded like fine theory, but it provoked some skepticism among those of us who had been teachers. What about teachers who do not have the patience to use such positive techniques? we asked. How do you deal with teachers who don't observe

For a child in China today, the experience of "multiple mothering" is very likely. If the mother elects not to leave her child in a nursing room where she works, chances are the child will be in the care of its grandmother or a neighbor.

the school's policy? The reply: "We all—teachers and leadership—have the same goal: to cultivate revolutionary successors. So we all work together and help each other. We study our profession together. We have regular criticism and self-criticism sessions, and sometimes we help each other on specific problems."

If we had not already seen many teachers in action here and elsewhere on our trip, we might have been dissatisfied with this answer. But we were constantly struck by the teachers' apparent love for their work in all the early child care institutions we

visited. These women, we learned (there were no men), were chosen for their jobs after having shown a particular interest in children, and "sensitivity and love for children" were the criteria most often cited for their recruitment. Credentials were secondary. Since the Cultural Revolution, the amount of training teachers receive has ranged all the way from university graduation to short-term training classes and "learning through practice."

Three of us in the group who were especially interested in child rearing and education often asked to see child care centers and schools under

normal operating conditions. Our guides accommodated these requests by arranging for us to stay behind after the formal tour or make a low-key visit to a kindergarten, say, without the rest of the group. Some of our most revealing insights occurred during our observation of everyday free playground activities.

One afternoon, for example, at the child care center serving workers of the Fan Ga Chong coal mine area near Tangshan, I spent nearly an hour outside among the four-and-a-half-to-six-year-olds and their teachers, or "nurses." Here was the one place where I saw what might be called a disruptive child—a little boy who, in the United States, would probably have been labeled hyperkinetic and put on Ritalin. While the other 50 or so children busied themselves with various games—rope jumping, drop the handkerchief, tricycle riding, playing with toys and each other— this boy ran constantly from place to place, trying to be in on everything at once and occasionally interfering with someone else's fun. The nurses, who themselves were taking part in the games, were obviously aware of the boy's actions, but they made no fuss over him. Instead, each time he ran by a nurse, she would reach out, place her hand on the back of his head, and gently guide him away from trouble or toward an activity he might like—usually with a few soothing words. Soon he was off again, and once or twice it was necessary to intervene when he began picking on another child. But always the adults acted cheerfully and patiently, and the boy never became a center of attention. His actions were the closest thing to aggressive or disruptive behavior among children that I saw on the entire trip.

After visiting several classrooms at the Pei Hai Kindergarten, a full-time kindergarten located in a park in Peking, I spent an even longer time on the playground watching free play. Once again I was struck by the way teachers enthusiastically joined in. The children, well over a hundred of them, had formed into a variety of play groups. Some played on slides, a merry-go-round, monkey bars, and swings. Some were organized into class-sized groups for games. Others were in smaller groups, jumping rope or kicking a ball around. There were kids in pairs and kids alone. One gleeful little boy, holding aloft a leafy twig, ran, danced, and twirled with it till he fell down from dizziness. And ranging over the whole playground, sweeping past and through everyone else's games, was a whooping pack of boys chasing a soccer ball, a laughing teacher in the lead.

In one group that especially caught my eye, seven or eight girls were jumping rope, taking turns at the ends of a pink plastic rope and lining up to jump one by one. No teacher was with them. They were very absorbed and used chants and songs to accompany each jumper. Several times while I watched, a minor controversy of some kind would erupt and everything would come to a halt. Maybe it concerned whose turn was next on the rope or how many times one had jumped before missing. Whatever it was, the whole group would come together and heatedly debate their points. With no single girl taking charge, they would quickly work out a settlement that seemed to satisfy everyone and then resume their jumping with all the gusto of before. These little girls were good jumpers, incidentally. So good that after a while they attracted an audience: six little boys found chairs, lined them up to form a small gallery, and proceeded to join in the jumping chants, applauding for each jumper. Great fun for all, highly organized, and by all indications spontaneous and undirected by adults.

In the United States the growing demand for facilities for the care of infants and preschool children has provoked a chorus of urgent questions: Doesn't a baby need a single individual to relate to and identify with as mother? How can a mother be sure that those to whom she entrusts her child will teach the same values she holds? Isn't it the mother's natural role to care for her own children? What is the effect of insitutionalized child care on the family?

Obviously, the answers the Chinese have found to these questions are not directly applicable to this country. Yet the insights they provide can be instructive as we seek our own solutions.

There is a strong likelihood that the average child in China will undergo "multiple mothering" of some kind. Even if the mother does not choose to leave her infant in the nursing room where she works, chances are the child will wind up in the care of a neighbor or the grandmother. Offsetting this diversity of "mothers," however, is the near-uniform consensus of values and methods of child rearing I have described. This consistency seems to go a long way toward providing young children with the kind of security we in the United States might normally associate only with single mothering.

Another aspect of multiple or "shared" mothering, as Ruth Sidel, author of the excellent recent book *Women & Child Care in China,* points out, "is that infants can thrive physically and emotionally if the mother-surrogates are constant, warm, and giving. Babies in China are not subjected to serial mothering; we were repeatedly told that aunties (i.e., nurses) and teachers rarely leave their jobs. And they are warm and loving with the children. The children show none of the lethargy or other intellectual, emotional, or physical problems of institutionalized children. Quite the opposite!"

"Everything is planned," and the position of mothers in China is the consequence of a society-wide effort to provide for the economic liberation of women. In keeping with Mao Tse-tung's edict calling for "genuine equality between the sexes," a broad series of programs, including birth control information and prenatal care with maternity leave, in addition to the system of child care facilities, is underway to assume the full participation of women in "building socialism." The objects of unspeakable oppression in prerevolutionary society, Chinese women today have been thoroughly integrated into the labor force, both in factory and commune. And a growing number of them are entering professions—for example, 50 per cent of the medical students are now women.

Despite the enormous progress, even the Chinese will concede that full parity with men is not yet a reality. Top governmental, military, and management posts continue to be mostly male preserves. However, women do wield considerable political and administrative power at the local level, where they often run the smallest governmental units, the neighborhood revolutionary committees.

But the key to liberation is still

4. OTHER FAMILIES, OTHER WAYS

economic independence, which depends on the availability of work. Since 1971 a new source of work for women has appeared: the so-called housewives' factories. These have been organized locally by women who live in housing areas like the Kung Kiang Workers' Residential Area in Shanghai, and whose husbands work in the various nearby factories. As they described it to us, the housewives were looking for ways in which they could contribute productively to the revolution without having to leave the residential area. So they set up their own light industries in workshops near their homes, and by working full- or part-time were able to produce needed commodities, such as flashlight bulbs or men's trousers, while earning extra money for themselves. The entire operation in each case was staffed and run by women.

Since nearly all working-age women in China today work and are no longer economically dependent on their husbands or families, one might well wonder about the effects of these conditions on the family.

By all available evidence the family is thriving in China, and the individual household continues to be the basic social unit. A featured item in every home we visited, as ubiquitous as a portrait of Chairman Mao, was a display of a great many photographs of family members, usually pressed under a piece of glass on top of a bureau or framed on the wall. Our host or hostess would invariably point this out with pride. Signs of active and full participation in family life were everywhere, and all generations were included. A man out with his children is a common sight, as is a child with a grandmother or grandfather.

Parents are obviously revered by children, and so are grandparents. In fact, the complete absence of a "generation gap" is a striking phenomenon to an American. Not only are grandparents well integrated into family life, but old people who have no family or who are disabled live in well-tended "respect for aged" homes and are given important functions that serve the neighborhood.

Far from undermining the family structure, we were repeatedly told, jobs for women and day care for children have made home life easier, having eliminated many former sources of friction and frustration. A major factor here is undoubtedly the mass commitment to working for the betterment of China. Personal gratification seems to derive from each individual's knowledge that he or she makes an important contribution, no matter how small, to the national effort and that the benefits of this contribution, and others like it, will be distributed to all.

Free Enterprise and The Ghetto Family

Jagna Wojcicka Sharff

Jagna Wojcicka Sharff is an urban anthropologist who teaches at City College and Columbia University in New York City. She completed her Ph.D at Columbia and is writing a book about the project discussed here, entitled Life on Dolittle Street: How Poor People Purchase Immortality.

Street life on Dolittle Street is a sleight of hand. The clumps of six to 10 young men who seem to be socializing daily on the corner from early morning until late at night are not there solely for convivial reasons. Nor is the little hole-in-the-wall cigarette store near the corner selling only tobacco cigarettes. Nor is the storefront several tenements down the block just the home of a popular bachelor with lots of friends continuously dropping by. The mechanic next door is not simply repairing cars. And the mothers conversing in small groups and calling out of the windows are not occupied with housework and child care. Nor are the children simply playing. All these places and activities are both what they are and something elso, too—and the something else is invariably aimed at adding to the meager resources of the neighborhood, often illegally.

From July 1977 to August 1979, an anthropological team of which I was project director rented a storefront on Dolittle Street, a fictitious name for a well-traveled street that cuts across Manhattan's Lower East Side. The block has provided shelter to successive ethnic groups in the same tenements that now house immigrant Hispanics.

Through earlier research, which included a socio-economic census of 168 blocks of the neighborhood, we knew a great deal about the area. It suffered from one of the highest fire rates in New York City, and its housing stock ranged from fair to almost uninhabitable. Like some areas of the south Bronx and Brooklyn, more than half the buildings had been abandoned or burned out. The area had one of the highest proportions of households with the lowest incomes in the city and an underemployment rate of about 60 percent. (Underemployment is a concept developed by some economists to provide a measure of worker discouragement, particularly in poverty areas; underemployment encompasses the number of unemployed as well as those who can find only part-time work or jobs at inadequate pay). Finally, about two-thirds of the households in the area had at some point received public assistance.

We also knew that the neighborhood was honeycombed with illegal economic activity and permeated with police undercover operations. Fierce competition between different drug-selling groups and frequent police raids often resulted in violence. There was a high death rate in the neighborhood (among young men in particular), as there is among other poor groups throughout New York City. Several definitive studies show that homicide accounts for more than 20 percent of the deaths among these groups.

Our general perspective followed the approach articulated by anthropologist Marvin Harris in his book *Cultural Materialism*—that human behavior is purposive and adaptive and deserves to be observed and recorded "on the ground." To pursue the strategy Harris had outlined we needed to see how the people of Dolittle Street actually lived their lives. The storefront became our means of integration into the social life of the neighborhood.

We explained our presence as an effort to learn "how people make a living in their neighborhood." We also explained that we were especially interested in the economic and social value of drugs. In turn, we made ourselves available to the residents as advocates, expecially in their dealings with the various public agencies that wield so much power over their lives.

It took a great length of time and a great deal of energy before the residents began to tolerate, accept, and finally trust us. But gradually we found our way from the street to the living quarters of the residents. As time passed, we became acquainted with the photograph albums of the households' past. We charted the starlike constellations of their kin, we compiled geneologies, household budgets (very important for our economic analysis), patterns of work and leisure; we participated in the residents' efforts to obtain sufficient food, to keep warm, and to raise their children.

We bore witness to many significant events, some joyful, many grievous. A sudden fire, a raid by the police, a street fair, an accident, a suicide, the birth of a child—all revealed the social and economic alignments that operate under the surface of public life on Dolittle Street.

For example, when a young marijuana dealer was murdered, we sat up with his family, drinking coffee, quietly conversing, while numerous members of the extended kin arrived from as far away as Puerto Rico. We took turns baby tending, cooking, and sleeping on the few available beds. Later we contributed to the neighborhood-wide collection to help the family pay for the funeral expenses. Burial ceremonies on Dolittle Street are a major expense, and the immediate family is expected to bear the financial burden of this rite of passage. (Aside from a modest baptismal party, a proper burial is the only ceremony a resident can look forward to with confidence). At the public wake in the funeral home we were part of a large throng of mourners—family, neighbors, and the dead boy's friends. It was by participant observation in such events that we began to uncover the networks that bind people together and to understand their behavior.

Most studies of poor people suggest that poverty results from some or all of the following: unwillingness to work, lack of skills, ignorance or apathy about contraceptives—hence large families, hence poverty and the perpetuation in the next generation of poverty-causing qualities through the so-called culture of poverty. Our research suggests the opposite, and our focus here will be on the strategies of survival among the Dolittle residents, especially their cultivation of that ostensible burden of the poor—the large family.

Briefly, we found that poor people are hardworking (no loose generality, as even the sketchy discussion below on the work efforts of the Dolittle people will indicate) and that they quickly develop requisite skills when reasonable work is available. Most

significantly, we found that having a large number of children is an immensely useful short-run option pursued by a majority of the households. The large family doesn't keep the poor in poverty, but rather serves as a mechanism for survival.

Essentially, the large-family option involves socializing the children into distinct social roles. We found four—the "street representative," the "young child-reproducer," the "wage earner," and the "scholar/advocate," each of which we will examine later. The aim of this network is to extend the domain of the household and help gather additional resources for the family. Indeed, the children of Dolittle Street can be seen as the "investment portfolio" of the mothers (and sometimes the fathers); a flexible resource for security in both the present and the future, one that will also help establish an economic base so that at least one child can move a step up the economic and social ladder.

THE ECONOMIC TIGHTROPE OF DOLITTLE STREET

Before we examine the social roles into which the young people are guided, we must briefly examine the economic context out of which these roles emerge. If the children can be considered a "strategy for survival," it is in part because the other strategies that are available to the adults have such severe limits.

The figures and facts that follow are based on detailed information about 36 households, consisting of 133 individuals. These households do not form a representative sample in a statistical sense. Yet their activities constitute a fair picture of the difficult and often dangerous economic balancing act that is performed by most of the households on Dolittle Street.

The households have three sources of income: regular work, public assistance, and what some economists call "irregular work"—quasi-legal or illegal activities.

Regular work is quite uncertain. The high rate of underemployment means that the residents can find only

sporadic and insecure jobs. Such jobs, when available, are usually in small, undercapitalized, and marginal business ventures. They offer low wages and no opportunity for advancement; they are usually non-unionized and often seasonal. Adding to the crunch in regular job opportunities is the fact that two-thirds of the manufacturing jobs in which Puerto Ricans worked have been lost during the past decade.

For the neighborhood's residents, the income from such jobs varies considerably. Factory workers earn $90 to $120 a week, when they are working. A handyman or janitor earns $40 to $60. A waitress in a restaurant or bar earns $60 to $140. But none of the work is steady.

Regular work is very important for the self-esteem and status of the adult males. The strains imposed by the condition of underemployment can lead to marital instability and worse. For example, over the course of a year, two of the 36 households in our group acquired husband/fathers, while four lost them. Of these four, one man committed suicide, another was murdered, a third was imprisoned, and the fourth, discouraged by his low-wage factory job, quit, and then, after a "grace period" of several months in which he did not find another job, was driven out of the house by his common-law wife.

It is this situation of constant economic and marital insecurity that prompts women with young children to apply for public assistance. The amount of assistance varies from household to household, but the general picture is simple to draw. In 1979, as an example, an average family of four—a mother and three children—received $258 in monthly assistance (called "Pre-Add Allowance"), a sum meant to cover gas, electricity, telephone, clothing, transportation, furnishings, cleaning materials, personal-care items, school supplies, leisure, and so forth. In addition, an average family of four received a limit of $218 a month as its shelter allowance—a sum that went directly to the landlord, who often charged more than that for a tiny, squalid apartment. And finally, a family of four in our sample received an average of $88 a month in food stamps. The purchasing power of this income is indicated by the fact that at the time of our research the cost of feeding a family of four in New York city, according to the Consumer Price Index, was $352 a month.

To understand the practical value of public assistance in more detail, we worked with our 36 households to itemize their annual budgets and learned that over the course of a year, the households spent an average of 87 percent of their public assistance (Pre-Add, shelter, and food stamps) for a combination of food and rent, which meant that the remaining 13 percent had to pay for utilities, clothing, furniture, transportation, and the rest.

The households used whatever strategies they could devise to close the gap between income and basic expenses. One of them was "doubling up" with unreported common-law husbands, whose contributions from regular work could make a difference between destitution and a very modest standard of living. Young adult children still living at home made similarly unreported contributions. But because regular work was so sporadic, even such contributions were often not enough to close the gap. In our households, the annual income derived from regular work ranged from $400 to $3,020, leaving deficits for many of the households in the area of $1,000 to $2,000 a year.

That is the background against which the residents turned to irregular work.

Contrary to popular belief, irregular work does not command large sums. A street vendor of drugs, for example, earns between $25 and $50 a week, a telephone operator for a "numbers" game earns between $75 and $90 a week. (In both cases, larger amounts are turned over to the outside groups running these operations). Yet these sums are vital to the households, and the residents engaged in irregular work—even the drug-selling street vendors—hand

over much of their income to mother and family.

There are three areas of irregular work. The least lucrative and most haphazard is what we call "freelance" work—stealing, mugging, fencing, and the like. Often, young adolescent boys who are not allowed to participate in more organized operations engage in such free-lance activities. Except in relatively smalltime shoplifting, they are not notably successful. They are often caught, arrested, and jailed.

A second source of irregular income is the *bolita*, the illegal lottery. This is the safest of the irregular jobs, but it involves only a small number of participants: a "street collector," a "telephone operator," a "cashier," and a "manager," all of them usually older adults.

The last source of irregular money involves the most people and is the most hazardous—the varied operations of the drug business. Like the *bolita*, the drug business is controlled by groups outside the neighborhood, who skim off the largest portion of the profits. The residents of Dolittle Street work mostly in the more visible, therefore more vulnerable, lower-level retail distribution jobs. For the residents of Dolittle Street, drug selling is a dangerous and low-paying profession that provides necessary income to the area's households.

Perhaps the most lucrative of the lower-echelon jobs is what we call the "drug-o-matic," an operation carried out through a hole in the door of an apartment. The customers, usually strangers to the neighborhood, are often steered to the location by local "touts." They knock on the door, give their order through the hole, pass their money through it, and receive their merchandise in return. The operation resembles automatic bank machines, and the greatest danger comes from competitors, not the police.

Participants in smaller home-operations, which include "shooting galleries," run a higher risk of arrest. Shooting galleries are apartments where users can buy heroin and then, for an additional payment (usually

$5), "shoot up" and rest in the apartment until ready to leave. There are also several operations that principally sell marijuana: the "drug stand," a small kiosk that also sells regular cigarettes, often by the piece; the "drug store," a storefront where people can buy and smoke marijuana; and "home sales," a kind of Avon-lady marijuana operation, in which women sell small amounts of marijuana to neighbors. Finally, there are street vendors, who have the most vulnerable and dangerous of the drug operation jobs.

This, then, in brief outline, is the harsh and hazardous economic life of the Dolittle neighborhood. But it is only fair to add one more element to the picture—a strategy of survival that conjoins with the economic scramble. Simply put, the residents of Dolittle Street help each other when they can. They are forced to compete for scarce jobs but often share goods and services with one another in regular acts of cooperation. We call this strategy "communal work." A typical example of such communality concerns the children. When the economic situation in one household is unusually low, the women of other households make a point of inviting the children to eat with them. The invitation is never offered in front of the children's mother, because it would embarrass her. Since every household experiences economic low periods, there is a continuous reciprocity in such meal sharing.

The most fascinating communal project we observed on Dolittle Street was that of "crabbing." Several families own crab traps, and during the summer, groups of adults and children set off in the late afternoon several times a week to catch soft-shell crabs in the waters of Coney Island. The group spends the entire night fishing from the pier. Early in the morning, usually in time for the employed men to get to their jobs, the crabbers return with full buckets. For the rest of the day, the women of the households clean and cook the crabs, and then send generous portions to other families and neighbors via the fire escapes and windows or in packages carried by the children.

The catching and sharing of crabs (the only source of seafood the residents can afford) was perhaps the most joyful community activity in the neighborhood.

In a sense, both the economic struggle and the communal work of the Dolittle residents help to maintain their lives from day to day. But it is through the children that they hope to purchase immortality.

THE YOUNG PEOPLE OF DOLITTLE STREET

Much of what the residents of Dolittle Street do to survive is clearly done for the sake of the children. Residents have a telling phrase to describe such efforts: *para el futuro*— for the future.

To the women of Dolittle Street in particular, almost any activity or action is legitimate if it is done for the children—*para el futuro*. So mothers falsely declare themselves as single to the representatives of welfare agencies. They do not see it as a form of cheating, but as a way of assuring their children regular allotments of money, since the insecure, dependent position of the men in the economic market makes the loss of a male a likely possibility. Similarly, the women will sometimes take a job with a "borrowed" Social Security card, especially in cold months, when expenditures are higher. It is, to them, only another effort to provide for their children.

As the children grow, they in turn provide valuable services for the mother and the household. They become, in effect, a human strategy for survival, the essence of which is a network in which the children adopt separate but interlocking roles.

To repeat: We have distilled four basic roles into which the children are socialized by their mothers and kin. Not every household has all four, of course. We are reporting *patterns* found in a majority of the households, patterns that seem to characterize the domestic strategies employed by a large segment of low-income Puerto Ricans in New York City. The roles are: the "street representative," the "young child-reproducer," the "wage earner," and the "scholar/advocate."

The most dangerous of the roles is that of "street representative," which is almost always filled by a young man. The street representative is the family's protector and avenger, and invariably undertakes irregular work, usually associated with the sale of drugs.

A boy who will become his household's street representative is socialized from an early age into this role by older boys and young men. By the age of six, he begins to participate in dangerous, risk-taking activities. As the young boys climb roofs and fire escapes, walk into the rushing traffic or bike and skate among cars, hitch rides on the backs of vehicles, and otherwise challenge, scuffle, and fight, they are in effect developing the requisite skills of a street representative. As they move into their teens, they join kinship-based male groups in which the older and more experienced members further train them in cooperative "raiding" from the open-air stalls in the neighborhood that sell clothes and food.

Around then, they also often become the physical protectors of their mothers, sisters, and young siblings, and they avenge any wrong done to them. As a defender/avenger, the street representative sees to it that the reputation of the women in his household is protected, and he intervenes in any premature flirtations of his sisters. If a young woman has a *novio* (a fiance approved by the family, which can happen when the girl is as young as 13), it is the defender's job to tag along on dates as a chaperon.

The learned aggressiveness of the street representative is not easily tolerated by the schools, which, instead of providing alternative skills, usually take active steps to have such students removed. This response encourages the boys to participate more fully in the activities for which their experience has been preparing them: fighting, defending, avenging, raiding, and contributing to their households with earnings from irregular work. Most street representatives begin playing hooky seriously in junior high school. They leave school completely at the age of 16 or 17, by which time they often have had unpleasant encounters with the police, the court system, and the jails.

As a rule, the boys then enter the highly competitive irregular economy, particularly that part of the economy concerned with drugs, and most often they become street vendors. They are on the street corners from mid-morning until well into the night, seven days a week, in all seasons, in all weather. Despite their low earnings ($25 to $50 a week), the job still enables them to contribute to the household's livelihood through work to which they have access and for which they have developed the requisite skills.

Few street representatives live to an old age. Their prospects are suggested by the fact that among our 36 households, six men between the ages of 19 to 30 were killed in drug-related incidents during the two and a half years of research. Because the life of a street representative is so uncertain, at any given time in the cycle of a household, a second young man is usually understudying the role. He is the "street-rep-in-waiting."

The certainty that some boys will not survive to maturity makes it important for households to raise several sons, which is the task the "young child-reproducer" takes over from her mother after the latter's reproductive years are terminated, either by age or tubal ligation. (It has been estimated that 30 percent of adult Puerto Rican women have been sterilized, sometimes against their will). The young child-reproducer is a girl who is socialized into the traditional feminine role of childbearer. She literally replaces lost household personnel. A 14-year-old girl that we knew, the sister of a young man who had been murdered, gave birth to a baby boy within a year of her brother's death. The baby was named after the dead brother.

The young child-reproducer helps with housekeeping and other facets of child care and contributes her assistance money to the pooled household budget. She usually drops out of school in her early teens. Like the street representative, she is destined to live and to die on Dolittle Street, or its equivalent.

The announcement that a woman is pregnant is greeted with great joy. But the pregnancy of a teenager sometimes brings other reactions, too. When it became known, for example, that a teenager just entering high school was pregnant (she had shown promise in the performing arts), several women told us privately that they had cried all night. "Now her life is going to be wasted, just like mine," they said. But within a few weeks, everyone was enthusiastic again about the prospect of a new child.

In addition to the two above roles, a household usually rears a "wage earner." The wage earner is sometimes a girl, but more usually a boy who has been socialized in a quasi-feminine mode. The macho training applied to the street representative is not applied to him.

We do not understand the dynamics of the process, but from our observations, it is apparent that a sizable minority of children, both boys and girls, are encouraged to develop differently from the stereotypical masculine and feminine roles. In the case of boys, we observed a youngster as young as eight years old being spoken of by the adults as a *pato* (colloquial for homosexual) and addressed as "wonderwoman" by some of the

children. He was an extremely gentle and affectionate person, and offered his cheek to be kissed by everyone. He seemed not to mind the teasing. We believe that the training of passive boys may be adaptive in preparing them to fulfill the requirements of subservient wage laborers.

These boys keep up a steady attendance in school, stay away from street action, help with household chores, and actively participate in their mothers' gossip groups. If they drop out of school, it is only in the last year, and they immediately begin work in wage-labor jobs. Most of their earnings are handed straight over to their mothers. They speak softly and shyly, and move with gentle body movements. Their earnings are essential to their households, and while they themselves might gradually rise out of Dolittle Street, more often a portion of their income is used to sponsor a younger, gifted child, often a girl, to improve her education and thus her career and marital possibilities.

This large hope for the future is the "scholar/advocate," usually a girl who has been encouraged to develop assertive skills normally associated with the training of boys. She is the nontraditional female in the sense that the quiet wage earner is the nontraditional male.

The "dominant" girls begin their contribution to the household by accompanying their mothers to welfare institutions and becoming their mother's articulate advocate. These girls usually complete their second-

ary education, and if the household has the luck to have an employed wage earner, they sometimes go on to college. They do not help with the housework, and if they do have children, they have them later in life and usually limit the size of their family. They are the most likely to obtain secretarial or other pink-collar jobs, the most likely to marry "up," and thus the most likely of any of the children to move up from and out of Dolittle Street, thereby adding to the domain and resources of their households.

In effect, the large family is a kind of social-security system for the present and future of the household. The members of the family are linked in an organic network, to which each contributes according to his or her talent and means, and on which all depend—the risks in the street representative role notwithstanding—for their day-to-day survival.

REFERENCES

deLone, Richard, *Small Futures: Children, Inequality and the Limits of Liberal Reform,* Harcourt, Brace, Jovanovich, 1979. $12.95

Harris, Marvin. *Cultural Materialism: The Struggle for a Science of Culture,* Random House, 1979, $15; paper, 1980, $4.95

Liebow, Elliott. *Talley's Corner: A Study of Negro Street Corner Men.* Little, Brown, & Co. 1967, out of print

Stack, Carol. *All Our Kin: Strategies for Survival in a Black Community.* Harper & Row, 1975, paper, $3.50

Valentine, Bettylou. *Hustling and Other Hard Work: Life Styles in the Ghetto,* Free Press, 1978, $12.95; paper, 1980, $6.95.

The Gypsies

William M. Kephart

The Gypsies are most incredible. For several years now, I have studied them, interviewed them, and—on occasion—mingled with them, but I still find it difficult to grasp their culture patterns. Other writers have experienced similar difficulties, for the Gypsies have a lifestyle that comes close to defying comprehension. On the dust jacket of Peter Maas' controversial and widely read *King of the Gypsies,* for example, the following blurb appears:

There are perhaps a million or more Gypsies in the United States—nobody knows exactly how many, not even the government. They no longer live in horse-drawn caravans on dusty roads; they live in cities, drive cars, have telephones and credit cards. Yet they do not go to school, neither read nor write, don't pay taxes, and keep themselves going by means of time-honored ruses and arrangements. Gypsies themselves recognize the contrast they make, and they are proud of it.[1]

Given the nature of modern journalism, can this statement be true? The answer is not a simple one, and each of the above points requires some explanation.

It is true that no one knows how many Gypsies there are in the United States, although the million figure commonly reported in the press may be too high. More reliable estimates place the figure closer to 500,000.[2] If the latter figure is correct, it would mean that only two other countries in the world have larger Gypsy populations: Yugoslavia (750,000), and Romania (680,000).[3]

Although 500,000 seems a reasonable estimate, it is unlikely that the real figure will ever be known. The fact of the matter is that Gypsies move about so much, have so many different names and aliases, and are generally so secretive that it is often difficult to pinpoint the numbers for a given city let alone for the nation at large.

Gypsies live in cities and drive cars? Indeed they do. They are not likely to be found on farms or in the suburbs. They will not be found on the water. They are urban dwellers—towns and cities—and they reside in nearly all of the fifty states. At the same time, Gypsies are, and always have been, great travelers. They may be the greatest travelers the world has ever known. (In England, the terms "Gypsy" and "Traveler" are often used interchangeably.) As we shall see, traveling serves as an integral part of Gypsy life-style.

As for the cars, Gypsies not only drive them but sometimes make their living repairing them. The days of the horse-drawn wagons and caravans have long since gone, but Gypsies—as is their wont—have adapted remarkably well to motorized transportation. Indeed, despite the fact that they are a low-income group, Gypsies often drive Cadillacs.

Gypsies do not go to school? Not very often—and not for very long. They feel that formal education is not germane to their way of life and that the American school system would tend to "de-Gypsyize" their youngsters. both claims are at least partially true, and the subject will be discussed later.

Gypsies neither read nor write? True. A large proportion of them are functionally illiterate. They cannot even read or write their own language, Romany, for it is a spoken rather than a written tongue. The literacy situation is improving, but so far progress has been slow. In spite of their self-imposed linguistic handicap, however, Gypsies have made a remarkable adaptation to their environment.

Gypsies do not pay taxes? Some observers would reply: "Not if they can help it." And it is true that many Gypsies do not pay property taxes because they have no taxable property. They often prefer to rent rather than to buy a dwelling-place. Also, many Gypsies work irregularly and have low—paying jobs, so that their income taxes would be negligible. A fair number are on welfare. On the other hand, at least some Gypsies are moving into white-collar occupations, and their tax payments are probably commensurate with those of other white-collar workers.

Gypsies keep themselves going by means of time-honored ruses and arrangements? A complicated question, surely, but then the Gypsies are a complicated people. As it true of all ethnic groups, there are honest Gypsies and there are dishonest Gypsies. Unfortunately, however, many Gypsies continue to believe that all *gadje** (non-Gypsies) are fair game. And more than occasionally this belief does culminate in ruses and petty swindles.

At the same time, Gypsy attitudes toward the *gadje* have been shaped in part by the *gadje* themselves. As will be shown, Gypsies have not been met with open arms by the various host countries. On the contrary, they have experienced near-universal prejudice and discrimination. Social distance studies in several countries, including the United States, simply confirm the obvious; namely, that Gypsies rank at the absolute bottom of the status scale.[4]

Through it all, the Gypsies have survived. Gypsies always survive. If they haven't exactly flourished, they have in many ways given a very good account of themselves. It is not easy to be a Gypsy. As one writer put it: "Only the fit need apply."[5] It is hoped that in the following pages the full implications of this statement will become clear.

WHO ARE THE GYPSIES?

Like so many other aspects of their life, Gypsy origins are draped in mystery. The word "Gypsy" derives from "Egyptian," for the Gypsies were mistakenly thought to have originated in Egypt. This was a belief that they themselves did little to discourage. In fact, some Gypsies still believe in their Egyptian roots, although it has now been rather well established that their original homeland was India. (Romany, the Gypsy language, has its roots in Sanskrit.)

*Interestingly enough, the Gypsy language has not been standardized. As a result, most of their terms have a variety of spellings. In the present account, spelling has been adapted to fit the pronunciation.

Exactly when the Gypsies left India—or what their status was—is still being debated. They have been variously described as being descended from the Criminal and Wandering Tribes, as being deported prisoners of war, and as being "a loose federation of nomadic tribes, possibly outside the Indian caste system entirely."[6] Rishi contends that "the majority of Gypsies, before migrating from India, formed a vital part of the upper strata of the Indian population, such as the Rajputs, Kshatriyas, and Jats."[7]

Whatever their class or caste origins, it seems likely that the proto-Gypsies left India at different times—and from different areas—perhaps during the first few centuries A.D.[8] By the fifth century, they seem to have settled in and around Persia and Syria. And although their early migration patterns are anything but clear, Gypsies were reported in Southeastern Europe (Greece, Hungary, Romania, Serbia) by the 1300s, and in Western Europe (France, Germany, Italy, Holland, Switzerland, Spain) by the 1400s.[9] Today there are Gypsies in practically every European country. They are also well established in North Africa, the Near East, South America, the United States, and Canada.

The term "Gypsy," incidentally, is not a Romany term. Gypsies refer to themselves as "Rom." (In the present account, the two terms will be used interchangeably.) And while there is much physical variation, the Rom tend to have dark hair, dark eyes, and medium to dark complexions. On the whole, they are of average or a little below average height. Several writers have noticed that Gypsies tend to become obese as they age.

(Some groups who are often thought of as Gypsies are not in fact true Gypsies, or Rom. These would include the Tinkers of Ireland and Scotland, and the Taters of Norway.[10] The Irish Tinkers, for example, are of Celtic origin, and they speak Shelte, a Celtic dialect.[11] In the present account, we are concerned only with the Rom.)

As they spread throughout Europe, Gypsies came to be—above all else—travelers. "A Gypsy who does not keep on the move," wrote Block just prior to World War II, "is not a Gypsy."[12] Actually, there have always been a fair number of sedentary Gypsies, or *Sinte.* Lockwood reports that in Yugoslavia there is currently a community of some 40,000 Gypsies.[13]

Nevertheless, *Sinte* or no *Sinte,* it was the horse-drawn wagons and gaily decorated caravans that seemed to strike a responsive chord in people of all ages. Jan Yoors, author of one of the most widely read books on Gypsy life, ran away as a young boy and lived for many years with a Gypsy group.[14] Webb, another writer, states that

for as long as I can remember, Gypsies have fascinated me. These dark-skinned strangers, indifferent to the rest of the world, mysterious in their comings and goings, traveling the roads with parades of highly colored raggedness, fired my imagination. I was curious about them and wanted to know more. But nobody, it seemed, could tell me more.[15]

The Rom themselves seemed captivated by the caravan style of life. Indeed, some still talk about the good old (premotorized) days. Whether, in fact, caravan life was all that good can be debated. Yoors himself writes as follows:

One year, for the first time, I stayed with the Rom throughout the winter. Lying half awake in the cold stillness of the long nights in Pulika's huge wagon, I heard the snapping noise of the nails in the boards as they creaked under the effect of the severe frost. The windows had been covered up with boards, old overcoats and army blankets, straw or pieces of tar paper, but the wind blasted through cracks too many to fill.

The dogs whimpered all night. The drinking water froze in the buckets, and washing in the morning became an ordeal. Hands chapped, lips cracked and bled. The men ceased to shave. The small children cried bitterly when they were put outside and chased away from the wagons near which they had wanted to relieve themselves. Clothes could not be washed. The air inside the wagons was thick and unbreathable, mixed with the coal fumes from the red-hot stove, from which small children had to be kept away.

During the winter months, not enough dead wood could be gathered outside to keep the fires going all day and part of the night, so the Rom were forced to buy, beg, or steal coal.[16]

No combination of elements, however, could dampen the Gypsy spirit—or their fondness for bright colors, especially greens, yellows, and reds. As one effervescent Gypsy put it, "I wear bright beads and bright colors because we're a bright race. We don't like anything drab."[17]

The Gypsy Paradox With their unusual life-style, there is no doubt that Gypsies have held a real fascination for the *gadje,* almost irrespective of the country involved. Novels, plays, operettas, movies, and songs have portrayed—and sometimes glorified—the romantic wanderings of the Gypsy vagabond. Popular pieces like "Gypsy Love Song" and "Play Gypsy, Dance Gypsy" have become part of the worldwide musical repertoire.

Yet side by side with the attraction and fascination has come harassment and persecution. This is the Gypsy paradox: attraction on the one hand, persecution on the other. The climax of persecution came during World War II, when the Nazis murdered between 250,000 and 500,000 Rom. Moreover, the extermination took place without the Gypsies even being given a reason!

Despite worldwide persecution, however, the Gypsies have managed to survive. Gypsies always survive. As Gropper puts it:

For 500 years Gypsies have succeeded in being themselves against all odds, fiercely maintaining their identity in spite of persecution, prejudice, hatred, and cultural forces compelling them to change. We may have something to learn from them on how to survive in a drastically changing world.[18]

The Modern Period Following World War II, urbanization and industrialization—together with population expansion—literally cramped the Gypsies' life-style. There was less and less room on the modern highway for horse-drawn caravans. Camping sites became harder to find, and the open countryside seemed to shrink. But—as always—the Gypsies adapted. Travel continued, albeit on a reduced scale. Caravans and wagons were replaced by automobiles, trucks, campers, and trailers. Somehow, by one method or another, the Rom managed to get by. And they did so without sacrificing their group identity or their freedom.

Their identity was not maintained without a price, however, for prejudice and harassment continued. Gypsy nomads were often hounded from one locale to another. The *Sinte* or sedentary Rom—whose proportion tended to increase—were also met by hostility and discrimination. "No Gypsies Allowed" signs came more and more to be posted in public places.

The issue was hardly one-sided. From the view of local authorities, Gypsies were using community services without paying their share of the taxes. Indeed, they were often not paying any taxes at all! Additionally, the Rom were dirty, they would not use indoor toilets, they lied, they cheated, and they stole. sometimes the charges were true; often they were unfounded. (Interestingly, the Rom have rarely been accused of crimes of violence.)

Fortunately, the Gypsies also had friends and supporters, and in a number of countries efforts were made to set up camping sites, establish housing facilities, provide legal assistance, and otherwise improve the lot of the Rom. By the 1970s, a number of national and international committees and councils had been organized—with Gypsy representation. The purpose of these groups has been not only to protect the interests of the Rom but to dispel stereotypes, combat false portrayals in the media, and act as a clearinghouse for information about Gypsies.

When all is said and done, however, there is not doubt that the Rom continue to have problems. According to Dodds, the idea of their having a carefree, romantic life is a myth. In reality, "the Gypsy's life is one of perpetual insecurity."[19]

And yet . . . contrast the foregoing statement with the following, by Clebert: "Gypsies themselves are Lords of the Earth. . . . All real Gypsies are united in their love of freedom, and in their eternal flight from the bonds of civilization, in their desire to be their own masters, and in their contempt for what we pompously call the 'consequences.' "[20]

Which of the two views if correct? Perhaps both are. In some ways, the Rom do indeed have a difficult life. Their relationship with the *gadje* often takes on the appearance of an interminable contest. At the same time, Gypsies show little inclination to assimilate. They are demonstrably proud that they are Gypsies, an attitude that is unlikely to change.

How many Gypsies are there in the world today? Estimates vary from five to ten million, with the latter figure probably being closer to the truth. (More than half are in Eastern Europe.) There is general—though not unanimous—agreement that the Rom are divided into four tribes or nations *(natsiyi):* the Lowara, Machwaya, Kalderasha, and Churara. While there are linguistic and cultural differences among the four *natsiyi,* surprisingly little has been written on this score. . . .

DIFFICULTIES IN STUDYING THE ROM

If you ask a dozen Gypsies the same question, you will probably get a dozen different answers. If you ask one Gypsy the same question a dozen times, you will still probably get a dozen different answers.
—*Anon*

Although there are many versions, this adage contains more than a little truth. Gypsies live—and always have lived—in alien cultures. The boundaries between Rom and *gadje* are sharp, and the Rom have every intention of maintaining the sharpness. Deception, avoidance, misrepresentation, and lying are part of the Gypsies' arsenal, and they have had hundreds of years to perfect and embellish their defenses. In many ways, investigating the Rom is like trying to penetrate a secret society. As Evans-Pritchard observes:

I am sure that it is much easier to enter into a primitive Melanesian or African community than that of the Gypsies. The Melanesian or African has not had to build his barricades as the Gypsies have had to do. . . . Gypsies have been for centuries living in societies in which they have not belonged.[25]

Perhaps the most formidable obstacle the researcher has to face is the avoidance syndrome. The Rom ordinarily do not mingle with the *gadje;* in fact, except for a possible visit to a fortune-teller, most Americans never come into contact with a Gypsy. Almost certainly they never see the inside of a Romany dwelling. Researchers face much the same problem. The fact that they are accredited university personnel means little to the Rom. Generally speaking, Gypsies have no intention of divulging their life-style and customs to social scientists or to anybody else.

Fortunately, we have some excellent American field studies such as those by Anne Sutherland[26] and Rena C. Gropper.[27] Both of these investigators are not only trained observers but spent several years among the Rom, learning the language and achieving a fair degree of acceptance. And even they experienced difficulties! Sutherland writes that

the first Gypsy I met was a young woman of my own age who smiled at me, talking soothingly and ingratiatingly, but when I asked to speak with her father, she lunged at me, grabbing my face with her fingernails, screaming and cursing, "WHAT DO YOU WANT?"

The second Gypsy I talked with vehemently denied that he was a Gypsy (what better technique for not answering questions), and the third feigned imbecility, mumbling to herself and staring wildly into space. . . .

It soon became clear that these are people who, through centuries of experience in avoiding the prying questions of curious outsiders, have perfected their techniques of evasion to an effortless art. They delight in deceiving the *gadje,* mostly for a good reason, but sometimes just for the fun of it or to keep in practice![28]

Although avoidance and deception serve as major impediments in studying the Rom, there are other difficulties involved—difficulties that make it hard to *generalize* about Gypsy life. To begin with, all four *natsiyi* or tribes are represented in the United States. Customs and practices that apply to one group might or might not apply to the others. (Actually, the Kalderasha and the Machwaya are by far the most numerous of the *natsiyi* in the United States, and most of the American studies have been done on these two groups. Little is known about the Churara, and there are relatively few Lowara in this country.)

Practices of the Rom also vary depending on their mobility patterns. Some Gypsies have lived in the same domicile for many years. Others move about constantly. Still others travel as the mood strikes them. And customs and life-style vary somewhat from one group to another.

Even if all Rom followed similar travel practices, their social structure would be difficult to analyze. Gypsies live in extended families (*familiyi*), which form part of a larger kinship or cognatic group called the *vitsa*. (The *vitsi*, in turn, are affiliated with one of the four tribes, or *natsiyi:* Lowara, Machwaya, Kalderasha, and Churara.) The point is that many Gypsy customs may vary from one *familia* to the next, and from one *vitsa* to the next, making it hard, again, to generalize.

In addition to these kinship and tribal affiliations, Gypsies in a given area often form themselves into economic units called *kumpaniyi*. A *kumpania* is a loose association formed for the purpose of organizing the labor force, parceling out jobs, and so forth. *Wortacha* are much smaller economic units, such as those involving friends, brothers, or father-son partnerships.

One final factor complicates the study of American Rom: their customs often depend on their country of origin. The Romnichals (English Gypsies), for instance, differ from the Boyash (Romanian), and both groups are culturally different from the Arxentina (Gypsies from Argentina and Brazil).[29]

In brief, American Rom do not present a uniform culture pattern. Because of their kinship structure, their social and economic organization, their geographical mobility, and their nationality differences, it would be difficult to generalize about Gypsies even if they were cooperative—which they are not. (And even the "cooperative" Gypsies pose a problem for the researcher. The Rom often have a working knowledge of their own particular group—but no other. Very few Gypsies have anything like a broad view or a historical picture of their own people.) . . .

MARIMÉ

Central to any understanding of the Rom is their concept of *marimé*. It is *marimé* that is the key to their avoidance of the *gadje*, and it is *marimé* that serves as a powerful instrument of social control.

Marimé means defilement or pollution, and as used by the Gypsies it is both an object and a concept. And since there is really no comparable term used by non-Gypsies, it is sometimes difficult for the latter to comprehend the meaning. "*Marimé*," writes Miller, "extends to all areas of Rom life, underwriting a hygienic attitude toward the world. . . . Lines are drawn between Gypsy and non-Gypsy, the clean and the unclean, health and disease, the good and the bad, all of which are made obvious and visible through the offices of ritual avoidance."[31]

The most striking aspects of *marimé* have to do with the demarcation of the human body. The upper parts, particularly the head and the mouth, are looked upon as pure and clean. The lower portions, especially the genital and anal regions, are considered *marimé*. As the Rom see it, the upper and lower halves of the body must not "mix" in any way, and objects that come into contact with one half must not come into contact with the other.

There are countless examples of this hygienic-ritualistic separation. Ronald Lee, who is himself a Gypsy, writes that

you can't wash clothes, dishes, and babies in the same pan, and every Gypsy has his own eating utensils, towels, and soap. Other dishes and utensils are set aside for guests, and still others for pregnant women. Certain towels are for the face, and others for the nether regions—and there are different colored soaps in the sink, each with an allotted function.[32]

Marimé apparently originated in the early caravan period, when—for hygienic purposes—it was imperative that certain areas of the camp be set aside for cooking, cleaning, washing, taking care of body functions, and the like. Also, within the close confines of the wagons and tents, it was important that rules pertaining to sex be carefully spelled out and enforced. As is so often the case, however, over the years the various hygienic and sexual taboos proliferated. Miller notes, for example, that at the present time:

Items that come into contact with the upper portions of the body are separately maintained and washed in running water or special basins. These items would include soap, towels, razors and combs, clothes, pillows, furniture like the backs of chairs and the tops of tables, tablecloths, aprons, sinks, utensils, and, of course, food itself, which is prepared, served, and eaten with the greatest consideration for ritual quality. . . .

Any contact between the lower half of the body, particularly the genitals, which are conceptually the ultimate source of *marimé*, and the upper body is forbidden. The inward character of the genitals, especially the female genitalia—which are associated with the mysteries of blood and birth—make them consummately impure. Items that have contact with this area are carefully segregated because they contain a dangerous threat to the status of pure items and surfaces. The most dreadful contact, of course, would be between the genitals and the oral cavity.[33]

Gropper states that "a woman is *marimé* during and after childbirth, and during her monthly period. . . . A *marimé* woman may not cook or serve food to men. She may not step over anything belonging to a man or allow her skirts to touch his things. Women's clothing must be washed separately from men's."[34]

Even such a natural phenomenon as urination may cause difficulties for the Rom. "One old lady called off a visit to a friend because she was indisposed and felt it would be too embarrassing to urinate frequently. Men often go outside to urinate rather than do so in their own homes, especially if guests are present."[35]

Interestingly and—given their conception of *marimé*—quite logically, Gypsy women attach shame to the legs rather than the breasts. Sutherland points out that it is shameful for a woman to have too much leg exposed, and that women who wear short skirts are expected to cover them with a sweater when they sit. On the other hand:

Women use their brassieres as their pocketbooks, and it is quite common for a man, whether he be the husband, son, father, or unrelated, to reach into her brassiere to get cigarettes or money. When women greet each other after a certain absence, they squeeze each other's breasts. They will also squeeze the breasts to show appreciation of a witty story or joke.[36]

Marimé vs Melalo Mention should be made of the distinction between *marimé* and *melalo*. *Marimé* is pollution or defilement, as just described. *Melalo* simply means dirty, or as Lee describes it, "dirty with honest dirt."[37] Someone who has not had a bath would be *melalo*, but not *marimé*. Hands that are dirty because of manual labor would be *melalo* rather than *marimé*—although they would be *marimé* if they had touched the genitals. (In actual practice, Gypsies tend to wash their hands many times a day—because they may have touched any number of objects or organs that are *marimé*. Miller states that "a working Rom also washes his face and hands whenever he feels his luck leaving him during the day; he washes again upon returning from his work.")[38]

The distinction between *marimé* and *melalo* explains why a Gypsy domicile often appears dirty to a non-Gypsy—and vice versa! Some of the Romany dwelling places I have been in, for example, are anything but spic and span. Food scraps, cigarette butts, paper, wrappings—all may be thrown on the floor, presumably to be swept out later. Such a condition is not *marimé* so long as the proper rules of body hygiene, food preparation, and so forth are followed. As one writer puts it: "Americans tend to be shocked at visible dirt, but Gypsies abhor invisible pollution."[39]

The *Gadje*: Definition of the Situation
Not all of the *natsiyi* follow the same rules and procedures regarding *marimé*. There are also some variations among family groups within the same *natsi*. (The Salos note that families who follow a strict observance pattern have a higher status than those who tend to be lax.)[40] But there is one point on which all true Rom are agreed: the *gadje* are *marimé*. Miller writes as follows:

The *gadje* are conceived as a different race whose main value is economic, and whose *raison d'être* is to trouble the Rom. The major offense of the *gadje*, the one offense that the Rom can never forgive, is their propensity to defilement. *Gadje* confuse the critical distinction between the pure and the impure. They are observed in situations which the Rom regard as compromising: forgetting to wash in public bathrooms; eating with the fork that they rescued from the floor of the restaurant; washing face towels and tablecloths with underwear at the laundromat; relaxing with their feet resting on the top of the table.

Because they do not protect the upper half of the body, the *gadje* are construed as *marimé* all over, head to foot. This condi-

tion, according to Rom belief, invites and spreads contagious disease. Rom tend to think of all illness and physical disability as communicable, and treat them accordingly.[41]

Since the *gadje* are *marimé*, relations with them are severely limited. In fact, Sutherland states that "interaction with the *gadje* is restricted to economic exploitation and political manipulation. Social relations in the sense of friendship, mutual aid, and equality are not appropriate."[42] The same author goes on to say that

not only the person of non-Gypsies but items that come into contact with them are *marimé*. Any time a Rom is forced to use *gadje* places or to be in contact with large numbers of *gadje* (for example, in a job, hospital, welfare office, school), he is in constant danger of pollution. Public toilets are particularly *marimé* places, and some Rom go to the extent of using paper towels to turn faucets and open doors.[43]

. . . The Amish [have a] concept [called] *definition of the situation* . . . ; i.e., "What men define as real is real in its consequences." And just as the Amish have defined the automobile as a threat to their social equilibrium, so the Gypsies have defined the *gadje* as *marimé*.

For example, the Rom ordinarily do not eat in *gadje* homes. Even in restaurants, they tend to avoid utensils, often preferring to eat with their hands.[44] Nor do they like to invite the *gadje* to their own homes. If they do—say, for political purposes—the *gadje* are given dishes and utensils that have been specially washed and kept separate.

Needless to say, Gypsies are prohibited from dating, marrying, or having sex relations with the *gadje*, even though all three of the prohibitions are occasionally broken. In fact, the Rom show a certain tolerance for a Gypsy male who marries a non-Gypsy female, particularly if the latter is given instructions in proper cleanliness. The Gypsy female, however, who is having relations with a *gadjo* is considered *marimé*. As long as she continues in the sexual relationship, she is treated as a social outcast.

Barrier to Assimilation Do not the various rules and prohibitions involved in *marimé* impose a hardship on the Rom?

In one sense, the answer is yes. The urban world, the Gypsies' major habitat, is seen as "pervasively *marimé*, filled with items and surfaces that are subject to use and re-use by careless *gadje*, polluted, diseased, and therefore dangerous."[45] To avoid the danger, Gypsies must take any number of daily precautions—and there is no doubt that these precautions are time-consuming and burdensome. Little wonder, as Miller points out, that "the home is the final bastion of defense against defilement, and the only place that the Rom feel altogether at ease."[46]

At the same time, *marimé* serves as an extremely effective *barrier to assimilation*. As used by sociologists, the term *assimilation* refers to the absorption of one population group by another, where the end result is a blending of culture traits. The so-called melting pot in America has boiled unevenly, some groups being assimilated much faster than others. The Gypsies, of course, would fall at the lower end of any assimilation scale—which is just where they want to be. As the Rom see it, assimilation would be tantamount to group extinction.

Nowhere is this resistance to assimilation more apparent than in their attitude toward the *gadje*. The belief that the latter are *marimé* not only serves as a barrier to assimilation but acts as an ever-present sustainer of pride and self-respect. In fact, so pervasive is their negative attitude toward the *gadje* that Gypsies will not assimilate even after death! Nemeth's analysis of cemetery plots and tombstones revealed that the Rom attempt "to maintain distance in the graveyard between themselves and non-Gypsies, and between themselves and outcasts from their own society."[47]

One further point should be mentioned regarding resistance to assimilation. The Gypsies are a markedly low-status group, and solidifying elements such as morale and esprit de corps are extremely important.

Categories of thought that rank the *gadje* as inferior to the Rom in purity and health have an obvious significance to pride and self-respect. . . . Despite demeaning life circumstances, which include frequent and irritating inequalities, morale is maintained at a favorable level.

When a Romni is arrested for telling fortunes, or a family is forced to move because the landlord has discovered that ten children, instead of the two or three expected, are living in one house, the aggravation can be lessened by a counter offensive of verbal abuse in Romany concerning the appearance of the skin, the odor, moral character, and personal habits of the gadje.[48]

Some Gypsiologists believe that the rules pertaining to marimé are softening. The Salos, in their study of Canadian Rom, found this to be the case.[49] In most areas of the United States, however, marimé still seems to be a potent force. When I asked an older Gypsy woman whether she felt that marimé was weakening, she shrugged and said, "Maybe. I hope not. Some of the young kids don't know it, but it's what holds us together."

FAMILY AND SOCIAL ORGANIZATION

Gypsies maintain a rather complicated form of social organization, and it is sometimes difficult to unravel the various kinship and community networks. It will simplify matters, however, if two points are kept in mind:

1. Gypsies are not loners. Their lives are spent in the company of other Gypsies. In fact, the term "individual Gypsy" is almost a play on words. In most of their communities, there are no single-person households, and no households of childless newlywed couples.[50]

2. The Rom are living in an alien culture, and they have no intention of assimilating. They are keenly aware of their position, and they are determined to keep an ever-clear line between the gadje and themselves. Their social organization is designed to enhance the process of boundary maintenance.

The Familia The heart of Gypsy culture is the familia. As Yoors points out: "The inner cohesion and solidarity of the Gypsy community lies in the strong family ties—which are their basic and only constant unit."[51]

The familia, however, is much larger and more complex than our own nuclear family. Whereas the latter is generally thought of as a husband-wife-children unit, the familia includes spouses, unmarried children, married sons and their wives and children, plus other assorted relatives and adopted youngsters. And since Gypsy couples often have six or more children, the familia may easily total thirty to forty members.[52] By the same token, since in many ways the Gypsy world is a man's world, the male head of the familia may wield considerable power.

The familia, then, appears to be an extended family, but it is actually more than that: it is a functional extended family. Members live together (or close by); they often work together; they trust and protect one another; they celebrate holidays together; they take care of the sick and the aged; they bury the dead. The familia, in brief, is close to being a self-sufficient unit. One of the few functions it does not perform is that of matrimony, since marriages between first cousins are frowned upon.

Although the Rom believe in private property and free enterprise, ownership is often thought of in terms of the familia rather than the individual. Traditionally, as Clebert notes, "the essential nucleus of the Gypsy organization is the family. Authority is held by the father. . . . property belongs to the family and not to the individual. But the family is not limited to the father, mother, and children. It includes aunts, uncles, and cousins."[53]

The familia is particularly effective as a supportive institution. Whether the problem is economic, social, political, or medical, the various family members unite in their efforts to provide aid. Should a police official, social worker, inspector, tax collector, or any other unwelcome gadjo appear on the scene, the intruder will be met with formidable—and generally effective—opposition. Should a family member fall ill, the familia will spare no expense in obtaining professional help, especially if it is a serious illness.

As hospital personnel can attest, a full-blown familia on the premises creates something of a problem. The Salos write that "illness, especially a terminal illness, requires the supportive presence at the hospital of the entire extended family. Hospitals often balk at the consequent waiting-room crowds."[54]

The very structure of the familia, of course, creates some problems—housing and otherwise. Landlords do not take kindly to rentals involving a dozen or more persons. Noise, sanitation disposal, complaints by neighbors—all must be reckoned with. Also, by virtue of its size the familia is cumbersome. It is one thing for a Gypsy couple to pack up and move; it is quite another for a large familia to "hit the road." And since the Rom obviously like to travel, the extended family presents a mobility problem.

(In an earlier period—during the days of the wagons and caravans—the familia probably made a better adaptation. Married sons and their families could sleep in adjoining tents, and the entire group could be packed and on the road in a remarkably short time.)

The familia has functional as well as structural problems. Disagreements and conflicts are bound to occur. Jealousies do arise. Living arrangements are sometimes felt to be unsatisfactory. In her study of Philadelphia Gypsies, Coker found that

there is constant slandering; rumors are started, and attacks and counter-attacks are made. Most of the rumors involve sex. Some reflect on the morals of young girls, implying that they are dating non-Gypsy men, or, as a particularly vicious accusation, that they are going out with Negroes.[55]

Despite the problems involved, the Rom show few signs of abandoning the familia. On the contrary, they seem to thrive on it! In some cases, the size of the extended family has been reduced. In others, the married sons may form their own households. Nevertheless, the familia continues to be the center of the Gypsy world. As long as the gadje are seen in an adversary context, the familia will remain the Gypsies' principal bastion of security.

The Vitsa Whereas the familia can be thought of as an extended family, the vitsa is a cognatic kin group made up of a number of familiyi. Some Gypsiologists refer to the vitsa as a clan or a band, but the important point is that the Rom think of it as a unit of identity. Members of the highly publicized Bimbalesti vitsa, for example, would identify with one another—feel a kindred relationship—even though they might all come together very infrequently.

Vitsi vary in size from a few familiyi

to a hundred or more households. Members of a smaller *vitsa* may live near one another and operate as a functioning group. The Rom have large families, however, and most *vitsi* tend to grow, The majority of American *vitsi,* therefore, function as a group on only two occasions: at a Gypsy trial *(kris romani)* and at a death feast *(pomana),* especially where the deceased has been a respected elder.[56]. . .

How are the various *vitsi* named? The process of nomenclature sheds some light on the Gypsy thought processes:

Each *vitsa* has a name which may be derived from a real or mythical ancestor (the descendants of Pupa will be called Pupeshti). A *vitsa* may also be named after an animal, object, or defining characteristic of the people in that *vitsa*. For example, Saporeshti comes from *sap* (snake), Kashtare from *kash* (wood, tree), and Bokurishti from *bok* (hunger, hence "hungry people").

Some names are supposedly given in jest, such as the Papineshti, who were so named because they were adept at stealing geese (*papin* means goose).[59]

Gypsies identify themselves—and other Rom—by their *vitsa* affiliation and by the liberal use of nicknames. However, they also have one or more names that are used in dealing with the *gadje.* These *"gadje"* names, according to Clark, are often popular American names such as John, George, and Miller.

The *gadjo* may find a John George, George John, Miller John, John Miller, Miller George, and George Miller. He may even find a Gypsy named Johnny John or Miller Miller. But he probably won't find the John George Miller he is looking for unless the man wants to be found.

The Rom deny that this is done deliberately to confuse the *gadje.* With broad smile, a Gypsy explained that these were just nice names and everybody liked them.[60]

Other writers have commented on the Gypsies' facility for changing their names, and their particular affinity for the use of John Miller. Silverman reports that

there are probably hundreds of Gypsies named John Miller. When a truant officer enters a home looking for John Miller, six boys may claim that title, hopelessly confusing the case. Furthermore, Gypsies use a multiplicity of names to avoid visibility. One Gypsy family may list their apartment under one name, the telephone under another, and the fortune-telling business under yet another. . . .

In Western society, a name is an indelible mark which rarely changes. For Gypsies, on the other hand, changeable American names are a strategy they use to remain invisible, concealed, and untraceable.[61]

According to their custom, Gypsies have the right to belong to either their mother's or their father's *vitsa.* In practice, most Rom choose their father's, although later in life they sometimes change their affiliation. Similarly, when a man marries a woman from another *vitsa,* the woman generally identifies with the husband's *vitsa.* Some *vitsi* grow to be large and powerful; other become ineffectual and die out. But the more prestigious a *vitsa* becomes, the greater the number of descendants and affiliates who will seek membership.

The status or prestige of a *vitsa* is determined by both variable and invariable factors. Variable factors would include size, reputation, leadership, wealth, and power. These factors can—and often do—change over time, so that in this sense the prestige of a particular *vitsa* may fluctuate. One *invariable* factor, however, is the *natsia,* or nation, to which the *vitsa* belongs. *Natsiyi* have their own status hierarchy, and this fact is reflected in the status accorded the various *vitsi.*

Although a number of considerations are involved, Sutherland gives the following rank order of the *natsiyi:*

1. Machwaya
2. Loware
3. Kalderasha
4. Churara

Sutherland goes on to state that in her Barvale, California, study, "even the wealthy Churara families usually have lower status than the poor Kalderash families, and the poor Machwaya families always remind the more powerful Kalderash of their superior status as Machwaya."[62]

Not all *vitsi* are able to provide the same services for their members. Those that are plagued by weak leadership and internal dissension may actually work to the detriment of their affiliated *familia.* A strong *vitsa,* however, is often able to protect its members against police harassment, provide economic and political assistance, aid in travel arrangements, and so on. One other very important *vitsa* function is to provide members with a ready supply of acceptable marriage partners.

ARRANGED MARRIAGES AND THE BRIDE PRICE

Gypsies may be the only group in America who follow the olden practice of arranged marriages! Indeed, such marriages seem to be a cornerstone of the Rom the world over. Matrimony is important to Gypsies, and they are reluctant to place their young people in Cupid's hands. This is not to say that the young are forced into marriage. Although Romany marriages may be arranged, the parents do not arbitrarily impose their will. However, parents do play a major role in the mate selection process, and the arrangements for the bride price, or *daro,* are entirely in their hands.

It must be kept in mind that Gypsy culture stresses the importance of group rather than individual activity. And as Gropper observes, "Marriage for the Rom is quite definitely more than a union of husband and wife; it involves a lifetime alliance between two extended families."[63]

Arranged marriages normally include a *daro,* a payment by the groom's family to the bride's family. The actual figure varies from less than $1,000 to $10,000 or more. The higher the status of the girl's *familia,* and the greater her personal attractiveness, the higher will be the asking price.

Although a *daro* of several thousand dollars is quite common, part of the money is spent on wedding festivities. The money is also used to pay for the bride's trousseau, to furnish the couple with household equipment, and so on. Additionally, part of the money may be returned to the groom's father, "as a sign of good will."[64]

Weddings themselves are private in that they involve neither religious nor civil officiants. They are, in a very real sense, *Gypsy weddings,* and are usually held in a rented hall. The festivities—involving ample food and drink—are fairly elaborate, and while formal invitations are not issued, all Gypsies in the community are welcome to come.[65]

The *daro* has traditionally served as a protection for the young wife. That is, if she should be mistreated by her husband or his *familia,* she can return home—whereupon the money might have to be forfeited.

Whether Gypsy wives are abused more than other wives is doubtful, but it is true that both sexes marry at a relatively young age. Marriages of eleven- and twelve-year-olds are known to occur, although the desired age range is between twelve and sixteen, and "not over 18 for the first marriage."[66] It seems likely, therefore, that many Gypsies are marrying under the legal age, although this fact would cause them no undue worry. The Rom are not overly concerned about marriage and divorce records, birth certificates, and other vital statistics.

While any two Rom can marry, most marriages involve partners from the same *natsia.* Young people are also encouraged to marry within the *vitsa,* provided the relationship is not that of first cousin or closer. The Rom feel that by having their youth marry someone in the same *vitsa*—a second cousin, for example—the prospects for a happy marriage will be increased. *Vitsa* members not only have blood ties, but follow the same customs, have the same *marimé* proscriptions, and so forth.

(Despite the fact that these endogamous unions are becoming more popular, Gypsy marriages seem to have a high rate of failure. While the reasons can be debated, one of my informants felt that the system of arranged marriages was simply not successful, and that too many of the Rom were marrying at too early an age. Whether or not this is the correct interpretation, it is true that in society at large, early marriages do show a relatively high incidence of divorce.)[67]

The Bori After the wedding, it is customary for the young wife to live with her husband's *familia.* She in now known as a *bori* and comes under the supervision of her mother-in-law.

The groom now has a wife who caters to his needs and whom he orders about, so his mother and sisters may devote less time to him. The bride, on the other hand, is now

a *bori,* to be ordered around by all. She is expected to be the first one to awake in the morning and the last one to go to bed.

She should do much of the housework as well as work as a fortune-teller, giving her earnings to her husband and mother-in-law. She should eat sparingly and only after everyone else has finished. She must ask neither for clothing nor for an opportunity to go out. She should be grateful if she gets either.[68]

It should be mentioned that contrary to our own culture pattern, Gypsy girls tend to be *older* than the boys they marry. As Sutherland explains, "It is important that the girl be older than the boy, since after marriage she must be able to perform her duties as a *bori* and make money for her husband; however, her husband need not take many responsibilities until he is fully mature."[69] . . .

The *bori,* naturally, is expected to bear children—lots of them. Birth control measures apparently are not utilized. On the contrary, childless marriages are looked upon as a great misfortune. Clebert states that according to Gypsy tradition, female sterility was believed to be caused by having coitus with a vampire.[71] At any rate, Andersen states that

The *bori* becomes a full-fledged woman when she bears her first child. Women I talked with in Philadelphia who are recently married, await the births of children eagerly, for they are aware of the improved status it will bring them. . . .

The *bori* then becomes a *romni,* a Gypsy woman and wife. Her ties to husband's extended family then become very strong, for if she decides to end the marriage for some reason and return to her parents' home, she may not be permitted to take the child with her.[72]

Once in a great while sex roles are reversed, and the boy lives with the girl's *familia.* This situation might occur because the boy was unable to meet the bride price, or because he possessed some undesirable physical or mental trait. Such a person is called a "house Rom," and because he is under the domination of his parents-in-law he loses the respect of the other men in the community.[73]

Changes in the System Although arranged marriages and the *daro* remain integral parts of Gypsy culture, the system may not be so rigid as it once was. Like society at large, the Gypsy world

is witnessing increased freedom on the part of its young people. The Salos note, for example, that at one time young Gypsies were not permitted to date without chaperones being present, a custom that is now often disregarded.

Parents are paying more heed to their children's wishes, and romantic love seems to be gaining in popularity. John Marks concludes that "parents still arrange the marriage, but now some young people fall in love whereas they used to marry without ever seeing each other beforehand."[74] Premarital chastity on the part of the girl, however, has always been highly regarded—and it remains so.

Elopements are reported to be increasing, and some of the young men "are willing to defend their wives against their mothers."[75] Some adults are openly critical of the traditional marriage system, although others stoutly defend it. Thus far, the number of families that have actually dispensed with the *daro* is relatively small. . . .

ECONOMIC ORGANIZATION

Gypsies are not the world's best workers. They have traditionally been involved in marginal and irregular occupations: horse trading, scrap metal, fortune-telling, blacktopping (repairing driveways), auto-body repair, and carnival work. Clebert adds the phrase "musicians and mountebanks,"[78] and Block contends that begging and stealing are among their principal occupations.[79]

Actually, as Hancock notes, the American Rom are to be found in a variety of pursuits, including "real estate, office work, acting, and teaching."[80] Nevertheless, as a group, Gypsies have not been noticeably successful in climbing the socioeconomic ladder, and it is doubtful whether this type of success has much appeal for them.

The Rom are quite willing to use banks, credit cards, charge accounts, and other appurtenances of a competitive economic system, but as a group they are loath to become involved in what they perceive to be the "rat race." Indeed, many Gypsies are quite adept at staying out of the race.

In his Chicago study, Polster found

that the Gypsy men did not have steady jobs but worked only when they felt like it.[81] In their Canadian investigation, the Salos concluded that the Rom saw work as a necessity and not as a goal or way of life.[82] The same writers go on to say that

although the Gypsy is ingenious in adapting occupationally, the true commitment of each man is to earn the respect of his people. The pursuit of social prestige among his fellow Rom makes up a significant portion of his life. The Rom must be free to visit, gossip, politick, arrange marriages, and to undertake journeys connected with these activities. The earning of a livelihood is a secondary though necessary activity.[83]

In his study of English Gypsies, Sandford found somewhat the same philosophy. The following remarks were made by one of his Gypsy informants:

The Gypsy philosophy is to live. Nothing else matters. Don't become clots, we say, like the *Gadje,* get up at 8, work till 5, watch television till 10, go to bed, get up at 8, back to work till 5. Their clocks is what they serve, the *Gadje,* they're automatons. Well, our people, we don't behave like that.

We get up when we feel like it, we eat and drink when we're hungry and thirsty, and we do what we want. We work to live rather than live to work. . . . When Gypsies go to work, it's the pleasure of the work. They enjoy what they do. The *Gadje* don't.[84]

It should be mentioned that the Rom face a number of economic and occupational handicaps. Many of their traditional pursuits have dried up. Horse trading has long been defunct. Metalwork, a traditional Gypsy standby (Kalderash actually means "coppersmith"), has largely been taken over by factory methods. Carnival work has been steadily reduced.

The Rom are also penalized by their lack of education, since all of the professional occupations require college and graduate training. And finally, a number of jobs—plumber, nurse, certain kinds of hotel and restaurant work— are off limits to the Rom because of their *marime* proscriptions.

All things considered, the wonder of it all is not that Gypsies have failed to climb the economic ladder, but that they have adapted as well as they have. In fact, one could argue—as one writer does—that the Rom "fill a gap, albeit

marginal, in the *gadje* system of production. They perform needed tasks, such as repair of shopping carts and seal-coating of driveways, that under usual economic conditions are too irregular or unprofitable to be attractive to larger, *gadje* economic enterprises."[85]

The *Kumpania* It is important to note that the Rom produce none of their own material needs. These must be procured from the *gadje.* And the procurement is often psychologically as well as materially rewarding:

Economic relationships of Rom with *gadje* are ideally exploitative. *Gadje* are by definition ignorant and foolish. The Rom value governing these relationships may be defined as "living by one's wits." The psychological satisfaction of "putting one over" on the *gadje* is often, at least in anecdotal retrospect, valued even more highly than the actual profit made.[86]

According to Sutherland, "The *gadje* are the source of all livelihood, and with few exceptions the Rom establish relations with them only because of some economic or political motive."[87] The same author points out that *economic relations among Gypsies* are based on mutual aid, and that they consider it immoral to earn money from other Gypsies. The only legitimate source of income is the *gadje,* and "skill in extracting money from them is highly valued in Rom society."[88]

The economic unit in this "extraction" process is not the *familia* or the *vitsa,* but the *kumpania.* Yoors believes that the *kumpania* was originally a group of wagons—a caravan—that traveled together for economic purposes, staking out a "territory" along the way.

Whenever another group, or even a single wagon, passed through an area not its own, it was the accepted custom to compensate the present Gypsy "owners." In exchange, the "owners" helped the new arrivals in their dealings with the authorities. . . . The Rom were aware that in rendering these services to other Gypsies they were building up good will and that in return they could hope for repayment in days of need.[89]

Although caravans and wagons have vanished from the American scene, the *kumpania* has persisted, especially in urban areas. Lee writes as follows:

The Gypsies of each town and city of the U.S.A. and Canada are organized into what

we call *kumpaniyi* or "unions." Each *kumpania* is composed of all the male members of the community inhabiting that particular town or city, and they together with their families are under the supreme authority of the *kris romani* (tribunal of Gypsy elders), which is their only authority in matters of Gypsy law and ceremonial behavior.[90]

The *kumpania* is thus an economic territory whose functions include regulating competition, providing police protection, settling competitive problems, and dealing with the *gadje.* Some *kumpaniyi* are small, loosely organized, and relatively ineffective. Others are solidified units, with substantial economic and political power.

An effective Kumpania would determine the number of blacktopping businesses or fortune-telling establishments to be permitted in the area, whether licensing or political protection was necessary, and so on. Such a *kumpania* would have the power to keep out unaffiliated *familia.* A loose *kumpania* would lack such power. *Familia* could come and go at will, making for an untenable social and economic situation.[91]

The *kumpania* takes on added meaning when seen from the vantage point of Gypsy culture. As part of their effort to maintain a sharp boundary between themselves and the *gadje,* the Rom avoid working with non-Gypsies. If necessary, they will accept employment in a factory or commercial establishment, but this is not their normal practice. Typically, Gypsies operate in terms of *wortacha,* small work units consisting of adult members of the same sex. Thus two or three men might engage in black-topping or auto-body maintenance. Women might work in small-sized groups doing door-to-door selling or fortune-telling.

This kind of territoriality has both advantages and disadvantages. On the one hand, it minimizes internal wrangling over resources and makes for a relatively smooth economic organization. On the other hand, as Gypsy population pressures mount, the struggle for territories becomes increasingly severe. Some writers feel that, because of this economic framework, Gypsies are having a more and more difficult time making a living. However, given their attitude toward the *gadje*—their definition of the situation—it is not easy for the

Rom to come up with a satisfactory alternative.

Welfare Practices A number of Gypsiologists have commented on the ability of the Rom to extract money via the welfare route. In Sutherland's study, for instance, virtually all the Rom in Barvale, California, were receiving some sort of aid from the Welfare Department.[92]

The Rom believe that acquiring welfare entails the same kinds of skills that other occupations require; that is, the ability to understand, convince, flatter, cajole, pressure, and manipulate the social worker. Welfare is not considered a hand-out; it is money that they convince the *gadje* to give them. . . .

They do not consider themselves a depressed minority having to beg for charity from the middle-class majority. On the contrary, welfare is to them an incredible stroke of luck, yet further proof of the gullibility of the *gadje*.[93]

Reporting on the New York City scene, Mitchell gives the following descriptive account:

The Gypsy women went into relief offices with their children following along behind and broke down and cried and said they were starving to death, and if that didn't impress the officials they screeched and fell on the floor and fainted and used foul language and swept papers off desks and stood in doors and wouldn't let people pass and brought everything to a standstill. They pretty soon got their families on relief.[94]

There is evidently some geographic variation in welfare practices, however, for none of the Gypsies in Coker's Philadelphia study were reported to be on welfare.[95] Similarly, in his article in the *Harvard Encyclopedia of Ethnic Groups,* Hancock makes no mention of Gypsy welfare proclivities.[96]

QUASI-LEGAL AND ILLEGAL ACTIVITIES

Although most of the economic activities of the Rom are legal in nature, some are quasi-legal while others are clearly illegal. Blacktopping and sealing of driveways, for instance, are perfectly legal operations. But when the asphalt is laid at only one-third of the required thickness, and when the sealer has been surreptitiously diluted, the legality becomes questionable. Similarly, auto-body repair is legal, but if instead of actually removing the dents a thick coating of "paint and putty" is used, the practice is obviously unethical.

Fortune-Telling Fortune-telling is a special case, for if there is one field that has been monopolized by the Rom it is certainly fortune-telling. Indeed, the terms "Gypsy" and "fortune-teller" seem to go hand in hand—and with good reason, as the following account by Andersen indicates:

The little girl is expected to be a fortune-teller or reader and advisor, as early as thirteen or fourteen, and as a child she is trained for this profession. Fortune-telling as a means of livelihood is a tradition among Gypsy women, and many little girls observe their mothers, aunts, and other female relatives performing within this tradition every day.

They are taught that they have a natural gift for the practice, that they received this gift from God, and that as fortune-tellers they will be performing a type of psychological counseling service for non-Gypsies.[97]

Fortune-telling is not a difficult occupation to learn, overhead expenses are negligible, and—depending on the location—business may be good. Clark cites the old Gypsy saying: "A fortune cannot be true unless silver changes hands."[98] And there have always been enough *gadje* who believe in this aphorism to make crystal gazing, palmistry, and card reading profitable ventures. Fees typically range from $2 to $5 per session, with a surprising number of repeat customers. Most of the latter are reportedly drawn from the lower socio-economic ranks. As Bercovici puts it: "The Gypsy fortune-teller is the psychoanalyst of the poor."[99]

Do Gypsies themselves believe in fortune-telling? The answer is yes and no. Despite what they may nominally teach their youngsters, all Rom realize that readings performed for the *gadje* are entirely fallacious. Paradoxically, however, some Gypsy women are believed to possess occult powers of prediction, at least when applied to other Gypsies. Older Gypsy women, therefore—who are felt to be experts in dream interpretation and card reading—are sometimes consulted.[100]

The specifics of Gypsy fortune-telling vary somewhat, though not a great deal. In a few areas, Romni still travel in pairs, telling fortunes on a catch-as-catch-can basis. The most common practice, however, is to set up a fortune-telling parlor, or *ofisa,* with living quarters in the rear. The actual location of an *ofisa* depends in good part on the availability of large numbers of shoppers or passers-by, which is why resort and vacation areas are considered choice places to set up shop.

I know one Gypsy fortune-teller who has been a fixture on the Atlantic City boardwalk for more than thirty years, although this is a rather exceptional case. In many instances, the life-span of an *ofisa* is relatively short-lived, some lasting for only a summer or winter holiday season. Another common practice is for the *ofisa* to remain at the same location, with the same decorations but with a series of different proprietors.

Although crystal gazing and palmistry are still seen, many Gypsy fortune-tellers prefer tarot cards. Trigg writes that "a tarot pack consists of 78 gaily decorated cards marked with a number of archaic symbols. . . . Each card has its own astrological, alchemical, numerological, and philosophical meaning. . . . There are, of course, many different methods which are used for interpreting the tarot cards."[101]

What do Gypsy fortune-tellers think of their customers? The following statement speaks for itself:

Gypsies cannot understand why the *gadje* take bogus readings so seriously; they assume that it is because non-Gypsies are stupid. What the Rom fail to take into account is that it is mostly the less intelligent or maladjusted who come to them for readings. Occasionally, the Gypsies are approached by younger people or a courting couple who want their palms read merely for a lark. . . .

In the large cities, fortune-telling stores are often seen in underprivileged neighborhoods; few are seen in affluent sections.[102]

The *Bujo* On occasion, Gypsy fortune-tellers have been accused—and convicted—of flimflam, or *bujo.* The *bujo* is nothing more than a swindle, whereby a gullible customer is cheated out of a goodly portion of his or her savings. One common ruse is called "switch the bag." In this instance, a bag of fake money or cut-up paper is substituted for a bag of real cash—which the customer had brought to the *ofisa* in order to have the evil spirits or curse removed. (In Romany, *bujo* means "bag.")

According to the New York police, *bujo* swindles in excess of $100,000 have occurred. And according to Mitchell, there are some Gypsy fortune-tellers "with a hundred or more arrests on their record."[103] Obviously, these are unusual cases; in fact, many Rom frown on the *bujo* because it causes bad community relations and is likely to bring police action.

At the same time, the *bujo* has occurred often enough to cause many areas to outlaw fortune-telling. Major cities like New York and Philadelphia, as well as most Canadian regions, have banned fortune-telling. Some observers feel that the illegalization of fortune-telling may be the Gypsies' biggest problem. (Interestingly enough, in 1985 the California Supreme Court, overruling a lower court decision, found that an ordinance prohibiting fortune-telling for profit violated the Constitutional right to free speech. The suit was brought by a *romni,* and the ramifications are as yet unknown. It is quite possible, however, that the case will eventually reach the United States Supreme Court!)

Legalities aside, the Rom continue to ply their trade, even though they are somewhat restricted in many areas. They often pose as "readers" and "advisors" rather than as seers. And this, in turn, may necessitate a measure of police "cooperation." But by one method or another, the Gypsies survive. Gypsies always survive.

Other Illegal Activities What about other types of crime—robbery, burglary, rape, murder, etc.—are the Gypsies not involved in these, also? The answer is yes and no. They are seldom involved in crimes of violence, such as assault, mugging, rape, and murder. Stealing is another matter, however, and the police are likely to have strong feelings on the subject.

The blunt fact is that law enforcement officers who come in contact with them believe that an undue proportion of American Gypsies are engaged in theft. District attorneys and prosecutors are likely to take a similarly dim view of the Rom, for it is both difficult and exasperating to try to send Gypsies to jail. To the Rom, time spent in prison means breaking a variety of *marimé* proscriptions. Consequently, an individual Gypsy will go to almost any length to avoid an actual jail sentence. Zucchino writes as follows on this point:

Prosecuting a Gypsy is a process as transient and bewildering as the Gypsy culture itself. Convictions and jail sentences are rare. In most cases, the several thousand Gypsies prosecuted in this country each year for burglary or theft jump bail or pay fines, according to national police estimates. . . .

Here the law enforcement system, splintered into thousands of local police agencies, is paralyzed by Gypsy transience. Here a court system based on due process provides time to post bond and disappear. . . .

"You end up taking their bail money and getting rid of them. Basically, you're sicking them on some other county," said a former district attorney. "That sounds bad, but the aggravation, the sheer frustration, is just unbelievable."

. . . The Gypsy language is another problem. Although Gypsies commonly speak English, they usually claim not to understand the language. Under the law, they are entitled to an interpreter, encumbering the already unwieldy court procedure. . . .

A Gypsy may have a history of burglary and bail-jumping, but arresting officers often do not know about it. Only a fingerprint check with the FBI in Washington can tell them exactly whom they have arrested, but that process takes several days or weeks. By that time, police say, the typical Gypsy under arrest would have posted bail and vanished.[104]

LIFE-STYLE

Although it is difficult to generalize about the life-style of any people, the Rom do have certain culture traits that set them apart from other groups. At or near the top of the list—and a trait that has been alluded to several times in the present account—is the Gypsies' indomitable love of freedom.

The Rom do not like to be tied down—by schools, businesses, material possessions, community affairs, financial obligations, or any other social or economic encumbrance. Their life-style not only reflects this predilection, but they are quite proud of it—as I was told by more than one Gypsy informant. Other writers, both Gypsy and non-Gypsy, have also commented on the matter. Ronald Lee, a Gypsy, says:

The Gypsy is invisible and he has many weapons. You have a name but he has two: one you will never know and one he is always changing. Today he is Tom Jones, yesterday he was William Stanley, and tomorrow he might be Adam Strong.

He can melt away at a moment's notice, which is his way of dealing with bill collectors. You cannot do this, for you have a name, an identity in the community, and a job which ties you down. You are a prisoner of your society, but he, existing beyond the pale of public morality, has only his wits, his cunning, his skills, and his faith in a just God.[105]

Gypsies also associate freedom with fresh air and sunshine, a belief that goes back to the days of the caravan. In this earlier period, the Rom linked illness and diseases with closed spaces. Fresh air was believed to be a cure-all. Clebert reports that at one time a Gypsy would not die in bed but would be moved outdoors so as not to pollute the home.[106]

Along with their love of freedom is the Gypsy tendency to live in the present rather than to plan for tomorrow. Perhaps the two traits go together; that is, it may be that "freedom" is reduced by the necessity to plan ahead. Webb writes that "the Rom live only for today. Why should a man hurry? Who knows what the morrow may bring? . . . Today is a happy time, and men grow old quickly enough. Why wish away life by looking for tomorrow?"[107]

Travel and Mobility Nowhere is the Gypsy love of freedom more apparent than in their fondness for travel. As Lee points out, the Rom may no longer be nomads, but they remain a highly mobile people.[108] One important reason for their mobility is the economic factor. While many Rom have a home base, job opportunities may arise elsewhere. Roofing, auto-body repair, carnival work, summer harvesting—all may require periodic travel. In at least some cases, overseas journeys are involved. The Salos report that

the dispersion of the Rom, coupled with an efficient system of communication provided by the *gadje,* allows them to be aware of economic conditions far afield. Some of the Canadian Gypsies have contacts in or first-hand knowledge of conditions in

Ireland, Wales, England, Belgium, France, Yugoslavia, Greece, U.S. (including Hawaii), Mexico, Australia, and South Africa.[109]

The Rom also travel for social reasons: to visit friends and family, to find a *bori* (bride), to celebrate Gypsy holidays, to attend weddings and death feasts. Illness is a special category, and Gypsies will travel long distances to be with a sick relative.

Predictably, the Rom frequently travel for tactical reasons: to avoid the police, social workers, school authorities, landlords, and the like. This sort of travel—coupled with their aforementioned name changes—makes it exceedingly difficult for the authorities to track down and identify "wanted" Gypsies. In fact, during their travels the Rom often pass themselves off as non-Gypsies. Silverman writes that

Gypsies deliberately conceal their ethnicity to avoid confrontations with and harassment by truant officers, landlords, the police, and the welfare department. They pass as Puerto Ricans, Mexicans, Armenians, Greeks, Arabs, and other local ethnics in order to obtain jobs, housing, and welfare. Gypsies usually report themselves as members of other groups to census takers, causing Gypsy census statistics to be extremely unreliable. Gypsies have developed these skills so well that many Americans are unaware that there are any Gypsies in America.[110]

A final reason for travel—and a very important one—is simply that Gypsies like to move about. It makes them feel better, both physically and mentally. Sutherland notes that the Rom associate traveling with health and good luck, "whereas settling down is associated with sickness and bad luck. . . . Barvale Rom all agreed that when they were traveling all the time they were healthy and never needed doctors, but now that they live in houses they are subjected to many *gadje* diseases."[111]

The Life-Cycle Gypsy children arrive in large numbers, and they are welcomed not only by their *familia* but by the entire Gypsy community. Although they are supposed to show respect for their parents, youngsters are pampered. As John Kearney points out, the maxim "Children should be seen and not heard" was surely never coined by a

Gypsy.[112] Corporal punishment is used sparingly—and reluctantly. A Romany child is the center of attention, at least until the next one comes along.

In many ways, Gypsy children are treated like miniature adults—with many of the same rights. Their wishes are respected in much the same manner as those of adults.[113] Subservience and timidity are not highly regarded by the Rom—and children are encouraged to speak up.

Gypsy children also spend much more time in adult company than do their non-Gypsy counterparts. This would almost have to be the case, since the Rom do not have much faith in formal education. While some government-funded Gypsy schools have been set up in various parts of the country, the Gypsy child's real training comes either at home or in what has been called "participatory education."[114] From the age of eight or nine, boys accompany their fathers on various work assignments, while the girls engage in household activities and start to observe fortune-telling routines.[115]

Although aggressiveness in children may be encouraged, adolescents—boys in particular—often need no encouragement. Like teen-agers the world over, Romany youth do cause problems. They misbehave, they are disrespectful, they sometimes mingle with the *gadje*. In fact, Clark believes that a major problem in the Gypsy world right now is their adolescents, "who want to be teen-agers first, and Gypsies second."[116] In most cases, however, maturity seems to serve as a panacea—with no harmful after-effects.

In Gypsy culture, both sexes tend to achieve higher status as they get older. A young man marries, matures, and has children. And as his children grow, "so does his status." When he is ready and able to marry his youngsters off, his position in the community is generally secure.

As he grows older, he will be expected to solve family problems and settle altercations. He also acts as a repository for Gypsy traditions and culture. He will spend increasing time and energy "on the affairs of the band rather than on those of his own immediate family.

He is becoming an Old One and a Big Man."[117]

A parallel sequence is followed in the case of the Gypsy female. As a young girl she is expected to assist in the housework. Later on—when she marries and becomes a *bori*—she is under the domination of her mother-in-law. But as she ages and has children of her own, she achieves a measure of independence and her status rises accordingly.

In many Gypsy communities, it is the woman rather than the man who deals with outsiders—school officials, social workers, and the like. And if she is successful in this regard, her position in the community becomes one of respect. She, too, is looked upon as a repository of wisdom, especially when it comes to dealing with the *gadje*.

Both sexes look forward to becoming parents, and both look forward to having grandchildren. The latter, it is said, dignify true independence, for now the Old Ones have both their children and their children's children to look after them. Gypsies do not maintain homes for the aged. The elderly are cared for by their own families, in their own homes.

Sex Roles The Rom have sharply defined sex roles. Indeed, one Gypsiologist states that "the male-female division is the most fundamental in Rom society." [118] The sex roles, furthermore, are characterized by separateness. Whether the occasion is a Gypsy function or simply day-to-day activity within the *familia,* men tend to gather on one side of the room, women on the other. The Rom are great talkers, but unless a special situation arises, the conversation will probably not be a mixed one.[119]

This separateness extends even to the marital sphere. Except for having a sex partner and someone besides his mother to cater to his needs, the groom's lifestyle changes very little.

Gypsy marriage is not predicated on romantic love, and the Rom frown on any display of affection between husband and wife. The husband wants the wife to perform services for him, but he continues to spend much of his time with his brothers and cousins. Husband and wife rarely go out together.[120]

Occupationally, also, sex roles tend to be definitive. Women tell fortunes; men are responsible for the physical layout of the *ofisa*. Women cook and take care of the household chores. Men are responsible for the acquisition and maintenance of transportation facilities. In many areas, the women bring in more money than the men. In fact, Mitchell claims that, economically, one Gypsy woman is worth ten men.[121] And while this may be an exaggeration, the women's income seems to be steadier and more reliable than the men's. It is the men, nevertheless, who normally hold the positions of power in the *familia,* the *vitsa,* and the *kumpania.*

SOCIAL CONTROL

Romania—not an easy term to define—refers to the Gypsy way of life and their view of the world. It embraces their moral codes, traditions, customs, rituals, and rules of behavior. In brief, as Hancock puts it, *romania* is what the Gypsies consider to be right and acceptable. [122] It is the glue that holds their society together.

Romania is not a set of written rules, however. It is, rather, a built-in aspect of Gypsy culture. And because it is not a written code, the Rom face two problems: (a) Who determines what is and what is not *romania?* and (b) How to handle those who knowingly or unknowingly fail to comply? These questions raise the whole issue of social control.

As used by sociologists, the term *social control* refers to the methods employed to "keep people in line." *Informal control* would include the application of gossip, ridicule, reprimand, and scorn. *Formal control* refers simply to the use of law, backed by physical force. Sociologically, informal control is considered more important than formal, and the Gypsies are a good case in point. The Rom have dispensed almost entirely with formal controls and rely largely on the informal variety.

Gossip, ridicule, and wisecracks, for example, are highly effective because the Rom are a closed society. Individual members cannot escape into anonymity—as is often the case in society at large. In any Gypsy community, therefore, reports and rumors of aberrant behavior lose no time in making the rounds.

LEADERSHIP: THE *ROM BARO*

In most groups, leadership serves as an important instrument of social control, but in this respect Gypsies are not so fortunate. The Rom are not known for their leadership qualities. For one thing, Gypsy leadership is a function of age; that is, the older one gets, the greater knowledge one has of *romania*—and knowledge of *romania* is a recognized source of power. Almost by definition, then, the Rom seldom have any young leaders.

Another drawback is the tendency for Gypsy leadership to be fragmented. Theoretically at least, each *familia,* each *vitsa,* and each *kumpania* has its own leader. And while there is some overlap—and some real harmony—there is also much bickering and infighting, especially when different *natsiyi* are involved.

Leadership starts in the *familia,* where the head is known as a *phuro.* As the *phuro* ages and as his *familia* grows in size and strength, his standing in the community—and his power—increase accordingly. Should his judgment prove sound, should he show genuine interest in the various members of his *familia,* and should he prove effective in his dealings with the *gadje,* the *phuro* might be come the leader of the *vitsa* or of a *kumpania.* He would then be known as a *Rom Baro* or "Big Man."

The Big Man has a dual function: to provide help and services for his followers, and to serve as a liaison with the non-Gypsy community, especially in a political sense. The following account of Big Mick, a *Rom Baro* from California, was provided by a social worker:

"Big Mick" now freely admits that he is the regional Gypsy leader and says his territory extends as far north as Santa Rosa and as far south as Oakland. He officiates at weddings and funerals, negotiates with the police on behalf of Gypsies who are in trouble, and takes up collections of funerals and to bail someone out of jail.

He has unsuccessfully attempted to set up a fortune-telling business in this area by negotiating with the police. Fortune-telling here is illegal. "Big Mick" has close contact with the police, and I suspect that he is an informant on occasions when he wishes to punish someone.[123]

A Big Man rules by persuasion and discussion rather than by coercion, and should his persuasive powers fail he may be replaced. Also, should he be convicted of a crime, his tenure as a *Rom Baro* may be terminated.

Although there are any number of Big Men in the Gypsy world, there really is no "King of the Gypsies," even though certain individuals often make the claim in order to ingratiate themselves with local authorities. For example, Silverman writes that the "status of King or Queen is invoked when securing hospital rooms or visiting privileges in funeral homes. One informant said, 'Any Gypsy who enters a hospital is automatically a King. They get better treatment. . . . There's no such animal in the Gypsy race as a King. But you go to the newspaper morgues in New York and get old papers, and every time a Gypsy died he was King. There has got to be 1,000 Kings.'"[124]

The same writer goes on to report the following eye-catching case:

Gypsies deliberately tend to perpetuate the stereotype of the King in order to inflate the power and romanticism of the Gypsies. The King is presented as the rightful and respected representative of the Gypsy people whenever there is some advantage in appearing as a unified, organized, and stratified society. For example, John Ellis of Portland was invited to Ronald Reagan's inauguration because he was "King of the Western North American Gypsies." He said he would use the opportunity to ask Reagan to place Gypsies on the same level as other minorities and make available grants and funds.[125]

The most famous (or infamous) Gypsy leader in modern times was Tene Bimbo, *Rom Baro* of the Bimbulesti *vitsa.* Tene Bimbo pursued power from coast to coast, and in the process he was reportedly arrested 140 times—for everything from petty larceny to murder! "If there are any charges that have not been brought against Tene Bimbo," one newspaper reported, "it is probably just an oversight."[126]

Tene Bimbo died in 1969 at the age of eighty-five, and there has been no *Rom Baro* like him since that time—and there probably never will be. Although his descendants speak fondly of him, and liken him to a modern Robin Hood, most Gypsies are glad that he is no longer on the scene. They feel that he brought unwanted notoriety to the Rom and was responsible for a distorted view of the Gypsy world. (Peter Maas' *King of the Gypsies,* mentioned earlier, was based on the struggle for power that erupted after Tene Bimbo's death.)

Marimé as Social Control Although Gypsy leadership may or may not be an effective source of social control, *marimé* has traditionally been a powerful instrument. Indeed, it may just be the most important factor in keeping the Rom in line. The reason is not hard to find, for *marimé* is more than a simple declaration that a person or thing is polluted. A Gypsy who has been declared *marimé* is ostracized by the entire group. Other Rom will have nothing to do with him or her.

It cannot be emphasized too strongly that within the confines of their own society, Gypsies are gregarious. They are never really alone. Practically all of their waking moments are spent in the company of other Rom. Talking, laughing, working, arguing, gossiping, and, most important perhaps, eating—all are considered group activities. To be declared *marimé,* therefore, effectively cuts a Gypsy off from the very roots of his existence. He brings shame not only upon himself but upon his family.

Sutherland writes that *marimé* "in the sense of being rejected from social intercourse with other Rom is the ultimate punishment in the Gypsy society, just as death is the ultimate punishment in other societies. For the period it lasts, *marimé* is social death."[127] A permanent *marimé* sentence is not only the most severe form of Gypsy punishment, but if there is no way to win reinstatement, the person involved may actually prefer to end his life by suicide.[128]

The Kris Romani Fortunately for the Rom, *marimé* need not be permanent. Accused Gypsies have the right to a trial in order to determine whether they are guilty as charged. The trial is known

as a *kris romani.* As used by the Rom, the term also refers to their system of law and justice, for they do not generally utilize American courts.

The *Kris romani* consists of a jury of adult Gypsies, presided over by an impartial judge. Certain judges, or *kris-atora,* are known for their wisdom and objectivity and are in great demand. No judge, however, will accept a case unless the litigants agree beforehand to abide by the verdict. In addition to allegations involving *marimé,* kris cases include disputes over the bride price, divorce suits, feuds between *vitsi,* allegations of cheating, and so on.

A *kris* is convened only for serious reasons, since Gypsy trials are time-consuming—and expensive. Personnel may come from other parts of the country, and it may be necessary to use a rented hall. In a lengthy trial, "courtroom" supplies may include food and liquor, payment for which must be made by the guilty party.[129]

Because of the above factors, a *kris romani* is not likely to be held until all other attempts at adjudication have failed. Ordinary disputes, for example, may be settled by the *Rom Baro* or by informal debate. And even if these efforts should fail, a *divano*—a public discussion by concerned adults—can be requested.

Is the *kris romani* an effective instrument of social control? It is hard to say. In most cases, probably yes—but there is a built-in weakness to the system. Presumably the disputants agree beforehand to abide by the decision. If they do not, theoretically at least they have no recourse but to leave the Gypsy world. In the last analysis, however, what can really be done with Gypsies who refuse to obey their own laws? As Acton observes, "It is difficult today for any Gypsy group larger than the extended family to exert effective sanctions on their members."[130] Yoors puts it as follows:

The *kris,* or collective will of the Rom, is a structure in flux. . . . The effectiveness of the pronouncements of the judges depends essentially on the *acceptance of their decisions by the majority of the Rom.* There is no direct element of coercion to enforce the rule of law. The Rom have no police force, no jails, no executioners.[131]

PREJUDICE AND DISCRIMINATION

Prejudice and discrimination are realities that virtually all Gypsies must learn to face—and live with. The sad fact is that the Rom have been persecuted in practically every county they have ever inhabited. As was mentioned, the Nazis murdered hundreds of thousands during World War II. Entire *vitsi* were wiped out. Furthermore, Kenrick and Puxon note that during the many months of the Nuremberg war crimes trial, not a single Gypsy was ever called as a witness![132] Nor was any monetary restitution ever made to the surviving Romany groups.

Although the wholesale slaughter ceased with the downfall of Hitler, Gypsy problems continued in both Western and Eastern Europe. About three-quarters of the European Gypsy population currently reside in Communist countries. Seeger writes about them:

In dozens of Budapest restaurants, Gypsy orchestras perform for foreign tourists and local citizens in Eastern Europe's most pleasurable city. These musicians, however, are the fortunate handful among tens of thousands of Gypsies who are an unassimilated, poverty-stricken, despised minority scattered across Central and Western Europe. . . .
Thirty years after the end of World War II, when thousands of Gypsies were exterminated by the Nazis along with the Jews, the Gypsy population is large enough to present Communist governments with major social problems.
At a recent session of the U.N. subcommission on the Prevention of Discrimination, Grattan Puxon, general secretary of the World Romany Congress, said that the five million Gypsies living in Eastern Europe were "at the bottom of the social pile despite 30 years of socialism."
The U.N. body responded to the plea by asking that "those countries that have Gypsies within their borders give them the full rights to which they are entitled."[133]

American Gypsies, too, continue to face prejudice and discrimination. Some large cities—like New York and Chicago—have special police assigned to the Rom. In the smaller towns, sheriffs will often escort Gypsies to the county line, glad to be rid of them. A recent issue of *The Police Chief* contains an article advising the police on how to keep their districts free of Gypsies.[134] Hancock reports that

various states have also directed laws against Gypsies. As recently as 1976, a family was expelled from the state of Maryland, where the law requires Gypsies to pay a licensing fee of $1,000 before establishing homes or engaging in business, and there is a bounty of $10 on the head of any Gypsy arrested who has not paid this fee.

In New Hampshire in 1977, two families were legally evicted from the state without being charged with any crime, solely for reasons of their ethnic identity.[135]

Why does the persecution continue? Some observers contend that it is a matter of ethnic prejudice, similar to that experienced by blacks, Chicanos, and certain immigrant groups. Others, however, simply feel that the Rom are perceived as non-productive troublemakers. As one police official put it, "they're nothing but economic parasites." The truth of the matter can be debated, but that is beside the point. If people *perceive* of Gypsies as non-productive dissidents, then unfortunately for all concerned, prejudice and discrimination might be looked upon as justifiable retaliation.

ADAPTABILITY: THE GYPSY TRADEMARK

It is doubtful whether the Rom spend much time thinking about the causes of discrimination. Being realists, they expect it. And being Gypsies, they learn to live with it. In fact, being Gypsies, they learn to live with a great many things they do not like or agree with. This, indeed, is the Gypsies' trademark: adaptability.

In addition to coping with discrimination, Gypsies have also had to adapt to a vast panorama of social change. Times change, customs change, governments change—sometimes it seems that nothing is permanent—but whatever the transformation, the Rom seem to make the necessary adjustments. *They adapt without losing their cultural identity.*

Examples of their adaptation are numerous. Gypsies have never had their own religion. In all their wanderings and migrations, they have simply adapted to the religion—or religions—of the host country. The same is largely true

of clothing styles, although as Polster observes, Gypsy women often do wear colorful outfits.[136] And aside from a seeming fondness for spicy dishes, the Rom adapt to the foods and cuisine of the country or area they are living in.

During the days of the caravan, Gypsy nomads camped outside the towns and cities—off the beaten track. When changing conditions forced them from the road, they took to the cities, where they have adapted rather well. Today, most of the American Rom are to be found in urban areas.

When horses were replaced by mechanized transportation, the Rom adapted. Instead of being horse traders, they learned auto-body repair and motor maintenance. When metalworking—long a Gypsy specialty—was superseded by factory-type technology, the Rom turned to roofing and blacktopping. When fortune-telling became illegal in various places, Gypsies became "readers" and "advisors." And when these latter efforts were challenged, the Rom resorted to bribery and police "cooperation."

Gypsies make no claim to being quality workers, or even to being industrious. But both in America and elsewhere they are versatile. *They adapt.* As one Gypsy remarked to Adams and her colleagues, "Put me down anywhere in the world, and I'll make a living."[137] . . .

FOOTNOTES

1. Peter Maas, *King of the Gypsies* (New York: Viking, 1975).

2. See Ian Hancock, "Gypsies," in Stephan Thernstrom, ed., *Harvard Encyclopedia of American Ethnic Groups* (Cambridge, Mass.: Harvard University Press, 1980), p. 441.

3. See William Lockwood, "Balkan Gypsies: An Introduction," in Joanne Grumet, ed., *Papers from the Fourth and Fifth Annual Meetings, Gypsy Lore Society, North American Chapter* (New York: Gypsy Lore Society, Publication No. 2, 1985), pp. 91-99.

4. Cited in Matt Salo and Sheila Salo, *The Kalderasha in Eastern Canada* (Ottawa: National Museums of Canada, 1977), p.17.

5. Rena C. Gropper, *Gypsies in the City* (Princeton, N.J.: Darwin, 1975), p. 189.

6. Donald Kenrick and Grattan Puxon, *The Destiny of Europe's Gypsies* (New York: Basic Books, 1972), pp. 13-14.

7. P.W.R. Rishi, "Roma Preserves Hindu Mythology," *Roma* (January 1977): 13.

8. See the discussion in T.A. Acton, "The Social Construction of the Ethnic Identity of Commercial Nomadic Groups," in Grumet, *Papers*, pp. 5-23.

9. See Gropper, *Gypsies in the City*, pp. 1-16.

10. Frederick Barth, "The Social Organization of a Parish Group in Norway," in Farnham Rehfisch, ed., *Gypsies, Tinkers, and Other Travelers* (New York: Academic Press, 1975), pp. 285-99.

11. For an interesting discussion, see George Gmelch, *The Irish Tinkers* (Prospect Heights, Ill.: Waveland Press, 1985).

12. Martin Block, *Gypsies: Their Life and Their Customs* (New York: Appleton-Century, 1939), p. 1.

13. William Lockwood, "Balkan Gypsies: An Introduction," in Grumet, *Papers*, p. 92.

14. Jan Yoors, *The Gypsies* (New York: Simon and Schuster, 1967).

15. G.E.C. Webb, *Gypsies: The Secret People* (London: Herbert Jenkins, 1960), p. 9.

16. Yoors, *Gypsies*, p. 86.

17. Jeremy Sandford, *Gypsies* (London: Secker & Warburg, 1973), p. 13.

18. Gropper, *Gypsies in the City*, p. 1.

19. Norman Dodds, *Gypsies, Didikois, and Other Travelers* (London: Johnson, 1976), p. 16.

20. Jean-Paul Clebert, *The Gypsies* (London: Vista, 1963), pp. xvii-xix.

25. E.E. Evans-Pritchard, quoted in Elwood Trigg, *Gypsy Demons and Divinities* (Secaucus, N.J.: Citadel, 1973), p. x.

26. Anne Sutherland, *Gypsies: The Hidden Americans* (New York: Free Press, 1975).

27. Gropper, *Gypsies in the City.*

28. Sutherland, *Hidden Americans*, p. 21.

29. See the discussion in Marcel Cortiade, "Distance Between Romani Dialects," *Newsletter of the Gypsy Lore Society, North American Chapter*, 8 (Spring 1985): pp. 1 ff.

31. Carol Miller, "American Rom and the Ideology of Defilement," in Rehfisch, *Gypsies*, p. 41.

32. Ronald Lee, *Goddam Gypsy: An Autobiographical Novel* (Montreal: Tundra, 1971), pp. 29-30.

33. Miller, "American Rom," p. 42. See also Trigg, *Gypsy Demons*, p. 64.

34. Gropper, *Gypsies in the City*, pp. 92-93.

35. Sutherland, *Hidden Americans*, p. 266.

36. Ibid., p. 264.

37. Lee, *Goddam Gypsy*, p. 244.

38. Miller, "American Rom," p. 47.

39. Gropper, *Gypsies in the City*, p. 91.

40. Salo and Salo, *Kalderasha*, p. 115.

41. Miller, "American Rom," pp. 45-46.

42. Sutherland, *Hidden Americans*, p. 258.

43. Ibid., p. 259.

44. Ibid.

45. Miller, "American Rom," p. 47.

46. Ibid.

47. David Nemeth, "Gypsy Taskmasters, Gentile Slaves," in Matt. T. Salo, ed., *The American Kalderasha: Gypsies in the New World* (Centenary College, Hackettstown, N.J., 1981), p. 31.

48. Miller, "American Rom," p. 46.

49. Salo and Salo, *Kalderasha*, pp. 128-29.

50. Ibid., p. 39.

51. Yoors, *Gypsies*, p. 5.

52. For an interesting account of the *Familia*, see Gropper, *Gypsies in the City*, pp. 60-66.

53. Clebert, *Gypsies*, p. 129.

54. Salo and Salo, *Kalderasha*, p. 19.

55. Gulbun Coker, "Romany Rye in Philadelphia: A Sequel," *Southwestern Journal of Anthropology*, 22 (1966): 98. See also Gropper, *Gypsies in the City*, pp. 60-66.

56. Sutherland, *Hidden Americans*, pp. 82-83.

59. Sutherland, *Hidden Americans*, p. 183. See also pp. 182-192 for information regarding the *vitsa.*

60. Marie Wynne Clark, "Vanishing Vagabonds: The American Gypsies," *Texas Quarterly*, 10 (Summer 1967): 208.

61. Carol Silverman, "Everyday Drama: Impression Management of Urban Gypsies," in Matt Salo, ed., *Urban Anthropology, Special Issue*, 11, Number 3-4 (Fall-Winter, 1982): p. 383.

62. Ibid., p. 198. See also the discussion, pp. 181-90.

63. Gropper, *Gypsies in the City*, p. 86.

64. Sutherland, *Hidden Americans*, p. 232.

65. Gropper, *Gypsies in the City*, p. 158.

66. Sutherland, *Hidden Americans*, p. 223.

67. William M. Kephart, *The Family, Society, and the Individual* (Boston: Houghton Mifflin, 1981), pp. 231-232.

68. Gropper, *Gypsies in the City*, p. 162.

69. Sutherland, *Hidden Americans*, p. 223.

71. Clebert, *Gypsies*, p. 161.

72. Ruth E. Andersen, "Symbolism, Symbiosis, and Survival: Roles of Young Women of the Kalderasha in Philadelphia," in Salo, *American Kalderasha*, pp.16-17.

73. Sutherland, *Hidden Americans*, p. 175.

74. Quoted in ibid., p. 219.

75. Gropper, *Gypsies in the City*, p. 163.

78. Clebert, *Gypsies*, p. 96.

79. Block, *Gypsies*, p. 142.

80. Hancock, "Gypsies," p. 442.

81. Gary Polster, "The Gypsies of Bunniton (South Chicago)," *Journal of Gypsy Lore Society* (January-April 1970): 142.

82. Salo and Salo, *Kalderasha*, p. 73.

83. Ibid., p. 93.

84. Sandford, *Gypsies*, pp. 77-78.

85. Beverly Nagel Lauwagie, "Explaining Gypsy Persistence: A Comparison of the Reactive Ethnicity and the Ecological Competition Perspectives," in Grumet, *Papers*, p. 135.

86. Matt T. Salo, "Kalderasha Economic Organization," in Salo, *American Kalderasha*, p. 73.

87. Sutherland, *Hidden Americans*, p. 65.

88. Ibid.

89. Yoors, *Gypsies*, p. 122.

90. Ronald Lee, "Gypsies in Canada," *Journal of Gypsy Lore Society* (January-April 1967): 42.

91. See Sutherland, *Hidden Americans*, pp. 34-35.

92. Ibid., p. 83.

93. Ibid., p. 78.

94. Joseph Mitchell, "The Beautiful Flower: Daniel J. Campion," *The New Yorker*, June 4, 1955, p. 55.

95. Coker, "Romany Rye," p. 89.

96. Hancock, "Gypsies," pp. 440-445.

97. Andersen, "Symbolism," in Salo, *American Kalderasha*, p. 14.

98. Clark, "Vanishing Vagabonds," p. 205.

99. Konrad Bercovici, *Gypsies: Their Life, Lore, and Legends* (New York: Greenwich House, 1983), p. 236.

100. See Silverman, "Everyday Drama," p. 394; Gropper, *Gypsies in the City*, p. 44; Yoors, *Gypsies*, p. 7.

101. Trigg, *Gypsy Demons*, p. 48.

102. Gropper, *Gypsies in the City*, p. 43.

103. Mitchell, "Beautiful Flower," p. 46.

104. David Zucchino, "Officials Say Gypsies Live by Their Own Rules," *The Philadelphia Inquirer*, February 1, 1982, pp. 1-2A.

105. Lee, "Gypsies in Canada," pp. 38-39.

106. Clebert, *Gypsies*, p. 187.

107. Webb, *Secret People*, p. 123.

108. Lee, "Gypsies in Canada," p. 37.

109. Salo and Salo, *Kalderasha*, p. 76.

110. Silverman, "Everyday Drama," p. 382.

111. Sutherland, *Hidden Americans*, pp. 51-52.

112. John Kearney, "Education and the Kalderasha," in Matt T. Salo, ed., *American Kalderasha*, p. 48.

113. Gropper, *Gypsies in the City*, p. 130.

114. Barbara Adams, Judith Okely, David Morgan, and David Smith, *Gypsies and Government Policy in England* (London: Heinemann, 1975), p. 136.

115. Gropper, *Gypsies in the City*, p. 138.

116. Clark, "Vanishing Vagabonds," p. 165.

117. Gropper, *Gypsies in the City*, p. 165.

118. Sutherland, *Hidden Americans*, pp. 149 ff.

119. Ibid.

120. Gropper, *Gypsies in the City*, p. 88.

121. Mitchell, "Beautiful Flower," p. 54.

122. Hancock, "Gypsies," p. 443.

123. Cited in ibid, pp. 106-107.

124. Silverman, "Everyday Drama," p. 385.

125. Ibid.

126. Cited in Maas, *King of the Gypsies*, p. 4.

127. Sutherland, *Hidden Americans*, p. 98.

128. Gropper, *Gypsies in the City*, p. 100.

129. See the discussion in ibid., pp. 81-102.

130. Thomas Acton, *Gypsy Politics and Social Change* (London and Boston: Routledge & Kegan Paul, 1974), p. 99.

131. Yoors, *Gypsies*, p. 174. (Italics added.)

132. Kenrick and Puxon, *Destiny of Europe's Gypsies*, p. 189.

133. Murray Seeger, "The Gypsies," *Philadelphia Inquirer*, October 9, 1977.

134. Hancock, "Gypsies," p. 44.

135. Ibid.

136. Polster, "Gypsies of Bunniton," p. 139.

137. Adams et al, *Gypsies and Government Policy*, p. 132.

SELECTED READINGS

Andersen, Ruth E. "Symbolism, Symbiosis, and Survival: Roles of Young Women of the Kalderasha in Philadelphia." In *The American Kalderasha: Gypsies in the New World*, ed. by Matt T. Salo, pp. 11-28. Hackettstown, N.J.: Gypsy Lore Society, 1981.

Beck, Sam. "The Romanian Gypsy Problem." In *Papers From the Fourth and Fifth Annual Meetings, Gypsy Lore Society, North American Chapter*, ed. by Joanne Grumet, pp. 100-109. New York: Gypsy Lore Society, 1985.

Clark, Marie Wynne. "Vanishing Vagabonds: The American Gypsies." *Texas Quarterly*, 10 (Summer 1967): 204-10.

Clebert, Jean-Paul. *The Gypsies*. London: Vista, 1963.

Cortiade, Marcel. "Distance Between Romani Dialects." *Newsletter of the Gypsy Lore Society, North American Chapter*, 8 (Spring 1985): pp. 1 ff.

Dodds, Norman. *Gypsies, Didikois, and Other Travelers*. London: Johnson, 1976.

Friedman, Victor A. "Problems in the Codification of a Standard Romani Literary Language." In *Papers From the Fourth and Fifth Annual Meetings, Gypsy Lore Society, North American Chapter*, ed. by Joanne Grumet, pp. 55-75. New York: Gypsy Lore Society, 1985.

Gmelch, George. *The Irish Tinkers*. Prospect Heights, Ill.: Waveland Press, 1985.

Gropper, Rena C. *Gypsies in the City*. Princeton, N.J.: Darwin, 1975.

Hancock, Ian. "Gypsies." In the *Harvard Encyclopedia of American Ethnic Groups*, ed. by Stephan Thernstrom, pp. 440-45. Cambridge, Mass.: Harvard University Press, 1980.

Kearney, John. "Education and the Kalderasha." In *The American Kalderasha: Gypsies in the New World*, ed. by Matt T. Salo, pp. 43-54. Hackettstown, N.J.: Gypsy Lore Society, 1981.

Lee, Ronald. *Goddam Gypsy: An Autobiographical Novel*. Montreal: Tundra, 1971.

Lockwood, William G. "Balkan Gypsies: An Introduction." In *Papers From the Fourth and Fifth Annual Meetings, Gypsy Lore Society, North American Chapter*, ed. by Joanne Grumet, pp. 91-99. New York: Gypsy Lore Society, 1985.

Maas, Peter. *King of the Gypsies*. New York: Viking, 1975.

Nemeth, David. "Gypsy Taskmasters, Gentile Slaves." In *The American Kalderasha: Gypsies in the New World*, ed. by Matt T. Salo, pp. 29-41. Hackettstown, N.J.: Centenary College, 1981.

Okely, Judith. *The Traveler-Gypsies*. New York: Cambridge University Press, 1982.

Pippin, Roland N. "Community in Defiance of the Proscenium." In *The American Kalderasha: Gypsies in the New World*, ed. Matt T. Salo, pp. 99-133. Hackettstown, N.J.: Gypsy Lore Society, 1981.

Polster, Gary. "The Gypsies of Bunniton (South Chicago)." *Journal of Gypsy Lore Society* (January-April 1970): 136-51.

Rehfisch, Farnham, ed. *Gypsies, Tinkers, and Other Travelers*. New York: Academic Press, 1975.

Salo, Matt, and Salo, Sheila. *The Kalderasha in Eastern Canada*. Ottawa: National Museums of Canada, 1977.

Salo, Matt T., ed., *The American Kalderasha: Gypsies in the New World*. Hackettstown, N.J.: Gypsy Lore Society, 1981.

Silverman, Carol. "Everyday Drama: Impression Management of Urban Gypsies." In Matt Salo, ed., *Urban Anthropology, Special Issue*, 11, Number 3-4 (Fall-Winter, 1982): 377-398.

Sutherland, Anne. *Gypsies: The Hidden Americans*. New York: Free Press, 1975.

Tong, Diane. "Romani as Symbol: Sociolinguistic Strategies of the Gypsies of Thessaloniki." In *Papers From the Fourth and Fifth Annual Meetings, Gypsy Lore Society, North American Chapter*, ed. by Joanne Grumet, pp. 179-187. New York: Gypsy Lore Society, 1985.

Yoors, Jan. *The Gypsies*. New York: Simon and Schuster, 1967.

———. *The Gypsies of Spain*. New York: Macmillan, 1974.

Sex Roles and Statuses

The feminist movement in the United States has had a significant impact on the development of anthropology. Feminists have rightly charged that anthropologists have tended to gloss over the lives of women in studies of society and culture. In part, this is because, up until recent times, most anthropologists have been men. The result has been an undue emphasis upon male activities as well as male perspectives in descriptions of particular societies.

These charges, however, have proven to be a firm corrective. In the last few years women and, more particularly, the sexual division of labor and its relation to social and political status, have begun to be studied by anthropologists. In addition, these changes in emphasis have been accompanied by an increase in the number of women in the field.

Feminist anthropologists have begun to critically attack many established anthropological truths. They have shown, for example, that field studies of non-human primates, which were often used to demonstrate the evolutionary basis of male dominance, distorted the actual evolutionary record by focusing primarily on baboons. (Male baboons are especially dominant and aggressive.) Other, less quoted primate studies show how dominance and aggression are highly situational phenomena, sensitive to ecological variation. Feminist anthropologists have also shown that the subsistence contribution of women has likewise been ignored by anthropologists. A classic case is that of the !Kung, a hunting and gathering people in southern Africa, whose women provide the bulk of the foodstuffs, including most of the available protein. Indeed, the article "Woman the Gatherer," by Eaton, Shostak, and Konner, shows the foraging way of life to be supportive of a more egalitarian relationship between the sexes.

Recent studies have concerned themselves with determining why women generally hold a subordinate status, as is illustrated in "Men and Women: The Warmth and Luxury of Male Dominance" by Jean L. Briggs. Such male domination seems to exist even where women are the economic mainstay of a society (clearly illustrated in "Women, Food, and Hospitality in Iranian Society" by Mayling Simpson-Hebert). In "What Keeps Women 'in Their Place'?" Anthony Layng points out that it is social custom and not biology that explains the differences in sex roles. In "Blaming the Victim," Maxine Margolis shows how ideology can be a very effective force in keeping women subordinate, even in modern America. When women try to challenge the status quo, they are faced with the dilemmas discussed in "A Matter of Honor" by Longina Jakubowska and in "Between Two Worlds" by Marilyn Stasio.

Looking Ahead: Challenge Questions

What is it about foraging societies that encourages an egalitarian relationship between the sexes? Why are the Eskimos an exception?

How may a culture's ideology serve to justify sex role differences?

What kinds of shifts in the social relations of production are necessary for women to achieve equality with men?

How are the relationships between men and women reflected in Iranian hospitality?

Why is elopement a breach of the "code of honor" among Bedouins?

What kinds of personal dilemmas do women face in a changing society?

Unit 5

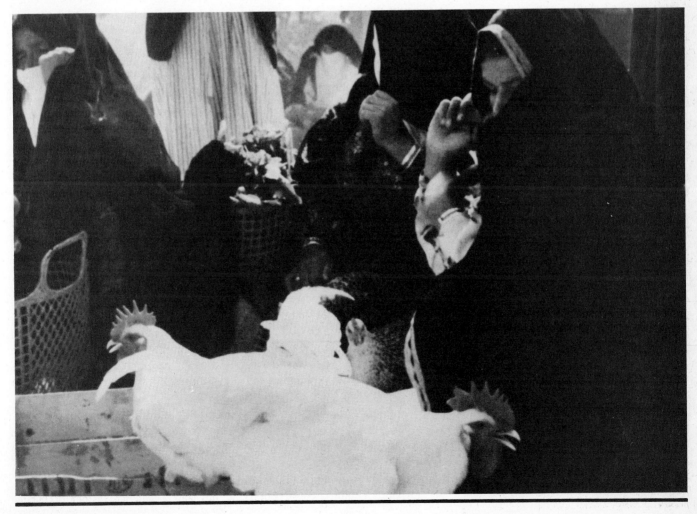

Woman the Gatherer

S. Boyd Eaton,
Marjorie Shostak,
and Melvin Konner

As the last rays of sunlight recede from a small village-camp situated on the northernmost fringe of Africa's Kalahari Desert, Naukha appears—a !Kung San woman in her mid-twenties, slight of build. She walks toward an insubstantial-appearing thatched grass hut and drops the firewood she has just collected. After clearing the ashes, she makes a new fire, then begins preparing food for the evening meal. Her younger sister, Chuko, soon appears with her own firewood. Naukha calls to her.

"Hey, Chuko! My stomach will surely rumble tomorrow and my family will complain if all we have to eat are these worthless leftover scraps. Why don't we walk west of the acacia grove to the *tsin* bean flat when the sun first brushes through the grass? That way, we can also see whether the sour plums are ready to be picked."

"Naukha, eh . . . how come my older sister's words always make sense? My mouth watered today when I smelled the roasting *sha* roots. My mother-in-law had brought them back. When she sent little Gau over with some for me, they were so sweet! Those women really did well! Did you see them? The ends of their leather pouches barely tied closed." She pauses, then adds, "What about little Nai? Will she come with us?"

"If she stays behind and plays with the other children, I'll worry that she will cry. If I take her along, it will be harder for me to gather as much food as I want. I suppose I'll ask Mother to tempt her into staying."

Chuko laughs. "Just like last time. Mother tried, and other children even asked her to play. But she wasn't satisfied until you took her along. You had to carry Nai and the baby until we almost reached the flats. Only then was she willing to walk on her own. Eh, children really are something!"

"Just wait until your next baby comes along. Then we'll see who does all the laughing!"

With different names, environmental features, and foods, a conversation such as this could have taken place just as easily 40,000 years ago most anywhere in the world as it might have 10 years ago among the !Kung San of Botswana. In most places and in most times women in hunting and gathering societies have known the importance of their work. Their labor was pivotal in keeping their families healthy and thriving; their efforts as gatherers of wild plant foods—together with the equally necessary contribution of game animals hunted by men—provided the original human diet.

Why has gathering—an activity so central to the lives of our ancestors—never really captured the imagination of most Westerners? Perhaps, because, if we think about it at all, we probably conjure up images of unpleasant, dull, tedious, and backbreaking work. After all, how many of us actually eat foods from the wild, and for those of us who occasionally do, would we not perhaps feel just a little more secure if the foods came wrapped in packages with assurances of edibility? As delicious as uncultivated berries or other wild plants often are, how many of us can imagine that such a diet would keep us satisfied meal after meal after meal? Even in the current vegetables-are-your-friends climate that most of us have been brought up in, we still believe that, while vegetables *are* good for us, they are a distant second to meat, which is far better.

Second to meat. Is this a biological determinant or a cultural construction?

Hunting has been, without question, central to human experience throughout time, attractive to the wealthy, to the poor, and to many other groups who have never had to hunt or gather for a living. Hunting, after all, has romance, the lure of the chase; it forges emotional connections between life and death, touching our deepest sensibilities as mortal, vulnerable, and transient beings. No wonder the hunt has been filmed and written about, its techniques—both ancient and modern—exhaustively described, and its importance to early human societies readily acknowledged. The concept of Man the Hunter is so widely held that it seems part of our collective unconscious.

Yet, without the continuing collection of wild plant foods, our species would not have been able to flourish to the extent that we have, settling, ultimately, all habitable regions of the earth. Because, in all but the most northern areas, plant foods have afforded a dietary stability and flexibility that have contrasted with the fluctuating availability of wild game. And in the majority of subtropical locations, plant foods have actually constituted the major dietary resource—a possible model for hunters and gatherers throughout vast stretches of human preagricultural life.

Naukha wakes just before sunrise, but stays in her skin blankets, savoring their warmth and waiting for the morning chill to soften. The baby stirs, expectant. At the taste of Naukha's warm milk, he settles into a familiar rhythm of nursing until, soothed, he goes back to sleep. Four-year-old Nai sleeps undisturbed beside him. As the first shadows are cast by the mounting sun, Naukha sits up. Rubbing the sleep from her eyes, she stokes the fire, takes some water she had carried back from the water hole yesterday, and washes. The rest she leaves for her family.

Daylight brightens, and the first sounds of people talking fill the camp. Her younger sister, Chuko, returns from her morning excursion to the surrounding bush, her skin cloth held snugly around her to protect her two-year-old—Nai's cousin—sleeping in a sling on her side. The sisters exchange greetings and agree to leave before the sun makes much more progress across the sky. Bereft of the warmth and softness of his mother's skin, Naukha's baby wakes again. This time little Nai soothes him, making baby sounds and funny faces until he starts to laugh. Naukha and Nai breakfast on roasted antelope, sha roots, and mongongo nuts while the baby nurses again.

Little Nai is called to her grandmother's hut and snuggles close as her grandmother also prepares food for her. Nai has just begun to play when she sees her mother and aunt preparing to leave—slipping infant and toddler into their slings, readying leather carrying pouches, and picking up digging sticks. She runs to them, pleading to go along. Naukha protests. Little Nai protests. There's a moment of hesitation, then, with a shrug and mock sigh of resignation, Naukha gestures to Nai the path they will be taking. Avoiding the amused twinkle sure to be in Chuko's eyes, Naukha starts off. Chuko follows. Little Nai darts ahead, skipping happily, singing softly to herself, triumphant.

Gathering is not for the weak, either of mind or body. It requires sophisticated knowledge of plant life and subtle understanding of the vagaries of the environment. Stamina, strength, visual acuity, memory, willingness to heed the advice of others, and a spirit of cooperation are the requirements for success. For such efforts, the rewards are great. Gatherers in many hunting and gathering societies provide the bulk of their family's food—adequate, varied, and satisfying. Nor is gathering considered drudgery, although, like hunting, it does demand considerable effort to walk the necessary miles and to carry the day's findings back to camp.

In most cases gathering is not a daily occupation. Even in less than ideal environments, women in many contemporary groups gather, on average, only a few days a week. Cuiva women of western Venezuela, for example, working two or at most three days a week, bring in enough food to feed themselves, their families, and other dependents. The rest of their time is spent maintaining their households, preparing food, sewing clothing, visiting nearby villages, or engaging in a variety of leisure activities.

The two women and three children reach the tsin bean flats within an hour and a half of leaving the village. They have traveled slowly, digging sha roots, collecting the last of the grewia berries, and pulling sweet lumps of sap from the bark of certain trees. The oppressive late morning heat permeates the dappled shade of the acacia tree where they sit to rest, so they feel little relief. Still, they light a fire to roast tsin beans, which they bury under a thin layer of hot sand beside some glowing coals.

Peeling the coarse, outer skin of a few sha roots, they eat the raw, sweet flesh, savoring its moisture. Little Nai drinks water from an ostrich eggshell container her mother has brought along, but is impatient to eat the tsin beans. She starts to fret; it seems contagious as her two-year-old cousin soon joins in. The women laugh, then begin a distracting and energetic round of singing, clapping their hands in complex rhythmic counterpoint that starts the two children dancing. By the time the tsin beans are cooked, the children stop only reluctantly, and sit down to eat.

The midday sun is ablaze. Little Nai and her cousin now sit beneath a different shade tree, watching their mothers collect tsin beans nearby. Naukha has left her powder shell, which dangled from her neck, for Nai to play with. Nai makes a doll—a tsin bean stuck on top of a small stick—and pretends it is a person who has just bathed. She takes the piece of tanned animal fur from the emptied tortoiseshell container, dips it deep into the fragrant powder ground from aromatic plants, and applies it to her doll. Another tsin-bean doll joins her play, then another and another. Her little cousin, enamored of Nai, holds the dolls dutifully while Nai gives directions.

The scattered piles of gathered beans, roots, and berries show that the two women have collected enough to fill their leather pouches. They join the two children at play, grateful to share the meager shade. Both women lie down, their little ones nursing; Nai looks wistfully on. Nestling beside her mother, she finds comfort. Holding her close, Naukha says as if to no one, "Maybe it's better Nai did come. If she hadn't, right now we'd be rushing through the heat to get home to her."

Small sounds of the bush surround them—a distant bird calling, flies humming, the dry underbrush crackling ever-so-slightly, a dung beetle moving busily beneath. The intense heat amplifies the stillness of the air, which settles like a dense, monochrome blanket on the broad untainted landscape, mile after mile after mile.

Naukha is the first to awaken. She sits up, looks at the steady progress the sun has made across the sky, then stands to brush off her leather coverings. Adjusting the baby so he can nurse while in the sling, she hums a refrain from the song they were singing earlier. She squats beside the piles she has left, opens her carrying pouch, and loads the food. When she joins the others, Nai and her cousin are already intent in play, tracking a little beetle like a game animal.

Chuko also collects her food, and they start their journey home.

Women are the primary food gatherers. True, men who live in contemporary hunting and gathering cultures have comparable knowledge of plant resources and are capable of gathering enough to feed themselves comfortably. But women are the ones responsible for the daily sustenance of their families. Their contributions include not only plant food, but some animal protein as well, brought back independently of men: small mammals, land turtles, snakes and other reptiles, birds, eggs, insects, some amphibians, and a variety of animals associated with water. Adept observers, women also survey all they see on their criss-cross journeys through the environment. They locate honey caches, make note of animals tracks, and mentally mark the position of valuable resources such as succulent water roots or reeds for arrow shafts to be harvested when needed.

Gathering is, ultimately, a satisfying way of earning a living. It is regarded as important and is personally rewarding. Every woman can learn the skills, and all have equal access to the foods available. The schedule and pacing of work is self-determined and flexible. Even though most food is collected primarily for one's family, sharing of food outside the family—while gathering or in the village—is typical: It is a kind of insurance against times of illness or other disability. Gathering is not isolating: women usually go with others, for protection as much as for companionship. They rely on their own courage and on each other, not on men's weapons, for safety as they traverse environments that are frequently dangerous, scaring off carnivores when necessary—leopards, lions, cheetahs, hyenas, jackals—and warning each other of poisonous snakes.

Gathering is challenging. It taps a woman's ability to identify, from among what may seem an infinite spectrum, a finite number of edible and seasonally variable plants. Gathering is also efficient. Unlike hunting, which has a variable rate of return, gathering is dependable and predictable. And because it requires only intermittent effort and women alternate their trips, gathering is a job compatible with motherhood; someone is usually in the village-camp, able to supervise children left behind.

Finally, unlike game, gathered foods are a woman's to distribute or to keep. Since success in gathering is universal, all women can provide food for their families and give presents. Personal circumstances and inclination may divide the generous from the selfish, but when obligations are incurred, they can be discharged quickly, if necessary. This is not always true for hunters who, perhaps down on their luck or lacking in skill, may wait weeks or even months before being in a position to return gifts of meat they have received from other men. Therefore, in these essentially egalitarian societies, women's work deflects status differentiation even more effectively than do most of the activities of men.

Sounds are brought by the wind; mere suggestions, at first, that quickly fade away. Yet, as the women walk, the rhythmic pounding of food preparation in the distant village-camp—"mortar-and-pestle talk," as the people call it—becomes clear. The two women quicken their pace and their movements become more energized, determined. Chuko is in the lead; Naukha trails behind, weighted down by both children, the food filling her leather pouch, and pieces of firewood she picks up as she nears the village.

This time the others watch *them*. Naukha and Chuko untie their leather pouches

and release their loads. Calls come from across the village-camp, speculating, commenting, teasing:

"Surely two women alone can not have collected so much food. Someone must have helped. Lovers, of course!"

And, "Oooh, I knew it! When just two decide to go off together, they are surely looking for some special food—the sweetest, most wonderful, most delicious food in the world."

And, "Who stays away all day and returns when dark just begins to sit? Without doubt, someone has tasted something as sweet as honey while away from the village-camp today."

Amid the burst of high-spirited laughter, another chides, "Oooh, women are clever!"

Naukha and Chuko shrug off the good-natured banter, accepting the women's barely concealed praise, pleased to be home and at rest. As Naukha separates piles of food to be given as presents—*tsin* beans, sour plums, and *sha* roots—her husband returns. Something small is slung over his shoulder—a guinea fowl caught in one of his traps—and she smiles in anticipation.

But that is all, he explains quietly. He had gone hunting, having left even before Naukha, and had followed what he thought was a promising lead. But although the tracks were quite fresh, he never came within sight of the animals. After a few hours, he finally turned back. Passing the traps he had set late the day before, he found the bird.

As he sits, slightly apart from the others, plucking and preparing the guinea fowl for cooking, Naukha tells him of her day. Little Nai joins her father, leaning against him, and pulls off a few feathers. She gives up, her attention now riveted by the gentle descent of the decorative black, brown, and white feathers she throws into the air. Naukha roasts and cracks some *tsin* beans and pounds them with nut meats and pungent leaves in her mortar. She takes a handful for herself and sets the rest beside them to eat. When the guinea fowl is cooked, others join for a taste, but no one expects much from something so small, and only Naukha and her family have a full share.

Naukha lies down, satisfied, grateful for the warmth of the fire, pleased to rest at last. As night deepens, a group of men sit at one fire, absorbed in the dramatic rendition of a hunting adventure. Chuko is sitting outside her hut, pressing for news of her parents from a woman at another hut who has just returned from their village. A few children burst into song, clapping dance tunes, hoping to entice the adults to join in, perhaps even to precipitate a healing dance. But although their voices are occasionally echoed by the women, enthusiasm is slight. They soon

give up, returning to their huts to play and then to sleep.

Amid the intimate circle of soft voices, Naukha drifts toward sleep. She barely notices little Nai slip quietly beside her and the baby, although almost reflexively she draws her near, pulling the leather blanket to cover her. Soon her husband joins them and lies down behind her, also close.

Quiet gradually descends, punctuated only by fires unwilling to give in to the dark—crackling, darting playfully, challenging, defiant—until the battle lost, they are at last subdued and become glowing embers covered by ash. Stillness is broken intermittently as one, then another stirs, filled with sleep, to add wood to the fire: brief bursts of light that seem to anticipate the new day, still hours away.

WOMEN'S LIVES

Imagine an infancy in which most of your needs for love and physical closeness were indulged, a childhood that—if you escaped serious illness—allowed you to flourish and mature at your own rate, absorbing and learning from role models only slightly older than yourself, a reasonably carefree adolescence that promoted individualism and self-confidence, assured you of your physical attractiveness, and didn't expect you to assume full adult responsibilities until you reached your late teens. Imagine, as well, an adulthood that essentially guaranteed marriage (with room for divorce and remarriage if necessary), that made it likely that you would have children, yet would not ostracize you if you couldn't or isolate you if you did, and that had social supports enabling you to balance family obligations with significant contributions to the economy. Although age, accidents, and infectious disease would gradually decrease your physical capabilities, your status within the community, especially within your family group, would be likely to increase. You would be turned to for the knowledge you possess about the past, highly relevant to a world that changes slowly, if at all. You would be the repository of stories told to you by your grandparents, entertaining to young and old alike. You would be vital to the life of your family.

A romantic fantasy of the noble savage? Twentieth-century pie-in-the-sky ideology? Given the unfortunate levels of mortality typical of foragers—and of all societies prior to the last hundred years—in some ways, of course, it is. But a version of life broadly similar to this one has been experienced by more generations of women than has any other. Even though there is and always has been marked diversity among hunting and gathering groups, certain elements affecting the way their lives progress are much more similar to each other than they are to ours today.

What follows, then, is a journey through a number of life stages as they would likely have been experienced by women in hunting and gathering societies.

Girlhood Among the Gatherers
As the toddler grows into a more independent child, play with a multi-age child group takes increasing amounts of time, but at first there is relatively little gender segregation. By age eight or nine, though, girls are more likely than boys to accompany their mothers on gathering expeditions, and so become trained and socialized in the art and science of plant food collecting. Before this age, boys exhibit more fighting behavior than girls, and the child in the play group most likely to be taking care of an infant or toddler is the baby's older sister; this role, however, is much less formal than in some agricultural communities in which young girls, or "child nurses" are responsible for much of the care of younger siblings. Because of demographic conditions (there are relatively few children in any one band so they all tend to play together), foragers have little opportunity for the extreme sex segregation during childhood that occurs routinely in many other societies.

Other features observed among recent hunters and gatherers also presumably characterized multi-age play groups of the past. With few peers, competition is minimized. Winning a game from someone much younger, or trying to beat someone much older is not very satisfying. Cooperation and nurturance is also fostered in children of both sexes. The inclusion of younger children means an expanded group, more diverse, and usually more interesting than solo or limited play.

Girls, as well as boys, spend a great deal of time in this group, which shifts in membership and size according to band composition, from toddlerhood to young adulthood. Much learning of adult skills takes place in this context; older children with more advanced knowledge are powerful role models for younger children. Older girls (and boys) eventually learn from adults as they gradually spend less time in play and more time refining their economic and social skills.

Puberty and Menstruation
The physical transformation from girl to woman is a dramatic occurrence, one that in many traditional societies occasions ritual celebration. First menstruation marks not only physical maturation, but entrance into the adult social world as well. In most societies this is a more important moment than the corresponding herald of male puberty—first seminal emission. The Siriono of eastern Bolivia, for example, celebrate puberty for girls but not for boys. Similarly, among California Indian hunters and gatherers, few groups had formal recognition of male puberty, while strong emphasis was placed on first menstruation.

As young girls in foraging cultures approach adolescence, they spend increasing amounts of time gathering with their mothers. Until puberty, however, their economic contribution is usually minimal. Among the Mbuti Pygmies of Zaire, children participate in all economic activities, including net hunting, where they help adults as "beaters," beating the bushes to drive animals into previously positioned nets. As a group, children also frequently prepare meals for themselves. But it is only after puberty that they actually begin to assume the responsibilities of adults. Among the Tiwi Aborigines of Melville Island in northern Australia, young girls also learn basic economic skills before puberty and are usually betrothed at birth. But only after puberty does a girl experience *ambrinua,* one of the most important rituals in her adult life: She is ceremonially introduced to the man who will become the husband of her yet-unborn daughters, her prospective son-in-law.

First menstruation generally occurs later in preindustrial societies than it does in our society. The adolescent period is therefore mostly free of the risk of pregnancy even though it is not free of sexual activity; this is especially true of hunting and gathering societies where restrictions on premarital sex tend to be less stringent than in other societies. More important, first birth does not come, on average, until the late-teen years: an average of age 20 for the Agta of the Philippines, 18.5 for the Aché of eastern Paraguay, and 19.5 for the !Kung San of Botswana.

Marriage
Romantic love is as ancient as the human race. The expectation of marrying for romantic love, however, is much more recent, especially in its Western form where it can occur independently of parental sanction. Marriage during the Paleolithic period must have varied widely, much as it does among recent hunters and gatherers, with differing emphasis placed on personal, economic, and political considerations.

Nevertheless Paleolithic marriage would probably have shared some of the features common to recent hunters and gatherers. Early marriage, for example, is virtually universal for women, and remarriage upon divorce or widowhood is fairly assured, especially for women in their reproductive years. Some are betrothed at birth, like Tiwi women of Australia; others, like the Agta of the Philippines, a few years before the onset of menstruation; still others marry sometime around first menstruation, which for the !Kung San of Botswana occurs at an average age of 16.5. !Kung girls who marry before menarche, however, are not expected to have sexual intercourse with their husbands, while premenstrual Tiwi and Agta wives may be introduced to marital sex earlier. Early marriages are often fragile, however, and divorce is frequent until after the birth of the first child.

While girls marry in their teens, men's marriage rates and ages are more variable. Some groups practice polygyny (the form of polygamy in which a man has more than one wife), enabling older men to monopolize a sometimes significant proportion of women. Other groups are more like the !Kung San. With a 5 percent polygyny rate, most !Kung men marry, although a young man's first marriage may be to an older woman, one recently divorced or widowed. More typically, however, men are older at first marriage than are the women they marry, affording them somewhat more control within the marriage relationship. (Men usually have to prove their worthiness as hunters before becoming eligible, which also helps account for the age difference.) At the other end of the life cycle, however, women often outlive their husbands, and "till death do us part" may translate into only a decade or two. But remarriage after divorce or death of a spouse is commonplace, and both men and women generally have a number of spouses if they live long enough. For the Tlingit of Alaska, for example, the clan of a deceased husband had to provide another spouse, although the woman was not forced to accept.

Where polygyny does occur, it effectively places a premium on young, marriageable girls. A young man may live with the bride's family and hunt for their benefit while waiting for the girl to mature. (The situation appears in Western tradition in the biblical story of Jacob, Rachel, and Leah.) Once the girl matures and if the marriage lasts, the couple will be guided by custom as to whether to stay with her relatives or move to be near his. Among the !Kung San, if the husband has no other wives, a young couple may divide their time between both villages, alternating one with the other until finally settling down with either.

For the Mbuti Pygmies, mutual affection between intended spouses is essential to the promotion of "real" as opposed to "empty" marriages. For the Tlingit of Alaska, a woman had to consent to a proposed marriage. After a formal ceremony, the couple lived together; if the relationship lasted four weeks, the marriage was considered permanent. For the !Kung San, marriages are usually arranged, especially first marriages, but early marriages are fragile and apt not to last. Subsequent marriages take place when a girl may be old enough to voice her own opinion and, depending on her age and the support she gets from other relatives, she may or may not be heeded. For both the Mbuti Pygmies and the !Kung San, however, divorce is accomplished more easily before a child is born than after.

Marriage is not only an affair of the heart, it is an arrangement between two groups of people. For hunters and gatherers, couples are not isolated units, but threads in a net thrown far and wide, connecting people in distant areas, involving them socially, politically, and economically in each other's lives. Marriage expresses interdependence, the mainstay of hunting and gathering existence. This interdependence offers a cushion against times of scarcity. A family or group can visit in-laws living in more bountiful areas for extended periods of time. Even within the village, the presence of relatives translates into having more people to count on in times of personal hardship, such as illness or accident.

The village-camp a couple lives in after marriage determines important aspects of their lives. Each knows the vegetation, terrain, and game-migration patterns in his or her territorial home. It is advantageous for women to live near their own relatives, especially in groups where husbands are more dominant, if only because of age. By living near her parents, a woman's position—both in relation to her husband and the social life of the camp—is strengthened. Although some foraging groups expect young married couples to reside with the husband's family, others expect them to reside with the wife's family, or have no set pattern at all and allow the couple to live with either family. However, even when the husband's family's residence is preferred, individual couples may be permitted the option of doing otherwise. In any event, the fluid nature of hunting and gathering bands usually translates into extended visits to both groups.

Birth

A woman feels the initial stages of labor and makes no comment, leaves the village quietly when birth seems imminent—taking along, if necessary, a young child—walks a few hundred yards, finds an area in the shade, clears it, arranges a soft bed of leaves, and gives birth while squatting or lying on her side—on her own. Unusual even for other hunters and gatherers, solo birth for !Kung San women is nevertheless an ideal: 35 percent of women attain it by their third birth and the majority do on subsequent births. Showing no fear and not screaming out, they believe, enhances the ease and safety of delivery. Cries of a newborn in the distance alert others, sending them running to the scene. They assist in the delivery of the placenta, cut the umbilical cord, clean the infant, and carry it back to the village. For the most stalwart, however, the first others learn of the birth is when they see the woman sitting near her hut, a small bundle in her arms.

Not all !Kung women attain this ideal, especially not those experiencing their first births. These women welcome the help and support of mothers, sisters, or other female relatives. Nor do most hunters and gatherers share this ideal. For the Siriono of Bolivia, for example, birth was a more public event. It took place in the village, and was attended by women and children; if it occurred at night, the prospective father would also be present. The actual birth, however, was left entirely to the woman to manage, since she received essentially no help throughout labor and delivery. She herself tied a rope above the hammock in which she would give birth, grabbing it when necessary for leverage. As she delivered the infant, it slid onto a pile of softened earth prepared a few inches below the side of the hammock. Birth for women among the Mbuti Pygmies also involves support from other women, not only by their presence but in the offering of help as well.

The experience of pregnancy and

birth for Paleolithic women, while certain to have varied widely in cultural expression and meaning, nevertheless must also have been constrained in a number of similar ways—many of which have been observed among recent hunters and gatherers. The rhythm of the menstrual cycle, for example, may have been charted according to lunar cycles. Marked bones that may have served as calendars have been found in European Upper Paleolithic archaeological sites; recording twenty-eight units, they are suggestive of an attempt to establish either the phases of the moon, the menstrual cycle, or both. !Kung San women start anticipating pregnancy when two lunar cycles pass without the onset of menstruation. Additional months confirm this, as do darker nipples, mood swings, and sometimes intense food preferences. Pregnancy doesn't mean coddling, however, either for !Kung San women or for other recent hunting and gathering women, who continue their usual work patterns until the very end and may resume them, like the Mbuti Pygmies and the Philippine Agta, within a few days after birth.

Whether with the help of other women or alone, women living in hunting and gathering societies have no choice but to give birth as nature intended. This means an inevitable and unfortunate loss of life, but the pattern is as typical of foragers as of agricultural and even early industrial peoples and continues in many parts of the world today. Attempts are made to prepare young women for the experience, and most girls see childbirth before they experience it themselves. But no amount of preparation can remove the risk. Indeed, our own security in this regard is unprecedented in human experience.

However bravely women may face childbirth, it is a risky affair that until about two generations ago took a dramatic toll on the lives of women and infants in all societies no matter when or where they lived. (In Europe, for example, from 1500 to 1900, about 25 percent of deaths of women ages fifteen to fifty were related to childbirth.) And, while the !Kung ideal of solitary

birth is atypical, beliefs and practices designed to minimize risk are widespread. For the !Kung (and for the Siriono), a solitary or unaided birth may have its positive side; minimizing the number of people present at the birth or who touch the woman throughout labor exposes a woman and her infant to fewer germs. But for the !Kung at least, solitary birth may also mean fewer dissenting voices in the rare cases when infanticide is being considered. Infants with serious deformities jeopardized an entire family's ability to survive, and twins—or children born too closely together—cannot both thrive on milk from nursing, the only kind of milk available.

In anthropological usage, "infanticide" refers to the abandonment or killing of an infant at birth or soon after. There is some dispute as to whether it has played (and continues to play), a large or small role in population regulation; either way, it is likely to have been part of our hunting and gathering past. Infanticide has been practiced throughout the world and over a wide span of time. Oedipus, Moses, Romulus, and Remus, like many other heroes in world mythology, were all abandoned; they survived only through extraordinary luck. In addition to its practice by the ancient Greeks and Romans, infanticide has been recorded in other societies both large and small: the Chinese, the Japanese, the high-caste Indians, the Aymara of Bolivia and Peru, the Yaudapu Enga of New Guinea, and the Ibo of Nigeria, as well as the Eskimo and the Australian Aborigines.

Infanticide has not been unknown in Western countries. Anthropologist Susan Scrimshaw writes:

In London in the 1860's, dead infants were a common sight in parks and ditches. In nineteenth century Florence, children were abandoned or sent to wet nurses who neglected them, while during the same period in France, thousands of infants were sent to wet nurses in the countryside, never to return.

On May 5, 1987, a baby was found in a dumpster in San Francisco—alive and fortunately saved, but a grim reminder of a common practice in our past.

Many studies of infanticide have calculated its incidence among human groups, both in the past and the present. One such study of 112 preindustrial cultures reported that 36 practiced infanticide commonly; an additional 13 practiced it occasionally. John Whiting and associates analyzed the literature on a group of 84 cultures and found similar results: one-third reported infanticide as a means of eliminating defective offspring, and 36 of a group of 72 cultures reported killing infants born too soon after the birth of an older sibling. This was more likely to occur in nomadic hunting, gathering, and fishing societies than in agricultural ones.

The practice of infanticide has had a long history. In trying to understand it, the drastic circumstances many of these people found themselves in have to be considered. Many of these infants would have died later from lack of food or general neglect. If allowed to live, a severely deformed infant could have jeopardized the survival of the entire family. Even normal children born too closely together endangered their siblings. This is not to justify the practice—even many hunters and gatherers do not. !Kung mothers suspected of it are bitterly criticized and their reasons closely scrutinized. As a Jicarilla Apache told anthropologist Morris Opler, "Sometimes unmarried mothers throw their babies away. But there is a strong feeling against it. To kill a child like this is to set yourself against life, and your own life will not be long after that." . . .

Motherhood

First motherhood is not often the occasion of special ritual and ceremony, but most cultures recognize it as the true dividing line between childhood and adulthood. The experience of first birth changes a woman. The !Kung San have an expression for the firstborn which applies to no other child, and after the baby comes, the parent is usually given a name derived from that of the baby: Susanna's-father, Adam's-mother (or the equivalents), a tribute to the change in status. Giving birth not only separates the women from the girls but, of course, the women from the men. The words of an Abyssinian woman recorded early in this century express this distinction, as applicable to hunters and gatherers as they are to ourselves:

How can a man know what a woman's life is? A woman's life is quite different from a man's. God has ordered it so. A man is the same from the time of his circumcision to the time of his withering. He is the same before he has sought out a woman for the first time, and afterwards. But the day a woman enjoys her first love cuts her in two. She becomes another woman on that day. The man is the same after his first love as he was before. The man spends a night by a woman and goes away. His life and body are always the same. The woman conceives. As a mother she is another person than the woman without child. She carries the fruit of the night nine months long in her body. Something grows. Something grows into her life that never departs from it. She is a mother. She is and remains a mother even though her child dies, though all her children die. For at one time she carried the child under her heart. And it does not go out of her heart ever again. Not even when it is dead. All this the man does not know; he knows nothing.

Becoming a mother entails a change of status for women in all cultures; among hunters and gatherers, it represents the assumption of full-fledged adult responsibility. The new demands now placed on a woman's time, however, do not contradict her role as economic provider. Mothering in the context of hunting and gathering societies not only provides ample opportunity for "dual careers," it requires them; it is also organized sensibly, and with many more social supports than it is for us. From the moment of birth, the differences are striking.

Infants in hunting and gathering societies are likely to be in frequent or even constant physical contact with others throughout the first year or more of life. They are carried wherever their mothers go during the day, often skin to skin in some form of sling, and they sleep beside or near their mothers at night. (North American Indians used cradleboards to comfort infants, but still maintained close

physical proximity.) Nursing is "on demand," a pattern of frequency unknown to most mothers in industrial cultures. The !Kung San believe that an infant cries for a reason. Mothers respond to a child's frets immediately—if not before, in anticipation—by putting it to the breast for as often and for as long as it wants—from a few seconds to several minutes. As a child gets older, it nurses whenever it chooses; it simply avails itself of its mother's breasts while being carried in the sling, when sitting near her on the ground, or while sleeping beside her at night. For the first two years or more of life, a !Kung child nurses an average of four times an hour. (One drawback of breast-feeding—that it drains calcium from the mother—is offset by exercise and high calcium intake.)

Few women in our own culture, even those committed to nursing on demand, have adopted a comparable level of frequency or degree of commitment to this mode of feeding. Work schedules and social patterns prohibit it. Breast-feeding in public is available only to the most stalwart, and even then social tension may interfere with it. Frequent breast-feeding also runs counter to the Western ideal of breast-as-sexual-object because of fears that it will hasten the transformation of an adolescent-shaped breast. Among hunters and gatherers, as among many preindustrial peoples, the breast is as much a symbol of nurturance and maternity as of nubility and sexual attractiveness, at least after adolescence.

Another practice common to hunting and gathering societies, sleeping beside the mother at night, seems to pose relatively few problems to the child or to the couple. A concern voiced frequently in the West—that a woman may roll over (also known as overlying) on a child and smother it while both are asleep—was not considered an issue for the !Kung. As far as they knew, no one had ever done that. In fact, infant death caused by smothering or strangling in a crib, away from the mother, is better documented in the medical literature than is overlying. Furthermore, when we consider how most of us sleep—on raised beds sev-

eral feet above the floor—why don't adults constantly fall our of bed? Because, despite our altered states of consciousness throughout the night, we are capable of making delicate calculations about our body position—the same made by mothers sleeping beside their children.

More problematic, to be sure, are a couple's sexual relations, which are likely to be more restrained in the presence of a sleeping child. Among hunters and gatherers, however, dwellings are often loosely constructed and set close together so that engaging in sex requires extreme discretion whether children are present or not. Sometimes a husband and wife meet like lovers in the bush for a less inhibited encounter. But even for these meetings a small infant would probably not be left behind.

Patterns of child rearing similar to these probably typify the Paleolithic period. Close contact with the mother promotes safety of infants and young children, and frequent nursing assures adequate water, nutrition, and at least some protection against infection. In an environment in which mortality within the first few years of life is high, close physical contact and frequent nursing also help cement a strong bond between a mother and child, maximizing the infant's care and thus its chance of survival.

As the child grows older, experiences unique to this way of life continue to affect its development. During the second year, for example, the child gradually turns its attention from the mother to the world beyond, but the initiation and circumstances of this separation contrast markedly with usual Western practices. As we have seen, because villages consist only of about a dozen families, children of all ages play together. For toddlers, the running, jumping, squealing, dancing, singing, rope jumping, cartwheeling, and all other variety of imaginative games played by multi-age child groups are so appealing that they attract even the youngest. An older sibling, cousin, or friend will pick up little ones eagerly crawling toward them or calling out to play, and include them in their games.

When the toddler tires, get hungry, or just wants more comfort than other children are willing or able to offer, the mother is usually nearby. In this setting it is primarily the child—not the mother—who controls the degree and timing of separation and social growth. The children's play group, therefore, relieves the mother of intensive child care for brief but frequent periods throughout the day.

A common complaint of mothers in the West was voiced by a young American woman caring for their first child. "I love being a mother and I love my son. I also enjoy playing games with him. But when he wants to repeat the same game fifty times the same way each time, I get so bored I can't stand it. I try to change the game, but he insists. Is there something wrong with me that I can't do it his way?"

The answer, from the perspective of our hunting and gathering past, is that nothing is wrong with her; something is wrong with the structure of Western child rearing. Mothers living in hunting and gathering societies are rarely faced with children who are bored, having to devise ever more elaborate strategies to entertain them. Other children are better at that. Other children, working out similar skills, perhaps at a somewhat higher but still immature level, *are* willing to repeat a game endlessly. Other children are also usually more fun. This does not mean that mothers in hunting and gathering societies are not playful with children, for indeed they are, especially with the very young. Their face-to-face and vocal interactions with infants are playful and tender, obviously a source of pleasure to infant and mother alike. But their primary role is to offer what they, and only they, are uniquely qualified to provide: food, nurturance, security, comfort, and, above all, love. Play is what other children do best.

Play also distracts young children from the pain of the ultimate separation from Mother: weaning. This probably took place relatively late among Paleolithic hunters and gatherers, since prolonged nursing provides the only form of milk available for growing children. It also helps maximize birth spacing. A four-year difference between successive children means that a second youngest child is able to walk on its own much of the time. Shorter birth spacing undermines a woman's capacity to work; instead of carrying only the youngest child on routine gathering expeditions (along with heavy loads of food), she has to carry the next oldest as well. The extra weight also severely limits her effectiveness as a provider and so profoundly taxes her energies that the prospects for all members of her family are diminished.

Motherhood is eased not only by the presence of a play group and by long birth spacing, but also by the social context in which it occurs: Other people are always around, adults whom one can rely on to take the baby for a few minutes at least. Fellow band members provide company, companionship, and conversation; they also act as a critical release valve for the tensions that motherhood often produces. All-day isolation of mother and children, so common in middle-class Western societies, is unusual among hunters and gatherers.

Unfortunately, the security and comfort of childhood provided by parents—especially mothers—in preagricultural societies has always been undermined by forces beyond anyone's control: diseases (primarily viral and bacterial infections of the respiratory and gastrointestinal tracts) and other medical problems which we can now control but which they couldn't. These caused high mortality for children of all ages, although the most vulnerable then, as now, must have been infants. Simple infections accompanied by diarrhea can fast become life threatening; dehydration can be swift and lethal in the absence of medical intervention. Having one's siblings, and later, one's children, die was an experience both men and women had to learn to cope with, to endure, and finally, to overcome. . . .

THE QUESTION OF EQUALITY

The battle between the sexes rages not only in our lives, but in the literature interpreting our lives. Not surprisingly, our hunting and gathering past is invoked by many as holding essential keys to the meaning of "male" and "female" as well as the possibilities and limitations of the two together. But, in contrast to diet and exercise, or even certain aspects of infant and child care, the relationship between men and women in hunting and gathering societies is more elusive; humans are forever innovative, and their social arrangements infinitely complex.

Disentangling the threads of the hunting and gathering adaptation from the fabric of culture may be difficult, but tracing a few common themes can provide useful insights and establish a range of possibilities and limitations that may have characterized our ancient past.

Perhaps the most intriguing finding, true in varying degrees of most hunters and gatherers, is one that defies the common "caveman" stereotype of our Stone Age past. Instead of being subservient and dependent, women are central to the economy, autonomous in their actions, and in positions of influence quite comparable to those of males. Relations between sexes, instead of resembling a battle, are usually more like a skirmish; and in at least one group, the Agta of the Philippines, the conflict may be almost nonexistent. If human societies were ranked along a continuum according the status of women, most foragers would be positioned near the end closest to full equality.

Another striking finding is that little in the structure of the foraging lifestyle requires male privilege. Instead, many features encourage an egalitarian system and a position of overall strength for women, along with men: (1) the importance of gathered food and the economic independence of women; (2) comparable mobility for men and women; (3) the absence of social or economic class structure; (4) leadership that is informal, nonheritable, and antiauthoritarian; (5) problem resolution that maximizes individuals' participation in group decisions; (6) an emphasis on cooperation, sharing, and generalized reciprocity; (7) minimal property ownership with little value placed on accumulation; (8) fluid band composition; (9) small living groups in which men and women mix freely; and, at least among recent groups, (10) a low frequency of war and of elaborate preparations for war.

Women's economic role is overwhelmingly as providers of gathered food. Depending on environmental factors, wild plants in the diet range from insignificant (for people such as the Eskimos, who live in extreme northern climates with little vegetation) to the vast majority (for people such as the Aborigines of the Central Australian desert, where game is scarce). Since foragers of the past lived in the most advantageous areas, it is possible that women's contribution of plant foods was less significant. However, contemporary hunters and gatherers such as the Hadza of Tanzania and the Tiwi of Australia live in environments rich with game, yet gathered foods still comprise at least 50 percent of their diets.

What about societies in which game *is* more prominent than plant foods? This probably typified some groups during the Late Paleolithic, especially those living near the receding glaciers, where game was abundant but plant growth was limited. High meat consumption also characterizes many contemporary groups living in northern latitudes, as well as some tropical forest dwellers such as the Aché of Paraguay. The status of women among the noncoastal, traditional "Caribou-Eater" Chipewyan Indians of Canada—whose diet consisted of more than 90 percent meat—has been described as being one of the lowest for any North American Indian tribe. Women participated only in food processing, not in food getting, which was almost entirely the responsibility of men.

A different picture emerges, however, among more recent tropical forest hunters and gatherers. Contrary to expectation, edible plant food is widely scattered and less available in the tropical forest than it is in mixed or open environments; the deep shade and high tree cover nevertheless provide ideal conditions for a wide range of game (as well as honeybees). For the Aché of

Paraguay, the Maku Indians of northwestern Amazonia, the Efe Pygmies of Zaire, and the Agta of the Philippines, meat and honey constitute more of their diets than does plant food. Among these groups, women's contribution to the economy is still significant, not only as gatherers, but also as hunters. Among Efe Pygmy net hunters, women participate in the hunt, driving animals into nets; among the Agta, women hunt as do men. Perhaps it is not coincidental that the relations between the sexes in these two groups are portrayed as being essentially equal.

Women hunters have also been described among the Tiwi of Australia, for whom the division of labor seems not so strictly dichotomized along sexual lines—at least in the economic sphere. Tiwi men and women both hunt and gather; their resources, not activities, are categorized into male domains (those of the sea and air) and female domains (those of the land). Men typically fish and hunt birds, aquatic reptiles, and mammals; women collect wild foods, shellfish, and hunt land animals with the aid of dogs. (The largest, strongest, and most-difficult-to-obtain land animals, however, are usually hunted by men.)

But in the social sphere, relationships seem less equitable, especially within marriage: Tiwi women are betrothed before birth into polygynous households (helping to establish their husbands as "big men" who command considerable power within the community) and they have little opportunity for divorce. As wives, they are "inherited" by other males when their husbands, who are much older, die. A woman eventually gains influence in this realm by the establishment of a formal relationship with a prospective son-in-law (the husband-to-be for all her female children) arranged even before she becomes pregnant. Age also brings increased status as she moves into the position of senior wife.

Work that equals or even exceeds that of men in practical value does not automatically lead to equality. Women in many small-scale agricultural societies also make significant contributions to subsistence, working hard in

the fields, often much harder than men, yet their status usually remains quite low. Perhaps the most significant difference is that for most foragers, food is gathered for use—not for exchange or for translation into forms of currency or prestige items. Women foragers control the conditions of their work, and the foods they gather are theirs to distribute. By being major participants in the food-procuring (as well as processing) part of the economy and by disposing of the fruits (literally) of their labor according to their will, women build strong social networks that lead to influence within the group.

The hunting and gathering economy also entails considerable time spent away from home base, with comparable mobility for men and women. Women leave camp often, usually with other women, and spend anywhere from a few hours to a full day away. (Men, who also leave camp frequently, are more likely to stay overnight in the pursuit of game.) The decision when and where to gather is a woman's to make, although when hunting strategies are considered, men become involved. Cohesion and cooperation among women are fostered in this setting, together with autonomy and mobility. Child care—the near-exclusive domain of women—takes place in the context of this economic contribution, not to the exclusion of it.

The absence of social classes and other forms of status hierarchies are additional features of the foraging lifestyle, ones that limit authority which might otherwise reside with males. Within a camp, just about everything enters the sharing network, be it food or material goods. Leadership itself is usually informal. With thirty or fewer people living together, always having the option to leave one camp for another, it is difficult to develop or maintain arbitrary leadership. Leaders do emerge, more often men than women, but their influence is informal at best; they listen, they suggest, and they argue. Their role is to reflect group consensus, not create it. People participate in the decision-making and conflict-resolution process freely, expressing their opinions and having their views considered.

Even ownership of resources is egalitarian. The land and its food are usually owned collectively, with all people in the group having equal rights of access, although "ownership" by one or more individuals is sometimes designated. !Kung visitors, for example, ask permission to exploit local resources and this permission will not be denied; granting use assures reciprocal access to the visitors' resources another time—an "insurance" policy against periods of local hardship or scarcity. Material goods owned by individuals are not hoarded since most items can be produced by individual families. More exotic ones invariably become part of an exchange network, so that there is no institutional separation of haves from have-nots. After all, when mobility and adaptability are at a premium, accumulation of goods becomes a liability. It is better to translate material advantage into obligations that can be "harvested" in times of stress than to be overburdened with coveted items during times of abundance.

Another feature that affects women's status is the site of residence after marriage. Many hunters and gatherers prefer a couple to live with the husband's group after marriage. The experience of living in the husband's village, quite common among agriculturalists, has been eloquently described by anthropologist Naomi Quinn:

Such a bride suffers the loneliness and the scrutiny of her affines [in-laws] which typifies the lot of all virilocally married women . . . , in addition she may find herself under the authority of a hostile mother-in-law, whose interests are opposed to hers in competition for the affection and loyalty of her husband. Her only claim to status rests on her success in bearing and raising sons and her eventual position as mother-in-law herself. Typically, women can only gain power in such households indirectly, through men, and their strategies for so doing may be characterized by gossip, persuasion, indirection and guile.

In Martin and Voorhies' sample of ninety foraging societies, nearly 65 percent either favor living with the woman's family or at least allow the option of living with them. By being based for at least some time with her family, a young woman has support for decisions that affect her life, and has the protection of family members in times of stress—physical, social, and even marital. Because there is a reasonable chance a girl may live with her parents' group after marriage, her value, even at birth, is not diminished. Just as a son may enhance his family's standing in the community by bringing in his bride, so can a daughter, by bringing in her husband. Among some Native American hunters, ownership of the home was seen as residing in the hands of the woman who built it; her husband was viewed as a long-term guest.

Within the family, women's standing is also enhanced by long birth spacing (only one small child to care for at a time), permissive child-rearing attitudes, and nonauthoritarian family structure. Together, these factors point to the hunting and gathering mode as one that maximizes mutual respect and easy dependence between the sexes—a lesson for our own times.

Yet a number of issues need further consideration. First, equality between the sexes is not universal among hunters and gatherers. Substantial diversity exists, ranging from groups in which women attain considerable influence and recognition (as among the !Kung San or the Philippine Agta) to those which are "less equitable" (as among some Eskimos and many Australian Aborigine groups). Second, among groups that *are,* for most practical considerations, egalitarian, men still invariably seem to have an edge. They are more likely to become leaders, both political and spiritual, more likely to use aggressive force against women (as well as against men), and, being generally older than their wives, are likely to be dominant in the marriage relationship, including exercising the option to have more than one wife. Men are also more likely to be *considered* dominant—by men and women alike.

Contemporary forces have been accused of being partly responsible for distorting what otherwise might be a more symmetrical male-female relationship. Some anthropologists condemn the colonial presence as having tipped the scales in favor of men. They argue that when hunters and gatherers were asked to present their "chief" to colonialists, it was made clear that a high-status male was to step forward. (For groups that downplayed "high status" anything, this was considered an affront to good manners.) Missionary influences often produced similar results—not only on foragers, but also on neighboring people with whom foragers had economic and cultural contact. Others criticize male observers (and most early observers were male) for concentrating primarily on male activities and for projecting their own sex-stereotyped images. This imbalance created an "androcentric," or male-oriented, view of hunting and gathering life.

Other influences have also inevitably clouded the picture. Recent hunters and gatherers live in a contemporary world; all have had contact with outside forces, some for hundreds of years. The Pygmies of Zaire, for example, only speak the language of their agricultural neighbors, having lost their original tongue. Others, like the Mashco-Piro of Peru, have remained more isolated, but none has been "untouched." In light of these circumstances, then, it seems all the more intriguing that a general pattern of high status for women characterizes most contemporary hunting and gathering groups—especially when they are compared to many agricultural and industrial societies in which extreme forms of female subordination often exist. Indeed, although not all agricultural societies should be implicated, the shift to agriculture generally heralded a decline in the overall status of women. This was probably due in part to an increase in the importance of war.

Archaeological evidence suggests that just before agriculture was introduced, areas with rich, abundant resources started supporting larger, more sedentary, and socially stratified settlements somewhat more oriented to war. A number of contemporary examples of this late hunting and gathering adaptation have been recorded, especially among various Native American groups living on the northwest Pacific coast. For the Tlingit of Alaska, in a good year the three-month salmon run could provide enough fish to last (when preserved) until the next season, twelve months later. Known for their rigid social classes, including slaves, and elaborate storage techniques, the Tlingit held widely publicized pot-latches—or social gatherings—during which large quantities of food and wealth were given away.

Yet anthropologist Laura Klein found that, historically, women's status was quite high in this stratified society. A report from 1874 reads, " . . . there are few savage nations in which the [female] sex have greater influence or command greater respect . . . the truth is that not only old men, but old women, are respected." And, "The women possess a predominant influence, and acknowledge superiority over the other sex." Indeed, she comments that in this society in which status was so important, "Women and men held similar positions in the ranking system." Not all stratified groups reflect this high degree of equality, but the Tlingit case makes clear that more complex societal organization didn't necessarily preclude women from enjoying privilege along with men.

That "true" equality between the sexes may have existed during the Paleolithic is clearly a theoretical possibility; many contemporary groups exhibit something quite close to it. Yet, contemporary analogues suggest that a balance of power favoring men also may have prevailed in many societies. What is least likely, however, is that the extremes of oppression experienced by women in many parts of the world today existed before the introduction of agriculture. Too many features of the hunting and gathering life-style guard against such conditions.

Contrary to popular belief, then, our remote past provides no precedent for extreme sexual or social inequality: It is not ubiquitous or inevitable. To survive during the long course of the Paleolithic period, humans had to be flexible more than anything else, so that they could freely adapt to diverse and variable conditions. Rigid social categorization would have undermined and limited their ability to fine-tune their social worlds to a wide range of environmental challenges. Gender roles were surely well elaborated, but must have existed in a variety of guises, responsive to the specific demands of a wide range of circumstances. Yet, the potential for human inequity—social classes, war, and the oppression of women—does seem part of the human makeup, never far below the surface. When the checks and balances against the extremes of its expression erode, inequality is only too quick to blossom.

But humans can clearly function quite successfully in an egalitarian framework. Recent hunters and gatherers are living proof: They discourage self-aggrandizement and encourage social equality. Thus the goal of an equitable and decent world order is not inconsistent with the original human condition.

(handwritten margin notes: "Men brothers & husbands of women"; "Women have their own trapline shorter & closer to camp than"; "One family men & women & children"; "in Contact with rest of world only when straight freezes"; "MAN COMMAND")

Men and Women: The Warmth and Luxury of Male Dominance

Jean L. Briggs

The easy conviviality that I saw among the members of the family in their private hours revealed an important aspect of the warmth that underlay the formal, somewhat distant, public relationships between the sexes. In a more literal sense, too, warmth was enhanced when the men and women of a family were together. "Iglus are cold when the men are away," people told me, but the words meant little to me until in January of my first winter Inuttiaq went to Gjoa Haven to trade.

The Utku looked forward to trading season. In late August the breeze began to bite and the ground to crunch underfoot; the drums of boiled fish bellies stored in the tent entries became granulated with ice, and the used tea leaves froze to the flat rock on which they had been piled to dry for re-use. Then the men, sitting flat-legged around their card games, and the women, rocking their babies on their backs and tucking stiff fingers into the hollows of their necks to limber them for sewing, began to talk about Gjoa Haven and what they would buy there when the strait froze in November and the men made the long sled trip in to trade. The lists were always the same: fresh tea to replace the jaded old leaves (and the weed-stalks that we brewed up as tea-substitutes when there was no life at all left in the old tea leaves); flour for bannock to supplement the staple fish; real tobacco and cigarettes to replace the bits of twig and trouser pocket that the people were smoking in thimble pipes; duffel for a new parka; cartridges . . . These trading trips were the events of the winter, the peaks of an otherwise even-flowing life. As Amaaqtuq, her eyes shining, told me once during my first autumn: "You will see: when the men come back from Gjoa Haven we stay up all night. It's *tiring!*" Feasting on bannock and more bannock, she meant; drinking tea, coffee, cocoa, one after the other, while listening to news of the world across the strait, a world accessible only during the winter. Any one Utku man would make the trip only once or twice in a winter, but somebody was always coming or going, and usually two or three traveled together, as without companions the journey of a week or two across jagged, empty sea ice would have been arduous and lonely.

The women appeared to look forward to the trips as eagerly as their men. They reported to each other again and again what their brothers and husbands had been overheard to tell the other men about their plans: how many sleeps they calculated the trip would take, and what they planned to trade their foxes for. If a woman was fortunate enough to have caught a fox or two on her own trapline—always shorter and laid closer to camp than a man's line—she, too, would outline her projected purchases, her pauses seeming to give weight to her choices as she listed each item thoughtfully against a finger: powdered milk for the children; jam; butter; embroidery thread for decorating cloth boots . . . On the eve of the trip, women sat late at night over their lamps, scraping and cleaning the foxskins, while the travelers prepared dogfeed for the trip, stuffing burlap sacks and ragged old caribou hides full of the woodenly frozen whitefish without which a trip was an impossibility.

Gear for the trip had to be settled too. "I'll take one of Yiini's primus stoves because mine is cached in my trapping shelter," Inuttiaq would decide. (He referred to the tiny iglu at the far end of his trapline, a day's journey from home, where he was accustomed to spend the night when he went to check his line.) "I'll take the frying pan so I can make bannock on the way home, and the big teakettle for the trip home, too, because I'm going to buy tea. The little kettle will be all right for you while I'm gone because you won't be in a hurry; when you want tea you can heat water several times in that little pot and it will be enough." Allaq never demurred at these decisions which always, I am sure unjustly, seemed to me so highhanded. Without comment she packed everything Inuttiaq designated in the wooden box that ordinarily served as a kitchen table. She seemed completely involved in the bustle and excitement.

Sleep was short on the night preceding a trip. On the morning of his departure, Inuttiaq always roused Allaq long before dawn had grayed the ice window. The sequence of events was almost always the same. "Allaaq! Make tea." Allaq, clumsy and speechless with sleep, dressed—parka and trousers—then pulled the primus toward her and filled its tray with alcohol. While the blue flame burned she pulled on her boots; and when the primus was roaring steadily under the kettle, Inuttiaq, still comfortably in bed with his pipe, spoke again: "Go out and look." Allaq, as on every other

From *Never in Anger: Portrait of an Eskimo Family* by Jean L. Briggs, 1971, pp. 96–108. Copyright © 1971 by Jean L. Briggs. Reprinted by permission of Harvard University Press.

winter morning, obediently went to test the weather, of which neither sight nor sound penetrated our snow walls. "It's still completely dark," she reported, ducking in again; "magnificent weather; no wind; no ground drift." "It makes one grateful (hatuq)!" Inuttiaq, suddenly electrically awake, threw off the quilts and pulled his parka on over his head. On the morning of a trip Inuttiaq never waited quietly in bed, as he usually did, to sip his first cup of tea in lazy relaxation. Fully dressed and booted, he gulped the tea as fast as its temperature allowed, then, catching his snow knife out of the wall by the door as he passed, he ducked out to see to the sled. Allaq, abandoning her tea, hurried to collect her husband's gear. Sometimes—I regret to say, not always—I, too, shamed into activity by the general bustle, dressed and helped Allaq. Together we pulled one of the two mattress hides out from under the sleeping children. Saarak stirred. "Kahla!" her mother whispered. "Careful! She's waking up." She laid a hand on Saarak's head, transferring quiet through her touch till the child once more slept securely. One mattress; one quilt pulled off the children and stuffed into a bag with Inuttiaq's Bible and prayerbook; the wooden kitchen box, which had to be hammered and wrenched free of the floor to which it was frozen—one by one I passed the things to Allaq, who shoved, tugged, and carried them along the passage to the slope outside where Inuttiaq waited to arrange them on the sled. Packing the sled itself was the driver's work. Allaq hurried, so as to be in time to lay out the harness in a neat pattern on the ground in front of the sled, before Inuttiaq should be ready for her to help him with the final tying-on of the load—tossing the rope back and forth to each other across the sled and hooking it firmly under the crossbars. The final job was harnessing, and this Inuttiaq and Allaq also did together, dragging and kicking the reluctant dogs one by one down the slope to the harness, while those still chained above clamored and leapt at their chains, their enthusiasm completely out of keeping

with the resistance they would show when their turn came to be harnessed. Most of the dogs had settled positions in the tandem harnesses, but Inuttiaq occasionally shifted two or three of the animals around. "Where to?" Allaq would ask, with difficulty collaring a wildly cavorting pup, and Inuttiaq would tell her.

I stood helpless and embarrassed during the hitching-up. In the beginning I had tried to learn, but, though unharnessing was easy, the reverse process I found impossible. Simple as the harness seemed when I helped to lay it out on the snow, as soon as I straddled a prancing dog the bands lost any semblance of pattern; the head went through the tail hole, the leg through the head hole; the poor dog yelped and struggled to escape. If I took off my mittens the better to unravel the puzzle my fingers started to freeze, and finally in the fury of frustration I roared, "Stand still!" and kicked the dog as brutally as my soft boots would allow, in emulation of Inuttiaq and Allaq. Several times Allaq had tried to demonstrate the proper technique, stretching the harness between her hands so that I could observe its pattern, moving her arm through it as if inserting the head of a dog so that my slow eye might follow, then with painstaking deliberation placing the dog in the harness. Emphasizing each move—"like this, like this"—she slipped one loop over the animal's head, raised the right leg and inserted it in the second loop, raised the left leg and inserted it in the third loop, and pulled the whole contraption straight over the tail. It was no use; I was all blind thumbs, my natural clumsiness with ropes aggravated by the atmosphere of haste. Then the others left me alone to struggle with my one dog while they dealt with the rest of the team, until finally, ready to start, Inuttiaq came, took the harness out of my hands, and expertly slipped it over the dog. He never commented on my ineptitude, but his silence humiliated me more than any joke or criticism could have done. I was grateful when he assigned me the far less taxing job of standing on the clawed anchor, which dug into

the snow beside the sled, adding my weight so that the dogs in their early morning enthusiasm could not run away with the sled before Inuttiaq was ready.

Meanwhile other iglu doors slammed, other teams yowled and leapt on their chains, and the frozen snow creaked underfoot as Inuttiaq's traveling companions—almost always Mannik, sometimes Putuguk or Ipuituq, more rarely Nilak—assisted by their households, made similar preparations for departure. There was never any farewell and rarely a backward glance; neither did any man wait for any other, but as soon as his last dog was in harness the driver leapt for the anchor, yanked it up out of the snow, shoved at the side of the sled to dislodge it, and breathing a hardly audible command to his team—"ai (be off)!"—flung himself sideways onto the sled and was off, careening at a gallop down the slope and out onto the flat river ice. Wives, sisters, and fathers, who had helped to harness, stood singly in front of their own iglus or moved to join one another, women to women and men to men. Full light was just growing on the southern horizon, infusing sky and snow alike with the soft winter brilliance of blue and rose. Arms withdrawn from their sleeves for warmth, women watched the sleds dwindle and be absorbed into the distant landscape. The old man Qavvik was a still silhouette alone on the hilltop by the farthest iglu, watching his adopted son, Putuguk, disappear. "Inuttiaq has climbed up," Allaq observed, her eyes intent on a moving speck that, veering to the west, had ascended the river bank and disappeared across the neck of land on the horizon. She stood silently for another moment. "On the far side of Sunday," she said, "we will see him coming again." She waved an imaginary greeting at the empty river and smiled at me. "Uunai!" she said. "It's cold. One feels like drinking tea." And she followed her sisters indoors.

From the beginning I shared in the excitement of these trips to Gjoa Haven, but I did not at first appreciate what life was like for those who stayed at home while the men were away. The events that should have given me my first insights into the chill discomfort of these occasions I misinterpreted. Two such misunderstandings occurred, the first at the very beginning of the autumn traveling season, about two months after my arrival at Back River. In need of a holiday and unaware that, except in the spring, the Utku ordinarily considered the trip to Gjoa Haven and back too arduous for women, I had asked and received from Inuttiaq permission to go along on the first trading trip that was planned in November. He was not going himself at that time, but he arranged for me to go with three other, younger, men. He said that when he went to trade in December, he would bring me back. Inuttiaq and Allaq supervised my preparations regarding equipment and provision: a sleeping bag, a mattress hide, sugar to drink in our tea—"for warmth," said Allaq. But when I mentioned that I planned to take my kerosene storm lantern and primus stove I thought I sensed a flicker of disconcertion pass between my parents. Perhaps I imagined the fleeting expression, it was almost nothing, but it moved me to explain that I would need these things in Gjoa Haven because I would probably be living by myself in an iglu there. I imagined simply that they did not like relinquishing the kapluna luxuries to which they had become accustomed since I had moved in with them. It did not occur to me that my independence in taking my own stove and lamp instead of using those carried by the men I was to travel with might be unusual behavior for a woman. Neither did it occur to me, since Inuttiaq and Allaq themselves owned both a primus stove and fish-oil lamp, that I might be working hardship on them. Because the Utku, when they felt cold, generally chose to stoke their own bodies rather than to heat the air around them, and stoves were therefore almost never run steadily throughout the day but were used only periodically for brewing tea, I was unaware how great a difference my equipment could make in the temperature of the iglu.

The second incident that I misinterpreted happened as I was returning

to Back River with Inuttiaq and Mannik after my holiday in Gjoa Haven. It was early in December; the dark and cold were bitterer than when I had traveled north three weeks earlier, and, after an interlude in overheated houses and warm beds, I was feeling somewhat less hardy than usual. Inuttiaq, having predicted that the trip would take three sleeps, was now pushing to cut it down to two, driving Mannik and me vigorously from dawn till long after dark each day. "Raigili and Saarak are cold," he explained. Resentful of being urged out into the black midwinter morning after only four hours' sleep, I privately accused him of using that unselfish pretext to cover his desire to rush home and display his new acquisitions. The meticulous honesty of Eskimos does not extend to public expression of one's motivations, and it is common practice to phrase one's own wishes in terms of concern for others.

Only when I was left for the first time with Allaq and the children in the iglu during Inuttiaq's absence in Gjoa Haven did I realize how genuine was the concern with warmth that I had crudely interpreted as an excuse for self-display. And then I realized, too, how complex were the causes of the chill that prevailed when the men were away.

My first experience of this chill was unusually impressive. It was, as I have said, in January of the first winter, when Inuttiaq, Allaq, the children, and I were living by ourselves. Though I enjoyed the cosiness of our life, the private family hours, and the conversations with Inuttiaq and Allaq, nevertheless I had looked forward to the trip Inuttiaq proposed making to Gjoa Haven in January as a much-needed opportunity to bring the typing of my fieldnotes up to date, unplagued by the changes in iglu temperature that Inuttiaq's presence caused. When he was there, it was impossible to maintain the iglu within the temperature range of twenty-seven to thirty-one degrees at which typing was feasible; either the iglu steamed and dripped so that my work was lost in a wet fog as a result of his demands for tea, boiled fox, ban-

nock, and soup in rapid succession, or my fingers and carbon paper froze as a result of his drafty comings and goings at jobs that seemed to necessitate propping the door open. Allaq never initiated eating orgies, never suggested that I interrupt my typing to cook just when the temperature had arrived at twenty-eight, rarely hinted that a contribution from my kapluna family's latest gift of soup might be welcome. She never came and went through the door with such abandon as Inuttiaq, nor sat in the open door to drink her tea. Many were the frustrated moments when I heartily wished him gone. But only when he was gone did I learn how essential his presence was to us, how dependent we were for warmth on the very demands I so resented.

In his absence that January, life seemed almost to be in abeyance. Perhaps it was partly the weather, of a solid, tangible cold that seized face and feet and hands in a burning, dry-ice grip. Indoors the cold, though much less intense than outdoors, had an aching, relentless quality that, in my first experience of it, I felt as a physical weight—the weight of the snow dome drawing down over me and numbing my energy. One of our two primus stoves had gone with Inuttiaq and one of our two kerosene storm lanterns; but it was not just the cold weather and the absence of some of our accustomed heating equipment that lowered the iglu temperature so spectacularly. It was Allaq's behavior, too. She became a different person; her passivity was beyond belief. She never boiled fish, rarely brewed tea, and never lit the lamp to dry clothes—any of which activities would have heated the iglu. Neither did she go out to warmer iglus to visit. She just sat in her corner of the ikliq, waved her feet, blew on her hands, and endlessly observed that the iglu was cold. She decided that one reason for its temperature was that she had not banked it thoroughly enough with loose snow when it was built; but she did nothing about it beyond pointing out to me the thin spots. She merely blew on her hands and remarked that they were too cold to sew, as she would like to do. One day when the temperature was eight degrees indoors (a full twenty-degrees lower than when Inuttiaq was home) Allaq spent the entire day searching for lice in Saarak's sweaters and her own and remarking that her knees were cold. We did not eat, because the fish on the floor were frozen too solidly to cut and Allaq did not light the lamp, which would have thawed them. I retreated to my sleeping bag during this period, and even so I froze the gloved fingers which, in order to hold my book, protruded from the sleeping bag. The children also stayed in bed most of the time, playing quietly and apparently happily under the quilts. Allaq never stayed in bed, even when there was no practical need for her to get up, a fact curiously out of keeping with her other behavior, I thought. She slept late—we all slept about sixteen hours as compared with the usual nine or ten—but then, having drunk her morning tea, she would say reluctantly but with a smile: "I ought to get dressed. The cold makes one lazy but one ought to get dressed." And she would pull on her parka and her thin boots and sit blowing on her hands and searching for lice.

But when the dogs' howling signaled Inuttiaq's return, bleak passivity vanished in a flash; the iglu filled with visitors come to share the feast and hear the news. Allaq made tea, coffee, bannock, tea and more tea, till the thawing dome dripped again, while Inuttiaq, enthroned on the ikliq with Saarak on his lap, recounted the Gjoa Haven news and the comic vicissitudes of the trip, and listed his purchases in detail to all comers.

Looking back on this incident, I find it even more puzzling than I did at the time, so contrary was Allaq's behavior to her usual quiet industry. Perhaps her pregnancy, then unknown to me, ate at her energy, intensifying the numbing effect of the cold and making it seem too effortful even to go next door for a visit and a cup of tea in Pala's iglu. She did visit, I thought, far less often than usual that winter, whether or not Inuttiaq was at home, and once she explained to me that she did not feel like visiting, because standing, as visitors

do, was tiring and made her feet cold. But this does not explain why she rarely visited in her father's iglu, where she was privileged to sit down familiarly on the ikliq. Allaq's failure to make more than the minimal morning and evening tea while Inuttiaq was gone was also puzzling. Perhaps it was because both the primus and the tea belonged to me; perhaps in the absence of her usual leader, Inuttiaq, Allaq, still a little shy of me, was waiting for *me* to give directions, as Inuttiaq usually did, concerning the use of my belongings. I, on the other hand, curious to find out to what extremes her passivity would go, had refrained from interfering or from taking the initiative myself.

In other camps and at other seasons the effect of Inuttiaq's absence was less dramatic. Whether that was because the weather was warmer on other occasions; or because Allaq had had her baby; or because in most other camps we lived in closer association with Pala's household, and Pala's requests for tea and food substituted for the absent Inuttiaq's, I do not know; in any event, I experienced then some of the pleasure I had anticipated in vain on the occasion of Inuttiaq's January trading trip. True, it was chilly because the primus or the Coleman had gone with the travelers; but life proceeded at a more relaxed and leisurely pace than normally. "We will sleep late when Inuttiaq is gone," Allaq said, smiling; and so we did, every day, undisturbed by Inuttiaq's early morning monologues and tea-brewing clatter. Inuttiaq never liked to be behindhand when the men went out to their morning tasks. When the men were gone, only a minimum of fishing and net-checking had to be done, because there were fewer mouths, human and canine, to feed.

Allaq, except on that first occasion, seemed closer to her own family during Inuttiaq's absences. Her sisters Amaruq and Amaaqtuq, always freely in and out of our iglu in any case, seemed at these times to visit longer and more talkatively, occupying Inuttiaq's place on the ikliq with comfortable familiarity. Once, during the

winter when we lived in a joint iglu with Pala, Amaaqtuq announced that she would spend the night on our side of the wall for the pleasure of it, and she did. She lay awake for a long time after we were in bed, gazing up at the dome and dreamily telling Allaq, as she had countless times before, the story of her household's recent trip from autumn camp to winter camp: ". . . It was very cold . . . the wind was blowing the snow along the ground, and then it began to storm . . . and one of the puppies climbed out of the box where we were carrying them and fell off the sled and we had to go back for him . . . it was funny *(tiphi)* . . ."

I enjoyed the enhanced conviviality of Allaq's family at these times: the family presided over by Pala, a benign patriarch, placidly puffing at his enormous curved pipe while he watched the activities of his children and grandchildren, laughed with them at their amusements, and periodically reminded Saarak of his love for her. "Ee ee! Did you mistakenly think you weren't lovable *(niviuq, naklik)*? Ee ee!" I enjoyed also the respite that Inuttiaq's trips gave me from what I perceived as his "domineering self-centeredness." I have mentioned already the difficulties I personally encountered when my interests clashed with his: when, for example, he destroyed the painfully achieved typing temperature of the iglu. In addition, I was irritated by his peremptory manner toward Allaq and the children and by the lack of consideration I felt he showed them. He seemed to have no compunctions about interrupting their activities, and occasionally even Allaq's sleep, to order them to do things for him: make tea, make bannock, fetch his pipe, help feed the dogs, chip the stalactites off the walls. If the wall developed a hole and snow began to accumulate on the bedding, or if a dog broke loose from its chain during the night, it would always be the soundly sleeping Allaq, not her wakeful husband, who had to go out and repair the damage.

Once I myself was unwittingly the occasion for Inuttiaq's disturbing Allaq's sleep. It was toward the end of my

OK FOR BE THE MEN TO BE the way they are because they have harder work

first winter when, frustrated to the point of desperation by the typing situation in the iglu, I had set up a double-walled tent behind the camp, a delightfully cosy cranny just large enough to hold the three boxes that served as desk, stool, and lampstand, and the primus with which I heated the tent. I often spent seven or eight hours a day there in January and February, trying to complete the notes that I had not been able to bring up to date, as I had hoped, while Inuttiaq was in Gjoa Haven. Coming home then late at night when the rest of the family was already asleep, I occasionally indulged in the luxury of frying my supper fish. Somehow, it was harder to eat it raw when I was alone than when I was surrounded by other raw-fish-eaters. Moreover, fried (as opposed to boiled) fish was a treat impossible to have during the day, both because the frying pan did not hold enough so that everybody could have a share and because the smoke from the frying smothered the other occupants of the iglu. In order not to disturb the sleepers on these midnight occasions, I used to carry the primus out into the unheated storeroom and cook there, jogging from foot to foot as I had been taught, to keep my feet from freezing while the fish fried. One such night when I came into the iglu bearing my smoking fish, I found Allaq sitting up in bed, eyes bleared with sleep, mixing bannock. Inuttiaq lay beside her, smoking a cigarette. He explained, "I told her to because I'm famished."

If Inuttiaq's intention was to make me feel the pinch of guilt for my pri-vate feast, he was successful; but I never found out whether his midnight demand for bannock was indeed a re-proach to me or whether he was merely awakened by the smell of fry-ing fish (very like that of frying ban-nock) and was, as he said, famished.

Inuttiaq rarely went so far as to make Allaq cook for him in the middle of the night; and most, if not all, of the demands he made were quite within the rights of a man in his position as independent head of a household. On one occasion I nonplussed Allaq by asking why it was that men "bossed" women and made all the daily deci-sions. Allaq, very resourceful when confronted with idiotic kapluna ques-tions, was silent for only a minute, then said: "Because the Bible says that's the way it should be." Wanting to know whether the situation was rationalized in terms of women's inferiority, I prod-ded her, telling her that some kapluna men also boss their women because they believe that women have less *ihuma* (judgment or mind) than men. She assured me that this was not the case among Eskimos: "It's just be-cause the Bible says women should obey men; that's the only reason." She did not, of course, mean that in pre-Christian days women obeyed men less. She meant that it is in the natural ordained order of things for men to boss women, and always has been.

Utku women, as far as I could tell, did not feel beleaguered by the de-mands of their men. A woman did not resent it when her husband took the best of the lighting and cooking equip-ment with him on his trips to Gjoa Haven, leaving her to suffer from the cold. She did not feel unjustly put upon when her husband waked her in bitter darkness to chase a loose dog, usually in vain, through the camp. She ratio-nalized these vicissitudes in terms of the feeling that it is the men who have the hardest work to do, going out in the coldest weather to fish or hunt and making long difficult sled trips under the most adverse conditions. "We want to do what we can to help them be-cause they take care of us," was the way Ikayuqtuq put it to me. She was not an Utku, but the latter also phrased their performance of everyday duties in terms of "wanting to help." When-ever Amaaqtuq abandoned a half-sewn seam or a half-written letter and rushed out at the sound of her brother's approaching team, it was because "I want to help Mannik unharness." And when Allaq, once achingly, wheezingly ill with a grippy infection, refused to take off her boots and lie down, it was "because I want to help Inuttiaq un-load," when he returned from a trap-ping trip.

Moreover, I had the impression that many of the demands men made were welcome for their own sake. A woman who would not have presumed to cook a rare delicacy like rice on her own initiative was delighted when her hus-band or brother told her to do so. Even tea was drunk in greater quantity when the men were around to order it. A woman herself would modestly claim to be satisfied with one cup; but if her husband were thirsty for a second ket-tleful, she would be more than happy to have a second cup.

→ Man irritates writer rough - unconsiderate orders wife around even when sleeping

men boss women around because the Bible says it's the way it should be not because women are inferior "The Bible says women should obey men"

What Keeps Women "in Their Place"?

"... Sexual equality will not be achieved until we face up to the fact that inequality is a product of our own behavior and attitudes."

[handwritten margin note: confusion re sex roles]

Anthony Layng

Dr. Layng is professor of anthropology, Elmira (N.Y.) College.

[handwritten annotations: Preference for male children · Exclusion from military · some socialization to keep women in their place · Exclusion from sacred rituals · Mythology, Menstruation seclusion · Segregation of male domains · Veneration of female virginity]

During the decade of the 1970's's, women in numerous nations called for the elimination of sexual discrimination. In the U.S., this latest feminist resurgence ambitiously attempted to end all inequalities between the sexes—including those involving employment, political participation, property rights, recreation, language, and education—and some reforms were achieved. An increasing number of women began to act like they were socially equal to men; there has been much talk about teaching girls to be more assertive; and there is now considerable confusion about what constitutes appropriate sex roles. Yet, judging by the fact that the Equal Rights Amendment did not pass and that it presently shows little promise of being resuscitated in the near future, many seem to have concluded that most American women are, by and large, content to remain where they are in relation to men. Further, since women in other industrialized nations have remained essentially "in their place," it appears that there are other formidable obstacles to overcome if we are to bring about such fundamental social change.

Why do sexual inequalities persist in the face of concerted feminist challenges? Is there any realistic basis for us to hope that sexual discrimination ever will be eliminated? What must be done to bring about full emancipation of women? What is it that keeps women "in their place"?

To understand fully how women have been kept "in their place," we first must learn how they came to be there. This requires consideration of the course of human evolution. Prior to 4,000,000 years ago, there was probably little social differentiation based on gender, because the two sexes were not economically interdependent; one could survive quite well without assistance from the other. It is likely that economic interdependence developed only after the evolving human brain reached a size that necessitated earlier birth, before the cranium of an infant was too large to pass through the birth canal. Giving birth earlier meant that the babies were less mature and would be more dependent on their mothers for a longer period of time. Prolonged helplessness of infants eventually created a need for mothers to depend on others for food and protection.

At the same time, more evolved brains enabled us to invent and use tools that resulted in our becoming effective hunters, in addition to being scavengers. Females with helpless infants still could gather and scavenge a variety of foods, but they were likely to be relatively handicapped hunters and so came to depend on males to provide them with a more reliable source of meat.

Increasing brain size and improved hunting skills also meant that some of our ancestors could begin to occupy northern regions where successful hunting was necessary for survival, since those foods that could be gathered were insufficient during some seasons. In such an environment, females with infants would not live long without food provided by others. Under these circumstances, a sexual division of labor made very good sense.

Although biological factors created the especially long dependency of human infants, the solution to this problem may have been entirely cultural. There is little evidence to suggest that any instinct developed at this time which led females to restrict their economic activities to gathering roots and fruits and men to go off in search of game, but doing so was sound strategy. Such specialization—encouraging females to learn and concentrate on gathering, and teaching only males to be hunters—was an efficient and realistic adaptation requiring only a change in our ancestors' learned behavior and attitudes.

So, a sexual division of labor emerged, but what about sexual inequality? The subordination of females was not brought about by this economic change alone, for, although economic specialization by sex made women dependent on men, it also

Reprinted from *USA Today Magazine*, May 1989, pp. 89-91. Copyright © 1989 by the Society for the Advancement of Education.

made men dependent on women. Where human populations subsist entirely by what can be hunted or gathered, most of the food consumed is provided by the gatherers—women. Meat acquired by hunters may be given a higher social value than nuts and berries and the like; but, if the technology employed in hunting is very primitive, meat is difficult to acquire and frequently absent from the menu. Thus, when men began to concentrate on hunting, an interdependence between the sexes emerged, each relying on the other to provide food that made survival possible.

BELIEFS AND CUSTOMS

The development of a sexual division of labor may have preceded and even facilitated social inequality, but it did not create male dominance. Although male dominance would be very difficult to achieve in the absence of a sexual division of labor, it takes firm beliefs and customs as well to retain a higher status for men. The following examples illustrate how societies in various parts of the world have directed the socialization of their children to assure that women will be kept "in their place."

• Mythology which justifies maintaining female subordination. Mythology and folklore are used in tribal societies to explain and justify the social *status quo*. The story of Adam and Eve illustrates how sexist myths can be, but some are even less subtle than Genesis in rationalizing male preeminence. Frequently found tales of Amazons or an era when our ancestors lived in matriarchal communities may be functionally equivalent to the Adam and Eve account; although they serve as inspiring models for some women, they may be far more instrumental in reminding men why they must be ever-vigilant in protecting their favored status. So, such tales become an important part of the conservative social learning of children.

• Seclusion based on the concept of pollution. In many horticultural societies, women must retire to a special hut during menstruation, since it is believed that their condition magically would jeopardize the well-being of the community. Their economic inactivity during these and other periods of seclusion serves to indicate symbolically that their economic contributions are of secondary importance. This subconsciously may suggest to children in the community that the labor of men is too important to be so restricted by taboos.

• Segregation of male domains. Many tribal societies have a men's house in the center of each village in which nearly all important political and ritual plans are made. Women are not allowed to enter this house, under the threat of severe punitive sanctions such as gang rape. Since this form of segregation effectively precludes the participation of women in the political arena, they are not likely to develop any political aspirations while growing up.

• Exclusion from sacred public rituals. Tribal societies customarily devote much energy to elaborate religious events, believing that the health of the community depends on these. With very few exceptions, men direct these rituals and play all the key roles; commonly, women merely are observers or participate only in a support capacity. A primary function of these public rituals is to reinforce social values. Since they even attract the full attention of young children, tribal members learn early that men are far more important than women, for they are the ones charged with magically protecting the people.

• Exclusion from military combat. As in the case of religious ritual in tribal societies, war is considered necessary to insure the survival of the community and almost always is conducted exclusively by men. Success as a warrior brings conspicuous prestige and admiration from women and children alike. Here again, the socialization process, instilling norms and attitudes of correct conduct, leads easily and inevitably to the conclusion that everyone's welfare depends on the performance of the men, and that the women should be suitably grateful.

• Exclusion from high-status economic roles. Women in most tribal societies are important producers and consumers, but their economic role is restricted largely to domestic concerns, producing food and goods for kinsmen. When it comes to regulating the exchange of goods between kin groups or with outsiders, men usually dominate such activities. This division of economic roles is fully consistent with the assumption that men are more important socially and more skillful politically. Given such an assumption, the economic differences between the behavior of men and women are likely to seem both proper and inevitable.

• Veneration of female virginity. If the religious, political, and economic activities of women are of secondary importance, then what, besides producing children, is their real value? One might be tempted to speculate that, because children in primitive societies are taught to venerate female virginity, this indicates that the status of women is not so lowly as might otherwise be assumed. However, it seems far more likely that this concern with virginity is an extension of the double standard and a reflection of the belief that the major value of women is their sexuality and fertility, their unexalted role as wife and mother.

• Preference for male children. When parents usually prefer that their next child will be a boy, this attitude may be considered as both a consequence of and contributor to the higher status of men. Before young children are mature enough to appreciate that one sex socially outranks the other, they can understand that their parents hope to have a boy next time. Impending childbirth in a home is given much attention and takes on real importance; this often may be the earliest opportunity for children to learn that males are more valued than females.

• Sexist humor and ridicule are used as important socialization methods in all societies and lend themselves quite effectively to maintaining a sexual hierarchy. Girls who behave like boys, and boys who behave like girls, almost inevitably inspire ridicule. Sexist jokes, particularly when they are considered to be good-natured, are

Most women accept sexual stereotypes

especially effective in this regard. Women who take offense or fail to find such jokes amusing are accused of having no sense of humor, thus largely neutralizing their defense against this social control mechanism.

• Sexual stereotyping. Stereotypes of any sort are likely to be of little use in teaching social attitudes to children unless they are accepted by the children as true images of nature. To believe that women and men behave differently because it is the way they were created helps to prevent misgivings from arising about the social inequality of men and women. To the extent that such status differences are believed to be imposed by human nature, the cultural supports of such inequality are not likely to be recognized and, therefore, will not be questioned.

DO WOMEN ACCEPT SUBJUGATION?

A society which effectively keeps women "in their place" need not employ all of the above techniques to do so; just a few will suffice, so long as there is general agreement throughout the population that the *status quo* of sexual inequality is both appropriate and natural. It is just as necessary that women accept this view as it is for men. Although some reformist writers argue that the subjugation of women was instigated by a male chauvinist plot forced upon unwilling victims, it seems amply evident that these social control mechanisms could not work effectively without the willing cooperation of women. They, too, must believe that they were designed by their creator to be subordinate; religious, political, and economic leadership are less suitable for them; and they have their own domains and should not be so immodest as to attempt to interfere where they do not belong. They, too, must consider military exploits as unsuitable for themselves.

Is this asking too much? Do not women value their virginity and that of their daughters as much as men do? Do they not condemn promiscuous women and at the same time tolerate promiscuous men? Is it not common for women to hope to have male children, in preference to daughters? Most women accept sexual stereotypes as an accurate reflection of nature to some degree, and they continue to encourage sexist humor by their laughter.

It seems clear that the "lowly" status of women was not brought about by a conspiracy, nor is it perpetuated only by men. There is no reason to view the above social controls as sinister or perverse where women willingly, even enthusiastically, teach their sons to be "real" men and their daughters to admire such men without wanting to be like them. In other words, in tribal societies, it is not male suppression which makes women subordinate.

It is only when we assume a missionary mentality, viewing such societies in light of our own society's values, that we think these women long for emancipation. Such an ethnocentric view fails to recognize that inequality, where it is accepted by all concerned as inevitable and proper, can be advantageous to lower-status individuals as well as to those who outrank them. Dominance hierarchies, like pecking orders, establish and maintain social order, a condition which tribal societies understandably prefer to disorder and uncertainty. Women in traditional societies do not contribute to their own subordination because they do not know any better or because they are forced to comply with the wishes of the men; they do so because they are socialized appropriately in an orderly society which is culturally well-adapted to its environment.

In tribal societies, sexual inequality is relatively high and protest against such inequality is relatively low. However, an increasing number of women in other societies are protesting sexual discrimination and their subordinate position. Most of this dissent comes from stratified and heterogeneous populations, where gossip, ridicule, and taboos are relatively ineffectual social control techniques. Social order in these more complex societies tends to be enforced by laws and specialized agencies, rather than depending upon voluntary compliance. Even in such complex societies, most may be wholly supportive of the social *status quo*, in spite of their own lowly status. Nevertheless, most of the discontent about sexual inequality comes from these populations.

In spite of such feminist discontent, sexual hierarchies still survive in even highly modernized societies like our own. American women have gained important rights in recent years, but many Americans continue to find Biblical justification for sexual discrimination. Many still think that our nation's economy appropriately remains under the domination of men, and, although the number of exclusively male domains (athletic teams, lodges, clubs, etc.) have been reduced greatly in recent years, a large number still find general endorsement and remain very much intact. Sexual stereotypes continue to enjoy robust health, the double standard is far from moribund, and sexist humor and ridicule seem to have recovered from their recent bout with militant feminism in the 1970's.

Today, in spite of a recent Gallup poll indicating that more than half the women in the U.S. consider themselves to be feminists, the most ambitious goals of the feminist movement have not been realized. However, it has grown increasingly difficult to convince American women that it is proper for them to be socially inferior to men, or that they should behave submissively. It seems that those customs and beliefs which deny opportunity to women in America are going to continue to be questioned by some who are very persuasive. Since a sexual division of labor has become largely anachronistic for our technologically advanced society, we may anticipate that efforts to preserve exclusive privileges for either sex will encounter increasing resistance.

Although tribal societies need to depend on a system of ascriptive statuses to maintain an orderly social structure, we do not. Tribal populations are not at risk in assigning economic roles strictly by sex, because not basing such assignments on individual aptitude and inclination is of little importance where the economy requires only a narrow range of tasks. In modern industrial society, however, where much highly skilled specialization is essential, selecting candidates for such positions from a limited talent pool, from only half of the adult population, places such a society at an unnecessary disadvantage, one which shows up very clearly if that society must compete with other nations which do not handicap themselves in this fashion. Also, traditional American values which exalt equality, opportunity, and achievement (matters of relatively little concern in tribal societies) are bound to give us increasing difficulty if we continue to deny equality to women and so restrict their ability to achieve the success that they desire and that our economy requires.

Since men have been politically dominant in all human societies, it is not surprising that many scholars have concluded that it is our nature, not our nurture, that has necessitated this inequality. Still, if sexual inequality is inevitable, given our nature, why must tribal populations resort to so many cultural methods to keep women subordinate and submissive?

Knowing how women have been kept "in their place" so long is essential if attempts to combat sexual inequality are to have some success. Just as the most effective medical cure is based on accurate causal diagnosis of an illness, so must social reform efforts take into account the nature of that which we would alter. If we recognize the various ways that our society uses cultural means to perpetuate differential socialization for boys and girls, we are prepared better to redesign that process to foster equality between the sexes. Similarly, if we are aware of the customary practices which encourage women to be submissive, we are more able to challenge and change such customs effectively. To fully understand how and to what extent women are kept "in their place" in the U.S., it is important that we understand how various societies effectively accomplish stable inequality.

Before all of this can enable us to eradicate male dominance, it may be that we first must learn why our society continues to deny equality of opportunity to women, for it is unlikely that we do so only as a result of cultural inertia. It may be that inequality is socially functional in ways that we do not understand fully.

Nevertheless, if women are to achieve total equality, if such a fundamental change can be brought about, it will require far more than passing the Equal Rights Amendment or changing discriminatory laws piecemeal. Since longstanding customs which encourage inequality thoroughly are ingrained in our culture, sexual equality will not be achieved until we face up to the fact that inequality is a product of our own behavior and attitudes. Only then might we discard this vestige of our tribal heritage.

- TO BE UPSET BY THIS State of affairs is missionary mentality (Ethnocentric)

INEQUALITY CAN BE ADVANTAGEOUS TO LOWER-STATUS INDIVIDUALS

- Dominant hierarchies maintain social order

- Most dissent comes from stratified heterogeneous populations where gossip, ridicule and taboos are relatively ineffectual control techniques

- U.S. not much change

- TRIBAL SOCIETIES CONTRARY TO OURSELVES need ascriptive statuses to maintain social structure NOT US

- WE ARE LIMITING OUR COMPETITION WITH ½ POPULATION CHOICE FOR skilled positions

- VALUES EQUALITY, OPPORTUNITY ACHIEVEMENT

Role of women in IRANIAN HOSPITALITY
WOMEN'S SUBORDINATION

Women, Food and Hospitality in Iranian Society

Foodways as reflection of culture & adaptation to an environment

DRY & WET SEASON

Mayling Simpson-Hebert

When first entering Iranian society, one is struck by three features of social interaction. First is the frequent invitations to dine, especially when greeted or when someone departs. Second, when the invitation is sincere the display of food is elaborate. Third, women are typically absent from the social event or they remain very much in the background.

The foodways of a society is a reflection of the culture and to some extent its adaptation to an environment. This is particularly true in the case of Iranian society, where the offering and displaying of food is a central feature of hospitality, and this hospitality, in turn, reveals much about the relative roles and statuses of men and women, Islamic values, and the society's adaptation to a desert-oasis environment.

The purpose of this paper is to describe Iranian hospitality, to describe the largely hidden but essential role that women play in it, and to offer some possible functional explanations for the importance of hospitality in Iranian culture. A key focus of the discussion is women's subordination and seclusion and how these factors make elaborate hospitality possible.

BACKGROUND

The information for this paper was gathered in the city of Dezful (pop. 135,000) in south-west Iran during two years of anthropological research. At that time, 1974–1976, which was prior to the revolutionary takeover of the government by the Islamic clergy, Dezful was a traditional city undergoing some government-sponsored changes, such as the establishment of schools, hospitals and clinics. Faith in Shia Islam was strong and women in general covered their bodies with *chadors* in keeping with Islamic values of female modesty. Although some women worked outside the home as nurses, midwives, teachers, social workers, and secretaries, the great majority remained confined to the home. High-walled courtyards protected women from being seen by those outside. Women would go out to shop and to visit friends and relatives covered by the *chador*, but mostly they spent their time cooking, doing the laundry, sewing, and taking care of children. To earn a little cash, some had small sidelines such as selling eggs and yogurt, spinning silk, and sewing or crocheting articles for sale.

The greater part of Iran occupies a high central plateau, characterized by large desert areas interrupted by oases around which villages, towns and cities have grown. Due to the dangers of the desert, travel in the past was usually by caravan. During the twentieth century, Iran acquired all the modern means of transportation so that even remote areas could be reached by car or landrover. Whereas the seasonal changes of the high central plateau are similar to those of Europe and North America, the Khuzistan valley, where Dezful is located, is outside this plateau and has very different climatic conditions. In that part of the country, summer (March to October) is quite harsh, with daily temperatures averaging 32 °C to 49 °C and almost no rainfall. Winter (November to February) is a cool rainy season during which most of the crops are grown.

DAILY EATING PATTERNS

The climate of south-west Iran to a large extent governs daily eating patterns, the timing and heaviness of meals. During the hot season (eight months of the year), people must rise early, at about 5.00 a.m., in order to complete their day's work before the extreme heat of midday arrives. Breakfast is usually a light meal of bread and tea with perhaps some eggs, goat cheese or butter. The midday meal is heavy and always includes rice. It is followed by an afternoon sleep. The evening meal is again light, often without rice.

Husbands and children expect a substantial and delicious meal when they return home each day for lunch. Among those who can afford it, the main meal should consist of plain rice (*chello*) or a rice pilaf (*pollo*), a fried meat or meat stew with vegetables, yogurt (*mast*), a raw vegetable salad and bread. Preparation for this meal begins early. Marketing for meat and vegetables occurs between 6.00 and 8.00 a.m., and cooking begins by about 9.00 a.m. Vegetables must be cleaned and finely chopped, fava beans must be split and stones removed from

 From *Canberra Anthropology*, Vol. 1, No. 1 (April 1987), pp. 24–34. Reprinted by permission of the author.

the rice. Stews are simmered for hours, and the rice is prepared in a special two-step process lasting more than one hour to ensure that every grain is separate and prepared to perfection. Due to the general lack of packaged foods and the high value placed on good cooking, the demands of food preparation on women's time is considerable. For these urban women, who have few opportunities for work or recreation outside the home, the time is available.

Although Iranian women must be covered with the *chador* when they go out, within their own compounds they have complete unveiled freedom as long as no unrelated male is present. Thus, at mealtime, all family members eat together around a large plastic tablecloth called a *sofreh* which is placed on the ground. Men are often served first but the women and girls usually join the men after a few moments. As will be shown, this pattern of interaction of males and females is quite different in the presence of guests, particularly male guests.

IRANIAN HOSPITALITY

Iranians are a very hospitable people. They entertain guests often, friends and strangers alike, and they enjoy doing so. The offering of food, even at the simplest level, is considered to be basic good manners. A glass of water or a piece of fruit is offered to all present before being consumed, even if a person is eating in the midst of total strangers and there is little to offer. Likewise, invitations to eat in someone's home are extended frequently in a free and easy manner as a sign of friendship and common good manners. Such invitations are a polite form of greeting and parting. Since they are almost always insincere, they are called 'making *ta'rof'*. An invitation should be extended three times in a row with an insistent tone of voice before it can be taken seriously. Iranians are very astute in perceiving whether or not an invitation is genuine, and they rarely make the mistake of accepting a false invitation. The following anecdote, told to me by an American engineer who lived in Dez-

ful, is an example of how Iranians 'make *ta'rof'*:

During my first few days in Dezful I was finding it difficult to shop and prepare my food. Every noon our research station jeep brought the staff members to their homes for lunch. All of my Iranian co-workers, males, were going home to a hot noon meal, while I returned to an empty house and no lunch. As the men would get down from the jeep, they would invite the others to join them for lunch. They, in turn, would decline, saying their own families were waiting for them. Then one day one engineer got down and invited all of us to lunch but with special reference to me. Since I was so new to the culture and believing that he was sincere, I accepted. He flushed in the face and said for the jeep to wait a moment to see if his wife would be prepared. While he was inside his house, another colleague told me that he was only 'making *ta'rof'* and that I should refuse the invitation. So when he returned, I refused and he seemed relieved. Later, when I knew these men better, I discussed *ta'rof* with them so that I would not make such mistakes in the future.

Sincere invitations are usually made a day or so in advance in order to give the women of the household ample time to prepare. This is because the quality of the meal is a measure of the guest's status. A poor quality meal or an inadequate quantity of food, as might happen if a guest were to accept an impromptu invitation, would also be a grave embarrassment to the family. So not only is the guest's honour at stake, but the family's honour and prestige is also at stake. The host wants to honour his guest so that his guest will, in turn, feel that the host is also honourable. On the other hand, a guest can never be turned away, for that would be even more dishonourable.

It is the men who usually extend invitations, and it is often they who will do the shopping for the meat, fruit and vegetables necessary for the meal. Men will sometimes plan the meal in advance with their wives, or at other times, simply buy the food and announce to her what will be served. Since menus for guests are usually fixed and predictable, the latter behaviour on the part of the husband is seen as expedient.

A typical midday meal for guests is similar to the family meal but is more

elaborate. It often consists of the following: chicken stock served as a soup, boiled then fried whole chickens surrounded by fried potatoes and peas, fried meat (lamb) patties, plain rice, fava bean pilaf (*baghala pollo*), bowls of yogurt (*mast*), a variety of fresh green salad vegetables, sliced tomatoes, green stew (*khoresht sabsi*) and fresh bread.

Proper preparation of rice is the single most important task. The rice is sorted, cleaned, and then soaked more than an hour before cooking. Then it is half-cooked in boiling salted water and drained through a sieve. The rice water is discarded. Ghee or oil is heated in the bottom of the pot and thin sliced potatoes are placed along the bottom. The rice is lightly spooned into the pot and mounded so as not to touch the sides. A few tablespoons of water are poured into the pot, and the handle of a long spoon is used to make a hole in the centre of the mound to allow steam to escape. The pot is covered with a pillow-like top and allowed to steam over low heat for about forty minutes. If the rice is to be served as a pilaf, then the spices, meat or fruit are added after the half-cooked stage. In the case of *baghala pollo*, for example, cooked fava beans, fresh finely chopped dill and chopped garlic pieces are lightly tossed into the rice. At the end of cooking and just before serving, hot sheep fat is poured over the rice. The rice is mounded lightly on long platters and should never be sticky, too wet or too dry. The potatoes (*tadik*: 'bottom of the pot') are mounded on top or served on a separate dish. The green stew, a second important item, consists of a variety of finely chopped green vegetables, beans and chunks of lamb meat. It is simmered for several hours over low heat and seasoned slowly as it cooks.

The meal is typically served on a long plastic tablecloth (*sofreh*) spread on the floor. The food is arranged with the rice dishes in the centre, a chicken at each end, and the other dishes arranged symmetrically throughout. A plate, fork and tablespoon are set for each person. A pitcher of water and one or two glasses are brought in to be shared among all guests.

In order that the women, who are in semi-seclusion, may not be seen, often the *sofreh* is set behind a curtain which is opened to reveal the food. The curtain is then again drawn at the end of the meal for the removal of all the dishes. If there is no curtain in a particular home, then the younger children may set the *sofreh*, or alternatively the women may do it, fully covered in their *chadors*. In cases where the guests include unrelated males, it is clear that the women are not to be noticed. When there are also female guests, some of the women of the household, particularly the elderly women, may join the company after the meal. The separation of women from guests is not true of all households. In middle-class and upper-class homes, where the adults are well educated and more cosmopolitan, the women will sometimes join the men and guests.

The preparation of food for guests is a time when a woman's worth is tested. She knows that the prestige of the entire family rests on how well she prepares and serves. Each dish must taste delicious and look appetizing. As the preparation of dishes in this region is culturally uniform rather than individualistic, girls learn at an early age how to prepare dishes in the acceptable way. Failure of the rice or stew, in particular, is considered to be a failure on the part of the woman (or women) to be competent in her female role. It is obvious, then, that the men of the household are constantly watching the reactions of their guests to the food served. Did they like it? How much did they eat? They listen for compliments and signs of satisfaction from their guests. The host may even ask his guest if the food was good or why he did not partake of a particular dish. The man whose wife has done well beams with contentment. He may walk back to the kitchen to say that nearly all the food is gone or directly say the meal was a success. If the guests did not eat heartily, he may feel disappointment or shame and may direct anger at the women of the household. But fail-

ure is unusual because most women recognize the importance of cooking well to their self-image and to the image of the family. An example of a fairly typical occasion is taken from my field notes:

After I had been in Dezful for about one week, my husband and I were invited to Mr M's home for dinner. My husband had met him some months before and they had struck up a friendship. The M's live in a newer part of town in a middle-class neighborhood. Mr M is an engineer technician and works in highway construction. He is 42 and his wife is 22. We were greeted at their gate by Mr. M, his wife and 2 children. We were ushered into the house through an entrance hall decorated with magazine pictures of modish men and women, and on into the parlour. A little later we were served dinner seated on the floor. A plastic tablecloth was spread and the food and plates were placed on it. M's wife and the children did not eat with us, although places had been set for them. We ate boiled chicken, chicken broth, rice, tomato, cucumber, and onion salad, whole cucumbers, Pepsies, and *duk*, a cold mixture of yogurt and water. I asked Mr M why his wife would not eat with us and he said that 'she is ashamed because she is illiterate'. The two small children, a boy aged 7 and a girl aged 4, came and went, bringing and taking food and dishes. After dinner, Mr M's wife joined us, bringing with her some bananas for dessert. Mr M encouraged his daughter to dance for us. He hummed a tune and beat on a tray while she danced a belly dance. Every movement was precise and stylized. The eyes were rolled back, the eyebrows were raised and lowered and always looking at us. M's wife kept covered by her *chador* and stayed in the background. And while the evening was lively and entertaining, she did not really participate beyond the elaborate preparation of the meal.

UNEXPECTED GUESTS

Occasionally the stressful situation of feeding unexpected guests arises. Sometimes husbands, sons, or other male members of the family, whether residing in that household or not, will invite guests for a meal without first informing the women. This can happen in a variety of ways. A man may extend a false invitation to lunch so many times and in such a convincing way that the invitee mistakes his inten-

tions as being sincere and accepts the invitation. This especially happens when the invited person is from out of town and must eat somewhere on the street; or when a person's other family members are out of town and that person has no one with whom to dine at home. Second, a man may extend an invitation some days in advance but forget to tell his wife or even forget himself. A third way is when a person brings friends, unannounced, to spend a day at his house. A fourth way is when travellers present themselves as needing a place to eat and sleep.

Since food preparation for guests, not to mention food preparation in general, usually takes hours and begins early in the day, women told to prepare a meal in an hour or so sometimes feel under great pressure. Since they know they cannot do a good job, they feel embarrassed and humiliated, but at the same time, they know it is their duty. They try to quickly thaw and fry or boil some meat or fish, cook rice and buy or borrow bread. I have seen women flushed red in the face while frantically trying to put a meal together at 11.00 a.m. or 12.00 midday. Another solution is to send someone out to a hotel or restaurant to buy stew, rice, yogurt and salad. This is also viewed as unsatisfactory because the food prepared in hotels and restaurants is believed to be inferior in quality. For example, on one occasion my research assistant insisted about six times that I go home with her for lunch because my husband was out of town. She seemed so sincere and I was afraid of insulting her, so I accepted. After I accepted, she seemed worried. She brought me to her home and spoke to her mother privately. About half an hour later a nice meal of green stew, rice, bread, yogurt and fresh green salad vegetables was served. My assistant immediately started apologizing for the low quality of the food, saying that her brother had gone out to a restaurant for it, but that if her mother had cooked the food it would have been much better. Her mother was also effusive with apologies about not having had enough food in the house ready for our lunch. Clearly I had been the one in error.

On another occasion, when visiting in another town, my husband and I telephoned a friend who promptly invited us to lunch and insisted we go straight to his home where his wife would prepare lunch for us. Since it was only 11.00 a.m., we went ahead to his house. His wife greeted us at their gate and soon after her husband telephoned to say she should prepare lunch for us. Flushed red in the face (and alone with five small children to care for), she quickly tried to thaw some ground meat, beating it with a knife, and to boil some spaghetti, all the while apologizing about the poor meal she would set before us. (She had no meal already prepared because her husband did not routinely come home for lunch as he worked some twelve miles away, and four of her children were under the age of six and had already been fed.) As we tried to extricate ourselves from this intrusion on her, she pleaded with us not to go because her husband would be so angry with her if we were to leave.

Whether the guests are expected or unexpected, the host tries to honour his guests by offering all that he has. For example, we were once invited by a family in the city to go on a picnic in a rural fruit garden owned by a village headman who happened to be their friend. We brought with us all the makings for our lunch: bread, kabob meat, vegetables, yogurt, soft drinks, and even the charcoal for cooking. As there were no telephones in the rural area, our arrival was a surprise to the headman, who graciously offered his garden to us and told us to wait, for the women in his household would prepare our lunch. We insisted we had brought our own. He showed us into his garden. A few moments later we heard gunshots. Our city friend predicted that the headman was shooting wild pheasant for our lunch. About an hour later, having finished our own meal, an entourage of four women came walking through the garden with trays of food. One dish was a real delicacy of the region, *fesenjun* (a very special stew made of pheasant, pomegranate, toma-

toes, potatoes and spices). The food was enough for a large gathering and we coaxed our satiated bodies to consume even more.

Even though one should be careful about accepting invitations that are only *ta'rof*, when travelling it is considered acceptable to present oneself as an unexpected guest. Once we were travelling by car with an Iranian friend, and we reached the city of Hamadan. We searched for a hotel but all were full. Evening was setting in and we were discussing sleeping in the car. Then our friend remembered that one of his friends had a relative who was a candy-maker in the bazaar. He had never met him but he was sure that if he could be found, his family would accommodate us. After some searching, we found the relative of the friend. He told us his address and said he would meet us there later. His son let us into their home. About the time the candy-maker arrived home, his family served us an elaborate evening meal and gave us mattresses to sleep upon. I saw his wife only once, when she brought a tray of food. Her *chador* hid all but one eye.

SOME INTERPRETATIONS

The exuberance of Iranian hospitality for the stranger, the friend and the traveller may not be unique, for some form of hospitality can be found in almost every society and it usually involves the sharing of food. While this very refined and gracious way of interacting with others may in part be a product of Iran's long history of civilization, some further observations and interpretations are possible.

First, hospitality is an expression of Muslim brotherhood. The practice is reported among Muslims from North Africa to China (Chatty 1978; Makhlouf 1979; Pillsbury 1978), but there is a dearth of detailed discussion on it. Pillsbury reports that Chinese Muslims offer open hospitality as an expression of Muslim brotherhood as well as a way Muslim travellers in a largely non-Muslim society (such as China) can obtain food without breaking the strict dietary rules, which in-

clude the avoidance of pork (1978). For Middle-Eastern Muslims, it must be less a matter of avoiding prohibited foods and more an expression of Muslim brotherhood, and this expression appears to be primarily among men. It is the men who are the more spiritual beings, the keepers of Islam, and it is also they who are free to travel and conduct commerce with one another.

That hospitality is an expression of Muslim brotherhood is supported by Mernissi's analysis of Moroccan society in general (1975). Mernissi explains that Moroccan Muslim society is divided into two sub-universes: the *Umma* and the family. The universe of men is the *Umma*; the universe of religion and power. The universe of women is the domestic universe of sexuality and family. The *Umma* is the community of believers, primarily male believers. 'Women's position in the *Umma* universe is ambiguous; Allah does not talk to them' (Mernissi 1975:81). The domestic universe, the family, is mainly women 'because men are not supposed to spend their time in the domestic unit' (1975:81). This dichotomy applies equally well to Iran.

Principles regulating relations among the *Umma*, according to Mernissi, are equality, reciprocity, aggregation, unity, communion, brotherhood, love and trust. Iranian hospitality can be seen as a practical application of these principles. Principles regulating relations among family members are inequality, lack of reciprocity, segregation, separation, division, subordination, authority and mistrust. These principles can be seen in the subordination of Iranian women to the task of elaborately preparing large amounts of food and their separation from the guests.

Iranian hospitality is for and about men, not women. Men use these occasions to build friendships by honouring the guest, to raise his own family's prestige by inviting higher status persons, and to build political and economic alliances. Teachers invite students they privately tutor, students invite teachers, employees invite their bosses, persons of lower economic level invite persons of a higher social status or economic level. Women form

Women are the labour force of hospitality which is a power builder

5. SEX ROLES AND STATUSES

the labour force and generally stay in the background, because they have little to gain. They perform their duties to their husbands. Only in a society where women are primarily confined to the home, have few economic and social opportunities outside the home, and are socially dominated by men, can such a feat be pulled off on a regular basis.

There may also be an ecological interpretation to the practice. 'Making *ta'rof*', the open hospitality and the free extension of invitations, may also be in part an adaptation to a desert-oasis environment. Giving refuge in the form of open hospitality to the traveller may have been a survival tactic on the societal level under harsh conditions: a mechanism any traveller could rely upon for survival in a geographical area full of perils. (In Iranian society, non-Muslims as well are given refuge.)

Even today in many parts of Iran there are few hotels and restaurants, and such places often are not clean and comfortable (except for the large expensive tourist hotels in big cities). In addition, it is not truly acceptable for women to eat in restaurants and lodge in hotels. (Perhaps because of the hospitality of the *Umma* and the segregation and seclusion of females, lodging and eating establishments were not profitable businesses.) If travellers need a place to stay, and strangers need a place to eat, then freely giving invitations benefits the society as a whole.

The understanding would be something like this: I will invite you or you can impose on me, because one day I may need to impose on others. It is not reciprocity in the usual sense, because the one to whom you are hospitable may never have a chance to pay back his debt (nor is he obliged to do so), but he may offer the same kindness to others in the future. If everyone has this understanding, then the system works well. Hospitality can incur a debt, but usually in Iranian society favours that incur a debt are of a different character (for example, the policeman who overlooks a traffic violation then asks for that person's help in getting his son into a university).

Thus, to summarize, it may be said that in Iranian society hospitality is a reflection of Muslim culture and values, an expression of the brotherhood of *Umma* and the subordination and segregation of the women. Being an activity that is for and about men, it is also used as a way to build men's social, political and economic alliances. By honouring and flattering the guest, the host raises his own prestige. And finally, it may be a cultural adaptation to an ecological zone characterized by desert-oasis geography.

Iranian women are enjoined by their society to be the hidden labour force in the expression of brotherhood among the *Umma*. If the women should ever refuse to continue to accept such subordination and segregation, the entire system of hospitality would collapse.

Thus, it is because of the women that Iranian hospitality is so generous and open, that the display is so impressive and that the food is so carefully seasoned and prepared. It may be the men who so freely make the invitations, but it is the women who make hospitality possible.

NOTE

This essay was based on two years of ethnographic fieldwork on infant feeding practices in Dezful, Iran (1974–1976). I am indebted to the many Iranian women who taught me their cooking methods and am grateful to the many Iranian families who graciously invited my husband and me to dine with them. I am also grateful to the Carolina Population Center and the National Institutes of Child Health and Human Development for their financial support of my work in Iran and to Dr John Gulick for critiquing an earlier version of this manuscript.

REFERENCES

Chatty, Dawn
1978, Changing sex roles in Bedouin society in Syria and Lebanon. In Lois Beck and Nikki Keddie (eds), *Women in the Muslim world,* pp. 399–415. Cambridge, Mass.: Harvard University Press.

Makhlouf, Carla
1979, *Changing veils: women and modernization in North Yemen.* Austin: University of Texas Press.

Mernissi, Fatima
1975, *Beyond the veil: male-female dynamics in a modern Muslim society.* Cambridge, Mass.: Schenkman Publishing Company.

Pillsbury, Barbara L. K.
1978, Being female in a Muslim minority in China. In Lois Beck and Nikki Keddie (eds), *Women in the Muslim world,* pp. 651–673. Cambridge, Mass.: Harvard University Press.

A Matter of Honor

Bedouin cultural codes and sense of honor persist despite the passing of the people's nomadic life-style

Longina Jakubowska

Longina Jakubowska teaches anthropology at the University of the Pacific in Stockton, California.

The world modernizes: Technology and consumerism spreads: a nomad hauls his herd in a truck; television antennas stick through tent roofs; a Walkman covers the ears of a shepherd. And today, no one is surprised. The Bedouin—pastoral Arab nomads who have roamed the deserts for centuries—hardly exist as such anymore. Most live in cities today.

The word *Bedouin* is derived from the Arabic *bada'* (desert). The Bedouin derived their livelihood from herding animals—camels, goats, sheep. Their life-style was a direct adaptation to the desert ecology; their movements and activities determined by the needs of their animals. Scarce reserves of underground water and sparse, unpredictable rainfall obliged movement over a large territory to ensure that herds had enough pasture and consequently people enough food. Nomads rarely consumed meat, considered a luxury, since doing so would deplete their capital. They mostly lived off animal byproducts (predominantly, processed milk), as well as dried fruits, dates, and some grains. There was a time when most of their needs were fulfilled by animal products—tents were woven from camel and goat wool, and gear was made from leather.

Given the limited resources of the desert, the nomads faced the constant challenge of maintaining a precarious balance between water supplies, pasture, and animal populations. Depletion of either meant demise. The land was sparsely populated and the lonely black tents of small Bedouin groups dotted the desert. Space and freedom of movement were essential to the nomadic existence, but the Bedouin nomads did not wander aimlessly; their movements were calculated, conducted seasonally, and limited to a territory they claimed as their ancestral tribal land. Territorial rights were closely guarded; infringements could, and frequently did, result in extended disputes or even an occasional war.

Fiercely independent, the Bedouin avoided involvement in the wars of others, even those conflicts that affected their own region. They remained disinterested in the politics of the entities surrounding them, until the middle of this century when the Bedouin became absorbed or encapsulated by the state structures. The process of settling the nomads in more permanent locations was strongly encouraged by all state governments in the Middle East and is now well under way. Nomadism is perceived as incompatible with modernity, and the nomads are also considered difficult to control. Yet the traditional Bedouin life-style still lingers in some areas, usually those which the state considers marginal.

"Settling-down" involves more than simply moving into houses. It necessitates a total restructuring of the society to be settled and a redefining of the sense of identity—which for the Bedouin is closely linked with the notion of honor.

The contrast between the Bedouin past and the present is striking. The change occurred rapidly, in less than one generation. Encased in the trappings of modernity, technological gadgets, and Western clothing, the Bedouin present a very different image today from that of the past. Most have moved to towns and adjusted to the market economy. They hold salaried jobs, work in construction, operate agricultural machines, and drive trucks. There is, however, continuity in their attitude toward employment. They prefer independence, the ability to set their own time schedule, and they frequently operate family businesses. Occasionally, forgetting the hardships of nomadic life, they reminisce nostalgically about when the Bedouin worried only about the rainfall and pasture, and tell stories to their children about the challenge and glory of *hel* (camel racing).

Contrary to expectations, settling-down has not greatly improved the quality of life for either Bedouin men or women. If anything, their behavior has become even more circumspect, and female honor is guarded even

The honor and authority of the father is central to Bedouin family and society.

closer. Compared with the sparsely populated desert, Bedouin towns are crowded, which greatly increases social interaction and potential sources of conflict. To maintain the code of modesty, women are forced to remain either inside their houses or to veil heavily, in a manner similar to peasant women. Since men are absent from the village most of the day, and since the behavior of women forms an intricate part of the honor code, there is even greater social control imposed on women. Furthermore, due to present patterns of employment, women are now completely excluded from involvement in the process of production, which diminishes their participation in decision-making and consequently harms their position in society.

So far the Bedouin exhibit considerable resiliency and cultural continuity. They remain the unquestionable ideal of the Arab ethos—honorable, pure, brave, independent, hospitable, and honest. It is widely believed that the Bedouin dialect is the untainted version of Arabic, the language in which the Prophet Muhammad spoke. Although highly praised, the Bedouin are also feared for their unequivocal honor code which does not allow for mistakes.

THE CONSEQUENCE OF AN ELOPEMENT

Changes in material culture and in the externals of life-style can be misleading: The beliefs and value systems taught to the generation of Bedouin born and brought up in the sedentary modern environment remain those of the nomadic tradition. The trial described below occurred a few years ago in southern Israel, but it could have happened in any other country in the Middle East, for the issues involved are of vital importance to the Bedouin cultural ethos. Despite the numerous changes that many of these societies experienced, the notion of honor has been altered little.

The trial took place early on a spring morning. The rains had stopped and the arid hills were, at least temporarily, green again. The busy morning activities in the small encampment of Sheikh Abu Rashid had subsided. Everything indicated that something unusual was about to happen. A long black tent, many times the size of the domestic tents that some of the Bedouin present remembered living in, had been erected. Firewood had been gathered in piles, animals stood nearby—unknowingly waiting to be slaughtered, and the rhythmic sounds of coffee mills could be heard. Everyone present awaited the arrival of the guests. The preparations that were under way in the camp (which consisted of tin shacks and wooden plank huts) were similar to those for a wedding, yet the joy of wedding preparations, usually marked by the shrilled ululations of women rejoicing because their sons were soon to become men, was missing.

There was another significant difference. Although Sheikh Abu Rashid was giving the last directions to his male and female kinfolk about the placement of the mattresses and pillows in the grand tent for the visitors to recline on, none of the implements—the tent, the firewood, the animals, nor the numerous other supplies including tea and coffee and even the mattresses, belonged to him. All were brought by the men who were to be tried, the family of Ataywah. A Bedouin court, or *manshed,* was about to be convened.

In a distant hut, surrounded by the sheikh's female relatives, a young girl called Azizah was anxiously awaiting the events of the day. Some weeks ago she and her boyfriend had run away to the Negev desert hoping their families would agree to their marriage. It occasionally would happen; elopements were rare but legitimate means of eliciting consent to marriage. According to tradition, marriage unions were arranged by the respective families of groom and bride, as marriage is not a matter for the individual but the family to decide. There were concerns about access to wells and pastures, previous marriage arrangements to finalize, and weakened ties that needed strengthening; in short, alliances to be made. In the absence of other forms of social integration, kinship and marriage serve as the primary means of political and social action. Women link families together. This link, however, is highly vulnerable, and women are placed under a constant cloud of suspicion regarding their loyalty (or suspected disloyalty) to either their paternal or husband's families.

Azizah did not rebel against the norms underpinning the Bedouin institutions, but rather against a particular choice of husband her father had made on her behalf. She miscalculated, however, the degree of his involvement in the marriage negotiations and the extent of his commitment. Once the agreement was made it became a matter of honor to keep it.

Whatever credits or discredits a woman earns reflect back on her paternal family. An unruly daughter can damage family reputation. Public disclosure of the inability to exert control over one's women is disgraceful. Fathers are aware of the inherent power in command of women and frequently mediate between daughters' preferences and their own goals. In this case, however, marriage to a man chosen by the daughter, a man from the Ataywah, was incongruent with the father's family politics. Public opinion is a double-edged sword. Mustering public sympathy could have turned events to Azizah's advantage, but it would also have exposed her father's honor. The only means of saving his and the family's face was to bring a legal case against the family of the offender, the young man she eloped with.

THE IMPORTANCE OF THE CODES OF HONOR

In the Bedouin social framework, an individual's actions reflect on his paternal kin. Family, which includes generations and can reach hundreds of members, is the strongest unit of identification. The farther the distance between kin, the "weaker the blood" between them, the lesser are the responsibilities toward one another and the accountability for each other's behavior. This system of organization, called the segmentary lineage system in anthropological literature, is best illustrated by the Bedouin proverb:

Me against my brother
My brother and I against my cousin,
My cousin and I against a stranger.

Family lineage, called *hamula,* places a person in the social structure, gives identity, and offers protection and security. It circumscribes, however, freedom of individual action and imposes obligations and strict rules of behavior. The price of misconduct on the part of an individual is paid by the group.

The behavior of the young man was irresponsible and implicated his hamula. The verdict of guilt was already pronounced and the result of the trial known beforehand. His family had few excuses to make on his behalf and had to carry the burden of the trial—including its costs—and reparations to the girl's family. The financial as well as social losses were considerable and would take years to repay. There were no possibilities of appeal—to maintain their respectability the family had to act in a socially prescribed responsible fashion. Serious transgressions of norms and recidivist behavior, which threaten the economic well-being and the social standing of the family, could result in the offender's expulsion from the larger group. This grave consequence served as the final safeguard for the family. It had happened only a few times in the living memory of the Bedouin present. Such an outcast, expelled from under the protective umbrella of the hamula, becomes a person without roots or identity; without kin, he loses his social existence. The Bedouin apply a very revealing term to such a person, *enshamma,* meaning literally and metaphorically "the one under the sun."

One may wonder why, knowing the serious potential repercussions, the young man risked public condemnation. The possibility of public exposure and confrontation at the beginning of the affair was rather small, and he had made every effort to avoid it. However, the girl's father was so unrelenting that the couple had sought refuge with the well-respected Sheikh Abu Rashid, leader of a powerful tribe, relying on his reputation in the Negev to mediate a noncontroversial settlement in the dispute.

On the surface, the issue concerned arranging a marriage. Using an important personality as a broker was common in such negotiations. However, this was no longer only a question of marriage; the problem now addressed a principle of honor. The girl's father had refused to grant his permission to the marriage both before and after the elopement and demanded restitution of his honor, insulted by an unlawful act of taking his daughter against his wishes. Since the offensive act, the elopement, was a public statement, so had to be the admission of guilt. The guilty party had to show humility and restore the honor of the offended.

Honor is the basis of the moral code of an individual in Bedouin society. It is inherently personal, but as the individual constitutes an integral part of the kinship group, his honor extends to the kin. Honor is obtained not by performing unusual acts but by the ability to live according to the ideal. Honor is maintained through a series of challenges and ripostes; success garnishes respect; failure to react entails disgrace. Even blood can be spilled in

Women's roles are closely defined, and their behavior, which can bestow honor or dishonor upon one's family, is under constant scrutiny.

defense of honor. "Blood can be washed only by blood," the Bedouin say. A wounding or killing is a stain on the family honor; restitution can be accomplished only through a similar retaliatory act.

Blood feuds are spectacular examples of the honor code binding Bedouin kin groups. Although they occur rarely in the extreme, they command attention, appeal to the imagination, and linger in Bedouin memories. Events that occurred in a distant past are handed down to each generation. The Bedouin culture always emphasized the oral tradition; skillful storytellers once held great respect. Historical time was changed; events of hundreds of years ago appeared as yesterday's happenings. Stories of blood feuds, of warriors fighting inadvertent circumstances told at the evening fires become relevant to the present. They form the integral part of the Bedouin ethos, the code of honor.

Sheikh Abu Rashid had little choice when the eloping couple approached him. He was expected to offer hospitality, protection, and to mediate in the dispute. Refusal would endanger his reputation. Heredity does not guarantee leadership among the Bedouin. So although Sheikh Abu Rashid came from a long line of tribal chiefs, he had to earn his title—by demonstrating charisma, powers of persuasion, and by gaining fame for his wisdom.

Hospitality among the Bedouin is proverbial. It also is the rule of the desert. Bound by ecological constraints and the frequent shortage of resources, the nomads customarily extend help to those in need. Visitors are fed, given shelter, and even clothing if necessary. Bedouin glorify hospitality. One is obliged by it even at the risk of starvation. Every Bedouin child can recall a tale that recounts the suffering of an impoverished nomad who, although his very life depended on it, slaughtered the last camel to feed the unsuspecting but

hungry guest. For his sacrifice he was held in the highest esteem. Furthermore, guests receive immunity and protection from their hosts. Hospitality is a sacred duty. Even one's enemies are granted this privilege and are entitled to safety of passage. Any attack on the guest would be perceived as an affront to the host.

It was common for eloped couples to seek refuge from their families at the powerful Bedouin houses. When Azizah and her young man arrived in the encampment of Sheikh Abu Rashid they were promptly separated from each other and housed in different places. Sheikh Abu Rashid could not afford, for his own sake, the reputation of his kin, and the proceedings of the case, to be placed under the slightest suspicion of fostering improper sexual behavior. He breathed easier upon learning that the girl's virginity was intact. Had the couple been involved

The "advantages" of modern life are affecting the core values of Bedouin society and could introduce an unprecedented separation between the generations.

sexually, the matter would have been even more grave.

The honor of Bedouin men is dependent upon the sexual conduct of women in their family. Male kin are required to protect female virtue. While male honor is flexible—depending on the man's behavior, it can be acquired, diminished, lost, or regained—female honor is rigid. A sexual offense on the part of a woman causes her honor to be lost, and it cannot be restored. Thus the core of male honor is the protection of one's female relatives' honor. According to the Bedouin ethical code, a transgression of sexual norms is a crime that may result in capital punishment.

Azizah's father pressed for court proceedings. *Manshed,* the highest Bedouin court, is convened extremely rarely, once in a few years or even a decade. Usually every effort is made not to escalate the conflict so that it can be resolved on a much smaller scale at lower levels of Bedouin social structure. Manshed deals with the most serious matters and achieves the greatest exposure, which was why the girl's father insisted on its taking place. As

one Bedouin said when addressing the sources of conflict in Bedouin society, Bedouin fight either over land or over women, and both concern honor.

THE TRIAL

Attendance at the manshed was enormous—over a hundred people arrived. As each visitor entered the tent, ceremonial greetings were exchanged and tea served. There were no women in sight, and adolescent boys quietly and busily attended to all the guests. The court was open to all men. Only the assailants' party, the family of Ataywah, was conspicuously missing. It was represented by Sheikh Abu Rashid. There was no set hour for the beginning of the proceedings, which began when all the important participants were present, notably the famous sheikhs of the area and authorities on Bedouin law. There was no set procedure either. All could voice their opinions. Knowledge and oratory skills prevailed in reaching the decision, which took until the late afternoon. The discussion of the case was inter-

twined with chatting about recent political events, questions about each other's families. It was interrupted by people taking leave for noon prayers and greeting those who were still arriving.

When a sense of consensus was reached, a tentative verdict was announced, the hearing of which could make an inexperienced observer shudder. The man's tongue was to be cut, for he talked to the girl; his hands were to be cut, for he touched her; his legs were to be cut, for he walked with her. Then a prolonged and heated bargaining started. It soon became clear that nobody had any intention of mutilating the culprit's body; the verdict was an expression of the severe nature of the crime committed. Instead the punishment was translated into monetary measures. The bargaining had all the makings of a ritual. There was more to follow. For every mile the man traveled with the girl, he was also to pay. All came to an enormous sum of 100 million lira, approximately $500,000. It was lowered considerably during further bargaining: in honor of the prophet Muhammad, on behalf of the people present and the costs of tea and coffee consumed by them, which they would have refused to drink otherwise.

A stream of new guests arrived in the afternoon. They came late intentionally, announced their names aloud, and refused to drink the customary cup of tea unless an additional sum of money was forgone. Only one representative of a hamula was allowed to make an appeal. The amount withdrawn from the one penalty depended on the respect commanded by his family. The family of the offender, although not present at the proceedings, kept a close watch over its developments. Through sending messengers and calling upon their allies, people were lobbied to make a plea on behalf of the Ataywah.

By the evening the sum was lowered to $100,000, but the bargaining did not cease yet. Dinner followed and this called for further negotiations. Meanwhile an elaborate meal was served,

for which fifteen sheep were slaughtered, but the guests refused to eat until the punishment was revised again.

It was late at night when the sheikhs pronounced their final verdict. Azizah was to come back to her family. The young man was found guilty of kidnapping, for such was the preferred interpretation of the affair, and had to pay 15 million lira ($75,000) to the girl's family. Also the family's car in which they eloped had to be returned to them. Sheikh Abu Rashid and two other prominent figures agreed to oversee the fulfillment of the sentence.

The punishment was severe. The young man, employed as a construction worker at the time, did not have the means to pay the penalty himself. The elopement proved to be a costly affair. The cost of materials and food supplied for the trial, together with the monetary amount of compensation, exceeded his probable lifetime earnings. These expenses were divided equally among his hamula, the members of

which from now on were obliged to commit their meager resources to paying the family debt, the debt of honor. The social costs were even greater. His family had to call upon old alliances and political favors, reserved for a time of crisis.

The girl returned to her father's household. Her future looked bleak. After causing so much discord, it was unlikely that she would still be welcomed as a match for the marriage her father arranged for her. Most probably Azizah would be married as a second wife, or else wedded to an elderly widower (which is certainly not regarded as the best option).

ADDITIONAL READING

Lila Abu-Lughod, *Veiled Sentiments: Honor & Poetry in a Bedouin Society,* University of California Press, 1986.

P. C. Dodd, "Family Honor & the Forces of Change in Arab Society," *International Journal of Middle East Studies,* 4 (1973): 40–54.

Emanuel Marx and Avshalom Shmueli, eds., *The Changing Bedouin,* Transaction Books, 1986.

Between Two Worlds

The women of Turkey straddle two worlds. In one, they are respected and forceful members of their society; in the other, they are restricted by Islamic traditions. An American woman's travels among Turkish women uncover a balancing act that echoes many of the problems of being a woman in any society.

Marilyn Stasio

Marilyn Stasio travels on assignment as a theater critic. Her book reviews are syndicated in newspapers nationwide.

How I got there is a long story. But there I was, in the plush lobby of a hotel in Istanbul, sipping *raki* (anisette) and nibbling *meze* (hors d'oeuvres) with several Turkish women in sleek coiffures and drop-dead evening dresses. Their laughter jingled like the gold bracelets we'd all bought that afternoon at the fabulous Grand Bazaar, and I remember feeling pleasantly awkward in their company, like a flower girl who had slipped into the bride's bedroom to watch her dress—and been welcomed.

Suddenly, the makeup froze on their faces.

Turning around, I saw that six people—four men and two women—had come into the lobby. The men were slender in black suits and ties, with shirts so white they stung the eyes. The women were even slighter and were completely shrouded in long, black robes and veils that covered all of their faces but their dark and luminous eyes. Without a glance at my gaping com-

panions, they swept through the lobby in arrogant silence and disappeared into a waiting elevator.

Glasses were quickly raised, and cocktail banter resumed in edgy earnestness. No one spoke a word about the curious scene that had just taken place . . . no one except Ayse, who had become my special friend during my stay in Istanbul.

"It's only the flight crew from Iran Air," she whispered. "Make nothing of it."

But I wouldn't leave it at that. Finally, my questions forced her to lead me out of the hotel and into a courtyard overlooking Istanbul. She pointed down at the Bosporus, the strait connecting the Black Sea and the Sea of Marmara that cuts through the city. "What do you see?" she asked.

I looked down at the fabled city, which wears its 3,000-year history like the encrusted jewels of a crown.

This was the city that the ancient Greeks called Byzantium, after a mythical sea god, and that the Arab world knew as Anthusa, "city of prosperity and bliss." The Romans renamed it Constantinople and made it

the seat of the Roman Empire. Among the people who fought over this ravishing city was Sultan Muhammad II, known as the Conquerer, who made it the capital of the mighty Ottoman Empire, which it remained for almost five centuries, until Turkey became a republic in 1923 and Ankara was made the capital.

Following Ayse's pointing finger, I looked down at the great ships rolling down the Bosporus, the fat-bellied ferries steaming through the straits, and the little fishing boats darting from shore to shore. My eye found the curve of water that clasps the city at its middle like a girdle of precious cloth; the Turks, in fact, call this inlet the Golden Horn, because at sunset its waters flash like the gold horn of a mythical bull.

"Look on this side of the river," Ayse's voice was saying. "What do you see?"

"I see the six slender minarets of the Blue Mosque pointing at the sky . . . the rounded domes of Aya Sofia . . . a glint of gold from the cupolas at Topkapi Palace."

"And on the other side, what do you

From *New Woman*, November 1987, pp. 103-105, 107-108, under the tital of "Behind the Veil." Reprinted by permission of NA Syndicate.

see there?" she pursued.

"The Villa Bosporus, I think—or is it the Beylerbeyi Palace? . . . and that boring modern suspension bridge, whatever it's called. . . . Ayse, what is it that you *want* me to say?"

"When I look out," she said, slipping her arm through mine, "I see a city trying to straddle two continents. On this side of the Bosporus, Europe. On the other side of the river, Asia."

I still didn't understand why the sight of the veiled Iranian women had so unsettled my companions.

"We Turks who live in Istanbul stand on the European side of the city and think ourselves the most cosmopolitan people in the world," she went on. "The women, especially. We make good money working for foreign firms. We speak many languages and go with our European friends to the theaters, to fine restaurants, and to the discotheques. We are so *proud* when people say how cosmopolitan our city is, how civilized is our way of life. Here in Istanbul, we like to pretend that the eastern provinces of our country don't exist. As modern women, we don't even like to *think* about women who still live the old way."

"So, the Iranians . . . " I began.

" . . . remind us of what's out there."

That same evening, I went to a performance of *I, Anatolia*, a theater piece that gave me a deeper insight into what Ayse had tried to tell me about modern Turkish women.

In this solo drama, distinguished Turkish actor Yildiz Kenter plays 16 women who represent the female contribution to the history of Anatolia. (Anatolia is the name that the nation of Turkey was known by in ancient times and the name by which its Asian provinces are known today.) In the audience were the same sophisticates who had cringed at the sight of the Iranians. Before the performance, I heard two women whispering (like all educated Turks, they spoke fluent English) that they didn't recognize half the characters in the program. By intermission the same women were cheering these national heroines.

"You see," Ayse leaned over to tease

me, "you are not the only foreigner here tonight."

Still, I wondered about the tone of amazement in which some of the cultured women had expressed their delight over their national heroines. It reminded me of those early consciousness-raising sessions of the seventies back home, where so many of us first discovered the meaning of sisterhood.

The first thing any educated Turkish woman will tell an American woman is they got the vote shortly after we did.

When Kemal Atatürk founded the Republic of Turkey and became its first president in 1923, he instituted numerous reforms that revolutionized overnight the position of women. He established the basic political principle of equal rights, not only giving women suffrage but also appointing them to official government posts and declaring them eligible for election to Parliament. Among other social reforms, he abolished the traditional veils and Muslim costume (the çarşaf) for women and championed monogamous marriage. (Today, only traditionally religious women still wear the veil). Women were also the special beneficiaries of the new educational system, which made schooling compulsory for both male and female children.

The position of women in Turkey stands out in sharp contrast to such Middle Eastern countries as Saudi Arabia, where women have not yet entered the labor market and where even upper-class women are not allowed to study abroad. The contrast is particularly keen in a fundamentalist Muslim country like Libya, where more than 7,000 women have been trained in the handling of rifles and surface-to-air missiles at the Women's Military Academy but where adultery is punishable by public flogging, abortion is illegal, contraception is forbidden, and unwed mothers can receive prison sentences.

The second thing a Turkish woman wants her American counterpart to note is her disappointment that we are so ignorant about these differences.

"Here we are with our good English and our Western clothing," said Ayse,

smiling, "and the Americans come and want to see the harem girls."

The deeper irony, of course, is what the Westernization of Turkey has meant to the women whom Atatürk "dragged kicking and screaming into the twentieth century," as one woman put it. While liberating them from political and economic inequities, the government reforms of the past half-century stopped short of giving women the *social* support to use their new opportunities. More than that, the country's headlong rush to embrace the ways of the West encouraged young Turks of both sexes to devalue the Asian side of their heritage.

I was beginning to understand Ayse's point about the modern Turkish woman who was trying to stand with each foot on a separate continent— without falling into the Bosporus.

Women of different nationalities have no trouble communicating: we just go shopping. It was on such a shopping excursion that I got to know Gungor.

Everybody rushes to the Kapali Carsi, the famous Grand Bazaar, when they come to Istanbul, and so did I. There is no shopping center on earth more magical than this vast labyrinth of shops laid out along narrow, tunnel-like streets that wind for miles and miles within the heart of the old city. The shops are arranged according to the products they sell—a stroll down the Street of Gold can cause instant blindness, as well as material lust—but the place is such a maze that even my Turkish friends kept getting lost.

The Spice Bazaar, where Gungor took me is fascinating. You can buy a book or a songbird at this raucous bazaar, but your nose will invariably direct you to bags of fresh-ground coffee beans and overflowing sacks of teas and spices.

"It is a hard thing to be a divorced woman in Turkey," Gungor told me.

I added that it was tough going through a divorce in any culture; but that isn't what she meant.

"Turkey is still largely a Muslim country, and the religion of Islam takes a very protective view of women," she explained. "Modern Turks no longer

[handwritten: Adapt to Western rules by making x-wives-pseudo wives thus maintaining polygamy]

[handwritten: fake virginity]

believe that we are a man's property, like a piece of goods; but we feel safer when we obey the laws of Islam and allow ourselves to be protected by men."

In Gungor's case, that means that she lives with her ex-husband's family—a common situation here—to maintain "a man's protection" for herself and her two children. Divorced women, who are no longer as rare as they used to be, may continue living in their ex-husband's homes—in private apartments, if space allows; if not, among other members of the family. Unlike in the United States, where woman-only households are common and acceptable, in Turkey such arrangements are frowned upon, and the woman is regarded as faintly disreputable. So although Atatürk long ago abolished polygamy, the prevailing social custom creates pseudo-wives of divorced women. These women have their freedom but are unable to fully exercise it in a society that takes a paternalistic view of them.

But what of the younger women? Surely all those keen-eyed women in their blue jeans and Madonna makeup are changing all that.

"Don't be taken in by our high-fashion labels," 32-year-old Burtul warned me. "Turkish women no longer wear the çarşaf, but in many respects we are still behind the veil."

I'd met Burtul, an associate archaeologist, at the Archaeological Museum and we walked together from the museum into the zoo for a chat.

"In the cities, we are very Westernized," Burtul told me. "Abortion is legal. So is divorce, and, officially marriages are no longer arranged. The groom's father no longer pays 'head money' to the girl's father, so the groom cannot sell his bride back if she isn't a virgin.

"But," she added, "much of this is only appearance."

In practice, she said, families of all classes still arrange their children's marriages, often to distant family branches, "to keep the money in the family." Men of position customarily keep mistresses, usually with the knowledge of their wives and families.

"Foreigners are very popular," Burtul told me, with an embarrassed smile. Women who hold down some of the most responsible jobs in the economy are still expected to keep the prevailing moral codes. "It's okay for a woman to be a bank president," is how Burtul put it, "but she still has to be a virgin when she marries."

Burtul had "solved" the double standard for herself, she said, by living with her parents and remaining single.

Somehow, that didn't seem like a satisfactory solution. So, when I got the chance—as I did on a Sunday afternoon visit to Topkapi Palace—I struck up a conversation with two young students.

Stefanie and her cousin, who was so shy I never got her name, had bicycled up to Topkapi hoping to meet their boyfriends, two fellow students at the university. Young people of the middle class are allowed to meet and talk on the grounds of the fabulous palace, they told me, because the former seat of the Ottoman sultans was now a respectable museum.

Unlike Burtul, both young women hoped to marry when they finished their studies. Stefanie, in fact, already had received the first of the three traditional rings that a Turkish man offers to the woman he hopes to marry. The first ring indicates both families have given the couple permission to date by visiting each other's homes. The second ring means they are officially engaged and may be seen together in public. The third ring is the wedding ring.

"You have to be very careful of your reputation," Stefanie explained. "If a photograph of a boy and girl together appears in a newspaper, it is like announcing that you're having an affair. The boy will have to marry you."

It sounded pretty odd to me, so I asked them to explain all the young people I had seen dancing at late-night discotheques.

"Rich kids," Stefanie's cousin sneered. "Rich kids can do what they want. They live differently from the rest of us."

"It is important for a girl to be a virgin when she marries," Stefanie said, with a shrug at my ignorance.

Her cousin chimed in with several stories about girls who had "put things up themselves" to replicate an intact hyman for their husbands.

Such artificial aids (made of rubber or natural membranes) are not uncommon here, where official decree says that women have equal rights with men but public opinion is still horrified by a bride who is "damaged goods." A local newspaper, in fact, recently published a highly controversial series of articles about the virginity issue, indicating that young women of all classes still feel honor-bound to stay "pure" for their husbands. Many readers wrote in to say that they approved of the use of artificial aids to simulate this state of purity.

"Rich girls use them," Stefanie and her cousin agreed.

A few nights before I had to leave Istanbul, I finally met a rich girl. Her name was Anna, and she was the daughter of a well-placed government functionary.

Anna was combing her long curls in the ladies' room of a smart restaurant in the fashionable area of Bebek. Like other women of her class, she was used to eating late—and extremely well—at Istanbul's celebrated dining spots. And, like many popular restaurants, this one turned into a discotheque at night, and the noise level had driven me to the ladies' room in search of aspirin. Anna had plenty of those in her purse. She also had a diaphragm tucked in there.

Within a few minutes, Anna was telling me in great detail about the double standard that the young daughters of well-off Turks are handed, along with their good educations and hefty allowances.

"It's the reputation, more than the act itself, that counts," she said, with bitterness in her voice. "My father would *kill* me if he knew I wasn't a virgin. But I don't think he would care at all if the man I married didn't make a big fuss about it. If nobody had to *know* about it."

The obvious question was why, indeed, anybody's father had to "know about it"—so I asked.

"It's the men!" she exploded.

[handwritten: No more arranged marriages because no "head money" but still arrange to keep money in family]

"They tell you not to be old fashioned . . . and then they say they can't marry you if you're not a virgin."

I said I'd heard that one before—that, in fact, it was a line used by men all over the world.

"It's different here," she insisted. "I had a friend who got pregnant from a married man, and her life was ruined. They threw her out of the house, just like they do in the villages. My friend became a prostitute. Rich, poor, what's the difference—you're still thrown out.

After a week in Istanbul, I finally realized what I had missed in my adventures. I had sailed down the Bosporus and sipped thick coffee in dark cafés; I had slipped barefoot into the Blue Mosque and bought a kilim at the Grand Bazaar; I had discoed in Europe and seen dancing bears in Asia; I had gawked at a jeweled dagger at Topkapi and spied on an old woman in a çarşaf chopping wood. But I had not met a married woman . . . until I met Ufuk.

Ufuk's young journalist husband happened to cover a theater production I attended with Ayse. Ufuk sat next to me, too shy to start a conversation but pleased to have someone to talk to while her husband scribbled notes during the long intermissions.

Before her husband transferred to a newspaper in Istanbul, the couple had lived in Ankara—a nine-hour bus ride away—where Ufuk's mother used to baby-sit for their daughter and help with household chores. With her help, both Ufuk and her husband could work full time. In Istanbul, where neither has family, Ufuk only works part time, so she can take care of her 3-year-old daughter and the housework. Turkish men, she said, are unfamiliar with the domestic sciences and are not about to learn.

"They didn't even have disposable diapers in Turkey until just a few years ago," she told me, "and it's impossible to get baby-sitters, except for the janitor's daughter. It is not considered proper for a young girl to take care of someone else's child; and besides, their own mothers do not want them out at night.

Factories and many businesses are required by law to have nurseries, and there are government-run day-care centers for working mothers in the city. But Ufuk said that they are always filled. Working mothers with no family nearby to help with the children have to pay expensive fees to private centers. Some of these centers are private homes, and mothers like Ufuk worry about the quality of the care their children receive.

"This so-called liberation for women is false," she said angrily. "Women are just free to work harder."

Ufuk loves her husband, her child, and her teaching job at the university. But she's so *tired* all the time. Indeed,

after intermission, she fell asleep in her seat.

"What did I learn, Ayse?" I asked crankily, on the way to the airport. "You learned, my curious American friend, that women have it tough all over," she said, laughing. "You discovered that it's still a man's world, even in the most sophisticated cities in the world."

I did learn something, of course, and it had to do with what Ayse had said that night we looked out over Istanbul, spread-eagled over the Bosporus, between Europe and Asia.

"The women are afraid to look back at the past, at Asia, aren't they?" I asked. "They're afraid that maybe the old ways might be best, after all, and that frightens them. They can't be modern women anymore if they go back to the old ways."

"And yet, how nice, how *warm* to have a husband, a father to take care of you, to treat you with respect," she said, surprising me.

In the quiet of the car "respect" sounded like the hiss of a snake—and I told her so.

"Ah, don't worry about me," Ayse said. "You know that scary precipice we hang over? Well, if I should ever lose my balance and fall into the Bosporus—I'll just *swim!*"

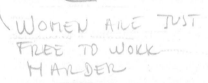

WOMEN ARE JUST FREE TO WORK HARDER

Blaming the Victim: Ideology and Sexual Discrimination in the Contemporary United States

Maxine Margolis

[handwritten annotations: Not the cause but the rationalization; CARDINAL RULE OF ANTHROPOLOGY: FUNCTION OF IDEOLOGY is TO PERPETUATE STATUS QUO; BLAMING THE VICTIM; FOCUS ON THE GROUP OR INDIVIDUAL BEING VICTIMIZED DISTRACTS ATTENTION FROM THE SOCIAL INJUSTICE; BLAMING THE VICTIM IS USED FOR BLACKS, 3RD WORLD & WOMEN]

Women are a problem not only as individuals, but collectively as a separate group with special functions within the structure of society. As a group and generally, they are a problem to themselves, to their children and families, to each other, to society as a whole.

Lundberg and Farnham
1947, p. 1

Only an equal society can save the victim from being the victim.

Gloria Steinem
PBS Program on wife beating
May, 1977

It has long been a cardinal rule of anthropology that one of the main functions of a culture's social and economic structure is the creation of ideologies that perpetuate, or at least do not threaten, the status quo. The need for system-maintaining ideologies is particularly acute in stratified societies where the divisions between haves and have-nots always present potential challenges to the established order.

Blaming the Victim is one such system-maintaining ideology. It helps to preserve the status quo in the United States and other stratified societies by attributing myriad social ills—poverty, delinquency, illegitimacy, low educational attainment—to the norms and values of the victimized group, rather than to the external conditions of in-equality and discrimination under which that group lives. According to William Ryan (1971:xii), who was the first to recognize and label this phenomenon, Blaming the Victim is "an ideology, a mythology" consisting of a "set of official certified non-facts and respected untruths."

The primary function of this ideology is to obscure the victimizing effects of social forces. Rather than analyzing the socially induced inequalities that need changing, it focuses instead on the group or individual that is being victimized. This results in distracting attention from the social injustice, thus allowing it to continue. To change things, according to the ideology, we must change the victims, rather than the circumstances under which they live.

In American society this ideology is most often applied to minority groups, particularly blacks. It is used to "explain" their low socioeconomic status, their "aberrant" family structure, and their general failure to reap the benefits of all—it is said—this society so freely offers. Then too, Blaming the Victim is a convenient tool used to account for the underdevelopment of the third world. According to the ideology, underdevelopment is due to some defect in the national character of the nations affected, to their people's lack of achievement motivation or openness to innovation.

Here I will argue that in the contemporary United States Blaming the Victim is also used widely to rationalize the continued economic, political, and social inequality of women. The application of this ideology to women is somewhat problematic in that, unlike other minority groups, women, at least until recently, have not regarded themselves as the objects of collective victimization. Moreover, through the process of socialization, most women have internalized victim blaming—they blame themselves and other female victims for their economic, social, and political problems. Essentially they ask: "What am I doing to make people discriminate against me?"

In writing this paper, I soon realized that women are blamed for a host of society's ills which, strictly speaking, only indirectly victimize women. Rather, in such cases, the victims are their children, their husbands, and their close associates who, it is said, are damaged by female behavior. The best known example of this type of thinking is the claim that women who work neglect their children and, therefore, are entirely responsible for

From *Researching American Culture*, 1982, pp. 212-227, edited by Conrad P. Koltak. Copyright © 1982 by University of Michigan Press.

whatever emotional and behavioral problems arise in their offspring. But this is simply a new twist of the victim-blaming mentality since its function is the same: to obscure the current social order's role in creating all manner of social and psychological problems by placing the blame where it is often not warranted.

Then too, it is sometimes difficult to distinguish the tendency to blame the female victim from outright misogyny. Is, for example, Philip Wylie's (1955: chap. 11) charge that men and boys are infantilized by their archtypical "Moms"—whom he describes as women who are "twenty-five pounds overweight," who have "beady brains behind their beady eyes," and who spend their time playing bridge "with the stupid voracity of a hammerhead shark"—simple misogyny or does it have an element of the victim-blaming mentality in it? It is clear why the line between the two is often blurred: it is far easier to victimize a group whom you dislike. By defining women as inferior, less trustworthy, more emotional, and less motivated than men, mistreatment or, at least, unequal treatment is justified and the status quo is preserved.

It is not particularly important to a great many working women whether or not they earn as much as men, or have equal opportunities for training and promotion. [Smuts 1974:108]

Blaming the female victim finds its widest application in the world of work. Here it comes in a variety of guises and is used to "explain" why women are paid less than men and have fewer opportunities for occupational advancement. Women, it is said, work only for "pin money" since they have husbands to support them and, therefore, do not really "need" their jobs. Similarly, it is claimed that women have higher rates of absenteeism and job turnover than men do, along with less interest in moving up the career ladder. These purported characteristics of the female labor force are then used to rationalize the fact that women are overwhelmingly confined to low-paying, tedious, dead-end positions.

According to the "pin money" argument, men must provide for their families, while women only work to supplement their husbands' income or for pocket money to buy "extras." Using this logic, employers rationalize paying women low wages on the grounds that they do not need their earnings to live on. And, lest it be thought that this justification for salary discrimination has succumbed to more enlightened thinking in this era of the Equal Pay Act and the feminist movement, the comments of a county commissioner in Utah should lay such hopes aside. When asked to explain why male employees had received a 22 percent wage increase and female employees a 5 percent increase, he replied: "We felt that with their husbands working, the ladies could stand the squeeze a little better" (quoted in *Ms. Magazine* 3 December, 1975).

This reasoning is specious since it misinterprets why women enter the labor force: the reasons are overwhelmingly economic. Of the nearly 38 million women employed in 1976, 84 percent were the sole support of themselves and their families, or were married to men whose 1975 incomes were under $15,000. Women's median contribution to family income was 40 percent, with 12 percent contributing one-half or more. Moreover, the only reason many families are able to maintain a middle-class standard of living is that they have two incomes. "Women flocking to work account for the vital margin between solvency and insolvency," says economic analyst Eliot Janeway (1977:66).

One of the most pernicious results of the pin money myth is the failure to take high levels of female unemployment seriously. The belief that women's jobless rates are less worrisome than those of "household heads" again belies the fact that most women work not for pocket money, but because they are the sole support of their families or because their earnings make up a substantial proportion of their household income. By ignoring these factors, a delegate to the 1976 Republican National Convention could pooh-pooh high unemployment rates.

The unemployment rate tells a dangerously false story for which women are particularly to blame. It's not an economic problem. It's a sociological problem. [Quoted in Porter 1976]

Another component of the Blaming the Victim mentality in the world of work is the purported tendency of women to have higher rates of absenteeism and job turnover than men. These supposed liabilities of employing female labor also have been used to justify lower wages for women as well as employers' reluctance to promote them to more responsible, better-paying positions. Here, it is argued that women are not attached to the labor force, that they just "up and quit their jobs" to get marries, or, if already married, to have babies. Why then, it is asked, should employers invest in expensive job-training programs for women or allow them to take on positions of responsibility?

Once again, the facts are ignored by the victimizers. A Department of Labor study of job turnover over one year found that 10 percent of male workers and 7 percent of female workers had changed jobs during that period (U.S. Department of Labor 1975). The number of women who leave work when they marry or have children has declined in the last two decades, and even with breaks in employment, the average woman now spends twenty-five years in the labor force.

It is also claimed that women miss work more than men do since they are subject to "female problems" and are more likely to stay home under the pretext of one minor ailment or another. Here too, the facts speak to the contrary. A recent survey by the Public Health Service found little difference in absentee rates due to illness or injury; women averaged 5.6 days annually and men averaged 5.2 days annually (U.S. Department of Labor 1975). Moreover, women over forty-five had a lower absentee rate than did men in the same age bracket.

Although ideas have changed since the early years of this century, when menstruation, pregnancy, and menopause were viewed as serious illnesses that disabled women and made them ill-suited for paid employment, many hiring and promotion policies still view women as baby makers who, if they are not pregnant, will soon become so. This assumption then becomes the employer's rationale for passing over women for promotion. Nor does the situation improve for older women since the belief that menopausal women suffer emotional disturbances is often used to justify denying them good jobs.

In a similar vein, Dr. Edgar Berman, a member of the Democratic party's Committee on National Priorities, received widespread publicity in 1970 when he questioned women's ability to hold certain responsible positions due to their "raging hormonal influences." "Take a woman surgeon," said the illustrious doctor, "if she had premenstrual tension . . . I wouldn't want her operating on me." Of course, Dr. Berman ignores the research which suggests that men have four- to six-week cycles that vary predictably and also seem to be caused by changing hormonal levels (quoted in Corea 1977:98–99).

Victim blamers also assert that women don't get ahead in their jobs because they lack the ambition to do so. They claim that women don't want promotions, job training, or job changes that add to their work load: "What they seek first in work," says sociologist Robert W. Smuts (1974:108), "is an agreeable job that makes limited demands. . . . Since they have little desire for a successful career," Smuts continues, "they are likely to drift into traditional women's occupations." George Meany offered a similar rationale in commenting on the lack of women on the thirty-three-member executive council of the AFL-CIO: "We have some very capable women in our unions, but they only go up to a certain level. . . . They don't seem to have any desire to go further" (quoted in *Ms. Magazine*, July, 1977).

Data regarding women's purported lack of ambition are difficult to come by, given that relatively few women have been offered positions of responsibility in the business world. Nevertheless, there is no evidence that the

5.1 million women who held professional and technical jobs and the 1.6 million who worked as managers and administrators in 1974 performed any less ably than men in comparable positions.

Yet another assertion made by Blaming the Victim ideologues is that women are "naturally" good at tedious, repetitive jobs; that they have an aptitude, if not an affinity, for typing, filing, assembling small items, packaging, labeling, and so forth. This view is clearly spelled out in a pamphlet entitled *The Feminine Touch* issued by Employer's Insurance of Wausau.

The female sex tends to be better suited for the unvarying routine that many . . . jobs require. Women are not bored by repetitive tasks as easily as men.

It was also echoed by the chief detective in the notorious "Son of Sam" case who, in a *New York* article, was quoted as saying that he sent two female detectives to the hack bureau to go through tens of thousands of licenses because they were "judged better able to withstand such drudgery than men" (quoted in Daley 1977).

These stereotypes lack any data to back them up and are simply rationalizations that allow men to assign women to such tasks without guilt. They also help justify the continued ghettoization of women workers in certain "appropriate" female occupations where their purported aptitude for tedium can be put to good use.

Many women . . . . exaggerate the severity of their complaints to gratify neurotic desires. The woman who is at odds with her biological self develops psychosomatic and gynecologic problems. [Greenhill 1965:154, 158]

Psychiatry and gynecology have provided lucrative settings for victim-blaming ideologues. Blaming the female victim is the unifying theme in the perception and treatment of such medically diverse spheres as depression, childbirth, contraception, abortion, menstruation, and menopause. The common thread in all is that women's psychological and medical complaints are suspect, that they exaggerate their ills to get attention, and

that most female ailments are of a psychogenic rather than a biogenic origin.

Most psychotherapists, wittingly or unwittingly, ignore the objective conditions under which female neurosis and depression arise, and help maintain the sexual status quo by suggesting individual rather than collective solutions to female discontent. The patient is encouraged to think that her depression, her neurosis, is unique, that they are conditions of her own making.

Nowhere is the Blaming the Victim syndrome more evident in the profession than in the diagnosis and treatment of female sexual problems. Lundberg and Farnham, in their misogynist tome *Modern Woman: The Lost Sex,* claimed that the failure of women to achieve sexual satisfaction is a neurosis that stems from a negative view of childbearing and from attempts to "emulate the male in seeking a sense of personal value by objective exploit" (1947:265). Similarly, Freudian psychoanalyst Helene Deutsch (1944) believed that frigidity in women resulted from nonconformity to the feminine role.

Blaming the individual woman for emotional problems that in many cases are related to her fulfillment of traditional, socially accepted female roles obscures the dilemmas inherent in these roles and relieves society of responsibility for her unhappiness. The psychiatrist Robert Seidenberg suggests that the housewife-mother role often gives rise to emotional problems in women who adhere to it. He found that the "trauma of eventlessness"— that is, the absence of stimuli, challenges, choices, and decision making, which characterizes many women's lives—can threaten their mental well-being as much as physical danger (quoted in Sklar 1976).

When women are used as guinea pigs—as in the case of the birth control pill and other contraceptive devices—their complaints of side effects are often dismissed as the reaction of neurotic females. For example, depression, a fairly common side effect of the pill, is discussed in a medical text in these terms:

Recent evidence suggests that a significant number of these depressive reactions are due to an unrecognized and deeply rooted wish for another child. [Ciriacy and Hughes 1973:300]

The fact that the development of birth control pills and other contraceptive methods has been largely aimed at women is the result of a number of assumptions made by the largely male research establishment. Not only do they believe that conception control is the responsibility of women, they fear the untoward effects of interfering with the male sex drive. Having a healthy supply of sperm is more important to men than ovulation is to women, claim these authorities.

Although the medical profession encourages women to employ problematic contraceptive techniques, it is far more reticent about permitting them to undergo early, medically safe abortions. The reasons are often of the victim-blaming ilk. A staff physician at a county hospital in Milwaukee compared abortions to such cosmetic procedures as face lifts and breast enlargements. "Women know what makes them pregnant and they should have responsibility," he is quoted as saying (quoted in the *Milwaukee Sentinel,* July, 1976).

Even pregnancy and childbirth do not escape the net cast by the medical victim blamers. Morning sickness, for example, is described in one gynecological text as possibly indicating "resentment, ambivalence, and inadequacy in women ill-prepared for motherhood" (quoted in Corea 1977:77). Thus, a condition that is experienced by 75 to 80 percent of all pregnant women, and seems to be related to higher levels of estrogen during pregnancy, is dismissed as a psychosomatic aberration. Others have claimed that many women exaggerate the pain of childbirth: "Exaggeration of the rigors of the process is self-enhancing and . . . affords a new and powerful means of control over the male," say Lundberg and Farnham (1947:294).

Menstrual cramps also are suspect. One gynecologic text writer (Greenhill 1965:154) argues that they often "reflect the unhealthy attitude toward femininity that is so predominant in our society." Other medical texts adopt a similar view. One attributes menstrual pain to a "faulty outlook . . . leading to an exaggeration of minor discomfort," while another states "the pain is always secondary to an emotional problem" (quoted in Lenanne and Lenanne 1973:288).

Victim blaming by the medical establishment reached a crescendo during Senate subcommittee hearings looking into unnecessary surgical procedures. There, the highest ranking staff physician of the American Medical Association argued that hysterectomy is justified—though the uterus was healthy—in women who feared pregnancy or cancer. The chief of obstetrics and gynecology at a Rhode Island hospital agrees: "The uterus is just a muscle" and "It's a liability after children are born because it's a cancer site." The doctor added that his reasoning "ideally" applied to breasts as well, but "this would be a hard concept to sell in this society" (quoted in *Ms. Magazine,* November, 1977). One fact little noted in these discussion is that while it is true that hysterectomy eliminates the possibility of later uterine cancer, the death rate from uterine cancer is lower than the mortality rate from hysterectomies.

Menopause is another medical area in which victim-blaming health practitioners have had a field day. The common medical depiction of menopausal women as aged hags suffering from hot flashes and severe depression has been adopted by the public at large. A judge in Toronto, for example, dismissed the testimony of a forty-eight-year-old woman, stating: "There comes a certain age in a woman's life . . . when the evidence is not too reliable" (quoted in *Ms Magazine,* July, 1977). This stereotype overlooks the fact that only between 20 and 30 percent of the female population have such symptoms. Moreover, it is usually assumed that depression is caused by the loss of reproductive capacity, while little attention is paid to the objective life conditions of many middle-aged women—their "empty nests," their husbands' inattention, their lack of challenging employment opportunities, and society's glorification of female youth and beauty. Surely these conditions do much to account for depression in middle-aged women. But rather than question traditional sex roles, or the unequal distribution of power between men and women in our society, the medical establishment appeals to the "empty uterus" as the source of female discontent.

Whether they like it or not, a woman's a sex object, and they're the ones who turn the men on. [Judge Archie Simonson, Dane County, Wisconsin, 1977]

Nowhere is victim blaming more pernicious than when it is used to rationalize sexual and physical aggression against women. The courtroom statements of Judge Archie Simonson of Wisconsin show that Blaming the Victim is still too often the norm in the perception of rape and the treatment of its victims. This is also true of wife beating. In fact, attitudes toward abused wives and rape victims are strikingly similar; just as the rape victim is supposed to be an irresistible temptress who deserves what she got, so, it is said, the abused wife provokes her husband into beating her. Then too, it is said that women secretly enjoy being beaten, just as they are supposed to be "turned on" by rape.

There are two components to victim blaming as a rationalization for rape. For one, it is assumed that all women covertly desire rape, and, for another, that no woman can be raped against her will, so that forcible rape doesn't really exist. In combination, these assumptions lead to the conclusion that if a woman is raped, she is at fault, or, as Brownmiller (1976:374) says: "She was asking for it" is the classic rapist's remark as he "shifts the burden of blame from himself to his victim."

Victim precipitation, a concept in criminology often used in rape cases, tries to determine if the victim's behavior contributed in any way to the crime. While an unlawful act has occurred, goes the argument, if the victim had acted differently—had not walked alone at night or allowed a strange male to enter her house—the crime might not have taken place. This point is illustrated by a court case in California in which the judge overturned the conviction of a man who had picked up a female hitchhiker and raped her. The ruling read, in part:

The lone female hitchhiker . . . advises all who pass by that she is willing to enter the vehicle of anyone who stops, and . . . so advertises that she has less concern for the consequences than the average female. Under such circumstances, it would not be unreasonable for a man in the position of the defendant . . . to believe that the female would consent to sexual relations. [*New York Times,* July 10, 1977]

Another example of this mentality is the minister who wrote in a letter to "Dear Abby" that a young girl whose father had sexually abused her had "tempted" him by "wearing tight fitting, revealing clothes." In light of these opinions, which reflect the deeply ingrained notion that women provoke rape by their behavior and dress, it is little wonder that rape victims often agonize over what they did to cause themselves to be raped.

These attitudes are also evident in the way rape victims are handled by the courts and the police: the victim is more often treated like the criminal than is the rapist. Some states still permit testimony about the victim's prior sexual experience and general moral demeanor, and Brownmiller (1976:419) cites a study of the jury system which reported that in cases of rape "the jury closely scrutinizes the female complainant" and "weighs the conduct of the victims in judging the guilt of the defendant."

Similar attitudes are reflected in a California police manual which states that "forcible rape is the most falsely reported crime," and Brownmiller (1976:408) notes that many police assume that rape complaints are made by "prostitutes who didn't get paid." If a woman is raped by a stranger, the charge usually is taken more seriously than if she is raped by a man she knows. The latter, the police claim, is a "woman who changed her mind."

No matter how women behave in rape cases they are still held responsible for the outcome. While popular opinions denies the possibility of forcible rape, a judge in England recently

suggested that a woman who was seriously injured fighting off a rapist had only herself to blame for being hurt. She should have given in to the rapist, said the judge. The *London Times* editorialized, "This almost suggests that refusing to be raped is a kind of contributory negligence" (quoted in *Ms. Magazine,* November, 1977). The accused rapist, a soldier in the Coldstream Guards, was freed pending appeal on the grounds that he has a "promising career"!

In dealing with sexual violence the victim blamers once again ignore the facts. As a whole, according to the National Commission of the Causes and Prevention of Violence, rape victims are responsible for less precipitant behavior than victims of other kinds of crimes (Brownmiller 1976:396). Nor are the vast majority of rape charges brought by "women who changed their mind"; a study showed that only 2 percent of rape complaints proved to be false, which is about the same rate as for other felonies (Brownmiller 1976:410). Finally, the idea that women secretly "enjoy" rape is too preposterous to take seriously. I heartily concur with Herschberger's (1970:24) remark that

the notion that a victim of sexual aggression is forced into an experience of sensory delight should be relegated to the land where candy grows on trees.

Since the evidence negates the widespread belief that rape victims are "responsible" for what happens to them, it is senseless to argue that if women took special precautions in their dress and behavior the problem would disappear. As Brownmiller (1976:449) convincingly argues: "there can be no private solutions to the problems of rape." Yet these attitudes persist since, by viewing rape as a "woman's problem" brought on by the victims themselves, both men and society are relieved of guilt.

As I suggested earlier, the explanation for and treatment of wife abuse are remarkably similar to that of rape, and the victim blaming is just as loud and clear. Police, who are notoriously loath to intervene in domestic disputes, too often take the attitude "well, if her

husband beat her, she probably deserved it." They often assume that women who accuse their husbands of beating them are vindictive, and will only prosecute if they are convinced that the wife is a "worthy victim." And in courtroom after courtroom, it is the battered woman's responsibility to persuade the judge that she is really a victim—a judge who may ask her what she did to provoke her husband's attack.

These attitudes are sometimes shared by members of the abused woman's family as well as society at large. In a newspaper article on wife abuse, a woman whose husband beat her while she was pregnant told of getting no support from her family or her doctor.

My mother said I must be doing things to make him mad, and my sister said it was all right for a man to beat his wife. I told my gynecologist that my husband was extremely violent and I was mortally afraid of him. Guess what he said? I should relax more. He prescribed tranquilizers. [*Gainesville Sun,* September 5, 1977]

Victim blamers have had a field day in looking for culprits in wife-abuse cases. A member of the New Hampshire Commission on the Status of Women, for example, suggested that the women's liberation movement was responsible for the increased incidence of wife beating and rape (reported on the "Today Show," September 16, 1977).

In fact that a mere two percent of battering husbands are ever prosecuted is clearly related to these attitudes. While assault and battery are quickly punished when they occur between strangers, punitive action is rare within a marital relationship. The extreme to which this can go is evidenced in a recent court decision in England. A man who killed his wife and pleaded guilty to "manslaughter" was sentenced to only three years probation on the grounds that his wife had "nagged him constantly for seventeen years." "I don't think I have ever come across a case where provocation has gone on for so long," said the judge (reported in the *Independent Florida Alligator,* October 20, 1977).

Many who are otherwise sympathetic to the battered wife are perplexed as to why she takes the abuse. But the reasons are not too difficult to discern. Not only are many women economically dependent on their husbands, but they also have been socialized to be victims. As Marjory Fields, a lawyer involved in wife abuse cases, has noted, "they not only take the beatings, they tend to feel responsible for them" (quoted in Gingold 1976:52).

Should something go wrong, as in the production of a Hitler, a woman is said to be at the root of the trouble—in this case Hitler's mother. [Herschberger 1970:16]

Victims blamers have devoted a good deal of their time and rhetoric to what can be termed "mother blame." In this category of victim blaming, it is not women themselves who are said to be adversely affected by their behavior, but rather their children and, ultimately, society at large. The psychiatric profession, in particular, has been responsible for popularizing the view that, in Chesler's (1972:378) words, "the lack of or superabundance of mother love causes neurotic, criminal . . . and psychopathic children." The absent or uncaring father and other forms of deprivation rarely are blamed for problem children and problem adults.

Mother blame is a natural outgrowth of the traditional, socially approved sexual division of labor that sees child rearing as exclusively "woman's work"; if something goes wrong, it must be mother who is to blame. Moreover, women are held responsible for their children's problems no matter what they do. If they work, they are accused of child neglect, while if they stay home and devote their time to child care, they are berated for smothering their offspring.

The theory that attributes juvenile delinquency and other behavior problems to maternal employment has been around for quite some time. During World War II, working mothers were widely criticized for rearing "latchkey children" who got into trouble for lack of supervision. Mother blame reached a peak shortly after the war with the publication of *Modern Woman: The Lost Sex.* In it, Lundberg and Farnham (1947:304–305) estimate that between 40 and 50 percent of all mothers are "rejecting, over-solicitous, or dominating," and that they produce "the delinquents, the behavior problem children, and some substantial proportion of criminals."

Some years later psychiatrist Abram Kardiner (1954:224) agreed with these sentiments when he wrote that "children reared on a part-time basis will show the effects of such care in the distortions of personality that inevitably result." After all, "motherhood is a full-time job."

Lest it be thought that mother blame is merely an artifact of the days of the feminine mystique, a recent newspaper editorial espoused it when attempting to explain the high crime rate.

Let's speculate that the workaday grind makes Mom more inaccessible, irritable . . . and spiteful, thereby rendering family life less pleasant . . . than the good old days when she stayed in the kitchen and baked apple pies. What could that be doing to the rising crime rate? Say fellows, could it be Mom's fault? [Editorial, *Gainesville Sun,* March 25, 1977]

These views, of course, ignore the studies that indicate that absent and low profile fathers are more responsible for delinquency in their children than are working mothers. Moreover, the most comprehensive study of maternal employment, *The Employed Mother in America* (Nye and Hoffman 1963), effectively rebuts the myths concerning the supposed ill effects of working mothers on their offspring, and concludes that "maternal employment . . . is not the overwhelming influential factor in children's lives that some have thought it to be" (Burchinal 1963:118; Siegal et al. 1963:80). But, as we have seen, victim blamers have little use for facts that contradict their strongly held beliefs.

What of the woman who stays home and devotes full time to child raising? She too is the target of the mother blamers who hold her accountable for an incredible variety of social problems. In his book *Generation of Vipers*, Phillip Wylie (1955) characterized such women as "Moms" who led empty lives and preyed upon their offspring, keeping them tied to their proverbial apron strings. This theme was also sounded by Edward Strecker (1946), a psychiatric consultant to the Army and Navy Surgeons General during World War II. In trying to account for the emotional disorders of 600,000 men unable to continue in military service, Strecker wrote, "in the vast majority of case histories, a Mom is at fault." But what causes "Moms" to be the way they are in the first place? In most cases, a Mom is a Mom because she is the immature result of a Mom, says Strecker (1946:23, 70).

If it weren't for Martha, there'd have been no Watergate. [Richard Nixon on David Frost interview, September, 1977]

Richard Nixon's statement holding Martha Mitchell responsible for Watergate is a timely reminder of the length to which victim blamers sometimes go. According to Nixon, Watergate occurred because "John Mitchell wasn't minding the store," but was preoccupied with his wife's emotional problems. This claim is particularly malicious given the often-noted fact that the large Watergate case was *all* male. A similarly absurd remark was made during the "Son of Sam" episode, when it was automatically assumed that a woman was at the root of "Sam's" problem. The killer "must have been terribly provoked by a woman," New York psychiatrist Hyman Spotnitz was quoted as saying in *Time* (July 11, 1977).

While Nixon's assertion was widely seen as self-serving, the opinions of psychiatrists and other authoritative victim blamers are taken quite seriously by the general public, including women. Women not only participate in this ideology, they often internalize it, blaming themselves and other women for a host of problems. This shows the effectiveness of the ideology in rationalizing subordination to the victims themselves. The very persistence of victim blaming, in fact, is partly due to the implicit participation of its targets. And men, of course, perpetuate the ideology since it is clearly in their own self-interest to do so. It helps maintain the status quo from which they benefit.

In recent years the ability of victim blaming to deflect attention from social institutions and obscure societal processes has been particularly valuable in "explaining" women's failure to make significant advances in employment and other realms. Despite the existence of the feminist movement and a plethora of equal opportunity laws, women still overwhelmingly remain in low-paid, low-prestige, female job ghettos. But, say the victim blamers, that is because they have no interest in getting ahead, they fear success, and don't want the added responsibility that comes with promotions. The goal of the victim blamers is clear: these purported qualities of the victimized group conveniently mask the fact of continued widespread sexual discrimination. But it must be emphasized that although the Blaming the Victim ideology does distort reality by covering up the inequalities in contemporary American life, it is not the *cause* of these deeply rooted social and economic inequalities: it is a rationalization for them.

Religion, Belief, and Ritual

The anthropological concern for religion, belief, and ritual does not have to do with the scientific validity of such phenomena, but rather the way in which people relate various concepts of the "supernatural" to their everyday lives. With this more practical perspective, some anthropologists have found that traditional spiritual healing is just as applicable in the treatment of illness as modern medicine, that voodoo is a form of social control, and that the ritual and spiritual preparation for playing the game of baseball can be just as important as spring training.

Every society is composed of feeling, thinking, and acting human beings who at one time or another are either conforming to or altering the social order into which they were born. Religion is an ideological framework that gives special legitimacy and validity to human experience within any given sociocultural system. In this way, monogamy as a marriage form or monarchy as a political form ceases to be simply one of many alternative ways in which a society can be organized, but becomes, for the believer, the only legitimate way. Religion renders certain human values and activities sacred and inviolable, and it is this "mythic" function that helps to explain the strong ideological attachments that some people have regardless of the scientific merits of their points of view.

While, under some conditions, religion may in fact be "the opiate of the masses," under other conditions it may be a rallying point for social and economic protest. A contemporary example of the former might be the "Moonies," while a good example of the latter is the role of the black church in the American civil rights movement, along with the prominence of such religious figures as Martin Luther King, Jr., and Jesse Jackson.

Finally, a word of caution must be set forth concerning attempts to understand the belief systems of other cultures. At times the prevailing attitude seems to be that "what I believe in is religion and what you believe in is superstition." While anthropologists generally do not subscribe to this view, there is a tendency within the field to explain that which seems, on the surface, to be incomprehensible, impractical behavior as some form of "religious ritual." The following articles should serve as a strong warning concerning the pitfalls of that approach.

"The Mbuti Pygmies: Change and Adaptation" involves ritual which is subtle, informal, and yet absolutely necessary for social harmony and stability. In contrast, what seems to be a highly formal circumcision ceremony in "The Initiation of a Maasai Warrior" is ultimately revealed to be a deeply personal experience. The emphasis in "The Secrets of Haiti's Living Dead" is upon both individual conformity and community solidarity.

Mystical beliefs and ritual are not absent from modern society. In fact, as Philip Graham shows in "A Writer in a World of Spirits," the spirit world of a rural African village is not unlike the author's imagination populated with fictional characters. "You've Gotta Have 'Wa'" shows Japanese baseball to have such a degree of seriousness about it that associated ritual must be performed precisely and correctly for a player to become accepted by the team. Finally, "Body Ritual Among the Nacirema" reveals that even our daily routines have mystic overtones.

In summary, the articles in this section will show religion, belief, and ritual in relationship to practical human affairs.

Looking Ahead: Challenge Questions

How does ritual contribute to a sense of personal security, individual responsibility, and social equality?

How has voodoo become such an important form of social control in rural Haiti?

In what ways is the spirit world of a rural African village similar in function to a fiction writer's imagination?

How important are ritual and taboo in our modern industrial society?

How would you prepare an American to play baseball in Japan?

Unit 6

The Mbuti Pygmies: Change and Adaptation

Colin M. Turnbull

THE EDUCATIONAL PROCESS

. . . In the first three years of life every Mbuti alive experiences almost total security. The infant is breast-fed for those three years, and is allowed almost every freedom. Regardless of gender, the infant learns to have absolute trust in both male and female parent. If anything, the father is just another kind of mother, for in the second year the father formally introduces the child to its first solid food. There used to be a beautiful ritual in which the mother presented the child to the father in the middle of the camp, where all important statements are made (anyone speaking from the middle of the camp must be listened to). The father took the child and held it to his breast, and the child would try to suckle, crying "*ema, ema,*" or "mother." The father would shake his head, and say "no, father . . . *eba,*" but like a mother (the Mbuti said), then give the child its first solid food.

At three the child ventures out into the world on its own and enters the *bopi,* what we mght call a playground, a tiny camp perhaps a hundred yards from the main camp, often on the edge of a stream. The *bopi* were indeed playgrounds, and often very noisy ones, full of fun and high spirits. But they were also rigorous training grounds for eventual economic responsibility. On entry to the *bopi,* for one thing, the child discovers the importance of age as a structural principle, and the relative unimportance of gender and biological kinship. The *bopi* is the private world of the children. Younger youths may occasionally venture in, but if adults or elders try, as they sometimes do when angry at having their afternoon snooze interrupted, they invariably get driven out, taunted, and ridiculed. Children, among the Mbuti, have rights, but they also learn that they have responsibilities. Before the hunt sets out each day it is the children, sometimes the younger youths, who light the hunting fire.

Ritual among the Mbuti is often so informal and apparently casual that it may pass unnoticed at first. Yet insofar as ritual involves symbolic acts that represent unspoken, perhaps even unthought, concepts or ideals, or invoke other states of being, alternative frames of mind and reference, then Mbuti life is full of ritual. The hunting fire is one of the more obvious of such rituals. Early in the morning children would take firebrands from the *bopi,* where they always lit their own fire with embers from their family hearths, and set off on the trail by which the hunt was to leave that day (the direction of each day's hunt was always settled by discussion the night before). Just a short distance from the camp they lit a fire at the base of a large tree, and covered it with special leaves that made it give off a column of dense smoke. Hunters leaving the camp, both men and women, and such youths and children as were going with them, had to pass by this fire. Some did so casually, without stopping or looking, but passing through the smoke. Others reached into the smoke with their hands as they passed, rubbing the smoke into their bodies. A few always stopped, for a moment, and let the smoke envelop them, only then almost dreamily moving off.

And indeed is *was* a form of intoxication, for the smoke invoked the spirit of the forest, and by passing through it the hunters sought to fill themselves with that spirit, not so much to make the hunt successful as to minimize the sacrilege of killing. Yet they, the hunters, could not light the fire themselves. After all, they were already contaminated by death. Even youths, who daily joined the hunt at the edges, catching any game that escaped the nets, by hand, if they could, were not pure enough to invoke the spirits of forestness. But young children were uncontaminated, as yet untainted by contact with the original sin of the Mbuti. It was their responsibility to light the fire, and if it was not lit then the hunt would not take place, or as the Mbuti put it, the hunt *could* not take place.

In this way even the children in Mbuti society, at the first of the four age levels that dominate Mbuti social structure, are given very real social responsibility and see themselves as a part of that structure, by virtue of their purity. After all, they have just been born from the source of all purity, the forest itself. By the same reasoning, the elders, who are about to return to that ultimate source of all being, through death, are at least closer to purity than the adults, who are daily contaminated by killing. Elders no longer go on the hunt. So, like the children, the elders have important sacred ritual responsibilities in the Mbuti division of labor by age.

In the *bopi* the children play, but they have no "games" in the strict sense of the word. Levi-Strauss has perceptively compared games with rituals, suggesting that whereas in a game the players start theoretically equal but end up unequal, in a ritual just the reverse takes place. All are equalized. Mbuti children could be seen every day playing in the *bopi*, but not once did I see a game, not one activity that smacked of any kind of competition, except perhaps that competition that it is necessary for us all to feel from time to time, competition with our own private and personal inadequacies. One such pastime (rather than game) was tree climbing. A dozen or so children would climb up a young sapling. Reaching the top, their weight brought the sapling bending down until it almost touched the ground. Then all the children leapt off together, shrieking as the young tree sprang upright again with a rush. Sometimes one child, male or female, might stay on a

little too long, either out of fear, or out of bravado, or from sheer carelessness or bad timing. Whatever the reason, it was a lesson most children only needed to be taught once, for the result was that you got flung upward with the tree, and were lucky to escape with no more than a few bruises and a very bad fright.

Other pastimes taught the children the rules of hunting and gathering. Frequently elders, who stayed in camp when the hunt went off, called the children into the main camp and enacted a mock hunt with them there. Stretching a discarded piece of net across the camp, they pretended to be animals, showing the children how to drive them into the nets. And, of course, the children played house, learning the patterns of cooperation that would be necessary for them later in life. They also learned the prime lesson of egality, other than for purposes of division of labor making no distinction between male and female, this nuclear family or that. All in the *bopi* were *apua'i* to each other, and so they would remain throughout their lives. At every age level—childhood, youth, adulthood, or old age—everyone of that level is *apua'i* to all the others. Only adults sometimes (but so rarely that I think it was only done as a kind of joke, or possibly insult) made the distinction that the Bira do, using *apua'i* for male and *amua'i* for female. Male or female, for the Mbuti, if you are the same age you are *apua'i*, and that means that you share everything equally, regardless of kinship or gender.

YOUTH AND POLITICS

Sometime before the age of puberty boys or girls, whenever they feel ready, move back into the main camp from the *bopi* and join the youths. This is when they must assume new responsibilities, which for the youths are primarily political. Already, in the *bopi*, the children become involved in disputes, and are sometimes instrumental in settling them by ridicule, for nothing hurts an adult more than being ridiculed by children. The art of reason, however, is something they learn from the youths,

and it is the youths who apply the art of reason to the settlement of disputes.

When puberty comes it separates them, for the first time in their experience, from each other as *apua'i*. Very plainly girls are different from boys. When a girl has her first menstrual period the whole camp celebrates with the wild *elima* festival, in which the girl, and some of her chosen girl friends, are the center of all attention, living together in a special *elima* house. Male youths sit outside the *elima* house and wait for the girls to come out, usually in the afternoon, for the *elima* singing. They sing in antiphony, the girls leading, the boys responding. Boys come from neighboring territories all around, for this is a time of courtship. But there are always eligible youths within the camp as well, and the *elima* girl may well choose girls from other territories to come and join her, so there is more than enough excuse for every youth to carry on several flirtations, legitimate or illegitimate. I have known even first cousins to flirt with each other, but learned to be prudent enough not to pull out my kinship charts and point this out—well, not in public anyway.

The *elima* is more than a premarital festival, more than a joint initiation of youth into adulthood, and more than a rite of passage through puberty, though it is all those things. It is a public recognition of the opposition of male and female, and every *elima* is used to highlight the *potential* for conflict that lies in that opposition. As at other times of crisis, at puberty, a time of change and uncertainty, the Mbuti bring all the major forms of conflict out into the open. And the one that evidently most concerns them is the male/female opposition.

The adults begin to play a special form of "tug of war" that is clearly a ritual rather than a game. All the men are on one side, the women on the other. At first it looks like a game, but quickly it becomes clear that the objective is for *neither* side to win. As soon as the women begin to win, one of them will leave the end of the line and run around to join the men, assuming a deep male voice and in other ways ridicul-

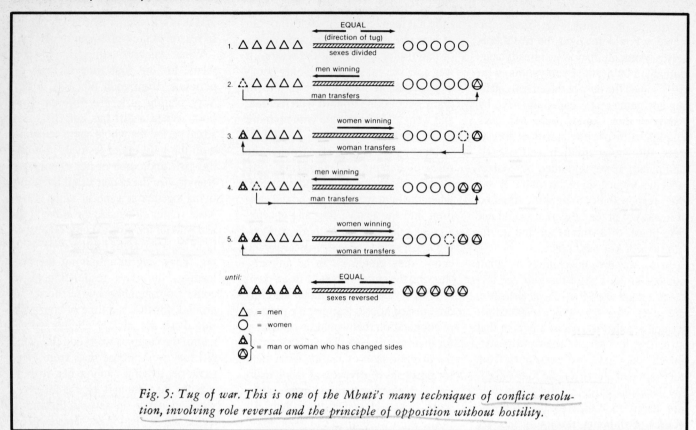

Fig. 5: Tug of war. This is one of the Mbuti's many techniques of conflict resolution, involving role reversal and the principle of opposition without hostility.

ing manhood. Then, as the men begin to win, a male will similarly join the women, making fun of womanhood as he does so. Each adult on changing sides attempts to outdo all the others in ridiculing the opposite sex. Finally, when nearly all have switched sides, and sexes, the ritual battle between the genders simply collapses into hysterical laughter, the contestants letting go of the rope, falling onto the ground, and rolling over with mirth. Neither side wins, both are equalized very nicely, and each learns the essential lesson, that there should be *no* contest. . . .

The Initiation of a Maasai Warrior

Tepilit Ole Saitoti

"Tepilit, circumcision means a sharp knife cutting into the skin of the most sensitive part of your body. You must not budge; don't move a muscle or even blink. You can face only one direction until the operation is completed. The slightest movement on your part will mean you are a coward, incompetent and unworthy to be a Maasai man. Ours has always been a proud family, and we would like to keep it that way. We will not tolerate unnecessary embarrassment, so you had better be ready. If you are not, tell us now so that we will not proceed. Imagine yourself alone remaining uncircumcised like the water youth [white people]. I hear they are not circumcised. Such a thing is not known in Maasailand; therefore, circumcision will have to take place even if it means holding you down until it is completed."

My father continued to speak and every one of us kept quiet. "The pain you will feel is symbolic. There is a deeper meaning in all this. Circumcision means a break between childhood and adulthood. For the first time in your life, you are regarded as a grownup, a complete man or woman. You will be expected to give and not just to receive. To protect the family always, not just to be protected yourself. And your wise judgment will for the first time be taken into consideration. No family affairs will be discussed without your being consult-

ed. If you are ready for all these responsibilities, tell us now. Coming into manhood is not simply a matter of growth and maturity. It is a heavy load on your shoulders and especially a burden on the mind. Too much of this—I am done. I have said all I wanted to say. Fellows, if you have anything to add, go ahead and tell your brother, because I am through. I have spoken."

After a prolonged silence, one of my half-brothers said awkwardly, "Face it, man . . . it's painful. I won't lie about it, but it is not the end. We all went through it, after all. Only blood will flow, not milk." There was laughter and my father left.

My brother Lellia said, "Men, there are many things we must acquire and preparations we must make before the ceremony, and we will need the cooperation and help of all of you. Ostrich feathers for the crown and wax for the arrows must be collected."

"Are you *orkirekenyi?*" one of my brothers asked. I quickly replied no, and there was laughter. *Orkirekenyi* is a person who has transgressed sexually. For you must not have sexual intercourse with any circumcised woman before you yourself are circumcised. You must wait until you are circumcised. If you have not waited, you will be fined. Your father, mother, and the circumciser will take a cow from you as punishment.

Just before we departed, one of my closest friends said, "If you kick the knife, you will be in trouble." There was laughter. "By the way, if you have decided to kick the circumciser, do it well. Silence him once and for all." "Do it the way you kick a football in school." "That will fix him," another added, and we all laughed our heads off again as we departed.

The following month was a month of preparation. I and others collected wax, ostrich feathers, honey to be made into honey beer for the elders to drink on the day of circumcision, and all the other required articles.

Three days before the ceremony my head was shaved and I discarded all my belongings, such as my necklaces, garments, spear, and sword. I even had to shave my pubic hair. Circumcision in many ways is similar to Christian baptism. You must put all the sins you have committed during childhood behind and embark as a new person with a different outlook on a new life.

The circumciser came the following day and handed the ritual knives to me. He left drinking a calabash of beer. I stared at the knives uneasily. It was hard to accept that he was going to use them on my organ. I was to sharpen them and protect them from people of ill will who might try to blunt them, thus rendering them inefficient during the ritual and thereby bringing shame on our family. The knives threw a chill down my spine; I was not sure I was sharpening them properly, so I took them to my closest brother for him to check out, and he assured me that the knives were all right. I hid them well and waited.

Tension started building between me and my relatives, most of whom worried that I wouldn't make it through the ceremony valiantly. Some even snarled at me, which was their way of encouraging me. Others threw insults and abusive words my way. My sister Loiyan in particular was more troubled by the whole affair than anyone in the whole family. She had to assume my mother's role during the circumcision. Were I to fail my initiation, she would have to face the consequences. She would be spat upon and even beaten for representing the mother of an unworthy son. The same fate would befall my father, but he seemed unconcerned. He had this weird belief that because I was not particularly handsome, I must be brave. He kept saying, "God is not so bad as to have made him ugly and a coward at the same time."

Failure to be brave during circumcision would have other unfortunate consequences: the herd of cattle belonging to the family still in the compound would be beaten until they stampeded; the slaughtered oxen and honey beer prepared during the month before the ritual would go to waste; the initiate's food would be spat upon and he would have to eat it or else get a severe beating. Everyone would call him Olkasiodoi, the knife kicker.

Kicking the knife of the circumciser would not help you anyway. If you struggle and try to get away during the ritual, you will be held down until the operation is completed. Such failure of nerve would haunt you in the future. For example, no one will choose a person who kicked the knife for a position of leadership. However, there have been instances in which a person who failed to go through circumcision successfully became very brave afterwards because he was filled with anger over the incident; no one dares to scold him or remind him of it. His agemates, particularly the warriors, will act as if nothing had happened.

During the circumcision of a woman, on the other hand, she is allowed to cry as long as she does not hinder the operation. It is common to see a woman crying and kicking during circumcision. Warriors are usually summoned to help hold her down.

For woman, circumcision means an end to the company of Maasai warriors. After they recuperate, they soon get married, and often to men twice their age.

The closer it came to the hour of truth, the more I was hated, particularly by those closest to me. I was deeply troubled by the withdrawal of all the support I needed. My annoyance turned into anger and resolve. I decided not to budge or blink, even if I were to see my intestines flowing before me. My resolve was hardened when newly circumcised warriors came to sing for me. Their songs were utterly insulting, intended to annoy me further. They tucked their wax arrows under my crotch and rubbed them on my nose. They repeatedly called me names.

By the end of the singing, I was fuming. Crying would have meant I was a coward. After midnight they left me alone and I went into the house and tried to sleep but could not. I was exhausted and numb but remained awake all night.

At dawn I was summoned once again by the newly circumcised warriors. They piled more and more insults on me. They sang their weird songs with even more vigor and excitement than before. The songs praised warriorhood and encouraged one to achieve it at all costs. The songs continued until the sun shone on the cattle horns clearly. I was summoned to the main cattle gate, in my hand a ritual cowhide from a cow that had been properly slaughtered during my naming ceremony. I went past Loiyan, who was milking a cow, and she muttered something. She was shaking all over. There was so much tension that people could hardly breathe.

I laid the hide down and a boy was ordered to pour ice-cold water, known as *engare entolu* (ax water), over my head. It dripped all over my naked body and I shook furiously. In a matter of seconds I was summoned to sit down. A large crowd of boys and men formed a semicircle in front of me; women are not allowed to watch male circumcision and vice-versa. That was the last thing I saw clearly. As soon as I sat down, the circumciser appeared, his knives at the ready. He spread my legs and said, "One cut," a pronouncement necessary to prevent an initiate from claiming that he had been taken by surprise. He splashed a white liquid, a ceremonial paint called *enturoto*, across my face. Almost immediately I felt a spark of pain under my belly as the knife cut through my penis' foreskin. I happened to choose to look in the direction of the operation. I continued to observe the circumciser's fingers working mechanically. The pain became numbness and my lower body felt heavy, as if I were weighed down by a heavy burden. After fifteen minutes or so, a man who had been supporting from behind pointed at something, as if to assist the circumciser. I came to learn later that the circumciser's eyesight had been failing him and that my brothers had been mad at him because the operation had taken longer than was usually necessary. All the same, I remained pinned down until the operation was over. I heard a call for milk to wash the knives, which signaled the end, and soon the ceremony was over.

With words of praise, I was told to wake up, but I remained seated. I waited for the customary presents in appreciation of my bravery. My father gave me a cow and so did my brother Lillia. The man who had supported my back and my brother-in-law gave me a heifer. In all I had eight animals given to me. I was carried inside the house to my own bed to recuperate as activities intensified to celebrate my bravery.

I laid on my own bed and bled profusely. The blood must be retained within the bed, for according to Maasai tradition, it must not spill to the ground. I was drenched in my own blood. I stopped bleeding after about half an hour but soon was in intolerable pain. I was supposed to squeeze my organ and force blood to flow out of the wound, but no one had told me, so the blood coagulated and caused unbearable pain. The circumciser was brought to my aid and showed me what to do, and soon the pain subsided.

The following morning, I was escorted by a small boy to a nearby valley to walk and relax, allowing my wound to drain. This was common for everyone who had been circumcised, as well as for women who had just given birth. Having lost a lot of blood, I was extremely weak. I walked very slowly, but in spite of my caution I fainted. I tried to hang on to bushes and shrubs, but I fell, irritating my wound. I came out of unconsciousness quickly, and the boy who was escorting me never realized what had happened. I was so scared that I told him to lead me back home. I could have died without there being anyone around who could have helped me. From that day on, I was selective of my company while I was feeble.

In two weeks I was able to walk and was taken to join other newly circumcised boys far away from our settlement. By tradition Maasai initiates are required to decorate their headdresses with all kinds of colorful birds they have killed. On our way to the settlement, we hunted birds and teased girls by shooting them with our wax blunt arrows. We danced and ate and were well treated wherever we went. We were protected from the cold and rain during the healing period. We were not allowed to touch food, as we were regarded as unclean, so whenever we ate we had to use specially prepared sticks instead. We remained in this pampered state until our wounds healed and our headdresses were removed. Our heads were shaved, we discarded our black cloaks and bird headdresses and embarked as newly shaven warriors, Irkeleani.

As long as I live I will never forget the day my head was shaved and I emerged a man, a Maasai warrior. I felt a sense of control over my destiny so great that no words can accurately describe it. I now stood with confidence, pride, and happiness of being, for all around me I was desired and loved by beautiful, sensuous Maasai maidens. I could now interact with women and even have sex with them, which I not been allowed before. I was now regarded as a responsible person.

In the old days, warriors were like gods, and women and men wanted only to be the parent of a warrior. Everything else would be taken care of as a result. When a poor family had a warrior, they

ceased to be poor. The warrior would go on raids and bring cattle back. The warrior would defend the family against all odds. When a society respects the individual and displays confidence in him the way the Maasai do their warriors, the individual can grow to his fullest potential. Whenever there was a task requiring physical strength or bravery, the Maasai would call upon their warriors. They hardly ever fall short of what is demanded of them and so are characterized by pride, confidence, and an extreme sense of freedom. But there is an old saying in Maasai: "You are never a free man until your father dies." In other words, your father is paramount while he is alive and you are obligated to respect him. My father took advantage of this principle and held a tight grip on all his warriors, including myself. He always wanted to know where we all were at any given time. We fought against his restrictions, but without success. I, being the youngest of my father's five warriors, tried even harder to get loose repeatedly, but each time I was punished severely.

Roaming the plains with other warriors in pursuit of girls and adventure was a warrior's pastime. We would wander from one settlement to another, singing, wrestling, hunting, and just playing. Often I was ready to risk my father's punishment for this wonderful freedom.

One clear day my father sent me to take sick children and one of his wives to the dispensary in the Korongoro Highlands. We rode in the L.S.B. Leakey lorry. We ascended the highlands and were soon attended to in the local hospital. Near the conservation offices I met several acquaintances, and one of them told me of an unusual circumcision that was about to take place in a day or two. All the local warriors and girls were preparing to attend it.

The highlands were a lush green from the seasonal rains and the sky was a purple-blue with no clouds in sight. The land was overflowing with milk, and the warriors felt and looked their best, as they always did when there was plenty to eat and drink. Everyone was at ease. The demands the community usually made on warriors during the dry sea-

son when water was scarce and wells had to be dug were now not necessary. Herds and flocks were entrusted to youths to look after. The warriors had all the time for themselves. But my father was so strict that even at times like these he still insisted on overworking us in one way or another. He believed that by keeping us busy, he would keep us out of trouble.

When I heard about the impending ceremony, I decided to remain behind in the Korongoro Highlands and attend it now that the children had been treated. I knew very well that I would have to make up a story for my father upon my return, but I would worry about that later. I had left my spear at home when I boarded the bus, thinking that I would be coming back that very day. I felt lighter but now regretted having left it behind; I was so used to carrying it wherever I went. In gales of laughter resulting from our continuous teasing of each other, we made our way toward a distant kraal. We walked at a leisurely pace and reveled in the breeze. As usual we talked about the women we desired, among other things.

The following day we were joined by a long line of colorfully dressed girls and warriors from the kraal and the neighborhood where we had spent the night, and we left the highland and headed to Ingorienito to the rolling hills on the lower slopes to attend the circumcision ceremony. From there one could see Oldopai Gorge, where my parents lived, and the Inaapi hills in the middle of the Serengeti Plain.

Three girls and a boy were to be initiated on the same day, an unusual occasion. Four oxen were to be slaughtered, and many people would therefore attend. As we descended, we saw the kraal where the ceremony would take place. All those people dressed in red seemed from a distance like flamingos standing in a lake. We could see lines of other guests heading to the settlements. Warriors made gallant cries of happiness known as enkiseer. Our line of warriors and girls responded to their cries even more gallantly.

In serpentine fashion, we entered the gates of the settlement. Holding spears in our left hands, we warriors walked proudly, taking small steps, swaying like palm trees, impressing our girls, who walked parallel to us in another line, and of course the spectators, who gazed at us approvingly.

We stopped in the center of the kraal and waited to be greeted. Women and children welcomed us. We put our hands on the children's heads, which is how children are commonly saluted. After the greetings were completed, we started dancing.

Our singing echoed off the kraal fence and nearby trees. Another line of warriors came up the hill and entered the compound, also singing and moving slowly toward us. Our singing grew in intensity. Both lines of warriors moved parallel to each other, and our feet pounded the ground with style. We stamped vigorously, as if to tell the next line and the spectators that we were the best.

The singing continued until the hot sun was overhead. We recessed and ate food already prepared for us by other warriors. Roasted meat was for those who were to eat meat, and milk for the others. By our tradition, meat and milk must not be consumed at the same time, for this would be a betrayal of the animal. It was regarded as cruel to consume a product of the animal that could be obtained while it was alive, such as milk, and meat, which was only available after the animal had been killed.

After eating we resumed singing, and I spotted a tall, beautiful *esiankiki* (young maiden) of Masiaya whose family was one of the largest and richest in our area. She stood very erect and seemed taller than the rest.

One of her breasts could be seen just above her dress, which was knotted at the shoulder. While I was supposed to dance generally to please all the spectators, I took it upon myself to please her especially. I stared at and flirted with her, and she and I danced in unison at times. We complemented each other very well.

During a break, I introduced myself to the *esiankiki* and told her I would like to see her after the dance. "Won't you need a warrior to escort you home later when the evening threatens?" I said. She replied, "Perhaps, but the evening is still far away."

I waited patiently. When the dance ended, I saw her departing with a group of other women her age. She gave me a sidelong glance, and I took that to mean come later and not now. With so many others around, I would not have been able to confer with her as I would have liked anyway.

With another warrior, I wandered around the kraal killing time until the herds returned from pasture. Before the sun dropped out of sight, we departed. As the kraal of the *esiankiki* was in the lowlands, a place called Enkoloa, we descended leisurely, our spears resting on our shoulders.

We arrived at the woman's kraal and found that cows were now being milked. One could hear the women trying to appease the cows by singing to them. Singing calms cows down, making it easier to milk them. There were no warriors in the whole kraal except for the two of us. Girls went around into warriors' houses as usual and collected milk for us. I was so eager to go and meet my *esiankiki* that I could hardly wait for nightfall. The warriors' girls were trying hard to be sociable, but my mind was not with them. I found them to be childish, loud, bothersome, and boring.

As the only warriors present, we had to keep them company and sing for them, at least for a while, as required by custom. I told the other warrior to sing while I tried to figure out how to approach my *esiankiki*. Still a novice warrior, I was not experienced with women and was in fact still afraid of them. I could flirt from a distance, of course. But sitting down with a woman and trying to seduce her was another matter. I had already tried twice to approach women soon after my circumcision and had failed. I got as far as the door of one woman's house and felt my heart beating like a Congolese drum; breathing became difficult and I had to turn back. Another time I managed to get in the house and suceeded in sitting on the bed, but then I started trembling until the whole bed was shaking, and conversation became difficult. I left the house and the woman, amazed and speechless, and never went back to her again.

Tonight I promised myself I would be brave and would not make any silly, ridiculous moves. "I must be mature and not afraid," I kept reminding myself, as I remembered an incident involving one of my relatives when he was still very young and, like me, afraid of women. He went to a woman's house and sat on a stool for a whole hour; he was afraid to awaken her, as his heart was pounding and he was having difficulty breathing.

When he finally calmed down, he woke her up, and their conversation went something like this:

"Woman, wake up."

"Why should I?"

"To light the fire."

"For what?"

"So you can see me."

"I already know who you are. Why don't *you* light the fire, as you're nearer to it than me?"

"It's your house and it's only proper that you light it yourself."

"I don't feel like it."

"At least wake up so we can talk, as I have something to tell you."

"Say it."

"I need you."

"I do not need one-eyed types like yourself."

"One-eyed people are people too."

"That might be so, but they are not to my taste."

They continued talking for quite some time, and the more they spoke, the braver he became. He did not sleep with her that night, but later on he persisted until he won her over. I doubted whether I was as strong-willed as he, but the fact that he had met with success encouraged me. I told my warrior friend where to find me should he need me, and then I departed.

When I entered the house of my *esiankiki*, I called for the woman of the house, and as luck would have it, my lady responded. She was waiting for me. I felt better, and I proceeded to talk to her like a professional. After much talking back and forth, I joined her in bed.

The night was calm, tender, and loving, like most nights after initiation ceremonies as big as this one. There must have been a lot of courting and lovemaking.

Maasai women can be very hard to deal with sometimes. They can simply reject a man outright and refuse to change their minds. Some play hard to get, but in reality are testing the man to see whether he is worth their while. Once a friend of mine while still young was powerfully attracted to a woman nearly his mother's age. He put a bold move on her. At first the woman could not believe his intention, or rather was amazed by his courage. The name of the warrior was Ngengeiya, or Drizzle.

"Drizzle, what do you want?"

The warrior stared her right in the eye and said, "You."

"For what?"

"To make love to you."

"I am your mother's age."

"The choice was either her or you."

This remark took the woman by surprise. She had underestimated the saying "There is no such thing as a young warrior." When you are a warrior, you are expected to perform bravely in any situation. Your age and size are immaterial.

"You mean you could really love me like a grown-up man?"

"Try me, woman."

He moved in on her. Soon the woman started moaning with excitement, calling out his name. "Honey Drizzle, Honey Drizzle, you *are* a man." In a breathy, stammering voice, she said, "A real man."

Her attractiveness made Honey Drizzle ignore her relative old age. The Maasai believe that if an older and a younger person have intercourse, it is the older person who stands to gain. For instance, it is believed that an older woman having an affair with a young man starts to appear younger and healthier, while the young man grows older and unhealthy.

The following day when the initiation rites had ended, I decided to return home. I had offended my father by staying away from home without his consent, so I prepared myself for whatever punishment he might inflict on me. I walked home alone.

The Secrets of Haiti's Living Dead

A Harvard botanist investigates mystic potions, voodoo rites, and the making of zombies.

Gino Del Guercio

Gino Del Guercio is a national science writer for United Press International, currently on leave studying television production as a Macy fellow at Boston's WGBH.

Five years ago, a man walked into l'Estère, a village in central Haiti, approached a peasant woman named Angelina Narcisse, and identified himself as her brother Clairvius. If he had not introduced himself using a boyhood nickname and mentioned facts only intimate family members knew, she would not have believed him. Because, eighteen years earlier, Angelina had stood in a small cemetery north of her village and watched as her brother Clairvius was buried.

The man told Angelina he remembered that night well. He knew when he was lowered into his grave, because he was fully conscious, although he could not speak or move. As the earth was thrown over his coffin, he felt as if he were floating over the grave. The scar on his right cheek, he said, was caused by a nail driven through his casket.

The night he was buried, he told Angelina, a voodoo priest raised him from the grave. He was beaten with a sisal whip and carried off to a sugar plantation in northern Haiti where, with other zombies, he was forced to work as a slave. Only with the death of the zombie master were they able to escape, and Narcisse eventually returned home.

Legend has it that zombies are the living dead, raised from their graves and animated by malevolent voodoo sorcerers, usually for some evil purpose. Most Haitians believe in zombies, and Narcisse's claim is not unique. At about the time he reappeared, in 1980, two women turned up in other villages saying they were zombies. In the same year, in northern Haiti, the local peasants claimed to have found a group of zombies wandering aimlessly in the fields.

But Narcisse's case was different in one crucial respect; it was documented. His death had been recorded by doctors at the American-directed Schweitzer Hospital in Deschapelles. On April 30, 1962, hospital records show, Narcisse walked into the hospital's emergency room spitting up blood. He was feverish and full of aches. His doctors could not diagnose his illness, and his symptoms grew steadily worse. Three days after he entered the hospital, according to the records, he died. The attending physicians, an American among them, signed his death certificate. His body was placed in cold storage for twenty hours, and then he was buried. He said he remembered hearing his doctors pronounce him dead while his sister wept at his bedside.

At the Centre de Psychiatrie et Neurologie in Port-au-Prince, Dr. Lamarque Douyon, a Haitian-born, Canadian-trained psychiatrist, has been systematically investigating all reports of zombies since 1961. Though convinced zombies were real, he had been unable to find a scientific explanation for the phenomenon. He did not believe zombies were people raised from the dead, but that did not make them any less interesting. He speculated that victims were only made to *look* dead, probably by means of a drug that dramatically slowed metabolism. The victim was buried, dug up within a few hours, and somehow reawakened.

The Narcisse case provided Douyon with evidence strong enough to warrant a request for assistance from colleagues in New York. Douyon wanted to find an ethnobotanist, a traditional-medicines expert, who could track down the zombie potion he was sure existed. Aware of the medical potential of a drug that could dramatically lower metabolism, a group organized by the late Dr. Nathan Kline—a New York psychiatrist and pioneer in the field of psychopharmacology—raised the funds necessary to send someone to investigate.

The search for that someone led to the Harvard Botanical Museum, one of the world's foremost institutes of ethnobiology. Its director, Richard Evans Schultes, Jeffrey professor of biology, had spent thirteen years in the tropics studying native medicines. Some of his best-known work is the investigation of curare, the substance used by the nomadic people of the Amazon to poison their darts. Refined into a powerful muscle relaxant called D-tubocurarine, it is now an essential component of the anesthesia used during almost all surgery.

Schultes would have been a natural for the Haitian investigation, but he was too busy. He recommended another Harvard ethnobotanist for the assignment, Wade Davis, a 28-year-old Canadian pursuing a doctorate in biology.

Davis grew up in the tall pine forests of British Columbia and entered Harvard in 1971, influenced by a Life magazine story on the student strike of 1969. Before Harvard, the only Americans he had known were draft dodgers, who seemed very exotic. "I used to fight forest fires with them," Davis says. "Like everybody else, I thought America was where it was at. And I wanted to go to Harvard because of that Life article. When I got there, I realized it wasn't quite what I had in mind."

Davis took a course from Schultes, and when he decided to go to South America to study plants, he approached his professor for guidance. "He was an extraordinary figure," Davis remembers. "He was a man who had done it all. He had lived alone for years in the Amazon." Schultes sent Davis to the rain forest with two letters of introduction and two pieces of advice: wear a pith helmet and try ayahuasca, a powerful hallucinogenic vine. During that expedition and others, Davis proved himself an "outstanding field man," says his mentor. Now, in early 1982, Schultes called him into his office and asked if he had plans for spring break.

"I always took to Schultes's assignments like a plant takes to water," says Davis, tall and blond, with inquisitive blue eyes. "Whatever Shultes told me to do, I did. His letters of introduction opened up a whole world." This time the world was Haiti.

Davis knew nothing about the Caribbean island—and nothing about African traditions, which serve as Haiti's cultural basis. He certainly did not believe in zombies. "I thought it was a lark," he says now.

Davis landed in Haiti a week after his conversation with Schultes, armed with a hypothesis about how the zombie drug—if it existed—might be made. Setting out to explore, he discovered a country materially impoverished, but rich in culture and mystery. He was impressed by the cohesion of Haitian society; he found none of the crime,

social disorder, and rampant drug and alcohol abuse so common in many of the other Caribbean islands. The cultural wealth and cohesion, he believes, spring from the country's turbulent history.

During the French occupation of the late eighteenth century, 370,000 African-born slaves were imported to Haiti between 1780 and 1790. In 1791, the black population launched one of the few successful slave revolts in history, forming secret societies and overcoming first the French plantation owners and then a detachment of troops from Napoleon's army, sent to quell the revolt. For the next hundred years Haiti was the only independent black republic in the Caribbean, populated by people who did not forget their African heritage. "You can almost argue that Haiti is more African than Africa," Davis says. "When the west coast of Africa was being disrupted by colonialism and the slave trade, Haiti was essentially left alone. The amalgam of beliefs in Haiti is unique, but it's very, very African."

Davis discovered that the vast majority of Haitian peasants practice voodoo, a sophisticated religion with African roots. Says Davis, "It was immediately obvious that the stereotypes of voodoo weren't true. Going around the countryside, I found clues to a whole complex social world." Vodounists believe they communicate directly with, indeed are often possessed by, the many spirits who populate the everyday world. Vodoun society is a system of education, law, and medicine; it embodies a code of ethics that regulates social behavior. In rural areas, secret vodoun societies, much like those found on the west coast of Africa, are as much or more in control of everyday life as the Haitian government.

Although most outsiders dismissed the zombie phenomenon as folklore, some early investigators, convinced of its reality, tried to find a scientific explanation. The few who sought a zombie drug failed. Nathan Kline, who helped finance Davis's expedition, had searched unsuccessfully, as had Lamarque Douyon, the Haitian psychiatrist. Zora Neale Hurston, an American black woman, may have come closest. An anthropological pioneer, she went to Haiti in the Thirties, studied vodoun

society, and wrote a book on the subject, *Tell My Horse,* first published in 1938. She knew about the secret societies and was convinced zombies were real, but if a powder existed, she too failed to obtain it.

Davis obtained a sample in a few weeks.

He arrived in Haiti with the names of several contacts. A BBC reporter familiar with the Narcisse case had suggested he talk with Marcel Pierre. Pierre owned the Eagle Bar, a bordello in the city of Saint Marc. He was also a voodoo sorcerer and had supplied the BBC with a physiologically active powder of unknown ingredients. Davis found him willing to negotiate. He told Pierre he was a representative of "powerful but anonymous interests in New York," willing to pay generously for the priest's services, provided no questions were asked. Pierre agreed to be helpful for what Davis will only say was a "sizable sum." Davis spent a day watching Pierre gather the ingredients—including human bones—and grind them together with mortar and pestle. However, from his knowledge of poison, Davis knew immediately that nothing in the formula could produce the powerful effects of zombification.

Three weeks later, Davis went back to the Eagle Bar, where he found Pierre sitting with three associates. Davis challenged him. He called him a charlatan. Enraged, the priest gave him a second vial, claiming that this was the real poison. Davis pretended to pour the powder into his palm and rub it into his skin. "You're a dead man," Pierre told him, and he might have been, because this powder proved to be genuine. But, as the substance had not actually touched him, Davis was able to maintain his bravado, and Pierre was impressed. He agreed to make the poison and show Davis how it was done.

The powder, which Davis keeps in a small vial, looks like dry black dirt. It contains parts of toads, sea worms, lizards, tarantulas, and human bones. (To obtain the last ingredient, he and Pierre unearthed a child's grave on a nocturnal trip to the cemetery.) The poison is rubbed into the victim's skin. Within hours he begins to feel nauseated and has difficulty breathing. A pins-

and-needles sensation afflicts his arms and legs, then progresses to the whole body. The subject becomes paralyzed; his lips turn blue for lack of oxygen. Quickly—sometimes within six hours—his metabolism is lowered to a level almost indistinguishable from death.

As Davis discovered, making the poison is an inexact science. Ingredients varied in the five samples he eventually acquired, although the active agents were always the same. And the poison came with no guarantee. Davis speculates that sometimes instead of merely paralyzing the victim, the compound kills him. Sometimes the victim suffocates in the coffin before he can be resurrected. But clearly the potion works well enough often enough to make zombies more than a figment of Haitian imagination.

Analysis of the powder produced another surprise. "When I went down to Haiti originally," says Davis, "my hypothesis was that the formula would

contain *concombre zombi,* the 'zombie's cucumber,' which is a *Datura* plant. I thought somehow *Datura* was used in putting people down." *Datura* is a powerful psychoactive plant, found in West Africa as well as other tropical areas and used there in ritual as well as criminal activities. Davis had found *Datura* growing in Haiti. Its popular name suggested the plant was used in creating zombies.

But, says Davis, "there were a lot of problems with the *Datura* hypothesis. Partly it was a question of how the drug was administered. *Datura* would create a stupor in huge doses, but it just wouldn't produce the kind of immobility that was key. These people had to appear dead, and there aren't many drugs that will do that."

One of the ingredients Pierre included in the second formula was a dried fish, a species of puffer or blowfish, common to most parts of the world. It gets its name from its ability to fill itself with

water and swell to several times its normal size when threatened by predators. Many of these fish contain a powerful poison known as tetrodotoxin. One of the most powerful nonprotein poisons known to man, tetrodotoxin turned up in every sample of zombie powder that Davis acquired.

Numerous well-documented accounts of puffer fish poisoning exist, but the most famous accounts come from the Orient, where *fugu* fish, a species of puffer, is considered a delicacy. In Japan, special chefs are licensed to prepare *fugu.* The chef removes enough poison to make the fish nonlethal, yet enough remains to create exhilarating physiological effects—tingles up and down the spine, mild prickling of the tongue and lips, euphoria. Several dozen Japanese die each year, having bitten off more than they should have.

"When I got hold of the formula and saw it was the *fugu* fish, that suddenly

Richard Schultes

His students continue his tradition of pursuing botanical research in the likeliest of unlikely places.

Richard Evans Schultes, Jeffrey professor of biology emeritus, has two homes, and they could not be more different. The first is Cambridge, where he served as director of the Harvard Botanical Museum from 1970 until last year, when he became director emeritus. During his tenure he interested generations of students in the exotic botany of the Amazon rain forest. His impact on the field through his own research is worldwide. The scholarly ethnobotanist with steel-rimmed glasses, bald head, and white lab coat is as much a part of the Botanical Museum as the thousands of plant specimens and botanical texts on the museum shelves.

In his austere office is a picture of a crew-cut, younger man stripped to the waist, his arms decorated with

tribal paint. This is Schultes's other persona. Starting in 1941, he spent thirteen years in the rain forests of South America, living with the Indians and studying the plants they use for medicinal and spiritual purposes.

Schultes is concerned that many of the people he has studied are giving up traditional ways. "The people of so-called primitive societies are becoming civilized and losing all their forefathers' knowledge of plant lore," he says. "We'll be losing the tremendous amounts of knowledge they've gained over thousands of years. We're interested in the practical aspects with the hope that new medicines and other things can be developed for our own civilization."

Schultes's exploits are legendary in the biology department. Once, while gathering South American plant specimens hundreds of miles from civilization, he contracted beriberi. For forty days he fought creeping paralysis and overwhelming fatigue as he paddled back to a doctor. "It was an extraordinary feat of endurance," says disciple Wade

Davis. "He is really one of the last nineteenth-century naturalists."

Hallucinogenic plants are one of Schultes's primary interests. As a Harvard undergraduate in the Thirties, he lived with Oklahoma's Kiowa Indians to observe their use of plants. He participated in their peyote ceremonies and wrote his thesis on the hallucinogenic cactus. He has also studied other hallucinogens, such as morning glory seeds, sacred mushrooms, and ayahuasca, a South American vision vine. Schultes's work has led to the development of anesthetics made from curare and alternative sources of natural rubber.

Schultes's main concern these days is the scientific potential of plants in the rapidly disappearing Amazon jungle. "If chemists are going to get material on 80,000 species and then analyze them, they'll never finish the job before the jungle is gone," he says. "The short cut is to find out what the [native] people have learned about the plant properties during many years of living in the very rich flora."

—G.D.G.

threw open the whole Japanese literature," says Davis. Case histories of *fugu* poisoning read like accounts of zombification. Victims remain conscious but unable to speak or move. A man who had "died" after eating *fugu* recovered seven days later in the morgue. Several summers ago, another Japanese poisoned by *fugu* revived after he was nailed into his coffin. "Almost all of Narcisse's symptoms correlated. Even strange things such as the fact that he said he was conscious and could hear himself pronounced dead. Stuff that I thought had to be magic, that seemed crazy. But, in fact, that is what people who get *fugu*-fish poisoning experience."

Davis was certain he had solved the mystery. But far from being the end of his investigation, identifying the poison was, in fact, its starting point. "The drug alone didn't make zombies," he explains. "Japanese victims of pufferfish poisoning don't become zombies, they become poison victims. All the drug could do was set someone up for a whole series of psychological pressures that would be rooted in the culture. I wanted to know why zombification was going on," he says.

He sought a cultural answer, an explanation rooted in the structure and beliefs of Haitian society. Was zombification simply a random criminal activity? He thought not. He had discovered that Clairvius Narcisse and "Ti Femme," a second victim he interviewed, were village pariahs. Ti Femme was regarded as a thief. Narcisse had abandoned his children and deprived his brother of land that was rightfully his. Equally suggestive, Narcisse claimed that his aggrieved brother had sold him to a *bokor,* a voodoo priest who dealt in black magic; he made cryptic reference to having been tried and found guilty by the "masters of the land."

Gathering poisons from various parts of the country, Davis had come into direct contact with the vodoun secret societies. Returning to the anthropological literature on Haiti and pursuing his contacts with informants, Davis came to understand the social matrix within which zombies were created.

Davis's investigations uncovered the importance of the secret societies. These groups trace their origins to the bands of escaped slaves that organized the revolt against the French in the late eighteenth century. Open to both men and women, the societies control specific territories of the country. Their meetings take place at night, and in many rural parts of Haiti the drums and wild celebrations that characterize the gatherings can be heard for miles.

Davis believes the secret societies are responsible for policing their communities, and the threat of zombification is one way they maintain order. Says Davis, "Zombification has a material basis, but it also has a societal logic." To the uninitiated, the practice may appear a random criminal activity, but in rural vodoun society, it is exactly the opposite— a sanction imposed by recognized authorities, a form of capital punishment. For rural Haitians, zombification is an even more severe punishment than death, because it deprives the subject of his most valued possessions: his free will and independence.

The vodounists believe that when a person dies, his spirit splits into several different parts. If a priest is powerful enough, the spiritual aspect that controls a person's character and individuality, known as *ti bon ange,* the "good little angel," can be captured and the corporeal aspect, deprived of its will, held as a slave.

From studying the medical literature on tetrodotoxin poisoning, Davis discovered that if a victim survives the first few hours of the poisoning, he is likely to recover fully from the ordeal. The subject simply revives spontaneously. But zombies remain without will, in a trance-like state, a condition vodounists attribute to the power of the priest. Davis thinks it possible that the psychological trauma of zombification may be augmented by *Datura* or some other drug; he thinks zombies may be fed a *Datura* paste that accentuates their disorientation. Still, he puts the material basis of zombification in perspective: "Tetrodotoxin and *Datura* are only templates on which cultural forces and beliefs may be amplified a thousand times."

Davis has not been able to discover how prevalent zombification is in Haiti. "How many zombies there are is not the question," he says. He compares it to capital punishment in the United States: "It doesn't really matter how many people are electrocuted, as long as it's a possibility." As a sanction in Haiti, the fear is not of zombies, it's of becoming one.

Davis attributes his success in solving the zombie mystery to his approach. He went to Haiti with an open mind and immersed himself in the culture. "My intuition unhindered by biases served me well," he says. "I didn't make any judgments." He combined this attitude with what he had learned earlier from his experiences in the Amazon. "Schultes's lesson is to go and live with the Indians as an Indian." Davis was able to participate in the vodoun society to a surprising degree, eventually even penetrating one of the Bizango societies and dancing in their nocturnal rituals. His appreciation of Haitian culture is apparent. "Everybody asks me how did a white person get this information? To ask the question means you don't understand Haitians— they don't judge you by the color of your skin."

As a result of the exotic nature of his discoveries, Davis has gained a certain notoriety. He plans to complete his dissertation soon, but he has already finished writing a popular account of his adventures. To be published in January by Simon and Schuster, it is called *The Serpent and the Rainbow,* after the serpent that vodounists believe created the earth and the rainbow spirit it married. Film rights have already been optioned; in October Davis went back to Haiti with a screenwriter. But Davis takes the notoriety in stride. "All this attention is funny," he says. "For years, not just me, but all Schultes's students have had extraordinary adventures in the line of work. The adventure is not the end point, it's just along the way of getting the data. At the Botanical Museum, Schultes created a world unto itself. We didn't think we were doing anything above the ordinary. I still don't think we do. And you know," he adds, "the Haiti episode does not begin to compare to what others have accomplished—particularly Schultes himself."

A Writer in a World of Spirits

Philip Graham

Philip Graham has published fiction in The New Yorker, *the* Washington Post Magazine, Chicago Review, *and elsewhere. He is the author of a collection of prose poems,* The Vanishings *(Release Press, 1978), and short stories,* The Art of the Knock *(William Morrow, 1985). He is currently completing a new short story collection,* Interior Design, *and is also collaborating with his wife on a nonfiction book about their African experiences. He teaches at the University of Illinois.*

Living in a rural west African village, I quickly discovered, was like living in an anti-artists' colony. I remember that first week, sitting with my wife at our desk in the open courtyard of our two-room mud hut, the center of a crowd of curious villagers. They whispered—almost certainly about us—in a language I knew I would have to learn. I tried not to think of that; instead, I gazed steadily at my typewriter, about to touch the keys. Then I felt a hand behind me tentatively stroke my hair, the cautious fingers intrigued by its smoothness. Trying to appear nonchalant, I proceeded to type.

This was in the fall of 1979, long before my first glimpse of the variegated ways of spirits. For the next fourteen months I struggled with a manuscript of interrelated stories I had brought with me—stories long in progress, stories that would not let me go—while my wife, the cultural anthropologist Alma Gottlieb, studied the social and religious systems of the Beng, a small and little-known ethnic group in Ivory Coast. Every day we sat outside at that desk, because in Beng culture all the ordinary, daily tasks are done outdoors: only witches, we were quickly told, stayed indoors for any length of time. So we were constantly surrounded by young girls laughing and arguing as they tressed each other's hair; mothers nursing and washing their babies; men in bright robes tying vine strips to make strong cord; gnarled old women roasting corn over an open fire; round-bellied children crying out a sudden, temporary grief or indulging in the simple pleasure of chasing themselves around our desk; and then there were the starers, those who just couldn't get their fill of us. (From the beginning it often seemed that *we* were being studied, because Alma and I were as strange to the Beng as they were to us.)

All this was the grist of anthropology: in a small village where everyone's history and daily behavior are known and shared, the more people around us, the busier Alma was. She quickly discovered that even a simple, halting question could open up worlds, and she dove eagerly into the confusing welter of kinship ties and food taboos. But I yearned for a solitude that I could no longer successfully imagine. The Beng didn't understand why I sat so quietly, rubbing my chin, pulling at my mustache, and intermittently scribbling marks on a piece of paper, and I didn't know how to tell them that with each interruption I felt the characters in my stories lose their outlines, their words becoming inaudible and my latest sentence evaporating, until the world I was trying to create was gone.

"I'm a storyteller," was the best I could manage when I tried to explain myself, but in their culture, which has a well-developed oral literature, stories are for *telling,* and I still made the simplest errors in daily conversation. Often Alma and I sat in on late night storytelling sessions and listened to uproarious tales, judging from the audience's reactions, told in a language we had difficulty following.

Once I was asked to tell one of my own short stories. I accepted, though it would be difficult, for Alma and I would have to translate from English to French, and Yacouba, a friend of ours in the village, would translate our French into proper Beng.

"My story," I began, looking at the dark faces lit by our lantern, "is about a man whose shadow left him."

An elder quickly asked, through our chain of translation, "Kouadio"—my Beng name—"was this the work of spirits?"

"No," I replied, a bit startled. Then I continued, saying that the man had stayed in his house for days, struggling with his fluid shadow.

"Inside all day? That man is a witch," a woman interrupted once my words were translated.

The elder interrupted again, triumphant. "The spirits *were* responsible," he said. "They took the man's shadow away because he was a witch."

We continued, though our tedious process of translation didn't make for compelling storytelling, and even sim-

Village of Kosangbe, where Graham and Gottlieb lived in 1979 and 1980

ple details such as a rocking chair or double-dating provoked elaborate discussions. I was reminded of the anthropologist Laura Bohannon's famous account of her difficulties telling the story of Hamlet to the Tiv of Nigeria. Here I was in my own small muddle: simply by being good listeners, the Beng were deconstructing and reconstructing my story before me, drawing me into their own foreign fiction.

Overwhelmed by the lack of common cultural categories and the need for an often unobtainable solitude, I found myself less and less able to write, and the still keys of my typewriter presented a silent, untranslatable reproach. Though each morning I treated villagers for fevers, infected cuts and other illnesses with our small supply of medicine and my limited knowledge, I still felt I had no identity the Beng could easily categorize. I realized I needed some sort of rite of passage, and suddenly it made sense to ask the very culture that afflicted me for a cure. Alma and I approached Kona, our village host, and we told him, in our best Beng, "Kouadio's

work isn't going well." This was the only translation we could come up with to describe my writer's block. And then we asked that I be taken to a diviner. Kona's polite face, always so patient during our awkward struggles with his language, stiffened, for the Beng were reluctant to discuss religious knowledge. But as our host, Kona couldn't deny our request.

Within a week we travelled to a distant village to meet Akissi, a noted diviner. I'm not sure what we expected, but we were surprised that Akissi looked no different from any other village woman—simple blouse and wrapped-cloth skirt, her hair bound by a scarf. We sat before her in her mud house, which was no different from any other mud house. A crowd of villagers gaped and jostled at the doorway, which was open, I suspected, because Akissi wanted to advertise her unusual clients.

Between us, on an animal skin, I placed a copy of my first book, a slim volume of prose poems; a copy of *The New Yorker* containing one of my stories; and a recent, unfinished manu-

script. Akissi examined all three piles, especially the glossy magazine ads. She then held a brass pan that contained a few black pebbles and a small amount of water made milky by the addition of white powder. She turned the bowl in her hands, watching how the pebbles settled. We learned much later that spirits were drawn by the powder—which was sacred—and they then spoke to Akissi. At the time, we hadn't felt ourselves in the presence of spirits; instead we simply saw pebbles circling in a bowl.

Once done, Akissi announced with quiet confidence that I was being bewitched by a jealous writer in my country who wished harm to come to me while abroad: if I sacrificed a white hen on the next sacred day, and then a goat once I began to write, I would be safe. We thanked and paid Akissi, and then we drank sweet and heady palm wine with her before leaving. Later that evening Alma and I lay in bed in our mud house and whispered about the "jealous writer," and we jokingly checked off a seemingly endless list of possible culprits.

Graham taking part in dance

Gottlieb sits with drummers during dance

But I was determined to go through with Akissi's cure. When the first sacrifice was performed, Alma took careful notes while the animist priest prayed and poured blood over the sticky, exposed roots of a sacred tree. I felt that with this public ceremony I was passing some uncharted boundary, because even though the Beng may not have known exactly what troubled me, it was now understood that I was cured. A few days later I began to write again.

As I worked at my typewriter in the morning, often a line of men, hoes in hand, would walk by on their way to work in the fields. "Kouadio! Come with us!" they shouted, most assuredly out of politeness, for whenever I worked in the fields I was a disappointment. I had once helped build long rows of yam mounds, digging with a hand hoe, but developed so many blisters that I couldn't type for days; another time I had helped harvest coffee but mistakenly worked too close to a nest of fire ants. As the men called to me again, I pointed to my typewriter and called back, as I always did, "This is my field." We laughed at our common, daily joke. And while I thought I had made my point, I was still interrupted again and again each day, as a farmer working in the fields would never be. Somehow my metaphor of the typewriter as farm didn't really address what was important to the Beng.

With my usual faith in the power of fiction, I turned to the books I'd brought with me to the village, hoping they would help make sense of my new world. My greatest disappointment was Conrad's Africa in *Heart of Darkness,* where "simple people" whose faces were "grotesque masks" spoke a language consisting of "short, grunting phrases." I was surprised and chagrined to read that Kurtz simply walked into the rain forest and took over a tribe with an ease that implied there was a cultural and linguistic vacuum he had no trouble filling. This was as far as possible from our own experience, for we had spent over a month just learning the seemingly infinite variations of how to say hello and

when to say thank you, and we still struggled with the difficulties of conjugating pronouns along with verbs in the Beng tonal language. Often we lay in bed in the mornings, listening to the heavy echoing throughout the village of women pounding yams with mortars and pestles, and we were reluctant to get up. We knew that our continued faltering in the local system of common sense placed us closer to the category of children than adults, and that before the day was over we would make fools of ourselves many times over.

Yet one book I had brought with me did convey the mood of my new existence. Ovid's *Metamorphoses,* with its constant transformations from the ordinary to the fantastic, echoed those interpenetrations of different realities that abounded in Beng daily life. There was a disturbing young girl in our village who behaved oddly, laughing while adults spoke, interrupting families while they ate together, running randomly through the village, her eyes and movements awkward, wild. She seemed to us, even given the different cultural context, mildly retarded. Once in passing we mentioned her to Amenan, a serious and sad-faced friend from another village.

"That girl's really a snake," Amenan said, and she proceeded to tell us how a pregnant woman, eating a yam while walking through the forest, might inadvertently drop a piece; if a snake is nearby it will eat the yam and be filled with an overwhelming desire for human food. The snake's soul will enter the woman's womb, possess her unborn child, and then be born into the human world. But this snake, unused to four limbs and language, must forever struggle through its new existence.

Though strange at first, such everyday beliefs, as invisible and all-pervasive as air, became the world we lived in, restricting our movements by the force of their gravity, but also allowing us, as we continued to breathe them in, to move with increasing grace. I began to feel myself in a vast novel written by Beng culture, a novel of uncountable chapters.

The Beng were Alma's subject, however, not mine, and I didn't want to write stories about village life because I knew enough of it to understand how ignorant I was of its complexities. Initially, I wasn't sure what in this unfamiliar culture might engage my imagination, or what within me might be drawn to it. I did know, however, that I wasn't interested in thinly disguised autobiography or the average adventure story that could be built from the surprise visit of a poisonous snake in our hut, the attacks of malaria, the invasion of an army ant horde. What my life among the Beng slowly gave me was an added respect for the extraordinary range of human inventiveness. I began to see my own culture and my ordinary American characters as alien. I began to glimpse what strange worlds *we* have within us.

But I struggled constantly to maintain this amphibious consciousness, to fuse the insistent call of my stories with the call of the odd and exciting events around me. Accompanying Alma to another village for a three-day funeral, while she took notes and I participated in the mourning dances, I found myself perversely longing to return my attention to the fate of a character in one of my stories. Yet when seated back at my desk, in the midst of the pleasure of trying to uncurl a stubborn sentence, I felt the need to walk around the village, to see if the unhappy snake child was up to some mischief, or to help a neighbor wash newly harvested kola nuts.

One day I left the desk and walked among millions of tiny, gray-green butterflies that had suddenly appeared and were flying about through the village. For the Beng, who experience this every year, it simply signalled the end of the dry season, a time to take out hoes and prepare for the coming planting. But I wandered about astonished, as the multitudes of butterflies parted before me like some ever-transforming, ever-receding curtain, a living metaphor of the protean Beng world shimmering before me and always retreating as I approached.

Once these two worlds did, frighteningly, meet. Kona, our village host, and I were bicycling together to a

191

funeral on the day of the annual yam festival, the most sacred day of the year. This was a day when spirits, who usually keep to the forests, are able to come out onto the roads, sometimes making travel dangerous. Unfortunately, I didn't yet know this last, essential bit of information, which was fine with Kona. He *had* to attend the funeral, being a close relative, and he was bringing me along so he wouldn't have to travel alone.

A short distance from our village we got off our bicycles to climb a steep hill. The bike I had borrowed was a wobbly affair, with only the left front brake working, but I didn't mind. I was happy to be alone with Kona, a knowledgeable elder, and I hoped he might tell me something interesting that I could report to Alma. With this in mind, as I pushed my bicycle along I casually mentioned the spirits who, I had heard, lived on the hill.

"No spirits live here," he said.

"Yes they do," I continued in my best Beng. "Remember the trucks?" Months earlier, in the rainy season, overloaded trucks had got stuck on the muddy, steep hill. The stranded drivers, on the advice of the villagers, made sacrifices to the hill spirits while they waited for rescue trucks.

"There are no spirits here," Kona nervously insisted, because, as he knew and I didn't, the spirits were out and listening.

What I *did* know was that Kona was normally cautious about speaking on any religious subject when other people were present, but since we were alone I continued to press him, recounting what little I knew of spirits, amazed that he denied it all.

He must have been relieved when we reached the top of the hill and climbed back on our bikes. Soon we were speeding down the other side of the hill. But a foolish stubbornness had taken hold of me.

"Kona," I said, "there *are* spirits here, can't you hear them? They're calling us!" And then I jokingly shouted out his name. The look of alarm on his face surprised me. At once I tried to reassure him, and as I called out my own name—"Kouadio!"—I realized I was

speeding down the hill too fast. I pulled on the brakes and they snapped. The front wheel twisted in and I was sent tumbling through the air.

Kona ran to me as I picked myself up. I had only cuts and bruises on my arms and legs, though I was quite shaken, and I dimly understood that I had received far less than I deserved. Kona accompanied me back the village, where word quickly passed around: "The hill spirits caught Kouadio." Slowly I began to realize that I had flown from one world into another, from a world of rickety bicycles and unreliable brakes to a world of angry spirits who meted out swift punishment.

Here indeed was a graphic example of my amphibious consciousness. As I limped about the village for the next few days, I was unwilling to explain away spirits as mere abstract "beliefs," though I was also unwilling to claim that spirits actually existed. Nevertheless, I remained silent whenever I again travelled over that hill, embarrassed by my concern that any possible spirits might recognize my voice. For the rest of our time among the Beng, and for years after we left, that split consciousness remained my own transforming curtain, endlessly parting inside me.

When we returned to Africa in the summer of 1985, this elusive curtain came to rest for me, in large part because Alma was now perceived by the Beng as an important chronicler of their culture. In the years since our first stay, a few bad harvests had driven a number of young Beng to the urban centers of Ivory Coast, and those who eventually returned brought city ways back with them. The elders felt that their traditions were in danger of fading, and Alma was now seen as an ally. She was taken on as an informal apprentice in Beng religion by Kokora Kouassi, a respected animist priest and the uncle of Amenan, Alma's best friend among the Beng. As for me, I typed out what I could, sometimes escaping the commotion of village life by tapping palm wine in the forest with Amenan's husband Kofi, an excellent teacher who was happy to have a

helper. More often, I sat beside Alma while she interviewed Kouassi.

Because Kouassi was imparting secrets, they worked in the empty room of a granary, enough out of the way to afford an almost unheard-of-quality among the Beng: privacy. Though I sat in a corner and scratched away at a manuscript, I often put is aside to listen, delighted, as Kouassi revealed to Alma, in greater detail than ever before, the world of spirits. He explained the downfall of the madwoman of the village, whose courtyard faced the back of our mud house. Each morning when we opened the wooden shutters of our bedroom she was the first person we saw, sometimes slapping the ground aimlessly with a stick, sometimes scandalously bathing in the open. During the rest of the day this sad, dazed woman wandered through the village, mumbling and mangling the various intricate greetings. Years ago she had had a bitter argument with her father. In anger he cursed her, and long after he died his curse worked in this manner: once while burning the underbrush in the forest as part of slash-and-burn farming, her fire went out of control and spread to a nearby and well-known invisible spirit village. Diviners later told her that the spirits cursed her for destroying their village, and soon after this she went mad.

We were told of the spirits who lived in the tall iroko tree dominating the nearby coffee fields and who sometimes could be heard singing at night, a whistling wind. A hundred yards farther away in the rain forest was another spirit village, the home of a polygamous spirit man who flew at night from one invisible village to another, visiting each of his two wives, and whose path was through our courtyard. The sound of the wind on those nights was the sound of his flight. Indeed, we discovered that the wind itself was the very movement and sound of all spirits, and in the forest encircling the village each swaying tree and shaking branch was their transfigured presence.

Soon Alma and I grew attuned to the order of invisible beings, as Kouassi carefully recounted to us the cosmol-

Gottlieb interviews Kokora Kouassi, animist priest, while stripping dried corn from cobs

ogy that was carried inside every person we passed on a village path or bargained with in the market: another universe in familiar bodies, and the multiplication, in a crowd, of strange, shared secrets. The spirits lived *within* the Beng and therefore around them as well, for those interior presences also filled up their outer world.

During one of their sessions, Kouassi told Alma of the different sorts of objects diviners can employ to attract spirits—red cloth, white powder, small statues. Drawn to these objects, spirits then speak to diviners, revealing the causes of an illness and who is bewitching whom. Diviners, Kouassi said, are the point where the spirit and human worlds communicate.

As Alma was writing this down, I remarked, "It sounds a bit like what a writer does. We hear voices too."

"Right," she agreed, turning to Kouassi. "That's like what Kouadio does."

"Kouadio?" he replied, his eyes squinting and skeptical in the dark room.

"Yes," Alma said, suddenly excited, "voices try to tell him their stories. And that's what he writes down."

"And my paper, and pen . . ." I said to her, and she understood.

"His paper and pen and typewriter," she repeated to Kouassi in Beng, "These are what he uses to draw the voices to him."

Kouassi watched me carefully, as I sat with my notebook in hand. I could see he understood. He had often seen me sitting silently in a corner and then suddenly scribbling furiously: a plausible enough sign of possession.

I turned to Alma, ready to speak, but she was ahead of me. "Yes!" she said to Kouassi, "That's why he shouldn't be interrupted when he's working, because then the voices leave, and their stories can't be written."

The next day when I sat at our desk in the middle of the compound, no one interrupted me while I wrote, for in the eyes of the Beng my typing was now a physical act that revealed a hidden world. I realized that in the past I had made the mistake of defending my writing solely as labor, my typewriter some sort of tiny, mechanical farm, each line of words another row of crops. But what the Beng understand best is the invisible, and for the rest of the summer, whenever I sat at my typewriter, I was both outside their world and within it: I wrote for hours, uninterrupted, visited by spirits the Beng could now see. I had finally found in this different society a complementary fit with my own culture, for what writer would disagree that we *are* possessed: by our imaginations, our interior voices, those gifts that surge up from within. Our characters call us, as we call them, and from that invisible, intuitive relationship our stories grow.

Back home in the United States, I write at a desk in a quiet, cloistered study, alone with my current marked-up manuscript. When I'm stalled before words that seem to harbor no revelations, I often think back to those pervasive spirits, and I wonder if I have too easily understood my relationship with them. Perhaps on our next trip to the Beng, their spirits will continue to reveal new secrets. But I'll have to wait to take any further, faltering steps in another round of knowledge, so I return to my struggles with the half-formed story before me that seeks to discover itself. Yet sometimes as I work I notice the wind rattling through the trees outside my window and then, like a strange dream dreamt again, I imagine another wind, one that takes the sound and shape of spirits.

Diviners between spirit & man — allows them to communicate

You've Gotta Have 'Wa'

*"Wa" is the Japanese ideal unity, team play and no individual heroes—
a concept that ex-U.S. major-leaguers playing in Japan
have had a lot of trouble grasping*

[handwritten: in Japan individualism is almost a dirty word]

Robert Whiting

"I don't know what it is they play here," grumbled former California Angel Clyde Wright after his first season as a Tokyo Giant. "All I know is, it ain't baseball." Wright had learned what many expatriates in the Land of the Rising Sun had known for years: baseball, Japanese-style, is not the same game that's played in the U.S. Since adopting the sport, the Japanese have changed it around to incorporate the values of samurai discipline, respect for authority and devotion to the group. The result is a uniquely Japanese game, one that offers perhaps the clearest expression among all sports of Japan's national character.

Like the American game, the Nippon version is played with a bat and ball. The same rulebook is also used, but that's where resemblance between the two ends. Training, for example, is nearly a religion in Japan. Baseball players in the U.S. start spring training in March and take no more than five or six weeks to prepare for the season. They spend three to four hours on the field each day and then head for the nearest golf course or swimming pool.

Japanese teams begin training in the freezing cold of mid-January. Each day they're on the field for a numbing eight hours, and then it's off to the dormitory for an evening of strategy sessions and still more workouts indoors. Players run 10 miles every day, and one team, the Taiyo Whales, periodically performs the "Death Climb," 20 sprints up and down the 275 steps of a nearby Shinto shrine.

That's only the beginning. The average Japanese game is more like a board meeting at Mitsubishi than an athletic event. As each new situation arises, there is so much discussion on the field among the manager, coaches and players that most games last three hours.

Unlike their counterparts in the States, losing managers in Japan are seldom fired outright. Instead, they go through an elaborate, time-consuming ritual designed to save face all around. It culminates with a public apology by the deposed skipper, his resignation and, often, an all-expenses-paid trip to the U.S. for him to "study baseball."

Such phenomena are the tip of the iceberg. Below the waterline are the concept and practice of group harmony, or *wa.* It is this concept that most dramatically differentiates Japanese baseball from the American game.

The U.S. is a land where the stubborn individualist is honored and where "doing your own thing" is a motto of contemporary society. In Japan, *kojinshugi,* the term for individualism, is almost a dirty word. In place of "doing your own thing," the Japanese have a proverb: "The nail that sticks up shall be hammered down." It is practically a national slogan.

In Japan, holdouts are rare. A player takes what the club gives him and that's that. Demanding more money is *kojinshugi* at its worst, because it shows the player has put his own interests before those of the team. Katsuya Nomura, the Nankai Hawk catcher who has hit 652 home runs in his career, said, upon quietly accepting a minuscule raise after winning yet another of his numerous home-run titles, "If I had asked for more money, the other players would have thought I was greedy."

The U.S. player lives by the rule: "*I know what's best for me.*" In Japan, the only ones who know what's best are the manager and coaches. They have the virtues Orientals most respect going for them—age and experience, hence, knowledge. Their word is law. In the interest of team harmony, they demand that everyone do everything the same way. Superstar Sadaharu Oh must endure the same pregame grind as the lowliest first-year player. At 38 Shinichi Eto, a three-time batting champion and a 10-year All-Star, found that 40 minutes of jogging and wind sprints before each game left him exhausted by game time. He asked to be allowed to train at his own pace. "You've been a great player, Eto-*san*," he was told, "but there are no exceptions on this club. You'll do things according to the rules." Eto lost weight, his batting average dropped, he spent the second half of the season on the bench and then reluctantly announced his retirement. Irrational? Perhaps, but any games lost because Eto was dog-tired were not as important as the example he set.

In the pressure-cooker world of U.S. pro sports, temper outbursts are considered acceptable, and at times even regarded as a salutary show of spirit. Unreleased frustrations, the reasoning goes, might negatively affect a player's concentration. Japanese players are expected to follow Sadaharu Oh's example. "When he strikes out," says an admirer, "he breaks into a smile and trots back to the bench." Oh has been known to be glum during a batting slump, but temper tantrums—along with practical joking, bickering, complaining and other norms of American clubhouse life—are viewed in Japan as unwelcome incursions into the team's collective peace of mind. They offend the finer sensitivities of the Japanese, and as many American players have learned the hard way, Japanese sensitivities are finer.

Michio Arito was the captain of the Lotte Orions, a 10-year veteran and the team's longtime batting mainstay. Because of a badly bruised hand he had been able to play only by taking a lot of painkillers, and before a crucial game that would, as it turned out, mean the pennant for the Orions, the manager decided to replace him with a healthier player. When Arito heard he'd been benched, he yelled, threw his glove and slammed his bat against the bench. Next day, at the Orions' victory party, Arito was summoned forth to atone for his sins. After bowing deeply to all, he said, "I am sorry for my childish actions yesterday. I have upset our team spirit and I deeply apologize."

Jim Lefebvre, a former Los Angeles Dodger infielder who spent five years in Japan, can still not quite believe what he saw there. "It's incredible," he says. "These guys are together almost all the time from January to October. They live together, eat together, play baseball together. I've never seen one fight, one argument. In the States, there's always somebody who mouths off and starts trouble."

If you ask a Japanese manager what he considers the most important ingredient of a winning team, he would most likely answer, *wa*. If you ask him how to knock a team's *wa* awry, he'd probably say, "Hire an American."

Former American major-leaguers have been an active part of Japanese baseball for 18 years. The somewhat lower level of play in Japan has given these *gaijin* (outsiders) a temporary reprieve from the athletic scrap heap. And although the Japanese have paid the *gaijin* high salaries, they have not been elated with the overall experience of having them on their teams.

Money is a particular sore point. Foreigners make two to three times as much as Japanese players of similar ability. This, combined with the free Western-style house and the other perks that the *gaijin* seem to view as inalienable rights, sets them too far above their teammates. And more than one American player has brought in an agent to negotiate his contract. That is considered to be in very bad taste. A contract discussion is regarded as a "family affair," with the official team interpreter, despite his obvious bias, acting as a go-between.

Avarice is only part of it, however. Deportment is the rest. Although few Americans hold a Japanese batting or pitching record, many have established standards in the area of bad conduct. For example, the amiable former Dodger Norm Larker set the Japan single-season high for smashed batting helmets, with eight. Joe Stanka, a 6'5", 220-pound behemoth, was ejected from games a record four times in his seven-year stay in Japan. Ken Aspromonte, who later managed the Cleveland Indians, was the first man in the history of Japanese baseball to be fined by his manager for "conduct unbecoming a ballplayer."

Aspromonte pulled off this feat during a sojourn with the Chunichi Dragons of Nagoya back in 1965. Furious after being called out on strikes, Aspromonte stormed back to the bench, kicked over chairs and launched the inevitable attack on the water cooler. He was just doing what comes naturally to many American players, but Dragon Manager Michio Nishizawa did not enjoy the show. He yanked Aspromonte out of the game and suspended him. An incredulous Aspromonte was fined $200 and required to visit Nishizawa's home and issue a formal apology to get back in his manager's good graces.

Other Americans have followed in Aspromonte's footsteps. Ex-Giant Daryl Spencer was one of the more memorable. Like most former major-leaguers, Spencer insisted on following his own training routine, and it was considerably easier than everyone else's. One night, as he was lackadaisically going through his pregame workout, his manager on the Hankyu Braves, Yukio Nishimoto, decided something had to be done.

"You don't look sharp, Spencer-*san*," he said. "You need a rest."

"What do you mean, I need a rest?" Spencer growled. "Who's leading this team in home runs, anyway?"

"I don't think you can hit this pitcher," Nishimoto said.

"I can't hit him? I'm batting .340 against that guy!"

"Not tonight. That's my feeling. You're out."

That was too much for Spencer to take. He was in the dressing room changing into street clothes when he heard his name announced in the starting lineup. Nishimoto had put Spencer down as the third batter, but only because he was planning to "fool" the opposition by inserting a pinch hitter in the first inning.

Now Spencer was smoldering. When the game began and he heard the name of the second batter over the loudspeaker, he decided to get even. Clad in his underwear and shower clogs, he headed for the dugout. Grabbing a bat and smirking in the direction of Nishimoto, he strode out to the on-deck circle to take a few practice swings.

Spencer's entrance delighted the fans, and his picture was in all the papers the next day. Nishimoto was not amused. He ordered Spencer off the field and slapped him with a suspension and a $200 fine. Spencer paid up, later reporting with a wide grin, "It was worth every penny."

In 1972, John Miller became the first American to be released solely for his misconduct. Miller, who played briefly for the Yankees and Dodgers, arrived in Japan in 1970 and soon became the most dangerous batter on the Chunichi Dragons. He was a battler. A U.S. coach once said, "Miller is the kind of guy I'd want on my team. He'll fight you with everything he has. He doesn't know how to quit."

However, Miller wasn't the kind of guy the Japanese wanted. He was seldom on time for practice. If a workout was scheduled for 2 p.m., Miller would arrive at 2:10. This was more serious than it sounds, because his teammates would invariably be raring to go by 1:50.

"He always had some excuse," says a team official. "One day it would be because the traffic was heavy. Another day, he missed the train. He never once said he was sorry."

When reprimanded for being late, Miller's response was most un-Oriental: "Japanese customs are too military. I do good in the games, don't I? What else matters?"

Miller's hot temper sealed his fate as a Dragon. The coup de grace came in the 12th inning of a big game. Miller had been slumping, and he had a bad game. He had been up four times without a hit. The fifth time, with the score tied, he was removed for a pinch hitter.

Miller blew his top. "You didn't have to take me out," he railed at his manager. "I've had it. I don't want to play for you anymore. I don't care if this team wins or not."

To Americans it would have been a fairly routine example of blowing off steam. To the Japanese, however, Miller might just as well have slit his throat. Although he later apologized and finished the year as the team leader in home runs, he was released at the end of the season. A second American on the team, Barton Shirley, who batted .190, was kept. He wasn't a battler.

Willie Kirkland, who had played for the Giants and Indians, was a happy-go-lucky sort who liked to tease his teammates. One day Kirkland was bemusedly watching an aging infielder who had recently been elevated to player-coach straining through a batting drill. "Hey, man, you're a coach now," Kirkland yelled playfully. "You don't have to practice anymore."

The player-coach took Kirkland's jest as a comment on his declining usefulness and he launched a roundhouse right that barely missed. It took half a dozen men to restrain him.

"I was just joking," Kirkland protested. "He was making fun of me," the unappeased coach retorted.

Kirkland left Japan with at least one enemy and considerable doubts about the Japanese sense of humor.

The Japanese didn't find Richie Scheinblum a barrel of laughs, either. A noted clubhouse wit in the U.S., Scheinblum spent his two years as a Hiroshima Carp baiting the umpires. Shane, as he was known on the club's official roster, was frequently agitated by the plate umpire's idea of Scheinblum's strike zone. It was considerably larger than the one Shane had in mind.

Scheinblum searched for a Japanese phrase to convey his sentiments to the men in blue, something that would really get under their collective skins. A Japanese friend came to the rescue, and soon Scheinblum was saying, "You lousy Korean" to arbiters who crossed him.

There is as much love lost between Koreans and Japanese as, say, between William Buckley and Gore Vidal. To the umpires, Scheinblum's taunts were

intolerable. To stop him, they imposed a stiff fine each time he uttered the dreaded epithet. When Scheinblum finally departed Japan for the last time, no cries of "Come back, Shane!" were heard—at least, not from the umpires.

It wasn't until Clyde Wright came along that rules of behavior for foreigners were finally codified. Wright, a pitcher of some note with the California Angels, made his first Japanese appearance, with the Yomiuri Giants, in 1976. A self-described "farm boy" from eastern Tennessee, Wright was regarded by those who knew him in America as a tough-as-nails competitor who didn't believe in hiding his feelings.

The Giants are something of a national institution in Japan. They are the oldest team, the winningest (12 pennants in the last 15 years) and by a million miles the most popular. Their games, all of which are nationally televised, get high ratings, and one out of two Japanese will tell you he is a Giant fan.

Their manager, Shigeo Nagashima, is the most beloved sports figure in the land. As a player he won a Central League-record six batting titles and was personally responsible for the most exciting moment in Japanese baseball history; a game-winning (or *sayonara*) home run in the only professional game Emperor Hirohito has ever attended. Sadaharu Oh plays for the Giants.

The Giants are the self-appointed custodians of national virtue. Popular belief has it that their players are neater, better mannered, more disciplined and more respectful than those of other clubs. Their *wa* is in better tune. In early 1977, when one writer, a former Giant player turned magazine reporter, suggested otherwise in print, he was forever banned from the team clubhouse. Among his blasphemous revelations were: 1) Some Giant players did not like other players on the team; 2) A few players thought Nagashima could be a better manager; 3) Some younger Giants did not especially care for the Saturday night 10 p.m. curfew at the team dormitory; 4) Some Giant wives objected to the season-long "energy-conserving" rule forbidding them to have sexual relations with their husbands. Tame material as far as exposés go, but to the *shoguns* of

Yomiuri, the Giant name had been desecrated, and someone had to pay.

Wright also faced the difficulty of being a foreigner on a team that traditionally liked to consider itself pure-blooded—Oh's Chinese ancestry and the few closet Koreans on the Giants notwithstanding. Wright was only the second non-Oriental *gaijin* to play for the team, and the sight of a fair-skinned American in a Giant uniform was a bit unsettling to the multitudes. Wright soon gave them reason to be even more unnerved. In the sixth inning of an early season game, with the score tied 1–1, Wright allowed the first two batters to get on base. Nagashima walked out on the field to take him out of the game. Few American managers would have removed him so abruptly. It was Nagashima's feeling, however, that Wright was getting weak, and that was that.

When Wright realized what was happening, he blew a gasket. To the horror of 50,000 fans at Tokyo's Korakuen Stadium and a Saturday night TV audience of millions, he brushed aside Nagashima's request for the ball and stalked off the mound, an angry scowl on his face. Halfway to the bench, he threw the ball against the dugout wall, cursed and disappeared into the clubhouse.

Once inside, he kicked over a trash can, ripped off his uniform, shredded it and flung it into the team bath. Amid a rapid-fire discharge of obscenities, he said something that the official team interpreter was able to understand, "Stupidest damn baseball I've ever seen. If this is the way the Giants treat their foreign ballplayers, I'm going. I've had it."

Nothing like this had ever happened on the Giants. Other teams had problems, but not the proud *Kyojin*. No one had ever shown this much disrespect for Nagashima. Crazy Wright, as he was instantly renamed by the press, became headline news in the sports dailies the next day. Letters, telegrams and phone calls poured into the Yomiuri offices. Outrageous! Inexcusable! Unforgivable! Wright should be sold. Released. Deported. Shot. Drawn and quartered. And not necessarily in that order.

Only Nagashima kept his cool. First, he patiently explained to his American pitcher that what he had done was not "stupid" baseball but simply the Japanese way of playing the game. It's a group effort. Then the manager faced the angry masses. There would be no disciplinary action. He was glad that Wright cared so much about winning. And he wished that some of his Japanese players would show as much fight.

Such benevolent words from the prince of Japanese baseball dissipated much of the public's antagonism toward Crazy Wright. It did not, however, pacify the front office. Management was not as eager as Nagashima-*san* to let Western ways penetrate their organization. They issued a set of 10 rules of etiquette that Wright and every other American player the Giants might henceforth deem worthy of their uniform would be obliged to obey.

The Japanese press quickly gave it a name: The *Gaijin* Ten Commandments. This is how they went:

1) Obey all orders issued by the manager.

2) Do not criticize the strategy of the manager.

3) Take good care of your uniform.

4) Do not scream and yell in the dugout or destroy objects in the clubhouse.

5) Do not reveal team secrets to other foreign players.

6) Do not severely tease your teammates.

7) In the event of injury, follow the treatment prescribed by the team.

8) Be on time.

9) Do not return home during the season.

10) Do not disturb the harmony of the team.

Willie Davis, then a practicing Buddhist, thought it would be different for him. Davis was perhaps the best all-round American player ever to come to Japan. He was a 17-year veteran of the major leagues and a former captain of the Los Angeles Dodgers. He had been an All-Star, he could run like a deer and hit and field with a grace and skill that few American big-leaguers, let alone Japanese, possessed. Even at 37, Davis could have continued to play in the U.S.—in fact, he has been a pinch hitter for the Angels this season—but when the chance to go to Japan came in 1977, he took it. Not for the money ($100,000), he insisted, but "for the good of baseball."

Davis was a product of his times, of America's "quest for meaning." While others were exploring the wonders of Transactional Analysis, est and the like, Davis was a devout member of the *Soka Gakkai,* the Nichiren Buddhist sect that had America chanting. Because Japan was the birthplace of the *Soka Gakkai,* Davis assumed he would be right at home. It was a misguided assumption.

The religion's sacred chant, *namu Myoho renge-kyo,* was an important part of Davis' daily life. He did it faithfully, because it brought him inner peace. When he joined the Dragons, he naturally continued this practice—in the morning, at night, in his room, in the team bath and on the team bus. When not intoning the chant himself, he would play tapes of it on a portable cassette recorder.

Davis reasoned that the chanting would be music to his teammates' ears. Instead, it drove them nuts. They complained: there was no peace and quiet on the team; they couldn't sleep. The incantatory chant that supposedly would bring inner harmony to anyone who regularly intoned it was rapidly eroding the Dragons' collective *wa*.

What particularly annoyed the Japanese players was Davis' locker-room chanting. Before each game, he would pull out his beads, and off he'd go, "*namu Myoho renge-kyo, namu Myoho renge-kyo, namu Myoho renge-kyo.*"

"He'd pray that he'd do well, that the team would win and that nobody would get hurt," his manager, a Japanese-Hawaiian named Wally Yonamine, says, "but it gave the others the feeling they were at a Buddhist funeral."

When the game began, Davis was a ball of fire—at least during the first half of the season. He was by far the most feared Dragon hitter, and on the base paths he displayed a flair the Japanese had never seen before. Nontheless the team was in last place. Key players were injured, and the pitching was subpar. Team *wa* was out of whack, and

197

many Dragons blamed their American Buddhist for it.

It was more than the chanting, which Davis soon modified to please his teammates. There was, for example, the matter of his personal attire. Davis liked his Dragon training suit so much he had a half a dozen made in different colors. He wore them in public, agitating club executives, who felt Davis was tarnishing the team's dignified image.

Davis would sometimes practice in stocking feet and he once appeared for a workout with his comely wife, who was wearing hot pants and who jogged with him on the field. "It's so . . . so unprofessional," one sportswriter observed. "Davis is destroying our team's spirit in training," grumbled a player. "We can't concentrate on what we're doing."

Several players complained that Davis had special privileges. They referred to him as "Davis, the King," and as "Davis, our precious black *gaijin*."

Yonamine was caught in the middle. "I'd try to tell them not to worry about it," he says. "Forget about how much money a man makes or how little he practices. What he does in the game is all that counts." Few Dragons were willing to accept that piece of American advice.

Davis' biggest liability was his gregariousness. "People didn't understand him," says a team official. "He was loud. He'd get excited. He'd yell a lot and wave his arms. It was all in English and people didn't have the faintest idea what he was saying, but it looked as though he was arguing."

Once he reproached a teammate for not attempting to score on a play that Davis had initiated. "Why didn't you try for home?" Davis shouted. That was the wrong thing to do, because the player was not only the team captain, but also a playing *coach*. In Japan, a player does not yell at a coach, much less question his judgment.

In August of 1977, when Davis had 25 home runs and a .306 batting average, he broke a wrist in a collision with the outfield fence. It put him out for the year. The Dragons immediately went on a winning streak. During the last two months of the season they had the best record in the league and missed finishing second by a hair.

"It's our pitching," Yanomine insisted. But if you listened to Dragon supporters and students of Japanese baseball, it was all because the team *wa* had been restored.

"I knew Willie as well as anyone," says Lefebvre, a teammate of Davis' on the Dodgers. "He had his quirks, but than we all do. He was named captain, and you're not chosen captain of a team like the Dodgers if you're a troublemaker. If you can't get along with Willie, you don't belong on a baseball team."

The Dragon front office apparently felt that it was Davis who didn't belong on a baseball team—at least not theirs. They traded him, and at the start of the following season the most exciting player ever to wear a Chunichi Dragon uniform was laboring in the backwaters of Fukuoka, contemplating the infinite and subtle mysteries of *wa* in between playing for the lowly Crown Lighter Lions.

Of course, not every American who comes to Japan wreaks havoc on his new team. There have been some, notably Felix Millan, Clete Boyer and George Altman, who did their best to please their Japanese hosts. In turn, the Japanese liked them, describing their demeanor as being *majime*. It means serious, sober, earnest, steady, honest, faithful. They did everything that was asked of them. They kept their mouths shut, their feelings to themselves.

Some, like Boyer, paid a substantial price for the goodwill they engendered. The former Yankee fielding whiz had three reasonably good seasons for the Taiyo Whales, but in his fourth year, when he began to reach the end as a player, he ran smack up against the cultural wall.

Boyer decided that he needed to be used more sparingly, and he asked the club to rest him every third game. "I hit in the first two, but then I get tired," he explained. "I'd do a better job with an extra day off."

The team trainer argued that what Boyer needed was not more rest but more training. Because he was older, the trainer reasoned, Boyer would have to work harder to keep up with the others. The team owner, after considering the probable reaction of the fans to an $80,000-a-year *gaijin* sitting on the bench a third of the time, agreed with the trainer. Boyer reluctantly acquiesced. In an effort to keep his energy level up, he took massive vitamin injections and worked very hard. Still, he finished the season hitting .230 and then retired to coaching. His goodwill, of course, remained intact.

Lefebvre, too, obeyed all the rules, yet he ended up incurring the largest fine in Japanese baseball history. His manager on the Lotte Orions, Masaichi Kaneda, Japan's only 400-game winner and the "God of Pitching," had personally recruited and signed Lefebvre—to a multiyear contract worth $100,000 a year—and had predicted that Lefebvre would win the Triple Crown. Lefebvre hit only .265 with 29 home runs his first season. Hampered by a leg injury, he fared even worse in succeeding years.

Kaneda was so embarrassed that he resorted to open ridicule of his "star" in an effort to regain lost face. Once, after Lefebvre had committed a particularly damaging error, Kaneda apologized to the other players for the American's "poor play." Another time, after a similar misplay, Kaneda temporarily relegated his *gaijin* to a farm team.

Lefebvre tried logic in appealing to Kaneda. "Look, you won 400 games, right?" he said. "That makes you the winningest pitcher in Japanese history, right?"

"Right," Kaneda proudly replied.

"You also lost 250 games, didn't you?"

"Yes."

"Then that also makes you the losingest pitcher in Japanese history."

"Yes, but. . . ."

"But, what? Don't you see? Even the greatest in the game have bad times. Give me a break, will you?"

But Kaneda kept up the pressure. And the unhappy Lefebvre endured it until his fifth season. After being summarily removed from the lineup in the middle of an important game, Lefebvre finally lost control. Walking back to the bench, he threw his glove at the dugout wall, producing a rather loud *whack*.

Kaneda, sitting nearby, assumed that

Lefebvre had thrown the glove at him. He sprang to his feet and raised his fists. "You want to fight me?" he yelled. Lefebvre, who saw his playing career rapidly coming to an end anyway, stepped forward to meet the challenge. Coaches intervened, but after the game Kaneda levied a $10,000 fine against his American "troublemaker" and suspended him.

"It was a big game, and I wanted to stay in it," says Lefebvre, "but what made me even madder was the way Kaneda took me out. He waited until I'd finished my infield warmups, then he came and waved me out. That's embarrassing. But I certainly wasn't trying to throw the glove at him. It missed him by *five* feet."

Kaneda wasn't interested in Lefebvre's version of the incident. If he had misunderstood his *gaijin's* intentions, perhaps others on the team had as well. What would they think if it appeared that the "God of Pitching" tolerated that sort of behavior?

Refused a private audience with Kaneda, Lefebvre took his case to the public. He called a press conference. Yes, he had lost his temper. That he regretted. But, no, he was not guilty as charged. A standard fine of 50,000 yen (about $250) he could understand. But there was no way he would pay the outrageous sum of $10,000. There was no way he *could* pay it. Kaneda was just getting back at him for his failure to win the Triple Crown. Or Kaneda was making him the scapegoat for everything else that was wrong on the team. Or, perhaps, Kaneda was simply taking this opportunity to demonstrate his skills as a "*gaijin* tamer." Whatever the reason, Lefebvre wasn't going to take it all lying down.

When Kaneda heard that he was being openly opposed, he called his own press conference and vowed that Lefebvre would "never, ever again wear the uniform of the Lotte Orions."

Lefebvre was in limbo for weeks, while the coaching staff and management covertly worked to find a solution. At one stage they suggested secretly dropping the fine but making an announcement that Lefebvre had paid it. As long as Kaneda, and his public,

didn't know the truth, they concluded, Kaneda's ego and image would suffer no damage. Lefebvre refused. He had his own ego and his own image to worry about. He appealed to a highly placed baseball official in the U.S., whom he refuses to identify. The official made a call to Kaneda and the next day the fine was quietly dropped. Lefebvre was allowed to put his uniform back on.

In the 18 years since Don Newcombe and Larry Doby became the first ex-major-leaguers to play in Japan, not a season has passed without a controversial incident involving a *gaijin* player. Last year's "villain," for example, was a former San Diego reserve infielder named John Sipin, who twice during the season took exception to deliveries apparently aimed at his person and engaged the offending pitcher in hand-to-hand combat. After the second melee Sipin was hit with a three-day suspension, fined 100,000 yen ($500) and castigated by the press for his "barbaric" behavior. One sports-page editorial likened his conduct to that of a *yakuza* (Japanese gangster), while another called Sipin a throwback to the days of the U.S. military occupation when, to hear some Japanese tell it, American GIs regularly roamed the streets beating up on the local citizenry.

"If Sipin doesn't want to get hit by the ball," said one commentator, "he should jump out of the way. There is no place for fighting on the field." In the face of such reasoning, Sipin had no recourse but to acknowledge his sins and promise to mend his ways.

Japanese team officials have understandably grown weary of the perennial conflicts wrought by their foreign imports and in recent years have tried to be more selective in signing Americans. Character investigations have become a standard part of the recruiting process, and more and more managers are going for those quiet, even-tempered types who keep their feelings to themselves and fit into the Japanese system. The 1979 crop of 24 *gaijin* (there is a limit of two per team) is the most agreeable, mildest-mannered group of foreign players ever to play in Japan. It includes Wayne Garrett, Felix Millan, Lee Stanton and Carlos May, as well as a

number of unknowns who never quite made it in the majors. There is even an American manager, Don Blasingame. Collectively they are so subdued that one American player's wife says. "This is the best-behaved bunch of ballplayers I've ever been around, either here or in the States. I just can't believe it."

Garrett, a former Met, is so obliging that he agreed to get up at 7:30 and join his teammates in their daily "morning walk." Stanton, late of the Angels and Mariners, amicably allowed the Hanshin Tiger batting coach to change his batting style. May, an ex-White Sox and Yankee, is so low key that some fans can't believe he's American.

Millan, a former Brave and Met, has been the quintessence of propriety. When he arrived last spring for his second year as a Taiyo Whale, he politely refused an offer to let him train as he wished and instead endured all the rigors of a Japanese preseason camp with his teammates. When he was benched on opening day, he sat quietly in the dugout, a shy smile on his face, intently watching the action. When he got his chance to play a week later, he went 4 for 4, won his spot back, and of late has been leading the league with a .354 average.

Davey Hilton, a former Padre, is setting new highs in cross-cultural "understanding." Last year's Central League All-Star second baseman and a hero of the Japan Series, he undertook an off-season weight-training program and arrived in camp this season a proud 20 pounds heavier. He was immediately accused by his suspicious manager of loafing during the winter, reprimanded for being "overweight" and told to reduce. A few days later he developed a sore arm and asked permission to ease up in fielding practice. He was coldly informed that no one got special treatment and was cautioned not to let his American head get too big for his Japanese cap. To top things off, after getting only two hits in his first three games of the season, he was benched and was ordered to take extra batting practice and to alter his batting stance. Through it all Hilton remained calm. "This is Japan," he told himself. "They do things differently here." Predictably, his average began to climb. By mid-season he was over .300, out of the doghouse and on his way to becoming an All-Star again.

Japanese observers are somewhat baffled by this outbreak of civility. One reporter speculated, "It must be the sagging dollar, the recession in the U.S. Americans have it good here, and they're afraid of losing what they have." American players, who pay both Japanese and U.S. income taxes and who

wince at such Japanese prices as $50 for a steak dinner, attribute their good manners to other factors: adaptability and a new awareness of cultural differences.

Whatever the reason, the new tranquility is certainly producing results. Americans are having their best year. Twelve of them are batting better than .300, and the affable Chuck Manuel, an ex-Minnesota sub, is leading the Pacific League in home runs, despite

having been sidelined for 58 days with a broken jaw.

Of course, a Reggie Jackson might look down his nose at the accomplishments of Manuel and his confreres—given the smaller parks and the slightly inferior level of play in Japan. But with his stormy background, it is doubtful that Jackson-*san,* in spite of his considerable abilities, will ever be invited to come over and prove he can do better.

Body Ritual Among the Nacirema

Horace Miner
University of Michigan

The anthropologist has become so familiar with the diversity of ways in which different peoples behave in similar situations that he is not apt to be surprised by even the most exotic customs. In fact, if all of the logically possible combinations of behavior have not been found somewhere in the world, he is apt to suspect that they must be present in some yet undescribed tribe. This point has, in fact, been expressed with respect to clan organization by Murdock (1949:71). In this light, the magical beliefs and practices of the Nacirema present such unusual aspects that it seems desirable to describe them as an example of the extremes to which human behavior can go.

Professor Linton first brought the ritual of the Nacirema to the attention of anthropologists twenty years ago (1936:326), but the culture of this people is still very poorly understood. They are a North American group living in the territory between the Canadian Cree, the Yaqui and Tarahumare of Mexico, and the Carib and Arawak of the Antilles. Little is known of their origin, though tradition states that they came from the east. According to Nacirema mythology, their nation was originated by a culture hero, Notgnishaw, who is otherwise known for two great feats of strength—the throwing of a piece of wampum across the river Pa-To-Mac and the chopping down of a cherry tree in which the Spirit of Truth resided.

Nacirema culture is characterized by a highly developed market economy which has evolved in a rich natural habitat. While much of the people's time is devoted to economic pursuits, a large part of the fruits of these labors and a considerable portion of the day are spent in ritual activity. The focus of this activity is the human body, the appearance and health of which loom as a dominant concern in the ethos of the people. While such a concern is certainly not unusual, its ceremonial aspects and associated philosophy are unique.

The fundamental belief underlying the whole system appears to be that the human body is ugly and that its natural tendency is to debility and disease. Incarcerated in such a body, man's only hope is to avert these characteristics through the use of the powerful influences of ritual and ceremony. Every household has one or more shrines devoted to this purpose. The more powerful individuals in the society have several shrines in their houses and, in fact, the opulence of a house is often referred to in terms of the number of such ritual centers it possesses. Most houses are of wattle and daub construction, but the shrine rooms of the more wealthy are walled with stone. Poorer families imitate the rich by applying pottery plaques to their shrine walls.

While each family has at least one such shrine, the rituals associated with it are not family ceremonies but are private and secret. The rites are normally only discussed with children, and then only during the period when they are being initiated into these mysteries. I was able, however, to establish sufficient rapport with the natives to examine these shrines and to have the rituals described to me.

The focal point of the shrine is a box or chest which is built into the wall. In this chest are kept the many charms and magical potions without which no native believes he could live. These preparations are secured from a variety of specialized practitioners. The most powerful of these are the medicine men, whose assistance must be rewarded with substantial gifts. However, the medicine men do not provide the curative potions for their clients, but decide what the ingredients should be and then write them down in an ancient and secret language. This writing is understood only by the medicine men and by the herbalists who, for another gift, provide the required charm.

The charm is not disposed of after it has served its purpose, but is placed in the charm-box of the household shrine. As these magical materials are specific for certain ills, and the real or imagined maladies of the people are many, the charm-box is usually full to overflowing. The magical packets are so numerous that people forget what their purposes were and fear to use them again. While the natives are very vague on this point, we can only assume that the idea in retaining all the old magical materials is that their presence in the charm-box, before which the body rituals are conducted, will in some way protect the worshipper.

Beneath the charm-box is a small font. Each day every member of the family, in succession, enters the shrine room, bows his head before the charm-box, mingles different sorts of holy water in the font, and proceeds with a brief rite of ablution. The holy waters are secured from the Water Temple of the community, where the priests conduct elaborate ceremonies to make the liquid ritually pure.

In the hierarchy of magical practitioners, and below the medicine men in prestige, are specialists whose designation is best translated "holy-mouth-men." The Nacirema have an almost pathological horror and fascination with the mouth, the condition of which is believed to have a supernatural influence on all social relationships. Were it not for the rituals of the mouth, they believe that their teeth would fall out, their gums bleed, their jaws shrink, their friends desert them, and their lovers reject them. (They also belive that a strong relationship exists between oral and moral characteristics. For example, there is a ritual ablution of the mouth for children which is supposed to improve their moral fiber.)

The daily body ritual performed by everyone includes a mouth-rite. Despite the fact that these people are so punctilious about care of the mouth, this rite involves a practice which strikes the uninitiated stranger as revolting. It was reported to me that the ritual consists of inserting a small bundle of hog hairs into the mouth, along with certain magical powders, and then moving the bundle in a highly formalized series of gestures.

In addition to the private mouth-rite, the people seek out a holy-mouth-man once or twice a year. These practitioners have an impressive set of paraphernalia, consisting of a variety of augers, awls, probes, and prods. The use of these objects in the exorcism of the evils of the mouth involves almost unbelievable ritual torture of the client. The holy-mouth-man opens the client's mouth and, using the above mentioned tools, en-larges any holes which decay may have created in the teeth. Magical materials are put into these holes. If there are no naturally occurring holes in the teeth, large sections of one or more teeth are gouged out so that the supernatural substance can be applied. In the client's view, the purpose of these ministrations is to arrest decay and to draw friends. The extremely sacred and traditional character of the rite is evident in the fact that the natives return to the holy-mouth-men year after year, despite the fact that their teeth continue to decay.

It is to be hoped that, when a thorough study of the Nacirema is made, there will be a careful inquiry into the personality structure of these people. One has but to watch the gleam in the eye of a holy-mouth-man, as he jabs an awl into an exposed nerve, to suspect that a certain amount of sadism is involved. If this can be established, a very interesting pattern emerges, for most of the population shows definite masochistic tendencies. It was to these that Professor Linton referred in discussing a distinctive part of the daily body ritual which is performed only by men. This part of the rite involves scraping and lacerating the surface of the face with a sharp instrument. Special women's rites are performed only four times during each lunar month, but what they lack in frequency is made up in barbarity. As part of this ceremony, women bake their heads in small ovens for about an hour. The theoretically interesting point is that what seems to be a preponderantly masochistic people have developed sadistic specialists.

The medicine men have an imposing temple, or *latipso*, in every community of any size. The more elaborate ceremonies required to treat very sick patients can only be performed at this temple. These ceremonies involve not only the thaumaturge but a permanent group of vestal maidens who move sedately about the temple chambers in distinctive costume and headdress.

The *latipso* ceremonies are so harsh that it is phenomenal that a fair proportion of the really sick natives who enter the temple ever recover. Small children whose indoctrination is still incomplete have been known to resist attempts to take them to the temple because "that is where you go to die." Despite this fact, sick adults are not only willing but eager to undergo the protracted ritual purification, if they can afford to do so. No matter how ill the supplicant or how grave the emergency, the guardians of many temples will not admit a client if he cannot give a rich gift to the custodian. Even after one has gained admission and survived the ceremonies, the guardians will not permit the neophyte to leave until he makes still another gift.

The supplicant entering the temple is first stripped of all his or her clothes. In every-day life the Nacirema avoids exposure of his body and its natural functions. Bathing and excretory acts are performed only in the secrecy of the household shrine, where they are ritualized as part of the body-rites. Psychological shock results from the fact that body secrecy is suddenly lost upon entry into the *latipso*. A man, whose own wife has never seen him in an excretory act, suddenly finds himself naked and assisted by a vestal maiden while he performs his natural functions into a sacred vessel. This sort of ceremonial treatment is necessitated by the fact that the excreta are used by a diviner to ascertain the course and nature of the client's sickness. Female clients, on the other hand, find their naked bodies are subjected to the scrutiny, manipulation and prodding of the medicine men.

Few supplicants in the temple are well enough to do anything but lie on their hard beds. The daily ceremonies, like the rites of the holy-mouth-men, involve discomfort and torture. With ritual precision, the vestals awaken their miserable charges each dawn and roll them about on their beds of pain while performing ablutions, in the formal movements of which the maidens are highly trained. At other times they insert magic wands in the supplicant's mouth or force him to eat substances which are supposed to be healing. From time to time the medicine men come to their clients and jab magically treated needles into their flesh. The fact that these temple ceremonies may not cure, and may even kill the neophyte, in no way decreases the people's faith in the medicine men.

There remains one other kind of practioner, known as a "listener." This witch-doctor has the power to exorcise the devils that lodge in the heads of people who have been bewitched. The Nacirema believe that parents bewitch their own children. Mothers are particularly suspected of putting a curse on children while teaching them the secret body rituals. The counter-magic of the witch-doctor is unusual in its lack of ritual. The patient simply tells the "listener" all his troubles and fears, beginning with the earliest difficulties he can remember. The memory displayed by the Nacirema in these exorcism sessions is truly remarkable. It is not uncommon for the patient to bemoan the rejection he felt upon being weaned as a babe, and a few individuals even see their troubles going back to the traumatic effects of their own birth.

In conclusion, mention must be made of certain practices which have their base in native esthetics but which depend upon the pervasive aversion to the natural body and its functions. There are ritual fasts to make fat people thin and ceremonial feasts to make thin people fat. Still other rites are used to make women's breasts large if they are small, and smaller if they are large. General dissatisfaction with breast shape is symbolized in the fact that the ideal form is virtually outside the range of human variation. A few women afflicted with almost inhuman hypermammary development are so idolized that they make a handsome living by simply going from village to village and permitting the natives to stare at them for a fee.

Reference has already been made to the fact that excretory functions are ritualized, routinized, and relegated to secrecy. Natural reproductive functions are similarly distorted. Intercourse is taboo as a topic and scheduled as an act. Efforts are made to avoid pregnancy by the use of magical materials or by limiting intercourse to certain phases of the moon. Conception is actually very infre-

quent. When pregnant, women dress so as to hide their condition. Parturition takes place in secret, without friends or relatives to assist, and the majority of women do not nurse their infants.

Our review of the ritual life of the Nacirema has certainly shown them to be a magic-ridden people. It is hard to understand how they have managed to exist so long under the burdens which they have imposed upon themselves. But even such exotic customs as these take on real meaning when they are viewed with the insight provided by Malinowski when he wrote (1948:70):

> Looking from far and above, from our high places of safety in the developed civilization, it is easy to see all the crudity and irrelevance of magic. But without its power and guidance early man could not have mastered his practical difficulties as he has done, nor could man have advanced to the higher stages of civilization.

REFERENCES

Linton, Ralph. 1936. *The Study of Man*. New York, D. Appleton-Century Co.
Malinowski, Bronislaw. 1948. *Magic, Science, and Religion*. Glencoe, The Free Press.
Murdock, George P. 1949. *Social Structure*. New York, The Macmillan Co.

Sociocultural Change: The Impact of the West

The origins of academic anthropology lie in the colonial and imperial ventures of the nineteenth and twentieth centuries. During these periods, many people of the world were brought into a relationship with Europe and the United States that was usually exploitative and often socially and culturally disruptive. For almost a century, anthropologists have witnessed this process and the transformations that have taken place in those social and cultural systems brought under the umbrella of a world economic order. Early anthropological studies—even those widely regarded as pure research—directly or indirectly served colonial interests. Many anthropologists certainly believed that they were extending the benefits of Western technology and society while preserving the cultural rights of those people whom they studied. But other representatives of poor nations challenge this view, and are far less generous in describing the past role of the anthropologist. Most contemporary anthropologists, however, have a deep moral commitment to defending the legal, political, and economic rights of the people with whom they work.

When anthropologists discuss social change, they usually mean change brought about in pre-industrial societies through longstanding interaction with the nation-states of the industrialized world. In early anthropology, contact between the West and the remainder of the world was characterized by the terms "acculturation" and "culture contact." These terms were used to describe the diffusion of cultural traits between the developed and less developed countries. Often this was analyzed as a one-way process in which cultures of the Third World were seen, for better or worse, as receptacles for Western cultural traits. Nowadays, many anthropologists believe that the diffusion of cultural traits across social, political, and economic boundaries was emphasized at the expense of the real issues of dominance, subordinance, and dependence that characterized the colonial experience. Just as importantly, many anthropologists recognize that the present-day forms of cultural, economic, and political interaction between the developed and the so-called underdeveloped world are best characterized as neo-colonial.

Most of the articles in this section take the perspective that anthropology should be critical as well as descriptive. They raise questions about cultural contact, and about the political economies of underdeveloped countries, that are both interesting and troublesome. In keeping with the notion that the negative impact of the West on traditional cultures began with colonial domination, this section opens with "Why Can't People Feed Themselves?" This article shows that the "progress" of the West meant poverty and hunger for peasant societies.

Each succeeding article emphasizes a different aspect of culture affected by the impact of the West. "Growing Up as a Fore" points to the problems of maintaining individual identity in a changing society, while "Dark Dreams About the White Man" reveals that even the dreams of natives are invaded by the white man. "Bicultural Conflict" and "Inuit Youth in a Changing World" describe the personal devastation inflicted upon people who are caught between two worlds, the traditional and the modern.

Finally, "The Aborigines' Search for Justice" and "Back on the Land" help us to understand that, even considering all that has happened to non-Western peoples, they have not been passive recipients of change. Rather, they have been actively adjusting, and to some degree directing, their responses to the new challenges facing them. With the advantages of new technology, some have even managed to salvage a part of their past.

Looking Ahead: Challenge Questions

What have been the effects of colonialism on formerly subsistence-oriented socioeconomic systems? What is a subsistence system?

Do cash crops inevitably lead to class distinctions and poverty?

What was it about the Fore culture that made it so vulnerable to the harmful effects of the change from a subsistence economy to a cash-crop economy?

How has culture contact affected the dreams of the Mehinaku?

What ethical obligations do industrial societies have toward respecting the human rights and cultural diversity of traditional communities?

Why Can't People Feed Themselves?

Frances Moore Lappé and Joseph Collins

Frances Moore Lappé and Dr. Joseph Collins are founders and directors of the Institute for Food and Development Policy, located in San Francisco and New York.

Question: You have said that the hunger problem is not the result of overpopulation. But you have not yet answered the most basic and simple question of all: Why can't people feed themselves? As Senator Daniel P. Moynihan put it bluntly, when addressing himself to the Third World, "Food growing is the first thing you do when you come down out of the trees. The question is, how come the United States can grow food and you can't?"

Our Response: In the very first speech I, Frances, ever gave after writing *Diet for a Small Planet*, I tried to take my audience along the path that I had taken in attempting to understand why so many are hungry in this world. Here is the gist of that talk that was, in truth, a turning point in my life:

When I started I saw a world divided into two parts: a *minority* of nations that had "taken off" through their agricultural and industrial revolutions to reach a level of unparalleled material abundance and a *majority* that remained behind in a primitive, traditional, undeveloped state. This lagging behind of the majority of the world's peoples must be due, I thought, to some internal deficiency or even to several of them. It seemed obvious that the underdeveloped countries must be deficient in natural resources—particularly good land and climate—and in cultural development, including modern attitudes conducive to work and progress.

But when looking for the historical roots of the predicament, I learned that my picture of these two separate worlds was quite false. My "two separate worlds" were really just different sides of the same coin. One side was on top largely because the other side was on the bottom. Could this be true? How were these separate worlds related?

Colonialism appeared to me to be the link. Colonialism destroyed the cultural patterns of production and exchange by which traditional societies in "underdeveloped" countries previously had met the needs of the people. Many precolonial social structures, while dominated by exploitative elites, had evolved a system of mutual obligations among the classes that helped to ensure at least a minimal diet for all. A friend of mine once said: "Precolonial village existence in subsistence agriculture was a limited life indeed, but it's certainly not Calcutta." The misery of starvation in the streets of Calcutta can only be understood as the end-point of a long historical process—one that has destroyed a traditional social system.

"Underdeveloped," instead of being an adjective that evokes the picture of a static society, became for me a verb (to "underdevelop") meaning the *process* by which the minority of the world has transformed—indeed often robbed and degraded—the majority.

That was in 1972. I clearly recall my thoughts on my return home. I had stated publicly for the first time a world view that had taken me years of study to grasp. The sense of relief was tremendous. For me the breakthrough lay in realizing that today's "hunger crisis" could not be described in static, descriptive terms. Hunger and underdevelopment must always be thought of as *a process*.

To answer the question "why hunger?" it is counterproductive to simply *describe* the conditions in an underdeveloped country today. For these conditions, whether they be the degree of malnutrition, the levels of agricultural production, or even the country's ecological endowment, are not static factors—they are not "givens." They are rather the *results* of an ongoing historical process. As we dug ever deeper into that historical process for the preparation of this book, we began to discover the existence of scarcity-creating mechanisms that we had only vaguely intuited before.

We have gotten great satisfaction from probing into the past since we recognized it is the only way to approach a solution to hunger today. We have come to see that it is the force creating the condition, not the condition itself, that must be the target of change. Otherwise we might change the condition today, only to find tomorrow that it has been recreated—with a vengeance.

Asking the question "Why can't people feed themselves?" carries a sense of bewilderment that there are so many people in the world not able to feed themselves adequately. What astonished us, however, is that there are not *more* people in the world who are hungry—considering the weight of the centuries of effort by the few to undermine the capacity of the majority to feed themselves. No, we are not crying "conspiracy!" If these forces were entirely conspiratorial, they would be easier to detect and many more people would by now have risen up to resist. We are talking about something more subtle and insidious; a heritage of a colonial order in which people with the advantage of considerable power sought their own self-interest, often arrogantly believing they were acting in the interest of the people whose lives they were destroying.

THE COLONIAL MIND

The colonizer viewed agriculture in the subjugated lands as primitive and backward. Yet such a view contrasts sharply with documents from the colonial period now coming to light. For example, A. J. Voelker, a British agricultural scientist assigned to India during the 1890s, wrote:

Nowhere would one find better instances of keeping land scrupulously clean from weeds, of ingenuity in device of water-raising appliances, of knowledge of soils and their capabilities, as well as of the exact time to sow and reap, as one would find in Indian agriculture. It is wonderful, too, how much is known of rotation, the system of "mixed crops" and of fallowing. . . . I, at least, have never seen a more perfect picture of cultivation."[1]

None the less, viewing the agriculture of the vanquished as primitive and backward reinforced the colonizer's rationale for destroying it. To the colonizers of Africa, Asia, and Latin America, agriculture became merely a means to extract wealth—much as gold from a mine—on behalf of the colonizing power. Agriculture was no longer seen as a source of food for the local population, nor even as their livelihood. Indeed the English economist John Stuart Mill reasoned that colonies should not be thought of as civilizations or countries at all but as "agricultural establishments" whose sole purpose was to supply the "larger community to which they belong." The colonized society's agriculture was only a subdivision of the agricultural system of the metropolitan country. As Mill acknowledged, "Our West India colonies, for example, cannot be regarded as countries. . . . The West Indies are the place where England *finds it convenient* to carry on the production of sugar, coffee and a few other tropical commodities."[2]

Prior to European intervention, Africans practiced a diversified agriculture that included the introduction of new food plants of Asian or American origin. But colonial rule simplified this diversified production to single cash crops—often to the exclusion of staple foods—and in the process sowed the seeds of famine.[3] Rice farming once had been common in Gambia. But with colonial rule so much of the best land was taken over by peanuts (grown for the European market) that rice had to be imported to counter the mounting prospect of famine. Northern Ghana, once famous for its yams and other foodstuffs, was forced to concentrate solely on cocoa. Most of the Gold Coast thus became dependent on cocoa. Liberia was turned into a virtual plantation subsidiary of Firestone Tire and Rubber. Food production in Dahomey and southeast Nigeria was all but abandoned in favor of palm oil; Tanganyika (now Tanzania) was forced to focus on sisal and Uganda on cotton.

The same happened in Indochina. About the time of the American Civil War the French decided that the Mekong Delta in Vietnam would be ideal for producing rice for export. Through a production system based on enriching the large landowners, Vietnam became the world's third largest exporter of rice by the 1930s; yet many landless Vietnamese went hungry.[4]

Rather than helping the peasants, colonialism's public works programs only reinforced export crop production. British irrigation works built in nineteenth-century India did help increase production, but the expansion was for spring export crops at the expense of millets and legumes grown in the fall as the basic local food crops.

Because people living on the land do not easily go against their natural and adaptive drive to grow food for themselves, colonial powers had to force the production of cash crops. The first strategy was to use physical or economic force to get the local population to grow cash crops instead of food on their own plots and then turn them over to the colonizer for export. The second strategy was the direct takeover of the land by large-scale plantations growing crops for export.

FORCED PEASANT PRODUCTION

As Walter Rodney recounts in *How Europe Underdeveloped Africa,* cash crops were often grown literally under threat of guns and whips.[5] One visitor to the Sahel commented in 1928: "Cotton is an artificial crop and one the value of which is not entirely clear to the natives. . ." He wryly noted the "enforced enthusiasm with which the natives. . .have thrown themselves into. . .planting cotton."[6] The forced cultivation of cotton was a major grievance leading to the Maji Maji wars in Tanzania (then Tanganyika) and behind the nationalist revolt in Angola as late as 1960.[7]

Although raw force was used, taxation was the preferred colonial technique to force Africans to grow cash crops. The colonial administrations simply levied taxes on cattle, land, houses, and even the people themselves. Since the tax had to be paid in the coin of the realm, the peasants had either to grow crops to sell or to work on the plantations or in the mines of the Europeans.[8] Taxation was both an effective tool to "stimulate" cash cropping and a source of revenue that the colonial bureaucracy needed to enforce the system. To expand their production of export crops to pay the mounting taxes, peasant producers were forced to neglect the farming of food crops. In 1830, the Dutch administration in Java made the peasants an offer they could not refuse; if they would grow government-owned export crops on one fifth of their land, the Dutch would remit their land taxes.[9] If they refused and thus could not pay the taxes, they lost their land.

Marketing boards emerged in Africa in the 1930s as another technique for getting the profit from cash crop production by native producers into the hands of the colonial government and international firms. Purchases by the marketing boards were well below the world market price. Peanuts bought by the boards from peasant cultivators in West Africa were sold in Britain for more than *seven times* what the peasants received.[10]

The marketing board concept was born with the "cocoa hold-up" in the Gold Coast in 1937. Small cocoa farmers refused to sell to the large cocoa concerns like United Africa

Company (a subsidiary of the Anglo-Dutch firm, Unilever—which we know as Lever Brothers) and Cadbury until they got a higher price. When the British government stepped in and agreed to buy the cocoa directly in place of the big business concerns, the smallholders must have thought they had scored at least a minor victory. But had they really? The following year the British formally set up the West African Cocoa Control Board. Theoretically, its purpose was to pay the peasants a reasonable price for their crops. In practice, however, the board, as sole purchaser, was able to hold down the prices paid the peasants for their crops when the world prices were rising. Rodney sums up the real "victory":

None of the benefits went to Africans, but rather to the British government itself and to the private companies. . . Big companies like the United African Company and John Holt were given. . . quotas to fulfill on behalf of the boards. As agents of the government, they were no longer exposed to direct attack, and their profits were secure.[11]

These marketing boards, set up for most export crops, were actually controlled by the companies. The chairman of the Cocoa Board was none other than John Cadbury of Cadbury Brothers (ever had a Cadbury chocolate bar?) who was part of a buying pool exploiting West African cocoa farmers.

The marketing boards funneled part of the profits from the exploitation of peasant producers indirectly into the royal treasury. While the Cocoa Board sold to the British Food Ministry at low prices, the ministry upped the price for British manufacturers, thus netting a profit as high as 11 million pounds in some years.[12]

These marketing boards of Africa were only the institutionalized rendition of what is the essence of colonialism—the extraction of wealth. While profits continued to accrue to foreign interests and local elites, prices received by those actually growing the commodities remained low.

PLANTATIONS

A second approach was direct takeover of the land either by the colonizing government or by private foreign interests. Previously self-provisioning farmers were forced to cultivate the plantation fields through either enslavement or economic coercion.

After the conquest of the Kandyan Kingdom (in present day Sri Lanka), in 1815, the British designated all the vast central part of the island as crown land. When it was determined that coffee, a profitable export crop, could be grown there, the Kandyan lands were sold off to British investors and planters at a mere five shillings per acre, the government even defraying the cost of surveying and road building.[13]

Java is also a prime example of a colonial government seizing territory and then putting it into private foreign hands. In 1870, the Dutch declared all uncultivated land—called waste land—property of the state for lease to Dutch plantation enterprises. In addition, the Agrarian Land Law of 1870 authorized foreign companies to lease village-owned land. The peasants, in chronic need of ready cash for taxes and foreign consumer goods, were only too willing to lease their land to the foreign companies for very modest sums and under terms dictated by the firms. Where land was still held communally, the village headman was tempted by high cash commissions offered by plantation companies. He would lease the village land even more cheaply than would the individual peasant or, as was frequently the case, sell out the entire village to the company.[14]

The introduction of the plantation meant the divorce of agriculture from nourishment, as the notion of food value was lost to the overriding claim of "market value" in international trade. Crops such as sugar, tobacco, and coffee were selected, not on the basis of how well they feed people, but for their high price value relative to their weight and bulk so that profit margins could be maintained even after the costs of shipping to Europe.

SUPPRESSING PEASANT FARMING

The stagnation and impoverishment of the peasant food-producing sector was not the mere by-product of benign neglect, that is, the unintended consequence of an overemphasis on export production. Plantations—just like modern "agro-industrial complexes"—needed an abundant and readily available supply of low-wage agricultural workers. Colonial administrations thus devised a variety of tactics, all to undercut self-provisioning agriculture and thus make rural populations dependent on plantation wages. Government services and even the most minimal infrastructure (access to water, roads, seeds, credit, pest and disease control information, and so on) were systematically denied. Plantations usurped most of the good land, either making much of the rural population landless or pushing them onto marginal soils. (Yet the plantations have often held much of their land idle simply to prevent the peasants from using it—even to this day. Del Monte owns 57,000 acres of Guatemala but plants only 9000. The rest lies idle except for a few thousand head of grazing cattle.)[15]

In some cases a colonial administration would go even further to guarantee itself a labor supply. In at least twelve countries in the eastern and southern parts of Africa the exploitation of mineral wealth (gold, diamonds, and copper) and the establishment of cash-crop plantations demanded a continuous supply of low-cost labor. To assure this labor supply, colonial administrations simply expropriated the land of the African communities by violence and drove the people into small reserves.[16] With neither adequate land for their traditional slash-and-burn methods nor access to the means—tools, water, and fertilizer—to make continuous farming of such limited areas viable, the indigenous population could scarcely meet subsistence needs, much less produce surplus to sell in order to cover the colonial taxes. Hundreds of thousands of Africans were forced to become the cheap labor source so "needed" by the colonial plantations. Only by laboring on plantations and in the mines could they hope to pay the colonial taxes.

The tax scheme to produce reserves of cheap plantation and mining labor was particularly effective when the Great Depression hit and the bottom dropped out of cash crop economies. In 1929 the cotton market collapsed, leaving peasant cotton producers, such as those in Upper Volta, unable to pay their colonial taxes. More and more young people, in some years as many as 80,000, were thus forced to migrate to the Gold Coast to compete with each other for low-wage jobs on cocoa plantations.[17]

The forced migration of Africa's most able-bodied workers—stripping village food farming of needed hands—was a recurring feature of colonialism. As late as 1973 the Portuguese "exported" 400,000 Mozambican peasants to work in South Africa in exchange for gold deposited in the Lisbon treasury.

The many techniques of colonialism to undercut self-provisioning agriculture in order to ensure a cheap labor supply are no better illustrated than by the story of how, in the mid-nineteenth century, sugar plantation owners in British Guiana coped with the double blow of the emancipation of slaves and the crash in the world sugar market. The story is graphically recounted by Alan Adamson in *Sugar without Slaves*.[18]

Would the ex-slaves be allowed to take over the plantation land and grow the food they needed? The planters, many ruined by the sugar slump, were determined they would not. The planter-dominated government devised several schemes for thwarting food self-sufficiency. The price of crown land was kept artificially high, and the purchase of land in parcels smaller than 100 acres was outlawed—two measures guaranteeing that newly organized ex-slave cooperatives could not hope to gain access to much land. The government also prohibited cultivation on as

much as 400,000 acres—on the grounds of "uncertain property titles." Moreover, although many planters held part of their land out of sugar production due to the depressed world price, they would not allow any alternative production on them. They feared that once the ex-slaves started growing food it would be difficult to return them to sugar production when world market prices began to recover. In addition, the government taxed peasant production, then turned around and used the funds to subsidize the immigration of laborers from India and Malaysia to replace the freed slaves, thereby making sugar production again profitable for the planters. Finally, the government neglected the infrastructure for subsistence agriculture and denied credit for small farmers.

Perhaps the most insidious tactic to "lure" the peasant away from food production—and the one with profound historical consequences—was a policy of keeping the price of imported food low through the removal of tariffs and subsidies. The policy was double-edged: first, peasants were told they need not grow food because they could always buy it cheaply with their plantation wages; second, cheap food imports destroyed the market for domestic food and thereby impoverished local food producers.

Adamson relates how both the Governor of British Guiana and the Secretary for the Colonies Earl Grey favored low duties on imports in order to erode local food production and thereby release labor for the plantations. In 1851 the governor rushed through a reduction of the duty on cereals in order to "divert" labor to the sugar estates. As Adamson comments, "Without realizing it, he [the governor] had put his finger on the most mordant feature of monoculture: . . . its convulsive need to destroy any other sector of the economy which might compete for 'its' labor."[19]

Many colonial governments succeeded in establishing dependence on imported foodstuffs. In 1647 an

observer in the West Indies wrote to Governor Winthrop of Massachusetts: "Men are so intent upon planting sugar that they had rather buy foode at very deare rates than produce it by labour, so infinite is the profitt of sugar workes. . . ."[20] By 1770, the West Indies were importing most of the continental colonies' exports of dried fish, grain, beans, and vegetables. A dependence on imported food made the West Indian colonies vulnerable to any disruption in supply. This dependence on imported food stuffs spelled disaster when the thirteen continental colonies gained independence and food exports from the continent to the West Indies were interrupted. With no diversified food system to fall back on, 15,000 plantation workers died of famine between 1780 and 1787 in Jamaica alone.[21] The dependence of the West Indies on imported food persists to this day.

SUPPRESSING PEASANT COMPETITION

We have talked about the techniques by which indigenous populations were forced to cultivate cash crops. In some countries with large plantations, however, colonial governments found it necessary to *prevent* peasants from independently growing cash crops not out of concern for their welfare, but so that they would not compete with colonial interests growing the same crop. For peasant farmers, given a modicum of opportunity, proved themselves capable of outproducing the large plantations not only in terms of output per unit of land but, more important, in terms of capital cost per unit produced.

In the Dutch East Indies (Indonesia and Dutch New Guinea) colonial policy in the middle of the nineteenth century forbade the sugar refineries to buy sugar cane from indigenous growers and imposed a discriminatory tax on rubber produced by native smallholders.[22] A recent unpublished United Nations study of agricultural development in Africa concluded that large-scale agricultural operations owned and controlled by foreign commercial interests (such as the rubber plantations of Liberia, the sisal estates of Tanganyika [Tanzania], and the coffee estates of Angola) only survived the competition of peasant producers because "the authorities actively supported them by suppressing indigenous rural development."[23]

The suppression of indigenous agricultural development served the interests of the colonizing powers in two ways. Not only did it prevent direct competition from more efficient native producers of the same crops, but it also guaranteed a labor force to work on the foreign-owned estates. Planters and foreign investors were not unaware that peasants who could survive economically by their own production would be under less pressure to sell their labor cheaply to the large estates.

The answer to the question, then, "Why can't people feed themselves?" must begin with an understanding of how colonialism actively prevented people from doing just that.

Colonialism
- forced peasants to replace food crops with cash crops that were then expropriated at very low rates;
- took over the best agricultural land for export crop plantations and then forced the most able-bodied workers to leave the village fields to work as slaves or for very low wages on plantations;
- encouraged a dependence on imported food;
- blocked native peasant cash crop production from competing with cash crops produced by settlers or foreign firms.

These are concrete examples of the development of underdevelopment that we should have perceived as such even as we read our history schoolbooks. Why didn't we? Somehow our schoolbooks always seemed to make the flow of history appear to have its own logic—as if it could not have been any other way. I, Frances, recall, in particular, a grade-school, social studies pamphlet on the idyllic life of Pedro, a nine-year-old boy on a coffee plantation in South America. The drawings of lush vegetation and "exotic" huts made his life seem romantic indeed. Wasn't it natural and proper that South America should have plantations to supply my mother and father with coffee? Isn't that the way it was *meant* to be?

NOTES

[1] Radha Sinha, *Food and Poverty* (New York: Holmes and Meier, 1976), p. 26.

[2] John Stuart Mill, *Political Economy*, Book 3, Chapter 25 (emphasis added).

[3] Peter Feldman and David Lawrence, "Social and Economic Implications of the Large-Scale Introduction of New Varieties of Foodgrains," Africa Report, preliminary draft (Geneva: UNRISD, 1975), pp. 107–108.

[4] Edgar Owens, *The Right Side of History*, unpublished manuscript, 1976.

[5] Walter Rodney, *How Europe Underdeveloped Africa* (London: Bogle-L'Ouverture Publications, 1972), pp. 171–172.

[6] Ferdinand Ossendowski, *Slaves of the Sun* (New York: Dutton, 1928), p. 276.

[7] Rodney, *How Europe Underdeveloped Africa*, pp. 171–172.

[8] Ibid., p. 181.

[9] Clifford Geertz, *Agricultural Involution* (Berkeley and Los Angeles: University of California Press, 1963), pp. 52–53.

[10] Rodney, *How Europe Underdeveloped Africa*, p. 185.

[11] Ibid., p. 184.

[12] Ibid., p. 186.

[13] George L. Beckford, *Persistent Poverty: Underdevelopment in Plantation Economies of the Third World* (New York: Oxford University Press, 1972), p. 99.

[14] Ibid., p. 99, quoting from Erich Jacoby, *Agrarian Unrest in Southeast Asia* (New York: Asia Publishing House, 1961), p. 66.

[15] Pat Flynn and Roger Burbach, North American Congress on Latin America, Berkeley, California, recent investigation.

[16] Feldman and Lawrence, "Social and Economic Implications," p. 103.

[17] Special Sahelian Office Report, Food and Agriculture Organization, March 28, 1974, pp. 88–89.

[18] Alan Adamson, *Sugar Without Slaves: The Political Economy of British Guiana, 1838–1904* (New Haven and London: Yale University Press, 1972).

[19] Ibid., p. 41.

[20] Eric Williams, *Capitalism and Slavery* (New York: Putnam, 1966), p. 110.

[21] Ibid., p. 121.

[22] Gunnar Myrdal, *Asian Drama*, vol. 1 (New York: Pantheon, 1966), pp. 448–449.

[23] Feldman and Lawrence, "Social and Economic Implications," p. 189.

Growing up as a Fore

E. Richard Sorenson

Dr. Sorenson, director of the Smithsonian's National Anthropological Film Center, wrote The Edge of the Forest *on his Fore studies.*

Exploring, two youngsters walk confidently past men's house in hamlet. Smaller women's house is at right.

Untouched by the outside world, they had lived for thousands of years in isolated mountains and valleys deep in the interior of Papua New Guinea. They had no cloth, no metal, no money, no idea that their homeland was an island—or that what surrounded it was salt water. Yet the Fore (for'ay) people had developed remarkable and sophisticated approaches to human relations, and their child-rearing practices gave their young unusual freedom to explore. Successful as hunter-gatherers and as subsistence gardeners, they also had great adaptability, which brought rapid accommodation with the outside world after their lands were opened up.

It was alone that I first visited the Fore in 1963—a day's walk from a recently built airstrip. I stayed six months. Perplexed and fascinated, I returned six times in the next ten years, eventually spending a year and a half living with them in their hamlets.

Theirs was a way of life different from anything I had seen or heard about before. There were no chiefs, patriarchs, priests, medicine men or the like. A striking personal freedom was enjoyed even by the very young, who could move about at will and be where or with whom they liked. Infants rarely cried, and they played confidently with knives, axes, and fire. Conflict between old and young did not arise; there was no "generation gap."

Older children enjoyed deferring to the interests and desires of the younger, and sibling rivalry was virtually undetectable. A responsive

sixth sense seemed to attune the Fore hamlet mates to each other's interests and needs. They did not have to directly ask, inveigle, bargain or speak out for what they needed or wanted. Subtle, even fleeting expressions of interest, desire, and discomfort were quickly read and helpfully acted on by one's associates. This spontaneous urge to share food, affection, work, trust, tools and pleasure was the social cement that held the Fore hamlets together. It was a pleasant way of life, for one could always be with those with whom one got along well.

Ranging and planting, sharing and living, the Fore diverged and expanded through high virgin lands in a pioneer region. They hunted out their gardens, tilled them while they lasted, then hunted again. Moving ever away from lands peopled and used they had a self-contained life with its own special ways.

The underlying ecological conditions were like those that must have encompassed the world before agriculture set its imprint so broadly. Abutting the Fore was virtually unlimited virgin land, and they had food plants they could introduce into it. Like hunter-gatherers they sought their sources of sustenance first in

one locale and then another, across an extended range, following opportunities provided by a providential nature. But like agriculturalists they concentrated their effort and attention more narrowly on selected sites of production, on their gardens. They were both seekers and producers. A pioneer people in a pioneer land, they ranged freely into a vast territory, but they planted to live.

Cooperative groups formed hamlets and gardened together. When the fertility of a garden declined, they abandoned it. Grass sprung up to cover these abandoned sites of earlier cultivation, and, as the Fore moved on to other parts of the forest, they left uninhabited grasslands to mark their passage.

The traditional hamlets were small, with a rather fluid system of social relations. A single large men's house provided shelter for 10 to 20 men and boys and their visiting friends. The several smaller women's houses each normally sheltered two married women, their unmarried daughters and their sons up to about six years of age. Formal kinship bonds were less important than friendship was. Fraternal "gangs" of youths formed the hamlets; their "clubhouses" were the men's houses.

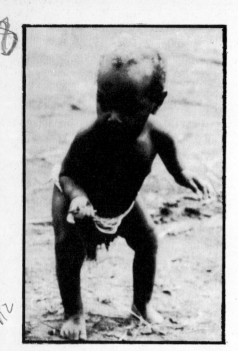

Learning to be a toddler, a Fore baby takes its first experimental steps. No one urges him on.

During the day the gardens became the center of life. Hamlets were virtually deserted as friends, relatives and children went to one or more garden plots to mingle their social, economic and erotic pursuits in a pleasant and emotionally filled Gestalt of garden life. The boys and unmarried youths preferred to explore and hunt in the outlying lands, but they also passed through and tarried in the gardens.

Daily activities were not scheduled. No one made demands, and the land was bountiful. Not surprisingly the line between work and play was never clear. The transmission of the Fore behavioral pattern to the young began in early infancy during a period of unceasing human physical contact. The effect of being constantly "in touch" with hamlet mates and their daily life seemed to start a process which proceeded by degrees: close rapport, involvement in regular activity, ability to handle seemingly dangerous implements safely, and responsible freedom to pursue individual interests at will without danger.

While very young, infants remained in almost continuous bodily contact with their mother, her house

mates or her gardening associates. At first, mothers' laps were the center of activity, and infants occupied themselves there by nursing, sleeping and playing with their own bodies or those of their caretakers. They were not put aside for the sake of other activities, as when food was being prepared or heavy loads were being carried. Remaining in close, uninterrupted physical contact with those around them, their basic needs such as rest, nourishment, stimulation and security were continuously satisfied without obstacle.

By being physically in touch from their earliest days, Fore youngsters learned to communicate needs, desires and feelings through a body language of touch and response that developed before speech. This opened the door to a much closer rapport with those around them than otherwise would have been possible, and led ultimately to the Fore brand of social cement and the sixth sense that bound groups together through spontaneous, responsive sharing.

As the infant's awareness increased, his interests broadened to the things his mother and other caretakers did and to the objects and materials they used. Then these youngsters began crawling out to explore things that attracted their attention. By the time they were toddling, their interests continually took them on short sorties to nearby objects and persons. As soon as they could walk well, the excursions extended to the entire hamlet and its gardens, and then beyond with other children. Developing without interference or supervision, this personal exploratory learning quest freely touched on whatever was around, even axes, knives, machetes, fire, and the like. When I first went to the Fore, I was aghast.

Eventually I discovered that this capability emerged naturally from Fore infant-handling practices in their milieu of close human physical

In infancy, Fore children begin experimental play with knives and other lethal objects. Sorenson never saw a child warned away or injured by them.

proximity and tactile interaction. Because touch and bodily contact lend themselves naturally to satisfying the basic needs of young children, an early kind of communicative experience fostered cooperative interaction between infants and their caretakers, also kinesthetic contact with the activities at hand. This made it easy for them to learn the appropriate handling of the tools of life.

The early pattern of exploratory activity included frequent return to one of the "mothers." Serving as home base, the bastion of security, a woman might occasionally give the youngster a nod of encouragement, if he glanced in her direction with un-

certainty. Yet rarely did the women attempt to control or direct, nor did they participate in the child's quests or jaunts.

As a result Fore children did not have to adjust to rule and schedule in order to find their place in life. They could pursue their interests and whims wherever they might lead and still be part of a richly responsive world of human touch which constantly provided sustenance, comfort, diversion and security.

Learning proceeded during the course of pursuing interests and exploring. Constantly "in touch" with people who were busy with daily activities, the Fore young quickly

learned the skills of life from example. Muscle tone, movement and mood were components of this learning process; formal lessons and commands were not. Kinesthetic skills developed so quickly that infants were able to casually handle knives and similar objects before they could walk.

Even after several visits I continued to be surprised that the unsupervised Fore toddlers did not recklessly thrust themselves into unappreciated dangers, the way our own children tend to do. But then, why should they? From their earliest days, they enjoyed a benevolent sanctuary from which the world could be confidently

5 *Babies have free access to the breast and later, like this toddler being helped to kernels of corn by an older girl, can help themselves to whatever food is around—indulged by children and grown-ups.*

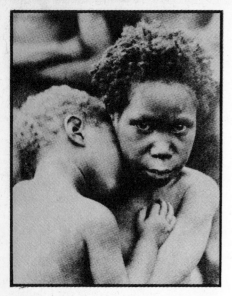

Close, constant body contact, as between this baby and older girl, creates security in Fore children.

viewed, tested and appreciated. This sanctuary remained ever available, but did not demand, restrain or impose. One could go and come at will.

In close harmony with their source of life, the Fore young were able confidently, not furtively, to extend their inquiry. They could widen their understanding as they chose. There was no need to play tricks or deceive in order to pursue life.

Emerging from this early childhood was a freely ranging young child rather in tune with his older and younger hamlet mates, disinclined to act out impulsively, and with a capable appreciation of the properties of potentially dangerous objects. Such children could be permitted to move out on their own, unsupervised and unrestricted. They were safe.

Such a pattern could persist indefinitely, re-creating itself in each new generation. However, hidden within the receptive character it produced was an Achilles heel; it also permitted adoption of new practices, including child-handling practices, which did *not* act to perpetuate the pattern. In only one generation after Western contact, the cycle of Fore life was broken.

Attuned as they were to individual pursuit of economic and social good, it did not take the Fore long to recognize the value of the new materials,

practices and ideas that began to flow in. Indeed, change began almost immediately with efforts to obtain steel axes, salt, medicine and cloth. The Fore were quick to shed indigenous practices in favor of Western example. They rapidly altered their ways to adapt to Western law, government, religion, materials and trade.

Sometimes change was so rapid that many people seemed to be afflicted by a kind of cultural shock. An anomie, even cultural amnesia, seemed to pervade some hamlets for a time. There were individuals who appeared temporarily to have lost memory of recent past events. Some Fore even forgot what type and style of traditional garments they had worn only a few years earlier, or that they had used stone axes and had eaten their dead close relatives.

Remarkably open-minded, the Fore so readily accepted reformulation of identity and practice that suggestion or example by the new government officers, missionaries and scientists could alter tribal affiliation, place names, conduct and hamlet style. When the first Australian patrol officer began to map the region in 1957, an error in communication led him to refer to these people as the "Fore." Actually they had had no name for themselves and the word, Fore, was their name for a quite different group, the Awa, who spoke another language and lived in another valley. They did not correct the patrol officer but adopted his usage. They all now refer to themselves as the Fore. Regional and even personal names changed just as readily.

More than anything else, it was the completion of a steep, rough, always muddy Jeep road into the Fore lands that undermined the traditional life. Almost overnight their isolated region was opened. Hamlets began to move down from their ridgetop sites in order to be nearer the road, consolidating with others.

The power of the road is hard to overestimate. It was a great artery where only restricted capillaries had existed before. And down this artery came a flood of new goods, new ideas

On the way to hunt birds, cuscus (a marsupial) or rats, Fore boys stride through a sweet-potato garden.

and new people. This new road, often impassable even with four-wheel-drive vehicles, was perhaps the single most dramatic stroke wrought by the government. It was to the Fore an opening to a new world. As they began to use the road, they started to shed traditions evolved in the protective insularity of their mountain fastness, to adopt in their stead an emerging market culture.

THE COMING OF THE COFFEE ECONOMY

"Walkabout," nonexistent as an institution before contact, quickly became an accepted way of life. Fore boys began to roam hundreds of miles from their homeland in the quest for new experience, trade goods, jobs and money. Like the classic practice of the Australian aborigine, this "walkabout" took one away from his home for periods of varying length. But unlike the Australian practice, it usually took the boys to jobs and schools rather than to a solitary life in traditional lands. Obviously it sprang from the earlier pattern of individual freedom to pursue personal interests and opportunity wherever it might lead. It was a new expression of the old Fore exploratory pattern.

Some boys did not roam far, whereas others found ways to go to distant cities. The roaming boys often sought places where they might be welcomed as visitors, workers or students for a while. Mission stations and schools, plantation work camps, and the servants' quarters of the European population became way-stations in the lives of the modernizing Fore boys.

Some took jobs on coffee plantations. Impressed by the care and attention lavished on coffee by European planters and by the money they saw paid to coffee growers, these young Fore workers returned home with coffee beans to plant.

Coffee grew well on the Fore hillsides, and in the mid-1960s, when the first sizable crop matured, Fore who previously had felt lucky to earn a few dollars found themselves able to earn a few hundred dollars. A rush to coffee ensued, and when the new gardens became productive a few years later, the Fore income from coffee jumped to a quarter of a million dollars a year. The coffee revolution was established.

At first the coffee was carried on the backs of its growers (sometimes for several days) over steep, rough mountain trails to a place where it could be sold to a buyer with a jeep. However, as more and more coffee was produced, the villagers began to turn with efforts to planning and constructing roads in association with neighboring villages. The newly built roads, in turn, stimulated further economic development and the opening of new trade stores throughout the region.

Following European example, the segregated collective men's and women's houses were abandoned. Family houses were adopted. This changed the social and territorial arena for all the young children, who hitherto had been accustomed to living equally with many members of their hamlet. It gave them a narrower place to belong, and it made them more distinctly someone's children. Uncomfortable in the family houses, boys who had grown up in a freer territory began to gather in "boys' houses," away from the adult men who were now beginning to live in family houses with their wives. Mothers began to wear blouses, altering the early freer access to the breast. Episodes of infant and child frustration, not seen in traditional Fore hamlets, began to take place along with repeated incidents of anger, withdrawal, aggressiveness and stinginess.

So Western technology worked its magic on the Fore, its powerful materials and practices quickly shattering their isolated autonomy and lifestyle. It took only a few years from the time Western intruders built their first grass-thatched patrol station before the Fore way of life they found was gone.

Fortunately, enough of the Fore traditional ways were systematically documented on film to reveal how unique a flower of human creation they were. Like nothing else, film made it possible to see the behavioral patterns of this way of life. The visual record, once made, captured data which was unnoticed and unanticipated at the time of filming and which was simply impossible to study without such records. Difficult-to-spot subtle patterns and fleeting nuances of manner, mood and human relations emerged by use of repeated reexamination of related incidents, sometimes by slow motion and stopped frame. Eventually the characteristic behavioral patterns of Fore life became clear, and an important aspect of human adaptive creation was revealed.

The Fore way of life was only one of the many natural experiments in living that have come into being through thousands of years of independent development in the world. The Fore way is now gone; those which remain are threatened. Under the impact of modern technology and commerce, the entire world is now rapidly becoming one system. By the year 2000 all the independent natural experiments that have come into being during the world's history will be merging into a single world system.

One of the great tragedies of our modern time may be that most of these independent experiments in living are disappearing before we can discover the implication of their special expressions of human possibility. Ironically, the same technology responsible for the worldwide cultural convergence has also provided the means by which we may capture detailed visual records of the yet remaining independent cultures. The question is whether we will be able to seize this never-to-be repeated opportunity. Soon it will be too late. Yet, obviously, increasing our understanding of the behavioral repertoire of humankind would strengthen our ability to improve life in the world.

Dark Dreams About the White Man

Thomas Gregor

Thomas Gregor, associate professor of anthropology at Vanderbilt University, is the author of Mehinaku: The Drama of Daily Life in a Brazilian Indian Village, *published by the University of Chicago Press.*

Last night my dream was very bad.
I dreamed of the white man.
A Mehinaku villager

In 1500 explorer Pedro Cabral landed on the coast of Brazil and claimed its lands and native peoples for the Portuguese empire. Since that time Brazilian Indians have been killed by European diseases and bounty hunters, forced off their land by squatters and speculators, and enslaved by ranchers and mine owners. Today the Indians, numbering less than one-tenth of the precontact population, inhabit the most remote regions of the country.

I have been privileged as an anthropologist to live among the Mehinaku, a tribe of about eighty tropical-forest Indians who have thus far escaped the destruction. The Mehinaku, along with eight other single-village tribes, live in a vast government-protected reservation in the Mato Grosso, at the headwaters of the Xingu River in central Brazil. Collectively called Xinguanos by the outside world, the Mehinaku and their neighbors speak dialects of four unrelated languages. In spite of their cultural differences, they have developed a peaceful system of relationships based on intermarriage, trade, and group rituals. This political achievement persists, thanks largely to the geographic isolation of the Xingu reservation. Even today, the Brazilian presence consists only of an outpost of the Brazilian Indian Agency and a small, dirt-strip air force base. Nearly 200 miles of forest and savanna separate the Xingu villages from Shavantina, the nearest permanent Brazilian settlement of any size.

Despite the remoteness of central Brazil and the traditional character of village life, even a casual visitor to the Mehinaku sees unexpected signs of Brazilian society: battery-operated shortwave radios (usually tuned to backwoods popular favorites), battered aluminum pots for carrying water, and discarded items of Western clothing. But these, and the other flotsam and jetsam of industrial society that drift to the center of Brazil, affect only the appearance of Indian culture. They catch the eye of the visitor, but they do not break the rhythm of traditional subsistence, ritual, and trade that are the heartbeat of Xingu life.

Although geographically and socially distant, urban Brazil peers nonetheless into the world of the Xinguanos. Popular magazines feature articles about their life in a "jungle paradise," and smiling Xingu faces adorn postcards sold at Rio newsstands. Recently, a film shot in the Xingu reservation was woven into a *novela,* an afternoon television soap opera. So heavily exposed are the physically handsome Xingu tribes that in the popular mind they *are* the Brazilian Indian.

Brazilian officials have their own use for the Xinguanos. Faced with charges of neglect and even genocide against its native peoples, the government has used the tribes of the area for public relations. Happy, well-nourished Xinguanos decorate government publications, and when necessary, the Indians themselves can be counted on to amuse visiting dignitaries. High consular officials from the diplomatic corps in Brasília and other international elite have flown out to the Xingu reservation for adventure and entertainment. Almost invariably their visits have been a success and they have returned home with an impression of idyllic relationships between the Brazilian authorities and the Xinguanos. But if such visitors came to know their hosts more intimately, they would learn that contact with the white man has had a profound and bitter impact on the Indians' inner life.

During my work among the Mehinaku I have become increasingly aware of the villagers' anxieties about the white man. The soldiers at the nearby air force base, whom they regard as powerful and unpredictable, are especially frightening to the Mehinaku. On one occasion a rumor swept through the community that a plane from the base was going to bomb the village because one of the Mehinaku had stolen a mosquito net belonging to an air force sergeant. This wild story was believable because it drew on a reservoir of anxiety and confusion about the white man. Recently, I have been studying the villagers' dreams as a way of learning about their unconscious fears.

According to the Mehinaku, dreams are caused by the wandering of the "shadow," or soul, which is conceived of as a tiny replica of the individual living within the eye. As the villagers demonstrate to children or to the inquisitive anthropologist, the soul's image can be seen as a reflection in a pool of water or even in the iris of another person's eye. The soul is said to leave its owner at night to wander about. "Far, far away my soul wandered last night," is the opening phrase that may begin a dream narration. In the dream world of the community and the surrounding forests, the soul meets the wandering souls of animals, spirits, and other villagers. These experiences come into the dreamer's awareness in a way the villagers do not fully understand. "Dreams come up," they say, "as corn comes up from the ground."

The nightly adventures of the soul through the nocturnal village and forest are interpreted with the help of an unwritten dream book, a collection of dream symbols and their deciphered meanings. To the Mehinaku, dream symbols (*patalapiri*, literally "pictures," or "images") represent events to come. Frequently, the predictions resemble the dream symbol in their appearance or activity. For example, since weeds are symbols of hair, a dream of a well-cleared path is symbolic of baldness in later life. Occasionally, the dream symbol is more abstract and poetic. A dream about collecting edible flying ants suggests bereavement, since the rain of ants that descends on the village in the fall of each year is likened to the tears that fall when a kinsman dies.

As the last example suggests, many Mehinaku dream symbols are gloomy forecasts of death or misfortune. The grimmest omens of all, however, are

those that deal with the white man. Any dream about a Brazilian is a bad dream. Even a dream prominently featuring an object associated with Brazilians, such as an airplane, is distressing. Dreams of the white man are, for the Mehinaku, "pictures" of disease. A person who has such a dream is likely to become sick. In support of this interpretation, the villagers point out that many illnesses—measles, colds, influenza—are brought in from the outside. These diseases have had a devastating impact on the community. In the early 1960s, nearly 20 percent of the tribe died in a measles epidemic, and the villagers continue to suffer from imported diseases for which they have neither natural nor acquired immunity. Dreams such as the following one reflect such concerns:

At the post a plane landed. Many, many passengers got off. It seemed as if there was a village in the plane. I was very frightened of them and the things they carried. I was afraid they would bring a disease to the village, the white man's "witchcraft."

The Mehinaku fear of the white man goes beyond the fear of disease, as I learned when I began to make a collection of their dreams. The villagers were willing collaborators in this effort since they regard dreams as significant and make a deliberate effort to recall them when they wake up. In the morning, as I circulated from house to house to harvest the previous night's crop of dreams, I would occasionally be summoned across the plaza ("Tommy, I have a dream for you!") by a villager with a particularly dramatic narrative. Altogether I collected 385 dreams, the majority of which (70 percent) were contributed by the men.

In thirty-one of the sample dreams, Brazilians were cast as the central characters. What is striking about these dreams is their high level of anxiety. While about half of the villagers' dreams show some level of anxiety, fully 90 percent of the dreams of the white man are tinged with fear. Furthermore, when I rated dreams on the basis of their frightening content

and the dreamer's own report of distress, I found that dreams of the white man were charged with more than double the average level of anxiety. This was higher than any other comparable class of dreams, even dreams of malignant spirits and dangerous animals.

Occasionally, the mere sight or sound of an outsider creates anxiety: "I heard them speaking on the radio at the post, but I could not understand. The speech and the language were frightening to me." Within the sample of dreams, however, I found a number of terrifying themes that repeatedly appeared in the villagers' narratives. The most prominent of these are heat and fire. In the dreams, Brazilian soldiers explode incendiary devices in the village, burning houses and people. Fiery planes crash and blow up in the central plaza, covering the villagers with flames. Even when the victims throw themselves in the river, the fire continues to burn their clothes and skin.

We went to the place where the canoe was moored. A plane came overhead and broke in the sky. It crashed in the water and everything caught on fire. The gasoline floated on the water. My mother caught on fire.

Fire and heat are appropriate symbols of terror among the Mehinaku. The villagers live in large thatch houses, often as much as 100 feet long, 30 feet wide, and 20 feet high. Two narrow doors in the middle of the house and a complete lack of windows minimize the intrusion of biting insects, but make the houses firetraps. On occasion, the Mehinaku deliberately burn abandoned houses and the resultant blaze is instructive. While the villagers watch, the house owner sets fire to some of the thatch at the base of the building. Within moments, white smoke pours through the wall, and suddenly an entire side of the house bursts into flame. Seconds later, the convection of air and heat turns the building into a blazing inferno. As the Mehinaku edge back from the wall of heat and flame, they consider what would happen if an occupied house caught on fire. "If the fire begins when the people are asleep," one of the villagers told me, "then everyone burns."

Less dangerous than house fires, but almost as frightening, are fires that are deliberately set to clear the villagers' gardens. The Mehinaku are slash-and-burn agriculturists who clear a plot of land in the forest, allow the vegetation to dry, and then set it on fire. The blaze sends up towers of white smoke that can be seen for miles. Once started, the fire is totally out of control. The villagers say that it is "wildly angry," and they tell myths of how men and spirits have gone to their death, trapped in the burning fields. This danger is more than fictional, since villagers have been badly burned when the wind shifted as they were firing their gardens. Dreams that link the white man to heat and fire thus associate him with one of the most frightening and destructive forces in the Mehinaku environment.

A second recurrent theme in dreams of the white man is assault. Villagers are shot with rifles, strafed from planes, pursued by trucks, and attacked with machetes. At times, as in the following dream of a young man, the assault is sexually motivated:

We were at the air force base, and a soldier wanted to have sex with my sister. He took her arm and tried to pull her away. We shouted at the soldier and at my sister. My aunt and I tried to pull her back. But the soldier was too strong for us. He was very strong. He said "If you don't let me have sex with Mehinaku women I will shoot you." I got a gun and shot at him, many times. But he was hidden and I couldn't see him.

Another dreamer described a similar situation:

A Brazilian doctor tried to take away my sister. . . . "If you don't let me, I will kill you," he said. . . . He shot and killed my two brothers. I cried in my dream, and I cried when I woke up.

Assault, like fire and heat, has an especially potent role in the Mehinaku symbolism of fear. In comparing themselves to other Indians and to whites, the villagers invariably point out that they are a peaceful people. There is no word for war in their language

other than "many flying arrows," nor is there a historical record of the Mehinaku having participated in organized, armed violence. When attacked by the Carib-speaking Txicão tribe in the 1960s, they responded by cowering in their houses as arrows whistled through the thatch walls. After the chief sustained a serious arrow wound in his back, they moved the village closer to the Indian post in the hope that they would not be pursued.

Within the village, strong sanctions bar interpersonal violence. The man who lets his anger get the best of him is slurred as a *japujaitsi* (literally, "angry man," but also a species of nearly inedible hot pepper). There are no *japujaitsi* in the village, and in my year and a half residence in the community, I never saw a fight between men. As one villager put it, "When we are angry, we wrestle, and the anger is gone. When the white men are angry, they shoot each other."

The menace of white society is real to the Mehinaku because of the accounts they have heard at the Indian post about Brazilian atrocities against Indians. They know that in the recent past Indians have been shot, poisoned, and enslaved by bounty hunters and, during one particularly shameful period prior to the establishment of the present Indian agency in 1967, by some government employees working for the former Indian agency. They know, too, that their lands are insecure and that the boundaries of the Xingu reservation can—and do—change according to the whim of bureaucrats in Brasília. A road has already penetrated the far northern end of the reservation and has brought tribes in that area into violent conflict with white ranchers. There is thus good reason to be wary of the Brazilian. As in the case of fire, dreams of assault and aggression link the white man to very real sources of anxiety in waking life.

A final theme of fear that permeates the villagers' dreams is perhaps the most poignant. In many of the narratives, the dreamer expresses a sense of disorientation in dealing with the outsiders. The white men lack

comprehensible motivation and perform capricious acts of malice and violence. They distract mothers from their crying infants, they give presents and demand them back, and they kidnap small children. They lure a man to a distant Brazilian city, cut off his head, and send it back to his horrified kin. Disguised as Mehinaku, they tempt the dreamer to give up his life as an Indian, and urge him to accompany them to distant cities from which he will never return. A mother dreams of losing her young children to the outsider:

My children said they would go to visit the Brazilians. They said they would go to São Paulo and Rio de Janeiro, and Cuiabá. I told them not to go. But they went, far off. We waited a long time, but they did not come back. I went to find them, but I could not. My mother's sister came to help me, and we looked all over. Then I heard them crying from a far way off, but still I could not find them. Then, I awoke.

Some of the dreams border on the Kafkaesque:

A guard pointed a gun at me. He told me to go through a door. I did. The room was filled with a beautiful light. The guard gave me a watch and told me I could come out at a certain time. He locked the door. I looked at the watch, and I realized I did not know how to tell time. There was a wind and a strange smell.

The confused portrayal of the white man stems from the Mehinaku's distorted view of Brazilian life. To the villagers, everyday Brazilian conduct and ordinary material objects are both alluring and strange. Tape recorders, radios, cameras, and other gadgets sported by visitors to the Xingu reservation fascinate the Mehinaku but also perplex them. Even when these objects are dismantled and inspected, they don't give up their secrets. "Are the white men wizards?" I was once asked by one of the Mehinaku.

Those villagers who have visited São Paulo and Rio de Janeiro return home with the same sense of fascinated puzzlement. A young man, the narrator of the dream text above, spent a summer living with a vacationing upper-class family in the beach resort of Guarujá outside of São Paulo.

He was intrigued and attracted by what he saw, but uncomprehending. The wealth of Guarujá seemed magically produced; certainly members of the family were not making their possessions with their own hands, as do the Xinguanos. On the same trip he saw impoverished beggars on São Paulo's streets, but once he was back in the tribe, most of his stories were about the magic and glitter of the city.

The outsider visiting the Mehinaku senses the gap of understanding in another way. Let a man arrive in the community and he is immediately questioned about his kinsmen. Does he have a wife? parents? sisters? Which of his kinsmen gave him his jacket? Was it his brother-in-law? The Xingu communities are kin based, and the questions are an effort to place the white man in the orbit of under-standable social relationships. If he remains within the community, the villagers probe further, often by teasing their guest. His appearance, gait, name, and speech become the object of semihumorous (and often painful) ridicule. This period of hazing has been reported by many researchers in the Xingu, and its predictability persuades me that it is part of the effort to make the powerful outsider knowable. If he has weaknesses and can be hurt, then he is human and understandable.

The many years of friendly but superficial contact with Brazilians have not made the white man more intelligible to the Mehinaku. As of my most recent visit in 1977, none of the villagers was able to explain why the Brazilians had come to the Xingu forests. "The white man is here," the chief told me in all seriousness, "to give us presents." The economic and political forces that led the Brazilian government into the interior of the continent to construct bases such as the Indian post are mysterious to the Mehinaku. The Brazilians and their impersonal society seem nearly as bizarre and disjointed in waking life as they do in the villagers' dreams.

Mehinaku lands and culture remain largely intact, but a part of their inner tranquility has been laid to waste. Neither geographic isolation nor heroic efforts at protection could save it. Contact with Brazilian society has taken a higher toll than we might have anticipated. Certainly the Mehinaku have paid dearly for their steel tools, their cast-off clothes, and the other "gifts of civilization." By day, all appears well. But each night, we outsiders visit the sleeping villagers and haunt them in restless dreams.

The Aborigines' Search for Justice

Descendants of Australia's ancient inhabitants see rays of success but not yet a full-blown dawn.

Ross Terrill

Ross Terrill, a writer and scholar in the field of international affairs, visited the Aboriginal communities in each state and territory of his native Australia while researching this article. He now lives in the United States.

On a brilliant spring evening in 1985 the Australian government gave Uluru, the nation's premier tourist site, back to the Aborigines. In the pink desert I watched an Aboriginal woman lift her child high in the air to see the governor general arrive through a cloud of dust. "Look, see the king," she said to the infant as the white-suited head of state handed over title to Uluru—called Ayers Rock by whites—to the Pitjantjatjara and Yankuntjatjara tribes.

The tribal blacks, for whom the huge monolith is a book of history from the Dreamtime—an epoch long ago when man and nature alike are believed to have been created—would now lease Uluru back to the federal government in Canberra.

On a makeshift platform draped with the Aboriginal flag, vibrant dances were performed by Aborigines painted in yellow and ocher and white. Then a dinner of buffalo steak was served on paper plates. To some, the long-awaited ceremony seemed to reverse history's sorry tide of whites forever pushing out blacks. To others, it was a mere token display to mask a retreat from turning back substantial land to Aborigines.

"The handover of Ayers Rock is a turning point in Australia's race rela-

tions," remarked Charles Perkins, then Australia's top black civil servant. "It's a recognition that Aboriginal people were the original owners of this country. Also it will save Australia hundreds of millions of dollars—in jails, murders, frustrations, anxieties."

But Galarrwuy Yunupingu, a militant Aborigine in Darwin who is the scourge of the Northern Territory's conservative government, didn't see the handover as a big victory. "I'd only call it a victory," he told me drily over breakfast the day after the handover, "if the governor general came and gave us title to the whole of Australia, and we leased *that* back to the Commonwealth."

Later events have cast doubt on Charles Perkins's optimistic reading that the shift of ownership of Ayers Rock marked a change in race relations. The deaths of Aborigines in police custody have been a dominant topic of news and conversation in Australia recently. Whether beaten by police, dangerously drunk, or demoralized to the point of suicide, 105 blacks—most of them in prison for minor offenses—have died in cells of the "Lucky Country" in the past six years. (The total black population is 250,000.)

Gerry Hand, the minister for Aboriginal affairs in the federal Labor Party government, said to me recently: "The handover of Uluru was the beginning of the awakening of Australians to the fact of genuine Aboriginal attachment to the land." Australia's Bicentenary in 1988 focused extra attention on the British settlers' dispossession of the Aborigines.

"Aborigines didn't tow Ayers Rock away and hide it," Hand commented, "though many people warned they would. Tourism is continuing to grow at Uluru."

Yet land rights have not been extended across the nation as supporters had hoped. Too many Australians have mixed feelings about handing over large tracts of land to Aborigines.

Prime Minister Bob Hawke has proposed a "treaty" between the Australian government and Aborigines: It would both carry forward the symbolic recovery of rights and transform the land-rights issue into a more general concept of Australia's debt to its original inhabitants.

But the treaty, and Hand's bold plan to make black "self-determination" a reality by establishing a structure of elected Aboriginal bodies—separate from existing elected state and federal parliaments—are eclipsed in the public mind by urgent social problems among the Aboriginal communities. Most haunting are the deaths while in policy custody.

Both scholars and ordinary Australians are beginning to realize how long the Aborigines have lived in Australia. It may well be, as Josephine Flood, author of the leading study "Archaeology of the Dreamtime," thinks likely, that the Aborigines came to Australia during the period of low sea level some 53,000 years ago—when it was easier to reach Australia than after the melting of Ice Age glaciers.

Where in Asia the Aborigines came from is unclear. Other intriguing questions beg answers. When did the southern isle of Tasmania develop its separate ways (its Aborigines gave up eating fish some 3,000 years ago; it never knew the dingo)?

Still, the past is yielding up some secrets. Archaeologists have found the stones and bones of a civilization at least 40,000 years old. The Aborigines created a viable, materially simple, leisured, but not easygoing society. They survived drought, flood, isolation, and other hazards. They grew no crops. Neither pig nor buffalo nor any other animal did they domesticate.

Subjugation of women, female infanticide, and other cruelties existed. Aboriginal law dealt less with the individual and his rights than with the clan and its subgroupings, and the responsibilities of these collectives.

In awe of nature, the Aborigines more or less equated the cosmic order and the social order. The existence of both man and matter was attributed to the activities of mythic Ancestral Beings who during the Dreamtime created the world and then withdrew from it.

Long after the Pilgrims reached America, then, the continent of Australia was peopled only by hunters and gatherers, who as local groupings had fitted themselves effectively into the natural order, in almost total isolation from the rest of the world.

Some 300,000 Aborigines existed when Captain Cook arrived in the 1770s. Blacks lost sources of food as whites caught fish and the new settlements drove away kangaroos. Blacks welcomed many accoutrements of the whites' life, but they could not cope with alcohol, and smallpox and venereal disease killed tens of thousands.

Aboriginal holy places—such as a mound, a hollow log, a rock of bizarre shape—were not taken seriously by whites because they seemed to be mere objects of nature. Christian shrines seemed trivial to blacks because they were merely man-made. Clergy did not react well when blacks, hearing the promise of Jesus to give them whatever they asked of him, requested boots and dresses.

Because the new settlers were the

Map by Dave Herring

more resourceful, they could give up their early attempts to understand the Aborigine and push him aside. Cook had taken a favorable view: "They are far happier than we Europeans," the sea captain said; while the "first parents" of the Europeans "saw themselves naked and were ashamed, these people are naked and not ashamed."

But misunderstanding chipped away at optimism. As Aboriginal workers failed to satisfy white employers, the Christian gospel made scant inroads into the Aboriginal soul, and rum worked its devastation, the whites increasingly doubted that the Aborigines could be "civilized," used to meet the labor shortage, or even saved from destruction.

A continent black for millennia rapidly turned white.

Fay Nelson, prominent in Aboriginal arts in New South Wales, told me that, during her school years, the only mention of Aborigines was that "Captain Cook saw some blacks and got speared by one. Nothing was taught of our life, art, culture."

In Adelaide, Johnny Moriarty, head of South Australia's Ministry of Aboriginal Affairs, told me how he was taken away from his tribal mother—his father was half Irish—at age 6 and

put in a foster home; half-castes were supposed to be "protected" from the black parent.

"With our upbringing, you went this way, or you went the other way," Moriarty reflected. "A few of us developed some tenacity, I suppose, from the experience. A number were destroyed—by alcoholism, lethargy, demoralization."

During my childhood in the Gippsland region of Victoria, Aborigines picked green beans in season and came door to door with woven baskets to sell. Camping under weeping willow trees by the river, they seemed to us kids more akin to the emus and the eucalyptus (gum) trees than to fellow Australians. I never had an Aboriginal friend and I don't think an Aborigine ever entered my schoolteacher parents' house.

The situation for blacks in those years of the late 1940s and early 1950s was basically as it had been for many decades. Not citizens but wards of the state, Australia's original inhabitants were forbidden to cohabit with a white, buy liquor, cross state boundaries without permission, or be a party in a civil court.

A referendum in 1967 gave the federal government power over Aboriginal issues, and thus began today's new era. Blacks gained civil rights, increased cultural respect, and government funds.

Yet this ancient people still lag even by fourth-world standards. Life expectancy is 20 years less than the Australian average. Aboriginal infant mortality is three times that of non-Aborigines. While 1% of Australians have never attended school, 11% of Aboriginal Australians have never done so.

As drink, disease, and the demoralization of the dole take their toll, an Aborigine is a dozen times more likely to be in prison than a non-Aboriginal Australian, and six times more likely to be unemployed.

The end of official programs aimed at assimilation, the subsequent pumping of vast sums of government money into Aboriginal services, and the recent environmental movement's respect for blacks' mystical ties to the land have together not been able to guarantee a future for the traditional Aboriginal way of life.

In Melbourne and Sydney the sparse Aboriginal population includes many militants. The whites—who have little experience of Aboriginal life—sometimes find Aboriginal traditions an appealing theoretical alternative to Western society's moneymaking and rule by the clock. And public policy tends to be generous toward Aboriginal causes and claims.

In the remoter cities, Perth and Darwin and Brisbane, and the rural areas beyond them, public policy is less "pro-Aboriginal." Whites are more inclined to criticize Aborigines as drunken, lazy, and dirty. The Aborigines—who are far more numerous in these regions than in the dominant states—are often moderate in outlook, ready to do business with miners and to compromise on the details of land rights.

In Perth I went to see Dame Mary Durack, a novelist and historian raised in the dry brown northwest. "We had a family relationship with the Aborigines on our stations," Durack recalled in the study of her sprawling home. "The Aborigines were our stockmen. It was a healthy, happy life, and the Aborigines felt important."

For Dame Mary, the coming of "equal wages" and Aboriginal access to the dole, after the referendum, ended the family relationship and brought to the blacks unemployment (as station owners could no longer afford to employ Aboriginal stockmen at the new wage rates) and alcoholism (fueled by dole money and idleness). "Now they've been told they ought to demand land rights," objected the veteran writer. "People are manipulating them."

I heard a militant view from Robert Bropho, longtime spokesman for the west's fringe dwellers, who holds to the traditional idea of the land as Mother to Aborigines. "We shared our Mother with you," he said. "But the white man won't share."

Bropho defended Aboriginal views of spirituality: "The white man calls our beliefs a myth, but can you, Mr. White Man, prove to us that your Ten Commandments are true and not a myth?"

Bropho, who was an alcoholic by age 15 and spent some 20 years in prison for stealing and other crimes, doesn't drink any more. "The day Aborigines won the right to go into a pub," he told me, "I had my last minty [drink] with my mates. I never looked back."

From Alice Springs I drove in a four-wheel drive toward pink hills dotted with mulga trees. Every 10 kilometers or so an abandoned Toyota sat by the road: Aborigines whose cars break down do not find it worthwhile to arrange repairs; they simply hitch a ride with someone else and leave the car to nature's hot embrace.

"There aren't any deserts in Japan," a companion from Alice Springs quipped, "but there's a lot of Japan in the desert."

We drove to the historic Lutheran mission of Hermannsburg. Gus Williams, its boss since the Lutherans handed control to Aborigines in 1972, recalled: "In the past the church made the decisions. They even thought for us."

Williams says the problems of the Hermannsburg community, which recently began to receive large royalties from Amadeus Basin gas, have grown in recent years. He blames automatic unemployment benefits. "Previously, if you didn't work, you didn't receive rations." Hermannsburg once boasted a tannery, a boomerang making industry, and cabbage and other vegetable plots, but all are gone.

Pride in their independence at times worsens the problems resulting from liquor and economic inertia. "The grog comes in because people say, 'It's our land now, we're going to do [on] it just what we want,' " explained Williams, who once worked as a tourist driver. "People say, 'No tourists, no white people here,' " and so Hermannsburg misses out on tourist dollars.

"SAD BOYS ARE SNIFFING," said a poster on a radio studio wall in Alice Springs, referring to the gasoline sniffing that kills many young Aborigines. Children of primary school age hang Coke cans filled with petrol from a string around their necks. Sniffing for escape or a thrill, they ignore the world around them, suffer brain damage and lead poisoning, and often die within a few years.

The Central Australian Aboriginal Media Association is a radio and TV station that broadcasts in English and five Aboriginal tongues to an audience that is 53% Aboriginal. Its director, Freda Glynn, said her mission is to enable Aborigines to "hear positive things about themselves" after having been taught for generations that they are "nothing but savages."

"I was a horrible ambassador to America," Glynn said of a recent trip to the United States. "I'm a bush person. I freaked out in New York and locked myself in my hotel room for five days. And I found black Americans just to be ordinary Americans with black skins."

"Aren't you an ordinary Australian with a black skin?"

"I suppose I am." She frowns. "No, I'm an Aborigine!"

No doubt the time will come—but it is not quite yet—when people with skins of all shades will be considered ordinary Australians.

For years, nature versus progress has been a vexed issue in Aboriginal affairs. Miners—more than 40% of

Australia's exports are from mining—are alarmed that 32% of the Northern Territory, whose tiny population of 140,000 is 24% Aboriginal, is under black control. In the public mind, Aborigines and miners seem pitted against each other.

I flew east from Darwin to Groote Eylandt (Dutch for "big island"; Abel Tasman named the island in 1644), where miners share a tranquil isolation with some of Australia's most traditional Aborigines. About 1,000 blacks and the 1,200 employees of Groote Eylandt Mining Company (GEMCO), which supplies some 12% of the world's traded manganese, cooperate and prosper in basic harmony.

The Groote Aborigines were taken in hand from 1921 by Anglican missionaries. They have a deep attachment to the island. Isolation has lent them security, and they have always viewed the whites as temporary visitors. Intermarriage here is uncommon and frowned on by the elders. Excellent bark art (it began as the decoration of the interiors of bark shelters) is produced, as are colorful parrot-feather montages.

Although only about 20 Aborigines work at GEMCO now—"sit-down money" (the dole) is too attractive—some 300 of them did so at one time. Their experience, plus royalties from GEMCO, provide skills, motivation, and funds to the nearby community of Angurugu.

Eighty miles away, Umbakumba, the second community on Groote, has less contact with GEMCO, more influence from government officials, and more readily available liquor. Umbakumba has been going downhill. One statistic tells much: The imprisonment rate in Umbakumba is more than 25 times the national imprisonment rate.

I watched a sad parade in Judge Stephen Hawke's courtroom in Alyangula as 92 offenses were described and the law dealt out penalties to 41 offenders. Nearly every case involved cars and liquor. "Failure to keep to the left . . . Unlawful entry with intent . . . Alcohol level above 0.8% . . . Driving manner dangerous."

Johnny Wurramarrba, who works

for GEMCO, took me to see Murabuda Wurramarrba, grandfatherly chairman of the Angurugu council. He and Johnny greeted each other calmly, and one would never have known that a few days before, after Johnny declined to seek a favor with GEMCO that Murabuda had asked for, Murabuda tried to strike him with a shovel-nose spear.

The tribal chairman's theme was black and white together. "At first when GEMCO began to take our manganese to another world, we were sorry. But now we think it's a good thing. Aborigines now learn the two ways, European and Aboriginal."

At the pretty township of Umbakumba, veteran nurse Connie Bush recalled being taken away from her mother as a child, 61 years ago, and brought to Groote. "It happened to everyone," she said as we sat under a brilliant sunset in a beached rowboat at the end of Umbakumba pier. "The police that had to do the job didn't like it either."

Did her father resist her removal? Bush laughed. "He couldn't—he was a [white] policeman!"

She regrets that the Anglicans broke down Aboriginal tradition, but she is nostalgic for the mission days when fruit and vegetable gardens flourished at Angurugu, prior to drink and the dole.

Traditional culture has revived to a degree on Groote in recent years, and Bush is pleased that she has been embraced as "one of them" by fullbloods. "But I do feel caught between two worlds sometimes," she confessed. "My mother's people would say I wasn't an Aborigine, and the missionaries would say I wasn't white. Now I'm older I understand that we halfcastes are a different race altogether from anyone else."

Connie Bush's situation as a half-caste is the situation of a majority—ever growing—of Australian Aborigines.

Amid the problems there are bright spots. There is much Aboriginal excellence in sport, painting, music, and theater.

Conscientious parents in many places try against high odds to keep alive in their children the traditional Aborigi-

nal philosophy of "sharin' and carin'."

Near Derby in the northwest, I found Ray Coonac, teetotal leader of the Mowanjum people, tackling the drinking problem by squatting down with the boozers, drinking a Coke, and saying (to their great embarrassment, for they were far gone on stronger beverages), "Where you drink, I should drink too."

Trade schools for young blacks are starting to offer the prospect of escape from the cycle of dependence and the dole. A dramatic rise in Aboriginal public service employment has occurred.

Some Aborigines are taking the all-important step of playing their own independent role in the capitalist economy. The self-help handicraft and tourism enterprises of the Bathurst and Melville islanders near Darwin are promising. Some quiet, mutually beneficial deals have recently been made between Aborigines and miners in the north.

The success stories amount to occasional rays of light rather than a full-blown dawn of recovery for Aborigines. What has been gained in general terms since the 1967 referendum is that Aborigines have a more secure sense of their rights and opportunities in Australian society, and white Australians have a greater respect of Aboriginal culture. Full civil rights, community councils, land councils, and an abundance of organizations channeling health, legal, and other services to Aborigines are all steps ahead.

What is generally absent, however, is economic self-reliance. Mendicancy is the sad norm; Aboriginal income consists overwhelmingly of pension, dole, and handout. Nearly $3 billion spent by the federal government in the past six years—more than $13,000 per Aboriginal person—does not seem to have solved basic problems.

The test of whether an enduring new deal lies in store for Aborigines will come in economics. The Aborigine as a producer will find his way. The Aborigine as a mendicant may not even hang on to the psychological and administrative gains of the recent past.

Many questions have been raised about self-determination. Will the treaty proposed by Hawke and Hand be an international document? Among the fragmented Aboriginal communities, who will sign it? Will the prime minister sign only for non-Aboriginal Australians?

Hand does not claim the treaty has great public support; the conservative opposition says it has little. The conservatives feel the treaty implies Aborigines represent one nation, while other Australians (of many races) represent another.

"We are one nation," the opposition spokesman on Aboriginal affairs, Chris Miles, insisted to me, "diverse, but united. A nation cannot make a treaty with itself." Miles wants people to focus on the present, not the past. His Liberal Party, the opposition to the Hawke government, stresses "one Australia" and warns against "separatism." Miles points out that the vast majority of Aborigines are more like the rest of the Australian population than they are like the Aborigines of pre-1788 Australia.

Few as the Aborigines are, they are a key to the nation's conscience and self-image. Yet as the economy has soured, special favors for Aborigines, however justified by history and by need, are less widely supported than in the 1970s.

The new cautiousness toward solving Aboriginal problems is understandable. Australia is huge, Aboriginal society is diverse, and national solutions easily come unstuck. No one speaks up for assimilation anymore, but a recovery of Aboriginal separateness is impossible. For most Aborigines, land rights are solving few problems.

Not land, but other forms of compensation, plus a general right of self-determination, and a focus on Aborig-

ines' motivating themselves, seem the themes for tomorrow.

The silence that befalls many urban Australians when the Aboriginal issue is raised suggests that it is a mirror for the white Australians. A consciousness exists—perhaps it is the root of Australians' ambivalence toward their harsh if beautiful terrain—that the nation was forged through the dispossession of its previous occupants.

The attempt of black Australians to recover some of their losses occurs in a historical period marked by a racial complexity new in Australian history. Long a British outpost under southern skies, Australia has begun to be multicultural, as millions of immigrants, first from Europe and more recently from Asia, have changed the nation's flavor. A reassessment of past treatment of Aborigines coincides with Australia's leap to racial and cultural pluralism.

All over Australia I heard Aborigines and immigrants—Asian and European alike—criticize each other. Many Aboriginal leaders want Asian immigration ended. A Greek-Australian demanded to know why *he* should feel guilt about past treatment of Aborigines.

Even the recent Asian immigrants outnumber the Aborigines. The Aboriginal population is young but very small, and the percentage leading a traditional life style gets ever smaller. In many ways Australia's ancient past and its beckoning future tug in sharply different directions. As Australia itself changes rapidly, the role of Aborigines in tommorrow's Australia becomes doubly uncertain.

A government report on black deaths in custody has made interim recommendations: Abolish criminal penalties for drunkenness; never leave an Aborigine in a cell alone; weed out racist

police and educate all police in Aboriginal culture; comprehensively combat alcoholism in the black communities.

To their credit, in the past year and a half Australians have done much soul searching about the factors involved in blacks dying in prison. But making the report's recommendations effective at the grass-roots level will not be easy. For in the country towns, the fringes of the cities, and the inner-city slums, the Aborigines are in poor morale, and white-black relations remain uneasy.

Each step a young Aborigine makes to advance his life seems to take him further from the magnificent myths of the past. Every Aboriginal leader I met believes earnestly in education as a way out of Aborigines' interlocking problems, but education is often an enemy of tradition. Programs embodying compensatory justice in the end yield their fruit in the life of the individual, and the Aboriginal individual is spinning steadily into non-Aboriginal society.

Like many other talented black women, tennis champion Evonne Goolagong married a white man. She typifies the Aborigine who "made it" through sport or the arts, and the tendency of such an individual to move away from the Aboriginal community and its traditions—she now lives in the United States.

"Rights" for Aborigines have not canceled out past wrongs, if by that is meant closing the gap between black and white. Measuring by results, rather than by rights, perhaps white Australia will never succeed in restoring black Australia's dignity.

Not Ayers Rock, not all the Crown land of Australia would be enough to recompense for what modernity's boot crushed out of vulnerable, unambitious Aboriginal society.

Bicultural Conflict

Chinese cultural traits conflict with those encountered in America, posing dilemmas for immigrant children

Betty Lee Sung

Betty Lee Sung, professor of Asian studies at City College of New York, is the author of many books and articles on Chinese immigrants in the United States.

The moment a child is born, he begins to absorb the culture of his primary group; these ways are so ingrained they become a second nature to him. Imagine for a moment how wrenching it must be for an immigrant child who finds his cumulative life experiences completely invalidated, and who must learn a whole new set of speech patterns and behaviors when he settles in a new country. The severity of this culture shock is underlined by Teper's definition of culture:

Culture is called a habit system in which "truths" that have been perpetuated by a group over centuries have permeated the unconscious. This basic belief system, from which "rational" conclusions spring, may be so deeply ingrained that it becomes indistinguishable from human perception—the way one sees, feels, believes, knows. It is the continuity of cultural assumptions and patterns that gives order to one's world, reduces an infinite variety of options to a manageable stream of beliefs, gives a person a firm footing in time and space, and binds the lone individual to the communality of a group.

The language barrier was the problem most commonly mentioned by the immigrant Chinese among whom I have conducted field research. Language looms largest because it is the conduit through which people interact with other people. It is the means by which we think, learn, and express ourselves. Less obvious is the basis upon which we speak or act or think. If there are bicultural conflicts, these may engender problems and psychological difficulties, which may not be immediately apparent but may nevertheless impact on the development of immigrant children.

This article will address some of the cultural conflicts that commonly confront the Chinese child in the home and, particularly, in the schools. Oftentimes, teachers and parents are not aware of these conflicts and ascribe other meanings or other motives to the child's behavior, frequently in a disapproving fashion. Such censure confuses the child and quite often forces him to choose between what he is taught at home and what is commonly accepted by American society. In his desire to be accepted and to be liked, he may want to throw off that which is second nature to him; this may cause anguish and pain not only to himself but also to his parents and family. Teachers and parents should be aware of these differences and try to help the children resolve their conflicts, instead of exacerbating them.

AGGRESSIVENESS AND SEXUALITY

In Chinese culture, the soldier, or the man who resorts to violence, is at the bottom of the social ladder. The sage or gentleman uses his wits, not his fists. The American father will take his son out to the backyard and give him a few lessons in self-defense at the age of puberty. He teaches his son that the ability to fight is a sign of manhood. The Chinese parent teaches his son the exact opposite: Stay out of fights. Yet, when the Chinese child goes to the school playground, he becomes the victim of bullies who pick on him and call him a sissy. New York's teenagers can be pretty tough and cruel. If the child goes home with bruises and a black eye, his parents will yell at him and chastise him. What is he to do? The unresolved conflict about aggressive behavior is a major problem for Chinese-American males. They feel that their masculinity has been affected by their childhood upbringing.

What do the teachers or monitors do? In most instances, they are derisive of the Chinese boys. "Why don't the Chinese fight back?" they exclaim. "Why do they stand there and just take it?" This derision only shames the Chinese boys, who feel that their courage is questioned. This bicultural conflict may be reflected in the self-hatred of some Asian-American male activists who condemn the passivity of our forefathers in response to the discrimination and oppression they endured. Ignorant about their cultural heritage, the activists want to disassociate themselves from such "weakness," and they search for historical instances in which Asians put up a brave but costly and oftentimes futile fight to prove their manhood. The outbreak of gang violence may be another manifestation of the Chinese male's efforts to prove that he is "macho" also. He may be

From *The World & I,* August 1989, pp. 670-679. Re-edition of Chapter 8, "Bicultural Conflict," from the book *The Experience of Adjustment: Chinese Immigrant Children in New York City.* Center for Migration Studies of New York, Inc.

overcompensating for the derision that he has suffered.

In American schools, sexuality is a very strong and pervasive force. Boys and girls start noticing each other in the junior highs; at the high school level, sexual awareness is very pronounced. School is as much a place for male/female socialization as it is an institution for learning. Not so for the Chinese. Education is highly valued, and it is a serious business. To give their children an opportunity for a better education may be the primary reason why the parents push their children to study, study, study. Interest in the opposite sex is highly distracting and, according to some old-fashioned parents, improper. Dating is an unfamiliar concept and sexual attractiveness is underplayed, not flaunted as it is according to American ways.

This difference in attitudes and customs poses another dilemma for both the Chinese boys and girls. In school, the white, black, or Hispanic girls like to talk about clothes, makeup, and the dates they had over the weekend. They talk about brassiere sizes and tampons. The popular girl is the sexy one who dates the most. She is the envy of the other girls.

For the Chinese girl, the openness with which other girls discuss boys and sex is extremely embarrassing. Chinese girls used to bind their breasts, not show them off in tight sweaters. Their attitude toward the opposite sex is quite ambivalent. They feel that they are missing something very exciting when other girls talk about phone calls from their boyfriends or about their dates over the weekends, yet they will shy away and feel very uncomfortable if a boy shows an interest in them.

Most Chinese parents have had no dating experience. Their marriages were usually arranged by their own parents or through matchmakers. Good girls simply did not go out with boys alone, so the parents are very suspicious and apprehensive about their daughters dating, and they watch them very carefully. Most Chinese girls are not permitted to date, and for the daring girl who tries to go out against her parents' wishes, there will be a price to pay.

It is no easier for Chinese boys. The pressure to succeed in school is even greater than for girls, and parental opposition to dating is even more intense. Naturally, the parents want their children to adhere to the old ways. Some children do not agree with their parents and have to carry on their high school romances on the sly. These children are bombarded by television, advertisements, stories, magazines, and real-life examples of boy-girl attraction. The teenager is undergoing puberty and experiencing the instinctive urges surging within him or her. In this society they are titillated, whereas in China they are kept under wraps until they are married.

The problem is exacerbated when teachers make fun of Chinese customs and the parents. I saw an instance of this at one of the Chinatown schools. A young Chinese girl had been forbidden by her parents to walk to school with a

Many Chinese immigrant parents walk their children to and from school, even as late as the junior high level. Some mothers come to the schools to feed their children lunch.

young Puerto Rican boy who was in the habit of accompanying her every day. To make sure that the parents were being obeyed, the grandmother would walk behind the girl to see that she did not walk with the boy. Grandma even hung around until her granddaughter went into class, and then she would peer through the window to make sure all was proper before she went home.

Naturally, this was embarrassing for the girl, and it must have been noticed by the homeroom teacher. He exploded in anger at the little old lady and made some rather uncomplimentary remarks about this being the United States and that Chinese customs should have been left behind in China. To my mind, this teacher's attitude and remarks could only push the daughter farther away from her parents. What he could have done was explain to the girl, or even to the entire class, the cultural values and traditions of her parents, so that she would understand how they thought and why they behaved in such a fashion. Putting down the parents and their customs is the worst thing he could have done.

SPORTS

The Chinese attitude toward sports is illustrated by an oft-told joke about two Englishmen who were considered somewhat mad. The two lived in Shanghai where they had gone to do business. In the afternoons, they would each take a racquet, go out in the hot sun, and bat a fuzzy ball across the net. As they ran back and forth across the court, sweat would pour from their faces, and they would be exhausted at the end of the game. To the Chinese onlookers standing on the side, this was sheer lunacy. They would shake their heads in disbelief and ask: "Why do these crazy Englishmen work so hard? They can afford to hire coolies to run around and hit the ball for them." The Chinese attitude toward sports has changed considerably, but it still does not assume the importance that it enjoys in American life.

Turn on any news program on radio or television, and you will find one-third of the air time devoted to sports. Who are the school heros? The football quarterback, the track star, the baseball pitcher. What are the big events in school? The games. What is used to rally school spirits? The games.

Yet in the traditional Chinese way of thinking, development of the mental faculties was more important than development of the physique. The image of a scholar was one with a sallow face and long fingernails, indicating that he spent long hours with his books and had not had to do physical labor. Games that required brute strength, such as football and boxing, were not even played in China. Kung fu or other disciplines of the martial arts did not call for physical strength as much as concentration, skill, and agility. In the minds of many Chinese, sports are viewed as frivolous play and a waste of time and energy. Add to this the generally smaller physique of the Chinese immigrant student in comparison to his classmates, and we do not find many of them on any of the school teams.

What does this mean to the Chinese immigrant students, especially the boys? On the one hand, they may think that the heavy emphasis upon sports is a displaced value. They may want to participate, but they are either too small in stature or unable to devote the time necessary for practice to make the school teams. If the "letter men" are the big wheels, the Chinese student will feel that his kind are just the little guys. But most important of all, an entire dimension of American school life is lost to the Chinese immigrant children.

Chinese-American students enjoy a break on the playground at Sun Yat Sen Intermediate School in New York City's Chinatown.

TATTLING

Should one report a wrongdoing? Should one tell the teacher that a schoolmate is cheating on his exam? Should one report to the school authorities that a fellow student is trying to extort money from him? The American values on this score are ambiguous and confusing. For example, in the West Point scandal a few years ago, most of the cadets involved were not cheaters themselves but they knew about the cheating and did not report it to the authorities. Their honor code required that they tell, but the unwritten code among their fellow cadets said that they should not tattle or "fink." If they had reported the cheating of their fellow cadets, they would have been socially ostracized. There is a dilemma for the American here as well.

This bicultural conflict was noted by Denise Kandel and Gerald S. Lesser in the book, *Youth in Two Worlds*, in which their reference groups were

Participation in sports—so heavily emphasized in America—frequently becomes a dilemma for Chinese immigrant students, who experience sharp contrasts in cultures when they come into contact with children from other ethnic groups in public schools.

Danish and American children. The Danish children, like the Chinese, feel duty bound to report wrongdoing. There is no dichotomy of consequences here. Authorities and peers are consistent in their attitude in this respect, and this consistency helps to maintain social control. The teacher cannot be expected to have four pairs of eyes and see everything. The parents cannot be everywhere at once to know what their child is doing during the day. If the siblings or schoolmates will help by reporting wrongdoing, the task of teaching the child is shared and made easier for the adults. But when social ostracism stands in the way of enforcing ethical values, an intense conflict ensues and contributes to the breakdown of social control.

DEMONSTRATION OF AFFECTION

A commonly voiced concern among Chinese children is, "My parents do not love me. They are so cold, distant, and remote." The children long for human warmth and affection because they see it on the movie and television screens, and they read about it in books and magazines. Because their experiences with mother and father and the other members of the family as well are so formal and distant, they come to the conclusion that love is lacking. In China, where such behavior is the norm, children do not question it. But in this country, where expressions of affection are outwardly effusive and commonly exhibited, they feel deprived.

This lack of demonstrative affection extends also to the spouse and friends. To the Chinese, physical intimacy and love are private matters never exhibited in public. Even in handshaking, the traditional Chinese way was to clasp one's own hands in greeting. Kissing and hugging a friend would be most inappropriate, and to kiss one's spouse in public would be considered shameless and ill-mannered.

Nevertheless, Chinese children in this country are attracted to the physical expressions of love and affection. While they crave it for themselves,

they are often unable to reciprocate or be demonstrative in their relations with their own spouses, children, or friends because of their detached emotional upbringing.

In the schools, this contrast in culture is made all the sharper because of the large numbers of Hispanics. In general, the Hispanics are very outgoing and are not the least bit inhibited about embracing, holding hands, or kissing even a casual acquaintance. The Chinese children may interpret these gestures of friendliness as overstepping the bounds of propriety, but more often than not they wish they could shed their reserve and reach out to others in a more informal manner.

On the other hand, the aloofness of the Chinese students is often wrongly interpreted as unfriendliness, standoffishness, as a desire to keep apart. If all the students in the schools were made aware of these cultural differences, they would not misread the intentions and behavior of one another.

EDUCATION

That education is a highly prized cultural value among the Chinese is commonly known, and the fact that Chinese children generally do well scholastically may be due to the hard push parents exert in this direction. None of this means, however, that these children do not experience a bicultural conflict regarding education when they see that the bright student is not the one who is respected and looked up to in American schools. Labels such as "bookworm," "egghead," and "teacher's pet" are applied to the intelligent students, and these terms are not laudatory, but derisive. When parents urge their children to study hard and get good grades, the children know that the payoff will not be social acceptance by their schoolmates. The rewards are not consistent with values taught at home.

Nevertheless, the Chinese immigrant high school students indicated in their survey questionnaire that they prized the opportunity to get an education. In fact, they identified the opportunity to get a free education as one of the most important reasons why they are satisfied with their schoolwork. Of 143 students who said that they were satisfied with their schoolwork, 135 mentioned this one factor. Education is not easily available to everyone in China, Hong Kong, or Taiwan. It is attained at great personal sacrifice on the part of the parents. It is costly and it is earned by diligence and industry on the part of the student. In this country, school is free through high school. Everyone has to go to school until sixteen years of age in New York, for example. It is not a matter of students trying to gain admittance by passing rigorous entrance exams, but a matter of the authorities trying to keep the dropout rates low that characterizes the educational system here.

This is ground also for conflict, however, since what is free and easy to get is often taken lightly. New York State's academic standards are lower than those in Hong Kong or Taiwan, and the schoolwork is easier to keep up with. As a result, there is less distinction attached to being able to stay in school or graduate. What the Chinese immigrant students prize highly has less value in the larger society, and again the newcomers to this country start to have doubts about the goals that they are striving for.

THRIFT

Twelve, perhaps thirteen, banks can be found within the small core area of New York's Chinatown. When the Manhattan Savings Bank opened a new branch in October 1977 it attracted to its coffers $3 million within a few months' time. Most of the large banks are aware that Chinatown is fertile ground for the accumulation of capital because the Chinese tend to save more of what they earn than other ethnic groups in America, in spite of the fact that their earnings are small.

Two major factors encourage the growth of savings among Chinese immigrants. One is the sense of insecurity common to all immigrants, who need a cushion for the uncertainties that they feel acutely. The other is the esteem with which thrift is regarded by the

Chinese. A person who is frugal is thought of more highly than is one who can sport material symbols of success.

I was once sent on an assignment to cover the story of a very wealthy Chinese man from Bangkok who was reputed to own shipping lines, rice mills, and many other industries. He was a special guest of the United States Department of State, and that evening he was to be honored at the Waldorf-Astoria. I found this gentleman in a very modestly-priced midtown hotel. When he extended his hand to shake mine, I saw that his suit sleeves were frayed.

The value placed upon thrift poses acute bicultural conflict for Chinese immigrant children who see all about them evidence of an economic system that encourages the accumulation and conspicuous consumption of material possessions. A very important segment of the consumer market is now the teenage population. The urge to have stylish clothes, a stereo, a camera, a hi-fi radio, sports equipment, and even a car creates a painful conflict in the child who is enticed by television and other advertising media, but whose parents reserve a large percentage of their meager earnings for stashing away in the banks.

In school, the girl who gets money to spend on fashionable dresses and the latest rock record feels more poised and confident about herself than do her less materially fortunate classmates. She is also admired, complimented, and envied. In the Chinese community, on the other hand, a Chinese girl who spent a lot of money on clothes and frivolities would soon be the object of grapevine gossip, stigmatized as a less-than-desirable prospective wife or daughter-in-law, whereas praises would be sung for the more modestly dressed girl who saved her money.

From my students I hear a commonly voiced complaint about their parents as "money-hungry." They give their children very little spending money. They do not buy fashionable clothing; rather, they buy only serviceable garments in which the children are ashamed to be seen. The Chinese home is generally not furnished for comfort

or aesthetics, so when Chinese children visit the homes of their non-Chinese friends and compare them with their own living quarters, they feel deprived and ashamed of their parents and their family. They certainly do not want to bring their friends home to play, and the teenagers may themselves stay away from home as much as possible, feeling more comfortable with their peers in clubhouses or on the streets.

The contrast in spending attitudes between the underdeveloped economy from which many Chinese immigrants have come and the American economy, which emphasizes mass and even wasteful consumption, is very sharp, and it creates many an unresolved conflict in the children, who do not realize that cultural differences lie behind it. They think that their parents value money more than they care for their children, and exhibit this by denying material possessions that give them pleasure and status in the eyes of their peers.

Credit is another concept foreign to immigrants from the Far East. If one does not have the money, one should not be tempted to buy. Credit is borrowing money, and borrowing should be resorted to only in extreme emergencies. The buy now, pay later idea goes against the Chinese grain. So the Chinese families postpone buying until they have saved up enough to cover the entire purchase price. This attitude is fairly common even when it comes to the purchase of a home. The family will scrimp and economize, putting aside a large portion of its income for this goal, denying itself small pleasures along the way for many, many years until the large sum is accumulated. To the Chinese way of thinking, this singleness of purpose shows character, but to the more hedonistic American mind, this habit of thrift may appear asinine and unnecessary.

DEPENDENCY

In her study, "Socialization Patterns among the Chinese in Hawaii," Nancy F. Young noted the prolonged period of dependency of the children commonly found in the child-rearing practices of the Chinese in Hawaii. She wrote:

Observations of Chinese families in Hawaii indicate that both immigrant and local parents utilize child-rearing techniques that result in parent-oriented, as opposed to peer-oriented, behavior. . . . Chinese parents maximize their control over their children by limiting their experiences with models exhibiting nonsanctioned behavior.

Analyzing and comparing the results of the Chance Independence Training Questionnaire that she administered to six ethnic groups and local (American-born) Chinese as well as immigrant Chinese, she found the mean age of independence training for American-born Chinese to be the lowest (6.78 years), while that for immigrant Chinese to be the highest (8.85 years). Among other ethnic groups in Young's study, the mean age of independence training ranged as follows: Jewish, 6.83; Protestant, 6.87 years; Negro, 7.23 years; Greek, 7.67 years; French-Canadian, 7.99 years; and Italian, 8.03 years.

Immigrant mothers exercise constant and strict supervision over their children. They take the children wherever they go, and babysitters are un-

heard of. They prefer their children to say home rather than go out to play with their friends. Friends are carefully screened by the mother, and the child is not expected to do things for himself until about two years beyond the mean age that a Jewish mother would expect her child to do for himself.

On the other hand, American-born Chinese parents expect their children to cut the apron strings sooner than any of the other ethnic groups surveyed. Young did not elaborate and explain why, but it seems that Chinese parents who are American-born have assimilated the American values of independence at an early age and may even have gone overboard in rearing their own children. There are areas of dependence and independence in which Young found divergence. The immigrant Chinese child is expected to be able to take care of himself at an earlier age, but he is discouraged from socializing with people outside the family until a much later age.

The extremes exhibited between the American-born and immigrant Chinese may be indicative of the bicultural conflict that the Chinese in this country feel. As children, they may have felt that their parents were overprotective;

this was frequently mentioned by the teachers to whom we talked. We saw evidence of this in the elementary schools—the previously mentioned practice of mothers coming to the school from the garment factories during their own lunch hours to feed their children lunch. Many walked their children to and from school, even as late as the junior high level, but it was not clear to us whether the parents were justifiably afraid for their children's safety from the gangs or whether they were being overprotective. The teachers thought the mothers were smothering the children and restricting their freedom of action. By adolescence, the children must have felt the same. They were chafing against parental control over what they presumed to be their own business, while the parents thought they were merely doing their parental duty.

Teachers and parents do not agree on this score, with the result that parental authority is often undermined by a teacher's scoffing attitude. A personal experience of my own reveals how damaging this can be to a parent's ability to maintain some kind of control over the growing teenager.

My seventeen-year-old son was

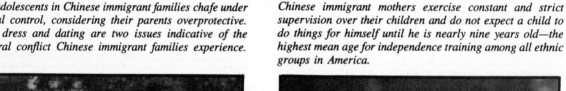

Many adolescents in Chinese immigrant families chafe under parental control, considering their parents overprotective. Stylish dress and dating are two issues indicative of the bicultural conflict Chinese immigrant families experience.

Chinese immigrant mothers exercise constant and strict supervision over their children and do not expect a child to do things for himself until he is nearly nine years old—the highest mean age for independence training among all ethnic groups in America.

coming home late at night, and I found it hard to fall asleep until he was home. I did not feel that he should be up so late, nor did I wish my sleep to be disturbed. My son objected strenuously to a curfew of midnight during the week and 1 A.M. on the weekends. His objection was based on the fact that no other teenagers he knew had such restrictions, that most get-togethers did not get going until 11 P.M., and that he would be the "wet blanket" if he left early. I understood his concerns and tried to get the parents of his friends to agree to a uniform time when the group should break up and go home to bed. I felt that if everybody had to go, my son would not mind leaving.

To my utter surprise, not one of the parents felt that boys or girls of seventeen years of age should have a curfew. They felt that I was being too strict and overprotective and that it was time for me to cut the apron strings. The worst part of it was that my conversation with the parents got back to my son, who immediately and gleefully confronted me with, "See, none of the other parents agree with you. You are the only old-fashioned, strict one." This lack of understanding on the part of the other parents in telling my son about our conversation undermined my authority. From that day, I was unable to set hours for him anymore.

The Chinese value of respect for one's elders and for authority is common knowledge and needs no further elaboration here. We have already mentioned that the Chinese immigrant children encountering the disrespect accorded teachers and school authorities for the first time in American classrooms find themselves extremely upset and dismayed. In our interviews with the students, this concern was voiced frequently.

Challenging established authority has been a notable feature of youth culture over the past two decades. The parents, the teachers, the police, the government, the church—all authority figures in the past—have been knocked down and even reviled. Violence against teachers is the leading problem in schools across the nation. If students

do not have respect for the teacher, neither will they have respect for the knowledge that the teacher tries to impart. The issue is a disturbing one, not only for the immigrant children but for the entire American society as well.

HEROES, HEROINES, AND INDIVIDUALISM

Who are the people who are praised, admired, looked up to, and revered? The idols of different cultures are themselves different types of people, and the values of a society may be deduced from the type of people who are respected and emulated in that culture. In the United States, the most popular figures are movie, television, and stage stars, sports figures, politicians, successful authors, inventors, and scientists; probably in that order. Who are the heroes and heroines of China? If we use literature as a guide, they are the filial sons or daughters, the sacrificing mother, the loyal minister, the patriot or war hero who saves his country, and revolutionaries who overthrow despotic rulers and set up their own dynasties. Even in modern China, the persons honored and emulated are the self-sacrificing workers who put nation above self.

Priests, ministers, and rabbis once commanded prestige in this country, but the status of these men of God has declined. In China, monks or priests have always occupied lowly positions. In contrast to the United States, in China actors were riffraff. Women did not act in the theater, so men had to play the female roles. Western influence has brought about changes in the pseudo-Chinese cultures of Hong Kong and Singapore and stage performers and movie stars are now popular and emulated, but this was not always so.

As a rule, Chinese heroes and heroines were people of high moral virtues, and they set the standards of conduct for others. In this country, the more sensational the exposé of the private lives of our national leaders or entertainment figures, the more our curiosity is aroused. How movie stars retain their popularity in spite of the

relentless campaigns to strip them naked is very difficult for someone not brought up in the United States to comprehend. An old adage says, "No man is a hero to his valet." Yet, the very fact that American heroes and heroines survive and thrive on notoriety and self-confession can only mean that the American people admire such behavior. One might say, Chinese heroes are saints; American heroes are sinners.

Noted anthropologist Francis L. K. Hsu has written extensively about individualism as a prominent characteristic of American life. According to Hsu, the basic ingredient of rugged individualism is self-reliance. The individual constantly tells himself and others that he controls his own destiny and that he does not need help from others. The individual-centered person enjoins himself to find means of fulfilling his own desires and ambitions.

Individualism is the driving force behind the competitiveness and creativity that has pushed this nation forward. Loose family ties, superficial human relationships, little community control, and weak traditions have given the individual leeway to strike out on his own without being hindered by sentimentality, convention, and tradition. Self-interest has been a powerful incentive.

In contrast, Dr. Hsu contends, the Chinese are situation-centered. Their way of life encourages the individual to find a satisfactory adjustment with the external environment of men and things. The Chinese individual sees the world in relativistic terms. He is dependent upon others and others are dependent upon him. Like bricks in a wall, one lends support to the other and they all hold up the society as a whole. If even one brick becomes loose, the wall is considerably weakened; interlocked, the wall is strong. The wall is the network of human relations. The individual subordinates his own wishes and ambitions for the common good.

Dr. Kenneth Abbott, in his book *Harmony and Individualism*, also points out that the Western ideas of creativity and individualism are not accented in Chinese and must be held within accepted norms. One of the reasons for this is the importance ascribed to maintenance of harmony. Harmony is the key concept in all relationships between god(s) and man and between man and man. It is the highest good.

To the Chinese, the sense of duty and obligation takes precedence over self-gratification. It is not uncommon to find Chinese teenagers handing over their entire paychecks to their parents for family use or for young Chinese males to pursue a course of study chosen for them by their parents rather than one of their own choosing. Responsibility toward distant kin is more keenly felt by the Chinese than by other Americans. Honor and glory accrue not only to the individual but to all those who helped him climb the ladder. This sense of being part of something

greater than oneself gives the Chinese a feeling of belonging and security in the knowledge that they do not stand alone. On the other hand, individual freedom of action is very much restricted.

Some of the better known problems that confront a Chinese immigrant to these shores, such as respect for elders, modesty and humility, and male superiority, were omitted here because they have been dealt with at length elsewhere. The foregoing examples—aggressiveness, sexuality, sports, tattling, demonstration of affection, education, thrift, independence training, respect for authority, heros and heroines, and individualism—represent other important areas of bicultural conflict that confront Chinese newcomers to these shores.

ADDITIONAL READING

Francis L. K. Hsu, "Rugged Individualism Reconsidered," *The Colorado Quarterly*, vol. 9, no. 2, Autumn 1960.

———— *Americans and Chinese: Reflections on Two Cultures and Their People*, American Museum of Science Books, New York, 1972.

———— "Culture Change and the Persistence of the Chinese Personality," in George DeVos, ed., *In Response to Change*, D. Van Nostrand, New York, 1976.

Denise Kandel and Gerald S. Lesser, *Youth in Two Worlds*, Jossey-Bass, Inc., San Francisco, 1972.

Richard Sollenger, "Chinese-American Child Rearing Practices and Juvenile Delinquency," *Journal of Social Psychology*, vol. 74, 1968.

Shirley Teper, "Ethnicity, Race and Human Development," N.Y. Institute on Pluralism and Group Identity of the American Jewish Committee, 1977.

Nancy F. Young, "Socialization Patterns among the Chinese in Hawaii," in *Amerasia Journal*, vol. 1, no. 4, February 1972.

Inuit Youth in a Changing World

Richard G. Condon

Richard G. Condon is an assistant professor in the anthropology department at the University of Arkansas and a research fellow of the Center for Northern Studies in Wolcott, Vermont. He is currently performing research for a follow-up study of Inuit adolescent development in Holman Island in the Northwest Territories of Canada.
The rapid social changes that have taken place in the Canadian Arctic over the past 20 to 30 years have created a host of challenges and dilemmas for young Inuit. The members of this younger generation are coming of age during a period of fundamental change in northern society. A previously nomadic population has been concentrated into centralized settlements and towns, resulting in population growth and increased economic security. More Inuit are exposed to southern values through travel, schooling, television and radio. Because of all these changes, young people have grown not only more autonomous but have been able to delay the acceptance of adult roles and responsibilities. As a result the patterning and sequencing of traditional Inuit life stages has altered significantly, creating a prolonged adolescent life stage that has up until now been absent in Inuit tradition.

Few regions of the world have experienced such a rapid pace of development and change as the Canadian Arctic. Recognition of the strategic significance and resource potential of Canada's arctic regions has led to an increase in government and corporate involvement with the North and its residents. Such involvement has had both positive and negative consequences for young Inuit. On the positive side, the economy is more secure and schooling and advanced vocational training are more available, creating opportunities for young people that did not exist just 10 to 20 years ago. On the negative side, however, young people face the significant social and psychological stresses incurred by rapid social change, as they strive to find a place in this newly emerging social order. Many young people lack sufficient employment opportunities, are inadequately prepared for advanced high schooling and are unwilling or unable to relocate to larger northern communities where jobs are more available. These adjustment dilemmas have contributed, in part, to the high rates of alcohol and drug abuse, suicide and juvenile delinquency which are characteristic of Inuit teenagers and young adults throughout the North (*Report on Health Conditions in the N.W.T.* 1983:35).

INUIT YOUTH: PAST AND PRESENT

The world of today's Copper Inuit youth is markedly different from that of their parents and grandparents. In the past, young people not only made a rapid transition into adulthood, but faced predetermined roles and responsibilities imposed by the demands of a harsh and unproductive habitat. The Copper Inuit of the Holman region occupied one of the most marginal environments within Canada's Arctic. Gender roles were narrowly defined, and options were extremely limited. A young man could aspire only to be a skilled hunter and provider for his family; a woman could strive to acquire the skills necessary to be an expert seamstress and household manager. Gender roles were learned through observation of and intense interaction with parents and other adult relatives. Because residential units were small and infant mortality rates high, young people had no peers to draw them away from the socializing influence of their parents (Jenness 1922:163–164).

In the past, parents made marriage arrangements, especially for young women, when the child was an infant, and in some cases even before a child's birth (Damas 1975:409).[1] Parentally

From *Cultural Survival Quarterly*, 1988, Vol. 12, No. 2, pp. 63-66. Cultural Survival Inc., 11 Divinity Avenue, Cambridge, MA 02138. Reprinted by permission.

arranged marriage and child betrothal were most adaptive in a society in which prospective spouses were few and far between and in which female infanticide reduced the number of marriageable females (Balikci 1967:616; Damas 1969:53; Riches 1974:358). As a result, parents sought marriage partners for their offspring through kinship and alliance networks. Most young women married at or just before their first menstrual period, and began bearing children three to four years later.

Young men, however, faced a different set of requirements. They were not considered old enough for marriage until they had proven themselves capable as hunters and providers. Until a man could develop the skills and strength necessary to build a snowhouse or hunt large game unassisted, he was not considered mature enough to take on and support a wife. In chronological terms, he would not reach marriageability until around 17 or 18 years of age. He then went through a period of bride service, during which he joined his future father-in-law's household, often while his betrothed was still pubescent. During this trial marriage period, the young man worked with his father-in-law for three to four years until the young couple was considered mature enough to establish a separate household (Damas 1972:42, 1975:409).

The rather rapid transition from childhood to adulthood in traditional Copper Inuit society stands in marked contrast to the situation today. In the past, Inuit teenagers were raised exclusively within the context of small family groups and spent much of the year in isolated hunting/fishing/trapping camps where there were few, if any, activities to distract them from participating fully in assigned chores. Today, a large adolescent peer group dominates the recreational activities of teens. Young people now have a great deal more autonomy than they ever had in the presettlement era. When they are not in school, they pass much of their time with their peers, more often than not engaged in social rather than work activities. The increased economic security of contemporary settlement life now makes it possible for teenagers to delay taking on the roles and responsibilities of adulthood. As a result, young people now make their own decisions concerning when and who to marry, often only consulting minimally with their parents.

DEMOGRAPHIC CHANGES

As of the early 1960s, the Canadian government sponsored population concentration in the Holman region, which significantly altered the demographic profile and social/physical context of contemporary Inuit society. Prior to this program, the regional population resided in isolated, scattered hunting and trapping camps. Through the construction of government-subsidized housing and a school, the government created a regional center from which it could more effectively deliver health care and social services.

Most importantly, the creation of settlements contributed to the unprecedented population growth of Holman and other northern communities. In 1963, for example, the population of the Holman region was 135 (Usher 1965:72). Since then, the Holman population has increased to its present size of more than 350. At present, children and teenagers comprise more than 52 percent of the population. Several factors have contributed to the rapid population growth since the early 1960s: (1) the introduction of bottle feeding, which has shortened birth intervals between offspring;[2] (2) improvements in prenatal and postnatal health programs, which have lowered the Inuit infant mortality rate; (3) improvements in nutrition, which have probably increased fertility by eliminating periods of nutritional stress; and (4) increased economic security, which now makes it possible for parents to support larger numbers of offspring.

One result of these demographic changes is that the teenage sector is much larger today than it ever was in the past; settlement existence has provided the social context for a large, active adolescent peer group.

ECONOMIC CHANGES

Since the creation of the settlement, residents of Holman and other Inuit communities have experienced a degree of economic security unheard of in either the traditional period or in the immediate post-contact period. Many of the uncertainties associated with a subsistence level of existence have been eliminated by the availability of wage employment, social assistance payments and government-subsidized housing. The introduction of firearms (in the 1920s) and snowmobiles (in the 1970s) has allowed the Inuit to hunt game more efficiently and over a wider area. Most wage-generating and subsistence-hunting activities have become highly individualized, thus diminishing the amount of cooperation and sharing between households. Today's young generation of Inuit is no longer socialized within a value system that emphasizes the importance of mutual cooperation and sharing.

The shift from a predominantly hunting-oriented economy to one based upon wage employment and government subsidy is not without some complications. Although the available wage employment increases economic security, the relative shortage of local employment opportunities limits the income prospects for Inuit teenagers and young adults. The little employment that is available tends to be only temporary or part time. As a result, even older youths who would prefer to be working end up with a lot of free time. Even though young men could go out trapping or subsistence hunting, most display little interest in these activities because the high investment in time and energy far outweighs the return. The anti-trapping and anti-sealing campaigns waged by southern-based animal welfare groups also have undermined the economic viability of such pursuits in Holman and other Inuit communities (Wenzel 1985). Many of the young people interviewed indicated that they preferred high-paying and highly skilled occupations such as carpentry, heavy duty equipment operation, mechanics, welding, teaching and nursing.

SOCIAL AND
ATTITUDINAL CHANGES

As Holman integrates with the outside world, its residents are exposed to southern lifestyles and behavioral standards. Much of this "attitudinal assimilation" is due to the introduction of formal schooling. The local school in Holman has been operating since the early 1960s and is staffed by southern teachers who use a predominantly southern Canadian curriculum. Since schooling is compulsory until age 16 (although, in fact, many students quit well before their sixteenth birthdays), children spend much of the day isolated from the socializing influence of parents and other adults. Thus, as expected, children learn more about the southern way of life than about their own cultural traditions. In addition, the Holman school has done much to create a whole category of individuals who, although physically mature, are chronologically labeled as teenagers (or schoolchildren) rather than adults.

In the fall of 1980, television was introduced in Holman and yearly school exchange trips to southern Canada were instituted. Both of these acculturation agents have increased young people's exposure to southern standards of teenage behavior, attitudes and expectations. Television is the most important source of increased knowledge and awareness of current events happening in the outside world. On the negative side, however, Graburn (1982) has gone so far as to suggest that television is a form of cultural genocide: it has reinforced use of the English language, disrupted social visiting patterns and contributed to a generation gap. Young people in northern communities have been profoundly affected by the assimilationist qualities of television programming; it has helped to alter their behavior, their outlook on life and even their language. The word *teenager*, in fact, was not used widely until *after* television was introduced in the community. Television not only is a window to the outside world; it is a window to the adolescent subculture of the US and southern Canada!

As a result of these demographic, economic and social changes in settlement life, parents and children interact much less than in the past. When children and teenagers are not attending school, they spend time with their peers. Many parents complain about this dramatic increase in adolescent autonomy, saying that they rarely see their teenage sons and daughters.

ASPIRATIONAL DILEMMAS

As Holman teenagers struggle to acquire the customs and values of Inuit society, they are also mercilessly inundated with the values, social expectations and behavioral norms of southern society. Exposure to southern value systems has raised young people's aspirations at a time when the northern economy is changing, but not expanding sufficiently to accommodate the employment needs of the new generation. Lack of local employment opportunities may partially explain the delay in social maturity among Inuit adolescents.

In school, young people learn within a value system that promises high-paying and challenging careers after high school. High schooling, however, is not provided on the local level; students must be prepared to spend three years attending the regional high school in the territorial capital of Yellowknife. Although an increasing number of young people in Holman recognize the importance of a formal high school degree, few have the skills to complete the required course of study. (It is not unusual for a ninth-grade student in Holman to discover, after taking the high school entrance exam, that he or she is operating at a fifth- or sixth-grade level of academic achievement.) In addition, the stress of being separated from family and friends, combined with the regimented life in the school's residence hall, simply adds to the students' sense of frustration and helplessness. As a result, many drop out after several months or even weeks. Many of those who remain cut classes or turn to drugs and alcohol, which are more readily available in Yellowknife than in Holman. As of the fall of 1987, only five

students from Holman had remained in Yelowknife long enough to complete their high school educations. The rest either did not try to attend or dropped out early, passing their time in Holman with casual work and hanging out with friends and peers.

Those Holman teens who are fortunate enough to receive either a high school diploma or vocational training often have to move to another community to find suitable employment, separating them from a close and supportive network of friends and relatives. As a small community, Holman does not have the employment base to support even a moderately sized work force; the young people who choose to stay in Holman have to settle for a combination of low-paying jobs and social assistance. The recent economic depression in the western Canadian Arctic, a result of the abandonment of oil and mineral exploration in the Beaufort Sea region, has made matters worse. With the promise of material wealth and job satisfaction unfulfilled, an increasing number of Holman's youth will turn to alcohol abuse, drug addiction and even suicide as a means of coping with their frustration. In addition, the lack of parental control and parental role models may further aggravate many youths' sense of alienation from the emerging social and economic order.

There is no doubt that further research, preferably of a longitudinal nature in a number of northern communities, is required to develop a full understanding of the wide-ranging impacts that rapid social change has had upon this new generation of Inuit. For example, many of the Holman youths studied in 1982–1983 have begun to raise families and assume important leadership and political positions within the community. How has their collective experience as a transitional generation affected their abilities to operate in a social environment increasingly oriented to the local control of political processes? Will recent settlement of land claims in the western Canadian Arctic and the subsequent creation of regional and village corporations increase local economic opportunities for young people in Holman and other small communities? Hopefully, as such economic and political opportunities become increasingly available, this transitional generation will find it possible to control the direction of their own lives and home communities.

ACKNOWLEDGMENTS

This research was conducted under the auspices of the Harvard Adolescence Project, directed by Professors John Whiting, Beatrice Whiting and Irven DeVore of Harvard's Department of Anthropology. Holman Island was but one field site in a larger cross-cultural study of adolescent development, which sent other post-doctoral researchers to Nigeria, Kenya, Romania, Morocco, Thailand and Arnhemland, Australia. The goal of the Harvard Adolescence Project was to collect comparable data on adolescent development from a sample of non-Western societies and, in so doing, assess the social and psychological impacts of modernization upon young people in these societies. These data are being published in a series of books by Rutgers University Press called "Adolescents in a Changing World." The first of these books, *Inuit Youth: Growth and Change in the Canadian Arctic* (Condon 1987), discusses adolescent behavior and socialization in the isolated Copper Inuit community of Holman Island.

NOTES

1. In traditional Copper Inuit society, as in most other Inuit societies, marriage did not imply the same legal, ceremonial or religious obligations as it does in Western culture. The term *marriage* is used here in a rather loose sense, for lack of a better word. A man and woman were married only after they had established a separate household and were recognized as husband and wife by members of the community. Even today, Inuit consider a young couple living together in a separate household married, even if they have not had a formal marriage ceremony.

2. Prior to the introduction of bottle feeding, Inuit mothers breastfed their offspring for three to four years, and sometimes up to five years (Jenness 1922:165; Graburn 1969:61). Recent studies have established that frequent and unrestricted suckling contributes to postpartum infertility (Kippley and Kippley 1977). For the Inuit, such prolonged suckling provided an ideal system of population equilibrium, whereby prolonged birth intervals maximized each child's chances of survival. With the introduction of bottle feeding in the 1960s, however, traditional birth spacing altered significantly, resulting in both a shortening of birth intervals and an acceleration in the livebirth rate (Schaefer 1959, 1973; McAlpine and Simpson 1975).

REFERENCES

Balikci, A. 1967. Female Infanticide on the Arctic Coast. *MAN* 2(4):615–625.

Condon, R. 1987. *Inuit Youth: Growth and Change in the Canadian Arctic.* New Brunswick, NJ: Rutgers University Press.

Damas, D. 1969. History, Environment, and Central Eskimo Society. In D. Damas, ed. *Ecological Essays.* National Museum of Canada, Bulletin 230:40–64.

_____ 1972. The Structure of Central Eskimo Associations. In L. Guemple, ed. *Alliance in Eskimo Society.* Seattle: University of Washington Press.

_____ 1975. Demographic Aspects of Central Eskimo Marriage Practices. *American Ethnologist* 2:409–418.

Graburn, N. 1969. *Eskimos Without Igloos.* Boston: Little, Brown.

_____ 1982. Television and the Canadian Inuit. *Etudes/Inuit Studies* 6:7–17.

Jenness, D. 1922. *The life of the Copper Eskimos.* Report of the Canadian Arctic Expedition, 1913–1918, Vol. XII, Part A, Ottawa.

Kippley, S. K. and J. F. Kippley 1977. The Relation Between Breastfeeding and Amenorrhea: A Report of a Survey. *Journal of Tropical Pediatrics* 23:239–245.

McAlpine, P. J. and N. E. Simpson 1975. Fertility and Other Demographic Aspects of the Canadian Eskimo Communities of Igloolik and Hall Beach. *Human Biology* 48:113–138.

Report on Health Conditions in the N.W.T. 1983. Yellowknife, N.W.T.: Chief Medical and Health Officer, Government of the N.W.T.

Riches, D. 1974. The Netsilik Eskimo: A Special Case of Selective Female Infanticide, *Ethnology* 13:351–362.

Schaefer, O. 1959. Medical Observations and Problems in Canadian Eskimos, Part II. *Canadian Medical Association Journal* 81: 386–393.

_____ 1973. The Changing Health Picture in the Canadian Arctic. *Canadian Journal of Opthalmology* 8:196–204.

Usher, P. 1965. *Economic Basis and Resource Use of the Coppermine/Holman Region, Northwest Territories.* Ottawa: Department of Northern Affairs and National Resources.

Wenzel, G. 1985. Marooned in a Blizzard of Contradictions: Inuit and the Anti-Sealing Movement. *Etudes/Inuit/Studies* 9: 77–91.

Back on the Land

Rejecting the comfort and security of settlement life, many of Canada's Inuit have chosen to return to the traditional hunting-and-gathering life-style of the Arctic

Bryan and Cherry Alexander

Bryan and Cherry Alexander are free-lance photojournalists based in England.

The five caribou seemed to sense the danger. They stopped grazing, raised their heads, and scented the air uneasily. Lying prostrate on a ridge of snow two hundred yards away, Augustine Taqqaugaq squeezed the trigger of his old and battered rifle. A shot rang out; the caribou began to run. One faltered, and then fell dead onto the ground. Taqqaugaq stood up and, brushing the snow from his caribou-fur clothing, walked back to his snowmobile, a smile of satisfaction on his face. He started the machine, revving the engine before setting off toward his fallen prey. By the time we reached it, what little blood that had spilled onto the snow had frozen, for this was early March and the temperature was minus thirty-six degrees Centigrade.

Taqqaugaq produced a pocketknife and set about skinning the caribou, a task he performed with remarkable speed. Within fifteen minutes, he had folded the skin and loaded the carcass onto a sled. The wind had picked up, and blown snow was snaking across the tundra. Taqqaugaq pointed to some

A group of hunters from the Iglurjuat winter camp take a tea break while out hunting.

small, narrow clouds near the horizon. "Maybe later there will be a storm," he said, as he pulled the starter cord of his snowmobile. After checking that I was firmly seated on the sled, he set off for camp.

"Camp" was at Iglurjuat on the west side of Steensby Inlet, Baffin Island. In March it didn't look like much, for the large wooden hut that Taqqaugaq had built was completely covered by snow. If not for some oil drums, a dog team, and a couple of snowmobiles, one would hardly have known it was there.

To describe the camp as remote would be an understatement. The nearest shop is the Hudson Bay Company store at Igloolik, more than a hundred miles away. That does not worry Taqqaugaq or the thirteen members of his family. Iglurjuat is their winter home, and has been since 1983 when, disillusioned with settlement life in Igloolik, Taqqaugaq and his wife took their kids out of school and returned to a life on the land.

The sound of our return brought Taqqaugaq's wife, Theresia, and several children out of the hut, all eager to see how we had fared on the hunt. The caribou carcass was unlashed from the sled and put up on a meat rack, while Theresia cast a critical eye over the skin. Keeping a large family in fur clothes means that she spends much of her time sewing skins. Back inside the warm hut, we removed our caribou-fur parkas and gradually thawed out over a mug of hot coffee. Theresia prepared a meal, putting walrus meat, a caribou haunch, and an arctic char, all raw, on a plastic sheet in the center of the floor. I joined the family as they gathered round to eat in traditional fashion, hacking off pieces of meat and fat with a knife and licking off any blood and fat that ran down their hands. Theresia's homemade bannock was one of the few concessions to white man's food.

Taqqaugaq's prediction of bad weather proved correct. We had barely finished eating when the plastic sheeting stretched across the hut's small window began to flap violently as the wind increased. Within minutes, blowing snow reduced the visibility to twenty-five yards. As darkness fell, Taqqaugaq called Igloolik and another outpost camp on his shortwave radio, his only link with the outside world. They too had wind—it seemed as though the bad weather was widespread. The evening was spent chatting and playing cards for matches by the light of a kerosene lamp. Luke, Taqqaugaq's son, won enough matches to keep his Coleman stove lit for the next year. It got late, and one by one the family stretched out to sleep on the communal sleeping platform that ran the width of the hut. As we settled down for the night, and the hut became quiet, I became very aware of the howling wind outside and was grateful for the snugness of the hut. "Maybe there will be fine weather tomorrow," said Taqqaugaq as he turned off the kerosene lamp.

This time his weather prediction proved optimistic. The storm raged for another two days, confining us to the hut, with odd brief excursions outside to collect ice. The hut was transformed into a busy workshop. Luke stripped down one of the snowmobile engines on the floor; Theresia cut pieces of sealskin for a pair of *kamik* (boots) for her grandson; and the two teenage daughters spent most of the time entertaining the younger children or thumbing through magazines while listening to Dire Straits on a Walkman. Taqqaugaq began work on a soapstone carving of a walrus, first chipping away at the stone with a grub axe, and later using a file and a pocketknife for the finer details. The carving would eventually be sold to the cooperative in Igloolik on a trip to buy more supplies.

Apart from Taqqaugaq and Theresia, the only other adults at the camp were a son and daughter with their respective partners. The nine children ranged from their sixteen-year-old son Marc to a two-year-old grandson. Only one son, who works in a mine at Nanisivik, was not with them. Theresia has no regrets about taking the children out of school. "They learn more useful things with us out on the land," she explained. She plays many roles herself, including hunter's wife, mother, teacher, and priest, for the family are Catholics and she holds a service at the camp each Sunday. She also acts as camp midwife and delivered her two grandchildren, who were both born at the camp.

Though they spend most of the year at Iglurjuat, in the spring they move to another camp at Ikpik Bay to hunt seal. Later in the summer they move again to a camp where they fish for arctic char. Cash for their everyday needs is raised by selling skins—mainly wolf, arctic fox, and seal—either to the Hudson Bay Company or to the cooperative store in Igloolik where they buy their supplies.

When the hunting is lean, and in periods of bad weather, Taqqaugaq carves soapstone figures to raise cash. He is an extremely talented carver. From the sale of three carvings to the cooperative the previous summer, he was able to buy a new outboard motor for his boat.

DISINTEGRATION OF INUIT CULTURE IN SETTLEMENTS

Some of the sites of camps like Iglurjuat have been used by the Inuit for four thousand years or more. Before the days of settlement living, camps were scattered right across the Arctic. Each northern community evolved its own seasonal cycle of life, following the movements of the animals they hunted from one area to another. Camps were formed at strategic points in good hunting areas.

Many of today's settlements in the Canadian north began with a trading post back in the pioneering days of the world-famous Hudson Bay Company. It was its role as the first trading company to establish itself in arctic Canada that gave rise to the joke that the company's initials stood for "Here Before Christ." In those days, it was acceptable to kill animals for their fur. Traders were anxious for every skin that the Inuit could provide.

The influence of the traders had a pronounced effect on the Inuit, who became no longer purely subsistence hunters, but came to be dependent on trading pelts. Missionaries followed hot on the heels of the traders, and after them came the administrators. Settlements began to be established, though many Inuit stayed at hunting camps. Hunger and starvation traditionally were always close at hand in Inuit life. Even as late as the 1950s, researchers found groups of Inuit starving in the Canadian north. Canada would not tolerate any of her people starving, and so the government began to pour vast sums of money into the north. Many Inuit were "persuaded"— and in some cases even forced—to abandon their traditional life at hunting camps for a more sedentary existence at newly formed settlements, housed in prefabricated bungalows. Many of these settlements were closer to a Hudson Bay Company store and a church than to good hunting grounds.

To begin with, all this seemed too good to be true to the Inuit: no more starvation, houses where heat and light came with the flick of a switch, medical facilities, and schooling for their children. None predicted the considerable problems to come. Large boarding schools were built in the main settlements like Iqaluit (formerly Frobisher Bay), and children from camps and small villages were sent to them to be educated and prepared for life in the modern Arctic. But insufficient jobs had been provided for the Inuit, and unemployment among the Inuit communities throughout the Arctic was high (in Igloolik, it is currently over 50 percent). The young Inuit found themselves caught between two cultures. Because they were away from their families so much during their formative years, they lacked the knowledge and skill necessary to become hunters. But the modern world had no work to offer most of them. They were faced with having to live on government handouts. In their frustration, many turned to alcohol, and later, to drugs.

By the late sixties, the Inuit culture seemed to be facing an inevitable disintegration. Some Inuit realized that living on government handouts in government settlements, with televisions and stores full of consumer goods and junk food, was doing more harm than good to many communities. An increasing number of families, disillusioned with modern settlements, gave

up their homes and moved back to the old hunting camps, in what became known as the back-to-the-land movement.

THE OUTPOST CAMP PROGRAMME

To its credit, the government of the Northwest Territories decided to assist those Inuit who wanted to return to a life on the land, and in 1975, it introduced the Outpost Camp Programme. Operated by the government's Department of Renewable Resources, it provides families who want to return to the land with both financial and material help. Each camp is provided with a grant for materials to construct a small single-room wooden hut, gas for snowmobiles and outboard motors, and four

gallons of heating fuel a day between September and May. Inuit can borrow a two-way radio and are provided with a basic medical kit. Loans are available to enable them to buy things like ammunition, tools, and other essentials to get started: after that, they are on their own.

Today, the Outpost Camp Programme operates in three regions of the Canadian Arctic: Inuvik in the west, Kiktikmeot in the central Arctic, and the Baffin region in the east. Some sites of traditional camps were never vacated, but many new camps formed as the back-to-the-land movement gathered momentum.

There is, of course, a certain irony in that the Canadian government, having spent millions of dollars over two decades to get the Inuit to move off the

Below: On the floor of the hut, Theresia Taqqaugaq works on a sealskin from which she will make a pair of boots. Inset: Theresia chews a piece of bearded seal skin to make it soft.

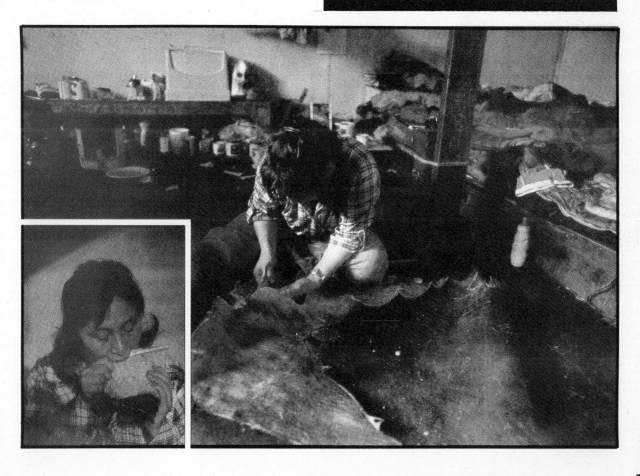

The Taqqaugaqs make a journey of over a hundred miles to purchase supplies at the Hudson Bay Company store at Igloolik.

land and into settlements, is now paying for them to move back again. Critics of the Outpost Camp Programme initially saw it as throwing away money in an attempt by some nostalgic members of the Inuit community to turn back the clock. They have been proved wrong, even though some Inuit, mainly the young, did not take to camp life. After their initial enthusiasm waned, many young Inuit returned to the rock music, videos, and coffee bars of the modern Arctic settlements. Many, however, did stay, and new camps were formed as interest in the program grew. In the early 1970s, before the start of the program, there were only three camps left on Baffin Island. By 1986 that figure had grown to twenty-nine, and there were a total of seventy-three camps in the three regions of the Arctic where the Outpost Camp Programme was in operation.

The program peaked in the early 1980s. Now, although there are more camps, there are fewer Inuit out on the land. In the early days of the program, there were a number of what Bob Decker of the Northwest Territories' Wildlife Management Department describes as megacamps, which had up to sixty Inuit at any one time. Now camps tend to comprise smaller family groups, and usually contain no more than twenty people. One reason for this decline is that in the last five years, it has become much harder to live as a hunter, though not because of any change in the Arctic.

The biggest threat to the Inuit and their culture in recent years has come from the emotional outcry over Canada's annual harp seal cull. A campaign mounted by Greenpeace and other conservation groups, illustrated with gruesome pictures of baby seals being clubbed to death on the ice, brought such a public outcry that the U.S. government banned all sea mammal products from its markets. Meanwhile, the European Economic Community took similar action, banning the import of all seal products.

Inevitably, the market for sealskins collapsed.

During the 1970s, a good-quality sealskin might have fetched sixty dollars or more at a fur auction. In the spring of 1985, the average price of sealskins at one European auction was $3.68. The collapse of the sealskin market meant that hunting communities throughout the Arctic faced economic disaster. Welfare officers throughout the north believe that the result of the "Save the Seals" campaign was that many more native people were thrown onto the dole. The Inuit are understandably bitter, for they had nothing whatsoever to do with the commercial seal cull. They mainly hunt adult ringed seals, the most common seal found in the Arctic. They take relatively few harp seals, and they certainly do not club baby "whitecoats" to death. Understandably, the Inuit feel aggrieved that self-righteous people did not consider the north's native people and the important part seal hunting plays in their existence.

The Inuit have a tradition of looking after their environment. They point out that it was not the Inuit who decimated the Arctic's great whale population. Neither are they responsible for polluting the arctic seas. They have always been concerned with preserving the wildlife they depend on. They have agreed with government ecologists on quotas for hunting polar bears and musk-oxen. They also have agreed with the government to vacate outpost camps if wildlife in the area is at all threatened—though this has yet to occur in the program's thirteen years of operation.

It is not surprising that Greenpeace is loathed throughout the Arctic, even though it halted its campaign against the fur trade (because, as one of its London spokesmen put it, "European cultures were again dictating to older cultures how they should live their lives"). Few people know that its campaign has ended; irreversible damage has already been done. In the north, memories die hard. In the Arctic, employment possibilities for native people are few. For most Inuit, the only real alternative to hunting is a life on the dole.

One of the most important things about the Outpost Camp Programme is that it gives the Inuit a choice. They no longer have to be part of the wage-earning community, and they can get away from the social problems of the settlements. Outpost camps also have the advantage of being in better locations for hunting and gathering food. Everyone contributes to the running of a camp, and by and large camps are relaxed and happy places. Above all, the Outpost Camp Programme is helping to preserve the Inuit culture. The children are able to travel with their parents and learn how to hunt and survive in the harsh Arctic environment. Camp life also cements the strong bond that exists between the Inuit and the land, and helps them retain their cultural identity. As one of Taqqaugaq's sons at the outpost camp at Iglurjuat told me, "When I am here, I feel like an Inuk; at Igloolik, I don't.

Index

Credits/ Acknowledgments

Cover design by Charles Vitelli

1. Anthropological Perspectives
Facing overview—United Nations photo.

2. Culture and Communication
Facing overview—United Nations photo.

3. Organization of Society and Culture
Facing overview—United Nations photo. 84—Photos by Jason Laure.

4. Other Families, Other Ways
Facing overview—United Nations photo by John Isaac. 97—Diagram by Joe LeMonnier. 102—Photo by Enid Schildkrout. 106—United Nations photo.

5. Sex Roles and Statuses
Facing overview—Israeli Tourist Office. 158, 160, 161—Photos by Longina Jakubowska.

6. Religion, Belief, and Ritual
Facing overview—Israeli Tourist Office. 189, 190, 193—Photos by Philip Graham.

7. Sociocultural Change
Facing overview—United Nations photo. 211-214—Photos by Dr. E. Richard Sorensen. 226-228, 230—Photos by Paolo Galli/The World & I. 237, 239, 240—Courtesy of Bryan and Cherry Alexander.

ANNUAL EDITIONS: ANTHROPOLOGY 90/91

Article Rating Form

Here is an opportunity for you to have direct input into the next revision of this volume. We would like you to rate each of the 40 articles listed below, using the following scale:

1. **Excellent: should definitely be retained**
2. **Above average: should probably be retained**
3. **Below average: should probably be deleted**
4. **Poor: should definitely be deleted**

Your ratings will play a vital part in the next revision. So please mail this prepaid form to us just as soon as you complete it.
Thanks for your help!

Annual Editions revisions depend on two major opinion sources: one is our Advisory Board, listed in the front of this volume, which works with us in scanning the thousands of articles published in the public press each year; the other is you—the person actually using the book. Please help us and the users of the next edition by completing the prepaid article rating form on this page and returning it to us. Thank you.

Rating	Article	Rating	Article
	1. Doing Fieldwork Among the Yąnomamö		21. Woman the Gatherer
	2. Doctor, Lawyer, Indian Chief		22. Men and Women: The Warmth and Luxury of Male Dominance
	3. Eating Christmas in the Kalahari		23. What Keeps Women "in Their Place"?
	4. Myth of the Man-Eaters		24. Women, Food, and Hospitality in Iranian Society
	5. Confessions of a Former Cultural Relativist		25. A Matter of Honor
	6. Language, Appearance, and Reality: Doublespeak in 1984		26. Between Two Worlds
	7. Shakespeare in the Bush		27. Blaming the Victim
	8. Social Time: The Heartbeat of Culture		28. The Mbuti Pygmies: Change and Adaptation
	9. How Not to Lose the Trade Wars by Cultural Gaffes		29. The Initiation of a Maasai Warrior
	10. The Blood in Their Veins		30. The Secrets of Haiti's Living Dead
	11. Memories of a !Kung Girlhood		31. A Writer in a World of Spirits
	12. Murders in Eden		32. You've Gotta Have "Wa"
	13. The Yąnomamis: Portrait of a People in Crisis		33. Body Ritual Among the Nacirema
	14. Mystique of the Masai		34. Why Can't People Feed Themselves?
	15. Potlatch		35. Growing Up as a Fore
	16. When Brothers Share a Wife		36. Dark Dreams About the White Man
	17. Young Traders of Northern Nigeria		37. The Aborigines' Search for Justice
	18. Child Care in China		38. Bicultural Conflict
	19. Free Enterprise and the Ghetto Family		39. Inuit Youth in a Changing World
	20. The Gypsies		40. Back on the Land

(Continued on next page)

ABOUT YOU

Name_____ Date_____

Are you a teacher? ☐ Or student? ☐

Your School Name _____

Department _____

Address _____

City _____ State _____ Zip _____

School Telephone # _____

YOUR COMMENTS ARE IMPORTANT TO US!

Please fill in the following information:

For which course did you use this book? _____

Did you use a text with this Annual Edition? ☐ yes ☐ no

The title of the text? _____

What are your general reactions to the Annual Editions concept?

Have you read any particular articles recently that you think should be included in the next edition?

Are there any articles you feel should be replaced in the next edition? Why?

Are there other areas that you feel would utilize an Annual Edition?

May we contact you for editorial input?

May we quote you from above?